FIFTH EDITION

A HISTORY OF MODERN PSYCHOLOGY

C. JAMES GOODWIN

Western Carolina University

WILEY

To Susan

VP & Executive Publisher	George Hoffman
Executive Editor	Christopher Johnson
Sponsoring Editor	Marian Provenzano
Project Editor	Brian Baker
Associate Editor	Kyla Buckingham
Editorial Assistant	Kristen Mucci
Editorial Assistant	Jacqueline Hughes
Marketing Manager	Margaret Barrett
Photo Researcher	James Russiello
Senior Production Manager	Janis Soo
Production Editor	Arun Surendar
Cover Designer	Kenji Ngieng
Cover Photo Credit	© Gordon Dixon/Getty Images, Inc.

This book was set in 10/12 Times Roman by Laserwords Private Limited and was printed and bound by R R Donnelley.

Founded in 1807, John Wiley & Sons, Inc. has been a valued source of knowledge and understanding for more than 200 years, helping people around the world meet their needs and fulfill their aspirations. Our company is built on a foundation of principles that include responsibility to the communities we serve and where we live and work.

In 2008, we launched a Corporate Citizenship Initiative, a global effort to address the environmental, social, economic, and ethical challenges we face in our business. Among the issues we are addressing are carbon impact, paper specifications and procurement, ethical conduct within our business and among our vendors, and community and charitable support. For more information, please visit our website: www.wiley.com/go/citizenship.

Copyright © 2015, 2012, 2008, 2005, 1998 John Wiley & Sons, Inc. All rights reserved. No part of this publication may be reproduced, stored in a retrieval system or transmitted in any form or by any means, electronic, mechanical, photocopying, recording, scanning or otherwise, except as permitted under Sections 107 or 108 of the 1976 United States Copyright Act, without either the prior written permission of the Publisher, or authorization through payment of the appropriate per-copy fee to the Copyright Clearance Center, Inc. 222 Rosewood Drive, Danvers, MA 01923, website www.copyright.com. Requests to the Publisher for permission should be addressed to the Permissions Department, John Wiley & Sons, Inc., 111 River Street, Hoboken, NJ 07030-5774, (201)748-6011, fax (201)748-6008, website http://www.wiley.com/go/permissions.

Evaluation copies are provided to qualified academics and professionals for review purposes only, for use in their courses during the next academic year. These copies are licensed and may not be sold or transferred to a third party. Upon completion of the review period, please return the evaluation copy to Wiley. Return instructions and a free-of-charge return mailing label are available at www.wiley.com/go/returnlabel. If you have chosen to adopt this textbook for use in your course, please accept this book as your complimentary desk copy. Outside of the United States, please contact your local sales representative.

Library of Congress Cataloging-in-Publication Data

Goodwin, C. James.
  A history of modern psychology / C. James Goodwin.—Fifth edition.
    pages cm.
  Includes bibliographical references and index.
  ISBN 978-1-118-83375-9 (pbk. : alk. paper) 1. Psychology—History. I. Title.
  BF105.G66 2015
  150.9'04—dc23

                                        2014039213

Printed in the United States of America

10 9 8 7 6 5 4

CONTENTS

CHAPTER 9   *GESTALT PSYCHOLOGY*   **244**

CHAPTER 10   *THE ORIGINS OF BEHAVIORISM*   **272**

CHAPTER 11   *THE EVOLUTION OF
BEHAVIORISM*   **302**

CHAPTER 15 *PSYCHOLOGY IN THE 21ST CENTURY* **429**

PREFACE

TO THE INSTRUCTOR

As you already know if you have taught the history of psychology course, it can be a tough sell. Students often come into the course with firm and long-standing negative preconceptions about studying history, prepared to agree that history is "just one d——d thing after another," as someone once said. And when they discover the last name of psychology's premier historian, E. G. Boring, they may nod their heads knowingly. This attitude is unfortunate, of course, because I can think of no more fascinating subject than the history of psychology. It is replete with extraordinary persons and events, and it yields insights into the basic questions still being asked in psychology today. More than any other course in the psychology curriculum, the history course gives students an overall perspective on their chosen field of study.

No one can be an informed psychologist without having some knowledge of the discipline's history. Our task as instructors is to show students how valuable a knowledge of psychology's history can be, help them connect psychology's present with its rich past, and get them to understand how exciting the journey from past to present has been. I hope that my textbook will aid in this process.

The book is titled a history of *modern* psychology, reflecting the decision about where to begin the course that faces everyone who teaches it. Psychology has deep roots in Western philosophical thought; hence, a full understanding of important and recurring themes requires some understanding of this heritage. Texts, however, differ in the depth of coverage given to our philosophical ancestors, tending to fall into two groups. Some books invest considerable effort in exploring philosophical issues and provide in-depth coverage dating back to the ancient Greeks. This certainly is a legitimate strategy, but not the one I have chosen to follow. Instead, my text belongs in the second grouping—that is, although not by any means ignoring philosophical roots, it devotes less space to them and more space to the recent history of psychology, especially that of the past 150 years. Like other "modern" histories of psychology, its treatment of philosophy will begin in the vicinity of Descartes and the British empiricists.

The decision about a starting point is partly pragmatic—it has been my long experience as a teacher of this course, which has to fit typically into a 15-week semester, that extensive treatment of philosophical thought between the time of the Greeks and Descartes makes it impossible to get very far into the 20th century ("It's December and we've just started Watson!"). I always remind myself that the course is not just a history or a philosophy course, but part of the psychology curriculum, and that if I want students to make meaningful connections between my course and their other psychology classes, an important goal for me, it is necessary to get to the 19th and 20th centuries as quickly as possible. The history course must teach students about the ideas and research of pioneer psychologists, especially those who worked within the past 150 years or so. Students have heard about some of these people in other courses (e.g., Hall in adolescent psychology, Watson in the learning course, Freud in personality, Binet in tests and measurements, Münsterberg in industrial/organizational psychology). The history course serves to build on that rudimentary knowledge and interconnect it.

As for the book's organizational structure, each chapter begins with a *Preview* and a set of *Chapter Objectives*, which set the stage for what is to come, and ends with a *Summary* of the chapter's contents. Each chapter also opens with a carefully selected quote that is also worked into the narrative at some point in the chapter. Words printed in boldface in each chapter are defined at that point in the chapter and in a Glossary found after the References. To enable the student to make some connections between psychology and the rest of the world, timelines are included at the end of the book after the index.

A password-protected online Instructor Companion Site includes

- A variety of assignments that I have developed over the years, as well as other assignments and activities culled from the journal *Teaching of Psychology*.

- A set of resources to help with lecture preparation; these resources include an annotated list of articles and books that undergraduates will find readable and can be used for a variety of course assignments.

- A Test Bank that includes multiple-choice, short answer, matching, short essay, and comprehensive essay questions.

To reach these resources, go to www.wiley.com/college/goodwin, and select "Instructor Companion Site."

New to the Fifth Edition

- The overall organization of the book remains about the same as in the fourth edition. I have worked through every line of the book, clarifying points that appeared unclear and elaborating when necessary. The file that I keep as I go along, which documents specific changes from the prior edition, runs close to eight pages (contact me at jgoodwin@wcu.edu, and I would be glad to send you a copy).

- I have tried to keep up with scholarship in the history of psychology, and that is reflected in a net increase of about 50 references in this edition.

- Although I have maintained a fair amount of biographical information because it adds interest and helps situate historical characters in their times and places, I have reduced this information somewhat and replaced the space with more information on psychology's important concepts, research, and theories.

- There is a new type of boxed insert, *From the Miles Papers ...*, which appears in 9 of the 15 chapters. These involve excerpts taken from documents in the Walter Miles papers, included to add depth to chapter topics and to give students some insight into the kind of material likely to be found in archival collections.

- Coverage of the following topics has been added or elaborated from prior editions: Triplett's study as origin myth, E. W. Scripture's postacademic life, Thomas Willis and brain anatomy, Luigi Galvani's research on electricity, the psychograph, the work of Johann Herbart, apperceptive mass, origins of stylus mazes, the Baldwin effect, the 1928 Carlisle conference, applying reaction time to football, European psychotechnics, the Nazi threat to Jewish researchers, Ivan Pavlov's lab as factory, the 1929 Yale conference, E. R. Guthrie's learning theory, medical approaches to mental illness (fever therapy, insulin coma therapy, metrazol shock therapy, ECT), shell shock and its treatment in England, Morris Viteles and his work in industrial psychology, Stanley Milgram's obedience research, and Henry Murray's personology.

TO THE STUDENT

One of the primary themes of this book is that understanding the present requires knowing the past. You know something about psychology's present state by virtue of the other psychology courses you have taken, but you are probably not aware of the many interconnections that exist among the different areas of psychology you have studied. One goal of a history of psychology course is to make those connections. For example, although I am sure that you know something about the nature–nurture issue, you probably are not knowledgeable about how our current understanding of it has been affected by Darwinian theory, by the search for tests of mental ability, and by the behavior of rats in mazes. I hope these connections, as well as many others, will be obvious to you after you have finished the course.

You are about to meet some fascinating individuals who helped shape the psychology that you have been studying in other courses. Although we tend to think of historical figures as being somehow remote and different from ordinary persons, I have tried to show that these individuals were real human beings, often struggling with the kinds of problems that affect the rest of us. In the pages that follow, you will be meeting some people whose efforts led to some extraordinary accomplishments, but who also dealt with some of the same issues that may be of concern to you. For example,

- Are you tired of school and ready to get out into the "real" world and learn things on your own? Read about René Descartes (Chapter 2).

- Are you fed up with the way things are, wish you could change them, and willing to take on the status quo?
  Learn about John B. Watson (Chapter 10), B. F. Skinner (Chapter 11), or Dorothea Dix (Chapter 12).

- Are you faced with major decisions about your future and worried about taking a big career risk?
  Refer to the discussion about E. B. Titchener (Chapter 7) or Wolfgang Köhler (Chapter 9).

- Are you fascinated by research and enjoy collecting and analyzing data?
  See Hermann Ebbinghaus (Chapter 4), Ivan Pavlov (Chapter 10), or Leon Festinger (Chapter 14).

- Do you have a strong desire to help others?
  Read about Mary Cover Jones (Chapter 10), William Tuke (Chapter 12), or Carl Rogers (Chapter 13).

- Do you have a strong desire to achieve but face a stacked deck because of racism or sexism?
  Learn about the determination of Francis Sumner, Mary Calkins (both in Chapter 6), or Eleanor Gibson (Chapter 14).

- Are you a slow starter, not doing well in school, and wondering if you have a future?
  Study the early life of Wilhelm Wundt (Chapter 4), Charles Darwin (Chapter 5), or Donald Hebb (Chapter 14).

- Are you concerned that health problems or a physical handicap will make it difficult for you to reach your goals?
Read about Lewis Terman (Chapter 8) or Clark Hull (Chapter 11).

I hope that you will enjoy reading this book, that you will learn something about psychology's present by learning about its past, and that you will gain some insight into human behavior in the process. At the end of the course, I hope that you will want to continue learning more about psychology's fascinating history.

To help you master the material in this text, I have prepared an online Study Guide. You can find it by going to www.wiley.com/college/goodwin, clicking on the book's image, and selecting "Student Companion Site" for this text. Among other things, it includes some practice tests that will help you ace the course.

ACKNOWLEDGMENTS

My graduate training was in the experimental psychology of memory and was typical in many ways: long hours in the lab, combined with joy whenever p was less than .05. What was a bit different for me, however, was the fact that my dissertation director, Darryl Bruce, was excited about psychology's history, and the feeling was infectious. While teaching me to be a good scientist, he was also convincing me of history's great truth—you cannot understand the present without knowing the past. So to Darryl, who died in 2011 from complications following a stroke, I owe a debt that I will never be able to repay.

In Chapter 1, you will see a photo of John Popplestone and Marion White McPherson of the Archives of the History of American Psychology (AHAP) in Akron, Ohio. AHAP was about a 90-minute ride from my house for a number of years, so I benefited from their hospitality and their eagerness to help an aspiring psychologist–historian on numerous occasions. Marion died in 2000, John in 2013. The Director of AHAP since 1999, David Baker, has also been immensely helpful to me and has become a good friend. I would also like to thank my colleagues in the Society for the History of Psychology (APA – Division 26), especially Ludy Benjamin, Don Dewsbury, Larry Smith, Al Fuchs, Wade Pickren, Alex Rutherford, Andrew Winston, and Chris Green, for their support and encouragement as I struggled to become knowledgeable as a historian of psychology.

The editors and staff at John Wiley continue to impress. Special thanks go to the psychology editor Chris Johnson, who has been consistently supportive of all three of my Wiley books. Thanks also go to Arun Surendar, who coordinated the production process with great precision and unusual speed.

Finally, I am grateful for the many thoughtful comments of the stalwart reviewers over the previous editions.

CHAPTER 1

INTRODUCING PSYCHOLOGY'S HISTORY

History isn't just something that's behind us; it's also something that follows us.
—Henning Mankill, 2011

PREVIEW AND CHAPTER OBJECTIVES

This chapter opens by describing why it is important to know about psychology's history. A contrast is drawn between traditional histories of psychology, which emphasize the contributions of distinguished psychologists, the outcomes of famous experiments, and the debates among adherents of different "schools" of psychology, and a newer approach, which tries to situate events and people in a broader historical context. This chapter also considers the methods used by historians to conduct research in history and the problems they face when constructing historical narratives from available data. After you finish this chapter, you should be able to:

- Describe the events during the 1960s that led to a renewed interest in psychology's history among psychologists
- Explain why it is important for everyone to have some understanding of history
- Explain why it is especially important for psychology students to understand psychology's history
- Distinguish between "old" and "new" history, as Furumoto used the terms
- Understand the concept of an origin myth, and explain the purpose such myths serve
- Distinguish between presentist and historicist views of history, and articulate the dangers of presentist thinking
- Distinguish between internal and external histories of psychology, and describe the benefits of examining each
- Distinguish between personalistic and naturalistic approaches to history
- Define historiography and describe the various selection and interpretation problems faced by historians when they do their work
- Explain how the process of doing history can produce some degree of confidence that a measure of truth has been attained

WHY TAKE THIS COURSE?

Psychologists have always been interested in the history of their discipline. Histories of psychology were written soon after psychology itself appeared on the academic scene (e.g., Baldwin, 1913), and at least two of psychology's most famous books, E. G. Boring's *A History of Experimental Psychology* (1929; 1950) and Edna Heidbreder's *Seven Psychologies* (1933) are histories. It was during the 1960s, however, that significant interest in the history of psychology as a specialized area of research began. Many people were involved, but the major impetus came from a clinical psychologist with a passion for history, Robert I. Watson (1909–1980). He began with a call to arms, a 1960 *American Psychologist* article entitled "The History of Psychology: A Neglected Area" (Watson, 1960), in which he documented a paucity of articles about history in psychology journals and urged his colleagues to renew their interest in psychology's history. Watson then mobilized a small group of like-minded psychologists within the American Psychological Association into a "History of Psychology Group." By the end of the decade, this group had accomplished the sorts of things that mark the creation of a new specialized discipline—they formed professional organizations (e.g., Division 26 of the APA, otherwise known as the Society for the History of Psychology), they created journals (e.g., *The Journal of the History of the Behavioral Sciences*), and they established institutional bases for the production of historical research (e.g., a graduate program at the University of New Hampshire; the Archives of the History of American Psychology at the University of Akron).

Today psychologists generally recognize the importance of knowing the history of their discipline, and a history of psychology course is offered in virtually all psychology departments and required for psychology majors in about half of those departments (Fuchs & Viney, 2002). Despite this consensus, students majoring in psychology are often surprised to find themselves in a course about the history of psychology. They check with their chemistry-major friends and find nothing comparable in that department. They examine the college catalog and discover that the closest course is one in the history of science, but the history department teaches it, not one of the science departments. What's going on? Why is there a history of psychology course taught by a psychologist, but not a history of chemistry course taught by a chemist?

The rationale for a history of psychology course is important, and will be considered shortly. First, however, let's examine the more general question of why it is important to study the history of anything. Is it true that "history is more or less bunk," as Henry Ford once said (quoted in Simonton, 1994, p. 3), or is it more likely, in the words of Swedish novelist Henning Mankill (2011), that "history isn't just something that's behind us; it's also something that follows us" (p. 220)?

Why Study History?

A typical answer to this question is that knowing history helps avoid the mistakes of the past and provides a guide to the future. These well-worn platitudes contain a germ of truth, but they are both simplistic. Concerning the "mistake" argument, rather than learning from the past, much of history appears to provide evidence that humans ignore the past. This possibility led the philosopher–historian G. W. F. Hegel to worry that the only true lesson of history is that people don't learn anything from history (Gilderhus, 2000). This almost certainly overstates the case, but it is also true that knowing the past provides, at best, only a rough guide, for history never really repeats itself because all events are tied into the unique historical context in which they occur. History is also a less than reliable guide to the future. Historians recognize this—as psychology's eminent historian, E. G. Boring, once wrote, "The past is not a crystal ball.... The seats on the train of progress all face backwards: you can see the past but only guess about the future" (1963a, p. 5)—but the acknowledgment seldom prevents them from venturing forecasts.

If knowing history is won't prevent repeating mistakes, and if history is an imperfect (at best) means of forecasting the future, then what is left? *The present.* In the sentence immediately following the one I just quoted from Boring, he wrote: "Yet a knowledge of history, although it can never be complete and fails miserably to foretell the future, has a huge capacity for adding significance to the understanding of the present" (1963a, p. 5). I believe the single most important reason to study history is that the present cannot be understood without knowing something about the past—how the present came to be.

Think of any current event, and you will recognize that it is impossible to understand the event adequately without knowing some of the history leading to it. For example, consider some recent history within psychology. I am sure that you have heard about APA, the American Psychological Association. You might also know about or at least have heard of APS—the Association for Psychological Science.[1] You might even know that the APS is a fairly recent creature—it was born in 1988. Perhaps you also recognize that the APS seems more focused on scientific research than the APA, but you might be wondering why there need to be two organizations for psychologists. Knowing some history would help you understand this. Specifically, your understanding of why APS exists and its purpose would be vastly enhanced if you knew of the long-standing tensions between research psychologists and psychologists whose prime interest is in the professional practice of psychology (e.g., psychotherapy). The problem traces to APA's very beginnings in the late 19th century and contributed to the formation of a separate group of "Experimentalists" in 1904 (the story of this remarkable group is elaborated in Chapter 7). Also, when the APA was reorganized after World War II, the divisional structure that exists today was designed in part to reconcile the conflicting goals of scientists and practitioners. The goodwill that accompanied the end of the war led those with different interests in psychology to unite, but the unity didn't last long. After decades of frustration with APA, researchers formed their own group—APS. Without knowing something of this history, you could never have a clear understanding of the APS, why it exists today, or why there is lingering tension between APS leaders and the APA's governing structure. And there are practical consequences. As a student, if you have an interest in becoming a psychologist, you will probably want to join one of these organizations as a student affiliate. Deciding which to join requires knowing something of the history—someone aiming for a career in the professional practice of psychology might be more likely to join APA, but a future experimental psychologist might be better served by joining APS.

Another aspect of the importance of the past for understanding the present is that knowledge of history helps us put current events in a better perspective. For instance, we sometimes believe that our current times are, as Charles Dickens wrote, "the worst of times." We complain about the seemingly insurmountable problems and the ever-present dangers (e.g., from terrorism) that seem to accompany life in the early years of the 21st century. We long for the "good old days," a simpler time when nobody locked their doors and a good house could be ordered as a kit from Sears (this is true). We think that there really used to be places like Disney World's Main Street, USA. But knowing history is a good

---

[1] In 2006, APS changed its name from the American Psychological Society to the Association for Psychological Science. The name change was designed to highlight the scientific focus of the organization, while at the same making it international in scope.

corrective here. Noted historian Daniel Boorstin, in an essay entitled "The Prison of the Present" (1971), described this fallacy:

> We sputter against the Polluted Environment—as if it had come with the age of the automobile. We compare our air not with the odor of horse dung and the plague of flies and the smells of garbage and human excrement which filled the cities of the past, but with the honeysuckle perfumes of some nonexistent City Beautiful. We forget that even if the water in many cities today is not spring-pure … , still for most of history the water of the cities (and of the countryside) was undrinkable. We reproach ourselves for the ills of disease and malnutrition, and forget that until recently, enteritis and measles and whooping cough, diphtheria and typhoid, were killing diseases of childhood, … [and] polio was a summer monster. (pp. 47–48)

Knowing history won't give us easy answers to current problems, but it certainly can immunize us against the belief that these problems are many times worse than they used to be. In fact, knowing the past can provide a comforting connection with it, and being aware of how others have wrestled with similar problems can provide us with some present-day guidance. There is at least the potential for learning from the past.

Besides making it possible for us to understand the present better, studying history provides other benefits. For example, it forces an attitude adjustment, keeping us humble in two ways. First, we occasionally delude ourselves into thinking we know a lot (especially true in my profession—university teaching). Studying history is a good antidote. For example, I grew up in southeastern New England, not far from Plymouth, and I thought I knew something about the Pilgrims. However, having read Nathaniel Philbrick's (2006) brilliant history of the Pilgrims, *Mayflower*, I am amazed by how little I knew—and by how much of what I thought I knew (e.g., about Thanksgiving) was dead wrong. Second, sometimes ignorance of the past can lead us to a kind of arrogance; we believe that the present is the culmination of centuries of progress and that modern-day accomplishments and thinking are more sophisticated and far surpass those of a crude and uninformed past. Knowing history, however, forces an understanding that each age has its own marvelous accomplishments and its own creative geniuses. Modern-day neuroscientists seem to make fascinating discoveries every day, but the importance of their discoveries and the quality of their scientific thinking do not surpass the elegance of Pierre Flourens's 19th-century investigations of the brain (Chapter 3), which disproved phrenology.

Finally, studying history ultimately means searching for answers to one of life's most fundamental yet perplexing questions: What does it mean to be human? To study the history of World War II is to delve into the basic nature of prejudice, aggression, and violence. To study the American Revolution is to examine the human desire for freedom and self-determination. To study the history of Renaissance art is to study the human passion for aesthetic pleasure. And to the extent that history involves people behaving in various situations, studying history means studying and trying to understand human behavior. For this reason alone, psychologists should be inherently attracted to the subject.

Why Study Psychology's History?

The preceding rationale for studying history is sufficient by itself to justify studying psychology's history, but there are additional reasons why psychologists should be interested in their ancestry. First, compared with other sciences, psychology is still in its infancy—not much more than 130 years old. Much of the content of the other psychology courses you have taken traces back through at least half of those years, and many of the so-called classic studies that you learned about (e.g., Pavlov's conditioning research) formed a major part of the first half of those years. Hence, modern psychology is closely tied to its past, so being a literate student of psychology requires knowing some history.

A second and related reason for an interest in psychology's history among psychologists is that the field is still grappling with many of the same topics that occupied it a century ago. Thus, an important issue today is the heritability of traits ranging from intelligence to shyness to schizophrenia. This nature–nurture issue, first popularized more than 140 years ago by Sir Francis Galton (Chapter 5) and pondered by humans for centuries, reverberates through the history of psychology. Seeing the parallels between the arguments made now about the interactive influence of heredity and environment, and comparing them with those made in earlier times, you will gain a more informed understanding of the issue.

Earlier, a question was raised about the presence of a history of psychology course and the absence of a history of chemistry course. Whereas an understanding of current research and related issues is essential in psychology, the situation is somewhat different in chemistry. Although the history of alchemy, with its stories of how people tried to transform lead into gold, is fascinating and can teach us a great deal about how science works and evolves, it doesn't inform today's students about the chemical properties of lead or of gold. Chemists, who tend to think (naively, as it happens) of their science as steadily progressing from the errors of the past to the truth of the present, aren't normally interested in cluttering their students' minds with "old" ideas. There is a small element of truth to this model of science as advancing through history (nobody tries to turn lead into gold anymore), but it is nonetheless unfortunate that many scientists don't see the value of studying the history of their discipline. At the very least, it would round out their education and teach them something about how scientific thinking has evolved. Indeed, there ought to be a history of chemistry course for chemistry students to take. Instead, they have to settle for a history of science course, typically taught in history rather than science departments. Psychology majors, on the other hand, are lucky—they get their own history course.

A third reason why the history of psychology course exists is that it can provide some unity for what has become a diverse and highly specialized field. Despite its youth, psychology in the early 21st century is notable for its lack of unity. Indeed, some observers (e.g., Koch, 1992a) have argued that a single field of psychology no longer exists, that a neuroscientist investigating the functioning of endorphins has virtually nothing in common with an industrial psychologist studying the effectiveness of various management styles. Yet all psychologists do have something in common—their history. For the psychology major who has taken a seemingly disconnected variety of courses ranging from developmental to abnormal to social psychology, the history course can serve as a synthesizing experience. By the time you reach the final chapter of this text, where the issue of psychology's increased specialization is again addressed, you will have learned enough to begin understanding the interconnectedness among the different areas of psychology.

Fourth, an understanding of psychology's history makes one a more critical thinker. By being aware of the history of various treatments for psychological disorders, for example, the discerning student is better able to evaluate modern claims for some "revolutionary breakthrough" in psychotherapy. A close examination of this allegedly unique therapy might reveal similarities to earlier approaches. The historically literate student also is aware that on many other occasions, initial excitement over a flashy new therapy (e.g., lobotomy) is tempered by a later failure to find convincing evidence that it works. Similarly, knowing history makes one skeptical about "large claims" (Helson, 1972), for example, the recent idea that all psychology can be known by understanding the brain and that neuropsychology, therefore, is the future of psychology. Those with an understanding of history will recognize the similarity to claims made in the 19th century about phrenology, will recognize that a brain scan showing activity in area X when a person is lying does not explain lying, and will understand why neuropsychology is sometimes referred to as the new phrenology (Satel & Lilienfeld, 2013).

Finally, the history of psychology course may be a history course, but it is also a psychology course. Thus, one of its goals is to continue educating about human behavior. Studying historical individuals as they helped develop the science of psychology can only increase our understanding of what makes people behave the way they do. For instance, our understanding of scientific creativity can be enhanced by studying the lives and works of historically creative individuals (e.g., Hermann Ebbinghaus, described in Chapter 4, who created nonsense syllabus to study memory). Some insight into the psychology of controversy and the rigid, dogmatic adherence to one's beliefs can be gained by studying the behavior of scientists engaged in bitter debate with their peers (e.g., the Baldwin–Titchener controversy, described in Chapter 7). In general, if all human behavior reflects a complex interplay between individuals and the environments they inhabit, then studying the lives of historical characters being shaped by and in turn shaping their environments can only increase our understanding of the factors that affect human behavior.

KEY ISSUES IN PSYCHOLOGY'S HISTORY

A common misconception of history is that historians simply "find out what happened" and then write it down in chronological order. As you will learn in the next two sections of this chapter, the process is considerably more complicated. When they are engaged in their craft, historians are affected by several important issues. These were nicely articulated by Furumoto, in a 1989 article distinguishing between what she referred to as "old" and "new" history.

The old history of psychology, according to Furumoto (1989), emphasizes the accomplishments of "great" psychologists and celebrates "classic studies" and "breakthrough discoveries." Within psychology, the preservation and retelling of these "great events" helped psychology secure an identity as an established scientific discipline. The milestones, whether accurately described or not, are passed down from history text to history text. Furthermore, previous insights or achievements are valued only if they somehow "anticipated" or led to some modern idea or research outcome. Old research or theory that is of no current relevance is considered erroneous or quaint and is either discarded or seen as an example of "how far we've come." Thus, from the standpoint of old history, the purpose of the history of psychology is to legitimize and even to glorify present-day psychology and to show how it has progressed from the murky depths of its unscientific past to its modern scientific eminence.

One effect of the old history thinking about the past is the creation of so-called **origin myths**. These are stories overemphasizing the importance of particular events in psychology's history. Their purpose is to highlight the contrast between what is said to be a prescientific approach to some psychological phenomenon and the emergence of a more scientific strategy. For example, modern social psychologists consider their field to be one in which scientific methods are used to establish certain laws about human social behavior. Fair enough. Holding this belief, of course, raises the question of when social psychology became "experimental" (i.e., real science, and therefore "worthy"). That is, when did it originate? The further back in history this origin can be placed, the greater the legitimacy of an experimental social psychology ("Oh yes, we have been around for a very long time, using science to explore social behavior."). If experimental social psychology could be said to originate in the 19th century, for instance, then the social psychologist can claim well over 100 years of research, suggesting that modern social psychology is (a) well established and (b) has been accumulating an extraordinary amount of scientifically based knowledge over the years.

These concerns led Haines and Vaughan (1979) to ask whether 1898 was a "'great date' in the history of experimental social psychology" (p. 323). Their answer: not really. This conclusion probably came as a surprise to many social psychologists because 1898 was the publication date for what has become a famous study by Norman Triplett, who wondered why cyclists seem to go faster when they race against others than when they ride alone. He created a simple apparatus that simulated racing and appeared to demonstrate that the presence of a competitor "facilitated" performance (Triplett, 1898). This is similar to a research phenomenon later called "social facilitation" and so, to social psychologists in the mid-20th century, Triplett's study seemed to be an early experimental demonstration of the phenomenon. Hence, some (e.g., G. Allport, 1954a) argued that Triplett was the founder of experimental social psychology, and the cycling study was the origin point. Now, the Triplett study was interesting one, but it is hard to justify it as the start of experimental social psychology. Triplett certainly did not think it originated anything like a new discipline—he was just interested in cycling. And a strong research tradition in social psychology did *not* begin to develop in the aftermath of the study, as one might expect if the Triplett study was a turning point. Deliberate efforts to make social psychology research based did not occur until the 1920s, with the work of Floyd Allport (1924), whose work is mentioned briefly in Chapter 14, and a significant push toward experimental research by social psychologists didn't occur until the work of Leon Festinger (also discussed in Chapter 14) in the 1950s. Yet modern social psychology texts still continue to trace the origins of experimental social psychology to Triplett, and the origin myth continues to be promoted.[2]

Old versus new approaches to psychology's history can be characterized in terms of three contrasts. Old history tends to be presentist, internal, and personalistic. New history, on the other hand, is more historicist, external, and naturalistic.

Presentism versus Historicism

Earlier, I argued that a major reason for studying history is to better understand what is happening in the present. This is indeed a valid argument. On the other hand, to interpret and assess the past *only* in terms of present understanding is to be guilty of **presentism**. In an editorial in the opening volume of the *Journal of the History of the Behavioral Sciences*, George Stocking (1965) contrasted presentism with an approach called **historicism**. As he described it, the presentist interprets historical events only with reference to modern knowledge and values, whereas the historicist tries to understand the same event in terms of the knowledge and values in existence at the time of the event. Because the historicist tries to place historical events within the overall context of their times, this approach is sometimes called a *contextual* approach to history. The danger of presentist thinking is that it misleads us into thinking that individuals in the past should have known better and that they ought to have foreseen what was coming. Consequently, we may be led to judge historical individuals more harshly than we ought to. "What were they thinking?" we say to ourselves.

To demonstrate the dangers of presentist thinking, consider some aspects of the history of intelligence testing. As you will learn in Chapter 8, in the years just before World War I, the American psychologist Henry Goddard was invited to Ellis Island in New York to help screen immigrants. Those deemed "unfit" for various reasons were returned to their country of origin. Goddard firmly believed that intelligence was an inherited trait and that it could be measured with a brand-new technology—something created in France and just beginning to be called an IQ test. Goddard used a version of this test to identify "feebleminded" immigrants, and his work contributed to the deportation of untold numbers of people. His conclusion that large percentages of immigrants were "morons" (a term he invented to describe

---

[2] A close reading of the Triplett study shows that the "social facilitation" explanation oversimplifies what he apparently found (Stroebe, 2012). Thus, only about half of the subjects in his study performed better in competition than by themselves. The others were unaffected or even adversely affected. Furthermore, subsequent statistical analysis (not available to Triplett in 1898) questioned whether the study found any differences at all.

a subcategory of feeblemindedness) might have contributed to the atmosphere that led Congress to pass restrictive immigration quotas in the 1920s. From today's standpoint, on the basis of an additional 75 years or so of research, we know about the need for caution when using and interpreting IQ tests. Hence, we find it difficult to believe that someone as smart as Goddard could have behaved with such obvious bias. "What was he thinking?" we might ask ourselves. But to understand Goddard's behavior, it is necessary to study it from the vantage point of the historical period in which it occurred instead of that of today. This means knowing about such things as (a) the powerful influence of Darwinian thinking and Mendelian genetics on the psychological testers of that day, which led easily to a belief that intelligence was a trait that had been naturally selected and enabled a physically weak species (humans) to adapt to their environment during the "struggle for existence" and was therefore inherited; (b) the nation's fears of being overrun with immigrants (large-scale immigration was a fairly new phenomenon at that time); and (c) the assumption, not yet brought into question by such inventions as atomic bombs, that any new technology (e.g., IQ tests) with the "scientific" seal of approval meant "progress" and was therefore good. The list could be continued but the point is clear. Goddard's work cannot be fairly evaluated by what we know today; it can be understood only in the context of its times. On the other hand, his work does have relevance for us in the present. Knowing about it can (a) help us better understand modern concerns about immigration—it's not a new problem; (b) inform us of the subtle influence of racism and other forms of bigotry, even in intelligent people; and (c) make us properly cautious about the alleged wonders of new technologies that arrive in our own day. Furthermore, just because we attempt to understand Goddard within the context of his own time, this does not mean that we cannot judge his actions; but our criticisms should be made with some caution, taking the form of arguments that were also made by others during the period in question. Thus, although the past can help us understand the present, our knowledge about the present should not be used to judge the past.

The Goddard episode illustrates how difficult it is for us to avoid a presentist orientation (Hull, 1979). After all, we are the products of our own personal histories, and it is perhaps impossible to ask us to think like a person who never experienced the events of 9/11 or the impact of digital technology. Nonetheless, for the historian and the reader of history it is important to at least be aware of the dangers of a presentist view of history and to constantly seek to understand historical episodes on their own terms. One must recognize, as pointed out by historian Bernard Bailyn (Lathem, 1994), that "the past is not only distant, but different" (p. 53). He went on to write that the major obstacle in overcoming presentism (or "anachronism," as historians often call it) is the problem of "overcoming the knowledge of the outcome. This is one of the great impediments to a truly contextualized history" (p. 53). As to how we might go beyond our knowledge of outcomes and overcome presentist thinking, Bailyn had this suggestion:

> Somehow one has to recapture, and build into the story, contemporaries' ignorance of the future.... One ... tries to avoid assigning the heroism or villainy that was unclear at the time but that was determined by later outcomes. And, if possible, one gives a sympathetic account of the losers. If one can, up to a certain point, work sympathetically with the losers, one can—in some small part at least—overcome the knowledge of the outcome. (pp. 53–54)

Let me close this section by giving you an example of presentist writing that I found while reading a biography of Sir Isaac Newton (White, 1997). Even good writers and historians can fall into the trap. One of Newton's strong avocations was alchemy, the quest to create gold from base metals. In describing the alchemy interests of one of Newton's predecessors, Paracelsus (famous in the history of medicine), the author wrote that "following many an alchemist in a stereotypical fixation with *finding the unattainable and achieving the impossible*, [Paracelsus] traveled Europe in search of the secrets of the ancients, squandering much of his talent and any money he earned along the way" (p. 120; emphasis added). This is a good example of writing from the standpoint of knowing the outcome (alchemy failed), while ignoring the importance of alchemy to the history of science and the historical context that made alchemy a respected endeavor for a time.

Internal versus External History

Histories of psychology are often written by psychologists who wish to trace the development of the theories and research traditions held by various psychologists. This kind of approach is referred to as an **internal history**—what is written occurs entirely within ("internal to") the discipline of psychology. Such an approach has the value of providing detailed descriptions of the evolution of theory and research, but it ignores those influences outside psychology that also influence the discipline. An **external history** considers those outside influences.

Internal histories are often referred to as histories of ideas. Typically, they are written by people trained in the specific discipline being analyzed, and they tend to be written by people with little or no expertise in history per se. They are inward looking, focusing on the development of ideas or the progression of research to the exclusion of the larger world. On the other hand, external histories take the broader view—they examine societal, economic, institutional, and extradisciplinary influences. An exclusively internal history is narrow and loses the richness of historical context, whereas an excessively external history can fail to convey an adequate understanding of the ideas and contributions of a discipline's key figures. A balance is needed.

The interplay between internal and external history is demonstrated nicely in the history of cognitive psychology, the study of such phenomena as attention, memory, language, and thinking. The story of cognitive psychology is told in Chapter 14, but for now a sketch of it provides a nice contrast between internal and external history. From the standpoint of internal history, cognitive psychology's rise in the United States is often seen in relation to the decline of behaviorism. Behaviorism was a force in American psychology throughout the 1930s and 1940s, and well into the 1950s. Part of its attraction was its seeming ability to explain, by means of conditioning principles, all that was important about behavior. Humans were a product of their conditioning history, so the argument went. One problem, however, became increasingly clear in the 1950s: Behaviorist accounts of human language were inadequate. The nature of language and the learning of language by children seemed to be inconsistent with conditioning principles. That is, *within psychology*, a shift began to occur from a behaviorist paradigm to one that emphasized cognitive factors.

External to psychology, there were several other forces at work that helped bring about what some called a cognitive revolution. First, it is no coincidence that interest in cognitive psychology occurred in parallel with the growth and development of computer science because psychologists began to see the computer as an interesting metaphor for the human brain. In both cases, information was taken in from the environment, "processed" in various ways internally, and then put in the form of some output. In memory research, for example, diagrams of memory processes looked just like computer flowcharts, tracking the flow of information through a system. Second, the momentum for a shift from behaviorist to cognitive models grew significantly in the 1960s, a decade of great disruption and change in American society. The cultural climate embodied by the phrase "change is the only constant" made it easier for psychologists to embrace change within their discipline. In sum, then, understanding the development of cognitive psychology requires knowing not just about the difficulties encountered by behaviorism (e.g., language) but also about developments in the wider world (computer science, the '60s).

Personalistic versus Naturalistic History

In addition to the presentist–historicist and internal–external distinctions, one additional contrast is worth noting. That distinction is between a personalistic history, one that sees the actions of individual historical characters as the prime movers in history, and a naturalistic history, one that emphasizes the overall intellectual and cultural climate of a particular historical era—what the German philosopher Hegel called the **zeitgeist**.

According to a **personalistic history**, the important events in history result from the heroic (or evil) actions of individuals, and without those individuals, history would be vastly different. Their actions are said to provide history's "turning points." This approach is often associated with the 19th-century historian and essayist Thomas Carlyle, whose "On Heroes, Hero Worship and the Heroic in History," written in 1840, is best remembered for this line: "The history of what man has accomplished in this world is at bottom the history of the great men who have worked here" (quoted in Boring, 1963a, p. 6). According to this view, people like Newton, Darwin, and Freud changed the course of the history of science; without them, the history would have been completely different. From this standpoint, the preferred method of writing history is biography. As a consequence of this approach, so-called **eponyms** (Boring, 1963a) are created. That is, historical periods are identified with reference to the individuals whose actions are believed to be critical in shaping events. Thus, we read of Newtonian physics, Darwinian biology, and Freudian psychology.

The personalistic approach has intuitive appeal. As individuals, we like to think of ourselves as agents—as individuals who have an effect on our world. It is not much of a leap from this type of thinking to an assumption that history is also profoundly affected by individuals: "Since we are agents, we have an interest in the efficacy of agency" (Menand, 2011, p. 69). Although Edwin G. Boring (featured in this chapter's Close-Up) favored a naturalistic model of history and argued that "history is continuous and sleek," he recognized that influential people "are the handles that you put on its smooth sides" (Boring, 1963b, p. 130). Boring argued that the persistence of a personalistic approach to history results from several factors, including a human need for heroes and the need of hardworking scientists for personal recognition (e.g., Nobel Prizes). More important, if history is continuous and sleek, then it is also immensely complex. In seeking to understand it, we try to reduce the complexity to understandable dimensions—categorization is a universal cognitive process, essential for achieving understanding. Our recall of concepts like the Freudian unconscious and Pavlovian conditioning is easier when the eponyms serve as retrieval cues.

CLOSE-UP

EDWIN G. BORING (1886–1968)

It is unfortunate that psychology's most famous historian has a name that students often associate with the general topic of history. In fact, E. G. Boring's writings are lively and elegant. His version of psychology's history has been criticized, but historians of psychology owe a great debt to Boring's pioneering historical work.

While an engineering student at Cornell University, Boring first encountered psychology in the fall of 1905 by taking an elective course in elementary psychology taught by the celebrated E. B. Titchener (Chapter 7). Boring described the lectures as "magic, so potent that even my roommates demanded, each lecture day, to be told what had been said" (Boring, 1961b, p. 18). He was not converted at that point, however; he continued his engineering studies and earned a master's degree in 1908. But after 2 years as an engineer for a steel company and as a high school teacher, he returned to Cornell and earned a PhD from Titchener in 1914. While at Cornell, Boring's research interests included (a) human maze learning, during which he met, fell in love with, and eventually married one of his research colleagues, fellow doctoral student Lucy May (who died in 1996 at the age of 109); (b) nerve regeneration, studied firsthand by severing a nerve in his arm and charting its recovery; (c) the learning processes of schizophrenics; (d) eyewitness accuracy; and (e) his dissertation topic, visceral sensitivity. Boring studied this last topic by learning to swallow a stomach tube to varying depths, then pouring various substances into the tube and noting the (often unpleasant) sensory effects (Jaynes, 1969b). Nobody could ever accuse Boring of not being involved in his work.

After finishing his degree at Cornell and staying on briefly as an instructor, Boring served in World War I in the Army testing program (Chapter 8), taught briefly at Clark University, and then went to Harvard in 1922, where he remained for the rest of his career. At Harvard, Boring spent the next decade building up the laboratory and trying to convince authorities that psychology should be a separate department, not just part of the philosophy department. This creation of a distinct psychology department did not occur until 1934. During the 1920s, he wrote his famous *A History of Experimental Psychology* (Boring, 1929), partly to further his political fight with the philosophers and administrators at Harvard, and partly to bolster basic research in experimental psychology at a time when most American psychologists seemed to be more interested in applied psychology (O'Donnell, 1979b).

In his years at Clark and Harvard, Boring's work habits, in imitation of Titchener, were legendary. In his words:

> [M]y friends, my children, and my students know how I have talked about the eighty-hour week in the fifty-week year (the 4,000-hour working year) and I have scorned those forty-hour academicians who take long summers off from work. I have no hobbies, except for a shop in my cellar. My vacations were never successful until I got a little study with a typewriter in it and could answer eight letters a day and write up the waiting papers. (Boring, 1961b, p. 14b)

Also in the tradition of Titchener, Boring taught the introductory course in psychology, believing that a student's first encounter with psychology should be from the master. He even became a pioneer in the video course: 38 half-hour programs on Boston's educational TV channel WGBH in 1960 featured Boring demonstrating various phenomena, but mainly sitting "on the corner of a table and talk[ing] in a friendly, enthusiastic, paternal manner to the red lights on whatever camera was on the air" (Boring, 1961b, p. 77; Figure 1.1).

APA's Division 26 was established in 1965, and some hoped that Boring would be its first president. According to Hilgard, Boring refused to run for the office but agreed to be named "honorary president." Boring's increasing deafness kept him away from the division's inaugural meeting during the APA 1966 convention, but he sent a note to be read, describing himself as the "ghost of History Past, when the interest in the history of psychology had not yet become as vigorous as it is now" (Hilgard, 1982, p. 310). Modern historians of psychology owe much to Boring's example.

Robert M. Pringle/Harvard Alumni Bulletin (now Harvard Magazine)

FIGURE 1.1 Teaching to the masses: E.G. Boring on educational TV in 1957, from Boring (1961b).

The alternative to a personalistic history is a **naturalistic history**, an approach emphasizing the forces of history that influence individuals. The Russian novelist Leo Tolstoy was a famous advocate of this determinist approach. One of his goals in writing the massive *War and Peace* was to demonstrate that history is moved by forces beyond the control of individuals. For Tolstoy, so-called great men like Napoleon were in reality mere agents of historical forces larger than themselves. In *War and Peace* he refers to kings and generals as history's slaves: "Every act of theirs, which appears to them an act of their own will, is in a historical sense involuntary and is related to the whole course of history and predestined from eternity" (Tolstoy, 1869/1942, p. 671).

Boring vigorously promoted a naturalistic view of history. Especially in his later years, he championed the zeitgeist concept, both in the second edition of his famous *A History of Experimental Psychology* (Boring, 1950) and in numerous essays. For Boring, understanding history meant understanding the historical forces that influenced the men and women living in a particular era. Although not denying Darwin's genius, for example, Boring argued that the concept of evolution was common in the 19th century and extended beyond just biology (to geology, for instance). Without Darwin, someone else would have produced a theory of biological evolution. Indeed, Darwin's theory might have been called the Darwin–Wallace theory, in recognition of Alfred Russel Wallace, a contemporary of Darwin's who independently developed virtually the identical theory (Chapter 5 tells this fascinating story). Great scientists can and do influence events, but simply focusing on individuals leaves unanswered the question of how those individuals were affected by the worlds in which they lived.

In support of the zeitgeist concept, Boring pointed to two kinds of historical events. In the first, called a **multiple**, two or more individuals independently make the same discovery at about the same time (Merton, 1961). Darwin and Wallace codiscovering natural selection at a time when evolutionary thinking was "in the air" is an example. Darwin's grandfather, Erasmus Darwin, illustrates the second type of event, a discovery or a theory that is said to be "ahead of its time." Like his more famous grandson, Erasmus developed a theory of evolution; but he did so in the 18th century, when belief in the immutability of species (i.e., each species is created in its finished form by God and doesn't change over time) was stronger than in the 19th century.

Relying on the zeitgeist as a way of explaining history can be problematic, however. For example, the uncritical observer might be tempted to *reify* (i.e., give a concrete and detached existence to an abstraction) the term *zeitgeist* and consider it a controlling force, independent of the historical persons who in fact give it meaning. That is, in answer to the question, "Why did event X occur instead of event Y at time Z?" one might be tempted to answer, "Because of the zeitgeist." But such an answer hardly explains the event in question. The concept of the zeitgeist invites one to examine the attitudes, values, and theories in existence at the time of some event to be explained, but it cannot exist by itself as some mysterious directing agent. As Ross (1969) pointed out with reference to the history of educational psychology:

> It has been stated, for example, that neither James, Dewey, Hall, Thorndike, Cattell, Galton, nor Darwin were necessary to the rapid development of educational psychology in America, for that was the trend of the "Zeitgeist." But certainly we only know what the Zeitgeist in fact *was* by the way in which James, Hall, Cattell, Darwin and others behaved. If they had not thought and acted the way they did, neither would the "Zeitgeist" they are said to embody. (p. 257; emphasis in the original)

Thus, a balanced view of history recognizes the complex interrelationships between people acting and the environments in which they act. The characters we will encounter shortly were all products of the world in which they lived, but they also made decisions that helped form and transform their world. Wallace might have been inspired to write a paper proposing a theory of evolution that matched the essence of Darwin's, but it is no accident that the term *evolution* is associated with Darwin and not with Wallace. It was Darwin who invested the years of research examining the intricacies of numerous species, and it was Darwin who followed up his initial writings with the monumental texts that brought evolution into its fullest development.

This Book's Point of View

This section of the chapter began with a reference to Furumoto's distinction between old and new history. Presentist, internal, and personalistic approaches typically go together and comprise what she referred to as the old history of psychology. It is a history that interprets events from the standpoint of the present, concentrates on the development of ideas within a discipline, and views progress as reflecting the accomplishments of important people. The new history of psychology, on the other hand, combines historicist, external, and naturalistic approaches. It tries to examine historical events on their own terms, with reference to the times in which they occurred, looks for the influence of extradisciplinary forces, and looks beyond great men and women to examine the contextual factors that helped to produce their ideas. Furumoto also pointed out that new history is more critically analytical than ceremonial and celebratory.

For historians of psychology conducting research, Furumoto's description of the new history of psychology provides a clear set of guidelines. The best historical research being published today is historicist, external, and naturalistic. For the author of a textbook and the teacher of the history of psychology course, however, the prescriptions about how to proceed are not quite as clear. As Dewsbury (1990b) pointed out in a review of several history of psychology texts, it is important to distinguish between "scholarly research directed at colleagues and … textbooks directed at introductory students" (p. 372). For the latter, the ideals of the new history need to be incorporated into the course, but they must be weighed against a need to inform students about content that is relevant to the psychology curriculum. This book presents a history of psychology that embraces the values espoused by Furumoto, but it is important to remember that the course for which this text is designed is a psychology course as well as a history course. Thus, although it is important to understand Pavlov's work within the historical climate of the early 20th century in Russia—especially the effects of the Russian Revolution of 1917—it is also important to understand the various classical conditioning phenomena that he investigated and how his work related to American behaviorism and influenced research on conditioning. It is important to understand the influence of computer science on the development of cognitive psychology, but it is also important for the psychology student to know about the difficulties that behaviorists experienced when trying to explain human language.

HISTORIOGRAPHY: DOING AND WRITING HISTORY

The simplest definition of **historiography** derives from the origins of the word itself—it means "to write history." But the term goes beyond the writing of historical narrative, referring also to theoretical issues like the ones just described, and to the methods that historians use when doing the historical research that eventually leads to written histories. Although the primary purpose of this book is to inform you about the history of psychology, a secondary goal is to give you some insight into the behavior of historians of psychology. That is, we will examine the kinds of data of interest to historians and the problems confronting historians as they do their work. At the outset, it is important to be aware of one crucial distinction. It might seem obvious, but accepting it allows one to realize that all history involves some degree of human interpretation. The distinction, pointed out by British historian Keith Jenkins (1991), is between "the past" and "history." They are not the same—as Jenkins pointed out, "the past is gone and history is what historians make of it when they go to work" (p. 8). Hence, the past refers to the infinite number of events that have occurred before the present moment, and the past can never be known because it is gone. What can be known is history—the manner in which *traces* of the past are selected, interpreted, and written into coherent narrative by professional historians. Whether those writings approach "truth" is an issue that is taken up at the end of the chapter. For now, let's examine these traces of history and what historians do with them.

Sources of Historical Data

Writers of psychology's history, especially textbook writers, have often relied on secondary sources to write their histories. A **secondary source** is a document that has been published and is typically an analysis or summary of some historical person, event, or period. These sources include books, articles published in journals, magazines, encyclopedia, and the like. Those doing research in the history of psychology, however, rely more heavily on **primary sources** of information, which are usually found in archives. An **archive** is normally an area within a university library that holds unpublished information. This primary source information includes university records, correspondence, diaries, speeches, minutes of the meetings of professional organizations, and documents donated by individuals connected in some way with the university. In addition to these separate university archives, historians of psychology often find primary source material at the Library of Congress and other governmental archives in Washington, D.C., and, especially, at the Archives of the History of American Psychology (AHAP), part of the Center for the History of Psychology at The University of Akron in Ohio. In general, primary source materials are items written or created at or near the time of some historical event, whereas secondary sources are written at some time after a historical event and serve to summarize or analyze.

AHAP was founded in 1965 by John Popplestone and Marion White McPherson (Figure 1.2), two clinical psychologists passionate about psychology's history; the founding was one of a series of

Rick Zaidan/Zaidan Photography

FIGURE 1.2 Marion White McPherson and John Popplestone, cofounders of the Archives of the History of American Psychology, The University of Akron, from Cohen (1991).

events mentioned earlier that sparked research interest in psychology's history in the 1960s. AHAP's collection includes the papers of more than 700 psychologists and professional organizations; more than 1,500 pieces of original laboratory apparatus; approximately 20,000 photographs, 6,000 films, and 4,000 audio recordings; and over 12,000 psychological tests.

What can you expect to find in an archive? Just about anything. When looking into the records of a professional organization, for instance, you would probably find lists of officers and correspondence among them, minutes of meetings, early drafts of position papers, and the like. When examining the papers of an individual psychologist, you might find (a) letters between that person and other psychologists; (b) personal diaries and/or appointment calendars; (c) course lecture notes and course schedules; (d) laboratory protocols, drawings of apparatus, data summaries, and other laboratory-related information; (e) early draft manuscripts of writings that eventually became secondary sources; (f) photographs and films of people, places, and research equipment; and (g) minutes of professional meetings attended by the psychologist. There will also be some surprises: One startling example was reported in *Civilization*, published by the Library of Congress. A researcher was studying the 19th-century Viennese physician Carl Koller, who was experimenting with the use of cocaine as an anesthetic in eye surgery. One of the folders contained a small pharmacist's packet containing, you guessed it, white powder. Federal authorities were called in to remove the drug, but the envelope remains in the archive collection, labeled as follows: "Remainder of the 1st dose of cocaine, which I used in my first cocaine experiments in August 1884. Dr. Koller" ("A Stash," 1996, p. 15).

How does a researcher interested in psychology's history know which archives to contact or visit when starting a project? Because their holdings are so extensive, AHAP is a good place to start. Even if it is not the primary repository for the papers of the person being studied, AHAP might hold some correspondence from that person in the papers it does have. Another good starting place is the university where the person in question worked. Third, bibliographic sources exist. Although a bit dated, the best known is *A Guide to Manuscript Collections in the History of Psychology and Selected Areas* (Sokal & Rafail, 1982). Suppose you are interested in the work of IQ researcher Henry Goddard, for instance. The guide briefly describes the contents of the Goddard papers, which happen to be held at AHAP. It also informs you of additional Goddard materials in the papers of Edgar Doll and Emily Stogdill at AHAP, and in the papers of developmental psychologist Arnold Gesell in the Library of Congress.

Historians also rely on their general knowledge to aid in their search. For example, some years ago I became interested in Edmund Clark Sanford (1859–1924), the first director of the psychology laboratory at Clark University (Goodwin, 1987). Through contact with the archivist there and two visits, I accumulated some information, but not a great deal. Sanford didn't seem to save very much, or if he did, the information didn't find its way to Clark. Some of the university records were helpful, however, in determining such things as laboratory purchases, and the papers of psychologist–university president G. Stanley Hall yielded some additional data, including one exciting discovery—a series of photographs taken in the laboratory in 1892, several of which are to be found in later chapters of this book. Many of them showed (or simulated, most likely) experiments in progress, thus providing a glimpse of what it was like to be doing research in psychology then. By searching through secondary sources, I knew about other psychologists who were contemporaries of Sanford. I also knew from his obituaries that Sanford was very close to E. B. Titchener of Cornell and Mary Calkins of Wellesley (Sanford died of a heart attack in 1924 on his way to give a talk at Wellesley). Visits to Wellesley and Cornell yielded more information. The Titchener papers were especially helpful—unlike Sanford, Titchener seemed to keep just about everything. I also wrote to about two dozen other archives that I guessed might be holding papers that Sanford might have written to his colleagues (this was before the days of e-mail). Copies of a few letters trickled in. At the same time, I was reading everything that Sanford published (not much, actually) and everything else that could shed some light on him and the world he inhabited (e.g., general histories of the decade of the 1890s, when Sanford was most productive at Clark).

Over the past decade, archival searching has been made considerably easier through electronic means. Archives frequently post "finding aids" (these are detailed listings of the contents of a particular collection) online, and sought-after documents are often available digitally. Other archival holdings can be discovered through Google searches. For example, as part of some research on the experimental psychologist Walter Miles, I was looking into his activities as a researcher at the Carnegie Nutrition Laboratory in Boston in the period from 1914 to 1922. From the Miles papers at AHAP, I knew that the laboratory's director was Francis Benedict. A Google search for Benedict yielded a connection to his papers at the archives of the Harvard Medical School, which in turn led to e-mail correspondence with a helpful archivist there and, eventually, to some important information about Benedict and the Carnegie Lab (e.g., the details of three different trips made by Benedict to Russia, where he visited Pavlov's laboratory and reported on Pavlov's research).

The Miles papers at Akron are a rich source of information for historians of psychology, mainly because Miles seldom threw anything away (Goodwin, 2003). The collection fills 128 boxes, which occupy 70 linear feet on the shelves; the detailed finding aid alone runs to 756 pages (in a searchable .pdf file, fortunately). To give you some idea of the range of materials that can be encountered in an archival collection, I will share some of the Miles documents with you at various places throughout the text. The first of these "From the Miles Papers …" pieces describes an event during a trip to Europe that Miles made while working as a researcher at the Carnegie Lab.

FROM THE MILES PAPERS...

MILES MEETS HIS ACADEMIC GRANDFATHER

From April until August, 1920, while a senior researcher at the Carnegie Nutrition Lab in Boston, Walter Miles (1885–1978) toured Europe, his first trip abroad (the Miles papers includes a postcard sent to his son of the steamship Miles travelled on, his cabin marked by an X). The purpose of the visit was to reestablish links between the Carnegie Lab and similar European laboratories that had been disrupted by World War I; for Miles, it was also a chance to become acquainted with some of Europe's leading scientists. During his trip, Miles visited 57 labs in 9 different countries. He also went to several conferences, including one for the British Psychological Society in London. There he met Edward Scripture for the first time. When Scripture was at Yale in the 1890s, his best known student was Carl Seashore. Miles, in turn, was a doctoral student of Seashore. In terms of their academic genealogy, then, Miles was a direct "descendent" of Scripture, his "academic grandson." Miles was therefore eager to meet Scripture, but was disappointed in the encounter, and it appears that the presence of Miles made Scripture less than comfortable. As described in a letter to Seashore shortly after returning to Boston, Miles wrote:

In England I attended a meeting of the British Psychological [Society] in Regent Park, London, Bedford College for Women. Dr. Spearman was in the chair. The first paper for lecture, somewhat over an hour long, was by Dr. E. W. Scripture on "Speech Inscriptions in Normal and Abnormal Conditions." I was very glad of an opportunity to see and hear Scripture .... Scripture looks and dresses the part of a wealthy consultant doctor of the Harley Street group of London. His hair was cut very short and worn pompadour, he has a Vandyke beard, and at first impression you would hardly think him more than forty-five years. He spoke with a great deal of gesture. I [illegible] his young wife with whom, according to what Spearman told me, he eloped from New York. I believe she was his former stenographer. Following Scripture's lectures, we had tea and at the end of this, while he was picking up his lantern slides, I introduced myself. The conversation which ensued was rather one-sided. I had to do most of it. He seems, I thought, a bit embarrassed. He spoke presently of you and he was pleased at the great success you had made. Very shortly after the meeting reassembled to hear the paper of Major Klein on the subject of camouflage in land warfare I saw Scripture and this very smartly dressed young woman slip quietly away. (Miles, 1920)

The Edward Scripture story is one that often has been made into a morality tale about the consequences of excessive conceit—someone who went from being a talented and creative yet excessively arrogant researcher to a disgraced and marginal bit player, whose obituary in the American *Journal of Psychology* appeared 20 years after he died because his death went unnoticed (Boring, 1965). Scripture founded one of the first psychology laboratories in the United States, at Yale in 1892, wrote a popular description of the "new psychology" (highlighted at the start of Chapter 8) in 1895, and had every reason to think that he would quickly rise to the top of his profession. Yet he was fired from Yale just after the turn of the 20th century after a series of conflicts; he was also accurately accused of plagiarism, with comparisons of his sentences and those of the original source made public; and he was divorced by his wife and more or less exiled to Europe. There he developed an expertise in speech pathology and, as seen in the Miles letter, made a living as a consultant on speech disorders in London.

Problems with the Writing of History

The journey from archive visits to a published paper or book is long, often tedious, occasionally exhilarating, but never easy. Along the way, the historian must confront two interrelated difficulties. First, there are problems associated with the collection of data. The historian must evaluate the validity of available data and select a subset of those data for inclusion in the historical narrative. The second problem concerns analysis. Historians are human, so their interpretations of the data will reflect their beliefs, their theories about the nature of history, and potentially, their biases.

Data Selection Problems Historians usually collect more information than will make its way into a historical narrative. Hence they must make judgments about the adequacy and relevance of the data at hand, and they must select a sample of the data while discarding the remainder. Sometimes, despite the large amount of data that might be collected during an archive visit, important pieces might be missing, further complicating the historian's life. For example, Titchener and Sanford wrote to each other frequently, but only Titchener saved his correspondence. The Titchener papers contain several hundred letters from Sanford to Titchener, but the Sanford papers include *none* from Titchener. In trying to piece together the Sanford–Titchener relationship, the historian gets only half the story.[3]

Sometimes information that could aid a historian can be lost through what insurance adjusters would call an act of God. For example, after painstakingly tracking down descendants of Mary Whiton Calkins (Chapter 6), the APA's first woman president, Furumoto discovered that many of Calkins's papers had been entrusted to her younger brother. Unfortunately, he put them in his cellar, where they were destroyed by flooding that accompanied a famous New England hurricane in 1938 (Furumoto, 1991).

Data might also be missing on purpose. In the last year of his life, John Watson, behaviorism's founder (Chapter 10), burned all his remaining notes, correspondence, and rough manuscripts. According to Watson's biographer, when "his secretary protested the loss to posterity and to history, Watson only replied: 'When you're dead, you're all dead'" (Buckley, 1989, p. 182). Similarly, on two separate

---

[3]More than half, actually. After about 1910, Titchener often made and kept carbon copies of his letters.

occasions Sigmund Freud also destroyed his papers, partly to make it difficult for others to trace the sources of his ideas (Chapter 12 details one of these episodes).

In addition to missing data, some information might be restricted by the donor and inaccessible to the historian. Even someone with the status of E. G. Boring could be denied. Writing to John Popplestone of AHAP, Boring indicated that even as a known historian and a faculty member at Harvard, he had been denied access to some papers at the Harvard archives. In his words:

> I trust the general atmosphere of the Archivists at Harvard. This is because I have been denied
> access to some things that are none of my business, graciously denied it because I am a Harvard
> professor. But, nevertheless, shut off from certain files of William James. (Popplestone, 1975, p. 21)

Beyond dealing with missing or incomplete information, the historian must make judgments about the adequacy of the available data. We know that eyewitness descriptions of everyday events can be wrong, that two witness accounts can differ substantially. If eyewitness unreliability can be demonstrated easily in modern psychology laboratories, then it is safe to say that the same lack of reliability exists for eyewitness accounts of historical events. A good example of this was experienced by Boring. While preparing a history of Titchener's Experimentalists (Chapter 7), Boring wrote to colleagues who had been to the meetings, asking for firsthand descriptions. There were numerous discrepancies among the letters, including one amusing example from a colleague who recounted to Boring in great detail a dinner conversation with Harvard's Hugo Münsterberg at the 1917 meeting at Harvard. Boring wrote back gently reminding his friend that Münsterberg had died in 1916 (Goodwin, 2005).

Information found in someone's correspondence or diary can also be of questionable value. Was the letter writer providing insight into the personality of a colleague or merely passing on unsubstantiated gossip? When the diarist described the meeting as meaningless and a waste of time, would others at the same meeting draw the same conclusion? Can letters and diaries be slanted by the writer's knowledge that historians might someday read his or her words? To what extent do the contents of letters and diaries reflect the personal prejudices of the writer? I think you can see the difficulty here.

Those who create the data that eventually occupy archives are human and therefore susceptible to the subtleties of human belief, preconception, and bias. Those who explore the archives and write the history are also human and subject to the same frailties. By virtue of their training, historians are more disciplined than laypeople; nonetheless, when making decisions about what information to select for historical analyses and narratives, the historian is not a machine. Boring expressed the problem eloquently in the preface to his 1942 text on the history of research in sensation and perception:

> Indeed, so much a matter of selection is the preparation of an historical text, that I am sobered by
> the responsibility. The [history] text of 1929 has existed long enough for me to see how *the mood
> that determined the choice of an afternoon's exposition can fix the "truth" of a certain matter upon
> graduate students for years to come.* With industry and patience one may avoid the falsification of
> facts, but those virtues are not enough to make one wise in choosing what to ignore. For that one
> also needs the wisdom and the integrity of objectivity, and who knows for sure whether he
> commands such? (Boring 1942, p. viii; emphasis added)

As you will learn in a few paragraphs, this passage from Boring is ironic. One of the themes of modern historiography within psychology is that Boring's writings reflect a strong bias for a specific brand of psychology. It also appears that he was motivated in part by the political and institutional context of his time.

Interpretation Problems Winston Churchill is alleged to have said history would be kind to him because he was going to be the person writing it. Historians normally try to be objective though, while realizing that all historical narrative will necessarily reflect something about the writer. Decisions about selection and about writing history both involve interpreting information, and those interpretations are influenced by the individual characteristics of the historian and by the features of the historical context in which the historian is writing. That is, historians will be influenced by their preconceptions, by the amount of knowledge they already have, as well as by the theories they hold about the nature of history (e.g., personalistic versus naturalistic emphases). In addition, even without necessarily being aware of it, historians can be influenced by the historical context in which their histories are being written. For example, you will discover in Chapter 4 that the work of Wilhelm Wundt has been reevaluated recently (e.g., Blumenthal, 1975), and many of his ideas have been found to be similar to those of modern cognitive psychologists. This similarity would not have been noticed before the advent of modern cognitive psychology—Blumenthal was writing at the height of the so-called cognitive revolution in psychology. Thus, historical characters are not the only ones influenced by the historical context in which they live; historians are affected as well.

The famous 1929 history written by Boring is a case in point. You know from this chapter's Close-Up that Boring was a devoted student of E. B. Titchener, and in the 1920s, he was a vigorous advocate for the development of a separate psychology department at Harvard that would emphasize "pure" laboratory research rather than application. Both of those facts played a role in the way he wrote his 1929 history text. First, his training as an experimental psychologist in Titchener's laboratory at Cornell surely affected his overall conception of psychology. More specifically, it influenced what Boring thought about Wundt, in whose laboratory Titchener earned a PhD in 1892. In general, Boring believed that Titchener's brand of experimental psychology, called structuralism, was virtually identical to Wundt's psychology, and that Titchener had merely imported it to America. In fact, Wundt's system was quite different from Titchener's system. Because of Titchener's influence on Boring, combined with the fact that Titchener translated much of Wundt's work and that Boring was not fully knowledgeable about some of Wundt's nonexperimental writings, the distinctions between Titchener and Wundt were lost. Thus, when writing his history, Boring's description of Wundt was filtered through Titchener's version and was consequently flawed. Because most psychologists trained in the period 1950 to 1980 learned their history by reading Boring's monumental *A History of Experimental Psychology* (1929; 1950), the mythological identification of Wundt's and Titchener's systems became conventional wisdom.

A second distortion in Boring's history relates to his emphasis on basic experimental psychology to the exclusion of applied psychology. As O'Donnell (1979b) has shown, Boring was disturbed by the growing status of applied psychology, especially mental testing. Believing basic laboratory research to be in jeopardy, he took several steps to restore its standing. One was writing the first edition of his history in 1929, which largely ignored the work of a substantial number of psychologists who were busily applying psychological principles to education, mental health, and the workplace. For instance, Boring (1929) began his brief section on mental testing by writing that "the history of mental tests can conveniently be excluded from the history of experimental psychology" (p. 545). The reader of his 1929 history could be excused for believing that applied psychology barely existed. In fact, as you will learn in Chapter 8, applications occupied center stage in America in the 1920s and 30s.

A common misconception of history goes like this: The events occurred in the past; now that they have been lined up chronologically and described in a historical narrative, that's the end of it. As the E. G. Boring case shows, however, historical analyses are in continual need of revision in the light of new information and new ways of examining old information. In recent years, for instance, scholars (e.g., Leahey, 1981) have taken a fresh look at the relationship between Wundt's and Titchener's ideas and the role of application in the development of psychology in America. As a result, newer histories describe the Wundt–Titchener differences more accurately and document the pervasive influence of applied psychology.

Comparing different editions of a history text can illustrate this reexamination process. For example, one popular history text, clearly influenced by Boring in its early editions, also shows the impact of the recent scholarship on Wundt in its later editions. In the book's third edition (Schultz, 1981), Wundt is described in a chapter that has *structuralism* in its title. The following chapter, on Titchener, refers to Wundtian psychology being "transplanted" to America by Titchener and includes this sentence: "A knowledge of Wundt's psychology provides a reasonably accurate picture of Titchener's system" (p. 87). Six years later, in the fourth edition, *structuralism* no longer appears in the title of the Wundt chapter, there is an explicit description of the problems with Boring's historical account, and the Titchener chapter opens by saying that the systems of Wundt and Titchener were "radically different," and that Titchener "altered Wundt's system dramatically while claiming to be a loyal follower" (Schultz & Schultz, 1987, p. 85).

The important lesson for the reader of history is to be alert to the dangers of assuming that if something is printed in black and white, it somehow must be true. Rather, it is important to read histories, including this one, with a healthy dose of skeptical awareness that other information might have been selected for inclusion in the narrative and that other ways of interpreting the historical record exist. As Bailyn (Lathem, 1994) put it, "there is no end to the writing of history—nor should there be, because new questions come up and new techniques develop, new data are discovered, and succeeding generations will and should tell the story differently" (p. 94). This raises an interesting question: Can history ever uncover the truth?

Approaching Historical Truth

From the foregoing discussion, you might be tempted to accept a version of historical relativism in which five historians make five different claims for truth and there is no reasonable way to decide among them. A degree of relativism among historians is an outgrowth of a reaction against traditional history, which held that the job of the historian is to search out the facts of "what really happened" and place them into a narrative with enough style to attract readers. The outcome was a tendency to write history from the standpoint of what happened to those in positions of power and influence, while ignoring the rich variety of alternative perspectives. Thus a traditional history of the American West, taught to American schoolchildren and grounded in a belief in Manifest Destiny, glorified the rugged pioneer who persevered in the face of daunting obstacles, including wild men who liked to shoot arrows. It is clear, though, that the very same history could be written from the standpoint of the Native American who valiantly defended the homeland against invasion by wild men who liked to shoot guns.

The critique of the narrowness and arbitrariness of traditional history has had the meritorious effect of enriching our knowledge of it. Thus we have come to recognize that history extends beyond the lives, deeds, and misdeeds of white males; it must be more inclusive. On the other hand, an unfortunate consequence of this broadening has been a relativism that, taken to extreme, can lead to absurd claims like the one made occasionally that the Jewish Holocaust in World War II never really happened but was merely "constructed" and exaggerated out of a few isolated events (said to have explanations other than genocide) by historians sympathetic to the Jewish movement who wished to encourage the creation of the nation of Israel following the war (Israel was created in 1948, three years after the close of World

War II). Those arguing for the "myth" of the Holocaust claim that their version is as valid as any other. Yet this example makes it clear that some versions of history are clearly better (i.e., closer to truth) than others. How does one decide?

To reach the truth through historical analysis requires an objectivity that recognizes the limits of one historian's views but also has faith in the notion that meaningful historical narrative and analysis can emerge from the combined efforts of many scholars, according to historians Appleby, Hunt, and Jacob. In *Telling the Truth About History* (1994), they argue for a historiography in which truth about history emerges from a Darwinian-like struggle between competing ideas held by historians, that "knowledge-seeking involves a lively, contentious struggle among diverse groups of truth-seekers" (p. 254). Some measure of truth, then, evolves from this struggle. Thus, just as individual variation within a species provides the basis for natural selection, so do different versions of historical episodes exist, subject to competing critical analyses that determine which version adapts best to the scholarly environment. This does not mean that the goal is a single version of truth that is then "settled" and immune to change. Rather, historical truth continues to evolve as new information is discovered and brought to light and as old information is subjected to new interpretations. Also, evolving historical truth includes a variety of perspectives. Multiple eyewitnesses to an event might give different versions of it, but all agree that the event did indeed occur. From their combined information, a complex truth might emerge that would improve on a single description from one perspective. If one historian of the Civil War period "sees an event from a slave's point of view, that rendering does not obliterate the perspective of the slaveholder; it only complicates the task of interpretation" (Appleby et al., 1994, p. 256).

Just as theories in science are temporary working truths that guide future research, their futures depending on the open and honest inquiry of scientists, so may historical truths be considered tentative yet valuable guides for further research by intellectually honest historians with open access to historical materials. And just as some theories in science are more durable than others, so are some historical truths: "All knowledge can be provisional, in theory, without eliminating the possibility of some truths prevailing for centuries, perhaps forever" (Appleby et al., 1994, p. 284).

Presumably, on the basis of the hard work of many historians of psychology, some degree of truth about the discipline's history has emerged, and I will try my best to describe it to you in this book. Many disagreements among historians of psychology exist, but Appleby, Hunt, and Jacob would consider that to be a good thing, the basis for future historical truths to develop during psychology's future. Placing the word *A* in the title of this book, rather than *The*, recognizes the fact that other histories exist now, and more will exist in the future. Nonetheless, I believe that what you are about to read contains some truth about the discipline you have chosen to study. To the extent that some of the truth might be tentative, I hope it will motivate you to continue learning about psychology's history long after you have finished with this particular version of it.

SUMMARY

Why Take This Course?

• Interest in the history of psychology has grown steadily since the mid-1960s, as reflected in the creation of professional organizations for historians of psychology, journals, archival collections, and graduate programs.

• Knowing history might occasionally help us to avoid mistakes of the past and to predict the future, but its most important value is that it helps us understand the present. Knowing history puts current events into a better perspective; without knowing some history, we cannot understand current events.

• Knowing history can immunize us against the belief that our current time has insurmountable problems, compared to the "good old days." Every age has its own set of problems. Knowing history also reduces the tendency to think that modern-day accomplishments represent a culmination of the "progress" we have made from the inferior accomplishments of the past.

• Because psychology is a relatively young science, much of its history is recent and of relevance for understanding psychological concepts and theories. Also, many issues of concern to early psychologists (e.g., nature–nurture) are still important.

• The history of psychology course can provide a synthesizing experience, tying together the loose threads that comprise the diverse specialties of modern psychology.

• Knowing about historical examples of supposed breakthroughs in psychological research or practice, or new theories that were shown to be pseudoscientific, the student of history is able to evaluate modern claims more critically.

• Because the history of psychology course informs the student about people behaving within their historical context, the course provides further understanding of human behavior.

Key Issues in Psychology's History

• The traditional approach to the history of psychology has been presentist, internal, and personalistic, and it tends to create what are called origin myths. Recently, historians have tended to be more historicist, external, and naturalistic.

• The presentist evaluates the past in terms of present knowledge and values, often passing judgment unfairly. The historicist tries to avoid imposing modern values on the past and tries to understand the past from the standpoint of the knowledge and values existing in the past.

• An internal history of psychology is a history of the ideas, research, and theories that have existed within the discipline of psychology. An external history of psychology emphasizes the historical context—institutional, economic, social, and political—and how this context influenced the history.

• A personalistic approach to history emphasizes the major historical characters and argues that history moves through the action of heroic individuals. When historical periods are labeled with reference to people, those labels are called eponyms (e.g., Darwinian biology). A naturalistic approach emphasizes the zeitgeist, the mood or spirit of the times, as the prime moving force in history. The existence of multiples, and of people with ideas said to be "ahead of their times," is consistent with a naturalistic view.

Historiography: Doing and Writing History

• Historiography refers to the process of doing research in history and writing historical narratives.

• Historians rely on both primary and secondary sources of information. A secondary source is a document that has been published. Primary source materials constitute the raw data for historians and include documents created at or near the time of the historical event in question (e.g., diaries, letters).

• Historical research often takes place in archives, which hold primary source information such as diaries, notes, original manuscripts, and correspondence, as well as secondary source information. The major archive for historians of psychology is the Archives of the History of American Psychology.

• Archival collections can be extensive, but they can also be incomplete and have important information missing for various reasons. The information that is available is subject to numerous sources of error (e.g., the biases of the diary writer; the vagaries of eyewitness memory).

• Historians are faced with two major problems: selection of information for their historical narratives and interpretation of the information at hand. These decisions can reflect bias on the part of the historian, and they can reflect the historical context within which the historian is writing. Nonetheless, most historians believe that some degree of truth can be reached through the open exchange of information and by examining historical events through a variety of perspectives.

STUDY QUESTIONS

1. Explain why "understanding the present" is a more compelling reason for studying history than the traditional arguments about avoiding the mistakes of the past and predicting the future.

2. Explain why it is important for students of psychology to understand psychology's history.

3. What is the point made by Boorstin in his essay "The Prison of the Present"?

4. Use Triplett's study as a way to explain the concept of an origin myth.

5. Define presentism, give an example of presentist thinking, and explain the dangers of this manner of looking at history.

6. Explain why a historicist approach to history is sometimes called a contextualized history.

7. Distinguish between internal and external histories. Use the example from cognitive psychology to illustrate the point.

8. What is a personalistic history, how is it related to the concept of an eponym, and what are its limitations?

9. What is a naturalistic approach to history, and what kinds of evidence are used to support this approach?

10. Distinguish between primary and secondary sources of information, and describe some of the primary sources likely to be found in an archive.

11. Distinguish between "the past" and "history."

12. Give examples from psychology's history that illustrate the data selection problems that all historians face.

13. Use the example of Boring's famous text to illustrate the interpretation problems that face historians.

14. In *Telling the Truth about History*, the authors describe the process of arriving at historical truth in Darwinian terms. Explain what they mean, and explain why they would argue that although absolute truth might not be reachable, some historical accounts are "truer" than others.

CHAPTER 2

THE PHILOSOPHICAL CONTEXT

Psychology has a long past, yet its real history is short.

—Hermann Ebbinghaus, 1908

PREVIEW AND CHAPTER OBJECTIVES

This chapter introduces you to the major philosophical issues and concepts that have been and continue to be important for psychologists. A working knowledge of these ideas provides a foundation for comprehending modern psychology. Although philosophers grapple with a wide range of problems, those especially relevant for psychology concern (a) whether mental and physical events are essentially the same or different and, if the latter, how the two kinds of events relate to each other; (b) whether our knowledge of the world is derived primarily from our ability to reason or results from the cumulative effects of our life experiences; (c) the extent to which our heredity and our environment shape the way we are; (d) whether the things we think, feel, and do result from our own free choices or are the result of deterministic laws of nature; and (e) whether or not complex phenomena can be best understood by analyzing them into their component parts. These issues are explored by examining the ideas of several well-known philosophers, giving special attention to René Descartes, history's most famous rationalist and the father of modern philosophy; John Locke, the founder of British Empiricism; and John Stuart Mill, a prominent 19th-century British empiricist/associationist. After finishing this chapter, you should be able to:

- Explain the meaning of the Ebbinghaus quote that opens the chapter
- Explain why Descartes is known as a rationalist, and describe his arguments concerning the mind–body issue
- Describe how Descartes would explain an involuntary movement of the foot (reflex) and a voluntary movement of the foot (i.e., requiring the mind)
- Describe Locke's ideas about how we develop our knowledge of the world and how he applied these ideas to education
- Distinguish between Locke and Berkeley on the question of primary and secondary qualities of matter
- Describe how Berkeley's philosophical system attempted to counter materialism
- Distinguish between Hume and Hartley on the question of the basic laws of association
- Distinguish between J. S. Mill and his father on the issue of atomism versus holism
- Describe how Mill's rules for inductive logic provided an underpinning for modern conceptions of research in psychology
- Describe the alternative to Locke's white paper metaphor proposed by Leibniz

■ Describe the mind–body solution proposed by Leibniz and how his ideas relate to the psychological concepts of the unconscious and thresholds

■ Describe Kant's arguments about the origins of knowledge

A LONG PAST

Most psychology students know Hermann Ebbinghaus as the inventor of the "nonsense syllable" and as the first person to study human memory experimentally (you will learn about this research in Chapter 4). Among historians of psychology, Ebbinghaus is also known for the opening sentence of a brief introductory textbook that he wrote in 1908. It is the "long past, short history" quote that opens this chapter.

By referring to psychology's "long past," Ebbinghaus was reminding readers that basic questions about human nature and the causes of human behavior are not new—they have been asked in some form or other since humans first started asking questions. More specifically, Ebbinghaus was pointing out that psychologists must recognize that their field has deep roots in philosophy. All the important issues that concern modern psychologists have been addressed by philosophers. In fact, you can notice the close association between psychology and philosophy the next time you go to the library—the place where you find the psychology books (BF ...) is sandwiched between general philosophy, logic, and knowledge (B, BC, BD) on one side and by aesthetics and ethics on the other side (BH, BL).

Does this close connection mean that psychology is just another branch of philosophy? No. In the last half of the 19th century, a number of converging forces produced an attempt to study human behavior and mental processes through the application of scientific methods rather than through philosophical analysis. Thus, what came to be called the New Psychology began to emerge as a separate discipline about 140 years ago—which led Ebbinghaus, just over 100 years ago, to proclaim that psychology's history as a new science had been relatively brief.

A thorough analysis of the long past referred to by Ebbinghaus requires much more content than this chapter can offer. It would take us through ancient Greece, deep into the writings of Plato and Aristotle and others, through the great medieval church philosophers such as Thomas Aquinas, who united Christian faith with Aristotelian logic, and into the Renaissance. Instead, we will begin with the 17th century and the multitalented René Descartes.

RENÉ DESCARTES (1596–1650): THE BEGINNINGS OF MODERN PHILOSOPHY AND SCIENCE

Descartes appeared on the scene at the end of the Renaissance and thus benefited from the changes that occurred during that remarkable time. The Renaissance lasted for approximately 200 years, during the 15th and 16th centuries. It derives its name from the rediscovery of ancient Greek and Roman texts, especially those of Plato and Aristotle, which had been lost to the Western world for hundreds of years. The period was marked by tremendous advances in the arts, starting in northern Italy, but quickly spreading throughout Europe. It was the time of Leonardo da Vinci (1452–1519), the prototypical "Renaissance Man," whose genius encompassed both art and science. His *Last Supper* and *Mona Lisa* are among the world's best-known paintings, and his scientific interests encompassed geology, astronomy, botany, anatomy, and the applied sciences of aeronautics, engineering, and weaponry. Another giant of the Renaissance was Michelangelo Buonarotti (1475–1564), who created artistic treasures ranging from a portrayal of the book of Genesis on the ceiling of the Sistine Chapel in the Vatican to the massive 17-foot-tall sculpture of David, now found in Michelangelo's home city of Florence.

In addition to rediscovering ancient texts and revolutionizing the arts, the Renaissance produced some notable advances in technology and science. In the 1450s, for instance, Johannes Gutenberg (c. 1394–1468) invented a new form of the printing press, enabling books to be created in larger numbers than ever thought possible, and at prices that brought literature, philosophy, and the Bible to more people than ever. Also during this time, clock makers improved on simple medieval instruments to produce the elaborate mechanical displays mounted on the cathedrals and public buildings of Europe. On the hour at the Wells Cathedral in England, for instance, viewers would be treated to a performance that included lifelike figures of armored knights in combat, one of whom would unhorse the other as another uniformed character struck the hour with a hammer (Boorstin, 1983). Knowledge about the inner workings of the human body was advanced significantly in 1543, when the Belgian physician Andreas Vesalius established his reputation as the founder of modern anatomical studies with his *Fabric of the Human Body*, which featured incredibly detailed illustrations (Klein, 1970). In astronomy in the 1540s, the Polish astronomer Nicolas Copernicus challenged the traditional **geocentric** view of the universe, which placed the earth ("geo") at the center of the universe, and suggested instead a **heliocentric** theory, which proposed that the sun ("helio") was at the center and the earth moved around it just like the other planets. Well aware of the religious controversy sure to result from the idea that "God's planet" was not in the center of the cosmos after all, Copernicus delayed publication until just before his death in 1543. The appearance of works by Vesalius and Copernicus in the same year led one historian of science to declare 1543 as the year when modern science was born (Singer, 1957).

The Copernican model of the universe, which appeared near the end of the Renaissance, is the clearest example of one of its themes—a questioning of authority, especially the authority of the church and the church's official philosopher, Aristotle. The ancient geocentric model placed God's greatest creation, man, at the focal point of the universe. Copernicus questioned this notion. An even greater challenge soon arrived in the person of the renowned Italian scientist Galileo Galilei (1564–1642), who supported Copernican theory with empirical observations aided by a telescope (20x power) that he constructed in 1609. Galileo's observations of things never seen before, such as the moons of Jupiter, further eroded traditional authority. How could Aristotle's view of the universe be correct when he was not capable of seeing what could now be seen? Galileo, a devout Catholic (his daughter was a nun), would eventually be charged with heresy by the church's Inquisition and forced to recant his claim of a heliocentric universe, but he did so with his fingers crossed. Even though his writings were placed on the Catholic Church's *Index of Prohibited Books* and remained there for nearly 200 years, his works continued to be published and read widely (Sobel, 2000). By the end of the 17th century, the geocentric model was, as they say, history.

Another threat to established authority occurred in England, during the time of Galileo, in the person of Sir Francis Bacon (1561–1626). Bacon was a strong advocate of an **inductive** approach to scientific inquiry. That is, he argued that scientists must observe nature as it presents itself, rather than follow the conclusions derived from a deductive analysis of Aristotle and other authorities. From many observations of individual cases, general statements about nature could be made. Bacon also believed that science should play an active role in controlling nature directly. Indeed, for Bacon, a true understanding of nature follows from the ability to create and recreate its effects at will (Smith, 1992). This, of course, is a plea for direct experimentation on nature to supplement careful observation. Bacon's insistence on acquiring knowledge through experience makes him an ancestor of British empiricism; his emphasis on induction and the control of nature made him a hero in the eyes of the 20th-century behaviorist B. F. Skinner (Chapter 11), who explicitly adopted a Baconian way of thinking.

Descartes and the Rationalist Argument

In the year that Galileo was observing the heavens with his telescope, René Descartes, a 13-year-old son of a prosperous French lawyer, was in his third year of study at the College de la Flèche.[1] The school was run by Jesuits, known for their skill as educators. The education Descartes received was in the **scholastic** tradition, combining the received wisdom of church authority with the careful use of reason. In particular, it relied on rational argument derived from the works of Aristotle to support the precepts of the church. Descartes quickly established himself as a star pupil, so good that he was granted special privileges—a private room and exemptions from regular class attendance and routine assignments.

Descartes left the college in 1614, not entirely satisfied with his Jesuit education. Like modern-day students surprised to learn that their formal education fails to give them answers to life's significant questions, he was dismayed to discover of philosophy that "it has been studied for many centuries by the most outstanding minds without having produced anything which is not in dispute" (Descartes, 1637/1960, p. 8). Consequently, he resolved to find things out for himself, rather than relying on authority. Reflecting a sentiment familiar to college seniors, he was ready to leave the classroom and enter the real world, "resolved to seek no other knowledge than that which I might find within myself, or perhaps in the great book of nature" (p. 8).

Because Descartes tried to keep his personal life private, the next few years are not well documented, but it appears that he spent some time sampling all that Paris had to offer (Vrooman, 1970). In 1619 he experienced what can only be called a conversion experience, in which a series of dreams told him, in effect, to quit fooling around and get serious about accomplishing something. He spent the next 10 years living in and around Paris, learning as much as he could about as many different topics as possible, especially the sciences. He firmly believed that he could produce a "unity of all knowledge" that would be grounded in mathematics.

Descartes's time, the early 17th century, is known as an era of revolutionary developments in science. It was the time of Bacon, Galileo, and in the latter half of the century, the incomparable Sir Isaac Newton. It featured Galileo's telescope and the microscope of the Dutch lens maker Antoni van Leeuwenhoek, tools that made it possible to observe things never seen before both in the heavens and in a drop of water (Boorstin, 1983). In medicine, systematic observation in 1628 by the British physician William Harvey refuted a widely held belief that the heart creates blood to be consumed by other parts of the body and demonstrated instead that it acts as a mechanical pump that recirculates blood. A gradual weakening of church authority, combined with an increasing faith in science and mechanics, created optimism among thinkers like Descartes that everything about the world could be known, perhaps in one's lifetime.

During the early 1620s, Descartes resembled a scientist more than a philosopher, studying physics, optics, geometry, and physiology. For example, he combined his interests in optics and physiology by extracting the eye of an ox and examining the properties of the lens, showing that retinal images are inverted (Vrooman, 1970). By 1633 he had written *The World*, designed to summarize his life's work to that point, demonstrating how the various disciplines could be united through the careful use of reason and grounded in mathematics. The section on astronomy, centering on a strong defense of the Copernican–Galilean heliocentric model of the universe, was a problem, however. Descartes was ready to publish *The World* when he learned that Galileo's work had been condemned by the church. Fearing a similar fate, and desiring to avoid notoriety and remain in the good graces of

---

[1]Descartes's birth date was March 31, 1596, a fact known only because it appeared below a portrait published after his death. During his lifetime, Descartes was secretive about his private life, refusing to disclose his birthday out of fear that it would lead to damaging speculation by astrologers (Vrooman, 1970).

Courtesy of Ludy T. Benjamin, Jr.

FIGURE 2.1   A French stamp featuring of Descartes's *Discourse on Method* (1637/1960).

the Catholic Church, Descartes suppressed publication—the book did not appear until after he died. Portions of it, however, appeared in various forms in several treatises that Descartes published during his lifetime, including his *Discourse on Method*, a book that eventually prompted the French to issue a commemorative stamp (Figure 2.1).

The Cartesian System   Although skeptical of the scholasticism he encountered as a student, Descartes was always grateful to the Jesuits for teaching him to be precise and logical in his thinking. His belief that truth could emerge from the careful use of reason became his modus operandi and marks him as a **rationalist**. In his *Discourse on Method* (1637/1960), he explained how he would accept as truth only that which could not be doubted. Thus, he rejected the evidence of the senses because the senses can deceive; he also questioned the plausible arguments of philosophers because equally plausible counterarguments existed. Yet he found that the one thing he was unable to doubt was that *he* was the one doing the doubting. As he put it in one of philosophy's most famous passages:

> I noticed that while I thus wished to think everything false, it was necessarily true that I who thought so was something. Since this truth, "*I think, therefore I am*" was so firm and so assured that all the most extravagant suppositions of the sceptics were unable to shake it, I judged that I could safely accept it as the first principle of the philosophy I was seeking. (Descartes, 1637/1960, p. 24; emphasis added)

For Descartes, then, the way to truth was through the unique human capacity to reason. In his *Discourse on Method*, he described four basic rules he used to arrive at the truth of some matter. First, he accepted nothing as true unless "it presented itself so clearly and distinctly to my mind that there was no reason to doubt it" (Descartes, 1637/1960, p. 15). Second, he used a strategy of analysis, breaking problems into subproblems. Third, he worked from the simplest of these subproblems to the more complex ones, and fourth, he carefully reviewed his conclusions to be certain of omitting nothing. Now to our modern way of thinking, these rules of method do not appear to be extraordinary. Descartes seems to be saying not much more than to think clearly, logically, and without bias; analyze problems carefully; work systematically from the simple to the complex; and check your work. Yet to conclude that these rules are ordinary is to fall prey to the kind of presentist thinking discussed in Chapter 1. In the context of Descartes's times, when the power of authority was weakening but still considerable, his rules of method were truly revolutionary. In effect, he was casting off authority completely. The only way to get to the certainty of truth is to *arrive at it oneself*, relying on the clear use of one's own reasoning powers. An indication of how unsettling this notion was to the authorities is the fact that after

Descartes's death, the Catholic Church put his writings in the *Index*, their list of books to be avoided by right-thinking Catholics (Vrooman, 1970).

An implication of Cartesian rationalism was that the ability to reason is inborn and that certain types of knowledge do not rely directly on sense experience, but result from our native ability to reason. For example, although we come to know the properties of wax (e.g., heat melts it) on the basis of our experience with it, there are certain things about wax that we know to be true simply as a result of a logical analysis, using our native reasoning powers. Thus Descartes would say that we can conclude, without doubt, that wax has the property of "extension"—it exists in space and, even though it may change form (e.g., through melting), it can never disappear. Because we can use our reason to arrive at our knowledge of the concept of extension, Descartes considered extension to be an example of an **innate idea**. Similarly, he believed that we have other innate ideas. These included the ideas of God, the self, and some basic mathematical truths. On the other hand, many of our concepts result from our experiences. These Descartes called **derived ideas**. Knowing that a wax candle of a certain size will burn for about 10 hours would be an example of such an idea. Descartes's position on innate ideas means that he can be considered a **nativist** as well as a rationalist. His distinction between innate versus derived ideas foreshadows one of psychology's recurring issues, the relationship between nature and nurture.

Descartes was also history's best-known **dualist**, arguing for a clear separation between mind and body. They can be distinguished, according to Descartes, by the aforementioned property of extension and by the additional property of movement—bodies take up space and move through it. Mind, on the other hand, possesses neither extension nor movement. The centerpiece of the unextended mind is the human ability to reason, whereas the body is in essence a machine. One implication of this dualism has come to be called the **Cartesian dichotomy**, which divides humans and animals. Descartes argued that animals were simple machines, incapable of reason and language, and therefore lacking a mind. Humans, on the other hand, combined a mechanical body with a reasoning mind. In addition to the labels *rationalist* and *nativist*, then, Descartes can also be considered a **mechanist**, for his belief that the body operates like a complicated machine. He was also an **interactionist**, believing that the mind could have a direct influence on the body (a decision to improve our health causes us to exercise) and the body could have a direct influence on the mind (a pulled hamstring causes us to redesign our exercise plan).

Descartes's use of the machine metaphor when describing the properties of bodies was no accident. We have seen that in the Renaissance, clock-building technology had advanced to the point where mechanical yet lifelike figures would put on hourly shows at the cathedrals and public buildings of Europe. Similarly, the wealthy of Europe created gardens that included elaborate mechanical fountains and statues that moved through the action of water-driven hydraulic systems. The unwary visitor to one of these 17th-century Disney Worlds might step on a hidden plate, thereby activating a system that caused a statue of Neptune to rise from the water in an adjacent pond. A less whimsical example of the mechanistic zeitgeist that infused Descartes's times was Harvey's demonstration of the heart as a mechanical pump.

Descartes on the Reflex and Mind–Body Interaction

In the year before his death, Descartes published *The Passions of the Soul* (1649/1969), which established his status as a pioneer psychologist and physiologist. Primarily a treatise on human emotions, it included an attempt to explain what we now call the **reflex**, an automatic stimulus–response reaction, and it provided a physiological model for Descartes's position on the mind–body question. Descartes opened the book with a characteristic attack on the traditional, authority-based approach to the study of the emotions, arguing in his opening sentence that "there is nothing in which the defective nature of the sciences which we have received from the ancients appears more clearly than in what they have written on the passions" (p. 331).

He then introduced his mind–body distinction and began a discussion of the "bodily machine," which included a reference to Harvey's discoveries about the mechanical heart and a description of muscle action. Muscles, in turn, "depend on the nerves, which resemble … little tubes, which all proceed from the brain, and thus contain like it a certain very subtle air or wind which is called the animal spirits" (pp. 333–334).

The **animal spirits** referred to by Descartes were said to be derived from the heat of the blood and were the driving forces behind movement. Descartes believed these spirits were tiny particles in constant motion and were found in the brain, the nerves, and the muscles. Muscle movement resulted from the action of animal spirits deriving from the brain, but what determined which muscles move? Two things, according to Descartes. First, the mind can initiate the movement of animal spirits in the brain by activating the nerves controlling certain muscles rather than others. That is, the mind can influence the body (more on this shortly). Second, certain muscles can move automatically in response to the results of certain sensory stimuli. That is, *reflexes* occur.[2]

Descartes explained reflexes by proposing the existence of thin wirelike "filaments" that existed within the nerves and extended to the brain. When the senses are stimulated, according to Descartes, these filaments move, causing "pores" in the brain to be opened. This in turn results in the flow of animal spirits that produces the reflex movement, as when we accidentally burn ourselves. Figure 2.2 shows a famous sketch by Descartes of this involuntary (i.e., reflexive) withdrawal of one's foot from a fire. The fire touches the foot, causing a tug on the filaments within the nerve there. These filaments extend all the way to the brain, where animal spirits are released into the nerve "tube." The spirits in turn are carried "partly to the muscles which pull back the foot from the fire, partly to those which turn the eyes and the head in order to regard it, and partly to those which serve to advance the hands and to bend the whole body in order to shield itself" (Descartes, 1637, quoted in Fearing, 1930, p. 24).

In addition to resulting in reflex action, the mind by itself can initiate action. That is, the mind can intervene between sensory stimulus and motor response. How to explain the nature of this interaction between mind and body was a problem, however. It is one thing to say that the mind can directly affect bodily movement and vice versa, but it is quite another thing to demonstrate just how this occurs. After careful analysis, Descartes concluded that the interaction occurred in a part of the brain called the **pineal**

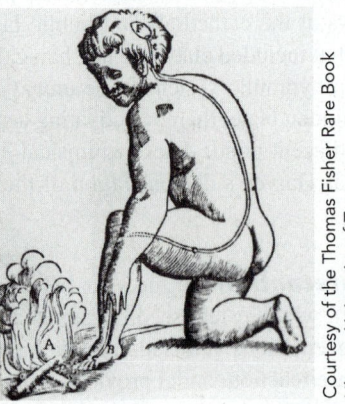

Courtesy of the Thomas Fisher Rare Book Library, University of Toronto.

FIGURE 2.2 Descartes's illustration of reflex action. From René Descartes, Lhomme et un traitté de la formation du foetus.

[2]Although Descartes was describing reflex action, he did not invent or first use the term *reflex*. That distinction belongs to Thomas Willis (1621–1675), a British physiologist, who named the phenomenon "reflexion" (Finger, 2000). Willis's work is elaborated in Chapter 3.

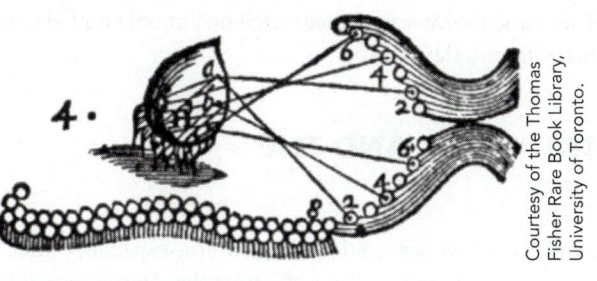

Courtesy of the Thomas Fisher Rare Book Library, University of Toronto.

FIGURE 2.3 Descartes's illustration of the action of the pineal gland. From René Descartes, Lhomme et un traitté de la formation du foetus.

gland, selected because he believed it was strategically located in a place where the flow of the animal spirits could be controlled. In Figure 2.3, Descartes showed how the pineal gland's movement could send animal spirits off in different directions (represented by the straight lines). The pineal gland was also a brain structure that was not duplicated on both the left and right sides of the brain. Because the mind was considered to be unitary, Descartes reasoned, it must exert its effect through a structure that was also a single unit. Descartes was not arguing that the pineal gland had its special function because it was a part of the brain found only in humans—he was well aware, on the basis of his own dissections, that other animals possessed the structure (Finger, 2000). Instead, he was arguing that the gland had a function in humans that would not be found in animals—the locus for mind–body interaction.

Descartes was not asserting that the mind was *in* the pineal gland, only that the gland serves as the place where mind and body influence each other. Thus sensations produce a stretching of the small filaments that open pores in the brain, thereby moving the animal spirits. These movements are felt by the pineal gland and result in the mental event of a "sensation." The animal spirits also continue their movement back down the nerve fibers into the muscles, producing movement. Movement can also be created by the direct action of the will. The decision to move causes the pineal gland to move, which in turn produces the movements of the spirits that eventually move the muscles.

Of course, despite the noble effort, Descartes was wrong about the physiology. For example, the pineal gland, which secretes the hormone melatonin and remains poorly understood today, is not a mind–body Grand Central Station. A more important problem, one pointed out almost immediately by critics in Descartes's own day, was that his proposal of the pineal gland as the point of mind–body interaction really did not explain *anything*, but merely restated the problem. If it is unclear how the unextended mind can influence and be influenced by an extended body in general, it is just as unclear how the unextended mind can influence, and be influenced by, the movements of a small, extended piece of the brain, the pineal gland (Cottingham, 1986). For psychology, the significance of Descartes's work is not that he made a serious yet flawed effort to solve the mind–body problem, but that in so doing, he created the modern concept of reflex action with its explicit distinction between sensory stimulus and motor response, and he tried to explain psychological concepts (e.g., memory) by using a physiological model.

Shortly after publishing *The Passions of the Soul* in 1649, Descartes was persuaded by Queen Christina of Sweden to move to Stockholm to be her tutor. The queen had a keen mind, was fluent in five languages, and was determined to make Stockholm a center of learning in Europe. To that end she created a world-class library and began inviting scholars to her court, Descartes included. He accepted with some misgivings and soon found himself conversing with and tutoring Christina for five hours a day, three days a week, beginning at 5 a.m., during a winter that was severe even by Swedish standards. For someone accustomed to lounging in bed until late morning while reflecting on the great issues of the day, the schedule was a killer. Sure enough, Descartes contracted pneumonia on February 1, 1650, and died 10 days later, just shy of his 54th birthday.

THE BRITISH EMPIRICIST ARGUMENT AND THE ASSOCIATIONISTS

Philosophy on the European continent has often been rationalist in spirit, especially after Descartes. In England, however, a different tradition arose at about the same time that Descartes's influence was spreading. This British tradition is strongly **empiricist**, based on the idea that our knowledge of the world is constructed from our experiences in it. Because this knowledge is woven together by the associations among our experiences and ideas, British empiricism is closely tied to the doctrines of **associationism**. Much of the history of British philosophy, from the 17th century on, has been concerned with the epistemological questions of how experience creates knowledge and how the rules of association work to organize that knowledge.

British empiricism has its roots in the inductive scientific thinking of Sir Francis Bacon and the social theories of Thomas Hobbes, a contemporary of Bacon and Descartes. We may conveniently begin with John Locke, however, usually considered the founder of this movement. We will then examine the work of other leading British empiricists and associationists, ending with the most important British philosopher of the 19th century, John Stuart Mill.

John Locke (1632–1704): The Origins of British Empiricism

John Locke spent most of his adult life in the academic environment of Oxford as a lecturer and tutor, but he mixed the contemplative life of a philosopher with an active political and diplomatic career. He was also trained in medicine, but he was primarily interested in the scientific aspects of it, and he seldom practiced as a physician. Locke is important to psychology for the concepts expressed in two books, *An Essay Concerning Human Understanding* (1690/1963a) and *Some Thoughts Concerning Education* (1693/1963b). The former explains Locke's views on how knowledge is acquired, how we as humans come to understand our world. The latter is based on letters to a friend, showing how empiricist thinking could apply to education.

Locke on Human Understanding Like Descartes, Locke was enamored of the science that was such a prominent feature of the 17th century. While a student at Oxford, he was drawn to the ideas of Sir Francis Bacon, and he rejected the same scholasticism that Descartes questioned. While studying medicine, Locke befriended other scientists, including Robert Boyle (1627–1692), one of modern chemistry's pioneers and a founder of the British Royal Society, established in 1662 to further the interests of science (Boorstin, 1983). Locke was also a contemporary of Sir Isaac Newton—his *Principia Mathematica* was published just three years before Locke's *Essay*. What Galileo, Harvey, Boyle, Newton, and others were doing for physical science, transforming it from the Aristotelian-based "natural philosophy" into an experimental discipline, Locke was determined to do for **epistemology**, the study of human knowledge and its acquisition.

Before describing how our ideas originate, Locke considered and rejected the existence of innate ideas. He granted that we have innate "faculties" such as the ability to think, but he did not accept Descartes's contention that ideas derived from reason (e.g., extension) could be considered innate ideas. Locke argued that there is no need to propose innate ideas because it can be shown that ideas originate from other sources, requiring only the use of our basic mental faculties. For instance, although our reasoning enables us to conclude that all physical objects have the property of extension, the conclusion is based on the fact that we have experienced lots of extended objects during our lifetimes. In the absence of such experiences, Locke believed that we would not arrive at the conclusion about extension being a property of all matter; indeed, it would not even occur to us to think about it.

Another argument for innate ideas was the belief that some ideas were universal, found in all people. If all cultures include the concept of the Deity, for example, it could be said that the concept of God does not require specific experiences, but is innate. Locke would not buy it. A universal belief in God does not necessarily mean the idea of God is innate to us, he argued. Instead, it could be that because all people die (i.e., a universal experience), they all worry about death and whether there is an afterlife, and proposing the idea of a supreme being is a natural consequence of this line of thought.

A final argument for innate ideas was that some ideas seem to appear so early in life that they must be innate. Locke rejected this argument also, pointing out that even before children can use language, they are already profiting from experience. Furthermore, in a tone similar to that taken later by American behaviorists in the 20th century, Locke pointed out that we often overlook the fact that a child has quite a few important experiences early in life.

Having rejected the concept of innate ideas, Locke turned to the question of how our minds develop ideas. In one of philosophy's most quoted passages, he declared that *all* of our knowledge about the world derives from experience:

> Let us then suppose the mind to be, as we say, white paper, void of all characters, without any ideas; how comes it to be furnished? Whence comes it by that vast store, which the busy and boundless fancy of man has painted on it with an almost endless variety? Whence has it all the materials of reason and knowledge? *To this I answer, in one word, from experience*; in that, all our knowledge is founded. (Locke, 1690/1963a, pp. 82–83; emphasis added)

The mind at birth, then, is an empty sheet of **white paper** (Locke was renaming an old Aristotelian metaphor of the mind as a blank slate or wax tablet), ready to be written on by experience. Furthermore, the ideas that result from experience and compose the mind have two and only two sources, according to Locke. He believed that every idea we have, without exception, originated from the two processes of sensation and reflection. *Sensation* refers to all the information taken in by our senses from the environment, and *reflection* refers to the mental activities involved in processing information from both the senses and from memory. Thus our concept of green derives from all our experiences with green objects, our memories of green objects, and our further reflections about "greenness." The reflection process also can produce new ideas not encountered initially by our senses. Even without encountering the Dr. Seuss story directly, we can conceive of "green eggs and ham" by combining, through the reflective processes of memory and imagination, our experiences of green, of eggs, and of ham.

Locke also distinguished between simple and complex ideas. **Simple ideas** resulted from experiencing basic sensory qualities such as yellow, white, heat, and so on, and from making simple reflections. A **complex idea** includes several other ideas, which can be a combination of simple and other complex ideas. The complex idea of a cold drink on a very hot day, for example, is composed of a number of simple ideas relating to color, temperature, shape, pleasantness, taste, and the additional complex idea of the good life. Complex ideas are compounds and can be ultimately reduced to simple ones, much as chemical compounds are composed of simple elements. This idea of the mind being an elaborate construction incorporating layers of ideas of varying complexity was a common feature of British empiricist thinking, and it reflects the influence of the other sciences, especially physics and chemistry. Just as water can be reduced to its elements and light can be broken down into the colors of the spectrum, so the mind could be analyzed into its fundamental units. The idea that complexity in nature can be understood by reducing objects to their most basic elements is sometimes referred to as **atomism**, and it is an assumption underlying many of the early systems of psychology, including E. B. Titchener's structuralism (Chapter 7) and John Watson's behaviorism (Chapter 10).

In the fourth edition of his *Essay*, Locke addressed the question of how simple ideas form compound ones, and in the process he introduced the concept of **association** into the discussion. Just as gravity was the central concept of Newtonian physics, holding together the elements of the universe, so would association be the glue that held together one's experiences in life. But although Locke discussed the concept of association to some extent, it was for the other British philosophers we will meet shortly to develop it more fully. As will become evident, British empiricism and associationism went hand in hand.

A final distinction worth noting is between what Locke referred to as the primary and secondary qualities of matter. This was a distinction well known in the 17th century and first popularized by Galileo. **Primary qualities** were said to exist as an inherent property of an object. Extension, shape, and motion are examples. These were the features Descartes believed to be innate ideas. To Locke, there was nothing innate about them. **Secondary qualities**, on the other hand, are not inherent attributes of objects, but depend on perception. The color, smell, warmth, and taste of objects are examples. Thus the redness of an object exists not in the object itself but in the perceptual experience of the observer. As it gets darker, the tomato in the garden does not change its shape; but its perceived color changes, gradually fading from red to almost black. The primary–secondary distinction raised questions that led, during the 19th century, to a direct examination by physiologists of how sensory systems actually work to create our "understandings." If "red" is not in the object but in the brain, how does it get there?

Locke's empiricist philosophy also suggested that those with different experiences would view the world differently. In the extreme case, someone with defective senses should have a distorted view of the world. This issue was posed to Locke in a letter from William Molyneux, a friend in Dublin. Molyneux asked what would happen if a man, blind from birth, whose experience of objects like cubes and spheres would be limited to the sense of touch, would recognize the objects if his sight was suddenly restored. Molyneux answered his own question in the negative, and Locke agreed. Once sight had been restored, the man would have to learn to distinguish cube from sphere all over again, by relating the information from the visual and the tactile senses. As early as the 18th century, congenital cataracts were being removed surgically, thus providing a direct test (and support) for this empiricist claim (Morgan, 1977).

Locke on Education   Another implication of Locke's empiricist thinking concerned how to raise and educate children. If the mind is shaped by experience, then a deliberate program of education based on empiricist principles should produce an ideal citizen. Locke's contribution to the issue was *Some Thoughts Concerning Education* (1693/1963b), a brief volume based on letters written to a friend who was seeking advice about educating his son. Locke's advice was wide ranging and included the following:

1. Trained in medicine, Locke believed in the importance of physical health, and he began the book by arguing that a sound mind requires a sound body. His specific suggestions reflected his own strict Puritan upbringing, which fostered simplicity, individual initiative and effort, and the belief that good outcomes require some degree of suffering. Children should have hard rather than soft beds, for example; the former toughens the person, whereas "being buried every night in feathers, melts and dissolves the body, is often the cause of weakness, and the forerunner of an early grave" (Locke, 1693/1963b, p. 22).

2. Training must begin early, because young children are more malleable, and if they don't develop good habits early in life, they will develop bad ones. Locke believed that one of the greatest mistakes made by parents was that their child's "mind [had] not been made obedient to discipline, and pliant to reason, when at first it was most tender, most easy to be bowed" (Locke, 1693/1963b, p. 27). Good habits also require practice. Children learn such habits by doing things repeatedly, not by learning rules, "which will be always slipping out of their memories" (p. 46).

3. Locke disliked punishment, especially for older children. The child who is beaten for not doing lessons soon comes to dislike learning (and tutors), he argued. Furthermore, although punishment might reduce unruly behavior, severe and repeated punishment carries the danger of "breaking the mind, and then, in place of a disorderly young fellow, you have a low-spirited moped creature" (Locke, 1693/1963b, p. 38).

4. Concrete rewards should be avoided. Giving a child candy for good performance produces a child interested only in obtaining candy. On the other hand, Locke recommended the use of rewards and punishments in the form of parental approval and disapproval. "If you can once get into children a love of credit, and an apprehension of shame and disgrace, you have put into them the true principle, which will constantly work, and incline them to the right" (Locke, 1693/1963b, p. 41).

Locke's views on education, and his empiricist philosophy in general, show a strong affinity with 20th-century behaviorism, as will be clear when you read Chapters 10 and 11. Although Locke was concerned with mental life and the behaviorists focused on overt action, strong resemblances exist. Like the modern behaviorists, Locke believed that complexity could be understood by analysis into component parts, that the environment directly shaped the mind and behavior, and that you can tell a great deal about a person if you know something of the person's experiences in life. Empiricism and behaviorism also share an emphasis on the importance of association, but as mentioned earlier, it was for empiricists subsequent to Locke to develop associationist doctrine to its fullest. It is to Locke's intellectual descendants that we now turn.

George Berkeley (1685–1753): Empiricism Applied to Vision

As the 17th century drew to a close, it was clear to the intelligentsia that the century had been marked by a steady decline in the authority of the church. This was accompanied by, and to a large extent precipitated by, enormous advances in science. From Bacon to Galileo to Harvey to Boyle to Newton, a zeitgeist evolved that envisioned the universe as a large machine, composed of material parts, and operating according to laws that could be discovered only by combining scientific methods with mathematical rigor. Although it was not until the 19th century that the "ism" called **materialism** would reach its full development, its roots were in the 17th century. Materialists are monists on the mind–body question, believing that the only reality is a physical reality, and that every event in the universe, including what we think of as mental events, involves measurable, material objects in motion in physical space. Materialism includes the aforementioned atomism, the idea that complex entities can be understood by reducing them to their component parts. Materialism also poses a threat to the concept of free will by implying **determinism**, the belief that all events have prior causes. If we are not free to choose, then perhaps we cannot be held responsible for our actions.

Such a materialistic and scientific worldview does not necessarily rule out religion (e.g., Boyle thought that to do science was to discover God's will), but it threatens the concepts of free will and moral responsibility, and so it was seen by some as a danger. One thinker who was especially concerned about the materialistic implications of 17th-century science was George Berkeley, a bishop of the Anglican Church in Ireland.

Berkeley (pronounced *BARK'-lee*) is important for psychology because of two books that he published in his mid-twenties: *An Essay Towards a New Theory of Vision* (1709) and *Treatise Concerning the Principles of Human Knowledge* (1710). Both were strongly empiricist and focused on analyzing sensory processes. Legend has it that Berkeley's interest in sensation had its roots in a hanging that he witnessed while a student. Curious about the sensations accompanying being hung, he arranged to have *himself* hung from the rafters in the company of friends who were instructed to cut him down after a few minutes. Berkeley apparently lost consciousness and almost died.

Berkeley's work on vision was the first clear example of how empiricist thinking could be applied to the study of perception. It was timely, written when advances in optics were producing new and improved telescopes, microscopes, and eyeglasses. In his book, Berkeley tried to show that perceptions of distance, size, and location are judgments depending entirely on *experience*. When judging distance, for example, Berkeley made use of what your general psychology book referred to as the monocular (only one eye needed) cues of overlap, relative clarity, and relative size:

> The estimate we make of the distance of objects considerably remote is rather an act of judgment grounded on experience than of sens[ation]. For example, when I perceive a great number of intermediate objects, such as houses, fields, rivers, and the like, which I have experienced to take up considerable space, I thence form a judgment or conclusion that the object that I see beyond them is at a great distance. Again, when an object appears faint and small, which at a near distance I have experienced to make a vigorous and large appearance, I instantly conclude it to be far off. (Berkeley, 1709/1948, p. 171)

Berkeley also examined the question of judging depth for relatively close objects and provided clear descriptions of phenomena today referred to as convergence and accommodation. In **convergence**, when objects move closer to us or farther away, "we alter the disposition of our eyes, by lessening or widening the interval between the pupils" (Berkeley, 1709/1948, p. 174). These eye movements are the result of muscle movements, which in turn create sensations that we come to associate with various distances. Similarly, objects are perceived clearly through **accommodation**, in which changes in the shape of the lens serve to keep objects focused on the retina. Closer objects produce a greater bulging of the lens than objects farther away. Again, these changes are accompanied by muscle action and sensations to be associated with different distances.

An important theme of Berkeley's theory of vision, made clear from the opening sentence of the monocular cues quote, is that we do not see objects directly; rather, we make judgments about them based on visual information and our experiences. This theme was carried into his other major work, *Treatise Concerning the Principles of Human Knowledge* (1710/1957), and provided the basis for Berkeley's attack on materialism. Just as we do not see "distance" directly, so it is that we do not see "material objects" directly. In both cases, they are "judged" on the basis of perception. Thus we cannot be entirely certain of the reality of material objects; the only certainty is that we are perceiving them. This position of Berkeley's is known as **subjective idealism** (sometimes "immaterialism"). It is in the empiricist tradition because experience is the source of all knowledge, but it denied Locke's distinction between primary and secondary qualities of matter. For Berkeley, everything was a secondary quality. Just as color depends on the perceiving person, so does extension. The only thing that has reality for us is our own perception.

Does this mean that we can never be sure about the reality of the world? Does a tree falling in the forest exist only if we hear it? No. Reality exists, according to Berkeley, because objects, including trees falling in forests, are *always* perceived by God, who Berkeley referred to as the Permanent Perceiver. We can be sure of the permanence of reality, but only through our faith in God. In this way, Berkeley sought to attack what he saw as a Godless materialism. Instead, faith in God becomes essential to our understanding of the world.

Berkeley was not successful in countering the trend toward materialism, as will be clear in the next chapter. By emphasizing the importance of perception in one's understanding of reality, however, and by directly attacking the question of how visual perception actually works, he furthered the cause of British empiricism while at the same time turning the issue of how knowledge is acquired from a purely philosophical question to a more psychological one. As Robinson put it, Berkeley "rendered epistemology a branch of psychology, and the two have never been divorced since" (1981, p. 228). Once the problem of human knowledge became a psychological one, people began asking different questions. Rather than asking a philosophical question like "How much can be known about the nature of reality?" thinkers now began asking questions like "Just exactly how does visual perception work to produce what we know?" This shift would eventually bring about a scientific psychology.

British Associationism

Like John Locke, Berkeley had little to say about how our sensory experiences and our reflections combine to produce the more complicated forms of our knowledge. That is, although both mentioned the issue of association of ideas, neither carefully examined the phenomenon. Association would soon occupy center stage for British philosophers, however, seen as a force organizing the events of mental life. Associationism is the doctrine that the mind can be understood as a complex set of ideas, related to each other by the force of the associations among them. Things become associated in our minds through our experiences in the world; thus, associationism is grounded in empiricism. The British philosophers David Hume and David Hartley both made important contributions to the understanding of how association operated.

David Hume (1711–1776): The Rules of Association Hume was born near Edinburgh, Scotland, entered the university there at age 12, and left after 3 years without finishing a degree. He tried studying law, hated it, then decided on a business career and hated it as well. Determined to become a scholar, he retreated to the French countryside[3] and wrote his first book, *A Treatise of Human Nature* (1739–1740/1969). Unfortunately, the book sold poorly, disappointing the ambitious Hume, who later said of the book: "It fell deadborn from the press, without reaching such distinction, as even to excite a murmur from the zealots" (quoted in Klein, 1970, p. 552). He later wrote shortened versions of the *Treatise* under different titles, but as a writer he was best known for writing a massive, five-volume history of England. Still highly regarded, Hume's history went beyond the usual military and political history and incorporated social and literary history into the narrative. Hume's exalted stature among the Scots is clear from Figure 2.4.

In good British empiricist tradition, Hume built his system on the basic premise that all our understanding is rooted in experience. To dissect human experience, Hume first tried to discover the mind's basic elements, analogous to the physicist's atoms. Upon reflection, Hume believed these elements were two in number: impressions and ideas. **Impressions** are basic sensations, the raw data of experience. We feel pleasure, see red, taste sweetness, and so on. **Ideas**, on the other hand, are "faint copies" of impressions. That is, although similar to impressions, and deriving from them, ideas are not as vivid.

---

[3]He chose the quiet town of La Flèche, known for the Jesuit school that trained Descartes.

© Edinburgh-Photos.com

FIGURE 2.4 Statue of Scotland's David Hume, portrayed as a heroic figure, found on Edinburgh's Royal Mile.

To support his contention that ideas emerge from impressions, Hume noted that it is possible to reduce all our ideas to impressions, even complex ideas that have never been experienced directly. Thus, even if we have never found a real four-leaf clover, we can have a complex idea of it by combining simple ideas (e.g., "four" and "clover" and "green") that can be traced to sensory impressions.

Note that Hume's analysis of impressions and ideas is mainstream British empiricism. If all ideas are faint copies of impressions, then all ideas come from the impressions we experience in life. Hence, there are no innate ideas. But how do impressions connect with ideas, and how are complex ideas formed? How does one idea lead to another? In a word, from *association*, the analysis of which Hume considered perhaps his major philosophical achievement.

Hume proposed three laws of association: resemblance, contiguity, and cause–effect. Sometimes an object reminds us of another because it has a **resemblance** to it. Thus, a photo of Yosemite's Half Dome resembles the actual structure and brings to mind memories (ideas), perhaps of a visit to Yosemite. **Contiguity** means experiencing things together. Thus, because purists eat lobster only in Maine, reading about lobster brings to mind the rugged Maine coast. Hume's third law of association concerned the relationship between **cause and effect**. If one event follows another with some regularity, we will develop an association between the two. Hume's example was a healed wound. The original wound "caused" us to experience pain; thus, when we now examine the old wound, we are reminded of the pain and the circumstances that produced it. But what determines causes and effects? Hume's answer made him a controversial figure in his day but might have been his most important contribution to modern psychology.

Hume believed that we can never be absolutely certain about the causes of events. Rather, all we can know is that events occur together with some regularity. To conclude that A causes B, he argued, we must know that (a) when A occurs, B occurs regularly; (b) A occurs before B does; and (c) B does not occur unless A does. Invoking empiricist thinking and aware of the basic problem of induction, Hume pointed out that we know about these regularities only because of our experience. Furthermore, because our experiences are limited, we can never be completely certain about the causes of events. Hume's conclusion that absolute certainty was unattainable labeled him a "skeptic" and brought him into conflict with sources of authority such as the church, which naturally took offense at the implication that the existence of God could be questioned.

It is important to note, however, that Hume did not deny the existence of reality, God, or the possibility of there being absolute causes of events. His point was that we as humans could never arrive at them with certainty. From the practical standpoint of day-to-day living, what is important, Hume believed, is to be able to accumulate enough experience to make the best possible predictions. Life is a probability estimate. If events occurred together reliably in the past, we have every reason to expect that they will continue to covary in the future. Thus, Hume was not denying causality; he was merely shifting it from a search for absolute causes to a search for greater-than-chance regularities. Modern psychologists searching for the "causes" of behavior are essentially following Hume's lead in this regard. They recognize that multiple factors contribute to all behaviors; the best one can hope for is to identify the factors that predict behavior with probabilities greater than chance.

David Hartley (1705–1757): A Physiological Associationism

Hume paid heed to the process of association, but the topic commanded an even greater share of David Hartley's attention. His *Observations on Man, His Frame, His Duty, and His Expectations* (1749/1971) summarized the essentials of British empiricist thought and added a forceful description of how association could be the guiding principle for a theory of how the human mind was organized. The book also attempted to describe the neurological correlates of the association process.

Hartley was a contemporary of Hume, but not influenced by him. He began preliminary drafts of his *Observations* in the early 1730s, before Hume's 1739 *Treatise*, and he seemed to be unaware of Hume's work (not surprising, considering the poor sales of Hume's book). Three years before producing the final *Observations*, Hartley published a version of the book as an appendix to a medical book on kidney and bladder stones. The appendix was written in Latin, under the tentative-sounding title of *Conjecturae*. Apparently, Hartley wished to preview his ideas to a restricted group of scholars before going public with it (Webb, 1988).

Hartley made it clear in the book's opening sentence that he was a dualist on the mind–body question: "Man consists of two parts, body and mind" (Hartley, 1749/1971, p. i). Unlike Descartes's interactionism, however, Hartley took a stance known as psychophysical **parallelism**. That is, he considered psychological and physical (physiological) events separately, but operating in parallel; he even structured the book as a series of propositions that alternated between the mind and the body. The widely quoted propositions 10 and 11 outline the core of his associationism, first on the mental side and then on the physical. Proposition 10 reads, in part:

> Any Sensations A, B, C, &c. by being associated with one another a sufficient Number of Times, get such Power over the corresponding Ideas a, b, c, &c. that any one of the Sensations A, when impressed alone, shall be able to excite in the Mind b, c, &c. the ideas of the rest.
>
> Sensations may be said to be associated together, when their Impressions are either made precisely at the same Instant of Time, or in the contiguous successive Instants. We may therefore distinguish Association into two sorts, the synchronous, and the successive. (Hartley, 1749/1971, p. 65)

For Hartley, then, the main law of association is *contiguity*, the experiencing of events together. If we repeatedly see Adam (A), Bess (B), and Chris (C) together, and each sensory experience produces the corresponding ideas of them (a, b, and c), then in the future if we see Adam (A), the ideas of Bess (b) and Chris (c) will occur to us. The chances of this happening relate to how often we have seen the three of them together. Thus the strength of an association relies on repetition. Furthermore, contiguity occurs either for events experienced simultaneously or in quick succession. Although Hartley used the terms *synchronous* and *successive*, these concepts are commonly referred to as **spatial contiguity** and **temporal contiguity**, respectively. Thinking of your house might lead you to think of your dog sitting by the front door (synchronous or spatial), whereas your dog's drooling might be the result of him associating your smiling face with the subsequent appearance of food (successive or temporal).[4]

There is no need to quote Hartley's Proposition 11 because it is identical to Proposition 10, except that the word *Vibrations* substitutes for *Sensations*, and the phrase *miniature Vibrations* replaces *Ideas*. This was Hartley's version of nervous system activity, taken from Newton, who suggested that all matter could be conceptualized as vibrating particles in space. Hartley had the advantage over Descartes in knowing that the nerves were not hollow; hence, there was no space for animal spirits to be flowing back and forth. Rather, nerves were tightly packed fibers, and he believed they conveyed sensory information by vibrating. In the brain, smaller nerves produced even smaller vibrations, which Hartley called "miniature vibrations." These correspond to ideas. Like Hume, who referred to ideas as "faint copies" of impressions, Hartley thought of ideas (miniature vibrations) as "less vigorous" than sensations (vibrations).

Hartley's model of the mind was a kind of building-block structure in which complex ideas were constructed from the individual component parts. He used the complex idea of a horse as an example, writing that "we could have no proper idea of the Horse, unless the particular Ideas of the Head, Neck, Body, Legs, and Tail, peculiar to this Animal, stuck to each other in the Fancy [i.e., occurred to us], from frequent joint Impression" (Hartley, 1749/1971, p. 71). These subparts can also be divisible into even simpler ideas (e.g., legs include hoofs). If we experience all these atomistic elements frequently enough, then seeing a part of a horse (e.g., a hoof) will make us think of the horse as a whole.

Hartley's analysis brings the issue of atomism versus "holism" into focus. Most of the British philosophers took an atomistic approach, and Hartley was perhaps the most explicit of the philosophers considered thus far. One problem with this approach is that it requires knowledge of the parts before one can know the whole. That is, complex ideas are built up from simpler ones. In his horse example, Hartley wrote of the parts "coalescing" into the whole animal. The whole is equal to the sum of its parts. **Holism**, on the other hand, argues for the primacy of the whole over its constituent elements, that the parts have no meaning without first knowing the whole. The psychologist G. F. Stout once used the example of a pyramid constructed of oval stones (Klein, 1970). Each element of the pyramid may be perfectly round, but the whole figure has an overall triangular shape not found in any of its parts. The holistic approach would eventually find a voice within psychology through the work of the Gestalt psychologists (Chapter 9).

Hartley, who was clearly in the atomist camp, had a direct influence on James Mill (1773–1836), another in the long line of British empiricists and associationists. The influence is clear from this

---

[4]As you can guess from the latter example, contiguity was an important concept for the Russian physiologist Ivan Pavlov, who you will encounter in Chapter 10.

often-quoted example provided by Mill in his *Analysis of the Phenomena of the Human Mind* (1829/1948):

> Brick is one complex idea, mortar is another complex idea; these ideas, with ideas of position and quantity, compose my idea of a wall. My idea of a plank is a complex idea, my idea of a rafter is a complex idea, my idea of a nail is a complex idea.
>
> These, united with the same ideas of position and quantity, compose my duplex idea of a floor. In the same manner, my complex idea of glass, wood, and others, compose my duplex idea of a window; and these duplex ideas, united together, compose my idea of a house. (p. 154)

Mill was another important character in British philosophy and, like Hume, was also well known as a historian; his *History of British India*, written in 1817, made him financially secure. James Mill was not as important as his son, however—an outcome that Mill, Senior, deliberately set out to produce. Read the Close-Up for more on the deliberate shaping of a philosopher.

CLOSE-UP

RAISING A PHILOSOPHER

James Mill was not content simply to write about the importance of experience for developing the mind. When his son was born, he was determined to put empiricism into action by filling the empty white paper of his son's mind with as much information as possible. John Stuart Mill experienced (endured might be a better term) an unusual childhood and described it later in a brief yet remarkable autobiography (Mill, 1873/1989).

Mill, Junior, never went to school with other children, but by his 12th birthday, he could match the intellectual accomplishments of any university graduate. Under his father's stern tutelage, he started learning Greek vocabulary at age 3, Latin at age 8, and by the time he was 10 he had read most of the classic Greek and Roman texts, ranging from *Aesop's Fables* to Plato's *Dialogues* to the Greek histories of Herodotus to Aristotle's *Rhetoric*. He also devoured art and literature and mastered algebra and geometry. For fun he read books like *Robinson Crusoe*, the *Arabian Nights*, and Shakespeare's history plays. The latter might have reflected a minor rebellion against his father, who "never was a great admirer of Shakespeare, the English idolatry of whom he used to attack with some severity" (Mill, 1873/1989, p. 35).

Young Mill spent the better part of each day in his lessons. His father tutored him directly, but he was also expected to learn a great deal on his own. A typical routine was for Mill to read a portion of some book, take notes, and then report on it to his father the following day, during prebreakfast walks through the countryside.

Mill later wrote that "my earliest recollections of green fields and wild flowers [were] mingled [with] the account I gave him daily of what I had read the day before" (p. 29). During the walks, his father would also lecture to him on "civilization, government, morality, [and] mental cultivation, which he required me afterwards to restate to him in my own words" (p. 30). But the education was not simply drill and practice. Mill came to value the fact that his father often challenged him with difficult material and forced him to learn as much as he could on his own. Concerning Mill's education in logic and political economy, for instance, he wrote:

> Striving … to call forth the activity of my faculties, by making me find out everything for myself, he gave his explanations not before, but after, I had felt the full force of the difficulties; and not only gave me an accurate knowledge of these two great subjects, as far as they were then understood, but made me a thinker on both.... Anything which could be found out by thinking, I was never told, until I had exhausted my efforts to find it out for myself.... A pupil from whom nothing is ever demanded which he cannot do, never does all he can. (pp. 44–45)

John Stuart Mill is often cited as an example of a brilliant child prodigy, one whose native intellectual gifts enabled him to learn so much so early in life. There is probably some truth in this, but Mill never believed it for a minute. Because he was not allowed to play with other children as he was growing up, he had no point of comparison except for his father. In fact, throughout his childhood he was under the impression, as he put it, that "I was rather backward in my studies, since I always found myself so, in comparison with what my father expected from me" (Mill, 1873/1989, p. 46). When he eventually realized how far advanced he was, he showed the empiricist spirit by crediting it to his experiences rather than to any innate ability. Indeed, he believed his "natural gifts [to be] rather below than above par" (p. 44) and that his advantages over others resulted from their inferior educations. In his self-effacing words, his accomplishments "could not be ascribed to any merit in me, but to the very unusual advantage which had fallen to my lot, of having a father who was able to teach me" (pp. 46–47).

John Stuart Mill (1806–1873): On the Verge of Psychological Science

Mill's adult life was no less extraordinary than his childhood. Following in his father's footsteps, he supported himself through Foreign Service work with the British East India Company, starting as a clerk and gradually rising through the ranks to an executive position. Royalties from the sales of his books eventually assured him a comfortable living. In his later years, he was elected to Parliament's House of Commons and served for 3 years. Very little else about his life was conventional. Raised by his father to be a "reasoning machine," he became a committed activist for political and social reform by age 15; but 5 years later, he suffered a mental collapse that today we might call an existential crisis—he wondered about the meaning of his life.

After several lethargic years, Mill emerged from this depression, partly as a result of discovering Wordsworth. The beauty of the Lake poet's words awakened Mill's emotional life for the first time, showing him there was more to life than cold rationality. His feelings were further developed when he met and fell in love with Harriet Taylor, a remarkable woman who combined beauty with intellect. Unfortunately for Mill, Taylor was married—and happily, it appears. Despite the impediment, a relationship between the two developed; Mill even lived with the Taylors for a brief time and tagged along on vacations. The alliance was evidently platonic, but it created a minor scandal nonetheless. They finally married in 1851, waiting a respectful 2 years after John Taylor's death. Harriet contributed significantly to Mill's work while she lived, especially to his most important political work, *On Liberty*, published in 1858. After she died unexpectedly in 1858, her daughter carried on the intellectual partnership with Mill. Helen Taylor (with Mill in Figure 2.5) contributed to Mill's classic feminist essay, *The Subjection of Women* (1869).[5] The book was written at a time when married women had almost no rights—they could not own property, they could not inherit, they could not vote, divorce was virtually impossible, and, if they managed to get a divorce, they had no child custody rights (Capaldi, 2004). Mill's essay challenged the prevailing mores and contributed a small step in increasing the rights of women. A year after the essay was published, Parliament (Mill was a member at the time) passed the Married Women's Property Bill, which gave married women the right to own and inherit property.

Mill's politics derived from and contributed to his psychology. As an empiricist, he believed that all knowledge came through experience and that under the proper circumstances, anyone could become knowledgeable. Thus he favored government support for education and was appalled at the traditional English system that favored the landed gentry, an elite minority. At the same time, he endorsed a meritocracy in which the vote would be given only to those men and women who had reached a certain

[5]Helen Taylor was more of an activist than her mother; she helped create Britain's first women's suffrage organization (the National Society for Women's Suffrage) and recruited such notable women as Florence Nightingale into the group.

The Granger Collection, NYC — All rights reserved.

FIGURE 2.5 John Stuart Mill and stepdaughter Helen Taylor. From Mazlish (1975).

level of education. In short, he aimed for a society that endeavored to fill everyone's blank slates to the maximum.

Mill's Psychology Mill's views on psychology can be found scattered in several places, including his *System of Logic* (1843/1987), which we examine shortly; in the extensive notes that he wrote for a republication of his father's *Analysis*, published in 1869; and in his *Examination of Sir William Hamilton's Philosophy* (1865). His attack on Hamilton is a good illustration of the strong connection between Mill's reforming zeal and his empiricist views. Mill criticized Hamilton's rationalism and his belief in innate ideas, arguing that the result was an antireform philosophy. As Mill put it:

> I have long felt that the prevailing tendency to regard all the marked distinctions of human character as innate, and in the main indelible, and to ignore the irresistible proofs that by far the greater part of those differences, whether between individuals, races, or sexes, are … produced by differences in circumstances, is one of the chief hindrances to the rational treatment of great social questions and one of the greatest stumbling blocks to human improvement. (Mill, 1873/1989, p. 203)

Mill subscribed to the basic tenets of British empiricism and associationism, but he extended the ideas of his father and others (especially Hartley) by using a chemical rather than a mechanical metaphor in his description of how complex ideas are built from simple ones. The earlier quote from James Mill ("Brick is one complex idea, mortar is another complex idea," etc.) portrays the mind as passively accumulating experiences in which the elements combine mechanically to form larger wholes. John Stuart Mill, however, believed the mind to be a more active force in synthesizing our experiences; he argued the holistic position that complex ideas are more than a passive combination of elements:

> When many impressions or ideas are operating in the mind together, there sometimes takes place a process of a similar kind to chemical combination. When impressions have been so often experienced in conjunction that each of them calls up readily and instantaneously the ideas of the whole group, those ideas sometimes melt and coalesce into one another, and appear not several

> ideas, but one . . . . [So] it appears to me that the Complex Idea, formed by blending together of several simpler ones, should, when it really appears simple (that is, when the separate elements are not consciously distinguishable in it), be said to *result from*, or be *generated by*, the simple ideas, not to *consist* of them. (Mill, 1843/1987, p. 39–40; emphasis in the original)

A wall, then, derives from the simple ideas of our experiences, but goes beyond the simple combination of brick and mortar and has properties all its own, just as water has its own properties even though it results from the simple elements of hydrogen and oxygen. To use the phrase later popularized by gestaltists, the whole is more than the sum of its parts.

Mill's Logic In 1843, Mill published *A System of Logic, Ratiocinative and Inductive, Being a Connected View of the Principles of Evidence, and the Methods of Scientific Investigation*. It described some of his beliefs about association and mental chemistry, and it included an argument for the creation of a scientific approach to the study of psychology, on the grounds that although it might not reach the level of precision of physics, it could do as well as some disciplines that were considered scientific at the time (meteorology was an example he used). The *Logic* also outlined a methodology for applying inductive logic while trying to determine causality in science. He called the methods Agreement, Difference, and Concomitant Variation. Descriptions of these methods remain popular today in modern research methods texts (although the labels are no longer used).

In the **Method of Agreement**, one looks for a common element in several instances of an event. For example, suppose a researcher suspects that a particular gene causes depression. Let X symbolize the proposed cause (the gene) and Y symbolize the effect (depression). To use the method of agreement, the researcher studies a sample of depressed people and looks to see if they all have gene X. If they do, then it can be said that X is sufficient for Y to occur: "If X, then Y." Does this mean that X caused Y? Not necessarily, and the example illustrates the problem with induction. Every depressed person in the sample might have X, but it is possible that some yet undiscovered person is depressed but does not have gene X. The method of agreement can both support some hypothesis and call it into question, but it cannot establish cause by itself.

Neither can the **Method of Difference**, in which one looks for evidence that the absence of an effect is always accompanied by the absence of a proposed cause: "If not X, then not Y." To stay with the depression example, this would mean examining nondepressed people and looking for gene X, hoping *not* to find it. If this outcome occurs, then one can say that gene X is necessary for depression to occur, because without X (the gene), nobody is Y (depressed). Again, there are problems. A sample of nondepressed people, none of whom have the gene, does not prove the case; there still could be some nondepressed people out there with gene X.

Combined, in what Mill called the **Joint Method**, the methods of agreement and difference have the potential for identifying cause, within the limits of induction (i.e., you will never study every case). Thus if it could be determined that every person with gene X is depressed, and that every person without gene X is not depressed, then it could be concluded that gene X is both sufficient and necessary for depression to occur (i.e., the gene causes depression). Of course, the conclusion about cause would be tentative, subject to potential disproof in the future.

The logic of the methods of agreement and difference underlie the use of the modern-day experimental method in psychology: The method of agreement corresponds to an experimental group and the method of difference corresponds to a control group (Rosnow & Rosenthal, 1993). Thus, a hypothetical experiment on the effect of gene (X) on depression (Y) would involve identifying two equal groups and implanting the gene in the experimental group but not in the control group. If everyone in the experimental group comes down with depression (if X, then Y), and if nobody in the control group gets depressed (if not X, then not Y), then you have evidence that X causes Y (again, within the limits of your study). Of course, you would have a hard time finding volunteers for this study. Mill recognized this ethical limitation, and along with a concern about precision of measurement and control, it made him skeptical of psychology becoming as rigorously scientific as physics.

Mill's third method, **Concomitant Variation**, is reminiscent of Hume and underlies today's correlational method. Using this approach, one looks to see if changes in X are associated with predictable changes in Y. The method is especially useful when either X or Y (or both) can be found in every person to some degree. For example, everyone gets at least some exercise, and everyone is more or less healthy. Using the method of concomitant variation, a researcher could see if those who exercise a great deal are healthier than those who exercise infrequently.

Unlike any of the philosophers considered thus far, John Stuart Mill did not attempt to write anything like an essay on human understanding (Locke), a treatise on human knowledge (Berkeley) or human nature (Hume), a series of observations on man (Hartley), or an analysis of the mind (his father). That is, none of his books can be pointed to and labeled as "J. S. Mill's psychology." Because he saw himself above all as a political and economic philosopher, this is not too surprising. Yet Mill is as important for modern psychology as any of those philosophers who did write a "psychology." He brought British associationism to its zenith, and he provided an analysis of scientific thinking that guides psychological research to this day. He was a key transition figure in the shift from the philosophy of the mind to the science of the mind.

RATIONALIST RESPONSES TO EMPIRICISM

Except for the section on Descartes, this chapter has focused on British empiricist and associationist philosophy. But other strong voices were heard during the times we have examined, and those voices also resonate with modern psychology. In particular, two German philosophers make a notable contrast to British empiricism and associationism. Gottfried Leibniz was a contemporary of Locke and responded directly to Locke's *Essay Concerning Human Understanding* with his own *New Essays on Human Understanding*, published posthumously in 1765. Immanuel Kant (1724–1804) lived during the same time as Hume and Hartley and wrote in response to them (especially Hume).

Gottfried Wilhelm Leibniz (1646–1716)

Leibniz had a remarkably wide range of interests, from politics to math to engineering to alchemy to philosophy. As a mathematician, he is best known as the coinventor (with Newton) of calculus, the event celebrated on a German stamp (Figure 2.6). His importance for psychology rests with his reply

FIGURE 2.6 German stamp commemorating Leibniz and the discovery of calculus.

to Locke, his approach to the mind–body problem, and his "monadology." He was a great admirer of Locke, agreeing that experience is essential to the formation of knowledge. However, he disagreed with Locke's "mind at birth = white paper" metaphor, proposing instead that the mind be seen as analogous to veined marble (Leibniz, 1765/1982). The sculptor can take a block of marble and shape it in many different ways, but the way the marble is veined limits the number of shapes that are possible. The veins in essence represent the innate properties of the marble, to be revealed by the artist's skill. Similarly, according to Leibniz, the mind has innate properties that help determine the limits and shape the effects of experience. The innate properties, such as reason, enable the individual to arrive at what Leibniz called "necessary truths," truths that are proven with reason and logic and not by direct experience. The fundamental principles of mathematics (e.g., the three angles of a triangle will always add up to 180°) are examples of necessary truths, he thought. Like Descartes, Leibniz agreed that animals lacked the innate properties found in humans, and thus could be considered pure "empirics."

On the mind–body question, Leibniz could not accept the Cartesian notion of direct and mutual influence because it led inevitably to a search for the manner of interaction and resulted in a fruitless hunt for such things as pineal glands. Instead, Leibniz proposed a psychophysical parallelism solution to the mind–body problem, similar to Hartley's idea. Thus, he proposed that mind ("psycho") and body ("physical") work in parallel to each other, kept in a "pre-established harmony," as Leibniz put it, by the hand of God. He illustrated his parallelism with a metaphor of two clocks that are constructed to be in perfect harmony. Like mind and body, they operate independent of each other, but in agreement. By implication, parallelism legitimizes the separate study of mental (psychological) and physical (bio-logical) events, thus providing a philosophical basis for "the eventual emergence of psychology as a separate science as distinct from physiology as a separate science" (Klein, 1970, p. 353).

The elements of both mental and physical reality were called **monads** by Leibniz. These were infinite in number and more like energy forces than material atoms. They were said to be arranged in a hierarchy, from rational to sentient to simple. Rational monads, according to Leibniz, form the essence of the human mind; sentient monads are found in all living beings that are not human; and simple monads make up physical reality. Rational monads account for consciousness, but Leibniz believed that awareness is not an all-or-nothing affair. Rather, he proposed a continuum of awareness, thus laying a foundation for two important developments in psychology. First, the continuum implies a level of unawareness, an idea leading to the concept of the unconscious, which was later to become the center-piece of Freud's theories. Leibniz distinguished between what he called apperception, perception, and petites perceptions. **Apperception** is the highest level of awareness, in which we focus our attention on some information, apprehend it fully, and make it personally meaningful. Perception is an awareness of something, but it is not as sharp as in apperception. **Petites perceptions** are below the level of aware-ness, but ultimately essential for enabling higher levels of perception to occur. To illustrate the latter, Leibniz used the example of an ocean wave or a waterfall. Petite perceptions are created by individual drops of water, which we never see or hear. Yet all the drops, taken together, are necessary for us to perceive or apperceive the larger reality of the ocean wave or the waterfall.

The second implication of the proposal about different levels of awareness is that there must exist points on the continuum of consciousness where one goes from unawareness to awareness. These points can be called **thresholds**, and as we will learn in Chapter 4, identifying and measuring thresholds became an important feature of the earliest experiments in psychology.

Immanuel Kant (1724–1804)

In his role as a diplomat, Leibniz traveled throughout Europe. In contrast, Immanuel Kant evidently never ventured more than 40 miles from his home in the eastern German city of Königsberg. He was born there, went to school there, eventually taught at the university there, and is buried there. Despite the apparent provincialism, Kant was a towering intellect in 18th-century German philosophy, doing for the rationalist view what Leibniz had done in the 17th century. Kant is best known to psychologists for three books published in his later years: *Critique of Pure Reason* (1781/1965), *Critique of Judgment* (1788/1952), and *Critique of Practical Reason* (1790/1959).

Kant agreed with the empiricists that our knowledge is built from experience; but, like Leibniz, he argued that the more important question was how the process occurs. That is, he wondered how experience itself was possible, and he concluded that it required the existence of some a priori (prior to experience) knowledge that helps shape the experiences we have. For instance, Kant pointed out that whenever we experience events, we organize them with reference to space and time. Thus we water the garden, which occupies space, and which takes X amount of time to complete. Our understanding of the concept "water the garden" is not possible without the a priori knowledge of space and time. The concepts of space and time, then, we know "intuitively," according to Kant; we don't have to "learn" about the concepts. To contrast Hume's view that we can never be certain of causality, Kant argued that the mind inevitably thinks in terms of cause and effect—everyone's experience of the world is that it operates according to causal laws (water poured on earth always goes down). Like space and time, cause and effect were considered by Kant to be innate properties of the mind.

Kant argued that psychology could never become a science like the physical sciences. He pointed out that compared with physical objects, mental phenomena could not be observed directly by an independent observer, nor could they be defined or measured with the precision of mathematics. As we shall learn, when German psychologists such as Wilhelm Wundt declared psychology a science in the 19th century, they had to disavow specifically their countryman's argument about the feasibility of the endeavor.

IN PERSPECTIVE: PHILOSOPHICAL FOUNDATIONS

This chapter only scratches the surface of psychology's "long past." Nonetheless, you should emerge from your reading with a basic understanding of some of the philosophical underpinnings of modern psychology. Furthermore, you should be starting to develop a sense of the continuity of ideas in our discipline's history. Psychology did not just pop out of the ground in the late 19th century. Rather, psychology's founders were wrestling with the same issues that concerned the people highlighted in this chapter. The founders chose to attack the questions from a slightly different angle than the philosophers, that of direct experimentation, but they were trying to answer the same questions: How do we accumulate knowledge? How is the mind organized? How do the senses work? Is any of our knowledge hard-wired (i.e., innate)? The founders of 19th-century psychology also had an ever-increasing knowledge of how the brain and the rest of the nervous system worked, and they were beginning to develop objective methods for studying the mind. In Chapter 3, we, encounter these developments in physiology and methodology.

Before closing this chapter, however, an important point must be made about presentism. From the standpoint of the early 21st century, knowing that psychology evolved into a scientific discipline, it is easy to look back at the early philosophers and wonder why they "failed" to take what might appear to us now to be an easy step—the one from careful observations and a close logical analysis of some mental phenomenon to an experimental investigation of it. That is, when we first read of people like Descartes and Locke and Mill, we tend to see them as gradually approaching but not quite reaching the "holy grail" of scientific psychology. It is a serious mistake, however, to think of these individuals as somehow falling short. In fact, they were clearly the best and the brightest of their day, going far beyond their peers in the brilliance of their insights. The proper way to view the philosophers in this chapter is to think of them as people living in the context of their times and grappling as best they could with the issues of their day. That these philosophers wrestled with the same questions that exist today is not an indication of steady progress upward from then to now, but of the universality of the issues. It is futile and simply wrong to criticize them for not doing what others did later.

SUMMARY

A Long Past

• The Ebbinghaus statement that psychology has a long past but a short history is a reminder that the issues that concern psychologists have been addressed by serious thinkers for thousands of years, even though psychology as a self-defined discipline is just over 130 years old. The "new psychology" that emerged in the late 19th century differed from philosophy in that the questions about human behavior and mental life were taken into the laboratory for the first time.

Descartes: The Beginnings of Modern Philosophy and Science

• Descartes lived during years of great advances in science and technology. It was a time when the authority of the church and of Aristotle came to be questioned, by Galileo's support for the Copernican heliocentric model of the universe instead of the traditional geocentric model, for example. Descartes's life also overlapped that of Sir Francis Bacon, who argued for an inductive scientific strategy for understanding the universe.

• Descartes was a rationalist, believing that the way to true knowledge was through the systematic use of his reasoning abilities. Because he believed that some truths were universal and could be arrived at through reason and without the necessity of sensory experience, he was also a nativist. In addition, he was a dualist and an interactionist, believing that mind and body were distinct essences, but had direct influence on each other.

• To explain mind–body interactionism, Descartes developed a model of nervous system activity that included the first model of reflex action. His concept of bodily action was a mechanistic one—the body was like a machine. According to the Cartesian dichotomy, animals are pure machines, but humans have a rational mind (soul) to complement their machinelike bodies.

The British Empiricist Argument and the Associationists

• The founder of British empiricism was John Locke, who rejected the nativist belief in innate ideas and argued that the mind was analogous to a blank piece of paper, to be written on by our experiences. Ideas that result from our experiences have two sources: sensation and reflection. Locke used an atomistic model, assuming that complex ideas were built from the basic elements of simple ideas. Primary qualities (e.g., extension) exist independent of the perceiver, but secondary qualities (e.g., the perception of color) depend on perception. Locke's beliefs led him to recommend that parents take an active role in educating their children, that children be encouraged with praise rather than concrete rewards, and that punishment be avoided as an educational strategy.

• George Berkeley wrote a detailed analysis of visual perception based on empiricist arguments, in the process describing visual phenomena such as convergence, accommodation, and depth perception. He rejected Locke's distinction between primary and secondary qualities; and to counter materialism, he proposed (subjective idealism) that we cannot be sure of the reality of objects except through our belief in God, the Permanent Perceiver.

• David Hume was an empiricist–associationist known for making a distinction between impressions, which result from sensation, and ideas, which he said were faint copies of impressions. He also identified the rules of association as resemblance, contiguity, and cause and effect. He believed that we cannot know causality absolutely; we know only that certain events occur together regularly.

• David Hartley is considered the founder of associationism because of his attempt to summarize all that was known about it and his argument that the essence of association was contiguity (both spatial and temporal) and repetition. He developed a model of nervous system action based on the Newtonian concept of vibrations, and his position on the mind–body issue was that of psychophysical parallelism.

• John Stuart Mill, a child prodigy, was the leading British philosopher of the 19th century. Compared with others (including his father, the empiricist philosopher James Mill), who described the mind in mechanical, atomistic, building-block terms, J. S. Mill used a more holistic chemical metaphor, arguing that complex ideas are greater than the sum of their individual simple ideas. Mill analyzed the logic of science and described several methods for trying to arrive at scientific truth: the Method of Agreement and the Method of Difference, which underlie today's experimental method; and the Method of Concomitant Variation, which is similar to the modern correlational method.

Rationalist Responses to Empiricism

• Gottfried Leibniz challenged Locke's white paper analogy and said the mind was more like veined marble, in which the veins were analogous to innate abilities that shape our experiences. He also challenged Descartes's interactionism, arguing for a parallelist position and using the metaphor of two synchronous clocks to make his point. His monadology provided a basis for the concepts of the unconscious and sensory thresholds.

• Immanuel Kant recognized the importance of our experiences for developing our understanding of the world, but he argued that experience itself was not possible without a basis in some a priori knowledge to provide the framework for our experiences. Kant believed that psychology could not achieve the status of a science because psychological events could not be observed objectively.

STUDY QUESTIONS

1. What did Ebbinghaus mean when he said that psychology had a long past but a short history?

2. How did a "mechanistic" zeitgeist influence Descartes's thinking?

3. Distinguish between a heliocentric and a geocentric model of the universe, and explain why advocating the former earned Galileo a charge of heresy.

4. Explain what it means to advocate a Baconian inductive strategy for gaining knowledge of human behavior.

5. Explain why Descartes is considered both a rationalist and a nativist.

6. According to Descartes, how does a reflex work? Use the example of the boy putting his foot in a fire.

7. In Descartes's model of the nervous system, how did mind and body interact, and why was the pineal gland chosen as the point of interaction? What was the essential flaw in the logic of identifying a part of the brain (pineal gland) as the point of mutual influence of mind and body?

8. What is meant by the "Cartesian dichotomy"?

9. Compare rationalist and empiricist explanations for how we arrive at our knowledge of widely held concepts (e.g., God).

10. Compare Locke's white paper and Leibniz's veined model metaphors, and relate them to fundamental epistemological questions.

11. Distinguish between primary and secondary qualities of matter, and compare the views of Locke and Berkeley with regard to these qualities.

12. Define materialism, and explain how Berkeley's subjective idealism attacked the concept.

13. Using Berkeley's depth perception examples, show how British empiricists applied their concepts to visual perception.

14. Compare Hume's and Hartley's laws of association. Explain why Hume's concept of cause and effect resonates with modern research psychologists.

15. Describe J. S. Mill's mental chemistry, and contrast it with his father's more mechanical view.

16. Show how Mill's rules for inductive logic relate to modern conceptions of the experimental and correlational methods.

17. Show how Leibniz's monadology relates to the concepts of the unconscious and thresholds.

18. Describe Kant's rationalist response to empiricist thinking.

CHAPTER 3

THE SCIENTIFIC CONTEXT

The entire doctrine of [phrenology] is contained in two fundamental propositions, of which the first is, that understanding resides exclusively in the brain, and the second, that each particular faculty of the understanding is provided in the brain with an organ proper to itself. Now, of these two propositions, there is certainly nothing new in the first one, and perhaps nothing true in the second one.

—Pierre Flourens, 1846

PREVIEW AND CHAPTER OBJECTIVES

Partitioning the philosophical and scientific antecedents to psychology into two chapters implies the presence of two nonoverlapping paths that eventually merged to form the new psychology during the late 19th century. There is a grain of truth to this—the British empiricists did not spend their time cutting into spinal cords or electrically stimulating nerves connected to frog legs, and the scientists to be encountered in this chapter did not write long philosophical treatises on "human understanding." But the distinction between philosophical and scientific antecedents to psychology is artificial, brought about by the decisions made when structuring a textbook. In fact, developments in philosophy and in the natural sciences proceeded apace, especially in the 18th and 19th centuries. Scientists were deeply concerned with philosophical issues; for physiologists, this concern focused on the epistemological questions about human understanding and the problem of the relationship between mental and physical reality (the mind–body problem). In turn, philosophers were well aware of, and in some instances contributed to, developments in physiology (e.g., Berkeley's work on vision), electricity, and the other sciences.

This chapter focuses on developments in physiology, especially 19th- and early 20th-century studies of the nature and functioning of the nervous system. We will examine (a) research that explored the physiology of reflexes and basic sensory-motor processes, (b) the issue of whether specific functions could be "localized" in different areas of the brain, and (c) the nature and functioning of the basic unit of the nervous system, the neuron. After you finish this chapter, you should be able to:

■ Show how Enlightenment thinking contributed to the idea that psychology could become scientific

■ Describe the contributions of Robert Willis to our understanding of the nervous system

■ Describe and explain the importance of Whytt's research on reflex action

■ Describe Magendie's research on sensory-motor function in the spinal cord, and explain why the Bell–Magendie law might have been misnamed

■ Describe the doctrine of the specific energies of nerves

■ Describe Helmholtz's research on nerve impulse speed, and relate it to the vitalism–materialism issue

- Understand the issue that Helmholtz referred to as the "problem of perception," and recognize that his solution was congenial to British empiricism
- Describe the essential tenets of phrenology, and explain why it ultimately failed scientifically
- Explain phrenology's widespread popularity, especially in America
- Describe the logic of the method of ablation, and show how Flourens used it to dispute phrenology
- Describe the clinical method and two different examples (Phineas Gage, Broca's "Tan") of how this method shed light on brain function
- Describe the method of electrical stimulation ("scientific phrenology") and the results it produced
- Describe neuron theory and Sherrington's research leading to the conclusion that synapses exist

HEROIC SCIENCE IN THE AGE OF ENLIGHTENMENT

As described in the last chapter, the years marking the end of the Renaissance were characterized by a gradual change from a reliance on authority as the source of truth to a belief that science and human reasoning could produce an understanding of the natural world. Bacon, Galileo, Harvey, and Descartes exemplified this shift in the beginning of the 17th century. Sir Isaac Newton solidified the change in the second half of the century. With the publication of his *Principia Mathematica* in 1687, serious thinkers began to take for granted the idea that objective truth could be gained through the methods of science and the unbiased use of reason. Because science and reason came to be seen as the way to shed light on the darkness of ignorance, this period became known as the **Enlightenment**. Scientists like Newton became heroic figures, searching for "objective" truth about the universe by applying scientific methodology to its study. Newton's influence on the philosophers was hinted at in the last chapter—his analysis of light into basic components and his theory of gravitation influenced the British empiricists, who tried to produce a similar analysis of the mind and conceived of association as a force analogous to gravity. Furthermore, Newton's vision of the universe as a vast machine resonated with philosophers and other scientists who developed mechanical models for various biological systems (e.g., Harvey's heart-as-pump idea).

Enlightenment thinking and Newtonian influence even spread into the political arena. America's founding fathers were passionate and knowledgeable about science, and Benjamin Franklin made substantial contributions to the theory of electricity, including the invention of the lightning rod. The Constitution itself borrowed from the Newtonian concept of equilibrium when developing the notion of a balance of powers among the executive, legislative, and judicial elements of government (Cohen, 1995).

The Enlightenment reached the height of its influence in the second half of the 18th century, but its ideals remained strong throughout the 19th and even into the 20th century. By the early 19th century, faith in science seemed to be paying dividends in the form of technological innovations that eventually produced the Industrial Revolution. Thus science seemed to lead inevitably to progress, and scientists were viewed as being objective, simply looking for the truth without imposing their values, and improving society through the inventions that derived from their science. It wasn't until such technological innovations as the poison gas that spread ominously over the battlefields of World War I, and the atom bomb of World War II that hinted at the end of civilization, that serious questions began to be raised: Could science be objective and value free, and did scientific discoveries always mean "progress"?

Nonetheless, during the period when the idea of a scientific approach to psychology began to take shape in the minds of such philosophers as the British empiricists, the model of scientist as hero held sway. If scientific thinking and human reason could enlighten the world about physics and chemistry, why not biology? If biology, why not psychology?

In the middle of the 19th century, scientific psychology evolved from the philosophical questions examined in Chapter 2 and the research on the nervous system to be described in this chapter. Physiologists trying to "shed light" on how the senses and the nervous system actually worked developed methods and made discoveries that were directly relevant to the epistemological questions about the nature and origins of human knowledge being raised by philosophers such as John Stuart Mill. This dynamic convergence of philosophy and physiological science created an atmosphere from which a "scientific" approach to psychology eventually emerged.

FUNCTIONING OF THE NERVOUS SYSTEM

In Chapter 2, we saw how Descartes developed a model of nervous system functioning as he sought answers to the mind–body question. His ideas fired the imaginations of others, and during the course of the next few centuries, our understanding of the nervous system steadily improved. Many of the advances resulted from the medical community dealing with the problem of brain and nervous system damage, which was quite common in the context of two European wars in the middle of the 18th century and both the American and French revolutions during the second half of that century. At a time long before the development of antiseptic surgical procedures and antibiotic drugs, the vast majority of those suffering head wounds died from infection. Many of those who lived, however, became case studies that increased our knowledge of the brain and nervous system.

One issue of interest was whether the brain was the center of consciousness and the controller of voluntary action. Decapitated soldiers often showed arm and leg movements for a brief time. How did this happen? The issue was directly investigated with reference to executions during the French Revolution at the end of the 1700s that used the invention of a noted French physician, Joseph Guillotin. The device, which bears his name, was said to be a marvelous improvement over large hairy (and often intoxicated) men with axes, who sometimes required several tries before completing their gruesome task of separating head from body. Although the guillotine was clean and quick and therefore considered humane, bodies continued to twitch for a brief time after execution. Eye movements and quivering facial muscles could also be seen. Did some level of awareness, and perhaps some perception of extreme pain, remain after a beheading? If so, then perhaps the instrument was not so humane after all. The problem was investigated in the early 19th century by Theodor Bischoff, who arranged to conduct tests on the decapitated heads of criminals immediately after execution. If consciousness remained, Bischoff reasoned, then the heads should react predictably to having fingers thrust toward its eyes, having smelling salts placed under its nose, or, cruelly, having "You're pardoned!" spoken in its ear. Bischoff tried all of these tests, but the unfortunate heads showed no reaction (Fearing, 1930). He concluded that consciousness ended with the moment of execution, thereby reinforcing the theory that consciousness resides in the brain, while at the same time reassuring investors in guillotines. The muscle twitches that occurred after death were therefore involuntary actions unrelated to consciousness. The question of why these movements occurred at all still remained, however, resulting in intensive research into the nature of basic reflex action and the role of the brain and spinal cord in these movements.

Reflex Action

As we have seen, Descartes was the first to develop a model of reflex action, part of his attempt to show that the body operated like a machine. After Descartes, and before the 19th century, two scientists made notable contributions to our understanding of the nervous system: Thomas Willis and Robert Whytt. One gave reflexes their name; the other completed the first systematic research on reflex function.

Thomas Willis (1621–1675) was an Oxford physician and professor whose students included the famous British empiricist John Locke. His life overlapped that of Descartes, and like the Frenchman, Willis had a similar passion for understanding how the brain worked. Unlike Descartes, however, who spent considerable energy hunting for the source of mind–body interactions (and settling, as we have seen, on the pineal gland), Willis was more interested in providing detailed knowledge about the range of brain and nervous system structures, without the added burden of trying to resolve thorny philosophical issues. In *The Anatomy of the Brain* (1664/1965), Willis carefully described these structures, based on many hours spent dissecting brains, most of them supplied from local gallows (Finger, 2000). He also conducted extensive dissections of animals, making him an important early comparative anatomist. A notable feature of the Willis book was the inclusion of numerous highly detailed and precise drawings by his close friend, Christopher Wren (better known for his subsequent career as a renowned architect—he designed St. Paul's Cathedral in London, for example). One of Wren's drawings, the underside of the brain, complete with midbrain and brainstem features, is shown in Figure 3.1.

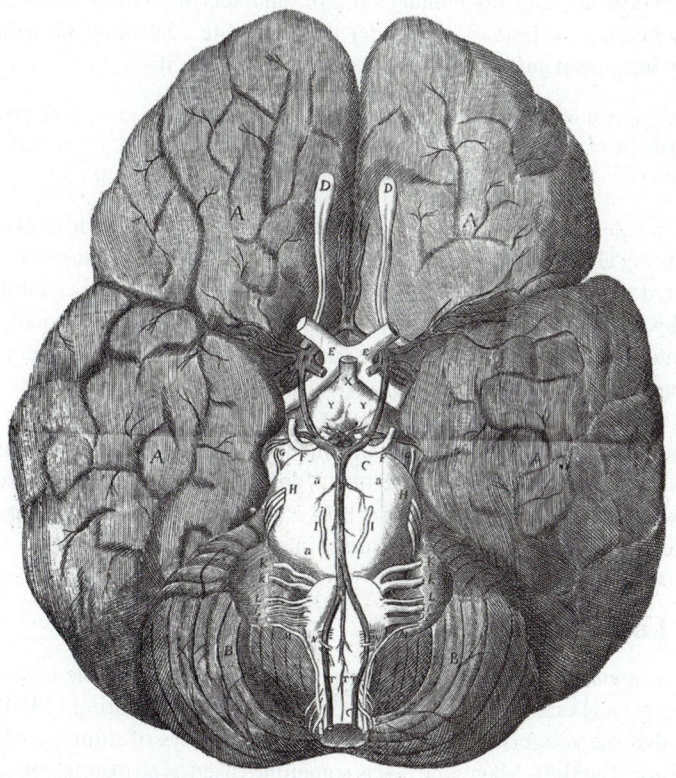

From Thomas Willis, Cerebri Anatome, 1664, drawing by Sir Christopher Wren, Courtesy of the National Institute of Health

FIGURE 3.1 One of Christopher Wren's drawings of the brain, in Thomas Willis's 1664 *The Anatomy of the Brain.*

In addition to extending our knowledge of the brain and nervous system, and noting the important differences between human and animal brains, Willis is also known for adding important terms to the general vocabulary of physiology—these included the structural terms *lobe*, *hemisphere*, and *corpus striatum* and the general term *neurologie*. Also, although we have seen that Descartes made the first attempt at describing the reflex, the term *reflex* (reflexion, actually) was coined by Willis (Finger, 2000). Crucial research on these reflexions, however, would not occur until Robert Whytt appeared on the scene.

The leading neurologist of his day, Robert Whytt (1714–1766; pronounced "*white*") of Edinburgh, Scotland, is famous in the history of pediatric medicine for being the first person to accurately describe tuberculous meningitis (Radbill, 1972). Among historians of psychology, however, it is Whytt's work on the reflex that takes center stage. His *Essay on The Vital and Other Involuntary Motions of Animals* (Whytt, 1751), summarizing years of research on the role of the spinal cord in mediating reflex action, was the first extensive treatment of reflexes to be based on experimental research (Fearing, 1930). Studying decapitated animals (mainly frogs), Whytt was able to show that leg muscles responded to physical stimulation—pinching the leg of a recently decapitated frog reliably produced a muscle contraction. On the other hand, if the connection between the leg and the spinal cord was severed, these "involuntary motions" of the leg failed to occur. Hence, Whytt demonstrated that the spinal cord played a crucial role in reflexive behavior.

Whytt distinguished between voluntary and involuntary actions, the former under the control of the "will," with the action originating in and requiring an intact brain, and the latter controlled through the spinal cord. In between voluntary and involuntary control, and serving to link them, was habit formation. Thus actions that begin as voluntary, and under the deliberate control of the will, become similar to reflexes when they have been sufficiently practiced. As Whytt put it:

> We not only acquire, through custom and habit, a faculty of performing certain motions with greater
> ease than we are wont to do them, but also, in proportion as this facility is increased, we become
> less sensible of any share or concern the mind has in them. (quoted in Fearing, 1930, p. 79)

Whytt also pointed out a consequence of the formation of habits—that the mere idea of a stimulus was sometimes sufficient to bring about a response. In a passage that will make you think of Ivan Pavlov (Chapter 10), Whytt illustrated the point with two everyday examples of what would eventually come to be called conditioned reflexes: "Thus the sight, or even the recalled idea of grateful food, causes an uncommon flow of spittle into the mouth of a hungry person; and the seeing of a lemon cut produces the same effect in many people" (quoted in Fearing, 1930, p. 80).

The existence of the kinds of reflexes documented by Whytt demands that a distinction be made between the sensory and motor components of the reaction, which in turn implies that some nerves may be for the purpose of conveying sensory information and others designed to pass messages along to the muscles, telling them to move. This distinction between sensory and motor nerves became established through the work of two scientists working at about the same time in different countries.

The Bell–Magendie Law

As you recall from Chapter 1, a *multiple* refers to a case in which two or more people make the same discovery during the same historical era, but do so independent of each other. Boring (1950) used the concept to support his idea that the zeitgeist affected the activities and ways of thinking of scientists during a particular historical era. The Bell–Magendie law is sometimes used as an example of a multiple: Two scientists, working in different laboratories (different countries, in this case) at about the same time and neither aware of the other's research, arrive at similar results. The situation was not quite that simple in the case of Bell and Magendie, however, and during the years following their work, there was a nasty fight over priority. The judgment of history is that Magendie should have been credited with the discovery; his research was more systematic, and he published it in the public forum of a journal. Bell's research, although occurring a few years earlier than Magendie's, was published in a private pamphlet with limited distribution and was based more on inference from anatomy than actual experimentation (Sechzer, 1983). Furthermore, Magendie got it right; Bell didn't. That Bell's name became paired with Magendie's is more of a tribute to the public clamoring of the politically influential Bell and his equally vociferous friends than to the quality of his research.

François Magendie (1783–1855), the son of a surgeon, grew up during the turbulent years of the French Revolution. Lacking much formal education, François used his father's influence to become an apprentice at a Paris hospital, where, at the tender age of 16, he was entrusted with the task of doing anatomical dissections (Grmek, 1972). After becoming a medical student and completing a degree in 1808, he quickly earned a reputation as a gifted scientist who distrusted theorizing in favor of inductively collecting "facts." This Baconian attitude he once described in this way: "I compare myself to a ragpicker: with my spiked stick in my hand and my basket on my back, I traverse the field of science and gather what I find" (quoted in Grmek, 1972, p. 7).

In 1822, Magendie published a three-page article summarizing the results of a study on the posterior and anterior roots of the spinal cord. From his earlier dissections he knew that nerve fibers exited the spinal cord in pairs before joining together: One type of fiber, the posterior root, was closer to the surface of the skin; the other (anterior root) was closer to the interior of the body. Different structures suggest different functions, and Magendie's research aimed at identifying these functions. Using a 6-week-old puppy as a subject,[1] Magendie exposed its spinal cord and cut the posterior fibers (i.e., those closer to the surface) while leaving the spinal cord intact. He sutured up the wound and observed the animal after it recovered. As he described it:

> I did not know what would result from this operation . . . . At first I believed the limb corresponding to the cut nerves to be completely paralyzed; it was insensitive to pricking and the hardest pressures and, further, it seemed immobile; but soon, to my very great surprise, I clearly saw it move, although sensibility remained completely absent. (Magendie, 1822/1965, p. 20)

Hence, the posterior roots controlled sensation. When this root was destroyed, the animal could still move the limb but had no sensation in it. Next, Magendie severed the anterior root in another animal, a task that required all of his considerable surgical skills. Because the anterior root lies below the posterior one, it is difficult to get to the former without damaging the latter. Nonetheless, Magendie worked out a successful procedure and managed to sever an anterior root cleanly (Bell, on the other hand, was never able to accomplish this). The results were clear: "There could be no doubt whatsoever; the limb was completely immobile and flaccid, although it retained an unequivocal sensibility. Finally, for completeness' sake, I cut both the anterior and the posterior roots; there was an absolute loss of feeling and movement" (Magendie, 1822/1965, p. 20). In summary, then, Magendie's finding, now known as the **Bell–Magendie law**, was that the posterior roots of the spinal cord controlled sensation, whereas anterior roots controlled motor responses. This was a major discovery, for it provided anatomical foundation for further study of the two sides of the reflex: sensation and movement.

---

[1] Magendie used puppies after having difficulty cutting through the tough protective covering of the spinal cord in older dogs. "A litter of eight puppies, six weeks old, ... seemed to me to be eminently suited for a new attempt at opening the vertebral canal. And, in fact, by using a very sharp scalpel, I was able with a single stroke ... to lay bare the posterior half of the spinal cord" (Magendie, 1822/1965, p. 19).

Furthermore, the distinction implied that nerves send messages in a single direction and that there are different sensory and motor tracts within the spinal cord and perhaps different sensory and motor regions within the brain.

As for Sir Charles Bell (1774–1842), his *Idea of a New Anatomy of the Brain: Submitted for the Observation of His Friends* had been written 11 years before the publication of Magendie's work, but it had been sent privately to about 100 colleagues. Bell was a prominent English anatomist with influential friends, however, and together they launched a campaign against Magendie when the latter's work was published in 1822. They accused the Frenchman of everything from unnecessary replication of Bell's original finding to animal cruelty. Bell went as far as to alter the wording of some of his work and republish it to make it appear that he had anticipated Magendie by a decade (Gallistel, 1981). Yet Magendie was unaware of Bell's work, which involved an analysis of anatomy of the spinal cord and an experiment on a "stunned rabbit." Bell deserves some credit for concluding that the posterior and anterior roots had different functions, but he mistakenly concluded that both roots had some sensory and motor function and that they were differentiated primarily by virtue of their connections to the cerebellum (posterior roots) and the cerebrum (anterior roots; Sechzer, 1983).

Magendie, personally affronted by the attacks from across the English Channel, recognized the value of Bell's research once he learned of it; but he refused to concede priority for discovering the critical (and correct) distinction between sensory and motor functions. In particular, while acknowledging Bell's priority concerning the strategy of segregating the spinal roots and the discovery that the anterior root influenced "muscular contractility" more than the posterior root did, Magendie vigorously asserted that "as for having established that these roots have distinct properties, distinct functions, that the anterior ones control movement, and posterior ones sensation, *this discovery belongs to me*" (quoted in Grmek, 1972; emphasis added).

The Specific Energies of Nerves

Another feature of Bell's 1811 pamphlet was his argument that different sensory nerves have different "qualities." Thus, "an impression made on two different nerves of sense, though with the same instrument, will produce two distinct sensations" (Bell, 1811/1965, p. 24). As an example, Bell pointed to the "papillae" on the tongue, some of which convey the sense of taste, others the sense of touch. When touching these latter papillae with a sharp steel pin, the resulting sensation is one of "sharpness." When touching one of the taste papillae with the same pin, however, the resulting sensation is one of a "metallic taste." Similarly, if two different types of stimuli affect a single type of nerve, then the sensation experienced will be determined by the type of sensory nerve stimulated. Thus light waves stimulate the optic nerve to produce a visual sensation, but pressing on the side of the eyeball also results in the sensation of a flash of light.

This idea of Bell's eventually became known as the doctrine of the **specific energies of nerves**, and although Bell's 1811 paper once again had chronological priority, credit went elsewhere, this time to the leading German physiologist of the first half of the 19th century, Johannes Müller (1801–1858). Müller, whose manic pace of work alternated with long periods of severe depression, was the first person ever named a professor of "physiology" at the University of Berlin, Germany's premier university. Müller elaborated on the specific energies doctrine and developed it more fully than Bell. In addition to making the point about different sensory qualities, Müller pointed out that in perception, we are not directly aware of the external world; rather, we are only aware of the action of our nervous system, which conveys information of the world to us. Thus our knowledge of the world is filtered through the physiology of the nervous system.

The doctrine of specific energies of nerves eventually became associated more with Müller than with Bell, mainly because Müller named it as such and presented it as a series of 10 related principles in his massive (eight books totaling more than 1,600 pages) *Handbook of Human Physiology*, which first appeared in 1840. This was the authoritative physiology text of the mid-19th century, and its stature guaranteed that Müller's name, not Bell's, would become attached to the doctrine (Boring, 1950).[2]

Helmholtz: The Physiologist's Physiologist

If Müller was the leading German physiologist of the first half of the 19th century, the honor for the second half goes to one of his followers—Hermann von Helmholtz (1821–1894; Figure 3.2). Shortly after he died, Helmholtz was eulogized by Carl Stumpf, another well-known German physiologist, as the person most responsible for building the "bridge between physiology and psychology that thousands of workers today go back and forth upon" (quoted in Turner, 1972). Helmholtz became *the* 19th-century authority on the sensory systems for vision and audition, developing theories still considered to be at least partly correct. He also provided a simple demonstration of nerve impulse speed that paved the way for one of psychology's most enduring methods, reaction time. And despite accomplishing more than any other 19th-century physiologist, his true love actually was physics, to which he also made original contributions.

Helmholtz was born in 1821 into a family of modest means in Potsdam, Germany. He quickly emerged as an academic star at the local gymnasium (high school), where he developed his lifelong love for physics, but financial straits prevented him from attending a university. The government was offering full scholarships for students to attend medical school in Berlin, however, and Helmholtz jumped at the

Library of Congress Prints and Photographs Division, Photoengraving of engraving by T. Johnson after a September 1893 photograph by Mathew B. Brady. Illustration from The Century Gallery of One Hundred Portraits Selected from The Century Magazine. New York: The Century Co., 1897, plate no. LXIV.

FIGURE 3.2 Hermann von Helmholtz (1821–1894), Europe's preeminent physiologist in the second half of the 19th century.

---

[2]After producing his famous handbook, Müller was less productive as a scientist and fell into a severe depression. Few of his friends believed that his death in 1858 was anything but a deliberate overdose of morphine (Steudel, 1972).

opportunity, even though it meant committing himself to 8 years of service in the army's medical corps. He left for Berlin in 1838, where he completed the 5-year program in 4 years. While enrolled at the medical institute, he also studied informally at the University of Berlin with the great Johannes Müller. Helmholtz quickly moved into Müller's inner circle and developed lifelong friendships with three other students destined to become leaders in the world of German science: Ernst Brücke (who will appear in Chapter 12 as Freud's mentor), Emil du Bois Reymond, and Karl Ludwig.

Although he was the leading physiologist of his day, Müller was already being challenged by his students in the 1840s, especially on the issue of **vitalism** versus **materialism**. Müller believed that in addition to the physical and chemical properties of physiological systems, there also existed a "vital force," a life force that could not be reduced further. It was an idea with deep roots and obvious theological connotations. Opposed to vitalism was a position that also had a long history but was becoming especially prominent in the 19th century—*materialism* (Chapter 2). According to this view, the vital force was a myth: Physical matter was the only reality, and all living organisms could be reduced to physical, mechanical, and chemical processes that eventually would be understood by applying scientific methods. Müller's students were committed materialists, with all the enthusiasm and confidence of youth (all were under 30), and they all made important contributions to physiology that supported the materialist position.

After finishing his medical degree in 1842, Helmholtz began his stint as an army surgeon, while at the same time maintaining his Berlin connections. During this time he made the first of his lasting contributions, one that simultaneously reflected his love of physics and his desire to support a materialist philosophy. It was a paper on the mathematical basis for a law of **conservation of energy**, first read to a scientific society in Berlin in 1847 and then published privately after being rejected for publication by a leading journal (Warren, 1984). Helmholtz is today considered one of the originators of this important principle in physics, which states that the total energy within a system remains constant, even if changes occur within the system. For Helmholtz, the principle was an important weapon in the fight against vitalism. He argued that body heat and muscle force could be explained by chemical energy accumulated during the oxidation process that accompanied digestion—there was no need to propose a special life force that could create its own energy. He supported his argument by showing that muscle contractions generated measurable amounts of heat (Turner, 1972).

Measuring the Speed of Neural Impulses   After being released early from his army commitment, Helmholtz was hired by the University of Königsberg in 1849, where he stayed for 6 years.[3] During this time, he completed a series of studies that had important implications for the study of the reflex and laid the groundwork for reaction time methodology.

When Helmholtz began studying the problem of nerve impulse speed in the early 1850s, physiologists' understanding of the nature of nerve impulses had come a long way from the animal spirits described by Descartes more than 200 years earlier. Alternatives to animal spirits, in the form of various types of fluids (one such theory was proposed by Thomas Willis), or by the action of vibrations and miniature vibrations (Hartley), gradually gave way to the idea that nervous impulses were in some way related to electricity.

The person most responsible for demonstrating the electrical properties of nerve impulses was the Italian physiologist/physician Luigi Galvani (1737–1798). It had been known for some time that

---

[3]Having well-connected friends helps. The position at Königsberg opened when Brücke, one of Helmholtz's Berlin friends, left a position there to take one at Vienna (where his prize student would be Sigmund Freud). The Königsberg job was first offered to Du Bois Reymond, who turned it down but apparently recommended Helmholtz, who accepted (Turner, 1972).

electricity could affect muscle action—one scientifically inclined abbot, for instance, connected a 900-foot line of Carthusian monks to a Leyden jar (device for storing and releasing electrical energy) and made them all jump simultaneously by completing a circuit (Finger, 2000). Galvani's contribution was to show that nerves were the means by which electricity resulted in muscle movement. He accomplished this by electrically charging a metal scalpel and touching it to the nerve that connected with muscle in a frog's leg. The frog's muscle contracted, moving the leg (Finger, 2000). Galvani extended the research and published his results in 1791. Although some of his conclusions were shown to be wrong (e.g., he thought the brain generated an "electrical fluid"), his work led to a dramatic increase in research designed to discover the precise electrical properties of the nervous system. As for Galvani, the importance of his discovery (along with the key role played by frogs) was celebrated in his hometown of Bologna with the creation of a monument to him in a plaza named after him. It features Galvani gazing fondly on a tablet holding a pair of frog legs.

By the 19th century, the electrical nature of nervous activity was well established, but there was disagreement concerning the extent to which the electrical activity in the nerves was similar to electrical activity outside the body. Authorities such as Johannes Müller believed that the nerve impulse might be instantaneous—or at the very least, it occurred too rapidly to be measured—but a study by Du Bois Reymond in 1850 suggested that the impulse was propagated along the nerve by an electrochemical process that would be slower than a pure electrical transmission. If so, then perhaps impulse speed could be measured. Enter Helmholtz, who succeeded in this measurement task by isolating a motor nerve and a connected muscle from a frog's leg. He then stimulated the nerve electrically at several different distances from the muscle and recorded the time from stimulus to response. Knowing distance and time, the calculation of rate was easy (rate = distance/time). It averaged about 90 feet per second (or just over 60 miles per hour), which was quite sluggish compared with estimates that placed it near the speed of lightning bolts. Helmholtz also roughly estimated impulse speed in sensory nerves by showing that human subjects took longer to respond to stimulation of their toe than their thigh.

For Helmholtz, the implications of the research were obvious. Here was more evidence that vitalism was wrong and materialism was right. Vitalists argued that the conscious decision to move an arm and the arm's movement were simultaneous, but Helmholtz had shown that the event took a measurable amount of time, a conclusion consistent with the idea that nervous action involved the movement of physical, material entities. For Helmholtz, this conclusion was enough: He was not interested in any further applications of the concept of reaction time. It would be for others to develop the idea into a technique for measuring the time of various mental activities. That story is told in the next chapter.

Helmholtz on Vision and Audition
During the Königsberg years, Helmholtz also began investigating the physiology of vision and audition and invented a tool that made him famous among eye doctors—the **ophthalmoscope**, a device for directly examining the retina. His research on vision culminated in a massive three-volume *Handbook of Physiological Optics*, published over an 11-year period from 1856 to 1867. During this same time he moved twice, first to Bonn and then to Heidelberg, where he spent 13 of the most productive years of his career (1858–1871).

Helmholtz is perhaps best remembered for elaborating a theory of color vision first proposed by the English scientist Thomas Young at the beginning of the 19th century. Sometimes considered an example of a *multiple*, it has come to be called either the Young–Helmholtz theory or, as Helmholtz called it, the **trichromatic theory**. It is based on the facts of color-matching experiments. If you shine a red spotlight against a wall and then shine a green light so that it overlaps the red, the colors in the area of overlap will "mix" and be seen as a new color, yellow. Both Young and Helmholtz demonstrated that by mixing various combinations of three colors (red, green, and blue) together, the resulting color could

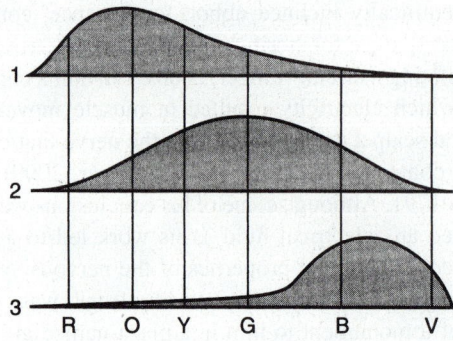

FIGURE 3.3   Relative sensitivity of the three color receptors proposed by Helmholtz, from his *Handbook of Physiological Optics* (1860/1965).

be made to match any other single color. On this basis, they concluded that the eye must contain three different kinds of color receptors, one for each of these so-called primary colors, red, green, and blue (or violet). Incoming light of a particular wavelength was said to stimulate these receptors to different degrees, resulting in the perception of a certain color. In Helmholtz's words:

> Suppose that the colors of the spectrum are plotted horizontally in Fig. [3.4] in their natural sequence, from red to violet, the three curves may be taken to indicate something like the degree of excitation of the three kinds of fibres, No. 1 for the red-sensitive fibres, No. 2 for the green-sensitive fibres, and No. 3 for the violet-sensitive fibres.
>
> Pure *red* light stimulates the red-sensitive fibres strongly and the two other kinds of fibres feebly; giving the sensation red.
>
> Pure *yellow* light stimulates the red-sensitive and green-sensitive fibres moderately and the violet-sensitive fibres feebly; giving the sensation yellow.
>
> Pure *green* light stimulates the green-sensitive fibres strongly and the two other kinds much more feebly; giving the sensation green.
>
> … When all the fibres are stimulated about equally, the sensation is that of *white* or pale hues. (Helmholtz, 1860/1965, p. 42; emphasis in the original)

Although Helmholtz's Figure 3.3 was hypothetical, it is similar to modern-day data plotted in spectral sensitivity curves, with three varieties of cones corresponding to the three main colors Helmholtz proposed. Thus the trichromatic theory has held up over the years.[4]

Color vision was only a small portion of Helmholtz's work on the visual sense. His love of physics, for example, led him to examine the basic question of optics: How does light become focused on the retina? Thus he provided a clear analysis of how light rays are bent, both by the cornea and through the process of *accommodation* that Berkeley had described (Chapter 2), in which the lens changes shape to alter the focus of objects at different distances. He also examined the perception of depth through the operation of **binocular vision**, and in the spirit of Bishop Berkeley, he took a strong empiricist stance on the question of how we come to perceive objects in space.

Helmholtz would be justly famous even if he had restricted his expertise to vision. In 1863, between the publication of volumes II and III of his *Optics*, however, he also published what quickly

---

[4]The trichromatic theory failed to account for certain color phenomena that were better explained by other theories, however, most notably the opponent process theory of Ewald Hering. Hering proposed that color-sensitive cells between the retina and the brain responded to opposing pairs of colors (i.e., red–green, yellow–blue, black–white). Today, theories of color vision integrate elements of both theories (Goldstein, 1996).

became the authoritative text on the sense of hearing, *The Theory of the Sensation of Tone as a Physiological Basis for the Theory of Music*. In it, Helmholtz presented his famous **resonance theory** of hearing, which proposed that different frequencies of sound were detected by receptors located in different places along the basilar membrane of the cochlea.

It is worth noting that both the trichromatic theory of color vision and the resonance theory of hearing were elaborations of Müller's doctrine of the specific energies of nerves. Whereas Müller proposed a single specific energy for each of the five basic senses, Helmholtz's theories amounted to proposing more than one specific energy for each sense: three for color vision and many for hearing.

Helmholtz and the Problem of Perception

As a physicist, Helmholtz was accustomed to look for precision in nature. Hence, he was perplexed by what he thought of as the **problem of perception**. On the one hand, it appears that the human sensory systems for seeing and for hearing are remarkably capable. On the other hand, the structures designed to deliver this sensory information seemed to him to be terribly flawed. In vision, for example, Helmholtz noted that aberrations in the cornea often distorted light waves; that the fluids within the eye distorted the perceptions of shape, motion, and color; and worst of all, that when light reached the retina, it had to pass through several layers of blood vessels and nerve fibers before reaching the receptors. Helmholtz once wrote that "if an optician wanted to sell me an instrument which had all these defects, I should think myself quite justified in blaming his carelessness in the strongest terms, and giving him back his instrument" (quoted in Warren, 1984, p. 257). Similar problems occurred for hearing with the structure of the ear.

Given such design flaws, Helmholtz asked, what accounts for the quality of our perception? The answer, he believed, could be found in the doctrine of the specific energies of nerves and in British empiricist philosophy. Thus, because our nervous system mediates between reality and the mind, we are only indirectly aware of the external world. As a result, the role of experience is central to perception, he argued. The raw information processed by the sensory systems is meaningless by itself, but takes on meaning only when a particular combination of sensory events becomes associated with specific consequences. Consider, for example, perceiving objects located at different distances. According to Helmholtz, we make what he called an **unconscious inference** about distance, based on our past experiences of various cues that are associated with distance (this should remind you of Berkeley). As a person gets closer to us, for example, the retinal image enlarges, but we perceive the person getting closer, not doubling or tripling in size. Helmholtz would say that because we know *through experience* that people don't actually grow as they approach, we conclude (i.e., unconsciously *infer*) that the person must be getting closer. All this occurs quickly and without our awareness, hence the term *unconscious inference*.

Despite being sickly as a youth, Helmholtz was strong and energetic in his later years. His favorite hobby was mountain climbing, for example, and he could often be found hiking through the Alps (Wade, 1994). The experience gave him a metaphor that summed up his approach to science. The elegance of his final theorizing contrasted with the messy and unpredictable day-to-day process of doing research. To explain how he proceeded, he compared himself to

> an Alpine climber who, not knowing the way, ascends slowly and with toil, and is often compelled to retrace his steps because his progress is stopped; sometimes by reasoning, and sometimes by accident, he hits upon traces of a fresh path, which again leads him a little further; and finally, when he has reached the goal, he finds to his annoyance a royal road on which he might have ridden up if he had been clever enough to find the right starting-point at the outset. In my memoirs I have, of course, not given the reader an account of my wanderings, but I have described the beaten path on which he can now reach the summit without trouble. (quoted in Warren, 1984, p. 256)

In 1871, at age 50, Helmholtz left Heidelberg for Berlin when he was offered a prestigious professorship in physics. Thus, in the last stage of his career he returned to his first love—physics. He traveled widely, even visiting the United States in 1893 to represent German science at the famous Columbian Exposition in Chicago. On the return voyage he suffered a severe concussion and prolonged double vision from a fall down a flight of stairs. He died of a cerebral hemorrhage the following year.

LOCALIZATION OF BRAIN FUNCTION

In addition to the advances in knowledge about sensory physiology, 19th-century scientists explored the nature of the brain, and argued over the issue of localization. The basic structures of the brain had been known for some time—as early as the mid-17th century, as described earlier, Thomas Willis had produced *The Anatomy of the Brain* (Willis, 1664/1965) with its precise and elegant Christopher Wren drawings (refer again to Figure 3.1).

Even a superficial visual inspection of the brain reveals obvious structural differences. There are clearly two hemispheres, the cortex subdivides further into a number of ridges (convolutions), the cerebellum is separate from the cerebrum, and the lower brain areas, an extension of the spinal cord, have their own distinct shapes and features. It is only natural to suppose that there are functional differences corresponding to these structures, and this raises the question of **localization of function**. To what extent do the different structural locations in the brain correspond to different physiological and psychological attributes?

The Phrenology of Gall and Spurzheim

The phrenologists proposed the first important theory of localization. According to advocates of **phrenology**, distinct human "faculties" could be identified and located in precisely defined areas of the brain.[5] When portrayed in today's introductory psychology texts, it is usually caricatured as a bizarre scientific dead end in which charlatans read a person's character by feeling around for the bumps on his or her head (i.e., lots of presentist thinking here). Actually, the story is considerably more complex, and much that is of importance to American psychology has its roots in the phrenological movement.

The origins of phrenology can be traced to a respected but eccentric Viennese physician, Franz Josef Gall (1758–1828). He was born in Tiefenbronn, Germany, into a devout Catholic family; his parents assumed that he would one day become a priest. Instead, Gall's theory about brain function came to be considered antireligious, his books were banned by the church, and on his death he was denied a Catholic burial (Young, 1972). Gall decided on a career in medicine early in life, earning an MD in Vienna in 1785. There he developed a successful practice and became a skilled anatomist. After his public lectures and surgical demonstrations were banned for promoting materialism (and by implication, immorality and atheism), he took the show on the road and lectured throughout Europe before settling in Paris in 1807, where he remained until his death.

Gall secured a place in the history of medicine with his careful anatomical work. He was the first to identify the fibers connecting the cerebral hemispheres (corpus callosum) and confirmed earlier

---

[5]Phrenology is often confused with the related doctrine of physiognomy, which also proposed a relationship between one's physical attributes (in particular, facial features) and character or personality. Physiognomy has a long history, dating to the ancient Greeks, but was most clearly spelled out in the work of Johann Kaspar Lavater (1741–1801), who published lavishly illustrated volumes on physiognomy in the mid-1770s. Lavatar's physiognomy related facial features (e.g., chins, noses, width between eyes, forehead height) to personality and character.

speculation that some fibers crossed from one side of the brain to the opposite side of the spinal cord, resulting in contralateral function, the notion that each side of the brain controls the opposite side of the body. Gall also compared the brain structures of different species and made a convincing argument that the mental abilities of different species correlated with the size and complexity of the brain, especially the cortex. And he was the first to argue that the brain's convolutions formed the same pattern within a given species; hence, the surface of the brain was not a random jumble of ridges and valleys, but had a reliable structure. His anatomical research was impeccable—the great French physiologist Pierre Flourens, phrenology's harshest critic (discussed later), reported that when he saw Gall dissect a brain, it was like seeing the organ for the first time. Unlike most anatomists, who dissected brains by slicing off segments from the top down, Gall worked from the brain stem up, removing structures one by one and thereby tracing the interconnections between structures with a precision not possible when starting at the top (Temkin, 1947).

Despite these notable accomplishments, Gall is remembered for originating phrenology. He began developing his ideas about localization early—as a youth, for example, he observed that schoolmates with protruding eyes seemed to have better memories than he did. This early experience began a lifelong pursuit of inductive evidence to support his theories. For example, Gall claimed that the impulse to steal resulted from an overdevelopment of the faculty of "Property" (later called "Acquisitiveness"), located in the temporal lobe of the cortex about an inch above and in front of the ear. According to Gall,

> I have constantly found this prominence, in all inveterate thieves confined in prison, in all idiots with an irresistible propensity to steal, and in all those who, otherwise well endowed with intellect, take an inconceivable pleasure in stealing, and even feel incapable of resisting the passion which forces them to theft. One of my friends … has this organ very large. When he sees scissors, knives, or other similar trifles, he feels a certain uneasiness … until he has put those objects in his pockets. (Gall, 1825/1965, p. 218)

This quote hints at Gall's modus operandi, which was to study the skull shapes of people with especially notable attributes. By examining exceptional cases, Gall believed it would be easy to relate skull contour with the person's special talent. The principles could then be generalized to others. By 1802, Gall had collected more than "300 skulls from individuals with well-documented mental traits ranging from literary talent to murderous tendencies [and] 120 casts from living persons who had distinguished themselves" (Finger, 2000, p. 127).

Gall's beliefs developed into the theory that his followers came to call phrenology, a term that derives from the Greek words for the study of ("ology") the mind ("phrenos"). The term was coined by Johann Spurzheim (1776–1832), who collaborated with Gall for a time but later broke with him. Spurzheim is the person most responsible for popularizing the theory, both in Europe and in America. As described in his *Outlines of Phrenology* (1832/1978) and elsewhere, phrenology's main principles reduced to five:

a. The brain is the organ of the mind.

b. The mind is composed of a large number (about three dozen) of abilities or attributes called "faculties"; some of these faculties are intellectual (cognitive), and some are affective (emotional).

c. Each faculty is located in a specific area of the brain; that location is the same for everyone.

d. For a given faculty, some people have more than others, and those with more of a particular faculty have more brain tissue in the corresponding location than those with less of that same faculty.

e. Because the skull corresponds roughly to the shape of the brain, the strength of various faculties can be inferred from the shape of the skull.

This last point came to be known as the **doctrine of the skull**, and for the phrenologists it was the key to measurement. If the size and shape of various brain locations reflected the strength of faculties, and if brain shape affected skull shape, then measuring the skull would yield a measurement of faculties. In short, everything of importance about people could be known by examining the shapes of their skulls. Figure 3.4 shows a typical phrenological skull with its faculties labeled (in this case, one used to entice subscriptions to a phrenological journal).

In the first two decades of the 19th century, phrenology was a legitimate attempt to identify the localized functions of the brain. By the time Spurzheim produced his *Outlines of Phrenology*, in the year he died while on an American lecture tour (1832), thousands of skulls had been examined with an eye toward correlating skull shape with ability and character. On close examination, however, it became clear that the evidence was questionable. As illustrated earlier in connection with the faculty of Property (Acquisitiveness), the phrenologists relied heavily on **anecdotal evidence**. That is, they looked for specific case examples to support their theory. This approach is not necessarily flawed—gathering lots of data and then looking for generalizations is a standard inductive strategy. The problem, however, is that the phrenologists tended to ignore or discount examples that did not support their case. Furthermore, their theory failed an important criterion of any good scientific theory: It must be stated precisely enough to be capable of disproof. But the phrenologists failed to do this. A thief with a small area of Property would be ignored, described as a potential thief ("he will start stealing any day now"), or explained away by referring to combinations of other faculties that would be said to offset the lack of Property.

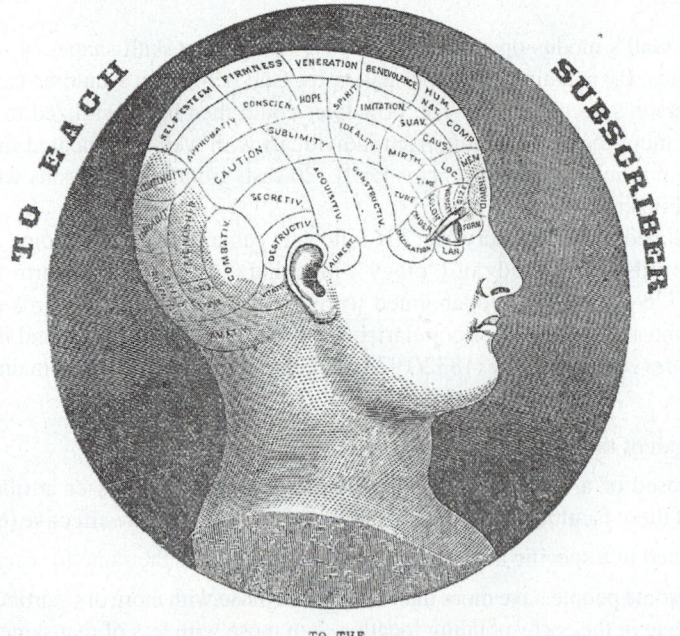

Courtesy of Dr. C. James Goodwin

FIGURE 3.4 A phrenological skull with faculties identified.

For instance, the thief might be described as having large faculties of Imitation and Self-Esteem, causing him to maintain his self-image by copying his pickpocket older brother, despite his lack of "natural" Property faculty. Perhaps the ultimate example of phrenological refusal to consider disproof was a comment attributed to Spurzheim on learning that Descartes's skull was rather small in the areas related to some of the intellectual faculties. Spurzheim was said to have suggested that perhaps Descartes wasn't so smart after all (Finger, 2000).

The failure of phrenology as a theory did not seem to bother phrenologists, but other scientists quickly recognized the flaws; by the middle of the 19th century phrenology was relegated to the status of pseudoscience. Unfortunately, it shared an important feature with other pseudosciences—the general public loved it. Phrenology became enormously popular during the 19th century. Gall and Spurzheim spread the faith throughout Europe, and Spurzheim and others exported it to the United States.

Phrenology reached its zenith of popularity in America. The version that was imported by Spurzheim and spread by him and others fit perfectly with the American culture of the "common man," especially during the middle and last half of the 19th century (Bakan, 1966). Although Gall believed the size of a person's faculties was an indication of native traits, Spurzheim argued that faculties could be affected by nurture. To Spurzheim, the brain was analogous to a muscle—its faculties could be exercised and strengthened through education and self-help. Thus phrenology provided a seemingly scientific basis for the traditional American belief that anyone, regardless of heritage, could "pull oneself up by one's bootstraps" and accomplish anything in life. The hopeful notion that children's brains and therefore their futures could be shaped by controlling their environments and improving their educations resonated with Americans. That same optimism would make behaviorism just as fashionable with the public in the 1920s. Phrenology also was consistent with the American idea that everyone is a unique person, possessing his or her own special talents. In phrenological terms, this translated into everyone having his or her own distinctive configuration of faculties, to be measured with proper phrenological tools. Thus phrenology was an important early example of a major theme of research in psychology that continues today: the search for ways to identify and gauge individual differences (Bakan, 1966). And if individual differences could be identified and measured, then a person's strengths and weaknesses could be known and he or she could be counseled about careers, mate selection, and so on. A final reason for phrenology's appeal, then, was in its promise to deliver practical applications to improve daily living.

Phrenology's popularity with the masses was enhanced through the energetic marketing efforts of the firm of Fowler and Wells. Although the scientific and more educated community rejected phrenology rather quickly, the public never seemed to tire of it. As you can see from this chapter's Close-Up, phrenology was big business in late 19th-century America, and even lingered well into the 20th century.

CLOSE-UP

THE MARKETING OF PHRENOLOGY

When Orson Fowler was a student at Amherst College in the early 1830s, he made pocket money by examining the heads of classmates for two cents a head (Joynt, 1973). Upon graduation, he joined with his brother Lorenzo and sister Charlotte to open a museum of phrenology in New York City that featured a large collection of skulls, casts of heads, and other phrenological tools of the trade. Admission was free, but once the museum goers were in the door, the Fowlers tempted them with a phrenological assessment that cost from one to three dollars.

When Charlotte married a medical student named Samuel Wells, the firm of Fowler and Wells was born. Located at 753 Broadway, with branches in Boston and Philadelphia, it dominated the phrenology business from its inception in 1844 to the turn of the 20th century.

Fowler and Wells published a seemingly endless list of pamphlets designed to bring phrenological insights into every home. They also began the popular *Phrenological Journal* (Figure 3.5), a subscription to which would produce the free phrenological bust pictured in Figure 3.4. They trained and "certified" phrenologists and, during an era when the public lecture was a primary means of communication, maintained a list of accomplished public speakers ready to spread the phrenological faith. To give you some idea of the range of topics addressed by the firm, consider these publications that could be ordered from Fowler and Wells:

> *The Indications of Character*, as manifested in the general shape of the head and the form of the face. Illustrated. 15 cents.
>
> *Wedlock*; or, The Right Relations of the Sexes. A Scientific Treatise disclosing the Laws of Conjugal Selection, Pre-natal Influences, and showing Who Ought and Who Ought Not to Marry. $1.50; in fancy guilt, $2.00.
>
> *Choice of Pursuits*; or, What to do and Why. Describing Seventy-five Trades and Professions, and the Temperaments and Talents required for each. 508 pp. $1.75.

As for the journal itself, each issue contained phrenological sketches of well-known individuals, articles on other hot topics of the day (e.g., hypnotism, spiritualism, physiognomy), and short pieces covering just about anything (e.g., "Why Bees Work in Darkness"). Although nothing quite like the *Phrenological Journal* exists today, the *Old Farmer's Almanac*, with its Down East commonsense wisdom, is similar.

A typical lead article in the journal featured some well-known person and showed how a phrenological assessment could "explain" that person's character and behavior. For example, the September 1873 issue included a piece about a notorious murderer. Here's how a phrenologist who interviewed the killer described him:

> I found his head to be 22 inches in circumference, 13.5 inches from Individuality to the occipital spine, and 14 inches from Destructiveness to Destructiveness, over the top of the head at Firmness. The animal portion of the brain predominates over all others. Destructiveness is the largest organ in his brain, the head swelling out enormously over the ears. The organ of Conscientiousness is, I think, the smallest I ever saw . . . . All the spiritual organs are small and inactive, while Cautiousness and Secretiveness are both below the average.

You will not be surprised to learn that the phrenologist knew that the person he was assessing was a murderer, knowledge that certainly biased his report.

The firm of Fowler and Wells had a long run, but interest in phrenology began to wane near the turn of the 20th century, as the general public became more informed about the workings of the brain and as other approaches to measurement (e.g., IQ testing) began to be popularized. In 1911, the *Phrenological Journal* published its last issue.

Phrenology experienced a brief revival in the early 1930s, however, when Henry Lavery, a hotel manager and entrepreneurial inventor from Wisconsin, created a device that came to be known as the "Psychograph" (Risse, 1976). As you can see in Figure 3.6, a helmet-like device covered a subject's head, enabling precise measurement of the skull at numerous points. The measurement points supposedly corresponded to phrenological faculties, and the measurements themselves were fed into a recording device (on the right) that produced a printout describing the subject's abilities and personality.

Lavery believed his device would rejuvenate phrenological analysis by making the process quick, objective (or so he thought), and inexpensive. He convinced Frank White, a wealthy Minneapolis contractor, to invest $33,000 to produce 50 machines a year (no more than 45 machines were actually produced, one of which resides today at Akron's Center for the History of Psychology), the ultimate goal being to market the devices to business and industry as a means of employee selection. The venture was a spectacular failure. The personality descriptions that emerged from the psychograph were no more accurate than astrological descriptions, the Great Depression ensured that few companies were willing to buy the device, and well-publicized attacks by local research psychologists at the University of Minnesota ridiculed the project. One of the psychograph's final appearances in public was at the 1933 Chicago World's Fair, where it "came to rest next to a trained flea show, Ripley's Believe It or Not, and a two-headed baby in a formalin-filled bottle" (Risse, 1976, p. 138).

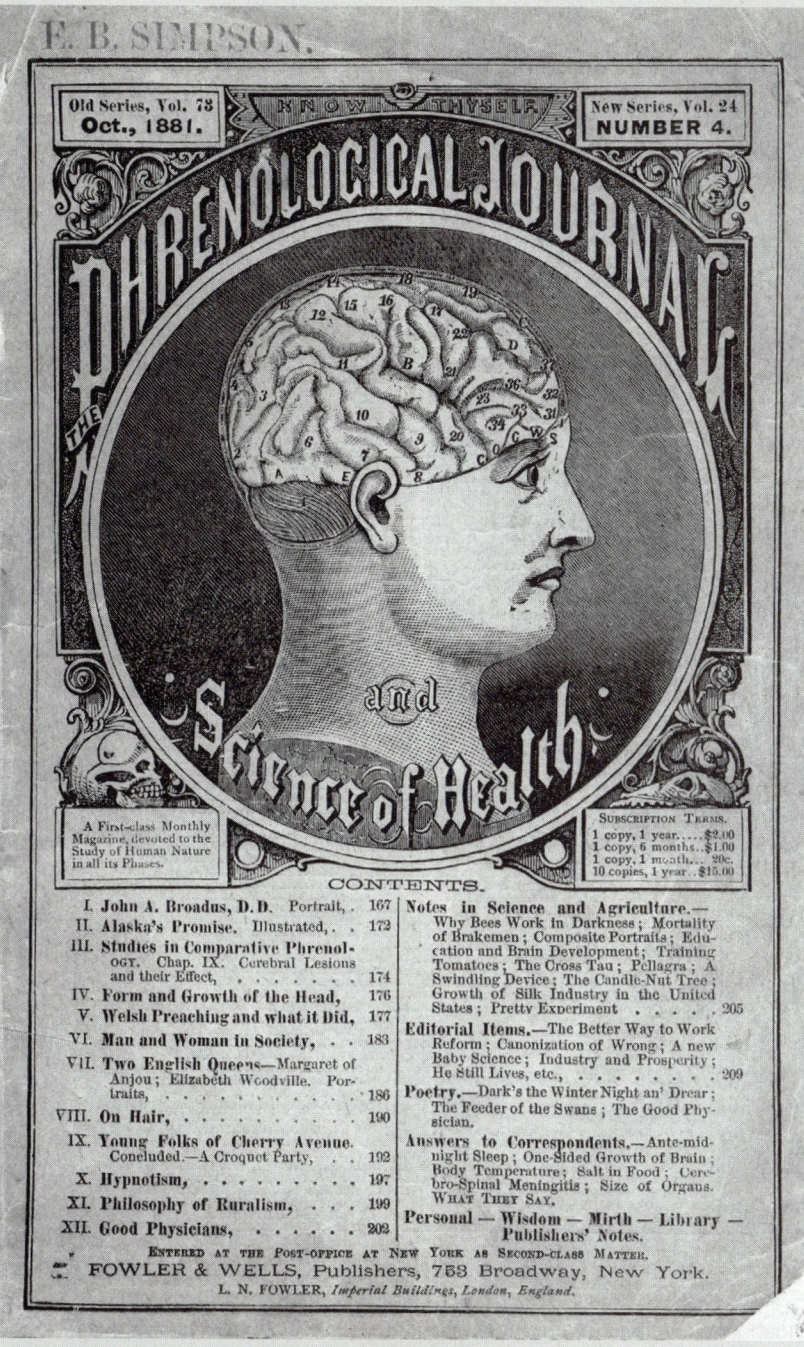

FIGURE 3.5 The October 1881 cover of Fowler and Wells's popular *Phrenological Journal*.

Courtesy of Dr. C. James Goodwin

© Bettmann/Corbis

FIGURE 3.6   Henry Lavery's psychograph in action, early 1930s.

Flourens and the Method of Ablation

Phrenology might have seemed like good science to Main Street America, but the real scientists were not fooled. As mentioned earlier, the scientific community rejected phrenology well before the middle of the 19th century. Phrenology's worst enemy was the distinguished French physiologist and surgeon Pierre Flourens (1794–1867). He reduced the doctrine to two main points: The mind is centered in the brain, and the mind is composed of numerous faculties, each located in specific places in the brain. In his sharply worded *Examination of Phrenology*, first published in 1843, he sarcastically observed that "of these two propositions, there is certainly nothing new in the first one, and perhaps nothing true in the second one" (Flourens, 1846/1978, p. 18). Flourens also reported an embarrassing example of the phrenologists' susceptibility to bias, describing a case in which Magendie presented a skull to Spurzheim for examination. Magendie told Spurzheim that the skull belonged to a famous French scientist (Simon-Pierre Laplace), but in fact the skull belonged to a severely mentally disabled man. As Flourens reported, "Spurzheim, who had already worked up his enthusiasm, admired the brain of the imbecile as he would have admired that of Laplace" (quoted in Finger, 2000, p. 134).

To disprove the phrenologists' claims directly, Flourens took an experimental approach, using the method of **ablation**. Although he did not create the procedure, he raised it to such a level of refinement that it is now associated with his name. Rather than wait for natural experiments to occur, in the form of accidental brain damage, Flourens created brain damage surgically, destroying specific sections of the brain and observing the effects (ablation derives from the Latin words for "carry away" or "remove"). If the result of an ablation was blindness, then presumably the removed portion had something to do with vision. Clearly, the method required animals as research subjects, and Flourens experimented on numerous species ranging from pigeons to dogs.

Flourens's attack on phrenology took the form of showing that areas of the brain that were alleged by the phrenologists to serve function X in fact served function Y, and that the cerebral cortex operated as an integrated whole rather than as a large collection of separate faculties located in specific places. One focus of his research was the cerebellum. To the phrenologists, this portion of the brain controlled sexual behavior and was the center of the "amativeness" faculty. Flourens had little trouble disproving this and demonstrating instead that the cerebellum is the center of motor coordination. Pigeons deprived of the organ were unable to coordinate wing movements to fly, and dogs were unable to walk properly and would be observed staggering and falling down. Also, the degree of abnormality in movement was directly proportional to the amount of cerebellum ablated.

Through his experiments in removing varying amounts of the cerebral cortex, Flourens found a similar relationship between the amount removed and the seriousness of the ensuing problem. He could find no indication of distinct functions residing in specific areas of the cortex, however, so he concluded that it operated as a whole and served the general functions of perception, intelligence, and will. Thus pigeons without a cortex or with most of it removed maintained some basic sensory functioning, but they showed no indication of the ability to learn from their experiences, and did not seem capable of doing anything except vegetating. The difference between a pigeon without a cerebellum and one without a cortex was that the first bird would attempt to fly but could not coordinate the movements, whereas it would never occur to the second bird that flying was one of life's options.

The general principles that the cortex acts as a whole and that the amount of disability is proportional to the extent of ablation were verified and extended by the discoveries of the great American physiological psychologist Karl Lashley in the 1920s, who referred to them as the principles of *equipotentiality* and *mass action*, respectively—Lashley's work is described in Chapter 14. Yet although Flourens was able to use these principles to attack phrenology in such a way that it never recovered, at least in the eyes of the scientific community, he overstated his case. He argued against any degree of localization in the cortex, a position soon to be shown inadequate by other brain scientists using other methods.

The Clinical Method

The results of ablation studies are not always easy to interpret, mainly because destroying one portion of a brain also influences connections to that portion, producing outcomes that are not always predictable or consistent. Also, ablation studies are sometimes impossible to do, as in the case of human subjects. It is one thing to systematically ablate portions of a person's brain for certain beneficial medical reasons (e.g., treating epilepsy), but destroying human brain tissue simply for the purpose of observing what happens is difficult to justify.[6] An alternative way to study human brain function is called the

[6]This ethical point was lost on Dr. Roberts Bartholow of Cincinnati. In 1874, he inserted electrodes into the cortex of an unwitting immigrant domestic worker who had come to him for treatment of an ulcerous scalp wound that exposed a portion of her brain. Mild stimulation produced muscular contractions, but when the curious Bartholow inserted the electrodes deeper and increased the strength of the current, the unfortunate woman went into severe convulsions and died (Hothersall, 1995).

clinical method. This involves either (a) studying the behavioral and mental consequences of brain injury, events such as strokes, war wounds, or illness; or (b) identifying people with some behavioral or mental disorder and examining their brains for structural abnormalities during autopsies. The person generally credited with developing the clinical method is Paul Broca, who we meet shortly, but there are numerous examples of famous clinical cases in the mid-19th century. Perhaps the best known concerned a respected Vermont railroad worker, Phineas Gage.

The Remarkable Phineas Gage   While blasting rock in preparation for a new railway line near Cavendish, Vermont, in 1848, Gage survived an accident that seemed certain to be fatal. After pouring gunpowder and placing a fuse into a hole drilled in rock that was about to be blasted, Gage accidentally ignited the powder while using a "tamping iron" (a metal rod a little over three feet long, about an inch in diameter, flat at one end, and pointed at the other) to compress the powder. The explosion converted the tamping iron into a missile that flew into the air and landed 20 meters away. Unfortunately for Gage, his head was in the flight path. The pointed end of the missile entered just below his left eye and exited from the top left of his forehead, taking a healthy portion of his left frontal cortex with it (Figure 3.7). Miraculously, Gage only briefly lost consciousness and, once he arrived back in town, he was able to walk with assistance to a doctor's office for treatment. Within two months he was sufficiently recovered to live independently,[7] but he had difficulty working productively again, and his personality apparently changed.

One of Gage's doctors, John Harlow, was amenable to phrenology and thought the case supported the phrenologist's localization beliefs. Harlow kept notes on the case and published accounts of it in 1848 and 1868. He described this case of frontal lobe damage as one in which

> the equilibrium or balance … between his intellectual faculties and animal propensities seems to have been destroyed. He is fitful, irreverent, indulging at times in the grossest profanity (which was not previously his custom), manifesting but little deference for his fellows, impatient of restraint or

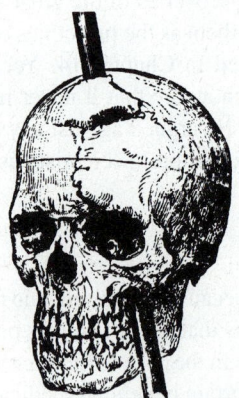

FIGURE 3.7   Sketch of Gage's skull, showing position of tamping iron. From the original medical report by Harlow 1868.

[7]That Gage survived at a time before the use of antibiotics to treat infection was nothing short of amazing. His recovery was probably aided because the entry wound provided a natural drainage area that prevented him from developing the kind of abscess that would almost certainly be fatal (Macmillan, 1986).

advice when it conflicts with his desires, at times pertinaciously obstinate, yet capricious and vacillating, devising many plans of future operation, which are no sooner arranged than they are abandoned. . . . In this regard his mind was radically changed, so decidedly that his friends and acquaintances said he was "no longer Gage." (Harlow, 1868, quoted in Macmillan, 1986, p. 85)

Although no completely accurate description of his personality before or after the accident exists (Macmillan, 2000), Gage evidently changed from a dependable, conscientious, respected worker (he was foreman of the railroad crew) into someone who was "no longer Gage." Descriptions have varied over the years, but he seems to have become less dependable and more prone to emotional outbursts.

Thus, although Gage survived the injury, he was altered by it—the brain damage resulted in changes to his personality and behavior. In terms of the localization issue, the Gage case seemed to indicate that the brain's frontal lobes served the function of rationality, helping to maintain control over the emotions. As for Gage, his whereabouts after his recovery have been a source of speculation and debate, but he died young (37), 12 years following the accident, after experiencing a number of increasingly severe convulsions. The tamping iron and Gage's skull can be seen today at Harvard's Warren Anatomical Medical Museum, and a Google search yields a photo of him after his recovery.

Broca and the Speech Center   In the Gage case, it was possible for Harlow to trace events from the initial brain injury to the resulting psychological outcome. Another type of clinical case occurs when a patient manifests some specific mental or behavioral problem, but it cannot be correlated with brain damage until a postmortem analysis. Such was the situation facing the French neurologist Paul Broca (1824–1880) in April of 1861, when treating a very unusual patient, known to history as "Tan," for reasons that will soon be apparent.

The patient had been in the Bicêtre hospital in Paris for a remarkable 21 years and had been incapacitated and in bed for the 7 years before 1861, when a severe case of gangrene brought him to Broca's attention. He first came to the hospital when, at the age of 30, he had lost the ability to speak coherently. In Broca's (1861/1965) account, the patient was

quite healthy and intelligent and differed from a normal person only in his loss of articulate language. He came and went at the hospice, where he was known by the name of "Tan." He understood all that was said to him. His hearing was actually very good, but whenever one questioned him he always answered, "Tan, tan," accompanying his utterance with varied gestures by which he succeeded in expressing most of his ideas. If one did not understand his gestures, he was apt to get irate and added to his vocabulary a gross oath ("Sacré nom de Dieu!"). (p. 224)

After 10 years (!) in the hospital, "Tan" began to lose control of the right side of his body, and over the next 11 years (!), his condition deteriorated. By the time he was brought to Broca's attention, he was near death. Broca reported that he hesitated to examine Tan because his general state of health "was so grave that it would have been cruel" (p. 225). Nonetheless, Broca proceeded with a physical exam that confirmed the paralysis of the right arm and leg, as well as with an examination of Tan's mental capacities:

His numerical responses, made by opening or closing his fingers, were best. . . . How many years had he been at Bicêtre? He opened his hand four times and then added one finger. That made 21 years, the correct answer. The next day I repeated the question and received the same answer. . . . Two days in succession I showed him my watch . . . [and] after having looked at the watch for a few seconds, he could each time indicate the time correctly. It cannot be doubted, therefore, that the man was intelligent, that he could think, that he had to a certain extent retained the memory of old habits. He could understand even quite complicated ideas. For instance, I asked him about the order in which his paralyses had developed. First he made a short horizontal gesture with his left index finger, meaning that he had understood; then he showed successively his tongue, his right arm, and his right leg. That was perfectly correct, for quite naturally he attributed his loss of language to paralysis of his tongue. (p. 226)

Broca guessed that Tan had a cerebral lesion that for the first 10 years of the illness remained confined to a fairly limited area in the left side of the brain, but then had spread. He did not have long to wait to confirm the diagnosis—Tan died 6 days after Broca examined him. Broca immediately performed an autopsy and removed the brain (which still resides in Paris's Musée Depuytren). As you can see from Figure 3.8, the damage is clear. The disorder suffered by Tan is known as expressive or **motor aphasia**, and it is characterized by an inability to articulate ideas verbally, even though the vocal apparatus is intact and general intelligence is normal. Over the next few years, Broca examined and autopsied at least eight other aphasic patients like Tan, found the same general pattern of left frontal lobe (third frontal convolution) damage, and concluded that the ability to produce speech was localized in the left frontal lobe. Others with a strong belief in localization of function had argued that speech production resided in the frontal lobe (e.g., Jean-Baptiste Bouillaud, a student of Magendie, as early as 1825, and Simon Aubertin, Bouillaud's son-in-law, who encountered a case similar to the Tan case and in the same year, 1861), but Broca generally gets credit for the discovery on the grounds of the level of detail of his description of the Tan case and his continuing research into other similar cases (Finger, 2000). In his honor, this part of the cortex is now called Broca's area.

Broca's research challenged Flourens's conclusions about the degree of localization to be found in the cortex. Broca joined a growing number of physiologists who were willing to argue for localization, even while they were rejecting the specific claims of the phrenologists. Additional evidence for localized language function came from clinical studies by the German neurologist Carl Wernicke (1848–1905). He studied a group of patients who had the ability to produce articulate speech, but the speech tended to be nonsensical; they also had difficulty comprehending the speech of others. He named the disorder **sensory aphasia**, to distinguish it from motor aphasia, and discovered consistent brain damage to an area of the left temporal lobe of the brain, several centimeters behind Broca's area.

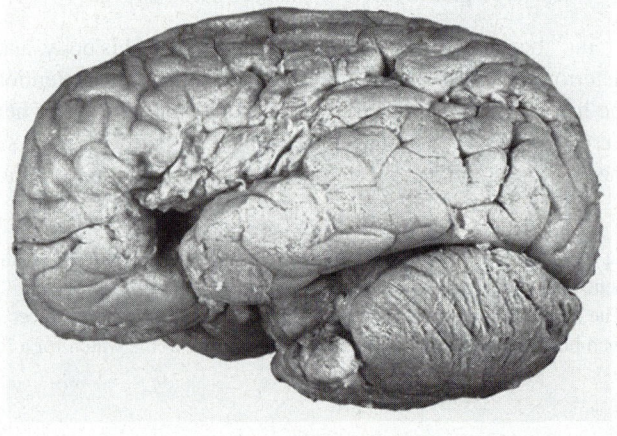

Courtesy of Musée de Dupuytren

FIGURE 3.8 Tan's brain—note damage in lower left.

Mapping the Brain: Electrical Stimulation

We have seen that in the 19th century, discoveries about the nature of electricity were being applied to research on sensory physiology, and the idea was evolving that neural activity was electrochemical in nature. In that context, two young German physiologists, Eduard Fritsch (1838–1927) and Edward Hitzig (1838–1907), lecturers at the University of Berlin, wondered whether the surface of the cortex would respond to mild electrical current. Hitzig had observed muscle movements when the exposed brain of a wounded soldier had been mechanically stimulated, but it was generally believed that touching the surface of the brain did not produce reliable effects. Using dogs as their subjects, Hitzig and Fritsch exposed the cortex and probed different surfaces. The stimulus was an electric current of "an intensity that just barely evoked a sensation of feeling on the tongue" (Fritsch & Hitzig, 1870/1965, p. 230), delivered using two thin wires placed 2 to 3 millimeters (mm) apart. Despite the relative crudeness of their procedures—the experiments were done in Fritsch's home—they contributed evidence of localization by identifying several motor centers in the front half of the brain. Stimulation of the areas marked in Figure 3.9 produced consistent movements in the right side of the dog's body, as follows:

Area 1: neck

Areas 2 and 3: anterior leg (extension and flexion, respectively)

Area 4: posterior leg

Area 5: face

The Fritsch and Hitzig research motivated a number of physiologists, who proceeded to map out motor areas in other species and with more precision. This activity became known as the "new" phrenology or "scientific phrenology": Localization was the goal, but now the brain's functions would be identified scientifically, rather than through the selected anecdotes of phrenologists. Just a few years after Fritsch and Hitzig published their work, the Scottish neurologist David Ferrier (1843–1928) wrote *Functions of the Brain* (1876), which included the map of a monkey's brain shown in Figure 3.10.

Comparing this with Figure 3.9 makes it clear how rapidly brain science was advancing. Ferrier also extended the localization search beyond motor functions, identifying several sensory areas. Using both electrical stimulation and ablation, Ferrier was able to identify the occipital lobe as the primary sensory area for vision and a portion of the temporal lobe as the center for hearing. It began to look like sensory nerves differed more in terms of their destinations in the cortex than in terms of "specific energies."

FIGURE 3.9 Motor centers of a dog's brain, identified via electrical stimulation by Fritsch and Hitzig (1870/1965).

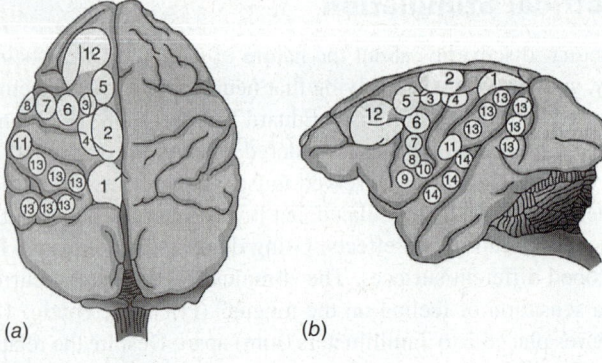

(a)   (b)

FIGURE 3.10 David Ferrier's map of the cortex of a monkey. From Ferrier, The Functions of the Brain, 1876.

NERVOUS SYSTEM STRUCTURE

As the 19th century drew to a close, knowledge of the nervous system in general and of the brain in particular was increasing rapidly. In addition to research on sensory physiology and localization of brain function, however, another line of research developed toward the end of the century and spilled over into the 20th century. This concerned the nature of the basic unit of the nervous system itself, the neuron. This is a long and complicated history, but a few of the highlights can be sketched here.

Neuron Theory

Identifying the neuron as the nervous system's basic element did not occur until the second half of the 19th century, when several important developments occurred in histology (the study of the structure of plant and animal tissue). Microscopes became more powerful, for instance, and techniques for studying brain tissue were perfected. Before it was discovered that the brain could be solidified by soaking it in alcohol, precise dissection was virtually impossible. Once it was known how to harden the brain, however, its nerve pathways could be traced with some precision. For example, in 1857, Louis Gratiolet was able to trace the optic nerve from the retina all the way to the back of the brain, where it radiated like a fan into the occipital cortex (Diamond, 1985).

It was also discovered that the brain could be immersed in paraffin, hardened, and then cut into very thin slices via a procedure called sectioning. Furthermore, if these sections were stained with various chemicals, identifiable structures could be observed in a microscope because the chemicals would collect within these structures. The Italian Camillo Golgi (1844–1926; Figure 3.11a) produced the first clear pictures of nerve cells in the 1870s when he immersed sections of brain tissue in silver nitrate. The silver stained about 3% of the cells in the section, which appeared as black images against a yellow background under the microscope (Finger, 2000). The silver staining technique earned Golgi a share of the 1906 Nobel Prize for medicine. He believed the nervous system was composed of these neurons, but he also argued that the cells were physically connected to each other in a "nerve network"—this position was eventually discarded in favor of the theory proposed by the other winner of the 1906 Nobel Prize for medicine.

Courtesy National Library of Medicine

From "Clark University, 1889–1899, Decennial Celebration" 1899. Story, William Edward 1850–1930; Wilson, Louis N., 1857–1937 Worcester, Mass.: Printed for the University, page 310

(a)   (b)

FIGURE 3.11   (a) Camillo Golgi (1844–1926), whose staining techniques made it possible to examine neurons in great detail; (b) Santiago Ramon y Cajal (1852–1934), who shared the 1906 Nobel Prize for physiology with Golgi; his theory of nerve networks trumped Golgi's theory.

Santiago Ramón y Cajal (1852–1934; Figure 3.11b) was a gifted and passionate Spanish neuroanatomist with a love of art; his research laid the foundation for the modern theory of the neuron (Taylor, 1972). Ramón y Cajal's artistic side can be seen in his eloquent description of the neuron as the "aristocrat among the structures of the body, with its giant arms stretched out like the tentacles of an octopus to the provinces on the frontier of the outside world" (quoted in Restak, 1984, p. 26). His passion for science can be seen in his comment that "all outstanding work, in art as well as in science, results from immense zeal applied to a great idea" (Ramón y Cajal, 1999, p. 7). Like Golgi, Cajal believed the neuron to be the nervous system's basic unit. In contrast with Golgi, however, he argued that each neuron was a separate unit, not physically connected with other units but merely in contact with them. Ironically, when he first proposed his neuron theory in 1889, he used a modification of Golgi's own staining techniques to make his case. The modification produced sharper images, and Cajal could find no evidence of neurons being directly connected with each other.

Thus, the cowinners of the 1906 Nobel Prize for medicine were at odds over the nature of neuron structure. To complicate matters further, Golgi the Italian and Cajal the Spaniard were both fiercely patriotic and convinced of the inaccuracy of each other's research. Hence, there was a certain amount of tension at the 1906 Nobel Prize ceremony, where they met for the first time. Golgi vigorously defended his nerve network theory (which, by 1906, had been discredited by the scientific community for several years) and sarcastically declared Cajal's neuron theory to be a fad (Finger, 2000). When it was Cajal's turn, he graciously credited Golgi for his pioneering work with staining technique while firmly asserting that Golgi's nerve network theory was of historical interest only.

Sir Charles Sherrington: The Synapse

Direct photographic evidence supporting Ramón y Cajal's neuron theory and refuting Golgi's would have to await the invention of the electron microscope, but empirical evidence supporting the existence of gaps between neurons was provided by a British contemporary of both men and a close colleague of Ramón y Cajal: Sir Charles Sherrington (1857–1952).[8] It was Sherrington who coined the term **synapse** (from the Greek word meaning "to join together") for this hypothesized space between neurons. He did not observe its existence directly; rather, he deduced it from a brilliant series of studies on spinal reflexes. The research was presented as part of a prestigious series of lectures at Yale University in 1904 and then published as *The Integrative Action of the Nervous System* in 1906 (dedicated to David Ferrier), the same year that Golgi and Ramón y Cajal shared the Nobel Prize. Sherrington would eventually win a Nobel Prize of his own, in 1932 (Swazey, 1972).

In the tradition of Robert Whytt, but with the advantages of improved technology, Sherrington examined reflex action in "spinal dogs," dogs with spinal cords surgically severed from their brains. As all dog owners know, stimulating a dog's side in the area of the rib cage will cause the dog's hind leg to produce a rapid and repetitive scratching reflex. The fact that Sherrington found these reflexes in spinal dogs replicated Whytt's basic finding about the role of the spinal cord in reflex action. Furthermore, the reflex was even more pronounced in spinal dogs than in intact dogs, which led Sherrington to conclude that the cortex has an *inhibitory* effect on reflex action. He also showed that excitatory and inhibitory action in the nervous system are closely coordinated with each other, producing **reciprocal innervation**, one of his most important discoveries. Although the concept had been known since the time of Descartes, Sherrington was able to demonstrate directly that pairs of muscles worked in conjunction with each other under the control of the nervous system—when one flexed, another extended. This action allowed such complex and coordinated actions as walking and balance (Finger, 2000).

Sherrington made several observations with his spinal dogs that led him to infer that synapses exist. First, the reaction time of the reflexes he observed was slower than predicted from what was known of the speed of neural transmission. This slowing would presumably not happen if the neurons were directly connected with each other, so something must have been slowing down the impulse. A second line of evidence came from the phenomena of temporal and spatial summation. Sherrington discovered that a single stimulation at a certain point on the skin might fail to elicit a scratch reflex, but if the point was stimulated many times in succession (at a rate of about 18 per second), the reflex occurred (Sherrington, 1906). This is **temporal summation**—stimuli separated in time combine to produce a response. **Spatial summation** occurred when two or more adjacent points on the skin were stimulated at the same time. Again, responses occurred only to the combined stimulation. Sherrington concluded that summation must occur where the endpoints of neurons met each other, the synapse. Each subthreshold stimulus caused some unspecified action at the end of neuron A that was by itself insufficient to fire the separate neuron B, but the combined action of information coming many times from A (temporal) or from other locations (spatial) triggered the firing of B. In effect, Sherrington predicted the later discovery of neurotransmitters, chemicals that we now know cross the synapse to promote (or inhibit) neuron firing. After Golgi, Ramón y Cajal, and Sherrington, then, the neuron was established as the fundamental unit of the nervous system, interrelated with other neurons through synaptic activity.

---

[8] Sherrington was described as being "gentle in criticism, whole hearted in admiration and appreciation of the work of others, embod[ying] the intellectual and physical serenity which appears so characteristic of the Victorian era" (Denny-Brown, 1952, p. 477). Yet this "serenity" did not keep him from his favorite sport during his youth—while a lecturer in physiology at St. Thomas's Hospital in London, he spent his Sunday mornings parachute jumping from the hospital's tower (Swazey, 1972).

FROM THE MILES PAPERS...

MILES VISITS SHERRINGTON IN OXFORD

In Chapter 1's excerpt from the Miles papers, we saw that during his 1920 tour of Europe, Miles went to a meeting of the British Psychological Society and encountered Edward Scripture, his academic "grandfather." Another memorable event for Miles during the England portion of the trip was a visit to Sherrington's lab at Oxford University. You will recognize Figure 3.12 in the following description of the lab. In the Miles narrative, note three points. First, Miles refers to a problem encountered by many researchers in England in the aftermath of World War I—many returning soldiers became students, which produced overcrowding and the conversion of laboratory space into teaching space. Second, in 1920, Miles was nearing the end of several years of work on the effects of alcohol, both physiologically and psychologically, and was pleased to learn of Sherrington's interest in the topic. Third, in the final paragraph of the narrative, Miles describes the selfless character of Sherrington, a description consistent with the sentiments expressed in footnote 8.

> In Professor's Sherrington's department, they had the same problem as found in the other universities in England, that is, overcrowding [with] students at the present time with the consequent interruption of research.... Although the laboratory building is old, it has been modified in certain particulars and is still quite adequate to the

teaching and research needs. The room in which the practical class works ... is lighted by large windows on two sides and also by a skylight which is really a continuation of the windows on one side of the room. There are six or seven long paper kymographs [note: a kymograph is a circular drum rotating at a constant speed while a pen records changes in some physiological activity] so that twelve or fourteen advanced students can be accommodated at the same time and the working conditions are especially excellent....

Sherrington is a member of the advisory committee of the Central Control (of the liquor traffic in England). He is quite keen on the subject of alcohol research and questioned me concerning the work at the [Carnegie] Nutrition Laboratory. He thought that a test of static control such as the standing test was a very good one to use in reference to alcohol investigations on human subjects. He made remarks about the changes in the gait of a man after being given alcohol, also concerning the influence upon vision and upon marksmanship....

One cannot help but be impressed with the genuineness and kindly eagerness of Sherrington. He is the very anthesis (sic) of self-assertion and so ready to point out things of interest in your work rather than discussing the importance of his own. (quoted in Goodwin & Royer, 2010)

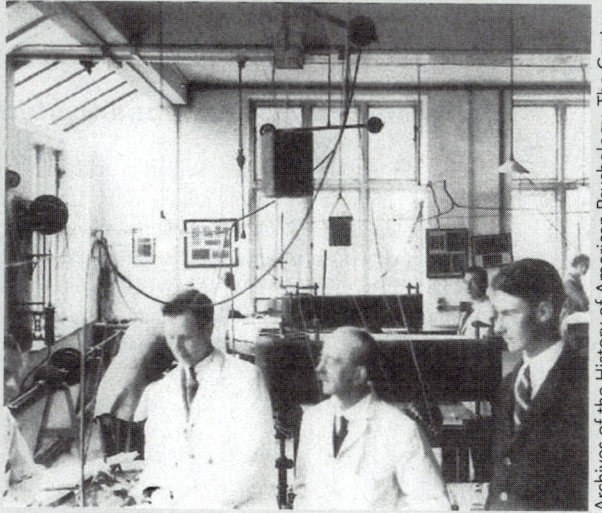

Archives of the History of American Psychology, The Center for the History of Psychology—The University of Akron

FIGURE 3.12   Sir Charles Sherrington (1857–1952; center) in his Oxford laboratory (photo by Walter Miles).

Sherrington's compliment about the "standing test" is a good example of how he would "point out things of interest" in the work of others. Miles was talented as an apparatus inventor, and one of his creations was called the ataxiameter, a device for measuring the amount that a person's head would move when instructed to remain perfectly still (Miles, 1922). As you can imagine, the amount of bodily sway increased under the influence of alcohol.

IN PERSPECTIVE: THE NERVOUS SYSTEM AND BEHAVIOR

During the 19th century, scientists made exciting discoveries about the nature of the brain and the nervous system. At the start of the 19th century, reflexes were generally understood (at least the fact that they could operate without requiring the brain), thanks to the work of Robert Whytt and others. But there was no understanding of how nerves actually worked, the concept of a "neuron" did not exist, and the most sophisticated notion about brain function was an emerging phrenological theory. Within 100 years, dramatic changes had occurred. Sensory and motor nerves were found to be distinct; neurons themselves had been identified and even seen, thanks to new staining techniques; the concept of a synapse was coming to be accepted; the physiology of nervous system function was starting to be understood; and knowledge of brain function had gone far beyond phrenology and identified areas responsible for language comprehension and production, as well as areas responsible for various sensory and motor functions. A remarkable century indeed.

In the last 30 years of the 19th century, as you are about to discover, several scientists who had been studying the physiology of the nervous system began to think that the scientific methods they were using to examine the brain and nervous system could be applied to questions that were distinctly psychological in nature. Could science shed light on how we perceive the world? On how we come to understand things? On the very nature of human conscious experience? One such person was Wilhelm Wundt, who served an important apprenticeship with the 19th century's most important physiologist, Hermann Helmholtz. By the early 1870s, Wundt was thinking that it was time for a brand new science—the science of psychology. This remarkable German scientist is the central figure in the next chapter.

SUMMARY

Heroic Science in the Age of Enlightenment

• The Enlightenment was a period during the 18th and 19th centuries when great faith existed in the ability of science and human reason to produce truthful knowledge about the natural world. Scientists were heroes, considered to be objective and value free, and Newton was the prime exemplar. Science was thought to lead inevitably to progress through technological innovation.

Functioning of the Nervous System

• From the time of Descartes, scientists had been interested in the nature of the simple reflex. In the 18th century, Whytt completed the first studies, showing conclusively that the spinal cord was sufficient for reflexes to occur (the term "reflex" had been created by Willis). Whytt also pointed out that stimulus–response connections could develop through habit, an idea similar to modern behaviorist accounts of conditioning.

• When Magendie severed the posterior root of a dog's spinal cord, the affected area could move but was insensitive to stimulation. When the anterior root was severed, no movement occurred. Magendie concluded that the posterior root controlled sensation, whereas the anterior root controlled motor movements. Bell made similar observations, but was not as methodical as Magendie. The distinction between the functions of the two roots is now known as the Bell–Magendie law.

• According to Müller's doctrine of the specific energies of nerves, (a) we are directly aware of our nervous systems, not the world; and (b) each of the basic sensory systems has nerve fibers designed for that specific sense.

• Helmholtz was opposed to vitalism and fought it through his doctrine of conservation of energy and by measuring the speed of the neural impulse. He was without peer as an expert on visual and auditory perception. He was known for the trichromatic theory of color vision, the resonance theory of audition, and his empiricist approach to perception, which emphasized unconscious inference.

Localization of Brain Function

• Phrenology, developed by Gall and promoted by Spurzheim, was the first serious theory of localization of brain function. Phrenologists believed that different parts of the brain served different faculties, that the portion of brain allocated to a faculty was proportional to the strength of the faculty, and that faculties and their strengths could be determined by measuring skull shape.

• Because it relied too heavily on anecdotal evidence and faulty logic, phrenology lost scientific credibility. It remained popular with the general public, however, being consistent with the American ideals of individuality, self-improvement, and the value of practical application.

• By developing the ablation method, Flourens was able to disprove phrenology while at the same time showing that the cortex operates as an integrated system.

• Evidence for localization came from clinical studies, in which those suffering from various forms of brain disease or damage were studied. The Phineas Gage case illustrated the effects of severe frontal lobe damage on judgment and personality. Broca's study of "Tan," who suffered from motor aphasia, showed that the ability to produce articulate speech depended on a fairly circumscribed area of the left frontal cortex.

• By developing the procedure of electrically stimulating the surface of the cortex, Fritsch and Hitzig in Germany and Ferrier in Scotland began to map the functions of the surface of the brain with a "scientific phrenology."

Nervous System Structure

• The identification of neurons as the basic units of the nervous system was made by Golgi, who thought they were physically connected to each other, and Ramón y Cajal, who thought they were physically separate from each other. Cajal's theory hinted at the presence of synapses.

• Ramón y Cajal's theory was verified by Sherrington, who is credited with naming the synapse and demonstrating its existence in his research on spinal reflexes and through the phenomena of temporal and spatial summation.

STUDY QUESTIONS

1. What was the Enlightenment attitude toward science, and how did this influence psychology's history?

2. Robert Whytt was able to demonstrate that reflexes required a spinal cord but not a brain. What was the research that led him to this conclusion?

3. What is the Bell–Magendie law? Explain why it should perhaps be called the Magendie law.

4. What was the vitalism–materialism issue, and how did Helmholtz provide support for the latter?

5. How did Helmholtz measure the speed of neural impulses, and what was the significance of this work?

6. Compare the color vision theories of Helmholtz and Hering.

7. According to Helmholtz, what is the "problem of perception"? Explain how his concept of unconscious inference was congenial to British empiricist thinking.

8. Describe the essential principles of phrenology, and explain why it eventually failed as science.

9. Explain why phrenology was highly popular in America. Why would the Spurzheim version be more popular with Americans than the Gall version?

10. Describe the method of ablation and how Flourens used it to assess phrenology.

11. Show how the two varieties of the clinical method for studying the brain are illustrated by (a) Phineas Gage and (b) Tan.

12. How did Broca establish that Tan had relatively normal mental capacity? What did Broca conclude on the basis of his postmortem examination of Tan?

13. Describe the importance of the late 19th-century research that came to be known as "scientific phrenology."

14. What was neuron theory, and what were the two versions proposed by the cowinners of the 1906 Nobel Prize for medicine?

15. Describe the work of Sherrington that led to the idea of the synapse.

CHAPTER 4

WUNDT AND GERMAN PSYCHOLOGY

The book which I here present to the public is an attempt to mark out a new domain of science.
—Wilhelm Wundt, 1874

PREVIEW AND CHAPTER OBJECTIVES

Chapters 2 and 3 described the context from which modern scientific psychology began to emerge in the 19th century. Philosophers, interested in the same fundamental questions about the human mind and behavior that occupy psychologists today, began to speculate about the need to examine these issues scientifically. At least one 19th-century British philosopher, John Stuart Mill, even proposed the development of a scientific approach to psychology. Meanwhile, European scientists made great strides in furthering our understanding of the physiology of the nervous system and, in particular, of the brain. This chapter examines how this experimental physiology combined with philosophical inquiry to create a new experimental psychology in Germany in the late 19th century. The chapter opens with a brief discussion of some aspects of German education that made it attractive to American students and then continues with a look at how the study of psychophysics set the stage for the creation of a "New Psychology" by examining sensory thresholds. The work of Wilhelm Wundt, usually labeled scientific psychology's "founder," forms the focus of the middle of the chapter. The chapter ends with consideration of three other important German researchers, Hermann Ebbinghaus, G. E. Müller, and Oswald Külpe. After you finish this chapter, you should be able to:

- Describe the philosophy of education in Germany that facilitated the development of the sciences, including psychology
- Describe Herbart's ideas about the nature of psychology and his concept of apperceptive mass
- Describe the early history of research on sensory thresholds, through the work of Weber
- Describe the methods of psychophysics developed by Fechner and how his work related to the philosophical position of materialism
- Describe Wundt's vision for his "New Psychology," distinguishing between his laboratory and his nonlaboratory approaches to psychology
- Describe the kinds of research typically completed in Wundt's laboratory at Leipzig
- Describe the logic of the complication experiment, and explain why it was valued so highly
- Compare the traditional description of Wundt and his work with more recent revisions, and explain why the discrepancies occurred

- Describe the methods developed by Hermann Ebbinghaus to study memory, his findings, and the importance of his research
- Describe the contributions to early experimental psychology made by G. E. Müller, and contrast his approach to memory with that of Ebbinghaus
- Describe the contributions of Oswald Külpe and his students at Würzburg, especially their elaboration of the concept of introspection

AN EDUCATION IN GERMANY

American students have always looked to European universities as a way to further their educations. Even today, a semester abroad is a valued experience. In the 19th century, Germany was an especially attractive location for young scholars; it has been estimated that in the 100-year span beginning in 1820, at least 9,000 American students enrolled in one German university or another (Sahakian, 1975), usually to study medicine or one of the sciences. By the end of that century, they were going there to study psychology.

One reason for the popularity of German universities was mere quantity. Between the time of the 1815 Congress of Vienna and the unification of Germany under Bismarck in 1871, Germany did not exist as a "country," but was a loosely organized federation of 38 autonomous "principalities" (e.g., Bavaria, Hanover, Saxony; Palmer, 1964). Each ministate wanted to keep up with its neighbors, of course, and one means of accomplishing this goal was to have its own university. Hence, universities proliferated. Although some of them were little more than a building with some classrooms and a few professors, several gained international stature and drew students from all over Europe as well as from America.

Circumstances in 19th-century Germany were especially conducive to the development of a new and more scientific approach to psychology. Beginning in the middle of the century, and originating at the University of Berlin, German universities developed a distinctive philosophy of education known as *Wissenschaft*. The term roughly translates as "scientific," and the philosophy encouraged scholars to take a scientific approach to the examination of nature. In addition, an academic culture developed that established academic freedom for professors to pursue their research interests without fear of administrative or political censure. Students were free to wander from one university to another, and earning a degree resulted more from passing special exams and defending a research thesis than from completing a specific curriculum.

For the professors who would create a new scientific psychology, many of whom you will meet in this chapter, the timing was perfect. The success of the physiologists reinforced the *Wissenschaft* emphasis on a research-based atmosphere and contributed directly to the growth of the new experimental approach to psychology throughout Germany, especially at Leipzig. As Blumenthal (1980) pointed out, the methods being developed by the physiologists, "involving measurement, replicability, public data, and controlled tests" (p. 29) were being applied to the study of the nervous system, but they might just as well be applied to other aspects of human behavior. Gradually the term *physiological* in German came to mean *experimental*. When Wilhelm Wundt referred to the new psychology as a "physiological psychology," he meant it in this broader sense of psychology being a discipline based on experimental methodology. He used the term *physiological* to refer to the fact that most of the methods in this new laboratory approach to psychology derived from the techniques first developed by the 19th-century physiologists (Greenwood, 2003).

FIGURE 4.1 Map of Germany, showing locations of the universities relevant for psychology's history.

For the American student of the 1880s who desired to learn about this new field of study first-hand, several choices were available (see map in Figure 4.1), including Wundt's laboratory at Leipzig. During Wundt's tenure there, approximately three dozen Americans completed doctorates under his supervision, and a number of others at least sampled the Leipzig environment (Benjamin, Durkin, Link, Vestal, & Accord, 1992). Before we consider Wundt and his influence on the development of experimental psychology, however, some important preliminaries are in order.

ON THE THRESHOLD OF EXPERIMENTAL PSYCHOLOGY: PSYCHOPHYSICS

A strong case can be made that scientific research on psychological topics began as a natural extension of the physiological research being done in the 19th century. Later in this chapter you will encounter one example of this in the connection between Helmholtz's physiological studies of nerve impulse speed and the psychological method of reaction time. In this section, we examine an association between physiological research on sensory processes and the development of **psychophysics**, the study of the relationship between the perception of a stimulus event ("psycho") and the physical dimensions of the stimulus being perceived ("physics"). Psychophysics derived from the logical and mathematical analyses of Johann Friedrich Herbart, began with the sensory threshold research of Ernst Weber, and became systematized through the research of the enigmatic philosopher/physician/physicist Gustav Fechner.

Johann Herbart (1776–1841)

Herbart began (earned a doctorate; taught for a few years) and ended (final 8 years of teaching) his academic career at the University of Göttingen, but he made his reputation during 24 years (1809–1833) spent at the University of Königsberg, where he succeeded the venerable Immanuel Kant (Chapter 2). Like Kant, Herbart did not believe that the mind could be studied using experimental methods—he thought of mental activity as an integrated whole, therefore resistant to analysis. Unlike Kant, however, Herbart believed that psychology could be scientific in the broad sense implied by the *Wissenschaft* philosophy of education just described. That is, he thought that an empirical psychology was possible, a psychology based on experience and reflection on that experience. He also thought that psychological principles could be established mathematically, and it is that contribution that places him on the list of those responsible for the gradual emergence of psychology as a science. His ideas were most clearly expressed in his *Psychology as a Science* (Herbart, 1824–1825). In German, the title is *Psychologie auf Wissenschaft*, reflecting the use of the term *science* as understood in Germany at the time.

On the assumption that different ideas in the mind have different strengths, Herbart assigned different mathematical weights to ideas. The mathematics need not concern us. Of importance, however, are some of the concepts that derived from this mathematical approach. From one of his intellectual heroes, Leibniz (Chapter 2), Herbart borrowed the concept of *apperception* and elaborated it into a concept of his own that he named **apperceptive mass**. After Leibniz, apperception had become a widely used term that generally referred to conscious awareness. If you are focusing on this paragraph and avoiding thoughts about what you'll be doing this weekend, then the paragraph's content is being apperceived. For Herbart, an apperceptive mass goes a bit further, referring to a group of related ideas that are at the forefront of consciousness. If you are working hard processing this paragraph, Herbart would say your apperceptive mass includes interrelated ideas about attention, apperception, idea strength, and mathematical analysis. Other ideas (e.g., the upcoming weekend) are out of your awareness, while remaining a part of your overall mental content. That is, the ideas related to "weekend" exist for you, but they are below the *threshold* of awareness. This concept of threshold is an important one because it requires the existence of a below-threshold unconscious—so Herbart is relevant for the history of Freudian psychoanalysis. Investigating the locations of these thresholds eventually became the heart and soul of psychophysics, as you are about to learn.

Herbart also believed the mind was a dynamic entity, actively organizing information in the apperceptive mass and actively preventing unrelated weaker ideas from interfering with the apperceptive process. He even used the term *repression*, later central to Freud's theories. Idea strength can change, however, through such factors as fatigue or distraction. Thus, the fact that I mentioned the upcoming weekend twice in the last paragraph, combined with the possibility that you have been reading for a while and are tiring of it, thoughts of the weekend might strengthen, and your apperceptive mass might shift from Herbart to the prospect of a nice cold beer.

For the purposes of this chapter, Herbart's importance is that he began to think about psychology as a discipline that was separate from philosophy and that did not necessarily require an understanding of physiology. Boring (1950) eloquently summed up Herbart's influence this way: "What Herbart gave to psychology was status. He took it out of both philosophy and physiology and sent it forth with a mission of its own" (p. 252).[1] One effect of this mission was the creation of techniques to

---

[1] Herbart is also considered to be a pioneer in the history of educational psychology (Boring, 1950). A key to good teaching, he argued, was to teach new material so that students can assimilate the content into an existing apperceptive mass. For example, preceding a chapter in a textbook with a preview and a set of objectives can be seen as a way of creating an apperceptive mass, preparing the student for the greater detail about to be encountered in the chapter. On a broader scale, requiring course prerequisites can also be seen as an application of Herbart's apperceptive mass concept.

examine the thresholds Herbart described, those separating events above and below the appercep-tive mass.

Ernst Weber (1795–1878)

Weber spent most of his academic career at the University of Leipzig, first as a student and then as a professor of anatomy and physiology from 1821 until his retirement in 1871. In the 1820s physiologists were beginning to learn a great deal about vision and hearing, but little was known of the other senses. Weber set out to correct the imbalance by becoming the leading authority on the tactile senses (Dorn, 1972). He made two major contributions: mapping the relative sensitivity of various locations on the skin, and demonstrating a mathematical relationship between the psychological and the physical that would establish psychophysics and later be known as Weber's law.

Two-Point Thresholds To examine tactile sensitivity, Weber used a technique in which he touched the skin's surface with a simple device resembling a two-point drawing compass. The distance between the points could be varied, and the blindfolded observer's task was to judge whether one or two points were being felt. For any specific area of the skin, there exists a **two-point threshold**—the point where the perception changes from feeling one point to feeling two of them. For skin areas of great sensitivity (e.g., the thumb), Weber found the threshold to be quite small. That is, the points didn't have to be very far apart before being noticed as two distinct points rather than one. On the other hand, for areas of less sensitivity (e.g., the upper arm), the points would have to be placed farther apart before they were perceived as being two separate ones.

Weber's Law Weber's second contribution derived from his interest in the "muscle sense," what we today call kinesthesis. He wanted to know how important this sense was for making judgments about comparative weights (Heidbreder, 1933). Picture two tasks: First, your hand is resting on a table and first one and then another weighted cylinder is placed in your palm. Your task is to judge which cylinder is heavier. Second, the two cylinders are on the table, and this time you lift each one before making the same judgment. In performing such an experiment, Weber found that observers could make finer discriminations when they lifted the weights than when the weights were just placed in the hand—that is, lifting brings the muscle sense into play. More important for the history of psychology, Weber also discovered that the ability to discriminate between two weights did not depend on the absolute difference between them in weight, but on a proportional relationship that became known as Weber's law.

In his weight-lifting experiments, Weber was dealing with thresholds again. For example, if observers could not distinguish between lifting 30 and 31 grams, or between 30 and 32 grams (they judged them to be the same weight), but *could* distinguish between 30 and 33 grams, then clearly some kind of threshold had been passed at 33 grams. Weber referred to the discrimination between 30 and 33 grams as a "just noticeable difference" or **jnd**. He discovered that the jnd depended not on the absolute size of the difference between the weights, but on the relationship between this jnd and the smaller of the two weights (called the "standard stimulus," or S). As the standard stimulus became heavier, a greater difference between it and the comparison weight was necessary before the difference was noticed. That is, **Weber's law** was this: $jnd/S = k$. So observers would notice a difference between 30 and 33 grams, but not between 60 and 63 grams. If the standard stimulus was 60 grams instead of 30, no difference could be detected until the second weight is at least 66 grams ($3/30 = 6/60$). Similarly, if $S = 90$ grams, the jnd was 9 grams. Hence, the jnd was proportional to the size of S.

The importance of Weber's law is threefold. First, as with the two-point threshold research, Weber was subjecting mental events (sensations) to measurement and mathematical formulation. This would eventually make psychophysics a key element of Wilhelm Wundt's new psychology, which claimed to be an experimental science. Science demands objective measurement, and threshold research seemed to fit the bill. Second, Weber showed that there was not a one-to-one relationship between changes in the physical world and the psychological experience of those changes. Increasing a weight by 3 grams does not always produce the same sensation. Sometimes differences are perceived (if $S = 30$), sometimes not (if $S = 60$). Consequently, understanding how the mind organizes its experiences requires knowing more than just the physical dimensions of the stimuli we are exposed to; it also requires an attempt to determine how the mind interprets those physical stimuli. Third, Weber's law showed that mental and physical events could be related mathematically. That insight would be developed more fully by another Leipzig scientist.

Gustav Fechner (1801–1889)

Weber's goal as a physiologist was to understand the tactile and muscle senses, and to do so he used methods that would eventually be known as psychophysical. His younger Leipzig colleague, Gustav Fechner, had an even more ambitious goal, however. Fechner was obsessed with the idea of resolving the ageless mind–body problem in a way that would defeat materialism, which he considered nothing short of evil, and he thought that psychophysics was the way to do it. A case can be made for calling Fechner the first experimental psychologist, even though he was trained as a physician; made his reputation as a physicist; and when he was in the midst of his pioneering research in psychophysics, thought of himself as a philosopher.

Fechner was born in a Lutheran parsonage in southern Germany in 1801; he was a precocious child, familiar with Latin by age 5. At 16 he entered the University of Leipzig to study medicine, and his education included a dose of physiology with Weber. Though Fechner earned an MD in 1822, he never practiced medicine. In the 1820s, his interests centered on math and physics, and he made original research contributions in the new physics of electricity.[2] His research was notable enough to earn him a position at Leipzig as professor of physics in 1834, the same year that Weber published his research on the sensation of touch.

Fechner's interests in science broadened in the 1830s to include the study of visual afterimages, the kind that occurs after a bright light is flashed on and off. He discovered a relationship between the brightness of the light and the strength of the afterimage, which led him to consider the quality of afterimages resulting from a quick glance at the brightest of all lights, the sun. Quick glances become longer glances, and even though Fechner wore filters to reduce the effects of looking at the sun, he damaged his eyes. The problem was serious enough to force him to resign his professorship in 1839 and accept a disability pension from the university.

Long before the afterimage episode, Fechner suffered from headaches and an occasional inability to control his thoughts, but the blindness triggered a descent into neurosis that lasted several years (Balance & Bringmann, 1987). Fechner became an invalid, forced to spend long periods of time in total darkness and plagued by a variety of anxiety, depressive, and somatic symptoms. His ascent to normality began in 1842 and was complete by the mid-1840s. It was accomplished largely through his

---

[2]Fechner's research on electricity reveals a connection with his father, a Lutheran minister, whose faith extended into the realm of science. The elder Fechner was aware of the famous electricity experiments of Benjamin Franklin and of Franklin's invention of the lightning rod. Knowing that church steeples were favorite targets of lightning bolts, the minister prudently installed one of Franklin's devices on his church steeple. Members of the church felt that their pastor was not showing much faith in God's ability to protect the church, but Pastor Fechner commented that the laws of physics also had to be considered (Boring, 1950). Pastor Fechner died when his son was only 5, but young Gustav apparently inherited his father's love of and respect for science.

efforts at regaining control over his life, but was facilitated by a steady improvement in his vision. After recovering, he turned his attention to philosophical matters and in 1851 was reappointed to the Leipzig faculty. During this period, he became immersed in the question of the relationship of mind to body and consumed with the idea of defeating materialism. As you recall from the last chapter, materialism, the belief that all events have causes that can be traced to physical and chemical changes, was favored by most of the younger physiologists of the day (e.g., Helmholtz).

Fechner referred to materialism as the *Nachtansicht*, or "night view," and he hoped to replace it with a contrasting *Tagesansicht*, or "day view." This day view derived from an idealism movement then popular in German philosophy, which held that the universe had a form of consciousness to it that went beyond the individual consciousnesses of the organisms within it. Upon death, one's personal consciousness merged with this cosmic consciousness. For Fechner, this meant that although mind and body could be considered two aspects of the same fundamental reality, the mind was the primary and ultimate feature of that reality. In searching for a way to conceptualize the exact mind–body relationship, he created psychophysics. He later claimed that he achieved the insight suddenly, upon waking on the morning of October 22, 1850.[3] It occurred to him that mind and body could be united harmoniously and with mathematical precision by measuring psychological sensations and the physical stimuli that produced the sensations. The resulting field of psychophysics he defined as "an exact theory about the functional relationships between body and soul and between the bodily, mental, somatic, and psychological world" (quoted in Meischner-Metge & Meischner, 1997, p. 102). Fechner's insight triggered a decade of intense work on sensory thresholds, resulting in the publication in 1860 of the *Elements of Psychophysics*, often considered the first book of experimental psychology (Fechner, 1860/1966).

Fechner's Elements of Psychophysics Fechner was aware of Weber's research on thresholds, but did not realize its significance until after his insight of 1850. The breakthrough for Fechner was the conviction that sensations could be subjected to exact measurement by assuming that jnd's were subjectively equal in magnitude. Thus weights of 30 and 33 grams are just noticeably different, as are weights of 60 and 66 grams. The differences in weight between the two pairs of stimuli are 3 and 6 grams, respectively. Psychologically, however, the difference between 30 and 33 *feels* the same as (i.e., is subjectively equal to) the difference between 60 and 66, according to Fechner.

Fechner's assumption of equal jnd's was challenged almost immediately, and the mathematical relationship he developed was shown to be true only under limited circumstances. No matter. The enduring legacy of his *Elements of Psychophysics* was his systematization of the methods used to establish thresholds, which are still in use both in the laboratory and in such applications as vision and hearing tests. These are known today as the methods of limits, constant stimuli, and adjustment.[4] Consider them in the context of a hearing test. In the **Method of Limits**, a stimulus is presented that is well above threshold and then gradually reduced in intensity until the subject reports that it can no longer be heard. This is called a *descending trial*, and it is followed by an *ascending trial*, in which the stimulus is first presented below threshold, and then increased until the subject hears it for the first time. Descending and ascending trials are alternated many times, and the threshold is calculated as the average of all trials. In the **Method of Constant Stimuli**, sounds of varying intensities are presented in a random order, and the subject's task is to indicate whether or not they are heard. This method solves a problem with the

---

[3]If you want to impress your psychology professors, send them a "Happy Fechner Day" card on October 22. To this day, experimental psychologists, especially those who study sensation and perception, take some time out on that day to raise a glass in honor of Fechner's insight, and modern psychophysicists plan an annual international conference around the date.

[4]Fechner referred to them as the methods of just noticeable differences, right and wrong cases, and average error, respectively.

method of limits, which is a tendency for the listener to anticipate the place where the threshold lies. In the **Method of Adjustment**, the subject directly varies the intensity of the stimulus until it seems to be at threshold. Ascending and descending trials can be used. Of the three techniques, a study using the method of adjustment takes the least amount of time, but is the least accurate; the method of constant stimuli is the most accurate, but takes the longest time (Goldstein, 1996). In an actual hearing test, the method of limits with descending trials is normally used; "catch trials" are inserted to prevent subjects from signaling ("I hear it") when there is in fact no stimulus presented.

Boring (1963b) referred to Fechner as the "inadvertent founder of psychophysics." He believed that Fechner's main purpose was philosophical—to establish his day view while defeating materialism (the night view). Unfortunately for Fechner, that goal was not reached, and the philosophical implications of his work were largely ignored. Fortunately for psychology, though, Fechner's efforts resulted in the creation of a research program and a set of methods that enabled others to see what Fechner did not—that psychological phenomena could be subjected to scientific methodology. By creating psychophysics in 1860, Fechner paved the way for another German physiologist, Wilhelm Wundt, to proclaim a New Psychology a few years later.

WUNDT ESTABLISHES A NEW PSYCHOLOGY AT LEIPZIG

The brief quote that opens this chapter comes from the preface of the epoch-making two-volume *Principles of Physiological Psychology*, published in 1873–1874. It was written by the German most often described as the "founder" of experimental psychology, Wilhelm Wundt. To claim, as Wundt did, that one is making an "attempt to mark out a new domain of science" is the kind of statement that separates founders from their contemporaries. Clearly, Fechner's work on psychophysics entitles him to a claim as the first experimental psychologist. We've seen, however, that Fechner had other, more philosophical, purposes—defeating materialism. Thus, as Boring (1950) pointed out, founders are promoters. They might not be the first to accomplish something, but they are the first to proclaim that their accomplishment breaks new ground. They make important scientific contributions, but they also have a talent for propaganda. Wundt had that talent.

Wilhelm Wundt (1832–1920): Creating a New Science

Experimental psychology's founder had a childhood of modest accomplishment. Marginal performance characterized his early school years, and it wasn't until his late teens that he began to show any interest in education. Despite a dismal academic record, family connections enabled him to begin medical studies at the University of Tübingen at the age of 19; after a year he switched to Heidelberg, where he finally began to show promise. By 1855, he had earned an MD from the University of Heidelberg and had finished first on a certifying exam (Bringmann, Balance, & Evans, 1975).

The Heidelberg years also saw the blossoming of Wundt's interests in science. The famous chemist Robert Bunsen (inventor of the Bunsen burner) made a lasting impression: When Wundt eventually became a professor himself, he copied Bunsen's technique of illustrating points in class through the use of visual displays and demonstrations. Bunsen also inspired Wundt's first independent research project, an examination of the effects of restricting salt input on the chemical composition of his urine. Wundt also conducted an experiment on the touch sensitivity of hysteric patients, using Weber's two-point threshold technique; this study served as his MD dissertation research.

Following completion of his degree in November of 1855, Wundt practiced medicine for a brief 6 months as a clinical assistant at Heidelberg's university hospital, but he was already beginning to think that a life of research was more appealing than a life of writing prescriptions and setting bones. He spent a semester in Berlin studying experimental physiology with the great Johannes Müller (Chapter 3), resolving to become a professor of physiology on his return to Heidelberg. In February 1857 he was given a position of *Privatdozent*, which in the German system meant that he was entitled to offer courses but that his salary depended on student fees. Wundt's first course attracted only four students and near the completion of the course he fell seriously ill, probably with tuberculosis (Bringmann, Bringmann, & Balance, 1980). After a yearlong recovery period, he applied for an opening as the assistant in the laboratory of the esteemed Hermann Helmholtz (Chapter 3), who had just begun his tenure at Heidelberg. Wundt got the job, a major boost for his career.

Wundt worked in Helmholtz's lab between 1858 and 1865, but he did much more with his time than just run the laboratory. He continued to offer courses as *Privatdozent*, and he began writing. In addition to several papers, Wundt published two important books that marked him as an emerging experimental psychologist. *Contributions to a Theory of Sensory Perception* appeared in 1862, followed a year later by *Lectures on Human and Animal Psychology* (Wundt, 1863/1907). The first book is noteworthy because it marks the first time that Wundt called for an explicitly experimental approach to basic psychological questions. Thus he was thinking about the possibility that psychology could be a science well before his famous pronouncement of 1873–1874. The second book repeated the call and described some of the early research in psychophysics and reaction time. Two full books in a short period of time was just the beginning of what became a remarkably prodigious output. Boring (1950) estimated that Wundt published 53,735 pages in his lifetime, an average of 2.2 pages per day.

Wundt left Helmholtz's laboratory in 1865 but remained at Heidelberg for another 9 years, setting up a private laboratory and earning a living through teaching fees and book royalties. In 1871, his efforts were rewarded by the university, which appointed him to the rank of Extraordinary Professor (similar to the associate professor level in American universities). This meant that for the first time in his life, Wundt had full faculty status and a salary that was not tied to student enrollment. Nearing the age of 40, he was finally secure enough to marry his fiancée of many years. During this time he wrote his famous two-volume *Principles of Physiological Psychology* (Wundt, 1873–1874/1904), which included this chapter's opening quote in its Preface. The book, which eventually went through six editions, earned him a professorship in "inductive philosophy" at the University of Zurich (academic year 1874–1875). And then, after just a year in Switzerland, Wundt was offered a similar position at the University of Leipzig, which he accepted immediately. Leipzig's university was more prestigious than the one at Zurich, and Leipzig itself was a center of German culture—home to the famous composers Bach, Wagner, and Mendelssohn, for example. Wundt remained at the University of Leipzig until his retirement in 1917. He died 3 years later.

We tend to associate Wundt only with his Leipzig years, but it is important to realize that when he arrived there in 1875, he was already in his mid-forties and had been an active scientist at Heidelberg for 17 years. He had already written three important books and numerous papers, more than most academics produce in a lifetime. Furthermore, he had announced that at least some aspects of psychology could become scientific, and he had set out a plan for establishing what quickly came to be called the New Psychology. Thus he had accomplished what would be a life's work for many. Yet Wundt still had more than *40* highly productive years left in him during his time at Leipzig.

During his years at Heidelberg, Wundt accumulated a private collection of laboratory apparatus, both for his own research and for demonstrating various phenomena during his lectures (in the spirit

Archives of the History of American Psychology, The Center for the History of Psychology—The University of Akron

FIGURE 4.2 An elderly Wilhelm Wundt (center) in his laboratory at Leipzig.

of his old chemistry professor, Robert Bunsen). Soon after his arrival at Leipzig, the university gave him some space to store the equipment. This modest space, a room with approximately 400 square feet, eventually became experimental psychology's first laboratory and the model for dozens of imitators. Wundt used the lab for demonstration purposes initially, but by 1879 he and his students were conducting original research in what he now called the *Psychologisches Institut*. Of course, calling 1879 the "official" founding date for experimental psychology's first laboratory is arbitrary—the room and its equipment were there before 1879. The designation is probably another reflection of the pervasive influence of Boring's 1929 history, which includes this sentence: "In 1879, four years after he had come to Leipzig, Wundt founded, as almost every psychologist knows, the first psychological laboratory in the world" (Boring, 1929, p. 318).[5]

Regardless of when it actually began, Wundt's laboratory quickly became a magnet, attracting curious students from all over Europe and from America. Additional rooms were added over the years, and in 1897 a new and more elaborate laboratory was built to Wundt's specifications. It was destroyed by an Allied bombing raid in 1943. An inside look at the workings of Wundt's laboratory, a glimpse of which can be seen in Figure 4.2, follows shortly. First, however, it is necessary to examine Wundt's vision for his new science.

Wundt's Conception of the New Psychology

The "new domain of science" that Wundt attempted to "mark out" in his *Principles of Physiological Psychology* was a vision first outlined 12 years earlier in his 1862 book on perception. This new psychology called for the scientific examination of human conscious experience, using methods borrowed from experimental physiology and supplemented by new strategies. Today, when we see a book with the label "physiological psychology," we are inclined to think the book will focus on the relationship between biology and behavior. Wundt, however, used the label *physiological* only in referring to the

[5]The identical wording appears on page 323 of the second edition of Boring's book (Boring, 1950).

fact that many of the methods for his New Psychology (e.g., reaction time) had been developed in physiology laboratories (Greenwood, 2003). As he put it:

> The introduction of the experimental method into psychology was originally due to the modes of procedure in physiology, especially in the physiology of the sense-organs and the nervous system. For this reason experimental psychology is also commonly called "physiological psychology." (Wundt, 1897, p. 1)

Wundt's new psychology included two major programs: the examination of immediate conscious experience using the experimental methods of the laboratory and the study of higher mental processes, using nonlaboratory methods.

Studying Immediate Conscious Experience To understand the contrast that Wundt drew between immediate experience and "mediate" experience, consider a simple example. If you look out the window at a thermometer and it reads 15°F, you are not experiencing the phenomenon of temperature directly. Rather, temperature is being *mediated* by a scientific instrument. On the other hand, if you then step outside without a coat, you have a direct experience of coldness. It is an immediate conscious experience. That is, there is no thermometer standing between you and the weather; you are encountering it firsthand. For Wundt, this immediate conscious experience was to be the subject matter of his laboratory psychology.

Wundt recognized the fundamental problem with studying immediate consciousness. To examine mediate experience objectively is simple. Because the temperature reading is a public event, two or more observers can agree on it; thus, it is a straightforward matter to apply scientific methods. Various aspects of the environment can be manipulated, and the resulting effects on temperature can be assessed with precision. Describing immediate experience is more difficult, however. How can you be sure that your experience of 15° compares with mine? Here Wundt made a critical distinction between *self-observation* and *internal perception*. The distinction has been blurred over the years, and both terms have been called **introspection**. Self-observation is the traditional philosophical attempt to analyze life's experiences through introspective reflection. This was unsystematic, and because such observations by definition take place some time after the experienced event has occurred, they rely heavily on faulty memory. Wundt rejected self-observation as nothing better than philosophical speculation. **Internal perception**, on the other hand, was like self-observation, but was a much narrower process of responding immediately to precisely controlled stimuli. The problem of memory was reduced by the immediacy of the response and by using observers trained to respond automatically and without bias. Such precision came with a price, however. Internal perception could yield valid scientific data only if its results could be replicated. For Wundt, this meant that laboratory research had to be limited to a narrow range of conscious experiences. In practice, this amounted to basic sensory/perceptual/attentional ones. Such experiences could be controlled by means of sophisticated apparatus used to present stimuli to observers, who in turn would give simple responses to these stimuli. In Wundt's lab, these types of introspective responses were "largely limited to judgments of size, intensity, and duration of physical stimuli, supplemented at times by judgments of their simultaneity and succession" (Danziger, 1980, p. 247). These, of course, are the kinds of judgments made in psychophysics experiments, which comprised a significant portion of the research in Wundt's laboratory. As we will learn, Wundt's conception of introspection as internal perception differed sharply from the "systematic experimental introspection" used by two of his better-known students, Oswald Külpe (discussed later in this chapter) and Edward B. Titchener (Chapter 7).

Studying Higher Mental Processes Although Wundt believed that laboratory investigation was necessarily limited to the immediate conscious experience of basic mental processes, he also had a broader aim for his psychology. He wished to examine other mental processes such as learning, thinking, language, and the effects of culture. But he believed that because these processes were so intertwined with an individual's personal history, cultural history, and the social environment, they could not be controlled sufficiently to be examined with precision in the laboratory. Instead, they could be studied only through inductive observational techniques, cross-cultural comparisons, historical analyses, and case studies.

These higher mental processes were a lifelong interest of Wundt's, first outlined in detail in his second major book (*Lectures on Human and Animal Psychology*, 1863/1907). They fully occupied the last two decades of his life; and during this time, he enhanced his reputation as a prodigious writer by publishing the massive 10-volume *Völkerpsychologie* (*volker* translates roughly as a combination of "cultural," "ethnic," "social," and/or "communal"). The books include detailed analyses of language and culture, and they encompass topics that would today be considered under the headings of psycholinguistics, the psychology of religion and myth, social psychology, forensic psychology, and anthropology. There were three volumes on myth and religion, two on language, two on societies, and one each on culture and history, law, and art (Blumenthal, 1975).

Wundt, like other thinkers of his time, believed that an implication of evolutionary theory was that cultures could be arranged on a continuum, from "primitive" (e.g., Australian aboriginal) to "advanced" (German, presumably). By studying the social customs, myths, religions, and languages of cultures differing in their level of sophistication, Wundt thought that an understanding of the evolution of human mental processes could be attained (Farr, 1983). He was especially interested in language. Much of what he wrote about language was ignored at the time, only to be rediscovered in the 1950s and 1960s, when psycholinguistics became a key element in the rise of cognitive psychology (Blumenthal, 1975). For example, Wundt distinguished between the idea to be conveyed by a sentence, the actual structure of the sentence itself, and the manner in which the listener took the sentence structure and inferred the speaker's meaning from it. The relationship between the idea to be conveyed and the sentence structure is similar to the distinction later made by linguist Noam Chomsky between the deep and surface structures of a grammar, and Wundt's belief that the listener would not recall the actual sentence but the meaning of it is similar to later research on memory for the "gist" of communicated messages.

Inside Wundt's Laboratory

Once Wundt's students began producing original research at Leipzig, the need for a way to publicize the work became apparent. Wundt solved the problem in 1881 by creating the journal *Philosophische Studien* (*Philosophical Studies*). It was the first journal designed to report the results of experimental research in psychology, and Wundt served as editor for its first two decades (1881–1903). The journal became a mouthpiece for the work done by Wundt and his students, so a look at its contents reveals the kind of research done at Leipzig during the last two decades of the 19th century. According to Boring (1950), who examined the 100 or so experimental studies published in the journal during this time, at least half of the research was in the area of sensation and perception. Of the remaining half, reaction time studies were the most popular, followed by studies on attention, feeling, and association.

Sensation and Perception Most of the basic information about sensory systems encountered in today's courses in sensation and perception was known by the turn of the century, and a fair amount of the research was carried out in Wundt's laboratory. As mentioned earlier, most of these "internal perception" studies were psychophysical in nature, examining such topics as the abilities to distinguish colors presented to different areas of the retina and tones presented in various combinations of pitch and loudness. In perception, Wundtians studied such topics as positive and negative afterimages, visual contrast, illusions, and the perception of size, depth, and motion (Boring, 1950).

Mental Chronometry When Helmholtz measured the duration of a nerve impulse and found it to be more leisurely than expected, he provided the impetus for a method that came to be known as **mental chronometry** in Wundt's lab. Today we call it reaction time. Wundt was aware of this research long before he arrived in Leipzig. He became Helmholtz's assistant at Heidelberg shortly after the nerve impulse studies had been carried out, and he became very interested in the problem of measuring mental speed in the 1860s. The problem had also been around for a number of years in the form of a practical difficulty faced by astronomers. The creation of tables for calculating longitude required knowing the precise positions of various stars and planets at specific times of a lunar cycle (Sobel, 1995). Identifying these positions involved a complicated procedure that measured the time taken for a planet to make a "transit" from one side of the crosshair of a telescope lens to the other. Humans were making the judgments, of course, and even though they were trained astronomers, their judgments of transit times tended to be different because of small differences in their reaction times. To solve the problem, an attempt was made to calibrate one astronomer against another by determining each one's **personal equation**. Thus, if astronomer A was regularly 0.12 second slower than astronomer B, their transit times could be made comparable through a personal equation: $A = B + 0.12$ second.

The individual who developed the reaction time procedure as it came to be used by the Wundtians and others was F. C. Donders (1818–1889), a Dutch physiologist. Donders reasoned that if nerve impulses take a measurable amount of time, and if mental activity is composed of nerve impulses, then the times taken by various mental events could be determined. Assuming that mental events could be combined in an additive fashion, Donders developed the **subtractive method** in the late 1860s. First, he would measure the time taken for a simple reaction, for example, by holding down a telegraph key and then releasing it as soon as possible after perceiving a light. The procedure would then be "complicated" by adding other mental tasks. For instance, the observer might be asked to respond only if a red light came on; if the light was another color, no response was to be made. This "discrimination reaction time" (DRT) was composed of everything involved in simple reaction time (SRT), *plus* the mental event of discriminating between the colors. Thus:

$$DRT = SRT + \text{discrimination time}$$
$$\text{discrimination time} = DRT - SRT$$

Hence, if a series of trials produced an average simple reaction time of 0.18 seconds and an average discrimination reaction time of 0.29 seconds, then the time for the mental event of "discrimination" was 0.11 seconds ($0.29 - 0.18 = 0.11$).

Similarly, "choice reaction time" (CRT) involved releasing one key if the light was one color and another key if the light was a second color. In addition to simple reaction time and the time taken to discriminate between the two colors, the observer had to choose which key to release. Thus:

$$CRT = SRT + \text{discrimination time} + \text{choice time}$$
$$\text{choice time} = CRT - (SRT + \text{discrimination time})$$
$$\text{choice time} = CRT - DRT$$

So if a series of trials produced an average choice reaction time of 0.42 seconds and an average discrimination reaction time of .29 seconds, then the time for "choice" was 0.13 seconds (0.42 − 0.29 = 0.13).

For reasons that are apparent, this procedure was also called the **complication experiment**, and studies using it flourished in Wundt's laboratory, especially in the 1880s. The procedure was eventually discarded, however, when it became clear that the subtractive assumptions underlying the method were simplistic. In the examples just described, for instance, more complicated reactions should always be longer than less complicated ones; in actual experiments, however, this outcome did not always occur. Wundt's student Oswald Külpe pointed out that complicating the procedure by adding discrimination and/or choice does not simply add elements; rather, it changes the entire psychological experience.

James McKeen Cattell (look ahead to Figure 7.8), perhaps the best known of the American students who studied with Wundt, was an enthusiastic advocate of the reaction time method (Garrett, 1951), using an experimental setup that probably looked something like the one in Figure 4.3. As Cattell described it, "[t]he observer sat in the dark, and looked through a telescopic tube at the point where the light was to appear" (1885/1948a, p. 323). Cattell examined the effects of stimulus intensity on reaction time, and he also studied individual differences in the times. His studies usually involved just two or three participants, including himself; those involved in the study took turns being experimenter and subject. This was common practice in early experimental psychology—very few participants, each person contributing a great deal of data, and no clear distinction between what in later years would be called the *experimenter* and the *subject* (Danziger, 1988). Furthermore, data from several participants would not be averaged together. Rather, all data from each subject would be reported, and additional participants served the purpose of replication.

Like Külpe, Cattell eventually became a critic of the complication experiment while continuing to see the usefulness of reaction time to test various hypotheses about mental processing. This led him to study such phenomena as recognition times for different letters of the alphabet and reaction times for verbal associations (e.g., Cattell, 1886). Cattell also left an intriguing account of day-to-day life in Wundt's laboratory, some of which is described in this chapter's Close-Up.

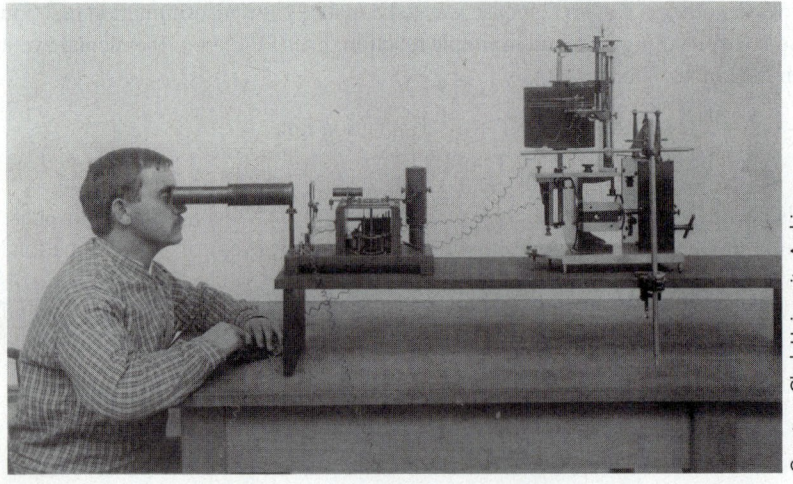

Courtesy Clark University Archives

FIGURE 4.3 Reaction time experiment in progress at Clark University, 1892.

CLOSE-UP

AN AMERICAN IN LEIPZIG

In 1886, James McKeen Cattell (1860–1944) became the first American to earn a Leipzig PhD in experimental psychology under Wundt's supervision (Benjamin et al., 1992). While at Leipzig, he kept a detailed journal and corresponded frequently with his parents in America. These materials were compiled and annotated in *An Education in Psychology: James McKeen Cattell's Journal and Letters from Germany and England, 1880–1888* (Sokal, 1981a). The book is a rich source of information about life in the early years of Wundt's laboratory.

Cattell first went to Leipzig as part of a European tour in 1881–1882. He then spent the 1882–1883 academic year at Johns Hopkins University in Baltimore, studying in the lab created by G. Stanley Hall (Chapter 6). He returned to Leipzig in the fall of 1883 and emerged with his doctorate 3 years later. Here are some of the observations he made about working in Wundt's laboratory.

Most of Cattell's research concerned the problem of reaction time. In a letter to his parents in 1884, he briefly described this research. Like others immersed in basic research that might seem trivial to Mom and Dad, Cattell apparently felt a bit defensive and believed it necessary to convince his parents that his reaction time work had value:

> *Letter to Parents, 8 October 1884* In [my research] I determine the time required by simple mental processes—how long it takes us to see, hear or feel something—to understand, to will, to think. You may not consider this so very interesting or important. But if we wish to describe the world—which is the end of science—surely an accurate knowledge of our mind is more important than anything else.... [I]f one thinks that knowledge for its own sake is worth the pursuit, then surely a knowledge of mind is best of all. Not only is the mind of man of infinitely more worth and importance than anything else, but on its nature the whole world depends.
>
> As to my special work—it is surely ... in itself interesting to know how fast a man thinks—for on this, not on the number of years he lives depends the length of his life. (Sokal, 1981a, p. 125)

Cattell's parents were apparently concerned that their son might overwork himself in the lab. To reassure them, Cattell described a typical research day with his colleague, Gustav Berger. Only a portion of it required the kind of focused attention that would be fatiguing, Cattell reported:

> *Letter to Parents, 26 November 1884* Berger began work with me again this morning. I do not think I shall hurt myself in working, if I keep taking ... constant exercise. It is undoubtedly true that making experiments on one's self is trying, but I do not do this continuously. If I spend six hours a day at this work, perhaps two must be given to looking after apparatus, preparing things &c. This is very easy work indeed. Then in two of the other four hours the other man is the subject and my work is not especially difficult. So you see I only spend two hours in work that strains. It were a pity if at twenty-five I could not stand that. (p. 141)

Cattell's observation about the 2 hours set aside for the apparatus illustrates the difficulty of developing a new science. Most of the apparatus had to be either adopted from the physics or physiology lab or invented on the spot. Apparatus maintenance was a constant irritant:

> *Letter to Parents, 5 January 1885* You have no idea how much one must fuss over apparatus. The trouble is not that one must know physics, but that he must be an original investigator in physics. For example Prof. Wundt thought that when a magnet was made by passing a current around a piece of soft iron, it was made instantaneously. I find with the current he used it takes over a tenth of a second. All the times he measured were that much too long. Now the time required for magnetism to be developed in soft iron has nothing on earth to do with psychology, yet if I had not spent a great deal of time on this subject all my work would have been wrong.... All this, getting the apparatus and running it, is very aggravating when one is in a hurry. (pp. 151–152)

Throughout his career, Cattell never hesitated to speak his mind and was not known for modesty or discretion. In the following comment, made near the end of his time at Leipzig, he made it clear what he thought of Wundt's laboratory.

Letter to Parents, 22 January 1885 I worked in Wundt's laboratory this afternoon probably for the last time . . . . Wundt's laboratory has a reputation greater than it deserves—the work done is decidedly amateurish. Work has only been done in two departments—the relation of the internal stimulus to the sensation [i.e., psychophysics], and the time of mental process [i.e., reaction time]. The latter is my subject—I started working on it at Baltimore [with Hall at Johns Hopkins] before I had read a word written by Wundt—what I did there was decidedly original. I'm quite sure my work is worth more than all done by Wundt & his pupils in this department, and as I have said it is one of the two departments on which they have worked. Mind I do not consider my work of any special importance—I only consider Wundt's of still less. (p. 156)

Rewriting History: The New and Improved Wilhelm Wundt

In Chapter 1, you learned that histories are continually being rewritten in light of new information, new ways of interpreting information, and so on. Wundt's psychology is a perfect illustration. If you had taken a history of psychology course about 50 years ago, you would have learned this about Wundt:

- He founded the first "school" of psychology and called it structuralism.
- The goal of Wundt's structuralist school was to analyze the contents of the mind into its basic structural components or elements, using a highly complex form of *introspection* of mental contents as the chief method.
- He was not really interested in cultural psychology; the 10-volume *Völkerpsychologie* was just a hobby for an old man.
- Wundt's intellectual son was E. B. Titchener, who spread the Wundtian gospel of structuralism in America.
- His model of the mind was similar to that of the British empiricists; that is, he did not believe in the concept of the mind as an active agent, but as the result of the buildup of passive associative experiences.

Today, the only time you read descriptions like this will be in narratives pointing out that each of these points is either a serious distortion or just plain wrong. In the 1970s, historians of psychology began taking a closer look at Wundt (e.g., Blumenthal, 1975; Danziger, 1980; Leahey, 1979), as part of the resurgence of interest in psychology's history, and they discovered that the traditional accounts were seriously flawed. Since that time, histories have begun to include more accurate descriptions of Wundt's life and work. Three questions arise: How did the distortions occur? Why were they not uncovered until the 1970s? What did Wundt really say?

The Source of the Problem Part of the difficulty derives from the fact that Wundt wrote more in his lifetime than most people read in theirs. Also, much of his work is either very difficult to read or has not been translated from German. Hence, there is a tendency for non-German speakers to rely on what others have written about Wundt, rather than on what Wundt actually said. Most psychologists before 1980 learned their history from E. G. Boring, Boring learned most of his from Titchener, and therein lies the root of the problem. As you will learn in Chapter 7, Titchener studied with Wundt for 2 years and earned a Leipzig PhD in 1892. He then spent his entire academic career at Cornell, where he spread the gospel of *structuralism*—his school of thought, not Wundt's. Titchener also translated several of Wundt's books and wrote a long obituary shortly after Wundt's death (Titchener, 1921b). In essence, Titchener took a portion of Wundt's work and exaggerated its importance, while downplaying or ignoring other parts of Wundt's work. The distortions were reflected in the way he taught about Wundt and in his translations of Wundt's writings. This was not a deliberate attempt to distort—Titchener was simply emphasizing what was most congenial to his own way of thinking. For example, Titchener's lack of interest in nonexperimental psychology led him to shrug off Wundt's interest in cultural/social psychology, making the remarkable comment in the obituary for his mentor that Wundt's 20-years-in-the-making, 10-volume *Völkerpsychologie* was little more than "a grateful occupation for his old age" (Titchener, 1921b, p. 175) and that "the dominant idea of Wundt's life … [was] the idea of an experimental psychology" (p. 175).

Boring was Titchener's best known student and psychology's most venerable historian (see Close-Up in Chapter 1). Boring's *A History of Experimental Psychology*, written in 1929 and revised in 1950, was the book that informed several generations of psychologists and until recently provided the model for other history texts. It was dedicated to Titchener (both editions), and the chapter on Wundt contains many of the distortions that originated with Titchener. The *Völkerpsychologie*, for instance, is barely mentioned. As for whether Boring might have probed more deeply and revised his treatment of Wundt in his second edition, "the chapter on Wundt … was republished unchanged in 1950," according to Blumenthal (2001, p. 124).

The Rediscovery of Wundt For two reasons, Wundt's ideas began to be reexamined in the 1970s. First, as you recall from Chapter 1, during the late 1960s and early 1970s the history of psychology as a discipline gathered new momentum under the leadership of Robert Watson and others. To some extent, new scholarship directed at Wundt's history reflects the increased interest in psychology's history. The second reason is more subtle and provides another justification for the continual rewriting of history. As you will learn in Chapter 14, during the 1960s, cognitive psychology happened. That is, psychologists became increasingly interested in the experimental study of mental processes, a topic that had languished in America between 1930 and 1960, due to the influence of behaviorism. Some scholars versed in the new cognitive research saw connections between the cognitive psychology of the 1960s and the earlier Wundtian psychology. Indeed, some of the cognitive research methods essentially duplicated research completed at Leipzig, even though modern researchers seemed unaware of it. Psychologist–historians began examining Wundt's work in light of the new cognitive psychology, producing papers that showed the connections between the two (Blumenthal, 1975; Leahey, 1979). The broader lesson is that histories can be strongly influenced by the context within which they are written. One effect of modern cognitive psychology was to view Wundt in a new light. In the days of behaviorism's dominance, such a reexamination of Wundt would not have occurred.

The Real Wundt The traditional but erroneous view of Wundt is that he was a structuralist. Now there is no question that one of Wundt's goals for his laboratory work was to classify the elements of immediate conscious experience. After all, he was originally trained in medicine and physiology and had a natural penchant for classification. Thus his experimental papers include descriptions of the basic elements of consciousness, which he decided were sensations and feelings. Moreover, each of these elements could be further categorized along certain dimensions. Sensations, for instance, were classified according to such dimensions as quality (e.g., different colors), intensity, and duration.

Analysis and classification, however, were only minor aspects of Wundt's overall system, and he was relatively uninterested in them. He was more concerned with the manner in which the mind actively organized its experiences through an act of will. He labeled his system **voluntarism** to reflect the active nature of the mind. A central concept of his voluntaristic system was the phenomenon of **apperception**, a term borrowed from Leibniz (Chapter 2) and Herbart (this chapter) and popular in the 19th century. As we have seen, to apperceive some event is to perceive it clearly and have it in the focus of one's attention. Other information (e.g., perhaps background music while you study) is in the periphery of your attention—Wundt would say that it is being apprehended, but not apperceived.[6] Thus, at any given time, there is information in the focus of attention and other information in the margins. Furthermore, apperception is a process that actively and vigorously organizes information into meaningful wholes. When we see the word *dog*, we do not perceive three separate letters; we perceive a single concept that has meaning for us. Our visual sense might be initially processing meaningless lines and symbols, but our mind creates a meaningful whole. Wundt referred to the apperceptive process as a "creative synthesis."

Wundt's concept of apperception is a far cry from a more passive associationism. Yet Wundt did recognize that some elements of conscious experience do combine as passive associations. As the British associationists said, if you see John and Mary together often enough, you will soon come to think of one when you see the other. This happens automatically because of a passively formed association. On the other hand, apperception is occurring if, when you see John and Mary, you bring them into the focus of your attention and perceive them as a special couple, or perhaps as two people who seem completely ill suited for one another. That is, you are going beyond the information given and perceiving them distinctly and meaningfully.

One final point about the historical misperception of Wundt concerns introspection. As described earlier, Wundt restricted verbal reports in the laboratory to simple responses to carefully controlled stimuli (e.g., "object A is heavier than object B"), a process he called *internal perception*. Titchener's approach to self-report, called *systematic experimental introspection*, was much more elaborate, involving detailed descriptions of mental experiences after some experimental task had been completed. From these descriptions, inferences would be made about human mental processing. Accounts of introspection based on Boring's history failed to distinguish between the two approaches, assuming that Wundt's strategy for self-report was the same as Titchener's (Danziger, 1980). It wasn't, and Wundt in fact was highly critical of Titchener's version, once writing that the method

> relies either on arbitrary observations that go astray or on a withdrawal to a lonely sitting room where it becomes lost in self-absorption. The unreliability of this method is universally recognized.... Clearly, Titchener has himself come under the influence of the deceptions of this method. (quoted in Blumenthal, 2001, p. 125)

The Wundtian Legacy

Because it was his intention to create a new way of conceptualizing psychology, Wundt is justifiably considered the first true experimental psychologist of the modern era. Although it is difficult to identify a single Wundtian among the early American psychologists, he had a strong influence on the origins of American psychology. The Americans who studied with Wundt may not have returned as disciples,

---

[6]The association/apperception difference was the key component of an important theory proposed by one of Wundt's more famous students, the psychiatrist Emil Kraepelin (1856–1926). Kraepelin devised a classification scheme for mental illness that produced the first clear description of what we call schizophrenia today. For more on Kraepelin and his system for diagnosing mental illness, see the Close-Up in Chapter 12.

and Blumenthal (1980) suggested that most came back with little more than a laboratory floor plan and an equipment list. Nonetheless, they emerged from Leipzig convinced that something new and exciting was in the air, and they wanted to be a part of it. American psychology quickly established its own distinctive and non-Wundtian shape, but much of the motivation for it derived from Wundt's example.

THE NEW PSYCHOLOGY SPREADS

It should not be surprising to learn that Wundt did not hold a monopoly on the New Psychology. As you recall from the opening of this chapter, the *Wissenschaft* environment created an atmosphere conducive to the creation of a scientifically based examination of psychological phenomena. Sure enough, several German contemporaries of Wundt were actively engaged in exploring this new approach to understanding the human mind. We will examine the work of three of them: Hermann Ebbinghaus, G. E. Müller, and Oswald Külpe.

Hermann Ebbinghaus (1850–1909): The Experimental Study of Memory

One indirect effect of Fechner's *Elements of Psychophysics* is that it helped launch the experimental study of human memory. This occurred sometime in the mid-1870s, when a young German philosopher named Hermann Ebbinghaus (Figure 4.4) stumbled on a copy of Fechner's book while browsing in a used bookstore in Paris. Fechner's demonstration that the mind could be subjected to scientific methods inspired Ebbinghaus, who was wrestling with the philosophical problem of the association of ideas at the time.

As a philosopher, Ebbinghaus was thoroughly familiar with the British empiricist–associationists and their analysis of association processes. As you recall from Chapter 2, the British philosophers

© Bettmann/Corbis

FIGURE 4.4 The pioneering memory researcher Hermann Ebbinghaus (1850–1909).

considered association to be an essential component of the mind's organizational structure, but they differed over the basic laws of association—for example, is contiguity sufficient to explain associations (Hartley), or are other principles necessary (Hume)? For Ebbinghaus, Fechner's scientific approach to the mind's sensory processes apparently triggered a creative leap. If sensations could be measured, why not other mental processes? Why not associations? Sometime during the late 1870s, Ebbinghaus became resolved to study the formation and retention of associations scientifically. By the middle of the next decade, he had produced *Memory: A Contribution to Experimental Psychology* (1885/1964). This brief book (123 pages in a 1964 reprinting) inaugurated a research tradition that continues today and includes results that are still described in textbooks of general psychology. As Ernest Hilgard pointed out in an introduction to the 1964 reprinting, "[f]or the experimental study of learning and memory there is one source that is pre-eminent over all others: this small monograph by Ebbinghaus" (Hilgard, 1964, p. vii).

Ebbinghaus (1885/1964) opened his memory book by considering the various forms of memory and the difficulty of studying the process experimentally. He pointed out that what little was known about memory was known through common sense and from anecdotes about "extreme and especially striking cases" (p. 4). As for more fundamental questions about the exact relationships between our experiences and our memories, however, he wrote that "these and similar questions no one can answer" (p. 5). He also recognized that studying the initial formation of associations required materials that would not be familiar. Memorizing meaningful materials like poems or prose would be a problem, for these materials already carried with them innumerable meaningful associations that could affect how quickly they could be learned. In one of psychology's more notable acts of creativity, Ebbinghaus hit on the idea of using materials that did not meaningfully relate to each other and were not especially meaningful themselves. That is, he originated **nonsense syllables** or CVCs, three-letter units comprised of two consonants with a vowel in the middle. He created about 2,300 of them.

Ebbinghaus recognized that some of the syllables would have meaning (i.e., would sound like words), but he was not overly concerned; his main interest was in how associations *between* syllables were first formed, not the relative meaningfulness of individual syllables. Individual syllables might have meaning, but the chances were quite remote that two successive syllables would be meaningfully related to each other. Gundlach (1986) has pointed out that one of Ebbinghaus's phrases was translated as a "series of nonsense syllables"[7] when a better translation might have been "meaningless series of syllables." That Ebbinghaus chose **serial learning** as his memory task is a further indication of his intent to analyze the buildup of associations between elements of a fixed sequence. Serial learning, in which correct recall includes accurately reproducing a set of stimuli in the exact order of their presentation, is well suited for examining associations between a "meaningless series of syllables."

How Ebbinghaus actually hit on the idea to use nonsense syllables is not clear, but Hilgard's (1964) analysis makes the most sense. Familiar with the mechanistic and atomistic assumptions of British empiricism–associationism, Ebbinghaus would have looked for the simplest possible unit that would still yield a large number of stimuli. Individual letters or numbers were too few, words too meaningful. Syllables of words comprise the simplest pronounceable unit in the language, so they would be a logical choice. The fact that Ebbinghaus called his stimuli nonsense "syllables" suggests that he was deliberately thinking of this reduction to a small functional unit.

Once he had created the stimulus materials, Ebbinghaus (1885/1964) set about generating lists of them and then memorizing the lists. He would read a list to himself at a constant rate, aided by a

---

[7]The phrase appears at the bottom of page 23, in the context of a comparison with memorizing poetry.

metronome (he later switched to a ticking watch), and he would consider the list to be learned "when, the initial syllable being given, a series could be recited at the first attempt, without hesitation" (p. 23). He also made "no attempt to connect the nonsense syllables by the invention of special associations of the mnemonotechnik type; learning was carried on solely by the influence of the mere repetitions upon the natural memory" (p. 25).

As you might have suspected, an important feature of this project was that Ebbinghaus was the *only* subject. He completed the research during two yearlong periods: 1879–1880 and 1883–1884, and used the second set of experiments primarily to replicate those of the first. Also, to become proficient at the task, he spent an unspecified "long time" (Ebbinghaus, 1885/1964, p. 33) practicing before he began the 1879–1880 studies. Thus, for more than two separate yearlong periods, he devoted a significant portion of his time to memorizing lists of nonsense syllables (about an hour or two per day), by his own admission a task tedious enough to occasionally produce "exhaustion, headache, and other symptoms" (p. 55). On just one set of experiments, the ones that produced his famous forgetting curve (Figure 4.5), Ebbinghaus memorized just over 1,300 different lists. One attribute said to characterize famous scientists is a total passion for their research. Ebbinghaus was certainly a case in point.

Ebbinghaus described the results of his research in several different chapters. For example, he examined how quickly a series of syllables could be learned as a function of the number of syllables per list. "Quickly" meant the number of repetitions needed before the list could be produced without errors. He reported the results in this table (p. 47):

Number of syllables in a series	Number of repetitions necessary for first errorless reproduction	Probable Error
7	1	
12	16.6	+/– 1.1
16	30.0	+/– 0.4
24	44.0	+/–1.7
36	55.0	+/–2.8

There are two things to note here. First, although it might not be surprising that it takes more repetitions to learn longer lists, this marks the first time that anyone had documented, with precision, the exact relationship between the length of material to be learned and the amount of effort required to learn it. Second, very little effort was needed when the list had just seven syllables. This result has recurred frequently during the history of experimental psychology, and George Miller's (1956) investigation of this "magic number seven" became a landmark paper in the rise of cognitive psychology (Chapter 14). You probably recall learning about the number 7 ± 2 in your general psychology course in the memory chapter under the heading "capacity of short-term memory."

After showing that it took more repetitions to learn longer lists, Ebbinghaus wondered whether increasing the number of *original* repetitions in a list of fixed length would strengthen memory. Thus he repeated lists of 16 syllables 8, 16, 24, 32, 42, 53, or 64 times and discovered that the ease of relearning the list 24 hours later was proportional to the number of original repetitions (he also discovered that 64 repetitions gave him headaches). Ebbinghaus also studied what today is called distribution of practice, finding that his memory performance was better if he spread his study over a period of time rather than cramming in all the study at once.

The Ebbinghaus Forgetting Curve The most famous of the studies completed by Ebbinghaus concerned the rate of forgetting for information that had already been learned. Here, Ebbinghaus relied on an ingenious measure of recall that he called the **savings method**, which enabled him to measure memory after the passage of time, even if, initially, nothing could be recalled after the interval. He described the logic of it early in the book:

> A poem is learned by heart and then not again repeated. We will suppose that after a half year it has been forgotten: no effort at recollection is able to call it back into consciousness. At best only isolated fragments return. Suppose that the poem is again learned by heart. It then becomes evident that, although to all appearances totally forgotten, it still in a certain sense exists and in a way to be effective. The second learning requires noticeably less time or a noticeably smaller number of repetitions than the first. (Ebbinghaus, 1885/1964, p. 8)

Notice the important implication of the savings method—information remains in our memory, to some extent, even if we cannot recall it.

To examine the effects of time on memory, Ebbinghaus memorized lists of syllables, tried to relearn them after the passage of a fixed amount of time, and applied his savings method to assess the outcome. Ebbinghaus recorded the total time for the original learning of the lists, which was typically about 20 minutes, and the time for relearning. Original learning minus relearning yielded a measure of savings, which was converted to a percentage by dividing by the time of original learning. Thus, if original learning took 20 minutes and relearning took 5 minutes, 15 minutes or 75% (15/20 x 100) of the original learning time was saved.

Ebbinghaus reported the results for each of the 163 separate experiments that he completed over the different retention intervals. The results of this study have made their way into almost every introductory psychology textbook. They are normally shown in a graph like the one in Figure 4.5 (in the book, Ebbinghaus presented the results in a table). The results are clear—the rate of forgetting was rapid at first and then slowed. Thus, after just 20 minutes (0.33 hour), Ebbinghaus's savings score was 60% (i.e., 40% lost). After an hour, 45% was saved (55% lost), and after just a day, about 33% (67% lost) was saved.

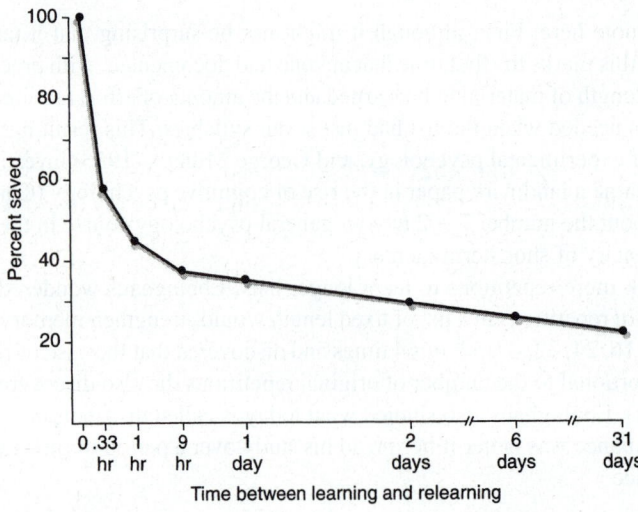

FIGURE 4.5 The Ebbinghaus forgetting curve, constructed from data he presented in table form. Redrawn by John Wiley & Sons, Inc.

In Chapter 14, you will learn about the development of modern cognitive psychology. One of its recent trends is a tendency to criticize the narrowness and artificiality of the "Ebbinghaus tradition." For modern cognitive psychologists, the memorizer is actively processing information, not passively strengthening associations through mindless repetition. Also, there is more emphasis today on **ecological memory**, memory for more realistic everyday events rather than for abstract lists. One prominent contemporary researcher lamented the "terrible struggle our field has had just to overcome the nonsense syllable" (Kintsch, 1985, p. 461). The criticism has some merit, but for the historian it clearly has the ring of presentist thinking. Considering the Ebbinghaus memory research in the context of its time, a more apt evaluation of its importance comes from a retrospective review of *Memory* by Roediger, written 100 years after the original publication:

> Considering that [Ebbinghaus] only began his research in the same year that Wundt founded his psychology lab and that he performed all experiments on himself and still produced such regular and compelling results, his achievement is nearly incredible. (Roediger, 1985, p. 522)

Other Contributions by Ebbinghaus The memory research was Ebbinghaus's greatest accomplishment, but not his only one. He was also a pioneer in the field of mental testing, inventing a sentence completion test in 1895 that was similar in spirit to the intelligence test soon to be developed in France by Alfred Binet (Chapter 8). Ebbinghaus held academic positions in the German universities at Berlin and Breslau and created the psychology laboratories at each university; he also worked at the university in Halle, where he rebuilt a lab. In 1890, he started the *Zeitschrift für Psychologie und Physiologie der Sunnesorgane* (*Journal of Psychology and Physiology of the Sense Organs*). Wundt's *Philosophische Studien* was primarily a means for publishing the work completed in his Leipzig laboratory, but Ebbinghaus's *Zeitschrift* filled its pages with research from laboratories throughout Germany. The journal's catholicity of interests and the prestige of its contributing authors (e.g., Helmholtz, G. E. Müller) led one historian to describe it as "the most important psychological organ in Germany" (Shakow, 1930, p. 509). Ebbinghaus also wrote two popular introductory psychology texts, including a brief version (just before his sudden death from pneumonia in 1909) that included the famous opening sentence, quoted at the start of this book's Chapter 2: "Psychology has a long past, yet its real history is short" (Ebbinghaus, 1908, p. 3).

G. E. Müller (1850–1934): The Experimentalist Prototype

Although Wundt is rightly given credit as the founder of experimental psychology, the psychology of the laboratory occupied only a portion of his interest. This is a theme that will be repeated: Many of the early pioneers of laboratory psychology actually spent little time in the laboratory. An exception was G. E. Müller,[8] an experimenter's experimenter, who devoted 40 years of his professional life to the psychology laboratory at the University of Göttingen. From 1881 to his retirement in 1921, Müller's laboratory rivaled the other German facilities in the quality of research produced. Studies completed in Müller's lab were known for their experimental control and meticulous attention to detail. That Müller is not well known today is primarily because little of his work was translated into English. Also, much of his research did not break radically new ground; rather, it systematically replicated and

---

[8] No relation to Johannes Müller, the famous physiologist you met in Chapter 3. Müller is a very common name in Germany, a bit like the German version of "Smith."

extended the research of others. Thus he made important contributions in extending Fechner's work in psychophysics,[9] Hering's work on color vision, and Ebbinghaus's work on memory. In this last area, Müller was a worthy successor to the venerable Ebbinghaus (Haupt, 1998).

During the decade of the 1890s, Müller and his students replicated and elaborated on many of the Ebbinghaus findings, developed a number of methodological refinements, and reached different conclusions about the formation of associations. Whereas Ebbinghaus concluded that associations were formed automatically and mechanically as a result of stimulus factors such as the number of repetitions and list length, and that the memorizer played a relatively *passive* role in the process, Müller believed that the individual forming the associations played a more *active* role. The conclusion resulted from a procedural modification—Müller added introspection to the memory process, and his observers reported that they engaged in a number of active strategies to learn the nonsense syllables. For example, they found themselves grouping nonsense syllables in clusters, organizing them by different degrees of meaning, and in general doing much more than just associating them by contiguity. This outcome foreshadows the modern view of memory, which assumes the learner is actively involved in the memorizing process.

Müller and his students also made some discoveries that went beyond what Ebbinghaus had found. For example, with Alfons Pilzecker he discovered that if a second list is learned between the learning of list 1 and the subsequent attempt to relearn list 1, the second list interferes with the relearning of list 1. They named the phenomenon **retroactive inhibition**, thus initiating a long line of research that eventually produced the interference theory of forgetting in the 1960s. Another of Müller's contributions was the invention of the **memory drum**, which automated the presentation of stimulus materials in memory studies. Müller and his assistant, Friedrich Schumann, cleverly altered a kymograph, a rotating drum normally used to record data (as shown in the reaction time photo of Figure 4.3). Stimuli were mounted on the drum, which revolved at a fixed speed, displaying stimuli through a small window for measured amounts of time and thereby adding precision to the procedure (Popplestone, 1987). Memory drums were standard laboratory equipment until 1990s, when computer presentation of stimuli became more efficient. Figure 4.6 shows an early version.

One final point is that although the University of Göttingen did not award advanced degrees to women, Müller welcomed several notable American women psychologists into his laboratory, including Christine Ladd-Franklin of Columbia (Chapter 6), Lillien Martin of Stanford, and Eleanor Gamble of Wellesley. As you will learn in Chapter 6, women faced numerous obstacles when trying to obtain graduate-level training. This was especially true in the United States, but it was also the case in Europe. Müller was ahead of his time in recognizing that women could be capable laboratory workers.

Oswald Külpe (1862–1915): The Würzburg School

After flirting with history and philosophy, Oswald Külpe became interested in psychology while taking a course from Wundt in the early 1880s. He then went to Berlin to study history and to Göttingen, where a year and a half in G. E. Müller's lab convinced him that experimental psychology was to be his career. He eventually returned to Leipzig and earned a doctorate with Wundt in 1887; he remained

[9]According to Boring (1950), E. B. Titchener held up publication of the second volume of his famous laboratory manual (Chapter 7) until Müller had published a handbook of psychophysics in 1903. Titchener had to rewrite the psychophysics portions of his manual after Müller's book appeared, and the second volume of the lab manual was not published until 1905, four years after volume 1. Margaret Washburn, Titchener's first graduate student, told experimental psychologist Walter Miles that Titchener was awed by Müller's research, and that Titchener "was always playing to an audience, usually G. E. Müller. T said that a postcard from G. E. M. was his best reward" (Miles, 1931).

Courtesy of Dr. C. James Goodwin

FIGURE 4.6 An early memory drum like the one developed in G. E. Müller's lab. On the left is the device as a subject would see it, displaying one item at a time. On the right is the inside of the drum. Stimuli were printed on the disc, which was rotated at a constant speed.

with his mentor for another 7 years, earning a living as a *Privatdozent* and as Wundt's assistant in the laboratory (he succeeded Cattell). Külpe also befriended E. B. Titchener (Chapter 7), who was at Leipzig for part of this time. In 1894 Külpe was called to Würzburg, where he created a laboratory sometimes considered second only to Wundt's and a match for Müller's at Göttingen. It was at Würzburg that Külpe created a brand of experimental psychology distinctive enough to earn the label "Würzburg school." It investigated topics and produced outcomes that put Külpe at odds with both his mentor Wundt and his friend Titchener.

Wundt had declared higher mental processes (e.g., memory, thinking) off limits for laboratory research, deeming them too complex and too heavily influenced by language and culture to be controlled adequately. Instead, such topics needed to be investigated with nonlaboratory methods, whereas the lab was to be restricted to such topics as sensation and perception. Yet Ebbinghaus and Müller had managed to control conditions in their studies of memory. It was up to Külpe, however, to challenge his former mentor directly by studying thought processes in the lab and by significantly elaborating on the Wundtian introspective procedure.

Külpe exercised close but congenial supervision over his students; he published little research under his own name, preferring instead to give his students the credit. In the words of his American student, Robert Ogden:

> [Külpe] was intimately engaged in all that went on in his laboratory. It was a matter of principle to him to act as observer in the experimental work of his students. In the instance of my own study … he came almost daily to the laboratory for what must have been weary hours of committing nonsense syllables to memory. His influence upon his students was never dominating. Instead, they were engaged together in a joint enterprise of scientific discovery. (Ogden, 1951, p. 9)

To study thought processes in the laboratory, Külpe found it necessary to expand what he thought of as the Wundtian limitations on introspection. Recall that Wundt distinguished between *self-observation*, in which someone experiences some event and then from memory describes the mental processes that occurred during the event, and *inner perception*, a more controlled introspective procedure in which simple stimuli are presented many times and responses are given immediately after stimulus presentation. For Wundt, only the latter procedure was appropriate in the laboratory. In Külpe's laboratory, however, introspection was more like what Wundt called self-observation. It came to be called **systematic experimental introspection**. Observers would experience more complicated events than in Wundt's laboratory and then give a full description of the mental processes involved. This created a potential memory problem because as Woodworth (1938) later pointed out, the mental experience of a 10-second event might take 10 minutes to describe. To deal with the fact that giving an introspective account of a complicated event might be distorted by memory, Külpe and his students developed a procedure called **fractionation**, a separation of the task into its components, each of which could be introspected many times. For example, in a study on word association by Watt (i.e., given a stimulus word, say the first word that comes to mind), the task was fractionated into "the preparation for the experiment, the appearance of the stimulus-word, the search for the reaction-word, and finally the cropping up of the reaction-word" (Watt, 1904, quoted in Sahakian, 1975, p. 162).

Külpe believed he was improving the introspective procedure, enabling it to be applied to higher mental processes; but Wundt rejected the Würzburg technique, calling it nothing but the unsystematic self-observation he had denounced years earlier. Thus, because he believed them to be built on unsound methods, Wundt dismissed the results of the Würzburg research. What were those results?

Mental Sets and Imageless Thoughts The Würzburg research on thinking produced several interesting outcomes. For example, in a study by Ach, observers were shown pairs of numbers after first being instructed that they would be performing some specific operation (e.g., add them, subtract them). Ach measured reaction time and also asked for introspections. He found that reaction time was the same, regardless of the type of operation asked of subjects, and that observers reported no conscious awareness of the instructions themselves once the task had begun. In other words, after receiving the instructions, their mind was "prepared" to function in a specific way (e.g., adding), so that once the number pair was presented, the addition occurred automatically and without further thought. Thus the instructions created what the Würzburgers called a determining tendency or **mental set**. This concept would eventually become important for the German Gestalt psychologists (Chapter 9). The absence of a difference in reaction time was also significant because Külpe used it to question the validity of the subtractive assumption underlying the mental chronography experiments that were such an important part of the Leipzig laboratory. Because instructions create a mental set, he argued, discrimination reaction time cannot be equal to simple reaction time plus the mental event of discrimination. Rather, DRT results from a different kind of "set" than SRT.

A second important finding of the Würzburg lab, and a controversial one, concerned the phenomenon of **imageless thought**. According to Titchener (and Wundt), a close analysis of thought processes reveals that the essential element in all thinking is an image of some form. In a psychophysics weight-lifting experiment, for example, the standard description was that the observer would lift one weight, form a kinesthetic image of it, and then lift the second weight and compare the sensation of it with the image of the first one to decide if the weights were the same or different. The judgment process was composed of sensory and image components from the two weights. In a weight-lifting study by Karl Marbe at Würzburg, however, no sensations or images occurred at the precise moment of judgment. Observers reported sensations and images while lifting the weights, but the judgment seemed to occur automatically and without images. That is, the judgment was an imageless thought. Furthermore, Marbe's observers reported other mental processes occurring just before the judgment, and these didn't seem reducible to sensations and images either. These processes included things like hesitation, doubt, and vacillation; collectively they were referred to as **conscious attitudes**.

The potential existence of imageless thoughts, mental sets, and conscious attitudes posed an especially serious threat to Külpe's colleague E. B. Titchener, who believed that all mental content under analysis would be found to contain the basic elements of conscious experience (more on Titchener and imageless thought in Chapter 7). If some thoughts occur without images, however, then not all thinking can be reduced to such basic elements. This imageless thought controversy was never resolved; its most notable side effect, however, was to raise questions about the validity of introspection as a method and to help pave the way for a radical new movement in psychology that you will learn about in Chapters 10 and 11: behaviorism.

IN PERSPECTIVE: A NEW SCIENCE

The new laboratory psychology that emerged in Germany quickly caught the attention of a number of American intellectuals, most notably William James, G. Stanley Hall, and James McKeen Cattell. All three either toured German labs, or, in Cattell's case, earned a PhD from one. You will learn more about these pioneers in Chapters 6 and 7. A number of other Americans followed in their footsteps, earning doctorates from Leipzig and other labs and then returning home enthusiastic about the idea of making psychology scientific. In addition, several American universities (e.g., Johns Hopkins, Clark, Chicago), with the German spirit of *Wissenschaft* clearly in mind, opened in the last third of the 19th century and developed laboratories in imitation of the German labs. American psychology, then, derives from the movement that started with Wundt. More generally, one could say that the new discipline of psychology had two clear sets of parents—the philosophers you learned about in Chapter 2 and the physiologists of Chapter 3. But parentage is sometimes a tricky business, and in the case of psychology, there was also a third parent—Darwinian biology. Darwin and his influence on modern psychology is the focus of Chapter 5.

SUMMARY

An Education in Germany

• In the 19th century, a large number of American students studied the sciences in Europe, especially in Germany. In the latter half of the century, many students went to Germany, in particular to Leipzig, to study a new approach to psychology that was developing there.

• The German educational system promoted a philosophy of *Wissenschaft*, which emphasized original research and the academic freedom to pursue that research. This created an environment conducive to new ideas, including the idea of a new scientific approach to the study of psychology.

On the Threshold of Experimental Psychology: Psychophysics

• Psychophysics is the study of the relationship between physical stimuli and the psychological reaction to them. The threshold concept was central to Herbart's mathematical psychology, but the first empirical research in this tradition was completed by Ernst Weber, who investigated the relative sensitivity of various areas on the surface of the body using the two-point threshold. In experiments in which observers made comparisons between two weights, Weber discovered that the ability to distinguish between them depended on the relative rather than the absolute differences in their weights (Weber's law).

- Gustav Fechner elaborated Weber's research, and his *Elements of Psychophysics* is considered experimental psychology's first text. Although more interested in using his research to defeat materialism, Fechner is known for developing several important psychophysics methods in use today (limits, constant stimuli, adjustment) and for the precision of his work in measuring absolute and difference thresholds.

Wundt Establishes a New Psychology at Leipzig

- Wilhelm Wundt is generally known as the founder of experimental psychology. He explicitly set out to create a new psychology that emphasized the experimental methods borrowed from physiology, and he created the first laboratory of experimental psychology and the first journal devoted to describing the results of scientific research in psychology.

- Wundt's new science involved studying immediate conscious experience under controlled laboratory conditions. Because they could not be subjected to experimental control and replication, higher mental processes (e.g., language), as well as social and cultural phenomena, had to be studied through nonlaboratory methods (e.g., observation).

- In Wundt's laboratory, most of the research concerned basic sensory and perceptual processes. The lab also produced a large number of "mental chronometry" studies, which attempted to measure the amount of time taken for various mental processes. James McKeen Cattell, an American student and Wundt's first official lab assistant, completed a number of these "complication" studies, which utilized a subtraction procedure developed by the Dutch physiologist F. C. Donders.

- Recent historical scholarship has uncovered serious distortions in the traditional accounts of Wundt's ideas. Rather than being a structuralist, seeking to reduce consciousness to its basic elements, Wundt was more interested in the mind's ability to actively organize information. One of his main interests was the process of apperception—an active, meaningful, and attentive perception of some event. He called his system voluntarism to reflect the active nature of mental processing. The distortions stem from Boring's famous history text.

The New Psychology Spreads

- One of the most important programs of research carried out in psychology's history involved the study of memory by Hermann Ebbinghaus. To investigate the development of new associations between unassociated stimuli, he invented nonsense syllables. Ebbinghaus measured retention in terms of the amount of effort "saved" in relearning. His famous forgetting curve showed that forgetting occurs at a very rapid rate shortly after initial learning and then tapers off.

- G. E. Müller and his students significantly extended contemporary research on color vision, the psychophysics research of Fechner, and the memory research of Ebbinghaus. By adding introspection to the nonsense syllable experiments, he argued that memory was an active process, not the passive buildup of associative strength. He was the first to identify retroactive inhibition (i.e., forgetting results from interference from events occurring between initial learning and recall), and he invented the memory drum.

- Oswald Külpe and his students created the Würzburg school of psychology, which defied Wundt by studying the higher mental process of thinking under laboratory conditions and liberalizing the method of introspection. In their research they found evidence for mental sets, imageless thought, and conscious attitudes.

STUDY QUESTIONS

1. Describe the *Wissenschaft* philosophy of education that developed in Germany in the 19th century. What were the implications for psychology?

2. Describe Herbart's ideas about the nature of psychology, and explain what he meant by the "apperceptive mass."

3. Show how Fechner's three psychophysics methods could be used to determine a two-point threshold.

4. Describe Weber's law and the concept of a jnd.

5. Wundt, rather than Fechner, is considered to be the founder of modern experimental psychology. Why?

6. Describe Wundt's contributions to psychology before his arrival at Leipzig.

7. Wundt's concept of psychology involved two major programs. Describe each of them.

8. Describe how Wundt (and others) used reaction time to measure the duration of various mental events. In what way was the method flawed?

9. Describe and criticize the traditional description of Wundt's "system." How did the misconceptions develop?

10. Explain why Wundt called his system voluntarism, and show how the concept of apperception was important to him.

11. What were nonsense syllables, why did Ebbinghaus use them, and what was the overall goal of his research project?

12. What was the method of savings, and why was it such a creative way to study memory?

13. Describe the method and results of the Ebbinghaus research that produced the famous forgetting curve.

14. Describe how G. E. Müller's view of memory differed from that of Ebbinghaus. Why was Müller described as the "prototype" experimentalist?

15. Describe Külpe's version of introspection and how introspection would occur for a complex mental process.

16. How was mental set investigated in Külpe's lab, and what were the implications of the findings for the complication experiment?

CHAPTER 5

DARWIN'S CENTURY: EVOLUTIONARY THINKING

This preservation of favorable individual differences and variations, and the destruction of those which are injurious, I have called Natural Selection.

—Charles Darwin, 1859

PREVIEW AND CHAPTER OBJECTIVES

Chapter 4 described the rise of scientific psychology in Germany in the 19th century. Preceding chapters examined the explosive growth of knowledge about the brain and nervous system in that same century and the maturation of British empiricist and associationist thought during that time. As remarkable as these 19th-century developments were, they were overshadowed by the impact of one man's theory about the nature of life itself. Biologists appropriately claim Charles Darwin as their most eminent historical figure, but his ideas also shaped psychology's history. This chapter examines Darwin's life and the development of his theory and then considers the impact of his ideas on psychology's history. His argument for continuity among species challenged the Cartesian distinction between humans and animals and led to comparative psychology, the study of animal behavior. His emphasis on the variability within species created interest in the study of individual differences, most clearly manifested in the work of his cousin, Sir Francis Galton. In Chapter 7 we will see how Darwinian thinking resonated with the functionalist school of thought in American psychology. After you finish this chapter, you should be able to:

- Describe the species problem and how the British theological community responded to it in the 19th century
- Describe how the concept of "evolutionary change" came to permeate 19th-century thinking in both geology and biology, thereby creating a zeitgeist conducive to Darwin's ideas
- Trace the influence of Darwin's education and the *Beagle* voyage on his developing ideas about evolution
- Show the effects of Malthus and of pigeon breeders on Darwin's thinking about evolution
- Describe the basic principles of Darwin's theory of evolution and explain why he delayed publishing for almost 20 years
- Explain how Darwin studied and interpreted the expressions of emotions in humans and animals
- Describe the work of Douglas Spalding, and show how it connects with modern ethology
- Describe and evaluate the comparative psychology of George Romanes
- Explain the importance of Lloyd Morgan's canon for the subsequent study of animal behavior

- Describe Sir Francis Galton's beliefs about the nature of intelligence, how he arrived at them, and how they led to his interest in eugenics
- Describe the logic of Galton's approach to mental testing
- Describe Galton's work on the psychological topics of association and mental imagery

THE SPECIES PROBLEM

From the time that Newtonian physics burst on the scene in the late 17th century, intellectuals became increasingly convinced that science was the way to truth, that it would shed light on our ignorance of the laws of nature, and that it would lead to the improvement of life through technological advancement. Thus, as we discussed in Chapter 3, the 18th and 19th centuries became known as an era of Enlightenment, in which science became religion, and scientists seemed heroic.

One manifestation of Enlightenment science was a questioning of the literal truth of the Bible's version of the origin of the earth's plants and animals. Global exploration was uncovering new species of plants and animals by the thousands. How did the earth come to be populated by such diversity? Why did some species seem to disappear, their existence known only from fossils? Why did some living species seem so similar to (but usually smaller than) species suggested by fossils? And for those accepting the literal truth of the Bible, how did all these species fit on Noah's ark?[1] Collectively, these questions became known as the **species problem**, sometimes referred to as the "mystery of mysteries."

The problem created great stress within the academic community in Great Britain, where the intellectual elite were also leaders of the Anglican Church, the Church of England. One solution was to turn the problem into an argument for the supreme power of the deity. This **argument from design**[2] is normally associated with the Reverend William Paley's 1802 *Natural Theology*, but it is also recognizable as one of the proofs for the existence of God suggested by the great medieval philosopher Thomas Aquinas (Scott-Kakures, Castagnetto, Benson, Taschek, & Hurley, 1993). The argument held that the very existence of precision and complexity in nature required a supreme being to create and to oversee it. Paley drew an analogy between the complex design of a watch, which necessitates a watchmaker to make it, and that of the infinitely more complicated human eye, which requires an "eyemaker," who is infinitely superior to the humans using those eyes (Ruse, 1979). (Paley was apparently more impressed with the human eye than Helmholtz was.) The argument from design enabled a minister/scientist to study the workings of nature while maintaining a belief in the Supreme Designer. There was no need to speculate about how species might develop; it was simpler to assume that God in his infinite wisdom had created each species and designed each to fit into its place in the world. Hence, the orderliness to be found in nature derived from explicit design, which in turn came from a mind greater than any found in nature, that is, from God.

Despite the power of this argument from design, several evolutionary ideas developed in the 18th and early 19th centuries. Two pre-Darwinian examples are worthy of note. First, Darwin was not even the first person in his family to propose an evolutionary solution to the species problem. A century earlier, his grandfather, Erasmus Darwin (1731–1802), a physician, rejected the biblical account of creation and proposed that all organic life evolved from a single living filament. Over time, new species developed from old ones, with later species being more "advanced" than earlier ones. The human species

---

[1] As early as the 15th century, a skeptical Leonardo Da Vinci wondered if the Biblical flood was worldwide or localized; if the former, he wondered where the water went after the flood receded (King, 1992).

[2] The modern version of this idea, in no way substantially different from it, is called "intelligent design."

represented the culmination of evolution, but there was no reason to assume that humans would not continue to improve.

The best-known pre-Darwinian theory of evolution belonged not to Darwin's grandfather, however, but to a prominent French naturalist, Jean Baptiste de Lamarck (1744–1829). Like Erasmus Darwin, Lamarck believed that all the species on earth could be arranged on a linear scale with reference to their complexity, an idea sometimes referred to as the **chain of being** (Ruse, 1979). Furthermore, each species is constantly evolving into a species that is more complex, he believed, and new life at the bottom of the scale is continually being created from inorganic life. Thus, at any point in time, a variety of species exist that could be ranked in terms of how much they had evolved from the first spark of life. Lamarck also believed that an important mechanism of evolution was the idea that changes occurring during the lifetime of an organism could be passed on to offspring. For instance, if during the course of its life an animal developed the ability to use simple tools, that new ability would be inherited by the next generation. This concept became known as the **inheritance of acquired characteristics**. It was taken seriously throughout most of the 19th century before being discarded, and it was included as part of Darwin's original theory. But we are getting ahead of the story.

CHARLES DARWIN (1809–1882)
AND THE THEORY OF EVOLUTION

There was little in the early life of Charles Robert Darwin (Figure 5.1) to predict the greatness to come—he appeared to be just an aimless and spoiled child of wealthy parents. He was born and raised in the rural west of England, in Shrewsbury. His father, Robert, was a successful and affluent country doctor, and his mother, Susannah Wedgwood, was heir to a fortune from the family that created the renowned Wedgwood china. Like most successful and ambitious men, Robert Darwin expected great things of his son, but he was frustrated by the boy's indifferent school performance and his apparent lack of purpose. By early adolescence, Darwin's wayward behavior drove his father to distraction. "You care for nothing but shooting, dogs, and rat-catching, and you will be a disgrace to yourself and all your family," he exclaimed (quoted in Desmond & Moore, 1991, p. 20), in a scene easily imagined by many parents of a smart but aimless adolescent boy.

The Shaping of a Naturalist

Determined that his son would follow in his footsteps, Robert Darwin sent Charles to study medicine at the University of Edinburgh, one of Europe's best medical schools. The experiment failed—Darwin's academic performance did not improve, and he was nauseated by the clinical procedures of the day. For young Charles, medicine would not do. He left Edinburgh in 1827. The next stop was Cambridge University, where Darwin studied for the clergy.

The Cambridge that Darwin encountered between 1828 and 1831 was not the fine academic university that we think of today. Rather, it was an institution under the firm control of the Church of England, its professors were Anglican priests who normally expected little scholarship on the part of their students, and its students (all male) tended to meet those expectations.[3] Most students were there to prepare for the clergy, but they were primarily concerned with learning how to become proper gentlemen. Honors programs for serious students did exist in classics and mathematics, but at a time when England was the most powerful nation on earth and was leading the Industrial Revolution, the university

---

[3]The same could be said at this time of England's other famous university, Oxford.

FIGURE 5.1 Darwin at three stages of his life: In 1840, 4 years after the *Beagle* voyage; in 1881, a year before his death; in 1854, when fully immersed in the research that would produce *Origin of Species*.

was strangely deficient in the study of science and technology (Ruse, 1979). Darwin never became a minister, of course. Nonetheless, he entertained the notion for several years, even after he had found his true vocation—natural science.[4]

    Young people growing up in rural areas often develop a love for the natural world, and Darwin was no exception. From his earliest youth, he avidly collected natural objects ranging from rocks to beetles to butterflies. It was at Cambridge that he realized for the first time that his love of the natural world could become his life's work. Darwin's model and mentor was the Reverend John Henslow (1796–1871), a professor of botany. In Henslow, Darwin saw his future—he could become an Anglican clergyman, use his wealth to acquire a quiet rural parish, and devote all his spare time to science. Darwin sat in on Henslow's classes, and his fervor quickly caught the botanist's attention. Before long, Henslow began including Darwin in weekly meetings in his home, at which a small group of like-minded enthusiasts, including some of Cambridge's leading scientists, debated the scientific issues of the day (including evolution). Between 1828 and 1831, Darwin continued to be an average student, but he was in regular contact with some of the leading scientific minds of the day, and he was making a favorable impression on them (Ruse, 1979).

[4]In his autobiography, Darwin reported that later in his life, a German phrenological society requested a photograph of his head. He complied, the photo was carefully examined, and a member of the society proclaimed that Charles had "the bump of reverence developed enough for ten priests" (Darwin, 1892/1958a, p. 18).

One of those scientific minds belonged to a noted geologist, the Reverend Adam Sedgwick (1785–1873). Sedgwick became a second mentor to Darwin, teaching him the basic methods of geology and sharpening his ability to make precise observations by taking him on a long geological field trip through the mountains of Wales in the summer of 1831. Darwin eventually rejected Sedgwick's views about the earth's formation, but he profited immensely from the experience.

After returning from the walk through Wales, opportunity knocked. A voyage to South America was being planned, and the captain, 26-year-old Robert FitzRoy, was advertising for an on-board dinner companion. It would also help if this person had some training in science, for there would be opportunities to collect specimens. Henslow recommended Darwin, Darwin's father eventually approved, and Darwin undertook the voyage of a lifetime aboard the *HMS Beagle*. It lasted 5 years and took him around the globe. In his autobiography, Darwin had this to say about the trip:

> The voyage of the *Beagle* has been by far the most important event in my life, and has determined my whole career....I have always felt that I owe to the voyage the first real training or education of my mind; I was led to attend closely to several branches of natural history, and thus my powers of observation were improved....(Darwin, 1892/1958a, p. 28)

The Voyage of the *Beagle*

Darwin's home away from home for 5 years was a small (90 feet long and 24 feet wide) three-masted brig that carried just over 70 officers, marines, geographer/surveyors, and crew. Darwin shared a small cabin at the rear of the ship with two of the survey officers, sleeping in a hammock with his face two feet from the underside of the main deck (Thomson, 1975). Some idea of the cramped living arrangements can be seen in Figure 5.2.

The primary purpose of the *Beagle's* voyage was to survey the southern coasts of South America, especially its port areas, thus allowing the powerful British merchant fleet to retain its edge in the competition for trade with developing South American countries. The ship would also circumnavigate the globe, using its chronometers to verify the longitude of various locations on the globe (Desmond & Moore, 1991). Once the *Beagle* reached South America, much of its time was spent going back and

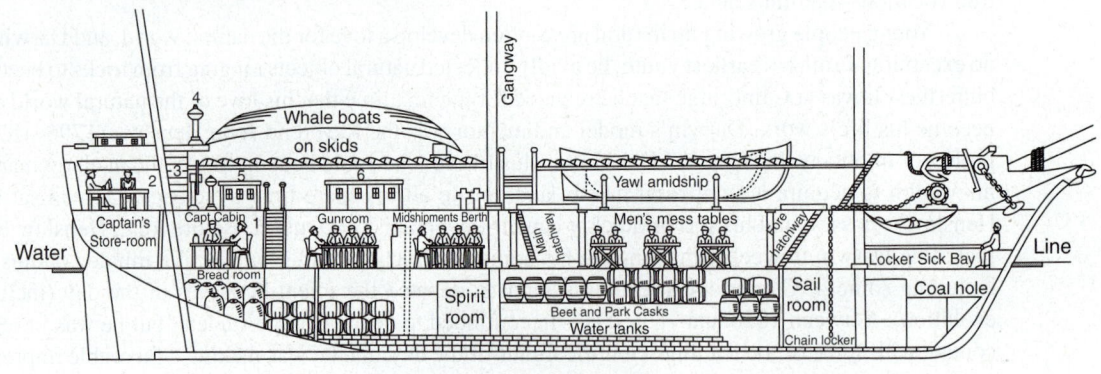

H. M. S. Beagle 1832

1. Mr. Darwin's seat in Captain's Cabin   2. Mr. Darwin's seat in Poop Cabin
3. Mr. Darwin's drawers in Poop Cabin   4. Azimuth Compass   5. Captain's skylight   6. Gunroom skylight

FIGURE 5.2 Cross-section of the HMS *Beagle*.

forth from one coastal region to another, enabling Darwin to spend months at a time ashore, exploring, observing, and collecting.[5] According to Desmond and Moore (2009), these periods ashore also exposed Darwin to the harsh realities of slavery, an experience that greatly affected him and contributed eventually to his motivation to develop an evolutionary theory that featured descent from a common origin. If everyone descended from a common species, it questioned the logical basis for slavery, he believed. Long periods away from the ship also benefited Darwin for a practical reason—he suffered from seasickness that lasted the entire trip. When aboard ship, he was constantly ill.

Darwin the Geologist   At the outset of the voyage, Darwin had a strong interest in geology. The field trip with Sedgwick was still fresh in his mind, and just off the press and among his possessions was the first volume of a book destined to have the same effect on geology that his own book eventually would have on biology. Its simple title, *Principles of Geology*, belied its revolutionary nature. Its Scottish author, Charles Lyell (1797–1875), took issue with the prevailing theory of geological change, called **catastrophism**. Much like the argument from design, catastrophism was an attempt to maintain the supremacy of God and the Bible while accounting for what scientists were discovering about nature. Catastrophists, including Darwin's geologist/mentor Sedgwick, argued that geological change occurred abruptly and dramatically as the result of major catastrophic events under the control of God. The flood in the Book of Genesis was the standard example. Lyell, on the other hand, argued that geological change occurred more slowly and involved forces that are constantly at work. These forces included such things as volcanic action, earthquakes, erosion, and the cumulative effects of weather. This view came to be called **uniformitarianism** because of the assumption that uniform laws of nature operated to produce gradual geologic change. The Swiss Alps were not thrust up overnight in some cataclysmic upheaval; they only arose gradually, over vast amounts of time, Lyell believed.[6]

Lyell's ideas about the origins and development of the earth's structures were never far from Darwin's thoughts. Indeed, although we now think of the trip as the event that gave Darwin the raw material for his theory of evolution of species, he also made important contributions to geology. For instance, he experienced, firsthand, the landscape-altering effects of an earthquake in Chile; he observed fossilized seashells high in the Andes Mountains; and during the Pacific portion of the trip, he was able to demonstrate that coral reefs were built on the rims of slowly sinking volcanoes. Darwin's immersion in Lyellian geology also convinced him that the earth had to be much older than previously thought. This idea would eventually be critical for Darwin's ideas about evolution because slow changes in species required vast amounts of time. Lyell's new geology supplied an earth that was sufficiently ancient for evolution to do its work.

Darwin the Zoologist   With the *Beagle* in South American waters completing its surveying work, Darwin collected specimens in earnest and kept encyclopedic notes. By the end of the voyage, he had compiled a 770-page diary, 1,383 pages of notes on geology, and 368 more pages on zoology. He also wrote a specimen catalog that included 1,529 species of animals that had been preserved in spirits and another 3,907 labeled items that were bones, fossils, skins, or dried specimens (Desmond & Moore, 1991).

[5]The *Beagle* spent 57 months at sea. Of these months, 42 were spent in South American waters, 27 on the east coast and 15 on the west coast (Browne, 1995).

[6]A modern form of catastrophism, minus the theological element, has become accepted since the accumulation of evidence that comets or large meteors have occasionally struck the earth. It is estimated that one such meteor destroyed 95 percent of all marine species when it landed about 250 million years ago. More recently (a mere 65 million years ago), a huge meteor produced effects leading to the rapid extinction of about 70 percent of the earth's species, including the dinosaurs (Monastersky, 1997).

For at least a year into the voyage, Darwin firmly believed that he would return to England and become the Anglican priest/amateur scientist that he so admired in Henslow. He also assumed that his work would have no bearing on the biblical account of creation; he was initially a believer in the argument from design. Yet his zoological observations gradually led to him to wonder about the species problem. It began to occur to him that just as the earth evolved slowly, gradually, and according to uniform geological laws, perhaps the same was true for the organisms populating the earth.

The Galapagos Islands   On September 7, 1835, more than 3 years into the voyage, the *Beagle* left South America and headed across the Pacific. A week later, it made landfall at a remote series of volcanic islands, located on the equator about 600 miles west of South America. They featured a variety of unusual species, including oversized, dinosaurlike lizards, and tortoises with shells up to 5 feet in diameter. The islands were named for the Spanish word for the giant tortoise, galápagos. They had little practical value, being used primarily as an Ecuadorian penal colony and as a stopping point for whaling vessels to replenish their stocks of food and water.[7]

The Galapagos were to give Darwin significant clues to evolution, although at the time of the visit, he had little idea of the importance of what he encountered there. During the 5 weeks spent on the islands, Darwin did some specimen collecting, but he was not as precise as he had been in South America. Nor did he pay much attention to the claim, made by the vice-governor of the penal colony, that he could tell the home island of a tortoise merely by observing its shell design. He did notice differences from one island to another in the various bird populations, however, especially what he thought were mockingbirds. And it appeared that many of the species of birds and plants resembled those from the mainland, while having their own unique qualities. He later discovered that the shapes of the beaks of several species of finch provided a clue to his theory, but while in the Galapagos he failed to notice these differences by mislabeling some of the finches as warblers, wrens, and "gross-beaks," and he was more intrigued by their coloration than their beaks (Sulloway, 1982).

After leaving the Galapagos, the *Beagle* sailed west across the Pacific, around Africa, and finally returned to England in October, 1836. Upon his return, Darwin was a changed man. He now seriously doubted that life as an Anglican priest was for him; a full-time devotion to science seemed more in the cards. During the voyage, he routinely shipped crates of specimens home to Henslow, and they had made a strong impression on the scientific community during his absence. By the time he returned, he was already a celebrity among zoologists and geologists and viewed as a rising young star.

The Evolution of Darwin's Theory

Upon his return, Darwin set out to organize his enormous collection of specimens, enlisting the help of other scientists and museum curators. In 1837, he moved to London, and 2 years later he married his cousin, Emma Wedgwood. Their union was a long and happy one, even though Emma's strong religious beliefs eventually conflicted with her husband's gradual loss of faith. Emma was destined to become the family's source of strength, caring for the 10 children she would bear and for Darwin, who became ill soon after his return. He was a partial invalid for the remainder of his life, suffering from a variety of chronic digestive, headache, and cardiac symptoms. For months at a time, he spent a significant portion of the day either in bed or being violently ill. The Darwins remained in London

---

[7]While accumulating the experiences that would eventually yield his classic novel *Moby Dick*, Herman Melville was aboard a whaling vessel that reached the Galapagos shortly after the *Beagle's* visit. Of the islands, Melville wrote, "Little but reptile life is here found; the chief sound of life is a hiss" (quoted in Moorehead, 1969, p. 187).

Courtesy of Ludy T. Benjamin, Jr.

FIGURE 5.3 Darwin's home and refuge at Down.

for 3 years, but the unrelenting street noise, coal-generated smog, and stench from the polluted Thames seemed to contribute to Darwin's declining health, so in 1842 they bought a country house at Down, about 15 miles south of London. Down became their permanent home and Darwin's laboratory. Today, Down House (Figure 5.3) serves as the Darwin Museum.

Despite his illnesses, Darwin produced. Within 10 years of his return to England, he published a journal of the voyage (Darwin, 1839); books on the geology of coral reefs, volcanic islands, and South America; and several technical reports that were read to various scientific societies in London. During this time he also formulated his theory on the evolution of species and wrote a brief abstract of it in 1842. Two years later he elaborated the sketch into a 200-page document, instructing his wife to publish it in the event that his chronic ailments proved fatal (Desmond & Moore, 1991).

Darwin's theory developed out of his reflections on the *Beagle* voyage, aided by hints that came from two distinct sources. First, in 1838 he read an essay on population by political economist Thomas Malthus (1766–1834), who championed the idea that government welfare for the poor would only increase their number, thereby decreasing Britain's overall standard of living. Instead, Malthus argued, society must recognize that life is a constant "struggle for existence" and only those best suited for survival will do so. He pointed out that although food supplies grow at a relatively constant rate, population growth, if unchecked, occurs at a much more rapid rate. Eventually, a population would outgrow its resources, and its members would begin to die until a level of stability occurred. For Darwin, this idea provided a model to be applied to species change. For any species, the time would come when unchecked population growth would result in food shortages, especially when growth combined with environmental change (e.g., prolonged drought). Under such circumstances, *only those best suited to survive would do so.* If those characteristics enabling survival could be passed on to offspring, the next generation would be better suited for survival and would be different from previous generations. Over time, might these changes be sufficient to create a new species? Darwin began to think so.

Darwin's second clue came from his reflections on what he knew of breeding by farmers and hobbyists. For instance, pigeon breeders had been able to produce breeds of pigeons that hardly resembled each other. The breeders accomplished this by observing tiny variations that occurred naturally within a breed of pigeons, then developing those differences through generations of selective breeding. The results were such that if these pigeon varieties had been encountered in the wild, zoologists would have judged them to be different species. If such differences could be created artificially by pigeon breeders,

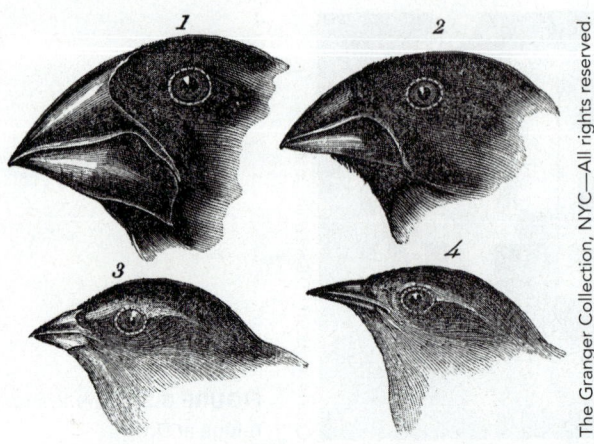

The Granger Collection, NYC—All rights reserved.

FIGURE 5.4 Darwin's finches—note the differences in beak size and shape.

could they not also be created naturally? Could there be a *natural* selection that was analogous to this *artificial* selection? Darwin began to think so.

In the midst of these ruminations about population and selective breeding, Darwin learned from the famous ornithologist John Gould, who was classifying some of his *Beagle* specimens, that there was something very interesting about the Galapagos birds. The birds that Darwin thought were finches, warblers, wrens, and "gross-beaks" were in fact all finches. Furthermore, Gould was "induced to regard them as constituting an entirely new group containing 14 species, and appearing to be strictly confined to the Galapagos islands" (Gould, quoted in Weiner, 1994, p. 28). These finch species were distinguished by their size and by clear differences in the shapes of their beaks. Wondering about these differences, Darwin reexamined his notes and saw a pattern—finches with specific beak shapes tended to cluster on islands that differed in terms of available food sources. For instance, finches living on islands with a large supply of certain types of hard shelled nuts and seeds had tough, blunted beaks, ideally suited for cracking open this food source. Other birds had thinner beaks, nicely designed to spear the insects that populated their islands (Figure 5.4) . This did not appear to Darwin to be accidental.

Darwin's Delay Much has been made of the fact that Darwin had outlined the essential features of his theory of evolution by the early 1840s, yet it took him almost 20 years to publish his *Origin of Species* in 1859 (Richards, 1983). Part of the reason was health—he was often incapacitated for months at a time. A second reason for the delay was that he was concerned about the reactions of his peers. When the anonymously authored and highly speculative *Vestiges of Creation* appeared in 1844, the same year that Darwin was entrusting his 200-page manuscript to his wife's care, it was ridiculed by the British community of zoologists, geologists, and botanists (including Lyell, now a close friend of Darwin's). Some of the reaction was to the vagueness of the proposed mechanism for evolutionary change in *Vestiges*. Darwin knew his model was better, but much of the negative response to *Vestiges* was to the idea of evolution itself. In a letter to the botanist Joseph Hooker, a close friend to whom he was confiding about his theory, Darwin wrote that proposing a theory of evolution was like "confessing a murder" (Colp, 1986). If he published in 1844, Darwin feared that his theory would be confused with *Vestiges* and condemned by association.

A third reason for Darwin's delay was his conservative scientific nature. He knew he had a good theory and some data to support it, but he also knew that he needed more evidence before he would be willing to go public. Thus, he spent years carefully gathering evidence to bolster the theory. For

From Marchant, James 1916, Alfred Russel Wallace—Letters and Reminiscences Vol. 1 ed., London, New York, Toronto and Melbourne: Cassell and Company, Plate between p. 36-37

FIGURE 5.5   Alfred Russell Wallace (1823–1913), whose 1858 letter to Darwin prompted Darwin to complete and go public with his evolutionary theory.

instance, in 1846 he began an intensive 8-year study of the evolutionary history of barnacles, eventually publishing the results in four volumes. He also joined a local pigeon fanciers club and did some of his own pigeon breeding. And at Down House, one could always find a dozen experiments going on at the same time. For example, to determine how seeds could be spread over large distances, he tested the idea that undigested seeds might be carried in the stomachs of birds. So he collected bird droppings, poking through them until he came across the occasional seed, which he planted. To his pleasant surprise, the seeds often germinated and grew.

Darwin's delay in publishing would have been even longer if not for a letter he received on June 18, 1858. It was from a fellow naturalist with an interest in evolution, Alfred Russel Wallace (1823–1913), who was at the time on the other side of the world in Malaysia. Wallace (Figure 5.5) asked Darwin's opinion on a brief paper that he enclosed with the letter—the paper outlined a theory of evolution that was remarkably similar to Darwin's. Darwin was shaken, writing to Lyell that "If Wallace had my MS. sketch written out in 1842, he could not have made a better short abstract!" (quoted in Desmond & Moore, 1991, p. 467).

After seeking the advice of Hooker and Lyell, Darwin agreed to a joint presentation at the July 1, 1858, meeting of the Linnean Society. Thus it occurred that the first public disclosure of Darwin's theory of evolution came at a professional meeting of botanists. The secretary of the society read Wallace's paper and an abstract of Darwin's 1844 essay. Neither Darwin (distraught—his youngest child died just before the meeting) nor Wallace (still on the other side of the world) attended the meeting, and neither paper attracted much attention at the time. The Wallace letter sent a clear message to Darwin, however. To establish his legitimate priority, he needed to publish. Despite continuing ill health and grief, Darwin completed the work over the next 15 months, and *On the Origin of Species by Means of Natural Selection or the Preservation of Favoured Races in the Struggle for Life* was published in late November 1859.[8]

Elements of the Theory of Evolution   After a brief introduction, in which Darwin emphasized the importance of the *Beagle* voyage and gave credit to Wallace, the *Origin of Species* opens with two chapters establishing the fact that members of a given species vary from each other. In the first chapter, "Variation Under Domestication," Darwin showed how individual differences within a species could be accentuated through deliberate breeding—artificial selection. This chapter prepared the way for him to argue later that just as there is deliberate selection by human breeders, there is also a "natural" selection by the conditions of everyday existence. In Chapter 2, "Variation Under Nature," Darwin noted the universality of individual differences within species found in nature. He made the connection to Chapter 1 by pointing out that these differences "thus afford materials for natural selection to act on and accumulate, in the same manner as man accumulates individual differences in his domesticated products" (Darwin, 1859/1958b, p. 59).

Darwin's third and fourth chapters, the "Struggle for Existence" and "Natural Selection," contain the core of the theory. Citing Malthus, Darwin first argued that in nature, species face a struggle to survive because they produce offspring at a rate that outpaces the food supply. That being the case, then those individuals having a variation that puts them at a slight advantage in the struggle will be "selected" by nature and live long enough to reproduce; those without the advantage will die. Over several generations, the "adaptive" variation will become more common. In Darwin's words:

> Owing to this struggle [for life], variations, however slight and from whatever cause proceeding, if they be in any degree profitable to the individuals of a species, ... will tend to the preservation of such individuals, and will generally be inherited by the offspring ....
>
> This preservation of favorable individual differences and variations, and the destruction of those which are injurious, I have called Natural Selection, or the Survival of the Fittest. (Darwin, 1859/1958b, p. 74, p. 88)

Darwin's finches illustrate the manner in which the struggle for existence and **natural selection** combine to alter species. Darwin believed that the original finches arrived as a single species from the mainland and settled in the various islands of the Galapagos. Because there is variation among members of a species in the wild, slight differences from one finch to another existed, including variations in beak shape. Suppose some of the birds happened to land on islands rich in certain types of seeds that are encased in hard shells. Those finches with slightly tougher and more blunted beaks would have an advantage in the hunt for these seeds. Finches with slightly thinner beaks would have a more difficult time getting at the seeds and would be more likely to die. Hence, the finches with the more "adaptive variation" would be "naturally selected" in the "struggle for existence." They would survive and pass on the advantage to their offspring. Over time, finches on that particular island would form a new species characterized by the specific beak shape. Similarly, on another island rich in insects, a species of finch with beaks thin enough to reach into small spaces would evolve.

---

[8]It is usually reported that all 1250 copies of the first print run sold out on the opening day of sales, but those books were all sold to booksellers, not to the general public; although the book soon attracted the public's attention, the impression of people making a mad dash to bookstores on the first day of sales is misleading (Reel, 2013).

Darwin believed that evolution by natural selection also explained extinction and the reason why modern species resemble fossils of extinct species found in the same geographical region. In South America, for example, Darwin had uncovered fossilized bones of animals similar to modern llamas but two to three times as large. Over time, he argued, the larger species had encountered environmental events (e.g., droughts) that reduced the food supply and favored the survival of smaller variations that did not need as much food.

In the remaining chapters of the *Origin*, Darwin described evidence in support of his theory and tried to answer the objections he knew would be forthcoming. He recognized that most people believed in the divine creation of every single species, but asked his readers to consider the evidence he had placed before them.

After the *Origin of Species*

Reaction to Darwin's theory was not long in coming. Although he did not discuss humans in the *Origin*, the implications were clear and threatened the Church of England. It might have been declining in power during the second half of the 19th century, but the Anglican Church was still capable of making its presence felt, and Darwin was denounced from pulpits throughout England. In the debates over evolution, Darwin himself stayed above the fray, preferring to have his case argued by others. One such ardent Darwinian was Thomas Huxley (1825–1895), who became known as "Darwin's bulldog" (Browne, 2002). In a famous debate at Oxford, during a meeting of the British Association for the Advancement of Science, Huxley defended Darwin against Samuel Wilberforce, an Anglican bishop and vocal opponent of evolution. Each made a series of complex arguments, but what is remembered is that at the end of his talk, Wilberforce, in jest, asked whether Huxley was related to an ape on his grandmother's or his grandfather's side of the family. Before beginning his reply, Huxley is said to have muttered "The Lord hath delivered him into my hands." He then began a point-by-point rebuttal of Wilberforce's arguments, ending with this response to the question about his lineage:

> If I would rather have a miserable ape for a grandfather or a man highly endowed by nature and possessed of great means and influence, and yet who employs those faculties for the mere purpose of introducing ridicule into a grave scientific discussion—I unhesitatingly affirm my preference for the ape. (quoted in Browne, 2002, p. 122)

Darwin's theory caused considerable consternation in the religious community, but the reaction in the scientific community was quite different. In his autobiography, Darwin argued that although there had been some initial resistance among some scientists (e.g., Lyell), general acceptance of the idea of evolution by natural selection came rather quickly. Although he rejected the idea that the success of his book demonstrated that the topic of evolution was "in the air," Darwin nonetheless recognized the importance of the zeitgeist: "What I believe was strictly true is that innumerable well-observed facts were stored in the minds of naturalists ready to take their proper places as soon as any theory which would receive them was sufficiently explained" (Darwin, 1892/1958a, p. 45).

As you recall from Chapter 1, one issue that pervades historical analysis is the extent to which people either move history or are themselves moved by historical forces—the personalistic versus naturalistic issue. The theory of evolution is a good illustration. From a personalistic standpoint, there is no question that Darwin had enormous influence. Regardless of whether the topic was "in the air," Darwin was the one who marshaled the evidence, developed a workable theory, and produced the book that made a compelling case for evolution. Indeed, the importance of Darwin's ideas eventually led some observers to begin using the phrase Darwinian evolution, an example of an *eponym*—identifying an idea with a person's name. The title of this chapter, borrowed from the title of a well-known book by Eisley (1958) on Darwin and evolution (*Darwin's Century: Evolution and the Men Who Discovered It*), emphasizes the personalistic. Yet it is also clear that Darwin was not the only intellectual who was thinking in evolutionary terms. Note that the title of Eisley's book suggests the involvement of more people than just Darwin. We have already seen that Lyell proposed an evolutionary theory for geology, that several earlier evolutionary models of biological change had appeared prior to Darwin's (Erasmus Darwin, Lamarck, *Vestiges*), and that the Wallace theory featured natural selection. There were others. For example, William Wells, an American physician, delivered an address to the Royal Society of London in 1813 in which he explicitly drew the same comparison that Darwin later made between artificial and natural selection, although he didn't use the same terms. And, in 1831, the Scottish botanist Patrick Matthew described what amounted to natural selection in an obscure book on trees. Neither Wells nor Matthews followed their writings with sustained research on evolutionary change, however, so their primary importance is to provide additional evidence that the idea of evolutionary change was not uncommon in the 19th century.

As for Darwin, despite his ever-present illnesses, and in the face of public criticism and religious condemnation, he worked vigilantly during his remaining years. He continued to collect evidence for his theory, publishing important works on topics ranging from orchids to earthworms. Although he avoided discussing human evolution in the *Origin of Species*, he addressed the topic head-on in *The Descent of Man, and Selection in Relation to Sex* (1871) and *The Expression of the Emotions in Man and Animals* (1872). In *Descent of Man*, Darwin added the idea of **sexual selection** to accompany his core idea of natural selection. Sexual selection entails the complementary processes of same-sex competition and female mate preference—the basic idea is that when males compete for female attention, any advantage they might have (e.g., larger antlers) will favor them in establishing dominance over other males and in the likelihood of being selected by females (Buss, 2009). Traits resulting from sexual selection are those that seem, by themselves, to have no direct survival benefit for the individual (e.g., a peacock's feathers), but do seem to favor the individual when competing for mates.

Darwin died on April 19, 1882. Although he wished to be buried quietly at Down, his cousin Francis Galton organized a successful campaign to have him interred among other British heroes at London's Westminster Abbey, just across the street from the Houses of Parliament. Today, the large rectangular stone marking Darwin's burial place can be found on the floor of the north side of the Abbey, just below the bust of Sir Isaac Newton.

Darwin and Psychology's History

In 1877, Darwin made a direct contribution to the history of developmental psychology by publishing an article in the British journal *Mind*, called a "Biographical Sketch of an Infant." It was based on extensive notes written years before on the physical and psychological development of his firstborn son, William. But Darwin's main contribution to psychology was his theory of evolution, which promoted a way of thinking among American psychologists that eventually became known as **functionalism**. This school of thought will be examined in Chapter 7; for now it is enough to say that the functionalists were interested in studying human behaviors and mental processes in terms of how they served to adapt the individual to an ever-changing environment (Green, 2009). Consciousness, for instance, was said to serve the adaptive function of enabling the individual to assess a problem and solve it quickly. Similarly, habits served to free the individual's limited consciousness to concentrate on unsolved problems.

Two specific aspects of the theory also have had a strong impact on psychology's history (Boring, 1963c). First, an obvious implication of the theory, which Darwin made explicit in *The Descent of Man* (1871), was that a continuity of mental processes existed between humans and other species. This led to an increased interest in what came to be called **comparative psychology**, the study of similarities and differences among all animal species. Second, the emphasis on individual variation prompted the study of **individual differences**, a research tradition that eventually led to the measurement of differences via intelligence and personality tests. These two developments need some elaboration.

THE ORIGINS OF COMPARATIVE PSYCHOLOGY

Studies of animal behavior preceded Darwin, but comparative research accelerated in the wake of Darwin's argument for continuity among species. Darwin himself may be considered one of the earliest comparative psychologists—many of the observations of animal behavior in his *Beagle* notebooks were comparative in nature (Armstrong, 1993). Comparisons among species also appear throughout his book on emotions—*The Expression of the Emotions in Man and Animals*, published in 1872. As the first scientific attempt to study emotional expressions, the book is Darwin's most important substantial contribution to psychology's history. It includes accounts of the circumstances producing the various types of emotional responses, descriptions of the manner in which these emotions are expressed by the facial musculature, and a theory of how the expressions might have evolved.

Darwin on the Evolution of Emotional Expressions

Darwin opened his book by arguing for an evolutionary approach to the study of emotional expressions, pointing out that for humans, things such as "the bristling of the hair under the influence of extreme terror … can hardly be understood, except on the belief that man once existed in a much lower and animal-like condition" (Darwin, 1872, p. 12). He then described the problems encountered when studying emotions in normal adults. First, although strong emotions certainly occur, most emotional expressions are muted. Studying one's own emotions is not easy either because the experience of a strong emotion is incompatible with a rational analysis of it. One cannot feel terror and dispassionately observe it in oneself at the same time. Investigating the forms and the causes of emotional expressions required a more creative strategy, and Darwin met the challenge by proposing several methods. For instance, he suggested studying children and the insane. Their expressions of such emotions as anger, joy, and fear, not restricted by normal adult inhibitions, would be more intense and their features more easily described as a result. Another method was to use a technique called galvanization. When electrodes passing mild current touched the surface of the skin, the stimulation produced recognizable muscle contractions. The idea was to establish exactly which muscles were involved in each emotional expression. Hence, if photos of a normal smile looked just like photos of a "galvanized" smile, one could assume that the galvanized muscles were the ones involved in smiling.

Darwin also reasoned that if emotional expressions were the result of evolution, then the same basic expressions would be found around the world. By using a large network of correspondents, including many encountered on the *Beagle* voyage, Darwin conducted the first cross-cultural study of emotional expressions. Darwin asked his correspondents to examine the facial expressions displayed in cultures far and wide and answer questions like the following:

> Is astonishment expressed by the eyes and mouth being opened wide, and by the eyebrows being raised? …
>
> When a man sneers or snarls at another, is the corner of the upper lip over the canine or eye tooth raised on the side facing the man whom he addresses? … (Darwin, 1872, pp. 15–16)

Darwin's final method, studying the emotional expressions of animals, gave him clues for a theory about the origins of emotional expressions. His theory involved three basic principles.

Principle one, the principle of **serviceable associated habits**, was the most important one proposed by Darwin. Incorporating the Lamarckian idea of the inheritance of acquired characteristics, Darwin argued that some emotional expressions were initially serviceable, or useful (Hess & Thibault, 2009). That is, they originated in bodily actions that served some adaptive function, helping the organism to survive the struggle for existence. Those actions then became associated with situations similar to the ones in which they originally occurred. These acquired expressions were then inherited. Consider the expression of contempt. In exaggerated form, it includes a pronounced intake of air through the nose, accompanied by a lifting and turning away of the head. According to Darwin, the characteristic expression of this emotion derived from a situation in which our evolutionary ancestors reacted to a physically offensive odor. Through habit and inheritance, the same reaction now occurs whenever a person is confronted with a person or situation judged to be offensive: "We seem thus to say to the despised person that he smells offensively, in nearly the same manner as we express to him by half-closing our eyelids, or turning away our faces, that he is not worth looking at" (p. 255). Similarly, the emotion of surprise includes raising one's eyebrows, which is a "serviceable habit." We wish to determine quickly the cause of that which surprises us, according to Darwin, "and we consequently open our eyes fully, so that the field of vision may be increased, and the eyeballs moved easily in any direction" (p. 281).

Darwin's second principle for explaining the form of emotional expression was based on the idea that emotions that are just the opposite of each other are expressed in bodily reactions that are similarly opposed. He called it the principle of **antithesis**. As examples, Darwin pointed to numerous animal expressions. When faced with a perceived threat, for instance, a dog will strike a pose designed to make it look bigger and more of a danger to a potential enemy (e.g., the hair on its back bristles). The opposite of this threat gesture, however, is a gesture of submission. Whereas a stranger might elicit the dog's threat gesture, the dog's master would elicit the gesture of submission.

Darwin called his third principle the **direct action of the nervous system**. In effect, these expressions are side effects of the physiological arousal that accompanies strongly felt emotions. As an example of direct action, Darwin cited the tendency to tremble, which could accompany any strong emotion and would therefore not be associated with any specific one.

A theme that runs through Darwin's book is the universality of emotional expression. His questionnaire results, similar to the findings of modern cross-cultural studies, showed that all over the world, basic emotions were expressed in the same manner. A smile means the same thing everywhere. If emotional expressions are universal, the implication is that they are instinctive and consequently, that human emotional behavior can only be understood by knowing its evolutionary past.

Along with Darwin's *Descent of Man*, the emotions book made it clear that humans shared traits with animals and that continuity in mental and emotional processes existed. Almost immediately, other naturalists began exploring this continuum. Many people were involved, but the best known were two Englishmen, George Romanes and Lloyd Morgan. Before reading about them, however, read the Close-Up, which describes the contributions of a third Britisher, Douglas Spalding, normally ignored in histories of psychology, but worthy of note.

CLOSE-UP

DOUGLAS SPALDING AND THE EXPERIMENTAL STUDY OF INSTINCT

An important but typically overlooked pioneer in the study of animal behavior was Douglas Spalding (1840–1877). Had he lived a full life, he might be known today as the founder of modern **ethology**, the study of instinctive animal behavior. Born in London to working-class parents, he did not have the luxuries of inherited wealth and an Oxford/Cambridge education to support his scientific work. Instead, he earned his keep by repairing slate roofs, and he was mostly self-educated. He did manage to complete a law degree in London in his early twenties, however, and it was during this time that he contracted the tuberculosis that would eventually kill him. While traveling for health reasons in southern Europe in the late 1860s, he met and came under the influence of the famous British philosopher John Stuart Mill (Chapter 2), who by then had retired to Avignon in the south of France. Mill recommended Spalding as a tutor for the two young sons of Lord and Lady Amberly, two ardent followers of Mill's liberal political philosophy. The younger son would become one of the best-known philosophers of the 20th century, Bertrand Russell.

Spalding apparently began his animal research in the 1860s, influenced by the evolutionary fervor that swept through the intelligentsia of the day. Although he never wrote a book and his studies were scattered throughout several popular magazines of the day, his research was noteworthy enough to catch the attention of the American psychologist/philosopher William James (Chapter 6). In a chapter on instinct in Volume II of his famous *Principles of Psychology*, James (1890/1950b) described "Mr. Spalding's wonderful article on instinct" (p. 396). He was referring to a piece that Spalding wrote for *Macmillan's Magazine* in 1873.

In that article, Spalding addressed the British empiricists' claim that such skills as depth perception and sound localization were learned very early in life as the result of direct sensory experience. Spalding's observations showed that experience was irrelevant, however—certain perceptual abilities, at least in animals, did not result from practice, but were the result of **instinct**. He also demonstrated several "species-specific" phenomena that later became associated with the work of 20th-century ethologists Konrad Lorenz and Niko Tinbergen.

Instinct

To determine whether experience is necessary for depth perception in baby chicks, Spalding developed a clever procedure. In his words, "[t]aking eggs just when the little prisoners had begun to break their way out, I removed a piece of the shell, and before they had opened their eyes drew over their heads little hoods" (Spalding, 1873, reprinted in Haldane, 1954, p. 3). The hoods remained intact for several days, preventing the chicks from having any visual experiences. Other hatchlings had "gum paper" inserted into their ears to eliminate auditory experiences. When the hoods were removed, the chicks showed no ill effects. For example, after spending just a minute or two adjusting to light, they had no difficulty pecking accurately at the insects provided by Spalding. Those with plugged ears responded similarly—when the obstruction was removed, they responded immediately to the call from an unseen mother hen and ran in the proper direction. Spalding concluded that raw instinct played an important role in animal behavior and that the British empiricists had overstated the importance of experience.

Imprinting

A famous picture, found in virtually all general psychology texts, shows a fatherly Konrad Lorenz, the modern-day founder of ethology, walking through a field followed by a string of young goslings. Lorenz showed that the young birds would follow the first object that they were able to detect moving, and he called the phenomenon **imprinting**. Although he did not label it, Spalding observed the same behavior.

> Chickens as soon as they are able to walk will follow any moving object. And, when guided by sight alone, they seem to have no more disposition to follow a hen than to follow a duck, or a human being.
>
> Unreflecting onlookers, when they saw chickens a day old running after me, and older ones following me miles and answering to my whistle, imagined that I must have some occult power over the creatures, whereas I simply allowed them to follow me from the first. (Spalding, 1873, reprinted in Haldane, 1954, p. 6)

Critical Periods

Spalding also described behavior illustrating the modern ethological concept of a **critical period**—certain behaviors must develop within a specific time frame, if they are to develop at all. For example, Spalding found that if chicks were prevented from hearing the call of the mother hen for 8–10 days, they would never recognize the mother. Also, while the chicks became attached to him when they were hooded for up to 3 days, those hooded for 4 days were afraid of him.

Spalding continued his animal studies when he began tutoring the children of Lord and Lady Amberly in 1873. The sprawling country house in England's Wye Valley was soon filled with a variety of species. The unconventional Lady Amberly, a strong advocate for women's equality, served as Spalding's research assistant, and according to some accounts (e.g., Boakes, 1984), she also tutored the naive Spalding in the human instinct of love. It was during this time that Spalding studied the flight instinct, demonstrating that birds did not have to learn how to fly. After hatching, he placed swallows and other nesting birds in wire mesh enclosures that prevented them from using their wings. Once released, they nonetheless flew immediately if sufficiently mature.

Spalding's idyllic life with the Amberlys came to an abrupt end in 1874, when both Lady Amberly and a young daughter died of diphtheria. A dispirited Lord Amberly also died within 2 years, naming Spalding as guardian to his sons. Amberly's parents successfully contested the will, however, and Spalding was on his own (Gray, 1962). He soon left England, and his tuberculosis reappeared. He was just 37 when he died in France in 1877.

George Romanes (1848–1894) and the Anecdotal Method

Like Darwin, George Romanes (Figure 5.6) was wealthy, stumbled through an adolescence of minimal accomplishment, appeared headed for the ministry but didn't get there, and became devoted to science as a result of his experiences at Cambridge (Lesch, 1972). A skilled researcher in physiology, Romanes became caught up in the prevailing excitement over Darwin's theory and decided to investigate the levels of mental ability that could be found in other species. Darwin apparently considered the younger man to be his protégé, often entertaining Romanes at Down House, and turning over some of his notes on animal behavior to the young scholar (Desmond & Moore, 1991).

Romanes combined Darwin's data with information he had been collecting on his own, and in 1882, shortly after Darwin's death, he published *Animal Intelligence* (Romanes, 1882/1886), a detailed catalog of animal behavior, from insects to primates. The book has earned Romanes the title of founder of comparative psychology, even though the term was introduced by Pierre Flourens (Chapter 3) in 1864 (Jaynes, 1969a), and several books similar to Romanes's effort preceded him or appeared about the same time (Johnston, 2003). Romanes gets credit because he made an effort to define the new field in a systematic fashion, doing so by drawing a parallel between comparative psychology and comparative anatomy. Romanes argued that just as the specialist in anatomy made comparisons among the anatomical features of various species, to examine the evolution of physical structure, so the comparative psychologist would study differences among the psychological (i.e., mental) features of different species to examine mental evolution.

Traditional accounts of Romanes's work focus on his overuse of uncritical stories about animal behavior supplied by others. **Anecdotal evidence**, as we have already seen in the discussion of phrenology (Chapter 3), has great potential for introducing bias and, in the case of comparative psychology, exaggerating the abilities of animals. Thus, Romanes's work has sometimes been discredited. This is unfortunate because Romanes was well aware of the problems with anecdotal evidence and took some care to include reliable reports of behavior in his book. For example, he tried to include accounts from observers known to be competent (e.g., Darwin), and he accepted unusual accounts of animal behavior only if they were reported independently by two or more persons. Nonetheless, Romanes himself

Courtesy of the Department of Psychology, Muskingum University

FIGURE 5.6   George Romanes (1848–1894), Darwin's protégé and usually considered the founder of comparative psychology.

recognized that the book, considered by itself, might seem to be little more than a collection of unusual animal stories. He expected that his subsequent books, outlining a theory of mental evolution, would be more important and that this initial "fact" book would come to be viewed as a preliminary step to the subsequent treatises (Boakes, 1984). Romanes indeed published his theory books, but they were largely ignored; his reputation, somewhat tainted, rests on the fact book.

Romanes took more precautions in his accounts of animal behavior than are usually attributed to him, but *Animal Intelligence* does nonetheless rely mainly on stories told by others and not on direct observation by Romanes. It also tends toward **anthropomorphism**, the attribution of human faculties to nonhuman entities. For instance, he argued that spiders have a "fondness" for music (Romanes, 1882/1886, p. 205), that scorpions feel despair and commit suicide when surrounded by fire or intense heat (p. 222), that birds show sympathy and conjugal fidelity (pp. 271–273), that beavers show "sagacity and forethought" when selecting sites for their lodges (p. 371) and have an intellectual appreciation for the architectural principles involved in dam-building (p. 376). Romanes was especially impressed with the intellectual capacity of dogs, arguing that they were capable of planning, bartering, recognizing information in pictures, and in this example, logical inference:

> Coming now to cases more distinctly indicative of reason … , dogs indisputably show that they possess this faculty. Thus, for instance, Livingstone [the African explorer] gives the following observation. A dog tracking his master along a road came to a place where three roads diverged. Scenting along two of the roads and not finding the trail, he ran off on the third without waiting to smell. Here, therefore, is a true act of inference. If the track is not on A or B, it must be on C, there being no other alternative. (p. 457)

Conwy Lloyd Morgan (1852–1936) and his "Canon"

The problems with Romanes's first book on animal behavior, with its emphasis on anecdotes and its excessive anthropomorphism, were noted by another British naturalist, C. Lloyd Morgan (Figure 5.7) . Son of a lawyer, Morgan attended the School of Mines at the Royal College of Science in London to be trained as a mining engineer. At the School of Mines, he came under the influence of the evolutionist Thomas Huxley (Darwin's "bulldog"). This led Morgan to an interest in zoology and geology and eventually to a lifetime position as a professor of these topics at University College, Bristol, starting in 1883. He published several books on geology, but he is best known for his work in comparative psychology, reflected in books with titles like *Animal Life and Intelligence* (1890) and *An Introduction to Comparative Psychology* (1895/1903). Just as Romanes was a protégé of Darwin, Morgan was a follower and admirer of Romanes, but he eventually developed a more sophisticated comparative psychology than his mentor, based more on direct observation than the compiling of anecdotes.

Morgan is known today for arguing that explanations for animal behavior should be no more complex than observational evidence allowed. This appeal came to be called **Lloyd Morgan's canon**. As he put it: "In no case may we interpret an action as the outcome of the exercise of a higher psychical faculty, if it can be interpreted as the outcome of the exercise of one which stands lower in the psychological scale" (Morgan, 1895/1903, p. 59). In response to the account you just read of a dog apparently using reasoning and inference (a "higher psychical faculty"), for example, Morgan would have noted that just because the dog chose the third path quickly does not rule out the use of scent ("lower on the psychological scale") as determining the choice.

Morgan did not rule out the use of anecdotes—after all, they often amount to careful observations. Yet Morgan believed that anecdotes needed to be interpreted with caution, and he had greater confidence in observation, especially if he was the one doing the observing. Two examples illustrate the point. First, before beginning his tenure at Bristol, Morgan taught in South Africa for 5 years, where he had the

University of Bristol, UK

FIGURE 5.7 C. Lloyd Morgan (1852–1936), whose approach to comparative psychology was more empirical and less anthropomorphic than that of Romanes.

opportunity to observe scorpion behavior firsthand. Thus, he had the opportunity to examine Romanes's anthropomorphic claim about scorpions feeling despair and committing suicide when surrounded by fire. Could there be a simpler explanation of the fact that scorpions occasionally sting themselves to death? Morgan thought so. What he observed was that scorpions regularly used their tails to remove foreign substances and other irritants (e.g., smoke) from the surface of their bodies. It was a simple reflex action, not a deliberate, calculated response arising out of "despair." Every once in a while, Morgan observed, the reflex action would be just a bit too vigorous, resulting in the demise of a scorpion. There was no need to propose a "higher psychical faculty" (a decision to commit suicide) when the behavior could be seen as the result of some factor "lower in the psychological scale" (a reflex action).

A second example used by Morgan is a famous one. Romanes had credited cats and dogs with the mental ability to understand simple mechanical principles and to plan, based on anecdotal examples of dogs opening gates and escaping from yards. Morgan, however, believed that such behavior had a simpler explanation, and he used his fox terrier, Tony, as a case in point. Tony could place his head through an opening in a gate and open the latch by lifting upward. The gate then swung open, and Tony was free to leave the yard and "get out into the road, where there was often much to interest him; cats to be worried, other dogs with whom to establish a sniffing acquaintance, and so forth" (Morgan, 1895/1903, p. 292). To a naive observer, it might appear that the dog rationally "understood" the mechanics of the gate operation and the concept of lifting the latch as a planned means to a desired end. To Morgan, however, the behavior was simply the result of a series of trial-and-error actions prompted by the dog's attempts to escape the yard for the romance of the road. He noted that before hitting on the correct solution, Tony had tried just about everything else, running back and forth along the fence, sticking his head between the bars at numerous locations, and eventually hitting upon the correct action by accident. After he had escaped, he soon abandoned the unsuccessful behaviors and learned to repeat the successful one.

Morgan's canon is sometimes used to highlight an important shift in how comparative psychologists thought about animal behavior and Darwin's notion of the continuity among species. It is often argued that prior to Morgan, naturalists were overly anthropomorphic and searched for evidence of varying amounts of cognition in virtually all species. After Morgan, so the story goes, researchers looked for simpler (i.e., more "parsimonious") processes to explain an animal's actions, gradually resulting in the behaviorist dictum that behaviors, even human ones, are best understood in terms of simple conditioning processes. Thus, B. F. Skinner wrote in the opening pages of his first book, *The Behavior of Organisms* (1938), "Lloyd Morgan, with his principle of parsimony, dispensed with [mental faculties in animals] in a reasonably successful attempt to account for characteristic animal behavior without them" (p. 4). And in a well-known book on "theories of learning," Hilgard (1948) stated that the canon, "which had seriously undercut the attributing of higher mental processes to animals had fairly well succeeded via behaviorism in excising them from humans as well" (p. 179). In short, Morgan is often seen as a pivotal figure in the "progress" from cute animal stories implying animal cognition to experimental research and a mechanical conception of animal behavior (including human animals) that eliminates the need for mental processes as explanations for behavior. Such an interpretation is mistaken, however. Morgan can indeed be credited for arguing that an understanding of animal behavior must go beyond the collection of anecdotes and embrace more precise observational strategies. Yet to say that Morgan wished to rule out the existence of animal consciousness and intelligence is wrong. As Morgan himself said, in the sentence immediately following the canon:

> To this, however, it should be added, lest the range of the principle be misunderstood, that the canon *by no means excludes the interpretation of a particular activity in terms of the higher processes*, if we already have some independent evidence of the occurrence of these higher processes in the animal under observation. (Morgan, 1895/1903, p. 59, emphasis added)

Thus, Morgan did not intend for his canon to be a prohibition against the idea of higher mental processes in animals—he was merely urging methodological caution. According to Costall (1993), Morgan's true purpose was to broaden the range of criteria on which to base continuity among species. Rather than relying exclusively on a search for sophisticated rational reflection on the part of a variety of species, other types of mental processes, differing in degrees of complexity, could be included. Put in evolutionary terms, Morgan proposed that animals exhibited many levels of cognition, reaching a level of complexity just sufficient to enable them to survive their own unique struggle for existence. The point of the canon was to argue that there was no reason to suggest levels of mental capability *beyond* that needed to survive. It is also wrong to say that Morgan rejected anthropomorphism as a means for understanding animal behavior. Although he thought Romanes might have been overgenerous in his anthropomorphic attributions, Morgan saw no problem with the basic logic of trying to understand animal cognition by looking for parallels in human cognition.

Comparative Psychology in America

It is not surprising that comparative psychology developed a firm foothold in Great Britain in the mid- to late 19th century, as reflected in the work of Darwin, Romanes, Spalding, and Morgan. Interest in the topic developed quickly in the United States as well, and you will learn about two prime examples in later chapters. First, an animal laboratory developed at Clark University in the mid-1890s, under the leadership of Linus Kline, Willard Small, and Edmund Sanford, the laboratory director there. As you will discover in the Close-Up for Chapter 6, they can be credited with creating one of psychology's enduring methods—maze learning. Also, Kline wrote an article entitled "Suggestions Toward a Laboratory Course in Comparative Psychology" (1899) that influenced instruction in comparative psychology for years. The second example occurs in Chapter 7—E. L. Thorndike's work on puzzle box learning. It is also worth noting that several American researchers developed interests in animal behavior and studied it in the British naturalist tradition. One, John Bascom, even wrote a textbook with "comparative psychology" in the title as early as 1878 (Johnston, 2003).

STUDYING INDIVIDUAL DIFFERENCES

A cornerstone of Darwin's theory, the raw material for natural selection, was the idea that individual members of a species varied from each other. For psychology, this fact led to the study of **individual differences**, a research tradition that includes the creation of techniques to measure those differences. Today's intelligence and personality tests are two outcomes of this tradition. The person most directly responsible for initiating the study of individual differences was Darwin's half-cousin, Francis Galton, whose obsession with measurement led one scientist to refer to him as the 19th century's "apostle of quantification" (Gould, 1981, p. 75).

Francis Galton (1822–1911): Jack of All Sciences

Like his more famous relative, Galton (Figure 5.8) thought for a time that his future was in medicine, but he was likewise put off by the experience of witnessing "grisly postmortems and assist[ing] at live operations performed without anesthetics" (quoted in Fancher, 2009, p. 86). Fortunately for his future prospects, though, inherited wealth enabled him to indulge a wide range of interests. His insatiable

© Bettmann/Corbis

FIGURE 5.8 The ever-curious Francis Galton (1822–1911).

curiosity, combined with a brilliant intellect,[9] resulted in a diverse set of accomplishments, only a small portion of which relates directly to psychology. For example, he became one of a number of famous British explorers of Africa during the Victorian era. His exploits won him a gold medal from the Royal Geographical Society, and he became a recognized public figure after publishing an account of his explorations and a popular (eight editions) travel guide for the inexperienced explorer.

In addition to geography and exploration, Galton made original contributions to several other fields. By gathering weather information from various locations at the same times during the day, for instance, he created the first weather maps, and he was the first to observe the relationships between high and low pressure systems and how they influenced the weather. By measuring the patterns of swirls on the fingertips of hundreds of different people, he demonstrated that every person had a unique pattern. Scotland Yard eventually started using this "fingerprinting" technique for identification purposes. This procedure, of course, is an example of looking for individual differences. Indeed, Galton's work in fingerprinting was just a small piece of his overall strategy of quantifying differences between people over a range of variables. And this leads to Galton's importance for psychology.

The Nature of Intelligence As a wealthy, upper-class, Victorian-era, British white male, living at a time when England was the most powerful nation on earth, Galton had little difficulty believing that he and his peers were superior to those from other classes, countries, races, or the other gender. Furthermore, more a product of his environment than he cared to admit, Galton shared the widespread assumption among his peers that this preeminence was no accident, but based on an inherited superiority. When his cousin published on evolution in 1859, humans were not discussed, but Galton immediately saw the ramifications. If inherited individual variation, acted on by natural selection, influenced the

---

[9]Galton resembled another child prodigy, John Stuart Mill, in this regard. Like Mill, Galton displayed adultlike abilities at a tender age. He could read and write English by age three, translate some Latin by age five, and quote from Shakespeare by his sixth birthday.

evolution of animal and plant species, it must have influenced humans as well. If human intelligence was a key trait enabling physically weak humans to survive the struggle for existence, then the more intelligent humans would naturally rise to the top of society. From this it was not hard for Galton to conclude that he and others of his class had achieved their lofty positions in society by virtue of their highly evolved and superior intellectual ability, rather than by the accident of being born to the right parents. He set out to collect evidence in support of his belief that intelligence was innate, producing *Hereditary Genius* in 1869 (Galton, 1869/1950).

To examine the question of whether intelligence was inherited, Galton relied on his penchant for quantification and statistical analysis. First, by examining the contents of biographical dictionaries, which profiled people who had achieved eminence in some field, and comparing the numbers therein with overall population data, he estimated that the "rate of eminence" in Great Britain was about 1 person in 4,000. He then looked at the family trees of these highly capable people and discovered that talent tended to run in families. Of those noted in the dictionaries, about 10 percent had at least one relative who was also so noted, a rate much higher than could be expected by the 1 in 4,000 probability for the general population. Also, talent within a family tended to be similar—lawyers related to lawyers, doctors related to doctors, and so on. Furthermore, if two relatives appeared in the dictionaries, they were four times more likely to be directly related (e.g., father–son) than related at a second level (e.g., uncle–nephew). Today, of course, we recognize that these patterns are just as likely to reflect environmental factors as genetic ones, but Galton was operating within the context of a social environment that was biased toward an assumption of inherited differences in ability and an intellectual environment that was dominated by the evolution discussion.

It is not that Galton failed to consider the effects of environmental circumstances. In fact, in *Hereditary Genius*, he granted that they played a small role, but he also went to great lengths to argue their overall irrelevance. Drawing an analogy between mental and physical prowess, for example, he pointed out that no matter how much one exercises, there is an upper limit to "the muscular powers of every man, which he cannot by any education or exertion overpass" (Galton, 1869/1950, p. 13). Similarly, a student learns to accept mental limits—"[h]e knows he can beat such and such of his competitors; that there are some with whom he runs on equal terms, and others whose intellectual feats he cannot even approach" (p. 14). Galton also pointed out that many people manage, through their natural ability, to overcome the effects of an impoverished environment. Conversely, he argued that an enriched environment could not overcome limited natural ability. He even used the United States to bolster his case, arguing that opportunity "is more widely spread in America, than with us, and the education of their middle and lower classes far more advanced; but, for all that, America certainly does not beat us in world-class works of literature, philosophy, or art" (p. 34). For Galton, then, all the signs pointed to the same conclusion—intelligence was part of human nature, the product of evolutionary forces.

Darwin responded enthusiastically to his cousin's work on natural ability, but not all of Galton's contemporaries agreed. In particular, there was dissent from Alphonse de Candolle, a distinguished Swiss botanist. He responded to Galton with a study of his own, which he believed showed the importance of environmental factors in paving the way for someone to achieve eminence. Candolle examined the lives of 300 European scientists, finding that a number of social, political, and economic factors were associated with scientific fame (Fancher, 1983). For instance, he found that eminence in science was more likely to occur in democratic than totalitarian countries (more academic freedom), and more likely to occur in countries with higher standards of living (greater opportunity, more funding for labs, etc.).

Following *Hereditary Genius*, and in response to Candolle, Galton sought to strengthen his argument about the inheritance of talent by pioneering two methodological techniques in use today: surveys and twin studies. Although his cousin was using a similar technique to study emotional expressions at about the same time, Galton is credited with being the first person to use the **survey method**, and right from the start, he had a good understanding of the difficulties involved in developing a good questionnaire, writing that "there is hardly any more difficult task than that of framing questions which are not likely to be misunderstood, which admit of an easy reply, and which cover the ground of inquiry" (Galton, 1883, quoted in Dennis, 1948, p. 279).

Sometime in the early 1870s, Galton wrote a questionnaire and distributed it to 180 fellows of the Royal Society, the scientific elite of England. The survey asked its respondents to describe their personalities, physical attributes, family characteristics, and the details of their upbringing; it also asked them to describe the origins of their scientific interests and to indicate "How far do your scientific tastes appear innate?" (quoted in Forrest, 1974, p. 126). Galton received about a hundred usable replies, and they formed the basis of his next book, which included a subtitle that popularized two words destined to become catchwords in the continuing debate over the origins of intelligence. The book was called *English Men of Science: Their Nature and Nurture* (Galton, 1874).[10] Although he granted that some of the replies demonstrated that the environment (nurture) helped to shape the scientists, Galton believed that his respondents overwhelmingly supported the idea that talent in science was inherited (nature). This he concluded from making the questionable assumption that scientific ability could be considered innate if a subject reported being interested in science very early in life and could not point to any particular set of circumstances bringing about such an interest. It just seemed to be there from the start. As one of his respondents put it: "As far back as I remember, I loved nature and desired to learn her secrets" (quoted in Forrest, 1974, p. 126).

Galton's second methodological innovation, **twin studies**, was on firmer scientific ground. He sent questionnaires to twins known to him, asking them to supply names of other twins; he eventually surveyed 94 pairs about their physical and psychological attributes. As might be expected, he found support for his hereditarian beliefs—many similarities between pairs of twins, even in their later years, after they had been living in different environments. He reported the data anecdotally, and both his questionnaire wording and his interpretation of the results were affected by his preconceptions about intelligence, but the twin studies method itself has proven effective over the years as a way to assess the interactive influence of nature and nurture.

The general conclusion that Galton reached on the basis of all these studies is clear from the opening sentence of *Hereditary Genius*: "I propose to show in this book that a man's natural abilities are derived by inheritance" (Galton, 1869/1950, p. 1). One implication of this statement, resulting from Galton's reading of Darwin's parallels between the artificial selection of the breeder and the natural selection of the wild, is spelled out in the book's second sentence. He wrote that just as it is possible "to obtain by careful selection a permanent breed of dogs or horses gifted with peculiar powers of running, ... so it would be quite practicable to produce a highly-gifted race of men by judicious marriages during several consecutive generations" (Galton, 1869/1950, p. 1). This suggestion eventually

---

[10]Galton is sometimes credited with inventing the label "nature–nurture issue," by virtue of the subtitle to his 1874 book. He had numerous predecessors, however, including Shakespeare (Conley, 1984), who described the notorious Caliban in the *Tempest* (Act IV, Scene 1) in these terms:

A devil, a born devil, on whose nature
Nurture can never stick.

led Galton to coin the term **eugenics** to promote the idea that society should take active steps toward improving its genetic material. This would include encouraging certain people to reproduce, known as "positive" eugenics. These individuals presumably would be those with great talent, people like Galton (ironically, Galton and his wife were childless). He founded a Eugenics Society in 1908, a journal a year later, and spent his remaining years promoting a eugenics-based society. Indeed, he came to think of eugenics as a new religion, as evidenced by this comment from his autobiography: "I take Eugenics very seriously, feeling that its principles ought to become one of the dominant motives in a civilized nation, much as if they were one of its religious tenets" (Galton, 1908, p. 232). As will be seen in the chapter on mental testing (Chapter 8), Galton found a sympathetic audience for his eugenicist views, both in Great Britain and in the United States.

The Anthropometric Laboratory   To breed selectively for the intelligence that would keep Great Britain in its position as a world power, Galton knew he needed a way to identify those best suited to improve the race. This meant developing ways to measure talent, a task close to Galton's quantitative heart and his interests in individual differences. His efforts reached their peak in the 1880s, when he established an Anthropometric Laboratory, initially as part of an international health fair held in South Kensington in 1884. It later moved to a nearby museum, where Galton collected data for another 10 years. Nearly 10,000 fair-goers were tested in 1884; about 17,000 were tested altogether (Forrest, 1974).

Each person entering the laboratory completed several tests, with many of the measuring instruments created by Galton. Many of Galton's measures were simple physical ones: height, weight, arm span, and breathing capacity. Others tested basic sensory/motor capacities: reaction time, auditory and visual thresholds, color naming, judgment of line lengths, and grip strength. After the lab moved from the health fair, head size was added as a measure. Although these might not appear to be valid measures of intelligence to us today, Galton argued that superior mental capacity was related to neural efficiency and sensory ability: "The only information that reaches us concerning outward events appears to pass through the avenue of our senses; and the more perceptible our senses are of difference, the larger is the field upon which our judgment and intelligence can act" (Galton, 1883/1965, p. 421). Galton also argued that women were intellectually inferior to men, a widely held 19th-century belief, and traced the deficiency to their inadequate sensory capacity. He noted that professions requiring sharp senses, such as piano-tuners, wine-tasters, and wool-sorters, were all populated by men. Deeply immersed in his times, of course, he failed to consider the fact that women would never be given the opportunity to learn these skills or the chance to be employed in these trades.

Galton's measures never proved to be useful indexes of intelligence and, as we shall see in Chapter 8, they were soon replaced by tests like those devised in France at the turn of the 20th century by Alfred Binet. Galton's effort is noteworthy, however, as the first serious attempt to measure individual differences in human ability. It is also important for the history of statistics—in his attempts to determine whether scores on his various measures were associated with each other, he invented the statistical concept of **correlation**. In an 1888 paper entitled "Co-relations and their Measurement, Chiefly from Anthropometric Data," Galton argued that the strength of association between any two measures could be stated mathematically. This idea was soon refined into the modern concept of the correlation coefficient by one of his followers, the mathematician Karl Pearson, whose name is associated with the most common expression of a correlation coefficient, Pearson's r.

Investigating Imagery and Association   Galton's major interest in psychological phenomena might have been in the area of mental ability, but he also studied two other psychological topics—mental imagery and association. As he had done for his project on the inheritance of intelligence, Galton turned to the survey to examine the use of visual imagery and the quality of the images seen. Respondents were asked to imagine their breakfast table and were asked these questions:

1. *Illumination.* Is the image dim or fairly clear? Is its brightness comparable to the actual scene?
2. *Definition.* Are all the objects pretty well defined at the same time, or is the place of sharpest definition at any one moment more contracted than it is in a real scene?
3. *Colouring.* Are the colours of the china, of the toast, bread-crust, mustard, meat, parsley, or whatever may have been on the table, quite distinct and natural? (Galton, 1883, quoted in Dennis, 1948, p. 279, emphasis in the original)

Galton's long-standing interest in scientists led him to survey a number of his scientist friends, but he also distributed the survey more widely (e.g., schoolchildren). He was surprised by the results. Compared to the general public, which reported imagery of varying degrees of vividness, most of his scientist friends appeared to report a virtual absence of imagery. As he described it,

> To my astonishment, I found that the great majority of the men of science to whom I first applied protested that mental imagery was unknown to them.... They had no more notion of its true character than a colour-blind man, who has not discerned his defect, has of the nature of colour. (Galton, 1883, quoted in Dennis, 1948, p. 279)

To the 21st-century observer, the lack of imagery among scientists seems like an odd result. This unusual finding led Brewer and his colleagues to attempt a replication of Galton's study (Brewer & Schommer-Aikens, 2006). They found that in fact modern scientists tended to show a relatively large amount of imagery. Intrigued, Brewer went back to Galton's original data and discovered that Galton had not reported his own results accurately. Perhaps overly influenced by some early questionnaire returns from a few prominent scientists who indeed reported a lack of imagery (Romanes was one of them), Galton evidently failed to carefully summarize his data accurately.

Concerning association, we have already seen that the topic was of great importance to philosophers and scientists in the 18th and 19th centuries, and Galton was no exception. He was aware of the long history of philosophical speculation about the nature of association, of course, but he was unaware of the work that Hermann Ebbinghaus (Chapter 4) was doing at about the same time. To examine associations systematically, Galton developed a **word association test**. He generated a list of 75 words and then looked at each one for a measured amount of time, noting any associations that occurred to him. He also tried to date his associations. Of the 124 associations the 75 words generated for him, 48 (39%) were from his "boyhood and youth," 57 (46%) from "subsequent manhood," and the remaining 19 (15%) from "quite recent events" (data and category labels from Forrest, 1974, p. 146). Galton's results also showed a tendency for associations to repeat themselves in one's mind. For example, after going through his list of 75 words four times, he found that in about 25% of the cases, the word gave rise to exactly the same association on all four trials. This led him to conclude that there was "much less variety in the mental stock of ideas than I had expected, and makes [me] feel that the roadways of our minds are worn into very deep ruts" (Galton, 1883, quoted in Dennis, 1948, p. 288). Galton also observed that we are only dimly aware of the course of our mental life, hinting at the unconscious mind that would shortly become the focus of another famous 19th-century mind, Sigmund Freud (Chapter 12).

It has been estimated that a mere 25 percent of Galton's research and writings were of direct concern to psychology (Forrest, 1974). Yet his contribution to our discipline is impressive: He pioneered the study of individual differences in human ability, he introduced research methods and statistical tools still in use, and he made some astute observations about human cognition. Galton's lifelong devotion to British science earned him a knighthood in 1909. He died 2 years later.

IN PERSPECTIVE: DARWIN'S CENTURY

Although Darwin's major influence has been on the biological sciences, modern psychology cannot be properly understood without knowing about his theory and its implications. The study of individual differences derives from his observation about individual variation within a species, and comparative psychology has its origins in an attempt to evaluate the claim of an evolutionary continuum. As will be seen in Chapter 12, Darwin's theory also had a direct effect on Freud's thinking about the importance of sexual motivation in directing the course of human behavior. Finally, functionalism (to be encountered in Chapter 7), which examined behaviors and mental processes in terms of their capacity for adapting the organism to the environment, also had its roots in evolutionary thinking. Darwin, in effect, naturalized the mind, causing it to be seen as the means by which the human animal survives in the struggle for existence.

In recent years, some psychologists have become even more explicit in looking toward evolution as a means to explain human behavior, and the result is a new field of study called **evolutionary psychology**. Advocates (e.g., Wright, 1994) argue that if evolutionary forces have been powerful enough to create the physical characteristics that make us human, then why not behavioral and mental characteristics as well? Evolutionary psychologists have paid special attention to social behaviors and to sexuality and sex differences in behavior, relying heavily on Darwin's theory of sexual selection. The general strategy is to describe some behavior that occurs regularly, then look for an evolutionary explanation for it, and then develop testable predictions about behavior. Evolutionary psychologists believe, for example, that much of the behavior that surrounds male–female relations reduces to an attempt to ensure that one's genetic material makes it to the next generation. Many of their ideas have been controversial, especially among psychologists who tend to emphasize the importance of the environment in shaping human behavior. Yet their increasing presence in the discussion about the causes of human behavior is just another indication of the lasting power of Darwin's ideas.

SUMMARY

The Species Problem

• During the Enlightenment, some scientists began questioning the biblical account of how species were created. The species problem concerned the question of how species originated, why there were so many, and how extinction could be explained. The argument from design enabled scientists to continue to examine nature scientifically while maintaining religious beliefs.

• An early theory of evolution that omitted reference to the deity was proposed by Charles Darwin's grandfather, Erasmus. A more important theory was proposed by the French naturalist Lamarck. His theory included the concept of the inheritance of acquired characteristics.

Charles Darwin (1809–1882) and the Theory of Evolution

• After several false starts, Charles Darwin found a vocation in science while a student at Cambridge. He initially thought of himself as a geologist, but he was also greatly interested in zoology. Two important mentors were the botanist John Henslow and the geologist Adam Sedgwick.

• During a 5-year voyage aboard the *Beagle*, Darwin collected evidence that made contributions to both geology and zoology. He made discoveries that supported Charles Lyell's uniformitarian model of geological change (the earth changes gradually according to known principles, rather than as a result of periodic geological catastrophes), and he collected data that would eventually provide evidence for his theory of evolution. Evidence from the Galapagos Islands (finches) was especially important.

- In developing his theory, Darwin was influenced by the views of Thomas Malthus, who pointed out that because populations tend to grow faster than food supplies, a struggle for existence occurs among members of those populations. Darwin also observed that hobbyists (e.g., pigeon breeders) and farmers were able to bring about dramatic changes in species by selective breeding.

- Darwin created the essence of his theory in the early 1840s, but did not publish for nearly 20 years. He was slowed by poor health, a concern over how his theory would be received by the scientific community, and a scientific cautiousness that led him to accumulate as much evidence as possible to support his theory. He was motivated to publish in 1859 by the appearance of a similar theory by Alfred Russel Wallace.

- Darwin's theory proposed that individual members of every species vary from each other; that some variations are more favorable in the struggle for existence than others, enabling the organism to adapt to the environment; and that nature "selects" (natural selection) those with the most favorable variations for survival.

The Origins of Comparative Psychology

- An implication of Darwin's theory was that continuity existed among species. This led to the development of comparative psychology, the study of differences and similarities among species on various traits (e.g., ability). Darwin was an early pioneer, examining the evolutionary history of emotional expressions and demonstrating that human expressions had evolutionary roots.

- George Romanes is considered the founder of comparative psychology, and he provided extensive descriptions of the behavior of many species. He relied on anecdotal observations and was too anthropomorphic in his interpretations of the behaviors he described. A more empirical approach was taken by Douglas Spalding, who demonstrated that certain behaviors were the result of instinct, not experience. C. Lloyd Morgan took issue with the excessive anthropomorphism shown by other comparative psychologists, favored empirical observations over anecdotal data, and argued that explanations of animal behavior could involve cognition processes, but only those processes just complex enough to enable survival. For example, some behaviors (e.g., dogs opening gates) were better explained as being examples of trial-and-error learning than rational planning.

Studying Individual Differences

- Individual variation is a cornerstone of evolutionary theory, and Francis Galton was the first to carefully examine these individual differences in humans. He studied individual differences in visual imagery, studying it through the first systematic use of the survey method (questionnaire). He also invented the word association method to study the nature of associations.

- Galton believed that intelligence was an inherited ability; nurture played a minimal role at best. As evidence, he pointed to the fact that certain abilities tended to run in families. He argued for a eugenics-based society—only those who are fit should be encouraged to reproduce. To identify those who were most fit, he set out to measure individual differences in ability. This resulted in the first widespread attempt to measure and classify human abilities. His measures relied heavily on basic sensory/motor processes and did not prove very useful.

STUDY QUESTIONS

1. What was the species problem, and how did the argument from design propose to answer the problem?

2. Describe Lamarck's ideas about evolution.

3. What were the important events leading to Darwin's appointment on the *Beagle*, and why did he consider himself as much a geologist as a naturalist at this time?

4. Distinguish between catastrophist and uniformitarian views of geology, and describe the evidence that Darwin collected relating to the issue.

5. Describe the example of Darwin's finches as a way of summarizing the essential features of his theory of evolution.

6. In developing his theory of evolution, what were the lessons that Darwin learned from (a) Malthus and (b) his pigeon breeder friends?

7. Darwin had his theory worked out in the early 1840s. Why did he delay publication, and why did he eventually publish in 1859?

8. Concerning the issue of whether his theory was in line with the zeitgeist, what were Darwin's thoughts?

9. Describe Darwin's contribution to comparative psychology. In particular, show how he applied evolutionary thinking to the concept of emotional expression.

10. Describe Spalding's research on instinct. How did his work demonstrate the phenomena that later came to be called imprinting and critical periods?

11. Describe and criticize the comparative psychology of Romanes. In what way has the criticism been unfair to him?

12. Describe Lloyd Morgan's canon, and apply it to the example of Morgan's terrier. Explain the important misconception about Morgan's canon that has developed over the years.

13. According to Galton, why is one person more intelligent than another? What kinds of evidence did he use to support his claim?

14. What is the connection between Galton's beliefs about intelligence and (a) eugenics, and (b) mental testing?

15. Describe Candolle's research on eminent scientists, and explain how it favored a nurture explanation.

16. Describe how Galton used the questionnaire method to study the mental imagery of scientists and others. What did he find that surprised him? What has recent research suggested about Galton's conclusions?

17. Describe the two different methods that Galton used to study the nature of his own associations. What did he discover and conclude?

CHAPTER 6

AMERICAN PIONEERS

Psychology is the Science of Mental Life, both of its phenomena and their conditions.

—William James, 1890

PREVIEW AND CHAPTER OBJECTIVES

Having considered the philosophical and scientific contexts out of which modern psychology emerged, its origins and early development in Germany, and the far-reaching importance of Darwin's ideas, we are ready to shift our focus to the development of psychology in the United States. This chapter opens with a discussion of the influence of faculty psychology in pre–Civil War America and a description of the development of higher education in America in the latter half of the 19th century. Considered in this section will be the limited opportunities available to women and minority students during this era. The chapter then examines the life and work of America's first major psychologist: William James. Although he eventually thought of himself more as a philosopher than a psychologist, his 1890 *Principles of Psychology* is perhaps the most important book written in psychology's history. The chapter also examines the careers and contributions of several other members of the first generation of American psychologists, especially G. Stanley Hall and Mary Whiton Calkins. Hall exemplified the pioneering spirit said to characterize Americans: He spread the gospel of the New Psychology by founding laboratories, journals, and the American Psychological Association. Mary Calkins was the best known of a handful of pioneering women psychologists who made their presence felt despite daunting odds. After you finish this chapter, you should be able to:

■ Explain what it was like to study psychology in America before the arrival of the New Psychology and the writings of William James

■ Describe the rise of the modern university and how the German model influenced education in America

■ Enumerate the obstacles facing women and minority students who tried to obtain higher education and graduate education in the late 19th and early 20th centuries

■ Describe the formative influences on William James, especially the development of his pragmatic philosophy

■ Describe James's definition of psychology and his attitude about the new laboratory approach to psychology

■ Provide a Jamesian description of consciousness and its attributes, and describe his ideas about the nature of consciousness, habit, and emotions

■ Explain why spiritualism was popular in late 19th-century America, and explain James's attitude about the investigation of spiritualism

- Describe the contributions of G. Stanley Hall to the professionalization of psychology in America
- Explain why Hall thought of himself as a "genetic" psychologist, and describe the importance of the idea of recapitulation to his thinking
- Explain why Mary Calkins is considered an important pioneer in memory research, and describe the difficulties she had in obtaining graduate education
- Describe the contributions of Margaret Washburn, Christine Ladd-Franklin, George Trumball Ladd, and James Mark Baldwin to American psychology in its formative years

PSYCHOLOGY IN 19TH-CENTURY AMERICA

E. G. Boring (1929) once described American psychology as the offspring of the new psychology created in Germany (i.e., Wundt) and of British biology (i.e., Darwin), and he asserted that American psychology did not really begin until William James appeared on the scene—"James began psychology in America with his recognition of the significance of the new experimental physiological psychology in Germany" (p. 493).[1] Boring influenced a whole generation of psychologists, of course, and one consequence has been the neglect of pre-Jamesian psychology. Although James was a towering figure during the formative years of modern scientific psychology in the United States, he was not the first American thinker to write about psychological issues or to teach psychology in an American university (Fuchs, 2000). Prior to James, psychology was taught in courses typically called "intellectual" or "mental" philosophy, and it was dominated by **faculty psychology**, which derived from a Scottish philosophical movement called Scottish Realism.

Faculty Psychology

As you recall from Chapter 2, empiricism and associationism, represented in the philosophies of Locke, Berkeley, Hume, Hartley, and Mill, were dominant intellectual forces in Great Britain during the 18th and 19th centuries. Empiricists argued that knowledge resulted from our experiences in the world, with the structure of our minds being organized through the laws of association. The Empiricists also addressed the concept of reality, with Locke distinguishing between primary and secondary qualities of matter, Berkeley arguing that only the secondary qualities were real, and Hume extending the argument by contending that we cannot be absolutely certain about the reality of anything. Thus, when we look at a tree, Locke would say that its basic shape and mass ("extension") are primary qualities that have existence independent of our observations, but that color is a secondary quality, depending for its existence on the perceiving person. Berkeley would deny the distinction and say that all aspects of the tree rely on the subjective perception of the observer, and we can only be sure of its existence by believing in God, the Permanent Perceiver. Hume would argue that we cannot even 100 percent sure about the reality of our perception of the tree—rather, we make our best guesses based on probability estimates.

The Scottish Realist philosophers, most notably Thomas Reid (1710–1792) in the 18th century and Thomas Brown (1778–1820) in the 19th, took issue with the extreme Humean view of reality on the grounds that such an idea simply violates common sense. They believed that humans have an intuitive understanding that a real world truly exists—daily human life would have no foundation otherwise. They also rejected the implication that the mind is little more than a collection of associated ideas

---

[1] The identical wording appears on page 505 of the second edition of Boring's book (Boring, 1950).

based on experience. Instead, the Scots argued that the mind had an independent existence in reality, was active rather than passive, and was composed of various interacting attributes that they called *faculties*. Reid divided these faculties into two broad categories—intellectual and active (Evans, 1984). Intellectual faculties included such things as memory, reasoning, and judgment, whereas active faculties concerned the emotions and the will. Understanding faculties required observation and inductive logic (i.e., a number of similar observations about how people memorize yields a general principle about the faculty of memory), making faculty psychology, in the words of one historian, "the first fully empirical psychology in history" (Albrecht, 1970, p. 36). If the concept of faculty sounds familiar, it is because you encountered it in Chapter 3; the phrenologists borrowed the concept of faculty and used it in their localization theory.

The Scottish influence in early American psychology arrived in the form of a wave of Scottish immigration in the 18th century. Many of the immigrants were educated—doctors, teachers, and ministers—and many played a role in the explosive growth of higher education in the United States in the years between the American Revolution and the Civil War. In the 140 years between the founding of Harvard in 1636 and the American Revolution of 1776, 9 colleges had been created; by the start of the Civil War in 1861, 85 years later, students could choose from 182 colleges. Faculty psychology dominated the curriculum of most of them.

American Psychology's First Textbook   Thomas Upham (1799–1872) of Bowdoin College in Maine is usually credited with authoring the first American psychology textbook when he organized his lecture notes and published them in 1827 as *Elements of Intellectual Philosophy*. The text eventually grew to three volumes and was given the broader title of *Elements of Mental Philosophy*. It quickly became the principal text in American colleges and universities for courses that today would be called introductory psychology (Evans, 1984). The book was organized along the lines of the Scottish faculty approach, although it included a healthy dose of associationism as well. It also made references to the deity, and morality was a recurring theme. This is hardly surprising, given the fact that prior to the Civil War, most professors at American colleges (including Upham) were Protestant ministers. As will be seen shortly, the postwar rise of universities like Johns Hopkins, with its emphasis on the German model of research, created a need for a new type of textbook.

Upham organized his book into three main divisions: the intellect (cognition), the sensibilities (emotion), and the will (action). This "trilogy of mind" (Hilgard, 1980) was not unique to Upham, but represented a theme that can be traced back to the Greeks and ahead to the present day. For Upham, the mind that he described in his book was an active one, and the book had a distinctly functional tone to it, emphasizing the purposes and uses of the various faculties (Fuchs, 2000). The topics covered were similar to those found in today's introductory psychology texts: The section on intellect included the topics of sensation, perception, association, and memory; the section on the sensibilities included instincts and the positive (e.g., love) and negative (e.g., anger) emotions; and the section on will described a wide range of behaviors.

Upham's text was a best seller on campuses well into the 1870s. By the end of the century, however, American psychology had changed dramatically, reflecting the midcentury influences identified by Boring: German psychology and British biology. The American system of higher education changed as well.

The Modern University

The steady growth of colleges prior to the Civil War was nothing compared with the revolution in higher education that occurred between the war and the start of the 20th century. During this time, the modern university was created, the result of a complex interplay of forces. One factor was the emergence of the public high school and the heightened expectation that education was a key to success. An increase in high school graduates in turn meant a greater number of students eligible to attend college, and attend they did. There were an estimated 67,000 students attending college in 1870, 157,000 in 1890, and 335,000 in 1910 (Hofstadter & Hardy, 1952). This expanding college student population produced a need for teachers with advanced degrees, thereby creating a demand for graduate education. Many students, as we have seen, went to Germany, where they encountered the *Wissenschaft* philosophy you learned about in Chapter 4. The decade of the 1880s was the high point for Americans studying in Germany, however. By the 1890s, several good American universities were available, and some of the second-level German universities were developing the reputation of being diploma mills (Veysey, 1965).

The modern American university began to develop shortly after the end of the Civil War. One major catalyst was the Morrill Land Grant Act of 1862, which gave every state a minimum of 30,000 acres of federal land. If the state built a university on the land within 5 years, it could keep the land; otherwise it reverted to the government. This produced the great state universities, run by laypeople rather than clergy, and emphasizing science and practical applications (e.g., applying science to improve agriculture and mining). Also during this time, several of the Ivy League schools developed graduate training: Yale in 1860 and Harvard in 1872, for instance. Another impetus was a consequence of the accumulation of great wealth by a handful of business tycoons in the second half of the 19th century. Several of them donated large amounts of money to found universities, motivated partly by a philanthropic desire to give something back to society, partly to blunt criticism of the exploitive manner in which they became wealthy, and partly to have their names associated with an enterprise that was universally valued. Four of the better-known schools created in this way were Johns Hopkins University (1876), Clark University (1887), Stanford University (1891), and the University of Chicago (1891). All but the last, which was created with Rockefeller money, was named for its major benefactor.

Johns Hopkins University in Baltimore became the prototype of the new university in America. It was explicitly modeled on the German example that emphasized research and the creation of new knowledge and, although it had a small undergraduate division from the start, its main focus was on graduate education. Endowed with $3.5 million by its founder, wealthy Baltimore merchant Johns Hopkins, it quickly became the most important American university of the 1880s, the only legitimate competitor to the German universities (Hawkins, 1960). Its innovative president, Daniel Coit Gilman, attracted good students by creating the competitive "university fellowship," which included a $500 stipend plus free tuition. He also encouraged the development of laboratory training and promoted use of the seminar to supplement the traditional lecture course. Gilman recognized the growing need to train educators, and Johns Hopkins became a leader in this area: During the school's first 10 years, 56 of its doctoral graduates were employed as professors in 32 different colleges and universities (Ryan, 1939).

Education for Women and Minorities The growth of opportunity for higher education was not equally available to all Americans; rather, it was mostly limited to middle- and upper-class white males. Women and minority group students faced significant barriers when trying to become educated.

Women in search of an education faced an entrenched set of beliefs about "the women's sphere"— an integrated set of concepts centering on the idea of woman as wife and mother. Nineteenth-century women were socialized to believe that they were created for the purpose of perpetuating the family. This meant getting married, having and raising children, and being content with those roles. Women who wanted to pursue higher education or to have a career were actively discouraged from doing so. For one thing, it was believed that pursuing a degree beyond high school would have adverse medical consequences. One Harvard medical school professor urged women to abandon education after reaching puberty; too much mental activity after that stage could retard the development of their reproductive organs, he warned (Scarborough & Furumoto, 1987). If education could reduce the chances of bearing children, then what would happen to the human species if too many women pursued higher education? And if undergraduate education could have such dangerous effects, education at the graduate level presumably would be even worse for a woman's health. As for pursuing a career, there was a zero-sum choice—it was considered to be out of the question for women to be both married and to have a career. It was one or the other. Furthermore, the unmarried woman, whether or not she had a career of some kind, had another family claim. She, not the brother(s) in the family, was the one expected to care for elderly parents.

In addition to the women's sphere, another impediment was the widespread belief that women were intellectually inferior to men. The belief had deep roots, even reflected in the biblical legend of women's creation—built from a piece of a man (a rib). The belief was maintained in part by the argument that women were intellectually incapacitated every month during menstruation. Evolutionary theory provided additional fuel. You recall from Chapter 5 that one of the cornerstones of Darwin's theory was the idea that individual members of a species differed from each other, and this variability provided the material for natural selection to do its work. Nature "selected" those individuals whose variations had high survival value. It follows that the greater the degree of variability for a particular trait, the better off a species will be. According to what was known as the **variability hypothesis**, men had a greater degree of variability than women on a number of traits, including intelligence. Although this presumably meant a higher proportion of mentally disabled men than women, it also meant that the brightest men would be more intelligent that the brightest women. One implication of the difference at the high end of intelligence was the belief that men were thought to be better suited for higher education and for graduate studies than women.

Despite these daunting barriers to women's education, some opportunities arose in the second half of the 19th century. At the land grant universities, for instance, women were admitted, although they tended to be enrolled in programs of study that "suited" them—home economics, for instance. But they also began to be trained to meet the increasing need for teachers, both at land grant schools and at colleges created for the purpose of teacher training, the so-called normal schools. Ivy League schools such as Harvard and Yale resisted efforts to have women enrolled, but attempted to achieve something of a compromise by creating women's schools affiliated with the men's school. At Harvard, for example, a "Harvard Annex" was created in 1879 and renamed Radcliffe College in 1894. The best opportunities for women to pursue a high-quality college education came with the creation of a new educational phenomenon—elite colleges created just for women. One of the first, Vassar College, was created in 1865 with a gift from Matthew Vassar, a man with ideas well ahead of his time. He endowed the college, he wrote, because "[i]t occurred to [him] that woman, having received from the Creator the same intellectual constitution as man, has the same right as man to intellectual culture and development" (quoted in Brubacher & Rudy, 1976, p. 66). Other women's colleges—Smith in 1871, Wellesley in 1875, and Bryn Mawr in 1885—soon followed, and by 1901, there were 119 of them in the United States (Brubaker & Rudy, 1976). These colleges produced the three important women psychologists highlighted in this chapter, as well as many others.

If educational opportunities for women were limited, they were even worse for minorities, especially African Americans in the wake of the Civil War. The slavery era had created a widespread belief among whites of the essential inferiority of blacks. This belief was strong enough to color the interpretation of research that might have suggested otherwise. For example, an early study by Bache (1895) comparing the reaction times of whites, blacks, and Native Americans found that whites had the slowest times. Ignoring the Galtonian idea that reaction time was assumed to be related to mental quickness and therefore to intelligence, the author concluded that the results provided evidence for the mental superiority of whites because it showed that whites, a "higher" human form, could be characterized as "reflective," whereas the swifter reactions of the more "primitive" blacks and Native Americans showed an immature and intellectually backward impulsiveness. Similarly, in a study comparing 500 white children with a like number of black children, Stetson (1897) found no differences in their ability to memorize poetry. Rather than drawing the reasonable conclusion that the groups were similar in this type of cognitive skill, Stetson decided that his study simply showed that memorization was useless as a test of intelligence. In short, strongly held prejudices rendered some scientists immune to data that might have called their beliefs into question.

One consequence of the prejudice against African Americans was inferior education and reduced opportunities for higher education. On the assumption that education would put ridiculous ideas like "freedom" into their heads, black slaves in the South were barred from formal education by "black codes" in the pre–Civil War years. After the war, conditions improved only marginally. Blacks were segregated into schools that were supposedly separate, but equal, and higher education was limited mostly to whites. Colleges and universities designed for African Americans began to be created in the second half of the 19th century, however, mainly in the South. By 1940, there were more than 100 such schools. They focused on training teachers, who usually returned to their communities to teach in the segregated schools there (Guthrie, 1976).

Psychology, especially as it applied to education, was typically part of the curriculum in the black colleges, but few of these schools offered a concentration in psychology. A 1936 survey on psychology at black colleges by Herman Canady, a psychologist at West Virginia's black college (West Virginia State College at Institute, WV), found that only 14 of the 50 schools he surveyed had psychology departments. Of those 14, only 4 offered majors in psychology (data from Guthrie, 1976, p. 105). Very few laboratory courses were offered, and aside from introductory psychology, the most popular courses were educational, child, social, and adolescent psychology. Thus, few black students had the background necessary to pursue graduate degrees in psychology. Those who did faced further obstacles. They were denied admission to graduate programs in the South, and although a handful of graduate programs in the North were more accommodating (Clark University, for instance), few African Americans could afford to travel that far from home.

For the African American who did manage to persevere and earn an advanced degree, the prospects for employment following graduate school were not good. About the only opportunity for a black psychologist with an advanced degree was to return to a black college to teach, where conditions typically included a heavy teaching load, minimal salary, no benefits, and poor research facilities, if any (Guthrie, 1976). Nonetheless, many bright young African Americans took this path, significantly enhancing the educations of countless black college students.

The best known of these pioneers was Francis Sumner (1895–1954). Sumner received most of his education at home—his father distrusted the quality of Virginia's segregated schools. In 1911, the 16-year-old Sumner was accepted "by examination" into Pennsylvania's Lincoln University, which had been founded in 1854 as the country's first black college. He earned a bachelor's degree in 1915, then a second bachelor's from Clark College in Massachusetts, the undergraduate counterpart of Clark University (both located in the same building on the Worcester campus). He then returned to Lincoln to teach psychology and German, while also completing the requirements for a master's degree. Sumner returned to Clark (University this time) in 1917 to study "race psychology" with G. Stanley Hall, financed by a university fellowship and strong moral support from Hall (Hicks & Ridley, 1979). Although Hall held stereotypical views about racial differences in intelligence, he welcomed "exceptionally talented" blacks at Clark. Sumner's doctorate came in 1920; he was the first African American to complete a PhD in psychology. His dissertation was a critical interpretation of Freudian and Adlerian psychoanalysis, which Hall praised by writing that Sumner had "shown unusual facility in mastering and even pointing out the limitations and defects of the great authorities in the field" (quoted in Guthrie, 1976, p. 182).

Like other black scholars, Sumner found his opportunities limited to teaching at black colleges, and he spent time at Wilberforce College in Ohio and West Virginia State College before finding his way to Howard University in Washington, DC, in 1928. Sumner remained at Howard as psychology department chair until his untimely death (heart attack while shoveling snow) in the winter of 1954. At Howard he established the country's leading psychology department at a black institution, offering both bachelor's and master's degrees in psychology. An indication of Howard's importance, and by extension Sumner's influence, is that of the 300 African Americans who held doctorates in 1975, 60 had earned their bachelor's and/or master's degrees at Howard (Bayton, 1975).

Two of those who earned both a bachelor's and a master's degree from Howard were Kenneth and Mamie Phipps Clark (Figure 6.1). As a research team, they played a role in what was perhaps the most important Supreme Court decision of the 20th century—the *Brown v. Board of Education* decision in 1954. In that 7–0 decision, the court ruled that "in the field of public education the doctrine of 'separate but equal' has no place. Separate educational facilities are inherently unequal" (quoted in Morison, 1965, p. 1086). Contributing to the decision was research showing that segregation in schools had adverse effects on minority children, and a key study was one by the Clarks, known as the

Library of Congress Prints and Photographs Division, New York World-Telegram and the Sun Newspaper Photograph Collection

FIGURE 6.1 Kenneth and Mamie Phipps Clark, coauthors of the famous "doll study" that documented the adverse effects of segregation on the self-esteem of black children.

"doll study" (Clark & Clark, 1947). Shown dolls with light- or dark-colored skin, black and white children were asked a series of questions (e.g., "Show me the doll that looks bad," quoted in Phillips, 2000, p. 147). The Clarks found that African-American children showed a preference for the white dolls and tended to consider the black dolls "bad." In some cases, the children even thought they looked more like the white dolls than the black ones. In a slightly different procedure, children were given dolls and crayons and told to color in the dolls. Black children consistently colored the skins of the dolls lighter than their own (Herman, 1995). The Clarks concluded that one insidious effect of segregation was that the self-esteem of black children suffered. And if childhood shapes the adult, these effects would have lasting effects.

After earning a doctorate in 1943, Mamie Clark took a position at the Riverdale Home for Children, providing psychological services for homeless black children. In 1946, she established and became the executive director for the Northside Center for Child Development in Harlem. The center provided counseling and therapy for the youth of Harlem and their families and was a model of an interdisciplinary team approach to treatment—Clark's staff included "psychiatrists, psychologists, social workers, case workers, teachers, and consulting pediatricians" (Lal, 2002, p. 25). During this same time, Kenneth joined the faculty of City College of New York and began a distinguished academic career that culminated in his election to the presidency of the American Psychological Association in 1971. He was the first, and so far the only, African American to hold the office.

WILLIAM JAMES (1842–1910): THE FIRST OF THE "NEW" PSYCHOLOGISTS IN AMERICA

The explosive growth of higher education at the end of the 19th century, accompanied by a willingness to experiment with new ideas, teaching methods, and the curriculum itself, made the new universities fertile ground for the creation of novel approaches to old problems. This was advantageous for psychology, which was undergoing a change from traditional faculty psychology to the new laboratory psychology. A major agent of this change was a troubled young man from a talented and wealthy Boston family.

William James did not establish a "school" of thought in psychology, produced no meaningful experimental research, and did not leave behind a dedicated group of students to "carry on his work." Indeed, near the end of his life, he insisted on being referred to as a philosopher rather than as a psychologist. When delivering an invited address in Princeton in 1896, for instance, he was adamant about not being introduced as a psychologist. In the closing pages of *Psychology: The Briefer Course* (James, 1892), a condensed version of his monumental *Principles of Psychology*, James made it clear that in his opinion at least, psychology had a way to go before it could claim the status of a genuine science—it was "no science, it is only the hope of a science" (p. 468). And when he was just finishing the briefer version of the *Principles*, he expressed his disenchantment with psychology in a letter to his former student Mary Calkins, writing that he was "sick of the association of ideas and all things connected with psychology" (James, 1891).

On the other hand, it is quite clear that James was crucial to the development of modern psychology in the United States and that his role was recognized not just by historians but also by his contemporaries. When James McKeen Cattell (Chapter 7) asked psychologists to rank their peers for eminence in 1903, James was ranked first. In fact, he was ranked first on *every* return (Hothersall, 1995). His peers also elected him to the presidency of the American Psychological Association twice

(1894 and 1904). Later, when second-generation psychologists wrote chapters for the series *A History of Psychology in Autobiography*, at least a dozen explicitly mentioned James and/or his *Principles* as the main reason for their initial interest in psychology (King, 1992). Today, James's star continues to shine brightly. Several biographies have appeared (e.g., Croce, 1995; Lewis, 1991; Richardson, 2007; Simon, 1998), and the 1990s saw the publication of two edited books celebrating the centennial of the *Principles* (Donnelly, 1992; Johnson & Henley, 1990). In a 1991 poll of historians, he ranked second (just behind Wundt) on a list of the most important contributors to psychology (Korn, Davis, & Davis, 1991). Who was this person who did not want to be called a psychologist, yet is high on everyone's list of "most important psychologists of all time"?

The Formative Years

William James was raised in an unusual family. His father, Henry James, Sr., had sufficient income from an inheritance to avoid working,[2] and he devoted himself to controlling the education and moral development of his five children, all born within 6 years of each other in the 1840s. In addition to William, the oldest, there was Henry, Jr., the celebrated American novelist, two younger brothers, and a sister, Alice, the intellectual equal of her brothers, but unable to develop her creativity into a professional career because of prevailing beliefs about the proper role for women (the women's sphere described earlier in this chapter). Henry James, Sr., who had been raised by a domineering father, was determined to raise his own children in a more liberal fashion, allowing them to study whatever they wanted whenever they wanted to, taking them to Europe frequently to expand their horizons, and caring little about their formal education. His primary expectation was that his children learn foreign languages, believing that "[t]o learn a language was not to enforce particular points of view, but to gain access to another realm of culture and thought; to be fluent was to see the world from another perspective" (Croce, 1995, pp. 43–44). Young William did not attend school formally before the age of 10 and attended only sporadically through adolescence. He made three trips to Europe before the age of 21 though, spending at least a year there each time. By age 18, he knew the essentials of Latin, had a reading knowledge of German, and was fluent in French. He would later add Greek and Italian to the list.

As he neared the end of adolescence, however, one other fact characterized William James—he had no idea about what to do with his life. He had a strong interest in art and some talent for it (Figure 6.2 is a self-portrait), but after a brief stint under the tutelage of the American artist William Morris Hunt, he realized that he would not achieve greatness (Simon, 1998). Despite abandoning a career in art, however, James never lost interest in it, and in some ways he remained an artist in temperament for the rest of his life (Leary, 1992).

A Life at Harvard

In the fall of 1861, James, then 19, enrolled in the Lawrence Scientific School of Harvard University, much to the delight of his father. Although his philosophy of child rearing prevented him from forcing careers on his children, Henry Sr. had always hoped that his oldest son would become a "scientist."[3]

---

[2]Henry's father lived the stereotypical American success story, an Irish immigrant who rose from store clerk to business tycoon, one of the wealthiest men in 19th-century America (Croce, 1995).

[3]He was also pleased that his son was able to avoid the Civil War, which began that same year. Henry, Jr., the novelist, also avoided the war, but the two younger brothers both fought for the North and one was severely wounded in the attack on Fort Wagner, near Charleston, South Carolina (the battle was dramatized in the 1990 film *Glory*).

published numerous articles based on it during the 1880s, and Holt began advertising it in 1881 (King, 1992). Shortly after its publication, James agreed to write a smaller version (referred to earlier in the letter to Calkins), which appeared in 1892 as *Psychology: The Briefer Course*.

In the *Principle's* opening sentence, James (1890/1950) defined psychology as "the Science of Mental Life, both of its phenomena and their conditions" (v1, p. 1). These phenomena of mental life included "such things as we call feelings, desires, cognitions, reasonings, decisions, and the like" (p. 1). By "their conditions" he was referring to the physiological processes that accompany these phenomena, as well as the social, personal, and environmental circumstances in which they occur.

On Methodology James was an eclectic, willing to include in his book the results of research using any methodological approach that could shed light on mental life. He was quite clear about what he believed to be the primary means of studying mental life, however: "Introspective Observation is what we have to rely on first and foremost and always" (James, 1890/1950, v1, p. 185). By **introspection** he meant careful self-observation, an examination and reflection on the states of consciousness that characterize one's mental life. He recognized the difficulties with the method—it was open to bias, one person's introspections could not be verified by a second person, and because it is impossible to experience a mental process and introspect to it at the same time, all introspection relies on memory. Nonetheless, he believed that careful self-reflection was essential to gain insight into the workings of the human mind. One consequence of this belief was that the book was reviewed harshly by psychologists enamored of the new laboratory approach that had emerged from Leipzig. Thus, Wundt thought it was more like literature than science, and G. Stanley Hall (discussed later), after writing that one's overall reaction to the book must be "gratitude and admiration" (Hall, 1890–1891, p. 578), criticized what he viewed as its "inconsistencies and incoherencies" (p. 589) and referred to James as an "*impressionist in psychology*" (p. 585, emphasis in the original).

James did not ignore the new experimental methods. He gave a thorough description of reaction time methodology, for example, and he referred to the results of psychophysics research in numerous places. Nonetheless, his personal dislike of the tedium of laboratory work led him to declare that the German psychophysics and reaction time research "taxes patience to the utmost, and could hardly have arisen in a country whose natives could be *bored*" (James, 1890/1950, v1, p. 192, emphasis in the original). He later created a phrase that came to sum up this laboratory approach, with its emphasis on precise laboratory apparatus often constructed using brass, when he referred to it sarcastically as a **brass instrument psychology**.

In addition to introspective and experimental methods, James listed the "comparative method" as a third approach. This involved learning about mental life by comparing normal human consciousness with that of "bees and ants, … savages, infants, madmen, idiots, the deaf and blind, criminals, and eccentrics" (James, 1890/1950, v1, p. 194) and included the use of data derived from the kinds of questionnaires pioneered by Darwin and Galton. Although James recognized the value of this kind of information, he disliked the tediousness of the survey, suspecting that the next generation of psychologists might rank these questionnaires "among the common pests of life" (p. 194).

Consciousness The chapter on **consciousness** shows James at his most eloquent. It is a key chapter, one in which James made it clear that he opposed any analytic approach that presumed to understand consciousness by reducing it to its elements. That strategy characterized "structuralism," which you will learn about in the next chapter, but it also formed the basis for the reaction time and lingering at the edges of his psyche for several years. He was completing a medical degree, but had no desire to actually practice medicine. He was trained in science, but hated the details. And as a reflective person, he was disturbed by the overwhelming determinism and materialism of the science that he was learning. If all life reduces to physical matter moving through space according to predictable laws, then what happens to free will? If freedom of choice is an illusion, then what is the basis for personal responsibility and morality? James was driven to the point of despair (Croce, 1995).

Salvation (temporary—he continued to suffer periodic bouts of depression throughout his life) came when James read an essay by the French philosopher Charles Renouvier. In an often-quoted diary entry from April 1870, James noted that his life had reached a crisis point when he encountered an essay by Renouvier and "saw no reason why [Renouvier's] definition of free will—the sustaining of thought *because I choose to* when I might have other thoughts—need be the definition of an illusion. At any rate I will assume for the present … that it is no illusion. My first act of free will shall be to believe in free will" (quoted in Simon, 1998, p. 126, emphasis in the citation). James later wrote to Renouvier, expressing his gratitude: "Thanks to you I have for the first time an intelligible and reasonable conception of freedom" (quoted in Richardson, 2007, p. 145).

The insight from Renouvier enabled James to continue studying physiology and psychology without being worn down by the materialist implications. Free will might be an illusion, but by choosing to believe in it, the concept became *useful* for him, enabling him to continue his scientific work without despair. This "pragmatic" approach to the concept of free will, in which the truth-value of the idea was a consequence of its functional value or usefulness, would become a cornerstone of James's philosophical position of **pragmatism** and a reason why he is considered a forerunner of those American psychologists who came to be known as functionalists.

In 1873, James accepted an offer from Charles Eliot, his old chemistry professor and now Harvard's president, to teach a course in physiology. Two years later, he taught his first psychology course, a class on the relationship between physiology and psychology. By incorporating the latest research from Germany, it differed radically from the typical mental philosophy course based on faculty psychology, thus inaugurating a new approach to the teaching of psychology in America. To help students understand some of the research he was describing, he set up some apparatus in a small room, thus creating in 1875 what would eventually become Harvard's laboratory of experimental psychology.[4] James remained at Harvard until his retirement in 1907. He died 3 years later of heart disease, 2 days after a return from one final trip to Europe.

Creating American Psychology's Most Famous Textbook

In July of 1878, a 36-year-old William James married Alice Howe Gibbens, a 29-year-old teacher at Miss Sanger's School for Girls in Boston. Alice would become a stabilizing force in William's life, with a mind sharp enough to make her an intellectual colleague. Indeed, on their honeymoon in New York's Adirondacks, she helped him begin writing his masterpiece, *The Principles of Psychology* (Lewis, 1991). A month before the wedding, James had signed a contract with an aggressive young Bostonian publisher named Henry Holt for a "manual" of psychology. Holt wanted the completed manuscript from James within a year, but the book took on a life of its own, eventually requiring 12 years before it finally appeared in 1890. It was encyclopedic, encompassing two volumes totaling nearly 1,400 pages. It was an immediate best seller, in part because the academic public knew what was coming—James

---

[4]This event has led some to argue that James created psychology's first laboratory, beating Wundt by 4 years. The lab was no more than a demonstrational adjunct to his lectures, however—Wundt's laboratory produced original research.

published numerous articles based on it during the 1880s, and Holt began advertising it in 1881 (King, 1992). Shortly after its publication, James agreed to write a smaller version (referred to earlier in the letter to Calkins), which appeared in 1892 as *Psychology: The Briefer Course*.

In the *Principle's* opening sentence, James (1890/1950) defined psychology as "the Science of Mental Life, both of its phenomena and their conditions" (v1, p. 1). These phenomena of mental life included "such things as we call feelings, desires, cognitions, reasonings, decisions, and the like" (p. 1). By "their conditions" he was referring to the physiological processes that accompany these phenomena, as well as the social, personal, and environmental circumstances in which they occur.

On Methodology James was an eclectic, willing to include in his book the results of research using any methodological approach that could shed light on mental life. He was quite clear about what he believed to be the primary means of studying mental life, however: "Introspective Observation is what we have to rely on first and foremost and always" (James, 1890/1950, v1, p. 185). By **introspection** he meant careful self-observation, an examination and reflection on the states of consciousness that characterize one's mental life. He recognized the difficulties with the method—it was open to bias, one person's introspections could not be verified by a second person, and because it is impossible to experience a mental process and introspect to it at the same time, all introspection relies on memory. Nonetheless, he believed that careful self-reflection was essential to gain insight into the workings of the human mind. One consequence of this belief was that the book was reviewed harshly by psychologists enamored of the new laboratory approach that had emerged from Leipzig. Thus, Wundt thought it was more like literature than science, and G. Stanley Hall (discussed later), after writing that one's overall reaction to the book must be "gratitude and admiration" (Hall, 1890–1891, p. 578), criticized what he viewed as its "inconsistencies and incoherencies" (p. 589) and referred to James as an "*impressionist in psychology*" (p. 585, emphasis in the original).

James did not ignore the new experimental methods. He gave a thorough description of reaction time methodology, for example, and he referred to the results of psychophysics research in numerous places. Nonetheless, his personal dislike of the tedium of laboratory work led him to declare that the German psychophysics and reaction time research "taxes patience to the utmost, and could hardly have arisen in a country whose natives could be *bored*" (James, 1890/1950, v1, p. 192, emphasis in the original). He later created a phrase that came to sum up this laboratory approach, with its emphasis on precise laboratory apparatus often constructed using brass, when he referred to it sarcastically as a **brass instrument psychology**.

In addition to introspective and experimental methods, James listed the "comparative method" as a third approach. This involved learning about mental life by comparing normal human consciousness with that of "bees and ants, … savages, infants, madmen, idiots, the deaf and blind, criminals, and eccentrics" (James, 1890/1950, v1, p. 194) and included the use of data derived from the kinds of questionnaires pioneered by Darwin and Galton. Although James recognized the value of this kind of information, he disliked the tediousness of the survey, suspecting that the next generation of psychologists might rank these questionnaires "among the common pests of life" (p. 194).

Consciousness The chapter on **consciousness** shows James at his most eloquent. It is a key chapter, one in which James made it clear that he opposed any analytic approach that presumed to understand consciousness by reducing it to its elements. That strategy characterized "structuralism," which you will learn about in the next chapter, but it also formed the basis for the reaction time and

(1894 and 1904). Later, when second-generation psychologists wrote chapters for the series *A History of Psychology in Autobiography*, at least a dozen explicitly mentioned James and/or his *Principles* as the main reason for their initial interest in psychology (King, 1992). Today, James's star continues to shine brightly. Several biographies have appeared (e.g., Croce, 1995; Lewis, 1991; Richardson, 2007; Simon, 1998), and the 1990s saw the publication of two edited books celebrating the centennial of the *Principles* (Donnelly, 1992; Johnson & Henley, 1990). In a 1991 poll of historians, he ranked second (just behind Wundt) on a list of the most important contributors to psychology (Korn, Davis, & Davis, 1991). Who was this person who did not want to be called a psychologist, yet is high on everyone's list of "most important psychologists of all time"?

The Formative Years

William James was raised in an unusual family. His father, Henry James, Sr., had sufficient income from an inheritance to avoid working,[2] and he devoted himself to controlling the education and moral development of his five children, all born within 6 years of each other in the 1840s. In addition to William, the oldest, there was Henry, Jr., the celebrated American novelist, two younger brothers, and a sister, Alice, the intellectual equal of her brothers, but unable to develop her creativity into a professional career because of prevailing beliefs about the proper role for women (the women's sphere described earlier in this chapter). Henry James, Sr., who had been raised by a domineering father, was determined to raise his own children in a more liberal fashion, allowing them to study whatever they wanted whenever they wanted to, taking them to Europe frequently to expand their horizons, and caring little about their formal education. His primary expectation was that his children learn foreign languages, believing that "[t]o learn a language was not to enforce particular points of view, but to gain access to another realm of culture and thought; to be fluent was to see the world from another perspective" (Croce, 1995, pp. 43–44). Young William did not attend school formally before the age of 10 and attended only sporadically through adolescence. He made three trips to Europe before the age of 21 though, spending at least a year there each time. By age 18, he knew the essentials of Latin, had a reading knowledge of German, and was fluent in French. He would later add Greek and Italian to the list.

As he neared the end of adolescence, however, one other fact characterized William James—he had no idea about what to do with his life. He had a strong interest in art and some talent for it (Figure 6.2 is a self-portrait), but after a brief stint under the tutelage of the American artist William Morris Hunt, he realized that he would not achieve greatness (Simon, 1998). Despite abandoning a career in art, however, James never lost interest in it, and in some ways he remained an artist in temperament for the rest of his life (Leary, 1992).

A Life at Harvard

In the fall of 1861, James, then 19, enrolled in the Lawrence Scientific School of Harvard University, much to the delight of his father. Although his philosophy of child rearing prevented him from forcing careers on his children, Henry Sr. had always hoped that his oldest son would become a "scientist."[3]

[2]Henry's father lived the stereotypical American success story, an Irish immigrant who rose from store clerk to business tycoon, one of the wealthiest men in 19th-century America (Croce, 1995).

[3]He was also pleased that his son was able to avoid the Civil War, which began that same year. Henry, Jr., the novelist, also avoided the war, but the two younger brothers both fought for the North and one was severely wounded in the attack on Fort Wagner, near Charleston, South Carolina (the battle was dramatized in the 1990 film *Glory*).

By permission of the Houghton Library, Harvard University

FIGURE 6.2 Self-portrait sketch of William James, completed in the early 1860s.

At Lawrence, William first studied chemistry with Charles Eliot, soon to be one of Harvard's most innovative presidents. He quickly learned to hate the subject, especially what he viewed as the tedium and obsession with detail that characterized laboratory work. It was an attitude that would later lead him to disparage much of the laboratory work of the new experimental psychology (Bjork, 1983).

After abandoning chemistry, James sampled several of the other sciences. One of his biology professors there was the famed Swiss naturalist Louis Agassiz, the acknowledged expert on the formation of glaciers, and a fervent believer in a close relationship between science and religion (Irmscher, 2013). A strong believer in the use of science to confirm religious truths, Agassiz was an advocate of the argument by design and an anti-Darwinian who believed that all species were created separately by God. James, of course, was a student during the height of the debates about Darwin's theory, which had been published in 1859. Although awed by Agassiz, James eventually became a firm Darwinian and realized that history would judge his professor to be on the wrong side of the argument over evolution. Accompanying Agassiz on a collecting expedition to the Amazon in 1865, James traveled 2,000 miles up the river (and 2,000 back), much of the journey in small boats and canoes. Agassiz was hoping to discover markedly different species of fish in different parts of the river, which he thought would support an argument from design. (Instead, although he refused to acknowledge it, he found similarities in species that would comfort a Darwinian). For James the trip was exhilarating, but he found the precise details of collecting and categorizing fish as much fun as chem lab. So he would not become a professional naturalist; as he wrote to his brother, "When I get home I'm going to study philosophy all my days" (quoted in Simon, 1998, p. 93).

In 1864, James enrolled in the Harvard Medical School, completing his medical training in 1869, but not before taking another trip to Europe, where he looked into the new experimental physiology that had been developing in Germany. His trip included stops at Heidelberg, where he met Helmholtz and learned of Wundt, and Berlin, where he attended lectures by the noted physiologist Emil du Bois Reymond. The experience was educational, but it also deepened a profound depression that had been psychophysics research imported from Germany, and it was an integral part of most British empiricist/associationist thinking. James believed that trying to identify the individual elements of consciousness, and then seeing how they could be constructed to form "mind," was a meaningless, artificial exercise. In one of psychology's more frequently quoted passages, he argued that consciousness is not a set of interconnected units:

> Consciousness, then, does not appear to itself chopped up in bits. Such words as "chain" or "train" do not describe it fitly.... It is nothing jointed; it flows. A "river" or a "stream" are the metaphors by which it is most naturally described. *In talking of it hereafter, let us call it the stream of thought, of consciousness, or of subjective life.* (James, 1890/1950, v1, p. 239, emphasis in the original)

The chapter in which this quote appears is titled "The Stream of Thought," and it is the first of several dealing with the nature of consciousness. Using an artistic metaphor, James told the reader that the chapter was introductory, with more detail to follow, describing it as being "like a painter's first charcoal sketch upon his canvas" (James, 1890/1950, v1, p. 225). His preliminary sketch described consciousness as personal, constantly changing, continuous while we're awake, selective in what it attends to, and active. Elaborating on this last attribute, James used an example that provides a compelling description of what later became known as the "tip-of-the-tongue" phenomenon (Brown & McNeill, 1966):

> Suppose we try to recall a forgotten name. The state of our consciousness is peculiar. There is a gap therein; but no mere gap. It is a gap that is intensely active. A sort of wraith of the name is in it, beckoning us in a given direction, making us at moments tingle with the sense of our closeness, and then letting us sink back without the longed-for term. If wrong names are proposed to us, this singularly definite gap acts immediately so as to negate them. They do not fit into its mold. (James, 1890/1950, v1, p. 251)

One final point about consciousness shows how James was affected by Darwinian thinking. In addition to describing the features of consciousness, he was interested in understanding the *function* of consciousness. How did it enable us to adapt to our environment? What was its survival value? For James, the answer was that consciousness served individuals by enabling them to adapt quickly to new environments, to learn new things, and to solve new problems that present themselves. Furthermore, in keeping with James's belief in free will, he argued that consciousness serves the function of selection—it enables us to choose one course of action over another (Richardson, 2007). Those making the best, most functional choices, adapt most efficiently to the environment.

Habit Habits also had an adaptive function, according to James. Because they occurred more or less automatically, they enabled the consciousness to focus attention on other, more important (i.e., survival-related) problems. On a broader scale, habits serve as:

> the enormous flywheel of society, its most precious conservative agent.... It alone prevents the hardest and most repulsive walks of life from being deserted by those brought up to tread therein. It keeps the fisherman ... at sea through the winter; it holds the miner in his darkness, and nails the countryman to his log-cabin and his lonely farm through all the months of snow.... It dooms us all to fight out the battle of life upon the lines of our nurture or our early choice. (James, 1890/1950, v1, p. 121)

In his typical pragmatic fashion, James also had some advice on forming good habits. The first was motivational, an admonition to "launch ourselves with as strong and decided an initiative as possible" (James, 1890/1950, v1, p. 123). For instance, he recommended making a public pledge about the habit to be developed. Second, we must not allow for any lapses to occur: "Never suffer an exception to occur till the new habit is securely rooted in your life" (p. 123). Third, he urged readers to arrange their lives to increase the opportunities to act on the new habit; mere good intentions are not sufficient.

Emotion James's theory about emotion is the idea most likely to be familiar to modern students. He acknowledged borrowing the theory from a Dutch physiologist, Carl Lange, and today it is known as the **James–Lange theory of emotion**. It appears in the emotion chapter of every modern introductory psychology text. James criticized contemporary thinking about emotion, which described emotions as following the sequence: perception of some emotion-arousing event (e.g., see a bear) → subjective experience of the emotion (e.g., fear) → bodily reaction (e.g., trembling, heart pounding, running away). James reversed the sequence, as he described it in one of psychology's most famous passages:

> Our natural way of thinking about … emotions is that the mental perception of some fact excites the mental affection called the emotion, and that this latter state of mind gives rise to the bodily expression. My theory, on the contrary, is that *the bodily changes follow directly the perception of the exciting fact, and that our feeling of the same changes as they occur IS the emotion.* Common-sense says, we lose our fortune, are sorry and weep, we meet a bear, are frightened and run; we are insulted by a rival, are angry and strike. The hypothesis here to be defended says that this order of sequence is incorrect, that the one mental state is not immediately induced by the other, that the bodily manifestations must first be interposed between, and that the more rational statement is that we feel sorry because we cry, angry because we strike, afraid because we tremble, and not that we cry, strike, or tremble because we are sorry, angry, or fearful, as the case may be. (James, 1892/1961, pp. 242–243, emphasis in the original)

James's argument was that the bodily changes that are the emotions are felt immediately upon the perception of an emotion-arousing stimulus, prior to the awareness of a cognitively recognizable emotion: Our heart pounds before we feel fearful. He also argued that we recognize different emotions because each one is associated with a unique pattern of bodily action. Thus, for James–Lange to work, each emotion must have its own unique pattern of bodily reaction and be recognized as such. We now know that although there are some physiological differences between emotions, most strong emotions are accompanied by similar patterns of physiological arousal in the autonomic nervous system. Of course, there was no way for James to be aware of the flaw, given the state of knowledge about the physiology of emotion in the 1890s.

As always, James was pragmatic. In the case of emotions, practical application was a natural consequence of his theory. If the emotion is, in essence, the physiological arousal, then a corollary is that if we could deliberately bring about the "bodily changes" associated with an emotion, we would experience the emotion. As he put it,

> There is no more valuable precept in moral education than this: … if we wish to conquer undesirable emotional tendencies in ourselves, we must assiduously, and in the first instance cold-bloodedly, go through the *outward movements* of those contrary dispositions which we prefer to cultivate. The reward of persistency will infallibly come, in the fading out of the sullenness or depression, and the advent of real cheerfulness and kindliness in the stead. Smooth the brow, brighten the eye, contract the dorsal rather than the ventral aspect of the frame, and speak in a major key, pass the genial compliment, and your heart must be frigid indeed if it do not gradually thaw. (James, 1892/1961, pp. 249–250, emphasis in the original)

The idea that forcing emotions to occur by deliberately producing specific bodily reactions has been supported by 20th-century research. For instance, people whose facial muscles have been arranged to match certain emotions will experience those emotions, at least to a degree (e.g., Izard, 1977).

James's Later Years

After completing the *Principles* in 1890 and the abridged version in 1892, James began to turn away from psychology and toward philosophy. In 1892, he convinced the research psychologist Hugo Münsterberg (Chapter 8) to emigrate from Germany to America and run the Harvard psychology lab, thereby separating James from the tedium of laboratory work. Although he continued to be involved in the APA and was elected its president in 1894 and 1902, James also supported the formation of the American Philosophical Association shortly after the turn of the century, and his publications after 1900 were mainly devoted to philosophy (e.g., *Pragmatism* in 1907) and religion (e.g., *Varieties of Religious Experience* in 1902).

Spiritualism In addition to the shift from psychology to philosophy during his final two decades, James also became fascinated with **spiritualism**, a popular movement in the late 19th century. Spiritualists believed that consciousness survived death and that those who died could be contacted by mediums, who in turn could convey messages from the dead to the living. Mediums were also said to be able to predict the future and to know details of people's lives through telepathic means. The movement began at midcentury, but gained momentum after the Civil War—the war's appalling death toll dramatically increased the number of people desiring to contact deceased relatives and acquaintances.[5] Furthermore, spiritualism was fueled by 19th-century technological advances such as the wireless telegraph. If living people could communicate over great distances via some mysterious invisible process, and if there was life after death, then why not a communication channel from the dead to the living (Coon, 1992)? Of course, not everyone was enthralled. The tough-minded British scientist Thomas Huxley (Darwin's "bulldog"—see Chapter 5) sarcastically commented that it would be "better to live a crossing-sweeper than to die and be made to talk twaddle by a medium hired at a guinea a séance" (quoted in Blum, 2006, p. 44).

The more open-minded James became seriously interested in spiritualism in the 1880s, after discovering the Society for Psychical Research while on a trip to London (Benjamin, 1993). He helped establish a similar organization in the United States and became a promoter of research into the phenomenon. He believed that psychologists, with their expertise in the powers of the mind and their training in scientific methodology, would be ideally suited for such investigations. And reflecting his pragmatic philosophy, in which the value of something is a consequence of its usefulness, he insisted on keeping an open mind about psychic phenomena—they might prove to be beneficial if they could be shown to be valid.

Starting in 1885, James began an extended study of Mrs. Leonore Piper, a popular Boston medium. Although most mediums, even in the 19th century, were easily shown to be frauds on careful investigation, James (and others) could find no trickery in Mrs. Piper's séances, writing that "knowledge appears which she has never gained by the ordinary waking use of her eyes and ears and wits. What the source of this knowledge may be, I know not, and have not the glimmer of

---

[5]To convince survivors of the possibility of communication with dead loved ones, the spiritualist newspaper *Banner of Life* often carried stories that were *supposedly* (the names did not appear on military lists) from dead soldiers giving "first-hand" accounts their deaths (Faust, 2008).

an explanatory suggestion to make" (cited in Lewis, 1991, p. 494). On the other hand, James was somewhat skeptical about some of the messages received by Mrs. Piper during seances. If the dead were truly communicating, surely they would have some rather important things to say—they might be expected to describe the afterlife for example. Instead, they tended to communicate inconsequential bits of information. In a letter to a colleague, James questioned Mrs. Piper's ability to reach the dead, pointing to the "extreme triviality of most of the communications. What real spirit, at last able to revisit his wife on this earth, [wouldn't] find something better to say than that she had changed the place of his photograph?" (quoted in Benjamin, 1993, p. 83). Furthermore, Mrs. Piper's spirit-control (the intermediary between her and the dead spirits) was supposed to be a French doctor, yet he was unable to respond when James asked questions in French (Murphy & Ballou, 1960).

James was not rewarded for open-mindedness by his scientific peers. Psychology was trying to establish its identity as a legitimate scientific discipline at the time, and it was embarrassing for one of its stars to be attending séances and publicly expressing interest in a medium (Coon, 1992). In a letter to James published in his journal *Science*, for example, James McKeen Cattell wrote that the "Society for Psychical Research is doing much to injure psychology" (quoted in Benjamin, 1993, p. 88); concerning James, Cattell pointed out that the psychological community "all acknowledge his leadership, but we cannot follow him into quagmires" (p. 88). Always independent, James was unmoved by the criticism, and in turn accused his critics of narrow and unscientific prejudgment. He continued to be fascinated by psychic phenomena for all of his remaining years.

Summing Up William James

In his lifetime, William James experienced the vast changes that characterized late 19th-century America. In his youth, America was an agricultural society, the western frontier was east of the Rocky Mountains, the possibility that Americans would kill each other in a Civil War was unthinkable, and higher education was limited mainly to the undergraduate college, which was aimed primarily at the training of ministers. In his last decade, America had entered the 20th century an industrialized power, the western frontier had been declared closed, the trauma of the Civil War was becoming a memory, and higher education, which now included universities devoted to graduate studies, was producing professionals and PhDs in a variety of disciplines.

Psychology in America also changed significantly during this time, from mental philosophy to an independent discipline with aspirations to be a science. Despite his reservations about the new psychology, William James was a prime mover in bringing about its emergence. Trained in physiology, he saw how advances in that field could make a new laboratory psychology possible. At heart an artist and philosopher, he could see the problems inherent in a purely scientific attack on the human mind. His monumental *Principles of Psychology* stands at the transition point, artfully blending physiology, philosophy, and the new laboratory psychology. James was the acknowledged leader of the first generation of American psychologists, but he was not alone.

G. STANLEY HALL (1844–1924): PROFESSIONALIZING THE NEW PSYCHOLOGY

G. Stanley Hall had none of William James's reluctance about psychology. Rather, he was a vigorous promoter of the new field and, more than any other American psychologist, responsible for its evolving identity as a distinct academic discipline. Like Wundt did in Germany, Hall professionalized psychology in the United States by founding laboratories and journals. In addition, he institutionalized psychology's professional status by creating the American Psychological Association. As a psychologist, Hall was a man of diverse interests, careening from one enthusiasm to another throughout his career, and aptly described by his biographer as a self-assured "prophet" for his zeal in promoting new ideas (Ross, 1972). He could be characterized as either creative and visionary or unsystematic and capricious. On the one hand, he pioneered the child study movement and the study of adolescence and aging, he demonstrated the importance of psychology to education, and he introduced Freud and psychoanalysis to America. On the other hand, a consequence of his catholicity of interests was a failure to contribute a substantial body of knowledge to any one of them. He also alienated his peers, including James, and some questioned his work. In a letter to Clark University librarian L. N. Wilson in 1906, for instance, this is what Cornell's E. B. Titchener (Chapter 7) thought of Hall's ability to prepare graduate students:

> You probably have no idea of the sort of contempt in which Hall's methods and the men trained solely by him are in general held in psychology, whether here or on the continent. Whenever his questionary papers get reviewed, they get slightingly reviewed.... He has made no impression on the men of scientific training. (Titchener, 1906)

You will discover in the next chapter that Titchener had a rather narrow concept of what scientific training should be like; the criticism might be overstated, but it was not far from the mark.

If there was a common thread and guiding principle to Hall's various interests, it was evolution. In his autobiography, Hall (1923, p. 357) wrote that "[a]s soon as I first heard it in my youth I think I must have been almost hypnotized by the word 'evolution,' which was music to my ear." Most of his work can be classified under the heading of **genetic psychology**, which in his day meant the study of the evolution and development of the human mind, and included comparative, abnormal, and especially developmental psychology.

Hall's Early Life and Education

Hall was born on a farm in western Massachusetts in 1844 and educated at nearby Williams College, graduating in 1867, and then enrolling in New York's Union Theological Seminary. New York was daunting for someone from rural Massachusetts, but Hall took advantage of the cultural, educational, and social opportunities available to him. After a year at Union, he was able to borrow enough money to go to Europe, and there he stayed until 1871, studying theology and philosophy, but also encountering scientific physiology. He then returned to New York and finished his education at Union. He was just going through the motions, however, and felt stifled by religious orthodoxy.[6] So the ministry was out—Hall wanted to teach philosophy.

While teaching for a few years at Antioch College in Ohio, Hall encountered Wundt's *Principles of Physiological Psychology* and resolved to return to Germany to study this new laboratory psychology. First, however, he moved to Cambridge to study at Harvard, feeding himself by teaching English composition to Harvard sophomores. He took courses with William James and completed a doctoral thesis on "the muscular perception of space" in 1878. It was primarily a philosophical piece, but it also included some experimental work in perception, completed in the physiology laboratory of H. P. Bowditch. Harvard had just begun offering the doctorate in philosophy, and Hall was the first person to

---

[6]Hall probably embellished the story he told about how Union's president reacted to Hall's trial sermon, supposedly the culmination of one's theological development at Union. According to Hall (1923), rather than critique the sermon, the president simply knelt on the floor and prayed for Hall's soul.

complete one. Because the topic was in the area that would eventually become known as experimental psychology, Hall's doctorate is sometimes considered to be the first one in psychology.

Doctorate in hand, Hall returned to Germany and found himself in Leipzig in 1879, the "official" year of the founding of Wundt's laboratory. He later claimed to be Wundt's first American student, but he actually had very little contact with Wundt, completed no publishable research, and was in fact preceded by at least one other American (Benjamin, Durkin, Link, Vestal, & Accord, 1992). Hall was disappointed with his experience in Leipzig and was later critical of Wundt, writing to James that he considered Wundt's experiments "utterly unreliable and defective in method" (quoted in Ross, 1972, p. 85). After Leipzig, Hall went to Berlin to study briefly with Helmholtz. While there, Hall became reacquainted with a young woman he knew from his days at Antioch, who was in Berlin to study art. They were married in Germany.

The Halls returned to Boston in the fall of 1880. Hall was 36 years old, highly educated, and devoted to his new bride. He was also unemployed. Yet within 10 years, he would be a university president and one of the acknowledged leaders of psychology in America. His big break was an invitation from President Eliot of Harvard to lecture on education. Hall had already given considerable thought to how psychology might contribute to the educational reform that was occurring in the late 19th century. His lectures, given on Saturday mornings so that local teachers could attend, were highly successful. The publicity caught the attention of President Gilman of Johns Hopkins, eventually leading to Hall's being asked to give a similar series of talks in Baltimore in January of 1882. Their success led to a job as part-time lecturer in philosophy. In 1884, Hall was hired as a professor at Hopkins at the generous (for the time) annual salary of $4,000 (Ross, 1972). At age 40, then, Hall had his first full-time job.

From Johns Hopkins to Clark

Hall did not stay long at Johns Hopkins, but while he was there, he significantly advanced the cause of psychology in America. In 1883, when still a part-time instructor, he created the first laboratory of experimental psychology in America and, with the help of talented students such as Cattell and John Dewey (Chapter 7), he began to produce experimental research. In 1887, he founded the *American Journal of Psychology*, the first journal for the new psychology published in the United States, designed expressly "to record the psychological work of a scientific, as distinct from a speculative character [and to] record the progress of scientific psychology" (Hall, 1887, pp. 3–4). It served partly as a mechanism for publishing original research from Hall's lab and elsewhere, but it also included summaries and reviews of the psychological literature and sections devoted to "Notes and News" about psychology and psychologists. Journal finances were aided by a $500 donation from an advocate of spiritualism, who apparently thought the journal would be devoted to "psychic" research. This was an understandable confusion—the terms "psychic" and "psychological" were used interchangeably in those days. Hall did not correct the donor's misperception and took his money. Over the years, articles on spiritualism occasionally appeared in the journal, but only to ridicule the scientific basis for it. Hall, for example, argued that what passed for telepathy, clairvoyance, and the like, was nothing more than magic tricks and other forms of deception (Ross, 1972). As you might guess, Hall received no additional funds from his original benefactor.

In the late 1880s, an economic slowdown created financial difficulties for Hopkins (Hawkins, 1960). Facing dwindling resources, Hall began to look for greener pastures and found them in Worcester, Massachusetts. Jonas Clark, a merchant made wealthy by selling supplies at inflated prices to prospectors during the California gold rush, had decided to buy respectability in his hometown by opening a college to educate its youth. Hall seemed the perfect choice for President—ambitious, knowledgeable about higher education, and with a record of accomplishment in his brief time at Johns Hopkins—and

Clark hired him in April of 1888. Clark wished to create a school for the youth of Worcester, but Hall had a grander vision, and managed to convince Clark that the school should offer graduate education, in the mold of Johns Hopkins, and that the focus should be on science. An undergraduate division could be added later. Thus, when Clark University opened its doors in the fall of 1889, it offered graduate training in five areas: psychology, biology, chemistry, physics, and mathematics. There were 18 faculty members and 34 graduate students in the initial group and almost all of the instruction took place by means of directed research—the teaching load was just two lectures each week (Ross, 1972).

For 3 years, Clark University approached Hall's vision of a true university. Faculty produced cutting-edge research, students came from as far away as Japan to join an elite group of scholars, and Hall developed an international reputation as a visionary leader in education. All was not well, however. At the end of the first year, Hall suffered a personal tragedy when his wife and 8-year-old daughter died in an accident. In the second year, faculty began to hear about new opportunities and larger salaries being offered at another new university being created in Chicago with Rockefeller money. And throughout these early years, Hall was constantly at odds with his faculty. Things came to a head in 1892, when a combination of financial problems, faculty unrest, and the lure of the University of Chicago almost closed the university. Approximately two thirds of the faculty and grad students left Clark that year, leaving psychology as the only viable graduate department (Koelsch, 1972).

Psychology at Clark

Psychology survived after the fiasco of 1892 in part because Hall was deeply involved in the work of the department and in part due to the loyalty of its two faculty members, Edmund Sanford (1859–1924) and William Burnham (1855–1941).

Both had been students of Hall at Johns Hopkins. In Clark's department of "psychology and pedagogy," Burnham was in charge of educational psychology and Sanford was in charge of the research laboratory. Hall was clearly the leader of the department, however, and dictated its general direction. He also directed the doctoral dissertations of most of the students, and his Monday evening seminars became legendary among Clark alumni. Held in the parlor of his home, they began at 7:30 and often lasted 3 hours. Students would make presentations, other students would contribute, and then Hall would have the final word:

> [F]or a half-hour or longer, depending on the importance he attached to the theme, he presented from his armchair in the central archway a masterly critique of the research just reported and added to it new illumination from fresh angles that sometimes left the [students] gasping....
>
> After the intellectually provocative evening was ended, many of the graduate students set off for their boarding-places but found themselves so moved by the galvanism of their emotions that only a long walk near midnight and a warm bath before retiring could relax them enough to permit them to sleep. (Averill, 1982, p. 342)

Implied in this quote is that Hall possessed an impressive awareness of the psychological literature of the day. Indeed, his knowledge was encyclopedic, based on a rigorous system he developed of voraciously reading everything available (in several languages), and then summarizing the material in a set of bound notebooks. As early as 1900, long before the end of his career, he had accumulated 30 of these notebooks (Leary, 2006).

During the early 1890s, the laboratory at Clark was a state-of-the-art facility, in part because when Hall left Johns Hopkins, he took most of the research equipment with him. Hall was also generous with expenditures in the early years, giving Sanford all he needed to equip the lab; the abundance of costly "brass instrument" technology is evident from Figure 6.3*a*. Figure 6.3*b* provides an inside look at the

(a) *(b)*

Courtesy of Clark University Archives

FIGURE 6.3 The Clark Lab in 1892: (a) "brass instruments," including timing devices and reaction time apparatus; (b) a voice reaction time study.

experimental psychology of the day—it illustrates a research project (voice reaction time) in action. Sanford gave students considerable leeway in the Clark laboratory; in addition, Hall was constantly suggesting ideas to students. Hence, although the experimental research from Clark was haphazard and scattered, it reflected the wide range of topics that interested American psychologists in the 1890s.

In the mid-1890s, as part of his deep interest in evolution, Hall began supporting research in comparative psychology. One consequence was the creation of the first studies using what would become a standard piece of laboratory equipment—the maze. For details on the origins of the venerable rats-in-mazes tradition, read this chapter's Close-Up.

CLOSE-UP

CREATING MAZE LEARNING

Ask psychologists to name famous pieces of apparatus in experimental psychology, and mazes will be at or near the top of the list. The maze reached its peak of popularity from about 1920 to 1950, especially in the research of behaviorists Edward Tolman and Clark Hull (Chapter 11), but the apparatus remains in use today. Hundreds of maze studies have been completed over the years, and one might ask how it all started. Credit is sometimes given to the British naturalist John Lubbock, who used crude Y-shaped mazes in the 1870s to study how ants followed scent trails, or to E. L. Thorndike (Chapter 7), who observed chicks escaping from simple mazes created by placing books on end. The research that launched the study of rats-in-mazes, however, was completed by Willard Small of Clark University at the turn of the 20th century.

Small arrived in Worcester in 1897 as a 27-year-old graduate student and was soon doing animal research with another student, Linus Kline. Kline completed the first general study of the abilities of rats (Dewsbury, 1984) and one of his interests concerned the rats' "home-finding" capacities. He discussed the problem with the lab's director, Sanford, who gave him the idea for a maze study and suggested a specific maze design. As Kline later told the story:

> I ... described to [Sanford] runways which I had observed several years ago made by large feral rats to their nests under the porch of an old cabin on my father's farm in Virginia. These runways were from three to six inches below the surface of the ground and when exposed during excavation

presented a veritable maze. Sanford at once suggested the possibility of using the pattern of the Hampton Court maze for purposes of constructing a "home-finding" apparatus. (Miles, 1930, p. 331)

One can only speculate about why the Hampton maze occurred to Sanford. That it was on his mind is clear from Kline's comment that "the readiness with which he directed my attention to the Hampton maze is presumptive evidence that he had thought of its use before" (Miles, 1930, p. 331). One possibility is that Sanford may have been in the Hampton Court maze himself just prior to the conversation with Kline. He was on sabbatical in the spring of 1898 and visited a number of laboratories in Europe (Goodwin, 1987). His last stop was in England, and it is at least conceivable that he visited Hampton Court, a favorite tourist stop, which is just 10 miles outside of London and includes England's most famous hedge maze.

It is not clear why Small did the first maze study and not Kline. Kline reported that other work prevented him from pursuing the idea, and it was perhaps natural for his friend and laboratory coworker to take up the project. At any rate, in January of 1899, Small constructed three 6 x 8 foot mazes with wire mesh walls, using the Hampton Court design but adjusting it to a rectangular pattern, as shown in Figure 6.4. He then began his historic research on the manner in which rats learn mazes.

Sanford reported on Small's study at the December 1899 APA meeting, and Small published a more detailed report in 1901. Modern accounts, perhaps inspired by Thorndike's rather caustic review (Thorndike, 1900), usually dismiss Small's description of the maze studies as a series of overly anthropomorphic comments about such things as the rat's alleged "disgust" over reaching a dead end. The criticism has some merit, but Small's report also gives a trial-and-error description of maze learning similar to other contemporary accounts by Thorndike (Chapter 7) and Lloyd Morgan (Chapter 5). Small also commented extensively on what he believed to be the mental processes involved, and he used blind rats to investigate the effects of sensory capacity on learning. These blind rats seemed to learn the maze as well as their sighted peers, leading Small to conclude that "tactile motor sensations furnish the essential data for the recognition and discrimination involved in forming the special associations" (Small, 1901, p. 237).

Small's work is less important for its conclusions than for the fact that it initiated a flood of similar research. In the next few years, versions of the Hampton Court maze were used by comparative psychologists to study species ranging from rhesus monkeys (Kinnaman, 1902) to English sparrows (Porter, 1904). With the white rat, research followed up on Small's ideas about the influence of the various senses on learning. The most famous of these were the studies by Watson and Carr at the

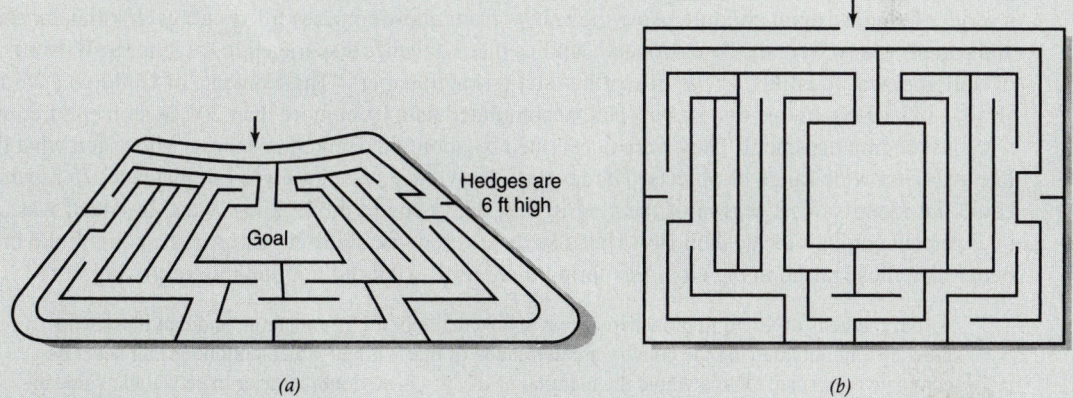

(a) (b)

FIGURE 6.4   (a) Design of England's Hampton Court maze; (b) Small's readjustment of the Hampton Court maze design to a rectangular configuration. Drawn by Dr. C. James Goodwin.

University of Chicago (described in Chapter 10); they concluded, like Small, that the kinesthetic sense was most critical. Subsequent research, and there were dozens of such studies completed by 1920, showed the process to be much more complicated, but it is worth noting that the animal maze literature began by investigating the sensory and mental processes involved in maze learning and by investigating how organisms adapted to their environment. These, of course, were topics clearly in tune with the psychology of the early 1900s, which was the psychology of mental life and reflected the pervasiveness of evolutionary theory.

In his remaining years at Clark University, Hall left his stamp on psychology in several ways. First, he continued to professionalize psychology by creating its first formal organization, the American Psychological Association (APA). He and about a dozen other psychologists held an organizational meeting in his study in July of 1892, at which time 31 charter members were named (Sokal, 1992); Hall was elected the association's first president. Eighteen of the charter members convened in December 1892, at the University of Pennsylvania, for the APA's first annual meeting. The organization grew rapidly: 74 members after 4 years and 127 by the turn of the century (Ross, 1972). It adopted a constitution in 1894, making clear its role in creating disciplinary identity for a scientific psychology. The purpose of the organization was to be "the advancement of Psychology as a science. Those are eligible for membership who are engaged in this work" (Cattell, 1895, p. 150). The APA also enhanced psychology's professional and scientific status by affiliating with older, more recognized associations, such as the American Association for the Advancement of Science (Camfield, 1973).

Hall and Developmental Psychology   In addition to activities connected with the journal and the APA, Hall contributed to American psychology by advancing his brand of genetic psychology. He was a pioneer in developmental psychology, promoting the child study movement, writing the first textbook on adolescent psychology, and near the end of his career, writing a book on aging. He also continued to champion the importance of psychology for education, in part by founding a second journal, *Pedagogical Seminary* (now the *Journal of Genetic Psychology*) in 1891.

Hall first became interested in child study while at Johns Hopkins, where he published the first in a series of studies about children using the results from questionnaires filled out by children, teachers, and parents (these were the "questionary" studies that Titchener disparaged in his letter to Wilson). His overall goal was identified in the title of his first research paper: "The Contents of Children's Minds" (Hall, 1883/1948). In this first survey, Hall accumulated data from more than 200 Boston children who were just beginning school. They were questioned by about 60 different teachers, who asked what they knew about a wide range of objects. The level of knowledge was not high. For instance, 75.5 percent could not identify what season of the year it was, 87.5 percent didn't know what an island was, and 90.5 percent couldn't locate their ribs. Hall also discovered that children reared in the country did much better than those raised in the city. As a farm boy himself, Hall did not find this surprising:

> As our methods of teaching grow natural we realize that city life is unnatural, and that those who grow up without knowing the country are defrauded of that without which childhood can never be complete or normal. On the whole the material of the city is no doubt inferior in pedagogic value to country experience. A few days in the country at this age has raised the level of many a city child's intelligence more than a term or two of school training could do without it. (Hall, 1883/1948, pp. 261–262)

This quote contains strong hints of Hall's philosophy of education. He ridiculed rote memorization and the rigid discipline of the classroom. Instead, he favored a more permissive approach that took for granted the child's "natural" curiosity about the world and encouraged what would be called "active learning" today—giving children problems to solve or activities to complete that would have some specific pedagogical value. His approach to education was profoundly influenced by his devotion to evolution. In his many talks to teachers, for instance, he urged as a strategy "one that would understand that the child's mind was a less evolved version of the mind of man, and would therefore emphasize mental development more than mental discipline" (Zenderland, 1988, p. 153).

Hall was not only interested in children. Some of his questionnaire studies collected data from teenagers, and he reported the results, along with everything else then known about that age group, in his encyclopedic two-volume *Adolescence* (1904). It was the first book devoted to the study of teenagers, and Hall is the person most responsible for identifying adolescence as a distinct stage of development. The description of adolescence as a period of "storm and stress," now generally recognized as overstating the case, has its origins in Hall's book. The book also contains the most thorough description of Hall's use of the theory of **recapitulation**. The theory originated with the German evolutionary biologist Ernst Haeckel, who proposed that an organism's stages of development, from cell to a fully formed individual, can be seen as a recapitulation of the evolution of the species. Thus, at one stage of development, the human fetus resembles a fish, reflecting that point in evolutionary history where the human species had aquatic ancestors. Hall and others extended the idea beyond biological development, into the area of psychological development, arguing the psychological development of the individual reflected evolutionary history (Arnett & Cravens, 2006). For example, Hall believed that the high level of recklessness and impulsiveness found in adolescence reflected a time in evolutionary history when humans were less "civilized" than they were in more modern times.

Hall has been criticized for his reliance on recapitulation theory, and some have dismissed the adolescence book on the grounds that it is tied to a failed theory. Yet Leary (2006) argued that such criticism is unfair to Hall and shows a lack of understanding of historical context. According to Leary, although recapitulation was under attack in the early 20th century, the scientific community did not wholly abandon it until 1930. Also, Hall was cautious in his use of recapitulation, relying on it merely as a general framework. He was also aware of and open to criticism of the theory—one of the scientists he invited to the 1909 anniversary celebration at Clark (below) was August Weismann, recapitulation's fiercest critic (Weismann declined the invitation). The key point is that recapitulation theory had the beneficial effect of stimulating Hall's interest in *all* stages of development, for testing the implications of recapitulation demands close attention to development across the life span (Youniss, 2006).

Toward the end of his life, Hall became interested in the middle and final stages of life, eventually writing about aging in *Senescence: The Last Half of Life* (1922). He once again relied on questionnaire data, asking the elderly their opinions about such topics as their fear of death and their ability to recognize the signs of aging. He also criticized the lack of retirement pension programs and recommended that the elderly organize politically (long before the advent of today's AARP).

Hall and Psychoanalysis   A significant portion of Hall's *Adolescence* concerned sexual behavior, including an entire 50-page chapter entitled "Adolescent Love." Hall also offered a course at Clark entitled "The Psychology of Sex" (Rosenzweig, 1992). Consistent with his ideas on education, he believed that the natural expression of sexual behavior should not be inhibited. This attitude raised eyebrows among his peers, leading one of them to wonder: "Is there no turning Hall away from this d___d sexual rut? I really think it is a bad thing morally and intellectually to harp so much on the sexual string, unless one is a neurologist" (letter from F. Angell to E. B. Titchener on March 19, 1990, quoted in Ross, 1972, p. 385).

FIGURE 6.5 Psychologists at the 1909 Clark Conference.

Hall's preoccupation with sex, combined with an interest in abnormal behavior, led him to become fascinated by Freud's theories. In 1909, to celebrate the university's 20th anniversary, Hall organized the Clark Conference; its centerpiece was a series of five talks given by none other than Freud himself.[7] Accompanied by his younger colleague Carl Jung, who lectured on his new word association technique, Freud made his first and only visit to America and delivered five lectures that were published in the *American Journal of Psychology* in 1910, and then separately in book form. The American psychologists in attendance had mixed reactions to Freud. William James, for example, was open to Freud's new ideas, writing to a colleague that Freud's ideas "can't fail to throw light on human nature" (James, 1920, p. 328). On the other hand, he was skeptical about Freud's dream theory and in the same letter wrote that Freud seemed to be "a man obsessed with fixed ideas" (p. 328). Nonetheless, a grateful Freud later said that the Clark Conference was an important point in the history of psychoanalysis, constituting the first international recognition of his theories. Figure 6.5 shows one of psychology's most famous pictures. In the front row, Hall is sixth from the left, Freud seventh, and Jung eighth; Ernest Jones, Freud's biographer, is in the second row, between Hall and Freud. Also in the front row, Titchener (Chapter 7) is second from the left and James is third; Cattell (Chapter 7) is just over the left shoulder of James. Halls' Clark colleagues Sanford and Burnham are also in the photo; Sanford is behind and just to the right of Jones, and Burnham is over Jung's left shoulder.

Hall retired from the presidency of Clark in 1920, but remained active in his remaining years of life. He published his book on aging in 1922 and an autobiography, *Life and Confessions of a Psychologist*, a year later (Hall, 1923). In 1924, he was elected to a second term as president of the APA, only the second person ever to be elected twice (William James was the other). He died before he could assume his duties, however.

---

[7]Hall originally hoped for an all-star cast of international psychologists, including not just Freud, but Wundt, Binet, and Ebbinghaus. Wundt and Binet declined to come, however, and although Ebbinghaus accepted the invitation, he died just before the conference began (Evans & Koelsch, 1985).

Before leaving Hall and Clark University, consider the following archival material from the Walter Miles papers. We have seen that animal maze learning had its origins at Clark. In a 1930 paper, Miles documented this maze history, in part by writing to the main characters and asking for their firsthand accounts. In the Chapter 1 discussion of archival research, you learned that archival collections are often incomplete, and this maze episode is an example. Despite the massive amount of information in the Miles papers, Miles apparently did throw some things away—the valuable letters on maze history from Small, Kline, and others are missing from the collection. What is there, however, is an interesting letter from E. G. Boring.

FROM THE MILES PAPERS...

MILES AND THE INVENTION OF THE STYLUS MAZE

While learning about the history of rats in mazes, Miles also became interested in the history of maze learning studies involving humans, in particular studies using so-called stylus mazes. These were typically rectangular pieces of wood or metal, about the size of a modern laptop, with the maze design imprinted in the form of a pattern of grooves. Blindfolded subjects moved a stylus (small rod about the size of a pencil) through the grooves, trying to navigate the maze successfully.

While a graduate student at Cornell, Boring spent the summer of 1912 at a mental hospital in Washington, DC, using mazes to study patients suffering from dementia praecox (today's term—schizophrenia). Miles knew of the study and wondered if perhaps this was when stylus mazes originated. He wrote to Boring asking about it and here is Boring's reply:

Your question about stylus mazes I cannot fully answer. I read over my own remarks and tried to reconstruct my mental state in 1912. It is plain that I had the idea of paper-and-pencil mazes through Franz from Miss Kent . . . . I had been working with animal mazes at Cornell and Lucia and I had built a big human maze that people could run through, and we were all full of the idea that they might do it mostly by kinesthesis. The stylus maze is such a tiny step of synthesis between these two things that I suspect I must have built it as a matter of course without thinking it original. I knew of a human maze at Chicago made by stretched wires, but not of a stylus maze. I believe Carr invented his stylus maze at just about this time. Certainly, if this should turn out to be the first stylus maze in print, it is an interesting case of where priority has little meaning. It would simply be priority and

nothing else. I never developed it, worked it hard, or emphasized the use or significance of it. I am quite clear however now that Franz did not contribute this idea. (Boring, 1928a)

There are several interesting points here. First, Boring makes it clear that to "get credit" for inventing some research method, a person cannot just do a single study. Instead, a program of research must ensue, and Boring was not interested in doing that with mazes. So he did not wish credit for inventing the stylus maze. Second, there is the hint of a *multiple* here—Harvey Carr (Chapter 7) of the University of Chicago created a similar maze at about the same time as Boring. Third, inventions seldom appear fully formed, unrelated to predecessors. In this case, Boring refers to the stylus maze as a reasonable next step from similar type of human maze, one in which a maze is printed on a sheet of paper and a subject uses a pencil to draw a line along the correct path to the goal. Boring was aware of research using these paper-and-pencil mazes being conducted by Grace Kent at the same Washington hospital where he was working in 1912 (also using subjects suffering from dementia praecox). Both Boring and Kent worked at the hospital under the supervision of S. I. Franz, who, as Boring recalled, "did not contribute" to the stylus maze idea.

One final note. Grace Kent was a doctoral student of Franz's at George Washington University, earning her degree there in 1911; her dissertation research was the paper-and-pencil maze study (Kent, 1911). She had a successful career as a clinician, working at several mental hospitals, and she was the coauthor of a well-known psychological test, the Kent Rosanoff Association Test (Kent & Rosanoff, 1910).

MARY WHITON CALKINS (1863–1930): CHALLENGING THE MALE MONOPOLY

Professional women in the early 21st century often face discrimination in the workplace and find themselves unable to rise above the proverbial "glass ceiling." As frustrating as the problem is for modern women, it was many times worse in psychology's early years. As described earlier in the chapter, women were widely believed to be intellectually inferior to men in the 1890s, and they had little standing in society (e.g., they could not vote until 1920). Combining marriage and a career was virtually impossible—marriage was assumed to be their career. Even if they didn't marry, they were expected to care for other members of their family, especially aging parents. Although women began attending college in increasing numbers in the late 19th century, higher education for women was looked on with skepticism by a male-dominated society. Hence, in the 1890s it was almost impossible for a woman to obtain a doctorate in psychology, a dilemma faced by Mary Whiton Calkins.

Calkins's Life and Work

Mary Calkins grew up in Buffalo, New York, the oldest of five children in a close-knit family headed by her Congregationalist minister father. He shared with William James's father a belief in the educational value of travel to Europe and in the importance of being multilingual. In fact, Mary's parents only spoke German in her presence during her first few years; by adulthood, Mary was fluent in English, German, and French (Furumoto, 1979). The Calkins family moved to the Boston area when Mary was 17, and soon after that she entered Smith College in western Massachusetts, one of the new women's colleges. She graduated in 1885 and then went to Europe with her family for 16 months where, among other things, she added Greek to her list of language competencies. Upon her return, she took a position teaching Greek at Wellesley College. Calkins (Figure 6.6) remained at Wellesley for the rest of her career.

Photo by Partridge, courtesy Wellesley College Archives

FIGURE 6.6 Mary Whiton Calkins (1863–1930) as a young instructor at Wellesley College, from Scarborough and Furumoto (1987).

By the late 1880s, Wellesley's leaders decided that to keep up with trends in modern science, the college needed to offer the new laboratory approach to psychology. Calkins had expressed some interest in teaching philosophy and had impressed her superiors in her first few years as a teacher, so she was given the opportunity to develop a course in laboratory psychology. It was understood, however, that she would take a year off to learn about this new field. Thus began her frustrating search for graduate education in psychology.

Graduate Education for Females Calkins quickly learned that opportunities for advanced training were quite limited for women. After considering Europe and a few American schools, she attempted to become a student at Harvard—it had William James to offer, and it was close to home. She also looked into Clark University, 30 miles to the west of Boston. At Harvard, she was grudgingly allowed to attend seminars with James and the philosopher Josiah Royce, both of whom supported her application vigorously, but Harvard officials made it clear that she was merely an unofficial "guest" of the university. It was the same story at Clark. Women were not allowed in officially, but Edmund Sanford welcomed her into his new laboratory. Calkins later credited Sanford, who contributed time, advice, and apparatus, with being the true founder of the psychology laboratory at Wellesley (Calkins, 1930).

Calkins entered Harvard in the fall of 1890 and immediately encountered the educational opportunity of a lifetime. She and four male students were enrolled in Philosophy 20a, Physiological Psychology, with William James, but the males, perhaps unnerved by the presence of a woman, dropped out within a few days. As Calkins (1930) later recalled, "James and I were left … quite literally at either side of a library fire. *The Principles of Psychology* was warm from the press; and my absorbed study of those brilliant, erudite, and provocative volumes, as interpreted by their writer, was my introduction to psychology" (p. 31).

After her year of study, Calkins returned to Wellesley, but her appetite for the new psychology had been whetted, and she was soon looking into further training. In 1892, when William James recruited Hugo Münsterberg (Chapter 8) from Germany to run the Harvard lab, Calkins returned to Cambridge, once more as an unofficial guest. For the next 2 years, Calkins worked in Münsterberg's lab part-time while continuing to teach 10 miles away at Wellesley. In the academic year 1894 to 1895, she took a leave from the college to complete her studies.

Calkins's Research on Association Under Münsterberg's direction, Calkins completed a brilliant series of experimental studies on association, publishing the research in two parts (Calkins, 1894, 1896), then writing an extended account as a *Psychological Review Monograph* paper in 1896. Traditional philosophical and introspective accounts often described how the strength of associations could be influenced by such factors as frequency, recency, vividness, and primacy. In the spirit of Ebbinghaus, Calkins was determined to go beyond "ordinary self-observation" and examine these factors experimentally. The procedure she developed is an important one historically; although she did not use the term, she invented **paired-associate learning**, later to become a standard method in memory research. Her subjects first studied stimulus-response pairs comprised of sequentially presented color patches and numbers (each shown for 4 seconds), then tried to recall the number responses when shown the color stimuli. Calkins manipulated frequency by presenting the same color several times, once with one number, then either two or three times with a second number. Here's how she described series #89:

I. Medium gray, 29; blue, 82; violet, 61 (n); red, 23; violet, 12 (f); peacock, 79; violet, 12 (f); strawberry, 47; violet, 12 (f); light brown, 53; dark gray, 34; light green, 72.

II. Peacock, red, green, violet, medium gray, brown, strawberry, dark gray, blue. (Calkins, 1894, p. 478).

Thus, during presentation (I.), violet was first paired with 61 (referred to by her as the "normal" pairing, or "n"), then three times ("f" = frequency) with the number 12. During recall (II.), violet was the fourth color presented, and the question was whether subjects would recall the number 61 or 12. In like manner, Calkins studied recency by comparing the recall of two numbers paired with the same color, one pairing in the middle of the sequence and one at the very end. Vividness was examined by presenting a critical pair in some way that made it stand out from the other pairs, such as by altering the size of the numbers. Primacy was studied by looking at performance for the first pair in a series. In general, her results showed that recall was enhanced by each of the four factors: frequency, vividness, recency, and primacy. In subsequent trials in which she directly compared these factors by combining them within the same list, Calkins found that frequency was the most critical factor. She also ran some trials in which the colors and numbers were presented together on the same card. This enabled her to compare "simultaneous" associations with the earlier "successive" ones, thus examining the old British Empiricist distinction between simultaneous and successive forms of contiguity. She found no difference.

Calkins (1896) summed up her overall results by emphasizing the importance of frequency, adding a caution that the laboratory results might not be completely "representative of ordinary trains of association" (p. 49). She even included a statement about the practical implications of her findings, referring to frequency as a "corrective influence . . . . The prominence of frequency is of course of grave importance, for it means the possibility of exercising some control over the life of the imagination and of definitely combating harmful or troublesome associations" (p. 49). Calkins was thinking along the same pragmatic lines as her teacher, William James, and her research can be seen as providing some empirical evidence for James's suggestions (discussed earlier) about how to firmly entrench a habit. Practice makes perfect.

Madigan and O'Hara (1992) closely examined Calkins's research on memory, including some studies completed after her dissertation research. They found clear indications that Calkins discovered a number of effects that would later be rediscovered half a century later, when psychologists once again became interested in studying cognitive psychology (Chapter 14). These included such immediate memory phenomena as the primacy, recency, and negative recency effects, the modality effect (stronger recency effect with auditory than with visual presentation), and the effects of interference.

Although it was unofficial, Calkins completed a defense of her thesis and a PhD examination in May of 1895. Münsterberg, James, and other examiners appealed to the Harvard authorities to grant her the PhD, with Münsterberg describing her as "superior . . . to all candidates of the philosophical PhD during the last years" and "surely one of the strongest professors of psychology in the country" (quoted in Scarborough & Furumoto, 1987, pp. 44–45). Harvard refused, though—after all, Calkins was a woman. Later, when Radcliffe College was created as a Harvard-for-women, Calkins was offered a Radcliffe PhD. This time it was Calkins who refused. She would have a doctorate from the school where she earned it or none at all. Although she would earn several honorary degrees, Harvard never did change its mind, and Calkins was never awarded a PhD.

From Psychology to Philosophy After completing her nondoctorate from Harvard, Calkins returned to Wellesley, continued building her lab with Sanford's help, and produced a string of research publications with her students through the turn of the century. In 1898, she turned over the laboratory to Eleanor Gamble, a new PhD from E. B. Titchener's lab at Cornell (one of the few institutions that admitted women doctoral students). From about 1900 on, her publications became less research-oriented as she developed her major theoretical contribution to psychology, **self psychology**. It was a system that clearly showed the influence of her mentor, William James. Calkins argued that psychology could be the study of mental life, as James had said, but that the central fact of psychology must be that all consciousness contains an element of the self (Strunk, 1972).

At a time when strong disagreements were developing over the proper direction for the new psychology, Calkins saw her self psychology as a means of resolving disputes. For example, as will be clear from the next chapter, one conflict was between structuralism, which emphasized analyzing consciousness into its basic elements, and functionalism, which focused on how consciousness served to adapt the individual to the environment. When her peers elected her the fourteenth president of the APA in 1905, the first female so honored, Calkins (1906) delivered a presidential address called "A Reconciliation between Structural and Functional Psychology." In it she argued that both views could be accommodated within a system that recognized the self as the fundamental starting point.

Like James, Mary Calkins gradually shifted her interests over the years from psychology to philosophy. Shortly after her APA presidency, for instance, she wrote *The Persistent Problems of Philosophy* (1907). In 1918, the American Philosophical Association elected her president of their organization, making her the first woman to be elected to the presidency of each of the APAs. Calkins retired from Wellesley in 1929 and died of cancer a year later.

Other Women Pioneers: Untold Lives

Calkins wasn't the only woman struggling against a male-oriented discipline at the turn of the century. In *Untold Lives: The First Generation of American Women Psychologists*, Scarborough and Furumoto (1987) documented the experiences of Calkins and several other pioneering women psychologists. Two of the better known were Christine Ladd-Franklin and Margaret Washburn.

Christine Ladd-Franklin (1847–1930) Like Calkins, Ladd-Franklin was educated at one of the new women's colleges, entering Vassar College in Poughkeepsie, New York, in 1866, a year after it had been founded. There she excelled in science and math and was inspired by the example of the astronomer Maria Mitchell, said to be the most eminent woman scientist in America (Furumoto, 1992). She graduated in 1869, then taught in secondary schools for several years before deciding to pursue graduate education in math at Johns Hopkins. There she encountered the same roadblock that faced Calkins—Hopkins did not admit women as official students. Nonetheless, she was allowed to attend classes and, by 1882, she had completed all the requirements for a doctorate in math. It would be 1926, however, before Johns Hopkins officially awarded her the degree, which she accepted in person, at age 79 (Scarborough & Furumoto, 1987).

While at Johns Hopkins, Christine Ladd met, fell in love with, and married a faculty member in the math department, Fabian Franklin, and became Christine Ladd-Franklin. With her husband's active support, she was able to continue her interests in math, and she published several scholarly papers. In the mid-1880s she became interested in visual perception, a shift that led her to the new psychology. Her first publication, on binocular vision ("A Method for the Experimental Determination of the Horopter"), appeared in 1887 in the inaugural issue of Hall's *American Journal of Psychology*. During her husband's 1891–1892 sabbatical in Europe, she was able to conduct research on vision in the Gottingen lab of G. E. Müller. As you recall from Chapter 4, Müller's lab was one of the best in Germany. She also spent time with Helmholtz in Berlin. It was during this time in Germany that she developed a theory of color vision that was grounded in evolutionary theory; it was influential for several decades.

Of the three pioneer women considered here, Ladd-Franklin was the most outspoken about the lack of professional opportunities for women. For example, she directly challenged the "men only" rule of a group of psychologists known as the Experimentalists (Chapter 7). Organized in 1904 by E. B. Titchener of Cornell, this select group met annually at various labs to discuss their current research. After being refused permission to attend in 1912, she wrote to Titchener that she was "shocked to know that you are still … excluding women from your meeting of experimental psychologists. It is such a very old-fashioned standpoint" (quoted in Furumoto, 1988, p. 107). Two years later her persistence wore Titchener down somewhat, and she presented her work on color vision at one of the Experimentalists' meetings. It was the only time a woman participated in a meeting during Titchener's lifetime.

Ladd-Franklin also vigorously campaigned for a faculty position at a research university, but never managed to obtain more than part-time lectureships, first at Johns Hopkins, then at Columbia when she and her husband moved to New York. Failure to land a university position also meant failure to have access to laboratory facilities; according to Furumoto, this explained why Ladd-Franklin's contributions to psychology were more theoretical than data based. Despite the obstacles, Ladd-Franklin persevered in her work as a mathematician and expert on visual perception, never giving in to the prevailing belief that science was for men only.

Margaret Floy Washburn (1871–1939)

In addition to Ladd-Franklin, Vassar College also produced Margaret Washburn, and then later reclaimed her. Washburn graduated from Vassar in 1890 with her interests divided between science and philosophy. She decided to pursue "the wonderful new science of experimental psychology" (Washburn, 1932, p. 338) because it seemed to combine her interests, so she applied for graduate studies at Columbia University, where she ran into the same problems faced by Calkins and Ladd-Franklin. She was welcomed as a serious student by Cattell, but (sound familiar?) was only permitted to attend his classes unofficially. Cattell saw her potential and encouraged her to apply to Cornell, which accepted women graduate students. There she encountered Titchener, who had just finished his doctorate with Wundt at Leipzig. Women might have been excluded from Titchener's Experimentalists, but they were accepted into his laboratory, and Washburn was Titchener's first PhD student. She became the first woman to earn a doctorate in psychology when she completed the degree in 1894, a study of visual imagery. It was one of the few studies published in Wundt's journal (*Philosophische Studien*) that was not completed at the Leipzig laboratory.

After leaving Cornell, Washburn held several teaching positions and then returned to her alma mater, Vassar, in 1903. She spent her remaining professional career there. Despite the heavy teaching load and inadequate research facilities that invariably accompany faculty life at small colleges, Washburn fashioned a remarkable career that included an APA presidency in 1921, coeditorship of the *American Journal of Psychology* for more than a decade, and election to the prestigious National Academy of Sciences in 1931. When the Experimentalists reorganized after Titchener's death in 1927, she was one of two women elected as a charter member of the new group, and she hosted a meeting of the reconstituted "Society of Experimental Psychologists" at Vassar in 1931 (Goodwin, 2005).

As a psychologist, Washburn published in the areas of perception, imagery, "social consciousness" (empathy and helping behavior) and developed a motor theory of consciousness, but she is best known for her work in comparative psychology. She contributed some original research (e.g., on the perception of color in fish) and summarized the field in a well-known text, *The Animal Mind*. First published in 1908, it went through three more editions (1917, 1926, 1936) and became the standard textbook of its day (Dewsbury, 1992). It was notable for including only the results of experimental research; anecdotal evidence was out. As implied by the title, its focus was on the cognitive processes of perception, attention, and consciousness, as exhibited by the behaviors of various species.

OTHER PIONEERS: LADD AND BALDWIN

James, Hall, and Calkins stand out among the early American psychologists, but of course there were others. Two notables were George Trumbull Ladd and James Mark Baldwin.

George Trumbull Ladd (1842–1921)

Ladd was a transitional figure, bridging the chasm between the mental philosophy of the early and mid-19th century and the modern laboratory-based psychology that took hold toward the end of the century. He was trained for the ministry and worked as a minister before taking a position, in 1879, as professor of psychology at Bowdoin College (where Thomas Upham had written the popular psychology text described earlier in this chapter). Two years later, Ladd was hired at Yale, where he remained for the rest of his career. He was the second person elected president of the APA, after Hall.

Ladd's reputation and his importance for early psychology rest on his work as a textbook writer. His best-known book, *Elements of Physiological Psychology*, appeared in 1887, and it was an immediate hit. It was the first detailed description of Wundtian laboratory psychology in English; hence it provided the introduction to this new psychology for most English-speaking psychologists (Mills, 1974). Titchener, a student at Oxford when the book first appeared, recalled his "excitement on finding this book in the library of the Oxford Union" (Titchener, 1921b), and argued that the book

> helped toward the establishment of laboratories and the recognition of experimental psychology as
> an academic study. Coming, as it did, from a professor of philosophy at Yale who had been a
> Congregational minister, it gave the young science an air of respectability. (p. 600)

Ironically, although he provided a faithful rendition of Wundtian laboratory psychology, full of descriptions of such topics as psychophysics and reaction time, Ladd was never a "laboratory man" himself, preferring a more philosophically based psychology that relied on introspection to study the mind. He never quite outgrew his early training in faculty psychology. In his APA presidential address, Ladd expressed concern over the direction that psychology was taking, that an introspective strategy for understanding the mind was being replaced by experiments with their quantitative measurements. His fears were realized.

The *Elements of Physiological Psychology* went through 10 printings and then was revised in 1911 by Ladd and Robert Woodworth (Chapter 7). During the 1890s, Ladd wrote no fewer than four other psychology textbooks, but by then James's *Principles*, along with its briefer version, was dominating the field. Although uninterested in laboratory work himself, Ladd established a state-of-the-art psychology lab at Yale in 1892 and brought in Edward Scripture (with a newly minted PhD from Wundt's lab in Leipzig) to run it. For the remainder of the 1890s, Scripture produced a steady stream of laboratory research. You might recall from Chapter 1's segment on the Miles papers that Scripture was Miles's academic grandfather. Unfortunately, Ladd and Scripture were equally strong-willed and often at odds over the direction that psychology at Yale should take; the conflict eventually cost both of them their jobs shortly after the turn of the century (Sokal, 1980).

James Mark Baldwin (1861–1934)

Like Ladd, Baldwin made important contributions to the new experimental psychology without being much of a laboratory researcher himself. Despite founding two laboratories and resurrecting another, his publications were primarily theoretical. In the words of E. G. Boring (1950), "while he was one of the 'new' psychologists, his skill was the philosopher's ability in speculative theorizing" (p. 529). Baldwin was among the leaders in American psychology from about 1890 until 1909, when scandal forced him out of academia and, in effect, into exile.

Baldwin earned his PhD in philosophy from Princeton University in 1889 and joined the faculty at the University of Toronto in that same year. The appointment produced some controversy because another candidate for the position was a Canadian, and Toronto newspapers and university alumnae could not understand why an American would be favored over a native son (Green, 2004). Yet Baldwin was hired (to placate Canadian concerns, the other candidate was also hired) and quickly made an impact—shortly after his tenure began, he founded Canada's first psychology laboratory. Four years later he returned to Princeton, founded his second lab, and began his most productive period as a psychologist. He staked a claim as pioneer developmental psychologist by writing *Mental Development in the Child and the Race* (Baldwin, 1895) and *Social and Ethical Interpretations in Mental Development* (Baldwin, 1897). As would be the case for Hall's 1904 book on adolescence, these books by Baldwin were much influenced by evolutionary thinking.

Baldwin's books had little in the way of empirical evidence, being based mostly on his application of evolutionary theory and the observations he made of his two daughters. Contemporary reviews of the books were mixed, and in an obituary for Baldwin, Washburn (1935) noted that the lack of empirical evidence to support his claims about development "accounts for the fact that the name of this brilliant thinker seldom if ever appears in present-day volumes on child psychology" (p. 169). Yet Baldwin's ideas about the origins of cognition influenced the theorizing of the famous Swiss developmental psychologist Jean Piaget (Cairns, 1994). For example, Baldwin used the terms *assimilation* (relating new concepts to already known concepts) and *accommodation* (developing new concepts) to refer to the processes involved in developing new ideas; Piaget used the same terms, and in the same manner. Along with Hall, Baldwin can justifiably be considered a founder of developmental psychology.

In addition to his work in developmental psychology, Baldwin also contributed directly to theories about the process of evolution itself, by proposing what came to be called the **Baldwin effect** (Baldwin, 1896). In essence, Baldwin proposed that a form of general learning ability, especially social learning involving imitation, could be selected for by natural selection processes. Those with high levels of the ability would be selected, allowing for the inheritance of abilities that could allow for the rapid learning of complex processes (e.g., nest building in birds). The Baldwin effect brought social learning processes into an evolutionary model without invoking the Lamarkian idea of the inheritance of acquired characteristics, which had been discredited by the end of the 19th century.

Baldwin also helped to promote psychology as a profession. He was a charter member of the APA and its sixth president in 1897. With Cattell, he founded *Psychological Review* in 1894, a journal that quickly began to compete successfully with Hall's *American Journal of Psychology* and remains today an important journal of theoretical psychology. *Psychological Index*, an important reference source identifying publications in psychology, accompanied the *Review*. Its first issue, listing everything published in psychology for 1894, had 1,312 entries; the *Index* lasted until the 1930s, at which time it was publishing about 6,000 references per year (Benjamin & VandenBos, 2006). It was replaced and improved on (i.e., brief summaries rather than just a reference listing) by *Psychological Abstracts*, the forerunner of today's electronic PsycINFO. In 1904, Baldwin helped launch another journal that continues to be prominent today, *Psychological Bulletin*. And shortly after the turn of the century, with the help of up to 60 different contributors, he began a huge project to create the definitive dictionary of psychology and philosophy. The final product, which appeared in 1901–1902 and was soon referred to as "Baldwin's Dictionary," occupied two volumes and had more than 1,500 entries (Wozniak, 2009). As a measure of Baldwin's eminence, he was ranked fifth on Cattell's 1903 survey of psychology's most prominent persons.[8]

In 1903, Baldwin accepted a new challenge, leaving Princeton for Johns Hopkins University, where he reestablished the laboratory that had been essentially moribund since the departure of Hall (with his suitcase full of laboratory apparatus) in 1888. There Baldwin remained until 1909, when he resigned abruptly, under pressure, after being arrested in a raid on a Baltimore house of prostitution that was just two blocks from his own home. Baldwin claimed it was a misunderstanding, that he had "foolishly yielded to a suggestion … to visit a house of a colored 'social sort' and see what was done there. I did not know before going that immoral women were harbored there" (quoted in Wozniak & Santiago-Blay, 2013, p. 228). Charges against him were dropped, but the embarrassment to him and to the university led to his resignation. His career effectively over, Baldwin spent his remaining years in Mexico and in Europe. Based on a series lectures delivered at the National University in Mexico City, his last substantial publication was a brief history of psychology that appeared in 1913 (Horley, 2001).

IN PERSPECTIVE: THE NEW PSYCHOLOGY AT THE MILLENNIUM

During the last 20 years of the 19th century, psychology in America changed dramatically. Prior to that time it had been dominated by faculty psychology and taught as "mental" philosophy. By the end of the century it was still being taught in philosophy departments for the most part, but it now reflected the influence of the new psychology of Germany and the revolutionary ideas of Charles Darwin. In the early 1880s there were no research laboratories of psychology in the United States, and most American psychologists wishing to study the new laboratory psychology had to travel to Germany. By 1890, laboratories had been established at 9 American universities, and by the end of the century, there were at least 41 (Hilgard, 1987). Although in the early 1890s a German PhD in psychology held higher status than one earned in the United States, this was no longer true by the end of the decade. The shift is reflected in the numbers: Between 1884 and 1892 the number of Americans earning PhDs in America (9) and Germany (8), was about equal, but from 1893 to 1899, 63 American psychologists earned their doctorates in the United States, whereas only 10 earned theirs in Germany (O'Donnell, 1985).

Hall's Clark University was a leader in the production of PhDs in psychology in the 1890s, but other young psychologists were being trained at several other up-and-coming universities. Foremost among them were Cornell, where students would find E. B. Titchener and a school of thought known as structuralism, and Columbia and Chicago, two leading centers of a uniquely American movement that became known as functionalism. The story of these "isms" will occupy the next chapter.

---

[8] As mentioned earlier, James headed the list. Rounding out the "top 10" were, in order, Cattell, Münsterberg, Hall, Baldwin, Titchener, Royce, Ladd, Dewey, and Jastrow.

SUMMARY

Psychology in 19th-Century America

• Prior to the Civil War, psychology in America was taught as mental philosophy. It was taught following the precepts of faculty psychology, which was based on Scottish Realist philosophy. Faculties were separate subcategories of the mind, normally falling into three categories: cognitive, affective (emotional), and behavioral.

• Thomas Upham's *Elements of Intellectual (Mental) Philosophy* is considered to be the first textbook of psychology, and it was organized around the concepts of faculty psychology.

• The post–Civil War period was one of great expansion in higher education. The modern university (e.g., Johns Hopkins), based on the German model that emphasized graduate education and independent research, began during this time.

• Although educational opportunities multiplied for white males in the second half of the 19th century, they were limited for women and minorities. Higher education was believed to harm women and keep them from their traditional roles, but opportunities existed at newly founded women's colleges. Opportunities for minorities were limited by entrenched beliefs about their abilities. Nonetheless, some persevered, including Francis Sumner, the first African American to earn a PhD (in 1920), who developed a highly successful psychology department at Howard University.

William James (1842–1910): The First of the "New" Psychologists in America

• Although he was an artist by temperament, was trained in medicine, and ultimately thought of himself as a philosopher, William James is considered America's first modern psychologist. He brought the new laboratory psychology to Harvard, and he published what is considered the most important book in all of psychology's history, *The Principles of Psychology*, in 1890.

• Disturbed by 19th-century materialism and determinism, James decided to believe in free will because it was a useful belief for him to hold. Out of this emerged his general approach to philosophy, called pragmatism.

• In the *Principles*, James took issue with those who would dissect consciousness into its elements. Instead, he argued that it was more appropriately conceived of as analogous to a stream. Consciousness was personal, constantly changing, continuous, selective, and active, and it served individuals by enabling them to adapt quickly to new environments and solve problems. Habit also had survival value, allowing individuals to avoid having to think about some activities so they could save their consciousness for more difficult and novel problems.

• According to the James–Lange theory of emotions, emotional responses were identified with the bodily reactions that accompanied the perception of some emotion-generating event. When trying to conceive of emotions without the physiological arousal, James argued, nothing remains. A problem with the theory is that it requires a recognizably different pattern of arousal to be associated with each different emotion.

• In his later years, James became interested in the possibility that there could be some validity to spiritualism. Despite criticism that he was harming the fragile scientific status of the new psychology, he believed that spiritualists and mediums should be investigated with an open mind.

G. Stanley Hall (1844–1924): Professionalizing the New Psychology

• Hall is best known for his efforts in professionalizing psychology. He founded the first psychology laboratory in America (at Johns Hopkins in 1883), America's first academic journal (the *American Journal of Psychology* in 1887), and psychology's first professional organization, the American Psychological Association (in 1892).

• As the first president of Clark University, Hall copied the German ideal of graduate education that he first encountered at Johns Hopkins. For several years, Clark was a leader in graduate education in several scientific fields. After 1892, however, only psychology remained as a prominent field of study at Clark.

• Hall was interested in a wide range of topics, which fell under the broad heading of genetic psychology, the study of the origins and development of consciousness and behavior. The importance of evolution was a consistent theme in Hall's work. At Clark, Hall encouraged research in developmental, abnormal, and comparative psychology. Under the direction of Edmund Sanford, Clark's laboratory produced important research throughout the 1890s, including the first maze-learning studies.

• As a developmental psychologist, Hall pioneered the child study movement and is responsible for identifying adolescence as a distinct stage of development. He characterized adolescence as a time of "storm and stress." Later in life he wrote about the developmental changes associated with adulthood and aging. He used the theory of recapitulation (the development of the individual organism is a mirror of the evolution of the species) as an overarching framework for his work.

• Hall's interests in development, sexuality, and abnormality led him to invite Freud to America for Clark's 20th anniversary in 1909. It was Freud's only trip to America, and he believed that the invitation was the first sign that his ideas were developing an international reputation.

Mary Whiton Calkins (1863–1930): Challenging the Male Monopoly

• Mary Calkins was barred from being an official student at Harvard, but nonetheless completed an important dissertation on association, during which she invented a memory procedure still in use, paired associate learning. In her thesis, Calkins investigated frequency, recency, vividness, and primacy as conditions that could strengthen associations and found that frequency was the most important for developing associative strength.

• In 1905, Calkins became the first woman elected president of the American Psychological Association; as her interests shifted to philosophy, she became (in 1918) the first woman elected president of the other APA, the American Philosophical Association.

• Calkins's major theoretical contribution was her self psychology, which was centered on the idea that all consciousness is personal. She used it as a way to reconcile competing theoretical schools of thought (e.g., structuralism and functionalism).

• Two other important women psychologists during this era were Christine Ladd-Franklin and Margaret Washburn. Both faced the exclusionary practices that made it difficult for women to become professional psychologists. Ladd-Franklin was a skilled mathematician and developed an evolutionary theory of color vision. Washburn was best known for her work in comparative psychology.

Other Pioneers: Ladd and Baldwin

• George Trumball Ladd, the second president of APA, was a transitional figure, bridging the gap between the old faculty psychology and the new psychology of the laboratory. He is best known as a textbook writer, and his *Elements of Physiological Psychology,* the first clear summary of Wundtian psychology in English, introduced the English-speaking world to Wundt's ideas.

• James Mark Baldwin founded two laboratories of psychology, resurrected a third, and was active in creating and developing important journals of psychology. He was also a pioneer in developmental psychology, publishing two well-known books on child development in the 1890s; his ideas later influenced Jean Piaget.

STUDY QUESTIONS

1. Describe the Scottish Realists' objection to British Empiricism and what they proposed instead.

2. Describe the barriers that made it difficult for women to obtain higher education, and describe what opportunities were available to them.

3. What were the barriers that made it difficult for African Americans to obtain higher education?

4. Describe the career and accomplishments of Francis Sumner.

5. Describe the "doll study" by the Clarks, and explain its importance.

6. Describe how William James overcame his concerns about materialism and developed a "pragmatic" philosophy.

7. What did James think of the "new psychology"? What did he propose as appropriate methodologies for psychology?

8. According to James, what is the best metaphor for consciousness? What did he believe to be the main functions of (a) consciousness and (b) habit?

9. Briefly state the essence of the James–Lange theory of emotions, using the example of meeting a bear in the woods to illustrate. What was the theory's fatal flaw? How did James use his theory to make some practical suggestions to improve one's life?

10. Why was spiritualism popular in the late 19th century? What was James's opinion about the phenomenon, and why was his view a cause for concern among his peers?

11. What does it mean to say that G. Stanley Hall was a genetic psychologist?

12. Describe Hall's contributions to the professionalization of psychology in America.

13. Describe the importance of maze learning research in psychology's history, and describe its origins.

14. Describe Hall's contributions to the study of human development, throughout the life span, but especially during adolescence.

15. Describe the difficulties encountered by Calkins when she tried to attain graduate training. What training was she able to accomplish?

16. How did Calkins study memory and association, and what did she conclude about the nature of the association process?

17. Describe the accomplishments of (a) Christine Ladd-Franklin and (b) Margaret Washburn.

18. What was Ladd's most important contribution to the new psychology? Why is he sometimes considered a transitional figure?

19. Describe the ways that Baldwin contributed to (a) the professionalization of psychology and (b) developmental psychology.

CHAPTER 7

STRUCTURALISM AND FUNCTIONALISM

The first object of the psychologist … is to ascertain the nature and number of the mental elements. He takes up mental experience, bit by bit, dividing and subdividing, until the division can go no further. When that point is reached, he has found a conscious element.

—E. B. Titchener, 1896

If you adopt as your material for psychological analysis the isolated "moment of consciousness," it is very easy to become so absorbed in determining its constitution as to be rendered somewhat oblivious to its artificial character. The most essential quarrel which the functionalist has with structuralism arises from this fact.

—James R. Angell, 1907

PREVIEW AND CHAPTER OBJECTIVES

This chapter begins with the story of a remarkable Englishman who came to a remote new university in America in 1892 and fashioned a unique but ultimately sterile system of psychology called structuralism. Cornell's E. B. Titchener was trained by Wundt at Leipzig but had his own ideas about the proper definition of scientific psychology. Its main goal was to analyze the adult mind into its structural elements, using a precise form of introspection that required extensive training. For Titchener, psychology was a pure positivist science that was centered in the laboratory; he was not interested in applications. Titchener was a commanding presence in academic psychology's early years in America, but most American psychologists rejected structuralist doctrine. Reflecting the influence of Darwin and traditional Yankee pragmatism, they were more interested in how the mind functioned than in its structure, and they knew that for psychology to succeed in America, it had to be applicable to everyday life. Whereas Titchener believed that the structure of mind had to be clarified before its functions could be studied, most American psychologists disagreed and adopted what came to be called functionalism. Functional psychologists were scattered throughout the academic landscape, but two schools became closely associated with the movement—Chicago and Columbia. The second half of the chapter examines how functionalism "evolved" at these locations through the efforts of James Angell, John Dewey, and Harvey Carr at Chicago, and James McKeen Cattell, Edward L. Thorndike, and Robert Woodworth at Columbia. After you finish this chapter, you should be able to:

- Distinguish between a structuralist and a functionalist approach to psychology
- Describe the general contents and the overall importance of Titchener's Manuals, and the content of a typical "drill course"

- Describe the impact of the Experimentalists and the effect of the group on opportunities for women in experimental psychology
- Explain Titchener's version of introspection and explain how he believed the limitations of introspection could be overcome
- Show how controversies over imageless thought and with Baldwin highlighted the limitations of introspection
- Evaluate the overall contributions of Titchener to experimental psychology
- Describe contributions to functionalist thought made by the Chicago functionalists Dewey, Angell, and Carr
- Describe Cattell's mental testing program and its fate
- Describe Thorndike's puzzle box research and his conclusions about animal learning
- Explain the importance of Woodworth's "Columbia bible" for the training of psychologists

TITCHENER'S PSYCHOLOGY: STRUCTURALISM

In 1898, a paper appeared in *Psychological Review* entitled "The Postulates of a Structural Psychology" (Titchener, 1898b). Its author, E. B. Titchener, was a young professor from Cornell University who had been in the United States for just a half dozen years, but already had a reputation as a talented laboratory psychologist with some clear and uncompromising ideas about the new psychology. In the article he labeled his approach a "structural" psychology, and he contrasted it with what he saw at other American universities, which he labeled a "functional" psychology. Drawing a parallel to biology, he wrote that **structuralism** is like anatomy—the purpose is analysis. Just as the anatomist organizes knowledge about the body into component structures, so would a structural psychologist analyze the human mind and organize it into its elementary units, basic sensations for example. **Functionalism**, on the other hand, is like physiology. The physiologist examines how the various parts of the body operate and the functions they serve to help keep people alive; similarly, the functional psychologist studies how the mind serves to adapt people to the environment. Although not rejecting a functional approach outright, Titchener used the biology metaphor to argue that it was futile to study function before structure had been fully described. Anatomy provides the foundation for physiology, Titchener contended. Similarly, a thorough understanding of the structure of the human mind was a necessary prerequisite to the study of its function. As Titchener had written 2 years earlier in *An Outline of Psychology*, the psychologist's goal "is to ascertain the nature and number of the mental elements. He takes up mental experience, bit by bit, dividing and subdividing, until the division can go no further. When that point is reached, he has found a conscious element" (Titchener, 1896/1899, p. 16). Structuralism was never widely popular in America, but, as we shall see, Titchener had an undeniable impact.

From Oxford to Leipzig to Cornell

Such a position of prominence in American psychology was a long journey from humble beginnings in southern England for Edward Bradford Titchener (1867–1927). His early years were unsettling—his father died when Titchener was 13, and the adolescent was raised mainly by his paternal grandfather. Titchener's grandfather, a stereotypical British country "gentleman," gave Titchener a set of attitudes and values that he never lost. Even after residing in America for many years, Titchener never stopped living according to the strict code of the behavior of a proper middle-class English gentleman (Leys & Evans, 1990).

Young Titchener was a talented student, good enough to win scholarships to attend Malvern, one of England's better public schools, and then Oxford University.[1] Titchener remained at Oxford from 1885 to 1890, where he excelled in the classics and philosophy. To strengthen what he perceived was a weak background in science, he spent most of his final year at Oxford in the physiology laboratory of John Scott Burdon-Sanderson. In that setting, Titchener showed himself to be just the opposite of William James in at least one respect—he discovered that he loved the precisely detailed work of the laboratory. For the rest of his life, he judged the quality of his peers by their standing as "lab men," which accounts for his derogatory comments about Hall (Chapter 6) and his paradoxically close friendship with John Watson (Chapter 10). Watson derided Titchener's structuralism and Titchener disliked everything about Watson's behaviorism, but Watson was a true laboratory scientist in Titchener's eyes, and that was sufficient grounds for respect and friendship. After first meeting Watson, Titchener wrote to a colleague: "I think that he has a big career, and I like him very much personally" (quoted in Larson & Sullivan, 1965, p. 340).

While at Oxford, Titchener learned of Wundt's new physiological psychology. Fluent in German and enamored of Germanic culture, he went to Leipzig, where he encountered like-minded laboratory devotees, including Oswald Külpe (Chapter 4), who was Wundt's assistant at the time (i.e., in charge of the day-to-day operation of the lab), and several Americans. Titchener completed a doctorate with Wundt in 1892, hoping to teach at Oxford or Cambridge, but neither school seemed interested in the new psychology. Fate then intervened on Titchener's behalf, in the form of an offer to cross the Atlantic and teach at Cornell University. Titchener was recommended by Frank Angell, one of the American psychologists Titchener befriended at Leipzig. Angell had created a small lab at Cornell, but was now leaving for the just-created Stanford University in California. Angell recommended his British friend as his replacement, the offer was made, and Titchener accepted.

Cornell University sits high on a hill in Ithaca, New York, overlooking Lake Cayuga, in the beautiful Finger Lakes region. In 1892, it was in the middle of nowhere, barely accessible by the occasional train. Even today, residents refer to their town as "centrally isolated." If you can imagine finishing your education and deciding to take a job somewhere in a remote area of Australia, then you have some idea of what the decision must have been like for the young Britisher with his new doctorate. Yet he took the risk, arrived in 1892, and never left.[2] Over the years, "Titchenerian psychology," "structuralism," and "the Cornell school" became interchangeable terms.

Promoting Experimental Psychology at Cornell

Titchener (Figure 7.1) moved quickly on his arrival at Cornell, expanding the laboratory (Figure 7.2), attracting students, and starting a research program—by the turn of the 20th century, he and his students

---

[1] In England, the term "public school" actually refers to a highly selective private high school. Only a small percentage of British schoolchildren attended public schools, but the majority of students at England's prestigious universities, Oxford and Cambridge came from the public schools. Oxbridge and Cambridge graduates thus represented a small elite group of the British upper and upper middle class.

[2] Titchener thought he would go to Cornell briefly and then return to Oxford when it came to its senses about laboratory psychology. Oxford didn't, and Titchener never returned to England, even to visit. In an 1898 letter to Hugo Münsterberg (then at Harvard), Titchener claimed that he wouldn't return even if offered a job, that in America he had "more money, more freedom, more power" (Titchener, 1898a). Titchener later considered offers from Clark University and Harvard, but turned down both.

Archives of the History of American Psychology, The Center for the History of Psychology —The University of Akron

FIGURE 7.1   E. B. Titchener (1867–1927) of Cornell, with ever-present cigar, from Popplestone and McPherson (1994).

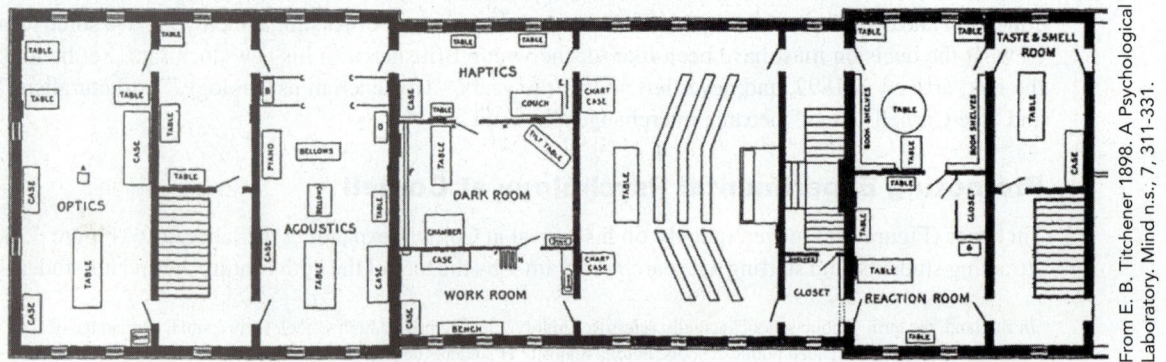

From E. B. Titchener 1898. A Psychological Laboratory. Mind n.s., 7, 311-331.

FIGURE 7.2   Floor plan of Titchener's domain in the top floor of Cornell's Morrill Hall, as of 1898.

had published more than 60 research articles (Boring, 1961a).[3] To ensure a forum for the research from the Cornell laboratory, he signed on with Hall in 1895 as editor of the *American Journal of Psychology*, enabling him to control one third of the journal's pages (Hall and Sanford, the other editors, controlled the remaining two thirds). In addition, Titchener spread the word about German psychology by translating books by Wundt and Külpe into English, and he began producing texts of his own.

His *Outline of Psychology*, first published in 1896, went through several revisions and was rewritten and expanded as *A Textbook of Psychology* in 1909. It was the clearest overall statement of his structuralist system. By 1900, Titchener was firmly established as a major player on the American psychological scene. His status was confirmed when he published "the Manuals."

The Manuals In German laboratories, students learned their craft mainly on their own, by participating in and running studies and by observing and questioning their more experienced peers. American universities, however, developed what came to be known as the **drill course**. Students in these courses did not produce original research but replicated classic studies, learned how to set up and work the "brass instruments," and in general became acclimated to the laboratory environment (Titchener, 1898a). At Cornell, for example, Titchener taught a yearlong drill course to undergraduates, typically juniors, after they had completed his introductory course. As the new laboratory psychology expanded, these drill courses proliferated, but Titchener worried about the quality and consistency of instruction. Thus, a need developed for a text that could explain how to train students in basic laboratory procedures. Edmund Sanford of Clark wrote the first one in the early 1890s, and it started the process of standardizing laboratory instruction in the drill course (Goodwin, 1987). Titchener recognized the value of Sanford's manual, but he also knew that it was just a beginning and that it had some weaknesses. For instance, it was not always clear about how the instructor should proceed in the laboratory, taking for granted more expertise than many instructors possessed. To remedy the problem, Titchener set to work on his own manuals and published them under the title of *Experimental Psychology: A Manual of Laboratory Practice*. They became his best-known work, serving for many years as the guide into the complexities of laboratory investigation.

The Manuals, as they came to be known, were published in two volumes, in 1901 and 1905, each containing separate texts for students and instructors. Because of Titchener's concern that teachers might need to have procedures worked out step by step, the instructor manuals for both volumes were almost twice the length of the student manuals. The 1901 volume was subtitled "Qualitative Experiments," and it included experiments on basic sensory, perceptual, and affective processes (Titchener, 1901). "Quantitative Experiments" filled the 1905 volume; these dealt mainly with psychophysics and reaction time procedures (Titchener, 1905a).

Students in drill courses worked in pairs, alternating between the roles of experimenter and **observer**, the latter being the person we would call the research subject today. Observers were so-called because while they were participating in the experiment, they would be observing their own mental processes and would give a description of these processes at the close of the experiment. This introspective procedure will be described more fully later in the chapter.

In the qualitative experiments, observers would experience some sensory, perceptual, or affective event, give an introspective account of it, and then answer some specific questions about it in

---

[3]Titchener developed very close mentoring relationships with his students and continued to advise them even after they had left Cornell. For example, in a letter to Walter Pillsbury, who had just started a new position at the University of Michigan, Titchener urged Pillsbury to "give your investigations to your students, and let them work out your ideas. Forget, so far as you can, the YOU have any part or lot in the work; let the students feel that they are making psychology" (Titchener, 1897, uppercase in the original).

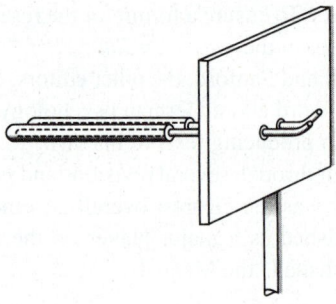

FIGURE 7.3 Sketch of an olfactometer, from Titchener's manual of qualitative experiments. From E. B. Titchener 1901. Experimental Psychology: A Manual of Laboratory Practice. Vol. 1: Qualitative Experiments. Part 1: Students Manual; Part 2: Instructors Manual. New York: Macmillan.

their notebooks. For example, olfactory sensations were studied with the use of a double olfactometer (Figure 7.3). The two thin glass tubes, each holding various odorous substances, were inserted into the nostrils. In a typical experiment, observers smelled pairs of substances (e.g., iodine, various herbs) with differing degrees of intensity, described the experience introspectively, and responded in their notebooks to questions about compensation ("Did one smell overwhelm the other?") and smell mixture ("Did the smells mix to form a new odor?").

The quantitative experiments involved numerical data, such as stimulus intensities identified as just noticeably different in psychophysics experiments or response times in reaction time studies. Figure 7.4 shows two different reaction time devices. The most common was an ordinary telegraph key (Figure 7.4a); it would be held down and then released when the observer detected a stimulus. The right hand of the observer in Figure 4.3 is using this type of key. The second device (Figure 7.4b) was a lip key, used in voice reaction time experiments. It is probably the same one shown in the Clark photo in Chapter 6 (Figure 6.3b). The right side of the key would be inserted into the closed mouth, and when observers opened their mouths to respond to a stimulus, the contacts separated from each other, breaking a circuit and stopping a clock.

Titchener's system of psychology faded rapidly after his death, but his encyclopedic manuals provided a lasting contribution to laboratory psychology. They remained in use well into the 1930s and trained several generations of experimental psychologists. Even today, they provide excellent demonstrations of a wide range of sensory and perceptual phenomena.

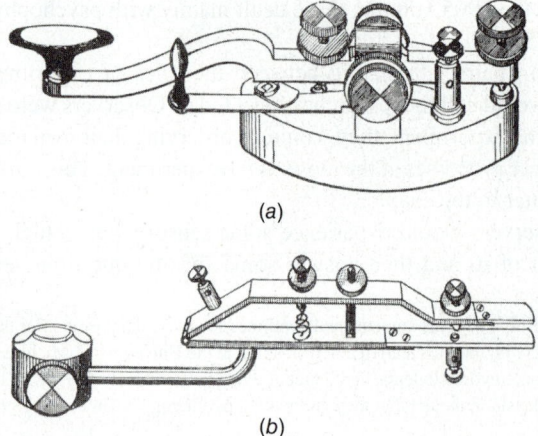

(a)

(b)

FIGURE 7.4 Reaction time apparatus: (a) a telegraph key; (b) a lip key, from Titchener's manual of quantitative experiments. From E. B. Titchener 1905. Experimental Psychology: A Manual of Laboratory Practice. Vol. 2: Qualitative Experiments. Part 1: Students Manual; Part 2: Instructors Manual. New York: Macmillan.

The Experimentalists Titchener was one of the charter members of the American Psychological Association. He quickly became disillusioned with the organization, however, and resigned his membership (he rejoined the organization on two later occasions, only to resign twice more). Part of the problem was personal. The British Titchener felt like an outsider in an "American" Psychological Association, and the organization violated his strict code of proper behavior when it refused to censure E. W. Scripture (academic grandfather to Miles, as you recall from Chapter 1), accused by Titchener, with good cause, of plagiarizing portions of his translation of one of Wundt's books. More important, the APA did not represent Titchener's vision for experimental psychology, and the format of its meetings did not advance psychology, he believed. In 1895, in a note for the *American Journal of Psychology*, he complained that the presentations of research were "hardly possible to follow intelligently … when method and results are thrown in lecture form and the lecture reduced to a compass of twenty minutes" (Titchener, 1895, p. 448). Instead, he suggested something similar to a modern poster session, with "the meetings allowed to take the form of a conversazione, the apparatus employed shown in their working, and the results made to speak for themselves in charts and diagrams arranged near the apparatus" (p. 448).

By 1904, Titchener was ready to fix the problem himself, and he proposed the creation of an informal "club" of experimental psychologists. He did not intend to compete with the APA, but to provide a better means for researchers to present their work to peers. Thus was born a group that came to be known as the Experimentalists (Boring, 1967; Goodwin, 1985). They met for 3 days every spring, rotating from one laboratory to another. They discussed research in progress, tinkered with apparatus, and in general tried to keep the spirit of pure laboratory psychology alive. No formal papers were allowed and published descriptions of the meetings were discouraged. Titchener generally dominated the group—for instance, hosts would often check with him about whom to invite. Figure 7.5 shows a group photo taken at the 1926 meeting at the University of Pennsylvania.

One important feature of the group was gender—all the Experimentalists were men. Part of the reason was the prevailing cultural norms of the day, as described in Chapter 6. In Titchener's mind,

Courtesy of the Society of Experimental Psychologists

FIGURE 7.5 The Experimentalists at Penn in 1926. Note the similarity (posture, cigar) between Titchener (front and center) and Boring (first row, far right), Titchener's most famous student.

however, the prohibition followed from his ingrained code of gentlemanly conduct. His desire was to have something like an English club, where men could converse freely on any subject without being concerned about behaving "properly" in the presence of women. This meant being able to argue vociferously about some issue without either party taking offense; Titchener and other males of his time took it for granted that women would take such arguments personally (i.e., they would be too emotional). The club atmosphere also included smoking, and the social mores of the day usually excluded women from rooms where men smoked. These sentiments were summed up in a letter from Sanford to Titchener just before the group was formed. Probably thinking of Calkins, Washburn, and Ladd-Franklin (Chapter 6), he pointed out that several women "on scientific grounds have full right to be there and might feel hurt (in a general impersonal way) if women are not asked. On the other hand they would undoubtedly interfere with the smoking and to a certain extent with the general freedom of a purely masculine assembly" (quoted in Furumoto, 1988, p. 104).

In defense of the charge that Titchener was antifemale, it has been pointed out that almost one half of his graduate students were women (26 of 60), his first doctoral student was Margaret Washburn, and on at least one occasion he argued for the hiring of a particular woman psychologist at Cornell over the objections of the administration (Leys & Evans, 1990). On the other hand, part of the reason for there being women in Titchener's laboratory was institutional—Cornell for years was about the only place for a woman to go to be an "official" student. At any rate, the exclusion of women from Titchener's Experimentalists created a barrier to advancement and contributed to their difficulty in securing major academic positions.[4]

Titchener's Structuralist System

For Titchener, a prime goal for psychology was to analyze human consciousness into its basic structural elements. Hence, Titchener's psychology was the science of the structure of the human mind, and a primary purpose of research was to determine this structure through experimental research. Analysis was not the sole purpose, however. Psychology must also understand the process of *synthesis*, how the mental elements combine and connect into more complex phenomena. In Titchener's words, the experimentalist "learns to formulate the laws of connection of the elementary mental processes. If sensations of tone occur together, they blend or fuse; if sensations of colour occur side by side, they enhance one another: and all this takes place in a perfectly regular way, so that we can write out laws of tonal fusion and laws of colour contrast." (Titchener, 1909, pp. 37–38). In addition to the goals of analysis and synthesis, Titchener argued that a third goal for psychology was explanation, by which he meant an understanding of how the nervous system produced the various sensory, perceptual, and cognitive phenomena that interested him. Very little of his research focused on this third goal, however.

To accomplish a thorough description of the analysis and synthesis of mental phenomena, Titchener developed a research program involving the kinds of qualitative and quantitative research described in the Manuals. To get a good idea of the topics that Titchener considered essential in an introductory course, consider his *Textbook of Psychology*, a text you would have used had you taken Titchener's introductory psychology course in 1909. There is very little about the nervous system in it, but a great deal concerning the descriptive goals of analysis and synthesis. Fully one third of the book is devoted to describing basic sensory processes (vision, hearing, etc.).

At the center of Titchener's system was a methodology that is often associated with his name—introspection. As you recall from Chapter 4, introspection was important in the Leipzig

---

[4]The noted physiological psychologist Donald Hebb (Chapter 14) resigned from the Society in 1953, mainly on the grounds that it seemed more like an exclusionary social club than a true honor society. His resignation letter included a handwritten note asking "Why no women? Charter admits them" (quoted in Glickman, 1996, p. 243).

laboratory, but Wundt called it *internal perception* and limited it to simple verbal reports of the results of psychophysics ("this weight is heavier than this other one") and other sensory studies. Wundt's student (and Titchener's friend) Oswald Külpe, however, elaborated the procedure into *systematic experimental introspection*, in which observers would give detailed reports of the conscious events occurring after completing some task (e.g., inhaling odors). It was this latter approach that was taken by Titchener and developed to a high level of sophistication.

Titchener was well aware of the essential problem of introspection—it is impossible to have a conscious experience and reflect on it at the same time. To deal with the problem, he suggested three solutions. The first was to rely on memory, delaying the introspection "until the process to be described has run its course, and then to call it back and describe it from memory" (Titchener, 1909, p. 22). Titchener's second suggestion for reducing the memory load was to break the experience into stages, using the fractionation method associated with Külpe's laboratory (Chapter 4). His third, and most important technique, was to acquire what he called the **introspective habit**:

> [T]he practiced observer gets into an introspective habit, has the introspective attitude ingrained in his system; so that it is possible for him, not only to take mental notes while the observation is in progress, without interfering with consciousness, but even to jot down written notes, as the histologist does while his eye is still held to the ocular of the microscope. (p. 23)

This is an important passage, for it is the main reason why Titchener insisted that his observers be highly trained. In effect, they were to become introspecting machines, behaving so automatically that problems of memory and any biasing influences would presumably disappear. The introspective habit is difficult for us to grasp today because this type of laboratory training no longer exists. This chapter's Close-Up, however, should give you some insight into what the habit was like.

CLOSE-UP

THE INTROSPECTIVE HABIT

The absence of Titchenerian introspection in contemporary psychology makes it difficult for us to grasp what an introspective description was really like. One way to find out is to read articles summarizing this kind of research because they often include verbatim introspective accounts. For example, consider the following study on attention. It was the doctoral thesis of Karl Dallenbach, one of Titchener's students and later a colleague on the Cornell faculty. Using procedures similar to those found in modern research on attention, Dallenbach (1913) was interested in what happens in consciousness when attention is divided and overloaded. In the study, observers listened to two metronomes set at different speeds and tried to count the number of beats occurring between coincident beats. At the same time, they completed a second mental task, such as continually adding numbers, singing, or saying the alphabet backwards. Each experimental trial lasted 90 seconds. Here is one observer's introspective account:

> The sounds of the metronomes, as a series of discontinuous clicks, were clear in consciousness only four or five times during the experiment, and they were especially bothersome at first. They were accompanied by strain sensations and unpleasantness. The rest of the experiment my attention was on the adding, which was composed of ... visual images of the numbers, sometimes on a dark grey scale which was directly ahead and about three feet in front of me. This was accompanied by kinaesthesis of eyes and strains in chest and arms. When these processes were clear in consciousness the sounds of the metronomes were very vague or obscure. (Dallenbach, 1913, p. 467)

Reading articles full of introspective accounts like this can be revealing, but they tend to be long, repetitive, and boring enough to make one understand why psychologists eventually abandoned the method. A more interesting way to gain insight into the introspective attitude is to read the letters that experimental psychologists wrote to each other during this era (Goodwin, 1991b). Introspective thinking was so much a part of their everyday thinking that their correspondence is liberally sprinkled with informal introspections relating to their experiences. After returning from a holiday in New Hampshire, for instance, Sanford wrote to Titchener about his fear of thunderstorms. He wrote that he had

> observed enough this summer to find that I cannot find anything in it but organic and other sensations unpleasantly colored and, on the cognitive side, a cramp of apperception towards a small group of ideas related to the thing dreaded with certain resultants in instinctive act and thought.... When the storm became imminent there would be cardiac and visceral symptoms to describe, etc. etc.—though when the thing was actually present these were as a general thing not so marked as in anticipation (Sanford, 1910)

A more dramatic example of how introspection was never far from the thoughts of turn-of-the-century psychologists comes from an 1893 letter from Lightner Witmer of the University of Pennsylvania to Hugo Münsterberg of Harvard. Witmer had been studying the psychology of pain firsthand in a rather unusual manner.

> I let a horse throw me from his back, allowing me to drop on my shoulder and head. I showed a beautiful case of loss of consciousness before the act....I not only do not remember mounting and the horse running, but I forgot almost everything that happened....[F]rom the time I got up in the morning till I regained complete consciousness..., I can form no continuous series of events. My head was bad for a while but is all right now, but my arm has served the purpose of quite a number of experiments as it still continues quite painful at times. Beside this, I have cut my foot badly and have a few other ills and aches. The psychological side of my afflictions will form the basis of at least three lectures next fall. (Witmer, 1893)

The Structural Elements of Human Conscious Experience

On the basis of his introspective analyses, Titchener identified three types of elementary mental processes: sensations, images, and affects. Sensations were the basic elements of the more complex process of perception, images were the elementary components of ideas, and affects (feelings) were the building blocks of our emotions. You should be able to detect all three elements in Dallenbach's sample introspective account. The basic elements could not be reduced further, but they did have various features or **attributes**. All sensations, for instance, had the attributes of quality, intensity, duration, and clearness. *Quality* is what distinguishes one sensation from another (e.g., red from green, cold from warm). *Intensity* refers to the strength of the stimulus, decibel level for example. *Duration* is self-evident—all sensations last for some measurable amount of time. And *clearness* "is the attribute which gives a sensation its place in a consciousness: the clearer sensation is dominant, independent, outstanding, the less clear sensation is subordinate, undistinguished in the background of consciousness" (Titchener, 1909, p. 53). According to Titchener, attention essentially amounted to this attribute of sensory clearness.

Images have the same four attributes, according to Titchener, but compared with sensations, the qualities are "relatively pale, faded, washed out, misty" (1909, p. 198). In addition, he argued that the intensity and duration of images were "markedly less" (p. 198) than sensations. Affective states, the elements of our emotional life, differ from sensations and images in two important ways. First, although there are literally thousands of different sensorial and imaginal qualities, Titchener believed that affect had only two fundamental qualities—pleasantness and unpleasantness. Second, affect had the attributes of quality, intensity, and duration, but they lacked clearness. If we want to experience pleasure at a concert, for example, we must attend to the sensory elements (i.e., the music), not to the feeling of pleasure itself; if we focus on the feeling, the pleasure disappears.

Titchener's structuralism continued to evolve over the years, and in the 1920s he moved away from an emphasis on elements and developed a more phenomenological model that described sensory processes in terms of dimensions. Thus, sensation shifted "from an observable entity to a classificatory term" (Evans, 1972, p. 172). Titchener was working on a major revision of his system along these lines, but his productivity dropped during the 1920s, possibly showing the early effects of the brain tumor that would kill him in 1927, and the final system was never completed.

Evaluating Titchener's Contributions to Psychology

Psychology for Titchener was a pure laboratory science aimed at discovering the basic structure of human consciousness. Systematic experimental introspection was its prime method, and because this form of introspection required extensive training, it was limited to highly motivated adult observers. Thus, according to Titchener, psychology was the science of the "generalized adult mind." Two immediate consequences of this rather limited definition of the field were that (a) Titchener was uninterested in individual differences between one mind and another, and (b) he excluded from his definition of psychology all research using children, animals, and the insane—they could never introspect properly. Also, because the discipline was to retain the purity of the laboratory, Titchener omitted such applied concerns as industrial and educational psychology from his definition of the field. Although his vision of psychology was therefore extremely narrow, it also led directly to his major contribution—the promotion of an experimental psychology that featured the tight controls found in the laboratory. Although his introspective methodology passed from the scene, his insistence on the value of basic laboratory research as the way to provide the foundation for psychological knowledge created a place for the laboratory in all colleges and universities with programs in psychology. As one historian put it, Titchener was "responsible for making psychology scientific—for setting psychology up in the laboratory and reaching his conclusions through experiment, under controlled conditions" (Hindeland, 1971, p. 28).

On the other hand, Titchener's narrow brand of psychology became as isolated from American psychology as Ithaca was from other centers of learning. Structuralism ultimately failed as a system, primarily because of the shortcomings of introspection as a method, but also because of Titchener's uncompromising insistence that his way was the only way. Despite Titchener's belief that highly trained observers gained the "introspective habit," thereby avoiding bias and allowing for replication of experiments to occur, it soon became apparent that serious problems existed with the method.

The introspection problem can be illustrated in two controversies. One was a conflict with Baldwin (Chapter 6) over reaction time (Krantz, 1969). At issue were some reaction time findings, with the crux of the matter concerning who was best able to provide reaction time data. Titchener, of course, believed that observers had to be highly trained, to avoid making errors and to avoid bias. With his highly trained observers, Titchener was able to demonstrate a distinction between what was called a sensory reaction time (when attention was focused on the stimulus in a reaction time task) and a motor reaction time (when attention was focused on the response). Baldwin could not replicate the finding, using relatively untrained observers, but he identified what he thought were individual differences in reaction time performance. Some people were "imagery types" and would respond faster given sensory RT instructions than motor RT instructions. Others, "motor types," would do the opposite. Because Baldwin's observers were not highly trained, Titchener considered the results meaningless. At a deeper level, the conflict concerns different ideals—Titchener's approach reflected his search for the generalized adult mind, whereas Baldwin's focused on a strong interest in how people differed from each other. As is the case with many scientific controversies, neither side "won," although a study by Angell and Moore (1896) provided a reasonable resolution by examining the effects of training—early in RT training, results like Baldwin's occurred; later, after more training, results like Titchener's occurred.

As for Baldwin and Titchener, as the controversy played out in print, their exchanges became increasingly acrimonious. In print, for example, Baldwin wrote that he could not "help thinking that Professor Titchener sometimes allows the dust of his machinery to obscure his vision" (quoted in Krantz, 1969, p. 11). Titchener replied that he had "no wish to emulate Professor Baldwin in the matter of name calling" and he chastised Baldwin's attitude as being neither "scientifically or ethically defensible" (p. 11).

A second issue that irked Titchener was the imageless thought problem, described briefly in Chapter 4. As you recall, introspectors in Külpe's Wurzburg lab discovered situations in which conscious thoughts occurred in the absence of images. In a psychophysics weight-judging study, for instance, images occurred at various points in the process, but not at the exact moment of judgment. The judgment itself seemed to be an "imageless" thought. This was a direct threat to Titchener's system, which held as dogma that images were the underlying elements of *all* ideas—imageless thoughts were simply not possible. To counter the assault, Titchener dismissed the Wurzburg outcome as a failure of experimental control and found that in *his* laboratory, observers were indeed able to detect images at all stages of the weight-judging experiment. Because of the inherently subjective nature of introspection, however, there was no independent means of determining who was right. It began to appear that introspection could not produce objective data.

Thus, psychologists eventually concluded that the extensive training insisted on by Titchener produced bias rather than eliminated it—the training began to look like indoctrination. In a 1913 paper that launched behaviorism, John Watson put his finger on the problem.

> Take the case of sensation. A sensation is defined in terms of its attributes. One psychologist will state with readiness that the attributes of a visual sensation are *quality, extension, duration*, and *intensity*. Another will add *clearness*. Still another that of *order*. I doubt if any one psychologist can draw up a set of statements describing what he means by sensation which will be agreed to by three other psychologists of different training . . . . I firmly believe that two hundred years from now, unless the introspective method is discarded, psychology will still be divided on the question as to whether auditory sensations have the quality of "extension," whether intensity is an attribute which can be applied to color, … and upon many hundreds of others of like character. (Watson, 1913, p. 164, emphasis in the original)

Hence, introspection was an Achilles heel, yet Titchener helped to establish experimental psychology as central to academic psychology in America. Shortly after his death in 1927, research psychologists met at an important conference in Carlisle, Pennsylvania, to discuss the current status and future prospects for their field. Walter Miles was there.

FROM THE MILES PAPERS...

MILES AND THE CARLISLE CONFERENCE

In the spring of 1928, Walter Miles made the long train journey from California (he was teaching at Stanford at the time) to Pennsylvania to attend what became known as the Carlisle Conference (Goodwin, 2010). Titchener had been dead for a year by then, or he certainly would have been a central figure at the conference. The meeting was organized by Knight Dunlap of Johns Hopkins University, who chaired the NRC Division of Anthropology and Psychology (the National Research Council, or NRC, was formed during World War I to provide government aid to science). Including Miles, 32 experimentalists went to Carlisle. One notable absence was Titchener's most famous pupil, E. G. Boring, who wrote grumpily to Miles that:

I am not going to Dunlap's conference. I am getting very tired of the NRC, which is always fixing up things that cost me time and even money for somebody else's research, or vague plans about someone else's research. (Boring, 1928b)

After Miles urged him to reconsider, especially because Boring happened to be APA president that year, Boring replied:

Nor had it occurred to me that I had any special responsibilities this year as President of the APA. If I have, then I think that they are not the responsibilities of a slave, but the responsibilities to uphold wisdom and to denounce foolishness. (Boring, 1928c)

Dunlap led off the conference with a talk in which he enumerated the problems existing for experimental psychology. Here are the notes that Miles recorded in his diary:

The situation in lab. Psy. Is not satisfactory, it is in fact depressing.
The war rush for application and aftermath.
Partly trained men.
Vol. of research great, but ? its quality.
Too much teaching by our young men.
Most of the lab course work given to elementary students is time wasted.
Large classes mean wasted time.

Grad. students do the PhD then die on job; many not research men to start with.
But in other cases he has no time, he teaches or must organize.
(Miles, 1928b)

Dunlap's solution was to create a National Laboratory with federal funding, where young researchers could form research teams and spend a sabbatical year devoting their time to research on specific topics. The idea never got off the ground, in part because federal funding for science dried up quickly with the onset of the Great Depression. But even at Carlisle there was skepticism among the attendees about nationalizing psychological science. One of the skeptics was Margaret Washburn, by then psychology's most prominent female psychologist. Dunlap had accompanied his invitation to the conference with a broad outline of what he had in mind, and he invited comments. After he gave his opening talk, he read some of these comments, in particular the favorable feedback he received. But Washburn had written a critical letter, prompting this diary entry from Miles, who was apparently sitting with his good friend Raymond Dodge:

Dunlap: "Dr. W has written a full letter of criticism of my whole point of view. I [wish] that I had that letter here to read to you but it seems to have been misplaced."
Dodge: "Freudian suppression."
(Miles, 1928b)

AMERICA'S PSYCHOLOGY: FUNCTIONALISM

Titchener might not have been interested in applying psychology, examining individual differences, or studying animals, children, or the insane, but practically every other psychologist in America was. Part of the reason for this derives from the historical context of late 19th-century America. During the final three decades of the century, following the Civil War, the United States entered a period of sustained growth. It was a time of reconstruction in the South, westward expansion, railroad building, technological innovation (e.g., telephone, typewriter), industrialization on a massive scale, and the amassing of great wealth by Gilded Age entrepreneurs with names like Rockefeller, Vanderbilt, and Carnegie. The evidence of this "progress" was put on display at a world's fair in Chicago in 1893—the Columbian Exposition. Timed to celebrate the 400th anniversary of the arrival of Columbus, but opening a year late because of construction delays, the Exposition was a massive undertaking. About 200 buildings were constructed, scattered over 600 acres near Lake Michigan, and housing exhibits depicting business, industry, science, and the arts.[5] It was estimated that 27 million people attended during the Exposition's 6-month run, about one in four Americans (Brands, 1995). It is important to keep in mind that this period in American history was also a time when Native American populations were uprooted from their land and decimated, workers endured long hours and unsafe working conditions for pitiful wages, women and minorities were considered mentally inferior to white males, and an enormous gap developed between the very few rich and the very many poor. Nonetheless, most (white, male) Americans came to develop a concept of their national character that placed a high value on taking individual responsibility for success or failure, making something of oneself regardless of one's background, competing and winning in the marketplace, and, of importance for our story, always thinking of the usefulness or practical value of objects and ideas.

This emerging prototype of American pragmatic individuality was consistent with evolutionary thinking, although most Americans would have denied that they were Darwinians. Nonetheless, Americans were attracted by the views of the British popularizer of evolution, Herbert Spencer (1820–1903), who promoted a brand of evolution congenial to Americans on the "winning" side. It was Spencer, not Darwin, who invented the phrase "survival of the fittest," but Spencer's idea of fitness was not the same as Darwin's.[6] Whereas any attribute that furthered the cause of survival (e.g., camouflage) would constitute fitness for Darwin, Spencer's use of the term implied that survivors were winners of fierce battles for limited resources. As Spencer used the phrase, survival of the fittest blended with and contributed to the developing American character of the 19th century. Spencer's system has come to be known as **social Darwinism**.

Social Darwinists believed that evolutionary forces were natural and inevitable and that any attempt on the part of humans to alter these forces was misdirected and harmful. Evolution must be left unchecked, Spencer argued, an attitude that had direct social, political, and economic implications. It meant, for example, that government should not interfere with business practices—losers in business failed simply because they weren't "fit." Those who accumulated enormous wealth, on the other hand, should not in any way be regulated or penalized (e.g., taxed): Their wealth was simply a sign of their fitness. Government also should not provide services to the poor: Their poverty was believed to result from a lack of fitness. If supported by the government, their lack of fitness would spread as they produced similarly unfit children. Thus, evolutionary fitness became a means of rationalizing the huge gap between rich and poor and of maintaining a belief in the superiority of the white male over all others (e.g., women). Most American psychologists, especially those interested in mental testing (next chapter), were generally agreeable to social Darwinist thinking.

As we shall see, the evolutionary mindset that psychologists found congenial led naturally to interests in studying individual differences, animal behavior, development, and abnormal behavior, and to the search for practical applications of psychological principles. This trend toward a more diverse psychology than Titchener's structuralism was clear from the work of James and Hall (Chapter 6), both of whom made important contributions even before Titchener arrived from Leipzig in 1892. The movement came to be called functionalism. Although it shared some common ground with structuralism (interested in studying human consciousness, willingness to use introspection), it represented a clear

[5]Two rooms in a science building were set aside to exhibit apparatus and mental testing materials from the "new" science of psychology. The exhibit was organized by Joseph Jastrow, one of Hall's first students at Johns Hopkins (Perloff & Perloff, 1977). Clark University sent a set of photos of its lab, several of which appear in this text (Figures 4.3 6.3*a*, and 6.3*b*).

[6]Another important difference between the men was that Darwin was scientifically conservative, unwilling to speculate in the absence of a large database. As discussed in Chapter 5, this unwillingness to go far beyond the data was one reason for his delay in publishing the *Origin of Species*. Spencer, on the other hand, did not hesitate to speculate. It was once said of Spencer that his "idea of a tragedy was a deduction killed by a fact" (quoted in Boakes, 1984, p. 10).

break with the structuralist goal of studying the contents of the "generalized adult mind." Instead, it was firmly grounded in evolutionary theory, which led functionalists to ask questions that would either not have occurred to Titchener or not have interested him (Green, 2009). These questions, as we shall see, led American psychologists to study the diverse range of topics that eventually would form the chapter titles of modern psychology textbooks.

Although functionalist thinking was widespread enough to be considered "America's psychology," it was especially associated with two universities, Chicago and Columbia. The remainder of the chapter will describe the work of psychologists at these schools. Chapter 8 will elaborate on the theme of application, a central component of functionalist thinking.

The Chicago Functionalists

In 1889, John D. Rockefeller, pockets bulging with Standard Oil profits, donated $600,000 to establish a Baptist university, contingent on the Baptists contributing an additional $400,000 (Ryan, 1939). It would be located in Chicago, a city already developing the reputation that would lead the poet Carl Sandburg to call it the "City of the Big Shoulders." Nearly destroyed by a famous fire in 1871 that burned 1,688 acres, consumed buildings valued at $192 million, and bankrupted 64 different insurance companies (Cashman, 1993), Chicago was one of America's fastest-growing cities in the late 1800s. Its hundreds of acres of cattle and hog pens, slaughterhouses, and packinghouses made it the center of the beef and pork industry, and its location made it a natural hub for railroads and a key location for industries (e.g., lumber, steel, agriculture) relying on transportation via rail and Great Lakes steamers. The new university was a bold enterprise, far removed from the East Coast academic community, and its success was entrusted to William Rainey Harper, a biblical scholar who had earned a doctorate from Yale at age 18. President Harper's main challenge was to hire a quality faculty, a task made easier by the troubles at Clark University. As you recall from Chapter 6, Harper filled a number of his faculty positions with disgruntled Clark University faculty and graduate students when financial problems and Hall's capriciousness led them to look for greener pastures.

The University of Chicago opened in 1892 and quickly became a leader in higher education, despite its remoteness. It included separate colleges of liberal arts, practical arts, literature, and science, as well as a graduate school and a school of divinity. It began with a large staff of 120 faculty, and within 3 years they were teaching 534 graduate students, more than Johns Hopkins and Clark combined (Ryan, 1939). Two years after the opening, Harper hired a young instructor from the University of Michigan to chair Chicago's philosophy department. Although he became better known for his philosophical writings on democracy and his innovative approach to education, John Dewey also wrote a paper that is often considered the starting point for American functionalism.

John Dewey (1859–1952): The Reflex Arc Born in Burlington, Vermont, John Dewey was raised in a setting that shaped in him the traditional Yankee values of hard work, respect for others, thrift, simplicity, and a love of democracy. After completing high school at age 15, Dewey enrolled in the nearby University of Vermont, graduating in 1879. While at Vermont, he studied the traditional curriculum of the classics and humanities, but he also sampled evolutionary thinking by studying the new sciences of geology and zoology (Barone, 1996).

After graduating, Dewey taught high school for several years and then decided to continue his education. Johns Hopkins University was a rising star, and Dewey enrolled there to study philosophy in 1882. The new psychology was included in the Hopkins philosophy curriculum, so Dewey's schedule included work in G. Stanley Hall's brand new laboratory. After earning his doctorate in philosophy in 1884, Dewey's next stop was Michigan, where he taught both philosophy and psychology, working his notes into a text, *Psychology*, in 1886. The book was used on numerous campuses for several years and was the standard text at Michigan for a decade (Raphelson, 1973), but met its demise upon the 1890 publication of William James's instant classic. Dewey himself readily acknowledged *The Principles of Psychology* to be superior to his own effort.

Dewey went to Chicago in 1894. His new department included traditional philosophy, laboratory psychology, and another area of great interest to Dewey—pedagogy. During his 10 years there, Dewey established Chicago as a center of functionalism, partly through recruiting colleagues sympathetic to the movement, but also through an article published in 1896 entitled "The Reflex Arc Concept in Psychology." In it, he took issue with the traditional manner of thinking about reflexes. Dating from Bell and Magendie's separation of the reflex into separate sensory and motor pathways (Chapter 3), physiologists thought of the **reflex arc** in terms of three separate elementary components: the stimulus producing sensation, central processing producing an idea, and the act or motor response. Dewey believed that dividing the reflex into these separate components was artificial, however, resulting in a reflex concept that was "not a comprehensive, or organic unity, but a patchwork of disjointed parts" (Dewey, 1896/1948, p. 356). Instead, Dewey proposed a model of the reflex that substituted a functional for a structural approach.

The reflex, Dewey argued, is best conceived of as an integrated, coordinated whole that serves the function of adapting the organism to its environment. Consider a child reaching for a candle flame, to use Dewey's example. Those using the traditional reflex arc model would analyze the event into a series of stimulus-response elements—seeing the flame, reaching for it, feeling the heat, and reflexively withdrawing. For Dewey, this analysis oversimplified a complex action. Reaching for something after seeing it, for example, can only make sense in the larger context of the child's learning history: "seeing and grasping have been so often bound together to reinforce each other, to help each other out, that each may be considered practically a subordinate member of a bigger coordination" (p. 356). The second part, being seared by the flame and withdrawing the hand, is also part of the larger coordination that produces a learning event; the flame now takes on new meaning for the child. From that point on, seeing a burning candle is "no longer mere seeing; it is the seeing-of-a-light-that-means-pain-when-contact-occurs" (p. 357). Hence, the child has adapted to the environment as a result of experience. Furthermore, the sight of a burning candle now has a specific meaning that differs from the same sight viewed by a different child with different experiences. Dewey argued forcefully that psychologists studying human action should not be concerned with microscopic analysis into elements, but with how the act functions to promote the organism's well-being in the struggle to adapt to its ever changing world. That is, Dewey was proposing a change in emphasis about reflex behavior, a shift in thinking from an emphasis on "what?" to a focus on "what for?"

America at the turn of the century was just entering the Progressive Era, a time of sweeping reform and the beginning of a reaction against social Darwinism. It was during this time that business monopolies were being attacked, and their leaders were as likely to be called robber barons as heroes of the struggle for existence. Labor unions made significant gains on behalf of workers, the federal government enacted regulations to protect ordinary Americans from a variety of abuses (e.g., child labor, unsanitary conditions in food production), and social reformers set out to improve the welfare of those who used to be written off as "unfit." John Dewey fit perfectly into this context, making significant contributions to educational reform by launching the movement that came to be known as **progressive education**.

As a schoolteacher, Dewey strongly disliked the conventional approach to education, which emphasized rote learning, drill and practice, and strict discipline. Such an atmosphere made the classroom a place to avoid rather than a place to learn. Yet education was the key to an effective democracy, Dewey believed, because it offered everyone an equal opportunity to advance. At a time when public education was growing by leaps and bounds,[7] educational reform was essential. Dewey responded by creating a "Laboratory School" at Chicago in 1896 to study how children learned best in the classroom and by writing *The School and Society* (1899), which established his reputation as a leading philosopher of education. He also implored psychologists to use their new knowledge of the mind to improve education, using his presidential address to the American Psychological Association in 1899 as a forum (Dewey, 1900). According to Dewey, children learn by interacting with their environment—they learn by doing. Consequently, the school must create an atmosphere that encourages children to explore on their own, to think critically and creatively, and to be actively involved in learning.

Dewey left Chicago for Columbia University in 1904, turning over departmental leadership to James Angell. At Columbia, he made no further contributions to psychology, but he continued to agitate for educational and social reform within the context of his democratic philosophy. He was a strong supporter of teachers' unions, helped found the American Association of University Professors, became a member of the American Civil Liberties Union, and actively campaigned for women's rights (Hilgard, 1987). He remained a committed activist for liberal causes well into his eighth decade.

James R. Angell (1869–1949): The Province of Functional Psychology Like Dewey, James Rowland Angell (Figure 7.6) was born in Burlington, Vermont, the son of the president of the University of Vermont. When his father took the same job at the University of Michigan in 1871,

Courtesy of Ludy T. Benjamin, Jr.

FIGURE 7.6 James R. Angell (1869–1949), the Chicago functionalist and Yale University president.

[7] Attending school was compulsory in just six states in 1871, but was virtually universal by 1900. Between 1890 and 1910, the number of students in public schools increased by a factor of four (Cashman, 1993).

the Angells moved to the Midwest, and James was raised in the academic environment of Ann Arbor. He went to school at Dad's university, studying philosophy, the classics, and the natural sciences. His introduction to psychology came in a course with Dewey, using the professor's new textbook. Angell graduated from Michigan in 1890, then stayed another year to earn a master's degree in philosophy. During this last year his courses included a seminar with Dewey that used James's new *Principles of Psychology* as the text. As he later recalled, the text "unquestionably affected my thinking for the next 20 years more profoundly than any other" (quoted in Raphelson, 1973, p. 120). To experience William James firsthand, Angell went to Cambridge and spent a year under James's tutelage. He then decided to earn a German doctorate. By this time doctoral training in America was as good as if not superior to training in Germany, but there was still a high prestige value to a doctorate from the Continent. That Angell was aware of this status benefit is clear—his cousin Frank, with Leipzig credentials paving the way, had just been lured from Cornell to Stanford by an offer that significantly increased his salary (O'Donnell, 1985).

Angell intended to follow his cousin to Leipzig, but Wundt's laboratory was full, so he studied briefly with Ebbinghaus in Berlin before settling into the University at Halle. There he completed the work for his doctorate, but never finished the final version of it after receiving an offer to teach at the University of Minnesota. The salary and the stability of real employment enabled him to marry the woman he had known since his Michigan days, and for the 24-year-old Angell, love and a new job were sufficient to offset the loss of what seemed to be a mere piece of paper. Thus, although he would go on to direct the doctoral projects of many prominent American psychologists, he never quite finished his own.

After Angell had spent a year at Minnesota, Dewey hired him to be in charge of the psychology portion of the philosophy curriculum, and the Angells moved to Chicago in 1894. When Dewey moved on to Columbia a decade later, psychology became its own department, separate from philosophy, and Angell was made department chair. He moved further toward administration and away from psychology by being named Dean of the Faculty in 1911. He eventually followed in his father's footsteps and became a university president, leading Yale University for most of the 1920s and 1930s. His stellar work as president (e.g., quadrupled the endowment) landed him on the cover of *Time* in 1936, just before his retirement the following year.

Angell's importance for psychology derives from his work in the period from 1894 to 1911. During this time he contributed valuable research in areas such as reaction time (e.g., the study with Moore mentioned in the context of the Baldwin–Titchener described earlier in the chapter), imagery, and sound localization,[8] and he built one of the top departments in the country. He also became the most visible spokesperson for functionalism by writing a popular introductory textbook (Angell, 1904) and by delivering a memorable address after being elected president of the American Psychological Association in 1906 (Angell, 1907/1948). Dewey's reflex arc paper might have been the foundation paper for functionalist thinking, but it was not a "Here is what functionalism means" type of paper. Angell's was—he called it "The Province of Functional Psychology."

Angell made it clear that functional psychology was not a dogmatic "school" of psychology, but rather "little more than a point of view, a program, an ambition" (Angell, 1907/1948, p. 439). He then drew a sharp contrast between functional and structural psychologies. Whereas a structuralist is interested in mental contents, the "what?" of conscious experience, Angell stated, the functional psychologist wants to study mental operations, the "how?" and "why?" of consciousness. If the structuralist

---

[8] Sound localization depends in part on sound waves reaching our ears at slightly different times. Angell, who was deaf in one ear, served as his own observer in a study on how localization was accomplished monaurally (Hunter, 1949).

is asking *What is consciousness*? the functionalist is asking *What is consciousness for*? Furthermore, with a dig at what he considered to be the highly artificial nature of the results from Titchenerian-style research, Angell argued that a minute analysis of some hypothetical "moment of consciousness" fails to capture the importance of consciousness for everyday life:

> If you adopt as your material for psychological analysis the isolated "moment of consciousness," it is very easy to become so absorbed in determining its constitution as to be rendered somewhat oblivious to its artificial character. The most essential quarrel which the functionalist has with structuralism arises from this fact. (p. 441)

Angell then explicitly rejected the analogy between psychology and biology that Titchener had used to argue for the primacy of his structuralist approach. As you recall, Titchener had likened structuralism to anatomy and argued that just as anatomy provides the basis for physiology, so must structuralism precede functionalism. Angell would have none of it. Anatomy involves material objects that can be manipulated, observed, and measured with precision, but mental contents are "evanescent" and "fleeting," Angell argued. With the analogy between anatomy and structuralism shown to be faulty, Angell believed the supposed primacy of structuralism over functionalism to be meaningless.

Angell's functionalist approach to consciousness had the same evolutionary flavor found in James. Like James, Angell described the function of consciousness to be in allowing the individual to solve problems and therefore to adapt to novel situations. Near the close of his article, he pointed out the connections between functionalist thinking and the interests of American psychologists. If the psychologist is interested in the functions of consciousness, then it is important to understand how those functions develop, both ontogenetically and phylogenetically. Therefore, the psychologist has legitimate interests in developmental and comparative psychology. Similarly, an interest in failures to adapt leads naturally to the study of abnormal psychology, an interest in how some individuals adapt better than others leads one to study individual differences and develop mental tests to measure those differences, and an interest in how individuals learn to adapt leads to the study of educational psychology and of learning in general. In short, virtually all the topics that were of interest to American psychologists could be gathered under the umbrella of functionalism. Furthermore, studying these diverse areas requires a liberal attitude about appropriate methods. Angell had no quarrel with introspection, but he believed that it had to be defined more broadly than Titchener would allow and that it must be supplemented with more direct observational methods.

In his productive years at Chicago, Angell mentored several individuals destined to become key figures in psychology's story. One was John Watson, the founder of behaviorism as a school of psychology (Chapter 10); another was Harvey Carr, Angell's successor as department head.

Harvey Carr (1873–1954): The Maturing of Functionalism Carr found his way to Chicago in 1902, after completing both a bachelor's and a master's degree in psychology at the University of Colorado. At Colorado, he learned of the new laboratory psychology from Arthur Allin, a former student of Hall and Sanford at Clark. While at Chicago, Carr developed lifelong interests in two diverse topics, the perception of space and maze learning. His doctoral dissertation in 1905 was on the former topic and eventually led to a book (Carr, 1935). Most of his research publications concerned maze learning, however, and a famous study with behaviorist John Watson is featured in Chapter 10. He was also interested in the general problem of maze standardization. In the early years of maze learning research, results often failed to replicate because the mazes used from one study to the next varied considerably. Carr improved the situation substantially by inventing a type of maze that came to be

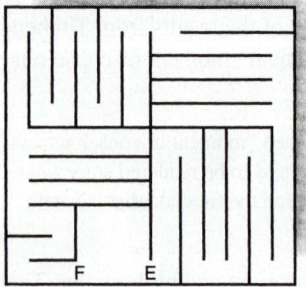 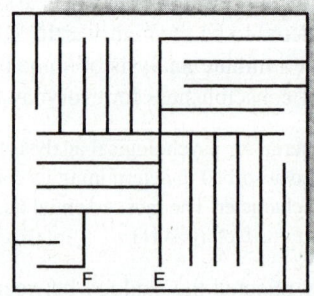

FIGURE 7.7 Designs for two Carr mazes. Redrawn by John Wiley & Sons, Inc.

called the "Carr maze" (Warner & Warden, 1927). Two examples are shown in Figure 7.7. Although each maze had a different solution, the number of choices per maze was constant, as was the length of each pathway and dead end.

After earning his doctorate in 1905, Carr taught elsewhere for several years and then returned to Chicago in 1908. With Watson leaving for Johns Hopkins that year, Angell hired Carr to run the psychology laboratory. Carr remained at Chicago until his retirement in 1938, chairing the department for the second half of his years there. He contributed to the evolution of Chicago functionalism through his influence on students and by the publication of a popular textbook in the mid-1920s—*Psychology: A Study of Mental Activity* (Carr, 1925). In his years at Chicago, Carr had a hand in the doctoral work of no fewer than 131 students, and he directed 53 dissertations, 18 in comparative psychology, 6 in space perception, and 29 in learning (Pillsbury, 1955). The 1925 text can be considered a statement of the "mature" functionalism, with the understanding that functionalism always remained more of an attitude than a precise theoretical position.

The Columbia Functionalists

Because functionalism was more of a state of mind than a rigorous system, it existed well beyond Chicago. Indeed, elements of functional thinking could be found throughout the academic landscape, with the possible exception of Cornell. Even there, however, Titchenerian orthodoxy occasionally relaxed. For instance, E. G. Boring once ran a human maze learning study that featured blindfolded humans navigating an outdoor maze, their pathways marked by trails of flour leaking from sacks attached to their backs; Boring reported that the only significant outcome of the study was that he became infatuated with one of the maze-runners, eventually marrying her (Jaynes, 1969b).[9] Beyond Chicago, however, functionalism at the turn of the century was associated with Columbia University in New York. In its formative years, James McKeen Cattell headed the psychology program there.

James McKeen Cattell (1860–1944): An American Galton   You met James McKeen Cattell briefly in Chapter 4. His research on reaction time in Wundt's laboratory was representative of the technique of estimating the duration of mental events by "complicating" the reaction time procedure. Cattell earned a doctorate from Wundt, although, as you recall from the Chapter 4 Close-Up, he did not hold a high opinion of Wundt's lab. After completing the doctorate, Cattell went to England and briefly

[9]Boring referred to this maze study in his letter to Miles, featured in the *From the Miles Papers* segment of Chapter 6.

studied medicine at Cambridge, where he was exposed to Galton's anthropometric testing, and his life was changed. Cattell never studied formally with Galton, but the two met, and for some time after they exchanged correspondence. Cattell later wrote that Galton was the greatest man he had ever known. The two shared the fundamental belief that the more one could measure, the more one would know.

Cattell (Figure 7.8) returned to America in 1889, after being appointed professor of psychology at the University of Pennsylvania. The title was unusual at a time when most psychologists were still considered professors of philosophy, and indicative of the changes starting to occur within departments of philosophy. He quickly established a laboratory and set out to continue his reaction time studies and to bring Galton's testing approach to America. In an 1890 article in the British journal *Mind*, he summarized the results of testing students on 10 different tests (Cattell, 1890/1948b). Some were borrowed from Galton, but Cattell eliminated the strictly physical measurements (e.g., height, weight, length of arm span), which led him to call his article "Mental Tests and Measurements." With this article, Cattell coined the term **mental test**.

The article's opening sentence revealed Cattell's inductive strategy: "Psychology cannot attain the certainty and exactness of the physical sciences, unless it rests on a foundation of experiment and measurement" (Cattell, 1890/1948b, p. 347). He did not propose any specific purpose for the tests, merely indicating in vague terms that people might "find their tests interesting" (p. 347) and that the results might somehow be "useful in regard to training, mode of life or indication of disease" (p. 347). The 10 tests, which Cattell estimated to take an hour, are summarized in Table 7.1.

Cattell spent 2 years at Penn before accepting (at a still youthful age of 31) an offer to head the psychology program at Columbia, where he remained until being fired in 1917. At Columbia, his testing plans became even more ambitious as he expanded the number of tests and reinstated some of Galton's physical measurements. Within a few years he was lobbying the authorities for permission to test every incoming Columbia freshman, suggesting that the results could be useful "to determine the condition and progress of students, the relative value of different courses of study, etc." (quoted in Sokal, 1987, p. 32).

Library of Congress Prints and Photographs Division, George Grantham Bain Collection

FIGURE 7.8   The irascible James McKeen Cattell (1860–1944).

TABLE 7.1 Cattell's Mental Tests

In his article on mental tests, Cattell (1890/1948b) described these procedures.

1. *Dynamometer pressure.* A measure of grip strength, which Cattell believed to be more than just a physical measure; mental effort and concentration were involved.

2. *Rate of movement.* How quickly one's hand could move across a 50-cm interval was determined; Cattell believed that mental effort and concentration also contributed to this measure.

3. *Sensation-areas.* Two-point thresholds on the back of the right hand were measured.

4. *Pressure causing pain.* The narrow (5 mm in radius) tip of hard rubber pressed into forehead until pain was reported.

5. *Least noticeable difference in weight.* Traditional psychophysics procedure involving the lifting of small boxes that differed slightly in weight.

6. *Reaction time for sound.* For Cattell, the most reliable variety of reaction time.

7. *Time for naming colors.* 10 colored papers pasted adjacent to each other, to be named as quickly as possible.

8. *Bisection of a 50-cm line.* A movable line vertically adjusted until it was at a perceived midpoint of a horizontal line.

9. *Judgment of 10-sec time.* Experimenter tapped a pencil twice, with 10 sec between; those being tested had to repeat the task.

10. *Number of letters repeated on once hearing.* This was an early version of a short-term memory test, to determine how many letters could be repeated verbatim.

For the rest of the 1890s, Cattell and his students accumulated masses of data, but the project collapsed shortly after the turn of the century. Cattell knew of Galton's correlational procedures and their development into the "coefficient of correlation" (Pearson's r). He asked one of his graduate students, Clark Wissler, to apply the new technique to the testing results, hoping to reveal strong relationships between the measures and to relate them to academic performance. Wissler completed the correlations, and the outcome was devastating—the tests were unrelated to each other (e.g., the correlation between reaction time and color naming was a meager +.15) and, more critically, they did not correlate with academic performance (e.g., a correlation of +.02 between reaction time and "college standing"). A student's performance in class (including gym) correlated more highly with overall academic performance than did any of Cattell's tests. In an understatement, Wissler (1901/1965) concluded that "correlations in … the foregoing tests are not of a degree sufficient for practical purposes" (p. 444).

After the Wissler debacle, Cattell turned his attention away from mental testing and toward another of his interests, the professionalizing of psychology. A charter member of the American Psychological Association, he was an active participant and, in 1895, its fourth president. In 1894, he helped to launch what would become one of psychology's more prestigious journals, *Psychological Review*, and a year later he took over the editorship of the financially ailing journal *Science*. By 1910, he had transformed *Science* into the most important scientific journal published in America (Sokal, 1981b).

After the turn of the century, Cattell devoted most of his time to editorial and departmental work. Always outspoken, he regularly irritated the Columbia administration by arguing for greater faculty participation in academic decision making and for increased academic freedom (i.e., a faculty member's right to investigate and teach about controversial topics). In 1917, he finally pushed the administration over the edge by publicly protesting the government's policy of sending conscientious objectors into combat in World War I. Columbia's president accused him of treason and fired him. Cattell also had alienated many of his peers over the years, so he received little faculty support (Sokal, 2009). Cattell sued for libel and won a large settlement, but his academic career was over. He continued his editorial work, though, and returned to applied psychology by founding the Psychological Corporation in 1921. Designed to be an organization of psychologist–consultants, it began at a time when American psychologists had high hopes for marketing their skills to business, industry, and education. Cattell proved to be a poor administrator, however; although the Psychological Corporation flourishes today, it barely survived Cattell's leadership (Sokal, 1981a).

Despite his myriad problems, Cattell created a vibrant department during his Columbia years. Dozens of well-known psychologists earned their doctoral stripes during his tenure as department head, and Cattell himself directed more than 50 dissertations (Jonçich, 1968). His two best-known students were Edward Thorndike and Robert Woodworth.

Edward L. Thorndike (1874–1949): Cats in Puzzle Boxes

Most of Edward Thorndike's impact was in the fields of educational psychology and psychological testing, but he is most often remembered among research psychologists for studying how cats learned to escape from puzzle boxes. For this reason he is considered a pioneer in comparative psychology, an example of what Lloyd Morgan had in mind as the proper way to do animal research. He also appears occasionally in chapters on behaviorism as a precursor to the conditioning work of Pavlov and Watson. In a certain sense, then, he was a transition figure from the early comparative psychologists to the later behaviorists.

Thorndike excelled at the Methodist-run Wesleyan University in Connecticut, graduating with honors in 1895. While there, he found his vocation by discovering James's *Principles of Psychology*, which electrified him as it had James Angell and countless others of that generation. Thorndike (1936) later described the book as more stimulating "than any book that I had read before, and possibly more so than any book read since" (p. 263). Like Angell, Thorndike entered Harvard's graduate program to experience James directly. It is not clear exactly how Thorndike's interests in animal behavior developed, but a seminar taken with James used Wundt's *Lectures on Human and Animal Psychology* , and he might have attended public lectures given by the visiting Lloyd Morgan, Britain's premier comparative psychologist (Chapter 5). Like every educated person of his day, he was thoroughly familiar with evolutionary thinking. With a characteristic self-confidence bordering on arrogance, Thorndike's explanation for his choice of research topic was simple: "My first research was in animal psychology, not because I knew animals or cared much for them, but because I thought I could do better than had been done" (quoted in Jonçich, 1968, p. 89).

Thorndike first studied instinct and intelligence in baby chicks by asking them to escape from simple mazes formed by placing books on end. Figure 7.9 shows three of the patterns he used. Chicks would be placed in the maze at location A, and then observed to see if they could find the exit. Thorndike reported that they initially jumped at the walls, made a lot of noise, and were just as likely to go more deeply into the maze than to escape from it. After several trials, however, they eliminated the useless

 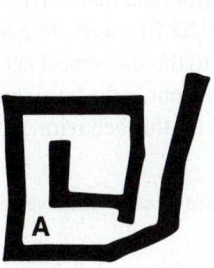 

FIGURE 7.9 Maze designs for baby chicks that Thorndike created by placing books vertically on a table. Thorndike, E. L. 2000. Animal intelligence: Experimental studies. New Brunswick, NJ: Transaction Publishers. Original work published 1911

behaviors and found their way out. Incidentally, some of this research was completed in the cellar of the William James household. Thorndike's landlord had evicted the animals, and James had taken them in after being unable to secure space for them on campus. Thorndike believed that the "nuisance to Mrs. James was … somewhat mitigated by the entertainment to the two youngest children" (Thorndike, 1936, p. 264).

For reasons partly financial and partly the consequence of a romantic relationship that seemed to be going nowhere (with the woman who would later become his wife, as it turned out), Thorndike applied for and received a fellowship to Columbia. Cattell was impressed with the young scientist, and Thorndike was awarded $700 a year in aid, more than the average annual income for most families at that time (Jonçich, 1968). At Columbia, he expanded his animal research to several different species, but his most famous work was done with cats in puzzle boxes, published as "Animal Intelligence: An Experimental Study of the Associative Processes in Animals" in 1898.

Thorndike was a strong critic of contemporary comparative psychologists, especially when they relied on anecdotal data to support claims of higher mental powers for animals. As he put it, rather sarcastically, "dogs get lost hundreds of times and no one ever notices it or sends an account of it to scientific magazines. But let one find his way from Brooklyn to Yonkers and the fact immediately becomes a circulating anecdote (Thorndike, 1911/2000, p. 24).

Thorndike knew he could do better, and the most important aspect of the puzzle box studies was the methodological rigor that he brought to the project (Galef, 1998). Disdaining anecdotes, Thorndike instead developed systematic procedures to test claims for animal intelligence—he would study more than a single case, he would repeat the experiments, and he would control the learning history and the environments of the animals he studied. The method he decided on was "to put animals when hungry in inclosures from which they could escape by some simple act, such as pulling at a loop of cord, pressing a lever, or stepping on a platform" (Thorndike, 1911/2000, p. 26). Their behavior, and the amount of time it took to escape, would be recorded.

Although Thorndike's research strategy was clear and logical, he was the exception to the rule that the early experimentalists were talented and creative apparatus builders. His books-on-end mazes for chicks hinted at a lack of mechanical aptitude, and his puzzle boxes confirmed the handicap.[10] Thorndike included a sketch of one of the 15 boxes he built (Figure 7.10). Although the drawing suggests a neat, clean design, his actual boxes were crudely built (Burnham, 1972). Nevertheless, there was a method to the apparent chaos in the box construction. Figure 7.10 (Box K), for instance, was designed to combine three responses that had been the only ones necessary in each of three other boxes. Box K was used with cats that had learned each of the individual responses, to see if they could combine the information and escape quickly. Thorndike used 13 different cats in his puzzle boxes. It is not clear from his description exactly how many cats were tested in each of the boxes, but it appears that each cat was tested in at least several of the boxes.

And how did the cats behave when placed in the boxes? At first, their behavior seemed random—a series of attempts to escape by any means possible (e.g., clawing at or biting the wood slats). Eventually, the correct response occurred, by accident at first. From trial to trial, the ineffective responses dropped out and the successful one occurred sooner. In Thorndike's (1911/2000) words, "the other nonsuccessful impulses will be stamped out and the particular impulse leading to the successful act will be stamped in by the resulting pleasure, until, after many trials, the cat will, when put in the box, immediately claw the button or loop in a definite way" (p. 36). Thorndike's explanation for this behavior, which also applied to

---

[10]Also, Thorndike never learned how to use a typewriter or how to drive a car, and his son could never recall seeing his father "fix" anything (Thorndike, 1991).

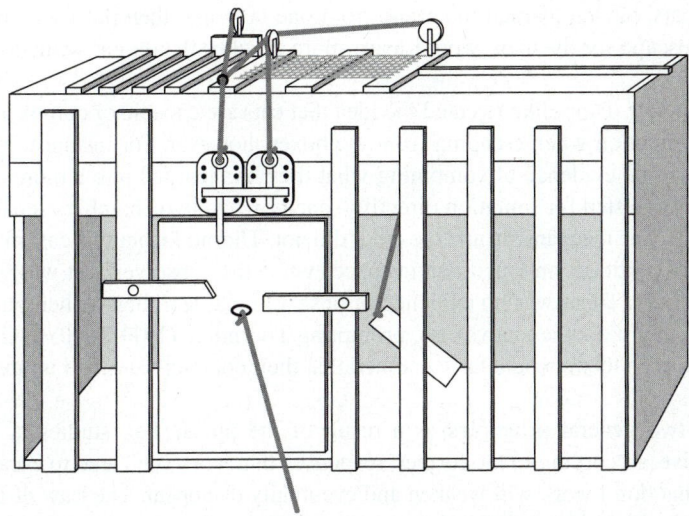

FIGURE 7.10 Thorndike's puzzle box K (required three separate responses). Thorndike, E. L. 2000. Animal intelligence: Experimental studies. New Brunswick, NJ: Transaction Publishers. Original work published 1911

his chicks-in-mazes experiments, was the same as that given by Morgan to explain the behavior of dogs opening gates to escape from yards—**trial-and-error learning** (Thorndike preferred the phrase "trial and accidental success"). Because he believed that the cat learned to make *connections* between stimuli in the boxes and successful escape responses during this trial-and-error learning, Thorndike's learning model is sometimes called **connectionism**. From trial to trial, then, unsuccessful behaviors drop out and the successful one is strengthened ("stamped in"). Figure 7.11 charts the gradually improving, if erratic, progress of one of Thorndike's cats.

To account for the fact that every situation encountered in life is unique, Thorndike applied the results of some research on transfer that he completed with Woodworth. He proposed that if a new situation had some elements in common with an old situation, then transfer would occur. For example,

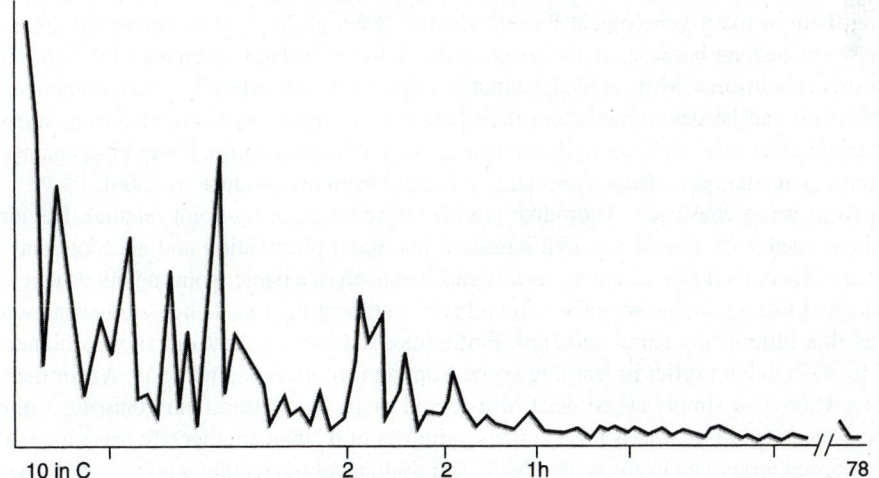

FIGURE 7.11 Performance of cat #10 in puzzle box C. On the *X* axis, the unlabeled vertical dash meant a day, "2" meant two days, "1 h" meant an hour, and "78" meant 78 hours. From E. L. Thorndike 1911, Animal Intelligence: Experimental Studies. Republished 2000 New Brunswick, NJ: Transaction Publishers.

he found that some of his cats, having learned to escape from one box, and then put into a box with a similar but not identical escape mechanism, would learn more quickly than a cat without such an experience.

While allowing for transfer, Thorndike rejected the idea that cats are capable of complex reasoning or able to benefit from imitation when escaping from the boxes, however. For instance, in Box K (Figure 7.10), the cats showed no evidence of combining what they had learned into a more complex sequence of behaviors. He also tested for imitation directly—one box had two chambers separated by wire mesh. One side had an escape mechanism, and the other did not. Thorndike put two cats in the box, one on either side of the wire partition, and recorded instances when the "observer" cat was watching the other cat escape successfully. There was no evidence of observational learning—when put to test, the observer cat behaved exactly like other, naive cats, prompting Thorndike (1911/2000) to conclude, "No one, I am sure, who had seen them, would have claimed that their conduct was at all influenced by what they had seen" (p. 89).

Thorndike proposed two general principles as a result of the puzzle box studies, a **Law of Effect** and a **Law of Exercise**. According to the former, responses that work (i.e., lead to escape) will strengthen, whereas those that don't work will weaken and eventually disappear. The Law of Exercise stated simply that the connection between stimulus situation and response would strengthen with practice. As will be seen in Chapter 11, Thorndike's Law of Effect bears a close resemblance to B. F. Skinner's concept of operant conditioning, and Skinner recognized his debt to Thorndike, referring to the Columbia psychologist's work as "[o]ne of the first serious attempts to study changes brought about by the consequences of behavior" (Skinner, 1953, p. 59).

Thorndike was excited about his research and willing to take on critics, writing to his future wife that his 1898 thesis was "a beauty....I've got some theories which knock the old authorities into a grease spot" (quoted in Jonçich, 1968, p. 146). One authority who was not amused by Thorndike's youthful exuberance was Wesley Mills, a comparative psychologist who dismissed Thorndike's research. Mills started by faulting Thorndike's lack of respect for his "elders," noting that "Dr. Thorndike has not been hampered in his researches by any of that respect for workers of the past ... which usually causes men to pause before differing radically from them, not to say gleefully consigning them to the psychological flames" (Mills, 1899, p. 263). More important, Mills rejected the study's conclusions because of the *artificiality* of the environment created by Thorndike. Cats placed in small enclosures, Mills argued, cannot be expected to act naturally. Thus, nothing about their normal behavior can be determined from their behavior in highly artificial, abnormal surroundings. Mills concluded that one might as well "enclose a living man in a coffin, lower him, against his will, into the earth, and attempt to deduce normal psychology from his conduct" (p. 266).

Far from being chastened, Thorndike (1899) offered a point-by-point rebuttal. He admitted to being unimpressed with animal research based on uncritical observation and anecdote and made no apology for it. He denied Mills's claim that his cats had been in a panic, pointing out caustically that if Mills had acted like a genuine scientist and bothered to repeat the puzzle box studies, he would have discovered that little if any panic occurred. Furthermore, those cats that did show a higher "fury of activity" (p. 412) did not differ in learning speed from their more sanguine peers. As for the charge of artificiality, Thorndike simply asked what Mills could mean by a natural environment. Animals constantly face new situations; who is to say one is more "natural" than another? To drive home the point, Thorndike turned around an example that Mills had used, a cat navigating a bookshelf. "The situation here coped with is as 'unnatural' as that in ... my experiments" (p. 414), Thorndike wrote.

The Mills–Thorndike exchange is a good illustration of a difference of opinion about the appropriateness of laboratory methods that continues to this day. On the one hand are those who argue that understanding animal behavior requires the precision afforded by a controlled laboratory environment.

In such a setting, the effects of various influences on behavior can be studied systematically. As will be seen, this approach was taken by the majority of American animal researchers who came to be known as behaviorists (e.g., Skinner). In contrast, other psychologists followed Mills and argued that animal behavior can only be understood if it is studied outside the structured confines of the laboratory. Most 20th-century European researchers took this route, creating a field known as **ethology**—the study of animal behavior in its "natural" surroundings. The best known of these scientists are Konrad Lorenz, Karl von Frisch, and Niko Tinbergen, who shared the 1973 Nobel Prize in biology for their work on instinctive animal behavior.

After earning his doctorate, Thorndike taught for a year at Case Western Reserve in Cleveland and then returned to Columbia's Teachers College, where he remained for the rest of his career. There he extended his research on learning to humans and became a leading educational psychologist. He also developed a series of aptitude tests for schoolchildren, thereby contributing to the psychological testing movement as well. Honors came his way in the form of an APA presidency (1912), election to the National Academy of Sciences (1917), and the presidency of the AAAS (American Association for the Advancement of Science (1934). Figure 7.12 shows Thorndike at the ceremony marking the end of his AAAS presidency; in the center is Thorndike's successor, noted physicist Karl Compton, and on the right is an aging Cattell, who had been the first psychologist elected to the AAAS presidency, in 1924.

Thorndike was a prolific writer, averaging about a dozen articles a year. He also wrote numerous textbooks, including a three-volume *Educational Psychology* in 1913, which made his name "practically synonymous with the field of educational psychology for many years to come" (Goodenough, 1950, p. 295). Like James, he followed this multivolume effort with a single-volume "briefer course" the following year (Thorndike, 1914). Most of Thorndike's texts were compilations of lecture notes, prompting Titchener to scold Thorndike for publishing "lecture courses as soon as the lectures have been delivered … [The practice] must inevitably show marks of hasty preparation and of immaturity of judgment" (Titchener, 1905b). The criticism didn't slow Thorndike down for a minute, however, and by the 1920s his royalty earnings far exceeded his Columbia salary. In 1924, for instance, his royalty

© Bettmann/Corbis Images

FIGURE 7.12 E. L. Thorndike (left) as retiring president of the American Academy for the Advancement of Science (AAAS); on the right is an elderly James McKeen Cattell.

income of $68,000 was five times his faculty salary (Jonçich, 1968). Thorndike retired from Columbia in 1940 and died in 1949.

Robert S. Woodworth (1869–1962): A Dynamic Psychology Woodworth (Figure 7.13), named Robert Sessions after an ancestor who participated in the Boston Tea Party, was born in the small western Massachusetts town of Belchertown. After graduating from nearby Amherst College, Woodworth taught high school science and math for few years and then discovered (who else?) William James and *The Principles* and decided to pursue a career in either philosophy or psychology. Like Angell and Thorndike, Woodworth wanted to experience the master directly, so off he went to Harvard in the fall of 1895. Woodworth stayed in Cambridge for 3 academic years, earning a second bachelor's degree, a master's degree, and serving as assistant in physiology at the Harvard Medical School. During this time he developed two lifelong friendships, one with the noted physiologist Walter B. Cannon, whose work would eventually yield a theory of emotion to rival the James–Lange theory (the Cannon–Bard theory), and a second with Thorndike. This latter friendship contributed to Woodworth's next stop after Harvard—Cattell offered him a fellowship to Columbia, partly the result of being pestered to do so by Thorndike (Jonçich, 1968).

Woodworth completed his doctorate at Columbia in 1899; after spending a productive year in England in the laboratory of the esteemed physiologist Charles Sherrington (Chapter 3), he accepted Cattell's invitation in 1903 to join the psychology department, where he remained until his retirement in 1939 at age 70. Retirement barely slowed him down, however, for Woodworth continued to teach part-time until he was 89 and to write until he was 91. Woodworth was a modest and unassuming man, remembered for (a) his research with Thorndike on transfer of training, (b) his "dynamic" psychology, with its emphasis on drives and organismic variables, and (c) his impact on students, both directly and

From Popular Science Monthly, Volume 74 (1909)

FIGURE 7.13 Robert S. Woodworth, author of the "Columbia bible." Woodworth is also in Figure 7.5, in the far left of the front row.

through textbook writing, especially the so-called Columbia bible. This latter achievement, by itself, was sufficient to ensure his lasting importance to 20th-century experimental psychology.

The research on **transfer** derived from a fundamental problem in higher education—the validity of claims made on behalf of the doctrine of "formal discipline." Rooted in faculty psychology, it was the mid-19th-century belief that the curriculum for higher education should be designed to "exercise" and strengthen the intellectual faculties. This was to be accomplished through the study of such disciplines as Latin, Greek, and classical literature. Once the faculties were "in shape," the skills that had been developed were assumed to transfer to other disciplines to be learned later. The doctrine came under fire near the end of the century, when several schools copied Harvard's radical concept of an "elective" curriculum, which enabled students to avoid Latin and Greek if they wished. The debate generated much rhetoric, but little evidence accumulated for or against the idea that learning topic A (e.g., Greek) made it easier to learn topic B (e.g., zoology). Thorndike and Woodworth, in a series of coauthored publications (e.g., 1901), set out to find evidence for transfer of training. Their subjects practiced one task, and then tried other tasks that varied in the degree of resemblance to the original task. After estimating the areas of rectangles, for instance, they estimated the areas of triangles (high resemblance) or the weight of objects (low resemblance). Briefly, what they found was that the amount of transfer occurring was directly proportional to the number of elements shared by the tasks. Although their tasks were quite different from curricular topics, Thorndike and Woodworth generalized their results to the issue of formal discipline, concluding that the doctrine had little merit. Because subjects like Greek bore minimal relationship to subjects like zoology, Thorndike and Woodworth predicted very little benefit to zoologists from studying Greek (except for some word origin information perhaps). As mentioned earlier, Thorndike also used the transfer concept to explain how cats that escaped from one box would find it easier to escape from a new box, especially if the two boxes shared similar escape devices.

Woodworth is often described as an *eclectic* when it came to theorizing, willing to incorporate the features of various diverse systems. In his popular introductory text, for example, he defined psychology as the study of both mental processes *and* behavior, thus blending behaviorism (Chapter 10) with the traditional psychology of consciousness. This definition continues to be found in virtually all general psychology texts. Woodworth also believed that psychologists should use a variety of methods, ranging from introspection to mental testing to the objective observation of behavior. He disliked those who would define psychology narrowly, naming both Titchener (structuralism) and Watson (behaviorism) as examples, and he revealed his basic philosophy by ending his popular history of psychology, *Contemporary Schools of Psychology*, with a chapter called "The Middle of the Road" (Woodworth, 1931, pp. 205–219). He was especially critical of a simple mechanistic, stimulus-response psychology, arguing for what he referred to as an **S-O-R model**. That is, he insisted that psychologists must understand not just the stimulus and response, but also the organism (O) that responds to the stimuli and produces the behaviors. This includes studying what motivates or drives the organism. In his *Dynamic Psychology* (1918) and *Dynamics of Behavior* (1958), Woodworth argued for the importance of studying motivational factors influencing behavior. As he wrote in an autobiography, "[m]otivation has always seemed to me a field of study worthy to be placed alongside of performance. That is, we need to know not only what the individual can do and how he does it, but also what induces him to do one thing rather than another" (Woodworth, 1932, p. 371).

Like his best friend Thorndike, Woodworth became wealthy by writing textbooks. His *Psychology*, with editions appearing in 1921, 1929, 1934, and 1940, introduced thousands of students to the field for over two decades. More important for research psychologists, his *Experimental Psychology* shaped the very definition the term *experiment*. When the book made its initial appearance in 1938, it was already so well known that no psychologist was perplexed when the publisher announced "The

Bible is out" (Estes, 1981). As early as 1909, Woodworth had been distributing mimeographed handouts for his course in experimental methods, and by 1920 these had grown into a 285-page handout called "A Textbook in Experimental Psychology." By 1938, the eagerly anticipated volume finally appeared and was an immediate success, selling more than 44,000 copies by 1954, when it was revised and a coauthor added (Woodworth & Schlosberg, 1954). By one estimate, between 1938 and 1959 more than 100,000 psychology majors learned about research in psychology from Woodworth (Winston, 1990).

Woodworth's 1938 text was encyclopedic, with more than 823 pages of text and another 36 pages of references. After an introductory chapter, it was organized into 29 different research topics, including such diverse topics as memory, transfer of training, maze learning, reaction time, hearing, visual perception, and thinking. Students using the text learned about the procedures related to each content area, as well as virtually everything there was to know in 1938 about each topic. They also learned some distinctions that you will recognize.

Prior to Woodworth, the term *experiment* had been used as a label for procedures ranging from the introspection of a mental event to a mental test to an observation under controlled circumstances. Woodworth, however, narrowed the definition and contrasted experimental research with what he referred to as correlational research. The defining feature of the experimental method was to be the manipulation of a factor that was the main focus of study, what Woodworth called an **independent variable**, and this variable would have its effects on some measure of behavior, or as he called it, the **dependent variable**. Woodworth did not invent the terms, but he was the first psychologist to use them in this manner. Although the experimental method manipulates independent variables, Woodworth wrote, the correlational method "measures two or more characteristics of the same individuals [and] computes the correlation of these characteristics. This method … has no 'independent variable' but treats all the measured variables alike" (Woodworth, 1938, p. 3). Furthermore, Woodworth originated the argument, now found in the methodology chapter of every introductory text, that the experimental method was the only technique allowing causal conclusions; no causation could be inferred from correlations. Although Woodworth argued that correlational research should have the same overall status as experimental research, he omitted correlational findings from the remainder of the text. The reader could be excused for thinking that the experimental approach was superior. Indeed, the consequences of Woodworth's distinction were sufficient to become the focus of a cautionary APA presidential address in 1957. In "The Two Disciplines of Scientific Psychology," Lee Cronbach argued for reestablishing the status of correlational research to that of the controlled experiment.

IN PERSPECTIVE: STRUCTURALISM AND FUNCTIONALISM

Traditionally, internal histories of psychology have been organized around the concept of "schools of psychology," a term referring to a broad conceptual framework that includes statements about psychology's definition, its preferred methods, and its important concepts. Thus, structuralism, functionalism, gestalt psychology (Chapter 9), behaviorism (Chapters 10 and 11), and psychoanalysis (Chapter 12) are normally considered to have been the predominant schools in psychology's history. This chapter has examined structuralism and functionalism, the former associated primarily with one man, Titchener, and the latter associated with just about everyone else in American psychology, at least during the period from 1890 to 1930.

Structuralism essentially died with Titchener, but the fact that it continues to occupy space in modern history texts is an indication of the strength of Titchener's influence. When Titchener died in 1927, E. G. Boring wrote this in an obituary for his mentor:

> The death of no other psychologist could so alter the psychological picture in America. Not only was he unique among American psychologists as a personality and in his scientific attitude, but he was a cardinal point in the national systematic orientation. The clear-cut opposition between behaviorism and its allies, on the one hand, and something else, on the other, remains clear only when the opposition is between behaviorism and Titchener, mental tests and Titchener, or applied psychology and Titchener. (Boring, 1961a, p. 246)

Boring's claim is inflated, the kind of language often found in obituaries, yet it has a ring of truth to it. Angell's "province of functional psychology" paper focused on a direct contrast with Titchener's structuralism. And as you read in the quote at the end of the structuralism section of this chapter and will learn in Chapter 10, John B. Watson described the advantages of behaviorism by contrasting them directly with structuralism.

Yet throughout psychology's history, psychologists have been less likely to call themselves structuralists or functionalists or behaviorists, and more likely to refer to themselves simply as psychologists. The "functionalists" illustrate this point perfectly. Angell, Woodworth, Thorndike, and others show why functionalism was not a dogmatic *school* of psychology, but rather a set of attitudes about psychology, attitudes rooted in American pragmatic thinking and firmly grounded in evolutionary logic. These same attributes characterize those functionalists who extended their laboratory research interests into the areas of applied psychology. Their work occupies the next chapter.

SUMMARY

Titchener's Psychology: Structuralism

- E. B. Titchener earned a PhD with Wundt at Leipzig, then came to Cornell University, where he established an approach to psychology called structuralism. The main goals for a structural psychology, were to achieve a complete analysis of the "generalized adult mind," show how elements could be combined into more complex phenomena (synthesis), and provide an explanation of mental processes by understanding the workings of the brain and nervous system

- Titchener promoted an experimental/laboratory approach to psychology by writing a series of highly detailed training manuals that introduced students and instructors to precise laboratory work and by forming a close-knit group of fellow male researchers called the Experimentalists, who met annually to share the details of their ongoing research.

- Titchener identified introspection as psychology's primary method and believed that introspections could yield valid data only if introspectors were highly trained and capable of the introspective habit.

- The main elements of conscious experience, according to Titchener, are sensations, images, and affects. Sensations and images have the attributes of quality, intensity, duration, and clearness, but images aren't as clear as sensations. Affects have but two qualities, pleasantness and unpleasantness, and they lack clarity.

- Titchener's primary contribution was to promote laboratory psychology, but his system omitted major topics of interest to most American psychologists, and his method of introspection was shown to be fundamentally flawed because of its lack of objectivity.

America's Psychology: Functionalism

- Most American psychologists, influenced by evolutionary theory and a generally pragmatic attitude, were interested more in the functions of consciousness than in its structure. Functionalism was widespread, but mainly associated with the University of Chicago and Columbia University.

- The origins of functionalism are often traced to a paper on the reflex arc by John Dewey of Chicago. Dewey argued against the analytic strategy of reducing the reflex to its elements and argued instead that the reflex needed to be seen in its broader context as a coordinated system that served to adapt the organism to its environment. Dewey was known primarily for his progressive views on education, believing that students should be active learners, and for his philosophical writings on democracy.

- The earliest clear statement of the functionalist philosophy came from the 1906 APA presidential address of James Angell, who explicitly compared structuralism and functionalism, pointing out that structuralists were more likely to ask the question "What is consciousness?" whereas functionalists were more concerned with the question "What is consciousness for?" This led them to study topics ranging from developmental to abnormal psychology and led them to be interested in individual differences and how psychology could be used to solve everyday problems.

- Harvey Carr was Angell's successor at Chicago, bringing functionalism to its maturity there. He was known for his maze learning research and for developing Chicago into one of the country's best graduate programs.

- Galton's approach to mental testing, which emphasized physical and sensory measures, was imported to America by James McKeen Cattell, who created the term "mental test" and developed a testing program at Columbia. The program failed when the measurements could not be correlated with academic performance, however. Cattell played an important role in the professionalization of psychology in America, primarily through his editorial work in rejuvenating (*Science*) or helping to found (*Psychological Review*, *Psychological Bulletin*) scientific journals.

- Edward Thorndike became a leading educational psychologist, but in his early years he was known for his studies of cats in puzzle boxes. He was highly critical of contemporary comparative psychology, which relied on anecdotal evidence and was overly anthropomorphic. He studied trial-and-error learning and proposed that learning occurred through the creation of connections between situations and responses that were successful in those situations (Law of Effect) and that connections were strengthened with repetition (Law of Exercise). His debate with Mills reflected a fundamental disagreement between those advocating laboratory methods and those who preferred to study animals in their daily environments.

- Robert Woodworth is remembered for his research with Thorndike on transfer, which called traditional educational practices into question; his dynamic psychology, which replaced an S-R model with an S-O-R framework and emphasized motivational influences on behavior; and his textbook writing, especially on methodology. His "Columbia bible" institutionalized the distinctions between experimental and correlational research and between independent and dependent variables in experimental research.

STUDY QUESTIONS

1. In his 1898 paper on structural psychology, what was the argument that Titchener made for studying structure prior to function?

2. Distinguish between German and American (drill course) methods for training students how to be experimental psychologists.

3. Describe the contents of Titchener's Manuals, distinguish between the qualitative and quantitative manuals, and explain the significance of the work.

4. What were the Experimentalists, why were they formed, what did they do, and why did they exclude women?

5. Describe Titchener's version of introspection, and explain why it was so important for introspectors to be highly trained.

6. Why did Titchener exclude the study of children, animals, and the insane from his definition of psychology?

7. What was the main issue behind the Baldwin–Titchener controversy?

8. Describe the imageless thought controversy, and show how it was a good illustration of the problems with introspection.

9. Show how the school of functionalism is related to evolutionary thinking.

10. Describe the main points of Dewey's reflex arc article and the significance of the article.

11. Use Angell's APA presidential address of 1906 to provide a comparison of structuralist and functionalist ways of thinking about psychology.

12. What was a Carr maze, and what was the importance of this apparatus?

13. Explain how Cattell's approach to mental testing was influenced by Galton, and describe any 5 of Cattell's original 10 mental tests.

14. Describe the Wissler study, and explain its significance for the Galton/Cattell approach to mental testing.

15. How did Thorndike describe the process by which cats escaped from his puzzle boxes? How did this illustrate the laws of effect and exercise?

16. Explain how Thorndike ruled out the idea that cats could learn the escape through reasoning and imitation.

17. What was the substance of the Thorndike–Mills controversy, and what was its significance?

18. What was the importance of Woodworth inserting an "O" between the "S" and the "R," when describing behavior?

19. What was the significance of Woodworth's "Columbia bible," and what distinctions did he make in the book that continue to be in use today?

CHAPTER 8

APPLYING THE NEW PSYCHOLOGY

Unless our laboratory results are to give us artificialities, mere scientific curiosities, they must be subjected to interpretation by gradual approximation to the conditions of life.

—John Dewey, 1900

PREVIEW AND CHAPTER OBJECTIVES

In the discussion of historiography in Chapter 1, I pointed out that E. G. Boring's famous 1929 text, *A History of Experimental Psychology*, was written in part as a way for him to return laboratory research to what he saw as its rightful place at the forefront of American psychology. Boring's concern about the threat to "pure science" was justified—American psychologists in the 1920s seemed to be obsessed with finding new ways to apply psychological principles to everyday life. Actually, interest in application existed from the earliest days of psychology in America, and this chapter will explore both the roots and the development of applied psychology. Its origins lie deeply embedded in the American character and in the economic, political, and institutional contexts of the late 19th and early 20th centuries.

This chapter will examine several examples of applied psychology, starting with the mental testing movement. We will learn how the Galton/Cattell approach (Chapter 7) was replaced by the strategy of Alfred Binet of France, how Binet's methods were brought to America, and how a hereditarian view of mental ability colored interpretations of intelligence. The major American mental testers discussed will be Henry Goddard, who brought Binet's test to America, where it quickly succeeded; Lewis Terman, developer of the Stanford–Binet test that institutionalized the concept of IQ; and Robert Yerkes, a comparative psychologist at heart, whose development of the Army testing program was a major reason for Boring's fear that the spread of applied psychology was a direct threat to "pure" experimental psychology.

A second major application of psychology took place in the area of business or industrial psychology. This part of the chapter will feature the work of the German psychologist Hugo Münsterberg. He earned a doctorate with Wundt, but became known for his applied work. Münsterberg also made contributions to other applied areas, especially forensic psychology. The chapter also includes briefer descriptions of the work of several prominent American industrial psychologists—Walter Dill Scott, Walter Van Dyke Bingham, Lillian Gilbreth, and Harry Hollingworth—as well as an account of "psychotechnics," the term used to describe applied psychology in Europe. Clinical psychology, a major area of application, will be considered in Chapters 12 and 13. After you finish this chapter, you should be able to:

- Understand why it was important for early American psychologists to show that their "new psychology" had practical applications
- Contrast Binet's individual psychology with a more "general" psychology
- Describe the origins, the content, and the original purpose of the Binet–Simon scales
- Describe Goddard's classification scheme for the different levels of feeblemindedness
- Describe and critically analyze the Kallikak study and Goddard's work at Ellis Island

- Explain the differences between the original Binet–Simon scale and Terman's revision, the Stanford–Binet
- Explain how Terman's belief in meritocracy led him to investigate gifted children; describe the findings of his research
- Describe the contributions of Leta Hollingworth to gifted education and to understanding gender differences in ability
- Describe the origins of the Army testing program, distinguish between Army Alpha and Beta, and explain why the program was controversial
- Describe the contributions made by Hugo Münsterberg to applied psychology
- Distinguish between the two general strategies used by Münsterberg to improve the employee selection process
- Describe the contributions to applied psychology of Walter Dill Scott, Walter Van Dyke Bingham, Lillian Gilbreth, and Harry Hollingworth
- Describe the scope of applied psychology in Europe in the years leading up to World War II

THE DESIRE FOR APPLICATION

In 1895, Yale's E. W. Scripture published *Thinking, Feeling, Doing*, a book intended to explain the new experimental psychology to the general public. He wrote in the preface that he hoped his effort would "be taken as evidence of the attitude of the science in its desire to serve humanity" (Scripture, 1895, p. iii). Perhaps to hold the reader's interest, he included 209 photos and drawings in the 295 pages of text. Most of the book described the basic laboratory procedures in vogue at the time—psychophysics, reaction time, basic sensory processes, and so on.

What was unusual, however, was Scripture's attempt to convince readers that basic laboratory methods could improve everyday life. For example, after describing reaction time research, Scripture pointed out that the method could be used to study the "psychological elements involved in sports, gymnastics, and all sorts of athletic work" (p. 57). He then proceeded to illustrate the point by adapting the reaction procedures to measure the reaction times involved in such activities as boxing, track, and even fencing (Figure 8.1), thereby making him an early pioneer in what would eventually be called sport psychology (Goodwin, 2009). Two decades later, another experimental-psychologist-by-training, Walter Miles also made a foray into sports, football in this case.

Scripture, E. W. (1895) Thinking, feeling, doing. New York, NY: Chautauqua-Century Press

FIGURE 8.1 Photo from Scripture's *Thinking, Feeling, Doing* (1895) designed to show how reaction time methodology can improve the performance of fencers.

FROM THE MILES PAPERS...

MILES AND STANFORD FOOTBALL

Walter Miles taught at Stanford during the 1920s, a time when the university's football team was among the best in the nation. The coach was the legendary Glen "Pop" Warner, who was known for being innovative (e.g., invented the screen pass, pioneered the use of shoulder and thigh pads), and was willing to try anything if it would improve the team. Miles became involved with the football program when B. C. Graves, a high school football coach who was a master's degree student in psychology at Stanford, became interested in how reaction time methods might be of value to a football team.

Warner was intrigued, as was Graves's teacher, Miles, who was known as an innovator in his own way—as the creator of interesting apparatus (Goodwin, 2003). The result was the construction of a device that Miles called a multiple chronograph because of its ability to measure several reaction times simultaneously (Figure 8.2). On a signal, the players would charge forward, their heads pushing on boards with strings attached to them, causing golf balls to drop on a drum revolving at a constant speed. Miles rigged the device to measure the exact time between the signal and the players' movements.

You can get a sense of Miles's love of apparatus-driven research in a letter he wrote on September 7, 1927, to his close friend Raymond Dodge:

During the last two weeks of September, I expect to take a try at collecting some data from the football men in their fall practice. I have rigged up an arrangement by which I can measure the charging time from signal to first movement of body on seven men at once. My preliminary results on 28 football players give pretty good correlation with the speed rating which the coaches independently made.... Our head coach, "Pop" Warner, has insisted that I canvass and rate the whole fall squad in this same manner. It is rather good fun, and I believe I can get some worthwhile data. (Miles, 1927)

Notice that, always thinking as a scientist, Miles made an effort to validate his device, showing that those football players rated as fast by coaches also tended to have the quickest reaction times on his device. Despite the apparent usefulness of the device (selecting players who reacted the quickest to signals), Pop Warner apparently lost interest. Miles and Graves published several studies on the research (e.g., Miles & Graves, 1931), and Miles in subsequent years had several inquiries from other coaches about the device, but the "rather good fun" that Miles had in 1927 seems to have been the main outcome.

Walter & Catherine Cox Miles papers, Archives of the History of American Psychology, The Center for the History of Psychology, The University of Akron

Stanford 1927

FIGURE 8.2   Walter Miles (in the suit) testing the quickness of Stanford linemen, 1927.

The interest in application among psychologists was partly the consequence of American pragmatism, combined with the progressive drive for reform that characterized the early 20th century. In an age of dramatic technological change, Americans were becoming accustomed to the idea that science should improve their lives. In the last few decades of the 19th century they had witnessed the arrival of such inventions as telephones, the telegraph, typewriters, electric lights (and chairs), skyscrapers, barbed wire, and the kinetoscope (for showing moving pictures). Railroads had expanded so dramatically that by 1900, virtually everyone in America lived within hearing distance of a train: The 35,000 miles of track that existed at the close of the Civil War had expanded to 193,000 miles by 1903 (Cashman, 1993). In the eyes of the public, technology meant progress, and progress meant a better life. For psychology to gain public support, it needed to be useful.

In addition to the public expectation that science ought to be practical, psychologists at the turn of the century faced institutional pressures for application. Most psychologists still taught within larger departments of philosophy, for instance, and although the philosophers needed little more than an adequate library budget, the psychologists among them needed funds for research apparatus and physical space for their laboratories. To justify the costs to skeptical administrators, psychologists had to show that their new science would bring credit to the university. One way to accomplish this was to show that psychology could benefit society.

The stress on application created strong internal conflicts for many research psychologists. Most had been trained to do basic laboratory research, conditioned to value the pursuit of knowledge for its own sake. They were also aware of the dangers inherent in promising more than they could hope to deliver. Yet reality forced them to adjust their activities toward application. For one thing, while laboratories proliferated in the decade just before 1900, those with doctorates in laboratory psychology grew at an even faster rate. O'Donnell (1985) pointed out that in 1894 the number of psychology PhDs just about matched the number of available American laboratories, thus providing adequate employment opportunities for psychological scientists. By 1900, however, the number of PhDs outnumbered labs by three to one (90 to 33 by O'Donnell's count). Thus, not everyone was going to find the ideal job—directing the university's psychology laboratory. Developing expertise as an applied psychologist enhanced the résumé and put bread on the table.

Some psychologists embraced the idea of using their laboratory training for applied purposes, but others were torn, believing that doing applied work meant they were somehow "selling out" their principles. Yet academic salaries tended to be painfully low, making it difficult to resist the financial rewards of applied work outside the university. Thus Floyd Ruch, a student of Walter Miles, wrote to his mentor in the mid-1930s that he had "a chance to leave academic work and go into a large advertising agency as a research man at a salary about twice my present one. I do not wish to leave academic work but sometimes I feel as though I should out of duty to my family" (Ruch, 1935). Fortunately for Ruch, he hit on a way to enhance his income while staying in academia. Not long after this letter to Miles, he wrote *Psychology and Life* (Ruch, 1937). It was a dramatic departure from other texts, the very first introductory textbook to be student oriented, featuring topics of interest to undergraduates (e.g., a chapter on "Psychology and Personal Problems") rather than dry summaries of research and descriptions of competing schools of psychological thought (Weiten & Wight, 1992). It became one of the best-selling introductory texts of all time, and its descendent, with new authors, exists today (as of this writing, it is in its 20th edition).

Not everyone managed to remain in academia, however. Many psychologists had to adjust their priorities and engage in the more remunerative activities associated with applied psychology. Others, of course, gravitated to applied psychology because it interested them more than teaching or research. Psychologists contributed their expertise to the areas of education, business, medicine, the military, and the law. One activity common to all of these areas is mental testing. Because psychological testing, especially intelligence testing, is a controversial issue even today, the early history of this movement is worth examining in some detail.

THE MENTAL TESTING MOVEMENT

Mental testing has its origins in the attempts by Galton to measure individual differences. As you recall from Chapter 5, one of his goals was to create measures that could identify those best able to further his eugenic vision. He believed that mental ability was inherited and that it was important to encourage procreation among the able and discourage it among those less capable. Galton's attitudes were shared by many American psychologists and later caused controversy that continues to this day. The strongest American supporter of Galton in the 19th century was Cattell. As we saw in the last chapter, the disappointing results of Wissler's study effectively ended the Galton/Cattell approach to mental testing, with its emphasis on tests that measured the physical and the perceptual more than the mental. But a new approach was on the horizon.

Alfred Binet (1857–1911): The Birth of Modern Intelligence Testing

An alternative to the Galton/Cattell philosophy, one focusing more on testing complex mental phenomena rather than physical measures, developed in Europe. One pioneer was Hermann Ebbinghaus, the famous memory researcher (Chapter 4), who developed a "completion test" in the mid-1890s as a way to assess the effects of mental fatigue in schoolchildren. He was responding to a practical problem—it seemed to the authorities in the German city of Breslau that the 5-hour uninterrupted morning school session was producing "fatigue and nervous irritability" (Ebbinghaus, 1897/1965, p. 433). City leaders appointed a commission to study how this 5-hour school day affected children. Some research in the Galtonian tradition used two-point thresholds as a measure, finding that changes in the thresholds occurred during the course of the school day. Ebbinghaus was unimpressed with the method, however, questioning the connection between skin sensitivity and school performance: "Are children who show a deterioration [in sensitivity] also to be regarded as mentally exhausted in other respects, or have they merely become incapable of performing that fixed, relatively insignificant task to which they are not accustomed?" (p. 435). If the goal was to assess mental fatigue, Ebbinghaus argued, then the measures ought to be of cognitive activities, not sensory ones. Assuming that an important aspect of intellectual ability involved taking incomplete information and forming it into a comprehensible whole, Ebbinghaus came up with the idea of giving students incomplete prose passages; they were shown sentences that had syllables missing from words and words missing from sentences and were asked to fill in the gaps to make the sentences complete and meaningful. Ebbinghaus found that his completion tests distinguished between strong and weak students, but he did not find any consistent differences in performance over the 5-hour school day, which remained intact.

Ebbinghaus did not develop his testing program further, but another European, Alfred Binet of France, took the same approach. Like Ebbinghaus, Binet was responding to an educational dilemma. Compulsory education had arrived in France, but some children lacked the ability to succeed in normal classes. By the turn of the century, school officials in Paris were faced with the problem of how to identify these children so they could be placed in what would later be called special education classes. In 1904, a commission was formed to study the problem; it included Binet, one of France's leading psychologists.

Binet's status among his peers was not always so high. In the mid-1880s, he published some dubious research on hypnosis, claiming that hysteric symptoms displayed in that state could be transferred from one side of the body to another by reversing the polarity of a magnet held next to the patient. More sober researchers showed that the effects were simply the result of suggestion, and an embarrassed Binet was forced to retract his claim. He gradually resurrected his reputation, however, becoming a research assistant at the Laboratory of Physiological Psychology at the Sorbonne in Paris in 1891. By 1895, he was the director, holding the position until his premature death in 1911 at the age of 54. While at the Sorbonne, Binet was involved in research ranging from the standard reaction time studies common at the time, to studies of exceptional individuals (e.g., blindfolded chess players; Nicolas & Sanitioso, 2012).

Even before starting his work at the Sorbonne, Binet had begun making careful observations of his two young daughters (Figure 8.3). The work shaped his belief in the value of conducting detailed case studies, and it contributed to his lifelong interest in studying and measuring individual differences. Binet was aware of Galton's work and used some of Galton's sensory tests on his daughters. He was surprised to discover that there didn't seem to be much difference between his daughters' scores and the scores reported for adults. Adults appeared to be superior only on tasks that involved *mental* processing that went beyond sensory capacity. For example, compared with adults, his daughters did quite poorly on color naming, a task requiring memory and language, but very well on color matching, a purely perceptual task. These and other similar results led Binet to conclude that Galton's sensory measures were inadequate to assess age differences in mental ability. He concluded that differences between the intellects of children and adults could be determined only by examining the more complex higher mental processes (Fancher, 1985).

Archives of the History of American Psychology, The Center for the History of Psychology —The University of Akron

FIGURE 8.3 Alfred Binet (1857–1911), with his wife and the two daughters whose development he studied, from Popplestone and McPherson (1994).

During his years at the Sorbonne, Binet coauthored an important paper with his assistant, Victor Henri, in which he contrasted his approach to psychology, an **individual psychology**, with a more general psychology. The latter is concerned with the discovery of laws that apply to some degree to everyone (e.g., repetition strengthens memory), whereas individual psychology "studies the properties of psychic processes that vary from individual to individual—it has to determine the various properties and then study how much and in what ways they vary with the individuals" (Binet & Henri, 1895/1965, p. 428). Studying these differences requires being able to measure them, of course, and that problem led Binet directly to his attempts to develop tests of mental processes. By 1904, when Paris school officials needed a way to identify students with low ability for special classes, Binet already had some definite ideas about what kinds of tests to use.

The term *retarded* did not exist as a category of mental disability in Binet's time. Instead, children with limited capacity were divided into three overlapping and poorly defined categories. *Idiots* were severely handicapped and not capable of caring for themselves; *imbeciles* were somewhat more capable but still not able to be independent; the third level included children capable of learning, but not in normal school classes. These were the children to be identified for special education, and Binet labeled them *débiles*, or "weak ones." He was appalled at the manner in which existing diagnostic labels were applied. Three doctors examining the same child, for instance, would often produce three diagnoses—idiot, imbecile, or débile. Determined to develop a more reliable way of differentiating these "weak" children from normal schoolchildren, Binet drew on his dozen years of research into individual psychology and created what became the first intelligence test.

The Binet–Simon Scales Along with his research assistant Theodore Simon, Binet published the first version of his test in 1905. They revised it in 1908 and again in 1911, just before Binet's death. Rather than starting with a preconceived definition of intelligence, they developed the test empirically by identifying two groups of students, one normal and one impaired, and then giving each group a series of tests that appeared to be conceptually related to intelligence, looking for tests that differentiated the groups. They eventually produced a series of 30 tests of increasing difficulty for their original 1905 test. By the 1908 revision, the number of tests grew to 58, and Binet and Simon incorporated age levels between 3 and 13. Table 8.1 lists some of the tests at different ages (note the contrast with Cattell's tests in Table 7.1).

Identifying average performance at different age levels was Binet's way of solving the diagnosis problem. He believed that subnormal children could be defined in terms of how far behind they were in years. Thus, a normal 5-year-old could solve the tasks at the 5-year level, but a subnormal 5-year-old might only be able to score at the 4-year level. The child's score identified what Binet called a **mental level**. He believed that children scoring at a mental level 2 years lower than their actual age, a group he estimated to include 7 percent of the population, should be considered débiles and placed in special classes (Fancher, 1985). In general, Binet defined mental ability in functional terms as the faculty of "judgment, otherwise called good sense, practical sense, initiative, the faculty of adapting one's self to circumstances. To judge well, to understand well, to reason well—these are the essential wellsprings of intelligence" (Binet & Simon, 1916, p. 44).

In light of how the concept of IQ evolved over the years, it is worth noting Binet's attitudes about intelligence and its measurement. First, he believed that intelligence was multifaceted, composed of a variety of skills. Thus, although he reduced the outcome of the tests to a single unit, mental level, he did so reluctantly. Had he lived, he would have been disturbed at the way in which the concept of IQ came to connote a unitary concept of intelligence. Second, he believed that within broad limits, mental levels could increase with training, and he developed a set of mental "orthopedics" to help children improve their mental levels. Binet was scornful of the prevailing opinion of his day, derived from evolutionary

TABLE 8.1   A Sample of Binet and Simon's Tests of Mental Levels

The 1908 revision of the Binet–Simon scale contained 58 different tests, arranged within 11 different age levels (3–13). Here are some of the tests.

Three Years
show eyes, nose, mouth
repeat 6-syllable sentence
name objects in picture

Five Years
copy a square
compare 2 boxes, different wts.
repeat 10-syllable sentence

Seven Years
copy written sentence
repeat five digits
indicate omissions in drawings

Nine Years
name days of week
retain 6 memories after reading
arrange five weights in order

Eleven Years
criticize absurd sentences[*]
place 3 given words in a sentence
give abstract definitions

Thirteen Years
differentiate word meanings
solve reversed triangle problem
solve paper cutting problem

[*]For example: The body of an unfortunate girl was found, cut into 18 pieces. It is thought that she killed herself.
Source: Dennis (1948)

thinking, that intelligence was a fixed and unchangeable trait. Third, Binet believed that his scale was useful only within the narrow educational context of identifying weak students. He would have been surprised at how quickly the tool became much more widely used, as we are about to see.

Henry H. Goddard (1866–1957): Binet's Test Comes to America

Henry Goddard (Figure 8.4) was a product of Hall's genetic psychology at Clark University, earning a doctorate there in 1899. After a few years of teaching, he accepted an invitation from the Vineland Training School for the Feeble-Minded in southern New Jersey to develop a research program there. His initial efforts reflected his training—he set up a laboratory in imitation of the one he knew at Clark and began testing the children using standard laboratory tasks similar to the ones being used by Cattell. Goddard quickly learned that in his new environment, using basic sensory tasks was easier said than done. His notes contain entries such as this: "A boy frightened at an insignificant thing so that it took six men to hold him could not squeeze a pound on the Dynamometer tho he clearly understood what was wanted" (quoted in Popplestone & McPherson, 1984, p. 242).

Archives of the History of American Psychology, The Center for the History of Psychology —The University of Akron

FIGURE 8.4 Henry Goddard (1866–1957), atop one of the pyramids of Egypt, from Popplestone and McPherson (1994).

In search of better methods, Goddard discovered Binet's work while on a European tour of institutions for the feebleminded in 1908. He brought the Binet–Simon scale back with him, translated it, and began administering it to the Vineland children. When the results matched expectations based on other observations of the children, Goddard became a convert. At a 1910 meeting of the American Association of the Feeble-Minded, he reported the results of testing 400 Vineland children and proposed a classification system based on Binet's mental level concept, which was now being called **mental age**. Idiots would now be defined as those scoring at mental ages 1 to 2 on the scale, and imbeciles would be those with mental ages between 3 and 7. As for the third category, Binet's débile, Goddard proposed a new name. These children had sometimes been called feebleminded, but that term was also used to describe the entire spectrum of mental disability. Yet it was important to have a clearly defined category for these children, Goddard argued, "to help the general public understand that they are a special group and require special treatment,—in institutions where possible" (Goddard, 1910, p. 395). Goddard proposed the term **moron**, from the Greek word moronia, which means "foolish." These would be individuals with mental ages between 8 and 12.[1]

Goddard's creation of the term *moron* and his promotion of its use helped to legitimize psychology as a professional discipline. Morons were believed to be responsible for many of society's ills, but to the average person they appeared to be normal, Goddard argued. To identify them, therefore, society needed the help of highly trained experts. Psychologists such as Goddard made it clear that they were the ones best prepared for the role, and mental tests were the proper tools to make the diagnoses.

[1]Clearly, a 12-year-old with a mental age of 12 would be normal. In assigning mental ages for his classification scheme, Goddard (1910) asked readers to assume the subjects involved were about age 20. Thus, a 20-year-old with a mental age of 12 or below would be subnormal.

Over the next few years, Goddard championed the Binet–Simon tests, and many others were soon using it to identify and classify those with limited mental capacity. Vineland distributed about 20,000 copies of Goddard's translated Binet–Simon test between 1910 and 1914 (Watson & Evans, 1991). Goddard's ultimate goals, however, were quite different from Binet's. Unlike Binet, Goddard was a strong believer in the notion that intelligence was inherited and represented a fixed quantity. Aware of the recent rediscovery of Mendel's work on genetics, Goddard came to believe that feeblemindedness was caused by a single recessive gene. To support his hereditarian case, he published the results of a seemingly conclusive study of the family roots of one of the Vineland children.

The Kallikaks Goddard made his case that feeblemindedness had a genetic basis in a brief 117-page book published in 1912 called *The Kallikak Family: A Study in the Heredity of Feeblemindedness*. In it he described a genealogical study of one of his wards at Vineland. "Deborah Kallikak" (Figure 8.5) was 22 at the time and had lived at Vineland for 14 years. She had been referred to Vineland when she was 8, supposedly because she "did not get along well at school and might possibly be feebleminded" (Goddard, 1912, p. 1).

In fact, the refusal of her mother's third husband to provide support for several of the woman's younger children, including Deborah, contributed to the placement. At Vineland, Deborah was tested periodically with the Binet–Simon scales, never achieving a mental age greater than 9 years. Goddard considered her to be an illustration of the person ideally suited for Vineland. Although she had learned to sew, cook, and do competent woodworking, she struggled to read or do math. If Deborah were to leave the safe and controlled environment of Vineland, Goddard believed,

> she would at once become a prey to the designs of evil men or women and would lead a life that would be vicious, immoral, and criminal, though because of her mentality she herself would not be responsible. There is nothing that she might not be led into, because she has no power of control, and all her instincts and appetites are in the direction that would lead to vice. (p. 12)

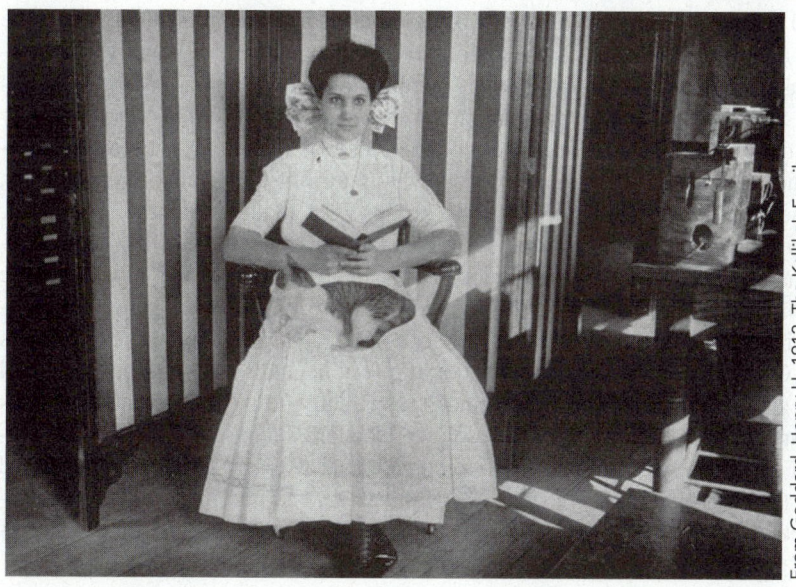

From Goddard, Henry H. 1912, The Kallikak Family

FIGURE 8.5 Deborah Kallikak at Vineland.

How could one explain such an individual? For Goddard the answer was simple: "'Heredity'—bad stock. We must recognize that the human family shows varying stocks or strains that are as marked and breed as true as anything in plant or animal life" (p. 12).

Goddard routinely sent workers into the field to gather information about the backgrounds of those referred to Vineland. In Deborah's case, many relatives lived close by, and the family was "notorious for the number of defectives and delinquents it had produced" (Goddard, 1912, p. 16). Goddard's diligent assistants were able to trace back several generations and "an appalling amount of defectiveness was everywhere found" (p. 16). On the other hand, field workers occasionally found themselves among relatives who were highly educated and living in comfortable environments—doctors, lawyers, and educators. Further digging yielded a tale of a family that had branched in two decidedly different directions.

It seemed that a distant relative, a soldier in the Revolutionary War, behaved like soldiers sometimes do and had a brief affair with a young "feebleminded" girl that he met in a tavern. The result was a feebleminded son, Deborah's great-great grandfather, and the start of a long line of mental deficiency, the "bad" Kallikaks. Meanwhile, the soldier, unaware of the havoc he had created by sowing his wild oats, settled down, married "a respectable girl of good family" (Goddard, 1912, p. 29), and began producing the "good" Kallikaks. Because the unfortunate girl at the tavern gave her young son the father's name, both sides of family bore the same surname.

Upon examining the Kallikaks, Goddard uncovered a stark contrast in the fates of those representing the two sides of the family. On the "bad" side, Goddard's field workers identified 480 descendants and on the basis of historical records, family histories, and some direct testing of living relatives, classified 189 of them; 143 were found to be feebleminded, while only 46 were normal. On the other hand, the descendants of the soldier and his respectable bride tended to be pillars of the community: doctors, lawyers, educators, and so on. Of 496 descendants, only 3 were found to be "somewhat degenerate, but … not [mentally] defective" (p. 29).

Despite the thoroughness of the Kallikak study, it was seriously flawed. The most critical problem was Goddard's failure to recognize environmental effects. Nutritional and health care differences alone could have accounted for the large differences between the groups in infant mortality: 82 (bad side) versus just 15 (good side). Rather than a case study of the genetics of feeblemindedness, then, the Kallikak study could just as easily represent a case study of the differential effects of poverty and privilege. Goddard himself was of course highly intelligent; his inability to believe that the environment was important in the Kallikak family histories says more about the powerful influence of the contemporary historical context than it does about his individual shortcomings. Indeed, the strong belief that intelligence level was a consequence of heredity, taken for granted by most turn-of-the-century psychologists, even led Goddard to argue that the environments of the two groups were about the same.

Goddard's bias also affected the way he interpreted his data. Much of the information about family members was secondhand and sketchy, with ambiguous events interpreted according to whether the person was on one side of the family or the other. Also, any Kallikak from the "bad" side with questionable morals or a criminal record, but without other evidence of feeblemindedness, was nonetheless classified as moronic by Goddard and his assistants. And at the very beginning of the story, Goddard merely assumed that the girl in the tavern was feebleminded, apparently on the questionable grounds that she was in a tavern and let herself be seduced by a soldier. Goddard claimed that he had independent evidence of the girl's feeblemindedness, but meticulous archival work by his biographer failed to substantiate the claim (Zenderland, 1998). In short, the Kallikak study, rather than being good science, is a classic illustration of how preconception can distort both the collection and the interpretation of data.

The name Kallikak was a pseudonym, as you might have guessed, constructed by Goddard to protect Deborah's identity. He chose the name from two Greek words—Kalos, meaning "good," and Kakos, meaning "bad." He thought the name nicely captured the two sides of the unfortunate Deborah's family.

Goddard's conviction about the cause of mental defectiveness led him to an obvious solution to the problem—eliminate the gene. Hence, Goddard became a confirmed eugenicist, arguing that the mentally defective should be prevented from breeding. If this social engineering could be accomplished, then feeblemindedness would be eliminated in just a few generations. Goddard's main recommendation was that states build more institutions like Vineland, so that idiots, imbeciles, and morons could be properly diagnosed, removed from society, and prevented from having children. He also supported other prominent psychologists, including Thorndike, Terman, and Yerkes, in recommending the sterilization of the mentally unfit, pointing out that "[t]the operation itself is almost as simple in males as having a tooth pulled. In females it is not much more serious" (Goddard, 1912, p. 108). Sterilization was a relatively new procedure, however, so Goddard advised caution until its long-term effects were better known.[2]

Thus, Goddard had a plan for dealing with feeblemindedness in America. But what about the importation of mental deficiency? In the early years of the new century, there was growing concern about an apparent threat to the American gene pool—rampant immigration. Goddard had a solution to this problem too.

Goddard and the Immigrants The United States has always been a nation of immigrants, but a regular feature of American political life is that immigrants who have lived in America for a few generations often seek to restrict new immigration. This was true at the turn of the 20th century when the number of immigrants increased dramatically, and these "new" immigrants seemed to be decidedly inferior to "old" immigrants. Throughout most of the 19th century, the majority of immigrants came from western and northern Europe. For instance, 788,992 hopeful men, women, and children arrived in 1882; of these 87 percent were from Germany, Great Britain, and Scandinavia, whereas a mere 13 percent were from southern and eastern European countries such as Italy, Poland, and Russia. By 1907, however, when the total number of arrivals grew to 1,285,349, the proportions had reversed—just over 80 percent now came from southern and eastern Europe (data from Cashman, 1993). Most of the immigrants settled in, and began to influence the nature of urban areas—by 1910, at least 70% of the populations of several large cities (e.g., Boston, Chicago, Detroit, New York) were immigrants and their children (Pegram, 1998). With this shift came increased fears among those whose ancestors had arrived earlier about the "quality" of the new immigrants. The old immigrants, generally Anglo-Saxon, Protestant, and at least moderately well educated, contrasted strongly with the new immigrants, who were generally poor and uneducated, had larger families, were more culturally diverse, and were likely to be Catholic or Jewish. Most Americans simply disagreed with the sentiments of the poet Emma Lazarus, who wrote that the Statue of Liberty, unveiled in 1886, symbolized a welcome to "your tired, your poor, your huddled masses yearning to breathe free."

New York was the main entry point for European immigrants, and to handle the growing numbers of huddled masses, the federal government in 1892 built a large immigration station on Ellis Island, a mile southwest of Manhattan and within sight of the Statue of Liberty. Immigrants arriving there, as many as 10,000 a day in the early 1900s, had to go through a series of evaluations before being allowed to

[2]The Kallikak study came under fire in the 1920s for its neglect of environmental factors, but the book (translated as *Die Familie Kallikak*) was quite influential in Nazi Germany in the 1930s. The Nazis, of course, were enthusiastic about eugenics, and when they started killing people, they started with the "feebleminded," not with the Jews.

enter the country.[3] Most immigrants passed through the Ellis Island inspections in a few hours, but about 20 percent were held for more detailed evaluations, and 1 to 2 percent were not allowed into the country (Schlereth, 1991). To be admitted, immigrants had to show that they were free from contagious diseases and mental illness, physically capable of working, not completely destitute, and not mentally defective. This latter criterion was difficult to measure, however, and Ellis Island examiners were concerned that "high-grade" defectives were slipping through the system. For Goddard, this problem represented a golden opportunity.

Anxious to demonstrate the diagnostic usefulness of the Binet tests, Goddard first visited Ellis Island in 1911 and then returned with two research assistants the following year. With one of his assistants picking out immigrants who "looked" defective and a second administering a version of the Binet tests, Goddard contended that his team could quickly identify mental defectives with about a 90 percent accuracy. In one instance, Goddard's workers selected a young boy suspected of being defective and gave him the test with the aid of an interpreter. The boy scored an 8 on the Binet–Simon scale. Goddard reported that the "interpreter said 'I could not have done that when I came to this country,' and seemed to think the test unfair. We convinced him that the boy was defective" (Goddard, 1913, p. 105). Because of his faith in the technology of testing, Goddard failed to consider that the immigrants were undoubtedly intimidated and confused by the entire Ellis Island experience and that they probably failed to understand why they were being asked to complete these odd tests.

Some physicians working at Ellis Island objected that the Binet tests, being highly verbal, were inadequate for detecting feeblemindedness (Richardson, 2003). Nonetheless, officials at Ellis Island were impressed enough to invite Goddard to expand his operation. In 1913, two female assistants spent two and a half months at Ellis Island. Through interpreters, they tested 165 Russian, Hungarian, Jewish, and Italian immigrants on the Binet–Simon and several other tests. Goddard found that a disturbingly large proportion, about 80 percent, scored at a mental level of 12 or below (i.e., morons). Even after readjusting the scores to take cultural factors into account, he estimated that about 40 percent of the sample was feebleminded and concluded that "one can hardly escape the conviction that the intelligence of the average 'third class' immigrant is low, perhaps of moron grade" (Goddard, 1917, p. 243).

As a result of Goddard's work, mental testing became a part of the screening process at Ellis Island, perhaps contributing to an increase in the percentage of deportations over the next few years. In 1913, for example, 555 people were deported on the grounds of being "feebleminded," triple the number deported in each of the previous 5 years (Richardson, 2003). No accurate estimate exists, but it is safe to say that during the second decade of the 20th century, hundreds of hopeful immigrants, tired, poor, and yearning to breathe free, were nonetheless sent back to Europe because they performed poorly on the Binet–Simon tests.

As for Goddard, he only remained at Vineland for a few more years. In 1918, the state of Ohio hired him to direct their Bureau of Juvenile Research, which had just been established to deal with the problem of juvenile delinquency. Four years later he became professor of abnormal and clinical psychology at The Ohio State University, where he remained until his retirement in 1938. While there, he broadened his interests by studying children at the other end of the spectrum from those at Vineland—gifted students. These later experiences led him to write a remarkable paper in 1928, in which he reversed many of his earlier views. He decided that a mental age of 12 did not necessarily mean feeblemindedness, that many of those diagnosed as morons could function in society and did not

---

[3]When ships carrying immigrants arrived in New York harbor, only those passengers traveling in "steerage" (i.e., poor) were transported to Ellis Island for examination. Immigrants traveling first or second class were given a brief examination in their cabins on board ship and then allowed to enter the city (Richardson, 2003).

need to be institutionalized, and that the danger of them producing feebleminded offspring had been overstated. He considered the problem of the moron to be primarily one of education and argued that "when we get an education that is entirely right there will be no morons who cannot manage themselves and their affairs and compete in the struggle for existence" (Goddard, 1928, p. 224). By the end of his career, then, Goddard had moved closer to Binet's original vision for educating those of marginal ability.

Lewis M. Terman (1877–1956): Institutionalizing IQ

Like Goddard, Lewis Terman was a product of Hall's psychology program at Clark University. He arrived there in 1903, just after finishing a master's degree at Indiana University, not far from his boyhood home on a large farm. Indiana was rather like a midwestern branch of Clark University—its philosophy department featured three psychologists, William Lowe Bryan, Ernest Lindley, and John Bergström, all Clark graduates. Lindley was especially influential, and in a seminar with him, Terman wrote papers on "degeneracy" and "great men." The projects brought him in contact with the writings of Binet and Galton and began to foreshadow his life's work (Minton, 1988). At Clark, his interests in intelligence and its testing deepened, and Terman's doctoral dissertation compared the mental and physical abilities of 14 preadolescent boys, "seven bright and seven dull" (Terman, 1906, p. 314). The former group outperformed the latter on all the mental tests, which included Binet-like procedures such as problem solving and memory, whereas the dull group did better on some motor coordination tasks. Perhaps influenced by his strong attraction to Galton's hereditarian ideas, Terman believed that his study supported "the relatively greater importance of endowment over training, as a determinant of an individual's intellectual rank" (p. 372). Terman never publicly wavered in his belief that heredity was the prime determiner of intelligence.

Terman suffered from periodic bouts with tuberculosis, leading him to search for warm-climate employment after completing his doctorate in 1905. He spent a year as a school superintendent in San Bernadino, California, and then landed an academic position teaching child psychology and pedagogy at Los Angeles State Normal School (later became UCLA). His big break came in 1910, when he was asked to move north to Palo Alto and join the faculty at Stanford University. The opening was sudden and unexpected—Terman replaced his former Indiana teacher, John Bergström, who went to Stanford in 1908, but died shortly thereafter (Capshew & Hearst, 1980). Within 12 years, Terman was chairing the psychology department, which he built into one of the premier departments in the country. Terman (Figure 8.6), three of his faculty recruits, and four of the doctoral students there during his tenure became APA presidents (Hilgard, 1957).

He was much admired as a teacher, especially for the stimulating Monday evening seminars held at his home, recreating the atmosphere he had experienced as a student in Hall's famous Monday seminars. Terman retired from Stanford in 1941, but remained professionally active until his death in 1956, just a few weeks before his 80th birthday. His legacy to psychology includes (a) developing one of the world's best-known IQ tests, and (b) conducting the longest-running psychology research project of all time.

The Stanford–Binet IQ Test Goddard translated the Binet–Simon scales into English and introduced them to America. Terman, however, went beyond translation, accomplishing a revision and the test's first real standardization. Terman added some new tests, revised others, and eliminated a few. Between 1910 and 1914, he standardized the test, using about 2,300 participants, mostly children and adolescents from middle-class environments, but also about 400 adults. He eventually arrived at a series

Courtesy of National Library of Medicine

FIGURE 8.6 Lewis Terman (1877–1956) in his office at Stanford University.

of 90 test items, compared with 54 in Binet's final (1911) version. Accompanied by a complete set of norms, Terman published in 1916 what he called the Stanford Revision of the Binet–Simon test. It became known as the Stanford–Binet, and it quickly dominated the market and earned Terman a healthy royalty income. Terman completely revised and restandardized it again in 1937. In a more recent version, it remains perhaps the best-known individual test of intelligence.

The 1916 Stanford–Binet included a concept that Binet would have found disturbing—IQ. Terman borrowed it from a leader of the testing movement in Germany, William Stern. Stern had pointed out that an average 5-year-old should score at a mental level of 5, whereas a very bright 5 -year-old might achieve a mental level of 6 or higher, and a slow 5-year-old would score lower than 5, 4 perhaps. He suggested that mental ability be capsulized in a "mental quotient" that represented the relationship between mental age and chronological age, found by dividing the former by the latter. For Terman, the idea meshed nicely with his norming procedures and with his growing belief that intelligence was a unitary trait. He changed Stern's "mental quotient" to **intelligence quotient** or IQ, multiplied the ratio by 100 to lose the decimal point, and built it into the revision. With the 1916 Stanford–Binet, then, IQ was born. Three 5-year-olds with mental ages of 4, 5, and 6 would have IQs of 80, 100, and 120, respectively. The message was clear—mental capacity could be represented in a single number.

Terman Studies the Gifted Binet's original purpose in developing his test was to identify children in need of special training. Terman went beyond this vision, however, and believed that his IQ test could identify special children at both ends of the continuum. His long-standing interest in students at the upper end of the scale led him to design his best-known research, a study of giftedness. His original intent was to identify a group of talented children, then follow up on their lives at some later time to see if their promise had been fulfilled. Instead, the project took on a life of its own, continuing long after Terman himself died. It became psychology's longest-running longitudinal study.

In formulating plans for the study, Terman was motivated by his hereditarian ideas about intelligence and his strong belief that America should be a **meritocracy**. That is, he believed its leaders should be those capable of leading, and IQ testing would be a good way to identify such people. With the possible exception of one's morals, he once wrote, "nothing about an individual [was] as important as his IQ" (quoted in Minton, 1988, p. 99). Terman's vision of a true democracy meant equal opportunity, but only for those with some minimum level of mental ability. Those with low IQs, which Terman referred to as "democracy's ballast" (p. 99), could also reach fulfillment in life if properly identified, trained, and placed in jobs suitable for them. Thus, large-scale IQ testing could produce a classification system that would result in different types of education for different levels of ability. Terman believed this system would "go far toward insuring that every pupil, whether mentally superior, average, or inferior, shall have a chance to make the most of whatever abilities nature has given to him" (quoted in Minton, 1987, p. 102).

With meritocracy in mind, Terman set out to identify a sample of gifted children in 1921. His aim was to select the top 1 percent of all California schoolchildren, but because of logistical and financial problems, his team of field workers concentrated on just a few large and medium-sized urban areas. Teachers were asked to identify the three smartest children and the youngest child in their classes. These children were then tested with a brief version of the Stanford–Binet. Those scoring highest were given the full Stanford–Binet.

The outcome was a group of 1470 children, 824 boys and 646 girls. Most were in elementary school, but the group included 444 from junior or senior high school (sample size data from Minton, 1988, pp. 114–115). The average IQ was 151 for the younger children and 143 for the high schoolers. The sampling procedures appeared to be reasonable, but the resulting sample was not representative. Students tended to be middle to upper class, Protestant, and white; their fathers tended to hold professional rather than working-class occupations. Jewish children were also overrepresented, whereas nonwhites and the poor were underrepresented (Cravens, 1992). The bias occurred in a number of subtle ways, from teacher selections to the reluctance of field workers, concerned for their safety, to go to some schools in urban areas. For example, one of Terman's workers omitted 14 Los Angeles schools that had been set aside by authorities "to handle children who had been found guilty of minor offenses" (Minton, 1988, p. 114).

Having selected a sample, Terman's team compiled considerable information for each child, the result being the 600-page *Genetic Studies of Genius: Mental and Physical Traits of a Thousand Gifted Children* (Terman, 1925). Terman retested the group in the late 1920s and conducted follow-ups 25 (Terman & Oden, 1947) and 35 years (Terman & Oden, 1959) after the original testing. When Terman died, Robert Sears, a member of the gifted group and by then a distinguished research psychologist himself, took over the project. He produced five additional follow-ups between 1960 and 1986 and was preparing *The Later Maturity of the Gifted* when he died in 1989 (Cronbach, Hastorf, Hilgard, & Maccoby, 1990).

The traditional view of gifted children is that although they are intellectually superior, they are physically weak, are socially inferior, and burn out at a young age, never quite fulfilling their childhood promise. Terman's research questioned this stereotype, however. In follow-up after follow-up, his group appeared to be not just smarter than others but more successful, productive, well adjusted, and physically healthy. Most entered professional life, but this was less likely to occur for the females in the group. Although more likely to be in a career and less likely to be married than their nongifted peers, the women of Terman's group tended to be frustrated by the lack of opportunities for women in America at mid-20th century (Minton, 1988).

One final aspect of the study worth noting is Terman's devotion to the group and the corresponding loyalty of those who came to call themselves "Termites." A typical problem in longitudinal research is **attrition**—as time goes by, subjects drop out of the study for a variety of reasons. Attrition was not a problem for Terman, however. Of those subjects who were alive for the follow-up studies done after 10, 25, and 35 years, the percentages of those participating were 92, 98, and 93, respectively (Minton, 1988). Terman corresponded regularly with his Termites and cared very much about their lives. This is not surprising, of course, for in Terman's mind, these were the meritorious people holding the key to America's future.

Terman is often credited with being the pioneer in the study of gifted children, and with reason. But there were others interested in the topic, Goddard for instance, and a woman whose work on the gifted preceded Terman's. She might not have studied them as thoroughly as Terman did, but a case can be made that Leta Hollingworth was the first advocate for specialized education for gifted children. This chapter's Close-Up examines her work on behalf of gifted children and also describes her research that debunked the idea that women were intellectually inferior to men.

CLOSE-UP

LETA HOLLINGWORTH: ADVOCATING FOR GIFTED CHILDREN AND DEBUNKING MYTHS ABOUT WOMEN

Near the end of this chapter, you will learn about the applied psychology of Harry Hollingworth. He was just half of one of psychology's dynamic duos, however, and his wife Leta (Figure 8.7) made contributions at least as important as her husband's. At a time when women faced the obstacles you learned about in Chapter 6, Leta Hollingworth (1886–1939) managed to earn a doctorate from Columbia, become the "mother of gifted education," in her biographer's words, and directly attack the belief

Archives of the History of American Psychology, The Center for the History of Psychology —The University of Akron

FIGURE 8.7 Leta Hollingworth (1886–1939), debunker of the variability hypothesis and early promoter of special educational opportunities for gifted children.

that men were intellectually superior to women (Klein, 2002).

Like her husband, Leta Stetter Hollingworth was a native Nebraskan, born and raised in frontier conditions and educated in the proverbial (and in this case literal) one-room schoolhouse. She graduated from the University of Nebraska in 1906 and then taught for 2 years before marrying Harry and following him to New York, where he was in his second year of graduate studies at Columbia. She immediately encountered one of the gender biases described in Chapter 6—the marriage versus career choice. Her plan was to teach in the New York school system, thereby supporting Harry in graduate school. What she discovered was a Board of Education policy prohibiting married women from being teachers (Hollingworth, 1943/1990). Instead, she started taking graduate courses and enrolled full time after Harry finished his doctorate. She earned a PhD from Columbia's Teachers College in 1916, under Thorndike's direction and was immediately hired there as an instructor.

In the spring semester of the academic year 1918–1919, Hollingworth began offering a new course, Education 254, which was designed to examine "fortunate variants, the generally and specifically gifted" (quoted in Klein, 2002, p. 120). It is believed to be the first course ever designed to study gifted children, and it marked the official beginning of Hollingworth's devotion to this group. The work culminated with her widely cited *Gifted Children: Their Nature and Nurture* (1926), the

first textbook of gifted education. The primary means of treating gifted children at that time was acceleration in grade, but Hollingworth argued that such a path could damage children who would not spend much of their time with age-related peers. Instead, she recommended a full-immersion enrichment approach. Gifted children, she argued, should be placed in classes with their gifted peers and given a curriculum that included the normal curricular topics, plus a level of enrichment that went far beyond what was taught to nongifted children.

Gifted education was her life's passion, but Hollingworth was also a determined feminist, and active in several groups advocating for, among other things, the right of women to vote (which came in 1920). Hollingworth's feminist beliefs were informed by data. In particular, two of her early studies challenged two widely held beliefs mentioned in Chapter 6. First was the *variability hypothesis*, the evolution-based idea that women showed less variation in traits than men and were therefore less suited for highly intellectual tasks and for careers requiring exceptional mental ability. Second was the idea that sex differences were due in part to the *periodic function*—women were intellectually incapacitated during menstruation (Poffenberger, 1940).

Hollingworth published several studies questioning both beliefs, and summarized her work in a chapter ("The Vocational Aptitudes of Women") she wrote for her husband's *Vocational Psychology: Its Problems and Methods* (Hollingworth, 1916). Concerning the variability hypothesis, Hollingworth discovered that the belief rested on very little empirical data, and what information that did exist was ambiguous. One study, which showed no differences among adult men and women in variability in physical traits, had been criticized by proponents of the variability hypothesis on the grounds that young children should have been investigated to get at "inherent or original differences in variability" (Hollingworth, 1916, p. 230). This prompted Leta and a pediatrician friend to study 2,000 newborns, half male and half female. Collecting a variety of physical measurements, they found that the boys were slightly larger than girls, but that the amount of *variability* in physical size was the same for both boys and girls (Montague & Hollingworth, 1914). Hollingworth was particularly incensed at the argument that the variability hypothesis accounted for the fact that

relatively few women had achieved eminence—the simple reason for that, she argued, was lack of opportunity in a male-dominated world (Shields, 1982).

As for periodic function, it was the subject of Hollingworth's doctoral dissertation. Prevailing opinion was that men and women were inherently unequal, and an important factor was that while men were capable "of sustained and regular hard labor, [a woman], for one quarter of each month, during the best years of life, is more or less sick and unfit for hard work" (Maudsley, quoted in Klein, 2002, p. 91). This irritated Hollingworth's social conscience, prompting her to comment:

> It is positively stated that women are on this account [menstruation] unfitted to pursue professional and commercial life; yet it is not proposed that cooks, scrub women, mothers, nursemaids, housekeepers, or dancers should be periodically relieved from their labors and responsibilities. (Hollingworth, 1916, p. 235)

In her dissertation, Hollingworth carefully studied 23 women and examined their performance on tests for "speed and accuracy of perception, controlled association, steadiness, speed of voluntary movement, fatigability, and rate of learning" (Hollingworth, 1916, p. 236), during all phases of the menstrual cycle. Data from several male "control" subjects were also collected. On all the tests she found no gender differences, and for the women, no differences traceable to periodic function.

Hollingworth recognized that at the time she wrote her chapter on women in her husband's book, little actual research had been done on sex differences. As she put it,

> All we can say is that up to the present time experimental psychology has disclosed no sex differences in mental traits which would imply a division of labor on psychological grounds.... So far as is ... known, women are as competent intellectually as men are, to undertake any and all human vocations. (Hollingworth, 1916, p. 244)

Leta Hollingworth's research on gifted education and on gender would have been even more substantial had she not become desperately ill with abdominal cancer during the last 10 years of her brief, 53-year life.

Robert M. Yerkes (1876–1956): The Army Testing Program

Yerkes (Figure 8.8) began his academic career as a promising comparative psychologist at Harvard, his love of animals tracing from his childhood on a farm (Carmichael, 1957). But Harvard's interest in comparative psychology was never great—research in the topic was expensive, the laboratory smelled, and it didn't seem especially relevant or useful (Reed, 1987). Thus, Yerkes was pressured to produce more on the "human side" if he expected to advance through the ranks. Although comparative psychology remained his first love, he compromised by writing a mainstream introductory textbook that centered on the study of consciousness and even included introspective exercises at the end of each chapter (Yerkes, 1911).

He further broadened his credentials by working part-time in the Psychopathic Department of Boston State Hospital from 1913 to 1917, where he first became familiar with intelligence testing by administering Binet tests to patients. Harvard still did not promote him, however, even though his reputation among peers was sufficient to get him elected to president of the American Psychological Association in 1917. In that same year, perhaps tired of waiting for Harvard to promote him, he accepted an offer to chair the psychology department at the University of Minnesota. Fate intervened, however, and Yerkes never made it to the upper Midwest.

In April of 1917, Yerkes was cohosting a meeting of Titchener's Experimentalists at Harvard when the United States declared war on Germany and entered World War I. The group held an impromptu meeting to discuss how psychology might help the war effort, and as APA president, Yerkes took the lead. He later said that he had no real desire to take on the Army project, but did so out of a sense of duty (Dewsbury, 1996). Nonetheless, he quickly demonstrated superb organizational and persuasive skills, convincing his colleagues and the Army that psychological testing could aid the war effort.

© Bettmann/Corbis

FIGURE 8.8 Robert Yerkes (1876–1956), in a photo reflecting his first love, comparative psychology.

By August of 1917, the Army had commissioned Yerkes as a major and placed him in charge of an elite group of psychologists (including Terman) charged with preparing mental tests. Their task was daunting. For one thing, the sheer number of people to be examined meant that traditional Binet-style testing, with examiners giving tests to one person at a time, had to be replaced by group testing procedures. Second, although one of the goals was in the Binet tradition of identifying those who were unfit, in this case for Army service rather than for normal schooling, Yerkes also had more ambitious plans. He hoped to create tests that would enable the Army to identify those with special skills so they could be placed where they could serve best. For instance, he hoped to be able to select candidates for officer training. The tests were pilot tested at four Army camps in October of 1917, and the program was in full swing by early 1918. By the time the war ended in November of that year, Yerkes and his team had tested 1,726,966 soldiers (Yoakum & Yerkes, 1920).

Army Alpha and Army Beta   Because nearly 30 percent of recruits could not "read and understand newspapers and write letters home" (Yoakum & Yerkes, 1920, p. 12), Yerkes developed two versions of his test. Recruits literate enough to read and follow written directions were given the **Army Alpha** test, while **Army Beta** was created for those with reduced literacy. Each test took just under an hour to administer. Any soldier failing Alpha was to be given Beta, and those failing Beta were supposed to be tested individually. Logistical problems and time pressures usually eliminated both levels of retesting, however.

Army Alpha comprised eight different tests, whereas Army Beta had seven (Table 8.2). Soldiers given Army Alpha were told at the outset that the purpose of the test was to "see how well you can remember, think, and carry out what you are told to do. We are not looking for crazy people. The aim is to help find out what you are best fitted to do in the Army" (p. 53). By contrast, those taking Army Beta were simply told to follow instructions and "ask no questions" (p. 82); they were not told why they were taking the exam.

To get an idea of what confronted soldiers, consider the first test in Army Alpha: the directions or commands test. Soldiers had the score sheet in Figure 8.9 in front of them and were told that in the Army it was important to be able to follow orders. The test would determine how well they could do so. For each of the 12 items, they were ordered to make specific marks on the page. Here are two of the commands:

> 4. Attention! Look at 4. When I say "go" make a figure 1 in the space which is in the circle but not in the triangle or square, and also make a figure 2 in the space which is in the triangle and circle, but not in the square.—Go! (Allow not over 10 seconds)
> 11. Attention! Look at 11. When I say "go" draw a line through every even number that is not in a square, and also through every odd number that is in a square with a letter.—Go! (Allow not over 25 seconds). (Yoakum & Yerkes, 1920, pp. 55–56)

TABLE 8.2 Subtests for Army Alpha and Army Beta

Army Alpha Subtests	Army Beta Subtests
Commands Test	Maze Test
Arithmetic Problems	Cube Analysis
Practical Judgment	X-O Series
Synonym–Antonym	Digit-Symbol
Disarranged Sentences	Number Checking
Number Series Completion	Pictorial Completion
Analogies	Geometrical Construction
Information	

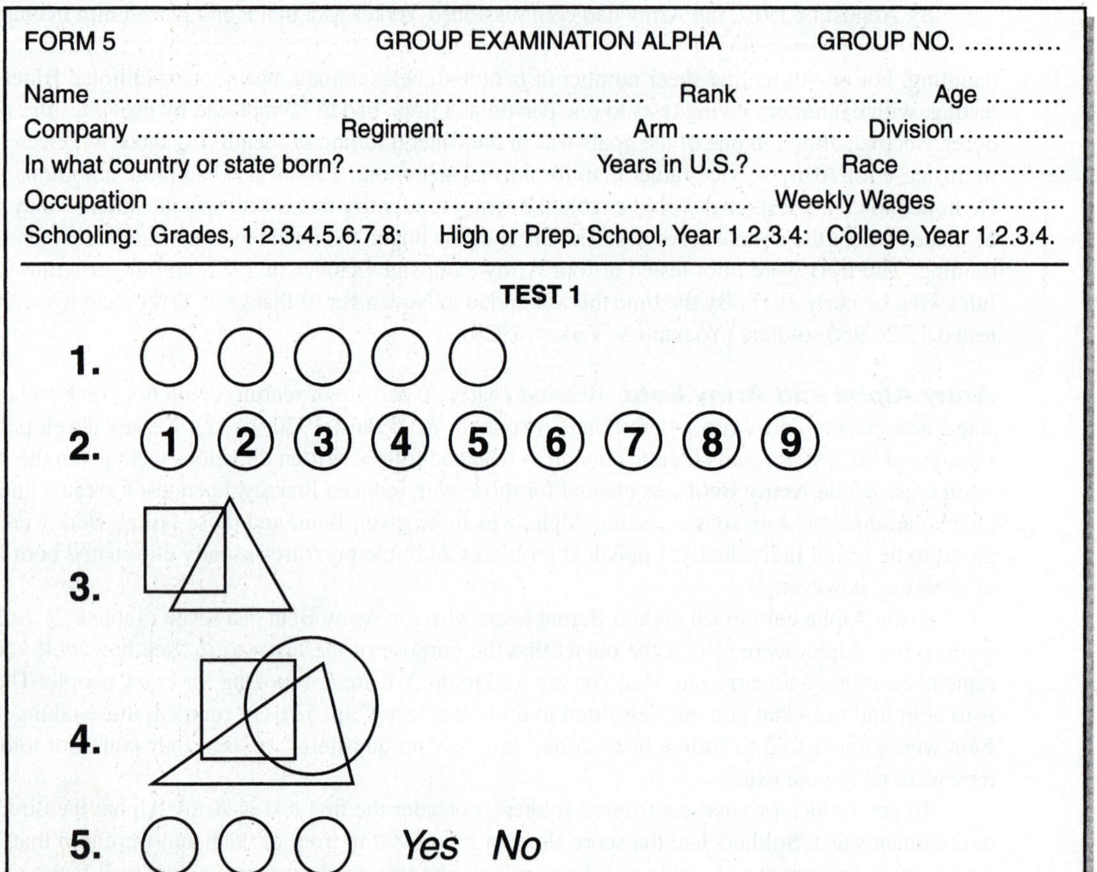

FORM 5   GROUP EXAMINATION ALPHA   GROUP NO. ....

Name .... Rank .... Age ....

Company .... Regiment.................... Arm .... Division ....

In what country or state born?........................... Years in U.S.?......... Race ....

Occupation .... Weekly Wages ....

Schooling: Grades, 1.2.3.4.5.6.7.8:   High or Prep. School, Year 1.2.3.4:   College, Year 1.2.3.4.

TEST 1

1. ○ ○ ○ ○ ○

2. ① ② ③ ④ ⑤ ⑥ ⑦ ⑧ ⑨

3.

4.

5. ○ ○ ○   *Yes No*

6. ○ ○ ○ ○ ○

7. **A B C D E F G H I J K L M N O P**

8. ○ ○ ○   *MILITARY GUN CAMP*

9. **34-79-56-87-68-25-82-47-27-31-64-93-71-41-52-99**

10. [| | | |]

11. [7F] △4 ③ △5A ⑧ [2] △6 ⑨B [3]

12. **1 2 3 4 5 6 7 8 9**

FIGURE 8.9 A test on following orders, part of Army Alpha, from Yoakum and Yerkes (1920).

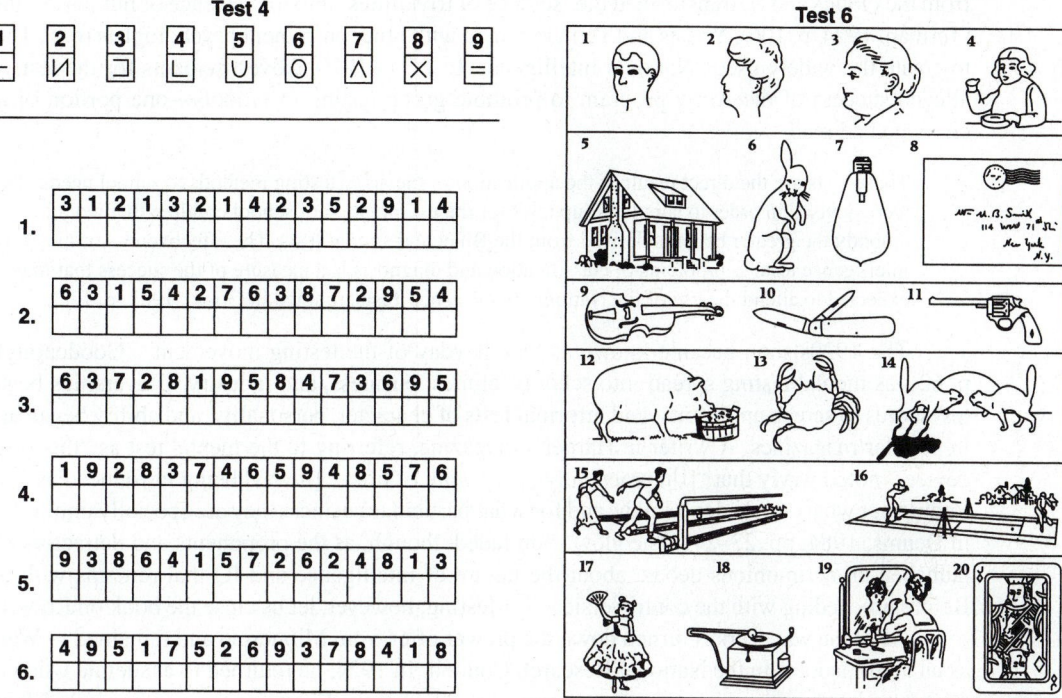

FIGURE 8.10 Digit-symbol and picture completion subtests from Army Beta, from Yoakum and Yerkes (1920).

Two of the Army Beta tests can be found in Figure 8.10. In test 4, digit-symbol, the symbols paired with each number had to be written into the blank spaces. In test 6, recruits were instructed to identify the missing elements of each picture. They had 2 minutes to complete as many digit-symbols as they could, and 3 minutes to do the picture completion test.

Despite the fact that almost two million soldiers took the tests, the war ended before they could be used effectively by the Army. Indeed, most historians conclude that the Army derived little if any benefit from the enterprise (Kevles, 1968). During the war, many within the military welcomed the tests as more efficient than traditional methods for placing soldiers. Yet others stubbornly refused to use the test results, some local commanders didn't cooperate with the examiners giving the tests, and testing conditions were often so poor as to render the results meaningless. At one point the Secretary of War polled camp commanders about the value of the testing program, and most of the 100 responses were negative (Gould, 1981). That the Army discontinued the testing shortly after the war ended suggests that its top brass were less than impressed with the program's utility. On the other hand, the testing program laid the groundwork for a scientific approach to Army personnel work, and a number of younger officers saw its potential benefits. And the program certainly gave psychology a boost. As Minton (1988) put it, "[w]hile testing may not have made a significant contribution to the war, the war had made a significant contribution to testing and as a by-product to psychology in general" (p. 74).

Yerkes believed the project showed that mental testing could be applied on a large scale, and after the war he spared no effort to propagandize the benefits of mass testing. Other psychologists soon climbed on the bandwagon. Terman, for instance, claimed that testing had "brought psychology down from the clouds and … transformed the 'science of trivialities' into the 'science of human engineering'" (Terman, 1924, p. 106). Yerkes and Terman joined with other prominent psychologists (e.g., Thorndike) to create the widely used "National Intelligence Tests" in 1920. Advertisements for the tests used the alleged success of the Army program to promote group testing in schools—one portion of a widely circulated ad read:

> These tests are the direct result of the application of the army testing methods to school needs. They were devised in order to supply group tests for the examination of school children that would embody the greater benefits derived from the Binet and similar tests. The effectiveness of the army intelligence tests in problems of classification and diagnosis is a measure of the success that may be expected to attend the use of the National Intelligence Tests. (quoted in Gould, 1981, p. 178)

The 1920s soon became known as "the heyday of the testing movement" (Goodenough, 1949, p. 62), as mental testing spread into schools, clinics, business, and industry. Universities began using test scores to screen applicants, and informal tests of character, personality, and ability began appearing in popular magazines. A writer in Harper's magazine, referring to the mental test as "this bright little device," noted wryly that "[i]n practically every walk of life … [it was] being introduced as a means of finding out what people don't know, and for what particular business they are specially unfitted" (quoted in Dennis, 1984, pp. 23–24). The glow soon faded, though, as the proponents and detractors of testing launched an acrimonious debate about the nature of intelligence and IQ that remains with us today. Before proceeding with the controversies over testing, however, let us close the book on Robert Yerkes.

After the war, Yerkes turned down the prewar offer from Minnesota and remained in Washington as an administrator in the National Research Council. In 1924, he returned to academia when his good friend, and now university president, James Angell, recruited him for the newly created Institute of Psychology at Yale (Dewsbury, 1996). There he returned to his first love, the study of animal behavior, and began a campaign to create a research center to study primate behavior. The eventual result was the "Anthropoid Experiment Station of Yale University," which opened in 1930 in Orange Park, Florida, near Jacksonville. When Yerkes retired in 1941, the center was renamed the Yerkes Laboratories of Primate Biology. It moved to Atlanta in 1965 and was renamed the Yerkes Primate Center (Dewsbury, 2006).

The Controversy over Intelligence

As leaders of the mental testing movement, Goddard, Terman, and Yerkes shared the beliefs that (a) mental capacity was primarily the result of genetic inheritance; (b) the environment had little if any effect on this overall ability; (c) intelligence might be composed of a variety of skills, but underlying all of them was a single, unitary capability;[4] and (d) this capability was what intelligence tests measured. In the 1920s, the tests were at the forefront of the "heyday" of mental testing. By the middle of the decade, however, mental testing was under assault from several directions, and Anne Anastasi, author of the best-known modern textbook on testing, would later write that "[t]he testing boom of the 1920s probably did more to retard than to advance the progress of testing" (Anastasi, 1993, p. 17). What happened?

An early sign of trouble was in Yerkes's 1921 report summarizing the Army testing program. Buried in the 890-page mass of detail was this statement: "It appears that the intelligence of the principal sample of the white draft, when transmuted from Alpha and Beta exams into terms of mental

---

[4]In this regard, most Americans agreed with the British psychologist/statistician Charles Spearman, who argued that although separate intellectual skills might exist, underlying all of them was a unitary intellectual ability, which he called "g," for "general" intelligence.

age, is about 13 years" (Yerkes, 1921, p. 785). Combining the widely held belief that the mental age of an average adult should be 16 and the Goddard scale of deficiency that considered those scoring between 8 and 12 to be morons, this was disturbing news. If the Army testing program was valid and the sample representative (at 1.7 million it was certainly big enough), then it appeared that the United States was becoming a nation of morons. Even though critics later pointed out that problems like the abysmal testing conditions and the failure to implement the retesting scheme made the results virtually impossible to interpret, the report reinforced existing biases and created alarm. Could the fears of the eugenicists be coming true? Could all those years of unrestricted immigration and the failure to control the breeding of feebleminded people be reducing the overall intelligence of America? To add fuel to the fire, Yerkes observed in the *Atlantic Monthly* that on the basis of the Army tests, no more than 10 percent of Americans "are intellectually capable of meeting the requirements for a bachelor's degree" (quoted in Degler, 1991, p. 168).

Yerkes also presented data on intelligence as a function of national origin and found higher scores for native-born Americans. And in support of prevailing fears about the new immigrants, he reported that for soldiers of northern European origin, mental age was higher than for those with roots in southern or eastern Europe. The average mental age for this latter group was about 11. Carl Brigham, who participated in the Army project, highlighted the immigrant findings in his *A Study of American Intelligence* (1923) and warned that continued immigration from southern and eastern Europe, combined with the tendency of these groups to have large families, would threaten the national IQ. In a theme that would echo ominously in Germany in the 1930s, Brigham suggested that the fair-haired Nordic races were intellectually superior to others.

All of this was happening at a time when the general political climate was characterized by an increasing **nativism**, a defensive nationalism that viewed outsiders with suspicion and alarm. It was exacerbated in the 1920s by several factors. Immigration, which had declined during the war years, was surging again. The new immigrants, already disliked, seemed increasingly unwilling to join into the mythical American melting pot. They retained their own communities and language, and a large proportion had no intention of remaining in America—their goal was to make a sufficient amount of money to return home. In addition, with the 1917 Bolshevik revolution in Russia creating headlines, the 1920s witnessed the first "Red Scare," and many Americans viewed immigrants from Russia as communist subversives rather than refugees from the harsh new Soviet regime. Thus, it came as no surprise when Congress passed the National Origins Act of 1924, which established immigration quotas with reference to 1890 data (i.e., before the shift from old to new immigration patterns).[5] The American psychologists who led the mental testing movement have sometimes been portrayed as leading the charge for restrictive immigration, but they reflected the context of their times as much as they contributed to it.

Although fears about immigration were widespread, not everyone was willing to accept the beliefs about IQ held by Goddard, Terman, Yerkes, Thorndike, and others. Although the popular press generated a continuous flow of articles about the dangers of immigration that suggested unity among social scientists, there was in fact considerable disagreement within the professional community (Satariano, 1979). Noted anthropologist Franz Boas, for instance, was a strong critic of the hereditarian view, arguing instead for the effect of culture on mental abilities (Degler, 1991). Within psychology, behaviorism (Chapters 10 and 11), with its emphasis on the powerful effects of conditioning, was beginning to have a moderating effect, shifting opinion from nature to nurture. Furthermore, numerous psychologists (e.g., Freeman, 1922) urged caution when interpreting the Army data, pointing out that mental testing was

---

[5] According to Okrent (2010), another factor contributing to the law's passage was Prohibition—drys wished to reduce the population of Catholics and Italians in particular, who tended to violate the Prohibition restrictions with impunity.

still in its infancy and that the effects of upbringing on IQ scores could not be ignored when interpreting IQ data. In the 1920s in general, psychologists and biologists tended toward hereditarian explanations of mental capacity, whereas anthropologists and sociologists leaned toward an environmental emphasis (Hilgard, 1987).

The most visible debate about intelligence and IQ testing in the 1920s resulted from a series of articles in the *New Republic* by its founder, the noted columnist Walter Lippmann, and replies from Terman. Neither Lippmann nor Terman minced words. Conceding that the tests might have some value in placing students or selecting employees, Lippmann ridiculed the notion that the tests were measuring innate general "intelligence," arguing that "[w]e cannot measure intelligence when we have never defined it, and we cannot speak of its hereditary basis after it has been indistinguishably fused with a thousand educational and environmental influences from the time of conception to school age" (Lippmann, 1922a, p. 10). Also, Lippmann was outraged at the possibility that testing could forever doom a child who happened not to perform very well for one 50-minute segment of his or her life. With the implications of Terman's meritocracy firmly in mind, he wrote that the result could be "an intellectual caste system in which the task of education had given way to the doctrine of predestination and infant damnation" (1922b, p. 298). Terman, who Lippmann mentioned by name when likening testing to other "fads" such as phrenology and palm reading, responded in an article that did not really answer Lippmann, but merely dismissed him as a rank amateur who should mind his own business and let the professionals deal with these complex issues. It was not one of Terman's better moments, and he later regretted writing the article (Minton, 1988).

Terman was one of the most vocal proponents of the hereditarian view of intelligence, but near the end of his life he had some second thoughts. In an autobiographical chapter for the series *A History of Psychology in Autobiography*, Terman wrote that differences in IQ could never be completely accounted for by environmental factors—heredity was the key. However, in Terman's personal copy of the volume, this section of his essay is circled, and he wrote in the margin on two occasions: "I am less sure of this now (1951)! And still less sure in 1955!—L. M. T." (quoted in Hilgard, 1957, p. 478). Questions about the relative influence of nature and nurture on intelligence, the existence of meaningful group differences in intelligence, the validity of IQ as a measure of intelligence, and the very nature of intelligence continue to be debated today.

APPLYING PSYCHOLOGY TO BUSINESS

Calvin Coolidge, U.S. president from 1923 to 1929, once said that the business of America was business. That being the case, and with psychologists desiring to be relevant for American life, it is not surprising that psychologists became interested in applying their knowledge to the business world. As early as 1895, in *Thinking, Feeling, Doing*, Scripture pointed out that advertisers could benefit from what psychologists knew about attention and memory. Shortly after the turn of the 20th century, Walter Dill Scott (1869–1955), a young professor at Northwestern University in Chicago who had been trained by Wundt at Leipzig, was asked to write a series of articles on the psychology of advertising by the head of a local advertising company. This must have seemed like just an interesting diversion to the young experimentalist, but instead it became the start of a distinguished career in what eventually came to be called industrial psychology. In 1903, Scott collected his magazine articles into a book, *The Theory of Advertising* (1903), and followed it 5 years later with *The Psychology of Advertising* (1908). Scott also wrote *Increasing Human Efficiency in Business* (1911), in which he applied psychological principles to suggest ways of increasing worker productivity. A main theme in Scott's work on advertising was that consumers were not rational decision makers and could be influenced by suggestion and appeals to emotion. He also applied what was known about memory—for instance, although he did not use the terms *primacy* and *recency*, he argued that "[t]he first and last advertisement in a magazine are the most effective. Likewise the first and last parts of any particular advertisement (unless very short) are the parts we remember best" (Scott, 1908, p. 16).

During this same period, Hugo Münsterberg, a young German psychologist, also a product of Wundt's laboratory and now at Harvard, was beginning to be involved in what he called "economic psychology." Although he became one of the most reviled public figures in America at the time of his sudden death in 1916, he was psychology's most visible applied psychologist in the first decade and a half of the new century.

Hugo Münsterberg (1863–1916): The Diversity of Applied Psychology

As one of Germany's rising stars in the new experimental psychology, Hugo Münsterberg (Figure 8.11) attracted the attention of William James at a time when America's premier psychologist was shifting his interests from psychology to philosophy and desiring to distance himself from the laboratory. Young Münsterberg had earned both a PhD with Wundt at Leipzig and an MD from Heidelberg, and he had established a productive laboratory of experimental psychology at Freiburg in the late 1880s. James was impressed with Münsterberg's research, citing it frequently in his *Principles of Psychology*. With promises of a well-equipped laboratory and minimal teaching, James lured Münsterberg to Harvard in the same year that Titchener arrived at Cornell, 1892. Münsterberg stayed for 3 years while on leave from Freiburg and then returned home to Germany, hoping to secure a professorship there. This was not forthcoming, however, and he came back to Harvard for good in 1897. There his career was nothing short

Picture History/NewsCom

FIGURE 8.11 Hugo Münsterberg (1863–1916), during his time as a controversial professor at Harvard.

of remarkable, including presidencies of both APAs (Psychological and Philosophical), a major position at Harvard as chair of the Philosophy Department, and status as a friend of the rich, the powerful, and the famous.

Although he could barely understand English when he arrived in Cambridge and it took him several years before he could lecture comfortably in it, Münsterberg managed to write more than 20 books between his arrival in America and his death. He also became a well-known public figure by writing extensively in popular magazines (e.g., *Harper's*, *Atlantic Monthly*) on such topics as hypnosis, gambling, lie detection, coeducation, and communicating with the dead (Benjamin, 2000). But he was a controversial figure. One of his goals was to explain the American temperament and personality to a German audience, and to an American audience, all the good qualities of Germans. His motives might have been pure, a simple desire to enhance intercultural understanding, and for a time his reputation as an ambassador of goodwill even earned him dinner at the White House with Teddy Roosevelt (Moskowitz, 1977). As World War I approached, however, his defense of German culture, and his attacks on what he saw as anti-German propaganda, changed public opinion about him. He was editorially condemned, hated by the general public, and even accused of being a spy (Landy, 1992). After an editorial in the *London Times* labeled Harvard a center for pro-German agitation, Münsterberg became an outcast even among his colleagues, and his sanity was questioned by former Harvard president Charles Eliot (Spillman & Spillman, 1993). The effects of this vilification can only be guessed at, but the resulting stress probably contributed to the cerebral hemorrhage that killed the 53-year-old Münsterberg in the middle of a lecture at Radcliffe on December 16, 1916.[6]

During his productive years at Harvard, Münsterberg contributed substantially to the growth of experimental psychology in America. His research interests were eclectic, and his students found him willing to direct research on a wide range of topics. He welcomed anyone with an interest in research, even students, like Mary Calkins (Chapter 6), whose gender prevented them from being there officially. By the turn of the century, however, Münsterberg was spending less time in the laboratory and more time developing his interests in applied psychology. One of these interests was in forensic psychology, which examines how psychology applies to legal issues. His best-selling *On the Witness Stand* (1908) included detailed descriptions of the reasons why eyewitness testimony often fails, many of which have been confirmed by modern research. He also warned against the use of hypnosis in the courtroom as a means of determining guilt or innocence, and in his final chapter on "The Prevention of Crime," he argued against the prevailing hereditarian view of human behavior and promoted the idea that the "prevention of crime is more important than the treatment of crime" (p. 233). For Münsterberg, criminals were made, not born.

In addition to writing about the law, Münsterberg contributed to abnormal psychology, taking an approach to the treatment of insanity that was based on suggestion. In essence, his strategy was to assume that if he suggested to patients how they should behave and think, the power of his authority would lead them to obey and be cured. In his *Psychotherapy* (1909), he was also critical of the newly popular Freudianism, with its belief in the importance of the unconscious. Münsterberg, often ahead of his times but behind them in this case, wrote that the subconscious mind had little if any impact on behavior. He did recognize the importance of Freud's emphasis on the early childhood determinants of later pathology, however.

---

[6]After Münsterberg's passing, psychology went into a decline at Harvard. Titchener was offered Münsterberg's position but declined, and Cattell sought the job but was rejected. Harvard brought the British psychologist William McDougall to America, but he quickly became isolated and left. The department only began to recover when E. G. Boring was induced to leave Clark and come to Cambridge in 1922 (Hilgard, 1987).

Münsterberg and Employee Selection   It was in the area of industrial, or "economic," psychology as he called it, that Münsterberg had his greatest impact. This influence resulted primarily from a book that he compiled from a set of lectures, published in German in 1912, and then in English a year later, with the title *Psychology and Industrial Efficiency* (Münsterberg, 1913). In his introductory chapter, Münsterberg made his feelings clear about the importance of applied work and responded to the claim, sometimes made, that application needed to wait until there existed a solid body of knowledge deriving from basic research. As he put it, "if the psychologists were to refrain from practical application until the theoretical results of their laboratories need no supplement, the time for applied psychology would never come" (p. 7). Münsterberg divided his book into three broad topics:

- "The Best Possible Man" → chapters on vocational guidance and how to select the best employees for the job
- "The Best Possible Work" → chapters on training, the effects of working conditions (e.g., fatigue), and worker productivity
- "The Best Possible Effect" → chapters on advertising and marketing

The first section of the book is the best known—here Münsterberg tried to show how psychological methods could help select workers. He argued for the importance of efficient selection of human resources by drawing an interesting parallel to the threats then existing to natural resources (which would soon lead to the creation of the National Park system). Just as the country was beginning to recognize "how the richness of the forests … and the rivers had been recklessly squandered without any thought of the future" (p. 38), so too were economists coming to believe that "no waste of valuable possessions is so reckless as that which results from the distribution of living force by chance methods instead of examining carefully how work and workmen can fit one another" (p. 38).

To show how psychology could contribute to the process of fitting work and workers together, Münsterberg described several examples. The first involved hiring driver/operators ("motormen") for the electric railways that provided the primary means of public transportation found in cities in those days, but now requiring a trip to San Francisco to experience anything comparable. The job was not easy, for the motorman had to stay on schedule while watching out for the carriages, motorcars, and pedestrians that filled the typical city street, often crossing in front of the rail car (no stoplights in those days). Mishaps were not uncommon—Münsterberg wrote that railway companies reported "up to fifty thousand accident indemnity cases a year" (p. 64)! Some operators had better records than others, and Münsterberg was asked by the Boston Elevated Railway Company to develop a way to distinguish between competent and accident-prone drivers. If he was able to do so, then the initial selection process could be improved.

Münsterberg believed there were two different ways to proceed, either by simulating, as a whole, the essential processes involved in successful work (driving in this case), or breaking the work down into subprocesses and developing tests for each. With regard to the "motormen," Münsterberg first considered using the second, more analytic approach. Competent workers might be expected to have faster reaction times, for instance. But when he tested drivers working for the company, he quickly discovered a ceiling effect: no differences in reaction time could be found between drivers with spotless records and those who had experienced some accidents—all were fast. As Münsterberg (1913) put it, "the slow individuals do not remain in the service" (p. 65) very long. Having rejecting the analytical approach, Münsterberg turned to his other method, simulation. After observing several motormen in action, he identified what he thought to be the critical process—an ability to attend simultaneously to an array of stimuli (e.g., pedestrians, horses, carriages), while making a continual series of decisions about whether these stimuli would affect the progress of the electric trolley.

To simulate the process, Münsterberg developed a clever procedure. He created cards 4.5 inches wide and 13 inches long, divided into half-inch squares. Two parallel lines ran down the middle, representing tracks. In the squares to either side of the "tracks" were random arrays of numbers representing people, horses, and automobiles, moving at different speeds, and moving either parallel to or perpendicular to the electric trolleys. Münsterberg rigged an apparatus so that the card was covered except for an area the width of the card and 2.5 inches long. By turning a crank, the motormen would successively expose various portions of the card and would be asked to identify objects that could end up being on the track, and therefore be dangerous. Figure 8.12 shows a sketch of the apparatus.

Münsterberg tested each individual on 12 different cards, then combined time and errors into a weighted measure when describing the results. Unfortunately, his description of the outcome is not clear. For example, the reader never learns how many men were tested, only that the company supplied "a number of the best motormen in its service," others "who had only just escaped dismissal," and a third group "neither especially good nor especially bad" (p. 74). Despite identifying these main groups, Münsterberg failed to report exactly how the groups differed in their performance on the simulation. That the simulation had some validity to it, however, was evident from (a) reports from the drivers that the procedure did indeed involve the kinds of decisions made while driving, and (b) some data showing that all the motormen, even the poor drivers, outperformed a group of Harvard students. Münsterberg (1913) considered the simulation a success and made a series of (arbitrary) recommendations about what score should be obtained before a potential motorman could be considered competent. He concluded by claiming that "an experimental investigation of this kind which demands from each individual hardly 10 minutes would be sufficient to exclude perhaps one fourth of those who are nowadays accepted into the service as motormen" (p. 81).

A study involving telephone operators illustrates Münsterberg's second research strategy—analyzing the job into specific subtasks and developing tests for each. These underpaid and overworked women handled up to 300 calls per hour, resulting in fatigue, errors, and what we would call burnout

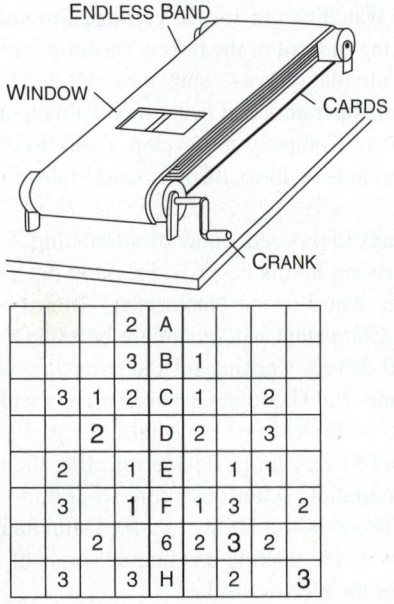

Copyright 1932 by W. W. Norton & Company, Inc. Copyright renewed 1960 by Morris S. Viteles. Used by permission of W. W. Norton & Company, Inc.

FIGURE 8.12 Sketch of Munsterberg's simulation to test the skills of "motormen" of the Boston Elevated Railway Company. From *Industrial Psychology* by Morris S. Viteles.

today. The Bell Telephone Company spent a lot of time and money on training, so they were looking for a way to screen out those most likely to have difficulty. Enter Münsterberg.

After observing operators for a time, Münsterberg (1913) was impressed with the complexity of their task, identifying 14 different "psychophysical processes" (p. 97); he selected several of them and developed tests. For example, memory was tested having operators recall lists of numbers, and attention was tested by having them examine a page of newspaper and cross out every example of a specific letter. They were also tested on word association, card sorting, and accuracy in touching a pencil to crosses drawn on a page (i.e., similar to hitting the correct hole in the switchboard). As with the motormen, Münsterberg failed to describe the results in any detail, but a sly move on the part of Bell Telephone, inserting some veterans into what Münsterberg had thought was a class of 30 novices, provided some unexpected validation:

> [T]he skeptical telephone company had mixed with the class a number of women who had been in the service for a long while and had even been selected as teachers in the telephone school. I did not know, in figuring out the results, which of the participants ... these particularly gifted outsiders were.... The results showed ... that these women who had proved most able in practical service stood at the top of our list. (pp. 108–109)

The "motorman" and telephone operator selection examples are the best known of the studies reported in Münsterberg's pioneering book, but there are dozens more, examining such topics as the effects of monotony and fatigue on productivity, whether magazines should place ads together in one section or spread them throughout the magazine, and the effects of the size of ads on memory for products.

Other Leading Industrial Psychologists in America

Münsterberg was far from alone in his involvement with business and industry. The commercial world provided fruitful opportunities for many psychologists needing to supplement meager academic salaries. This part of the chapter began by mentioning one of them, Walter Dill Scott. Other prominent industrial psychologists included Walter Van Dyke Bingham, Lillian Gilbreth, and Harry Hollingworth.

Walter Van Dyke Bingham (1880–1952) Bingham's career found him in direct contact with many of the psychologists who are or soon will be familiar to you. He was a graduate student at functionalist Chicago from 1905 to 1908, where he completed a dissertation on the perception of tones under James Angell and worked as John Watson's student assistant. In 1907, he traveled briefly in Europe, where he met the gestaltists Köhler and Koffka, then spent some time at Harvard getting to know James and Münsterberg while acquiring a minor in philosophy. His shift to applied psychology began to occur after he went to Columbia in 1908 to start his academic career. There he encountered Cattell and Thorndike, who sparked his interests in mental testing and educational psychology, respectively. After 2 years he moved to Dartmouth College, where he remained until 1915. For the next 9 years, he presided over a unique academic enterprise, the Division of Applied Psychology at the Carnegie Institute of Technology, a school founded 10 years earlier and now known as Carnegie-Mellon University.

It was in Pittsburgh that Bingham established his reputation for applying psychological principles to business. With the aid of generous funding from local business executives (e.g., Westinghouse, Heinz), he established units within his division specifically oriented to business psychology. One example was the Bureau of Salesmanship Research, and Bingham recruited Walter Dill Scott to direct it. On temporary leave from Northwestern University, Scott is believed to be the first person ever given the title of Professor of Applied Psychology (Landy, 1993). The bureau produced a useful guide for personnel directors called *Aids in the Selection of Salesmen*, which included a standardized application form, a set of questions for interviewers, and recommendations for tests to be given to applicants (Bingham, 1952). The sales bureau soon spawned a related enterprise, the Research Bureau for Retail Training. It was also generously underwritten, this time by department store magnate Edgar Kaufmann.[7] The bureau "prepared employment tests, training manuals, merchandise manuals, and specific procedures for correcting defects of sales personality and of supervision" (Bingham, 1952, pp. 15–16). A third Bingham innovation was the School of Life Insurance Salesmanship, which trained a legion of sales reps to convince people that they were underinsured. Many of the staff and students that Bingham attracted to Carnegie became leaders in the field of industrial-organizational psychology (Vinchur, 2007).

In addition to his work at Carnegie from 1915 to 1924, Bingham was also a key player in establishing the credibility of the Psychological Corporation. He replaced Cattell in 1926 when the temperamental founder was ousted as president of the corporation by its board (Sokal, 1981a). He also served with Yerkes in World War I, helping with the Army testing program, and he played a similar but even larger role in World War II. Given the title of Chief Psychologist by the War Department, he chaired a committee that produced the Army General Classification Test (AGCT), which was eventually given to 10 million soldiers (Hilgard, 1987). From the mid-1920s through the end of World War II, Bingham consistently promoted industrial psychology, making him the discipline's most visible advocate.

Lillian Moller Gilbreth (1878–1972) The career of Lillian Gilbreth (Figure 8.13) can be divided into two segments by the early death of her husband, Frank. Prior to this unfortunate event, she was able to combine the roles of mother and professional in ways seldom seen before or since. Frank

FIGURE 8.13 Lillian Gilbreth (1878–1972), mother of 12 and pioneer in ergonomics and industrial psychology.

© UPI/Bettmann/Corbis

[7]Kaufmann is also known for hiring Frank Lloyd Wright to design a house, outside Pittsburgh, that could be used as a getaway from the hustle and bustle (and pollution from wall-to-wall steel mills) of Pittsburgh. The result was one of Wright's best-known creations—Fallingwater.

Gilbreth, a former bricklayer without the benefit of a college education, was a pioneer in the field of time-and-motion study. By carefully observing bricklayers, for instance, he identified wasteful motions and recommended more efficient ones, thereby increasing worker productivity. Lillian collaborated with this work, contributing equally to their successful consulting business, Gilbreth, Inc. In the process, she completed the requirements for a doctorate at Berkeley by writing a dissertation called "The Psychology of Management," but was not given the degree because she could not meet residency requirements. After the Gilbreths moved to Rhode Island, she finished a second doctorate at Brown University, with a dissertation on how worker efficiency principles could be applied to the teaching profession. Her PhD, awarded in 1915, was the first ever granted in industrial psychology (Perloff & Naman, 1996). During this time she also published her initial dissertation in book form, after reluctantly bowing to pressure from her publisher to disguise her gender by having the book attributed to "L. M. Gilbreth." Together, the Gilbreths published books on ways to eliminate fatigue (Gilbreth & Gilbreth, 1916) and on the uses of time-and-motion study (Gilbreth & Gilbreth, 1917).

These achievements, remarkable by any measure, approach the incredible when one realizes that during the 20 years of their marriage, Frank and Lillian Gilbreth had a dozen children, six boys and six girls. You might be familiar with this part of the story from the book or the movie *Cheaper by the Dozen*; two of the children wrote the book (Gilbreth & Carey, 1949). It is a marvelous tale about living in a large family run by principles of worker efficiency (e.g., "shave" a few seconds off the morning's whisker removal by using two blades, one in each hand). Their family also became the focus of a paper written by one of Terman's students in 1923 called "IQ Farming." With both parents and all the children testing in the "gifted" range, the Gilbreths were the prototypical example of the kind of family destined to lead Terman's meritocracy (Minton, 1988).

After her husband's fatal heart attack in 1924, Lillian Gilbreth's accomplishments increased, even though she was now raising 11 children on her own (one of the dozen died in infancy), while continuing to run the consulting business and teaching part-time. She became a pioneer in the field of **ergonomics**, the study of how systems and products can be made efficient for human use. Her ideas included the redesign of household tasks, based on her own ample experiences. For instance, she became largely responsible for modern kitchen design, creating what she referred to as the "practical" kitchen; pop-up trash cans and side-door shelves for refrigerators were among her innovations (Perloff & Naman, 1996). She was also a major force in helping people with physical handicaps become productive citizens—she considered this her most important work. When she died in 1972 at age 94, Gilbreth had added 16 honorary doctorates to her 2 earned ones.

Harry Hollingworth (1880–1956) Hollingworth was one of a number of psychologists who came to applied psychology reluctantly, needing to put food on the table. As an undergraduate at the University of Nebraska, Hollingworth encountered the new psychology in a laboratory course taken with T. L. Bolton, a student of Hall's at Clark University. He left Nebraska in 1907 to pursue graduate studies at Columbia, where he studied with Cattell, Thorndike, and Woodworth. After a year, Hollingworth married fellow Nebraskan Leta Stetter, who you met in this chapter's Close-Up.

Hollingworth finished his doctorate in 1908 and then took a position as instructor at nearby Barnard College, but barely managed on his $1,000 annual salary. Meanwhile, as you read in the Close-Up, Leta was unable to teach in the New York School system because she was married. Salvation came in the form of an offer from the Coca-Cola Company, which hired both Hollingworths in 1911 to conduct research on the effects of caffeine. The company had been charged by the government with adding an element to its formula (caffeine) that had what were believed to be unhealthy stimulant properties. The Hollingworths completed a series of studies, using careful double-blind procedures, and Harry was able to testify in court that the amount of caffeine in the cola had no discernible adverse effects, except that relatively large amounts taken late in the evening could interfere with sleep (Benjamin, Rogers, & Rosenbaum, 1991).

The Coca-Cola project was lucrative for this financially strapped young couple. It provided enough money to finance 3 years of graduate education at Columbia's Teachers College for Leta, enabled the couple to spend the summer of 1912 touring Europe, and launched Harry onto the path of applied psychology (Benjamin, 2003). He became inundated with consulting opportunities from businesses ranging from railroads, which wanted to know what color to paint their cars, to city planners, who wanted to know how to improve the legibility of traffic signs, to chewing gum manufacturers, who wanted some evidence that gum chewing was relaxing (Benjamin, 1996). He took advantage of many of these requests, and he made a name for himself as a prominent applied psychologist, but he claimed that he did the work reluctantly, seeing himself first as a "psychologist," and only secondarily as an applied psychologist, writing that "[i]t has been my sad fate to have established early in my career a reputation for interests that with me were only superficial" (quoted in Benjamin, 1996, p. 134).

Applied Psychology in Europe—Psychotechnics

The focus of this chapter has been on applied psychology in the United States, from the turn of the 20th century to the decade of the 1920s. Application certainly meshes with the American national character, but it is important to note that applied psychology flourished in other countries as well. This was especially true in Europe, where the field of applied psychology developed its own label, **psychotechnics**, a term implying the use of special "techniques" for the purpose of workplace improvement. One pioneer was Münsterberg, of course—his *Psychology and Industrial Efficiency* was published in Germany a year (1912) before it was translated and published United States. Another was William Stern. In addition to developing the concept of the intelligence quotient that Terman incorporated into the Stanford–Binet, Stern created the term psychotechnics and invented several memory tests that could be used to assess eyewitness memory.

Psychotechnics in Europe came into its own in World War I and then, mirroring the progress of applied psychology in the United States, became immensely popular with business and industry in the 1920s. During the war, psychologists in several countries became involved in military applications. These typically involved developing tests to select individuals for highly skilled specialties (e.g., pilots). Most of these tests measured such variables as reaction time and hand–eye coordination, but at least one device, used in France, was based on the idea that good pilots would remain calm under pressure. To assess "the stability of the nervous system," examiners for the French Air Force fired pistols behind the heads of unsuspecting pilots-in-training, measuring changes in breathing, heart rate, and hand steadiness in response (van Drunen, 1997).

In the 1920s, especially in Germany but throughout Europe, business and industry began using psychotechnic specialists to improve the bottom line. In Germany, according to Viteles (1932), 22 different corporations had laboratories at their worksites by 1922, and more than 100 firms were using psychotechnical methods in various ways. The main activity was employee selection, but the approach in Europe was quite different from that taken in the United States. In America, employee selection procedures in the 1920s were predominantly in the form of paper-and-pencil tests or simple laboratory procedures (e.g., reaction time). In Europe, however, selection procedures were more often tied to elaborate apparatus that had been especially designed for the particular job at hand, or, inspired by Münsterberg's "motormen" project, simulations of the skills assumed to be needed for the job (van Strien, 1998). For instance, those applying to be drivers in the Dutch Postal Service had to take a "sensitivity to movement" test. The device consisted of two hand cranks that were connected by a belt and separated by a partition. On one side of the partition, the examiner turned one of the cranks in a specific sequence. The person being tested had to sense the sequence of turns and then mimic them. It was assumed that the postal driver "had to be sensitive to the movements of his car in order to react appropriately" (van Drunen, 1997, p. 482).

Just as the testing craze waned in the United States in the late 1920s and early 1930s, psychotechnics came under critical scrutiny in Europe. For one thing, validation research was either nonexistent or based on crude measures or anecdotal evidence. In addition, the use of specialized apparatus for selection was costly. Different devices were needed for different jobs, so construction costs could be high. Also, individuals usually had to be tested individually, a more costly procedure than the group testing available to those in the United States using paper-and-pencil tests. Nonetheless, psychotechnics thrived in Europe in the period between the world wars. As one indication, an international conference on psychotechnics was held in Geneva, Switzerland, in 1920. During the next 15 years, there were more international conferences throughout Europe devoted to psychotechnics (eight) than there were devoted to general psychology (five; van Strien, 1998). After World War II, the term psychotechnics fell out of use, and in 1955 the International Association of Psychotechnics (formed at the 1920 Geneva conference) was renamed the International Association of Applied Psychology (Warr, 2007).

IN PERSPECTIVE: APPLIED PSYCHOLOGY

Research methods textbooks typically make a distinction between basic and applied research. Basic research is normally done in a laboratory setting and investigates fundamental psychological processes (e.g., memory, perception, conditioning). Applied research, on the other hand, normally (but not necessarily) occurs outside the laboratory and is focused on solving real-world problems (e.g., how to select the best worker). The texts will point out that both forms of research are necessary and that they complement each other. In reality, however, basic research in its purest form, the kind of research that would make Titchener smile, is a hard sell. Modern-day psychologists, for example, often find it difficult to win grants for basic research, unless they can somehow show that the results can be applied in some way. In an interview after being elected president of the APS (Association for Psychological Science), for example, noted experimental psychologist Richard F. Thompson noted that "[m]any of us who have been basic scientists have come to feel that to justify our existence we, too, have really got to try to develop applications to the problems of society" (Kent, 1994, p. 10).

After reading this chapter, you now know that Thompson's concern is not a new one. Right from the start, many psychologists, even though they had been trained for the laboratory, believed it was necessary to make their work relevant. Indeed, in the United States at least, this focus on application existed even before the advent of the New Psychology—consider the popularity of phrenology (Chapter 3), for example, which can be considered a form of applied psychology.

Harry Hollingworth is the prototype of the psychologist, trained to be a "pure" researcher, who nonetheless found himself forced by circumstance into applied work. Benjamin (2003) has argued that Hollingworth might have been protesting too much when he claimed that all he really wanted to be was a laboratory psychologist—he never seemed interested in abandoning the applied work that made his life comfortable. And for the most part, Hollingworth's nonapplied research has been forgotten. His doctoral dissertation on motor accuracy in reaching, however, which emphasized the importance of the overall environment within which the reaching behavior occurred, did catch the notice of at least one prominent figure. The gestalt psychologist Kurt Koffka once told Hollingworth that the study had been a "cornerstone" of the Gestalt psychology movement, the topic of our next chapter. As we shall see, the gestaltists had a lasting impact on American psychology, especially in the areas of perception and thinking. Yet their influence was never as strong as they would have wished, in part because they never appreciated the lesson of this chapter—the importance of application.

SUMMARY

The Desire for Application

• From the time when the new psychology first appeared in America, in the late 19th century, psychologists have been concerned with how psychological knowledge could be put to good use. The concern over application was partly a natural consequence of American pragmatism and the belief that scientific progress should result in beneficial technology.

• Psychologists also experienced institutional pressures to justify their existence within departments of philosophy, with their needs for expensive fully equipped laboratories.

The Mental Testing Movement

• Modern intelligence testing, with its emphasis on measuring cognitive rather than sensory processes, originated with the Ebbinghaus completion tests and the creation of the Binet–Simon tests. Binet's goal was to identify students who were academically weak (débiles), so that special programs could be developed for them. The test was scored in terms of mental level (later called mental age), and children in need were considered to be those scoring two levels below their actual age. Binet's approach to psychology, which he called individual psychology, was to emphasize the study of individual differences rather than the search for general laws of behavior.

• The Binet tests came to America when they were translated by Henry Goddard of Vineland Training School. Goddard used the tests to classify degrees of feeblemindedness in terms of mental age and created the term moron to identify those with mental ages between 8 and 12. He believed that mental deficiency was inherited and supported his case with the methodologically flawed and biased Kallikak study, which traced the lineage of one of the Vineland children. Goddard also used the tests to help officials at the Ellis Island immigration center try to identify the mentally unfit. His results added to the perception that immigrants from southern and eastern Europe were inferior to those from northern and western Europe.

• Lewis Terman institutionalized intelligence testing by revising and standardizing the Binet tests, thereby creating the Stanford–Binet, one of the best-known modern tests of intelligence. The test was scored in terms of William Stern's concept of IQ, a ratio of mental age to chronological age. To support his belief in a meritocracy, Terman conducted an extended study of gifted children, finding that they broke the stereotype that such children are intellectually superior but socially and physically inferior.

• Robert Yerkes, a comparative psychologist at heart, became involved in mental testing in World War I by organizing the Army testing program. He and his team developed two group intelligence tests, one for literate soldiers (Army Alpha) and one for illiterates (Army Beta). The program was minimally useful to the Army, but launched intelligence testing as big business and made testing a popular enterprise in the 1920s. After the war, Yerkes's report on the program, which suggested that the typical American soldier scored barely higher than moron level, generated much controversy over mental testing, IQ, and the question of how much intelligence resulted from nature and nurture.

Applying Psychology to Business

• The first psychologists to apply psychological principles to business were Walter Dill Scott, who wrote pioneering books on advertising and how to improve business practices, and Hugo Münsterberg, who came from Germany to run the laboratory at Harvard, but soon developed interests in several applied areas, including forensic psychology, psychotherapy, and industrial ("economic") psychology.

• Münsterberg's *Psychology and Industrial Efficiency* included several examples of how psychological principles could be used to select employees. He recommended two approaches to measurement: simulations of critical features of the worker's task, as in driving an electric trolley car, and analysis into component skills, as in being a telephone operator. The book also included research-based advice on improving the workplace and marketing.

- Other pioneering industrial psychologists include Walter Van Dyke Bingham, whose Division of Applied Psychology at the Carnegie Institute developed programs for training people in sales and retailing; Lillian Moller Gilbreth, an efficiency expert and one of the first to study ergonomics; and Harry Hollingworth, a reluctant applied psychologist, but an effective one who applied sophisticated experimental design to applied problems such as the effects of caffeine on performance.

- Applied psychology was known as psychotechnics in Europe, and it flourished there during World War I (e.g., pilot selection) and in the 1920s. Compared with Americans who tended to rely on paper-and-pencil tests for employee selection purposes, Europeans often developed simulations and used elaborate apparatus to test job applicants on skills assumed to be relevant for the job.

STUDY QUESTIONS

1. What was the significance of Scripture's *Thinking, Feeling, Doing*, which included numerous examples of how laboratory methods had a wider use?

2. Why was it important for advocates of the "new psychology" to show that their work had applications?

3. When testing for fatigue in schoolchildren, what was the approach taken by Ebbinghaus? Explain.

4. Binet's approach to psychology has been referred to as "individual" psychology. Explain and contrast his approach with an alternative research strategy.

5. What was Binet's idea about the reason for developing mental tests, and what did he conclude about the placement of schoolchildren?

6. Had Binet learned of the subsequent history of IQ testing after his death, he might have turned over in his grave. Explain.

7. According to Goddard, define the term moron, and explain why Goddard thought it was critically important to study and be able to identify this type of person.

8. Describe and criticize the Kallikak study. Explain why it is an example of how preconceived bias can influence research.

9. Describe and criticize Goddard's work at Ellis Island.

10. Describe the origins of the term intelligence quotient.

11. What was Terman's contribution to the measurement of intelligence?

12. Explain how the concept of a meritocracy led Terman to complete psychology's longest longitudinal study. On the basis of his research, what did Terman conclude about gifted children?

13. According to Leta Hollingworth, what was the best strategy for educating gifted children?

14. Describe the research reported by Leta Hollingworth that raised questions about gender differences in intellect.

15. Describe the Army testing program, being sure to distinguish between the two forms of the test. Why were the results controversial?

16. Use specific examples to illustrate the two primary methods used by Münsterberg to accomplish employee selection.

17. In Münsterberg's study of telephone operators, an unexpected validation procedure occurred. Explain.

18. Aside from his work in industrial psychology, what other contributions did Münsterberg make to applied psychology?

19. Describe the contributions to applied psychology made by Walter Bingham and Lillian Gilbreth.

20. Using the Coco-Cola study as the example, describe how research psychologists brought special expertise to the area of applied psychology.

21. Describe how industrial psychology in Europe differed from its counterpart in the United States.

CHAPTER **9**

GESTALT PSYCHOLOGY

> There are wholes, the behavior of which is not determined by that of their individual elements, but where the part-processes are themselves determined by the intrinsic nature of the whole.
>
> —Max Wertheimer, 1924

PREVIEW AND CHAPTER OBJECTIVES

Advocates of a new way of thinking often find that they must speak loudly to be heard. Such was the case for those who became known as gestalt psychologists. With missionary zeal, these German psychologists promoted an approach to psychology that objected deeply to the prevailing analytical strategy that characterized certain aspects of other German psychologies, Titchenerian structuralism, American behaviorism, and any theory derived from British associationist principles. The gestaltists argued that understanding mind and behavior could not be achieved by trying to dissect conscious experience into its sensory elements, or by reducing complex behavior to elementary stimulus-response units. Rather, their emphasis was on phenomenologically whole experiences, and before long their movement came to be identified with this catch phrase: The whole of an experience is greater than the sum of its individual parts. The first section of this chapter highlights the work of three Germans who established the gestalt movement in the early years of the 20th century: Max Wertheimer, normally considered the founder by virtue of his elegant yet simple demonstrations of apparent motion; Kurt Koffka, who introduced gestalt concepts to an American audience and extended gestalt ideas into developmental psychology; and Wolfgang Köhler, whose research on learning and problem solving in apes challenged behaviorism.

All three gestalt pioneers emigrated from Europe and came to the United States, two of them (Wertheimer and Köhler) as a consequence of Hitler's dismantling of the German academic environment in the 1930s. The gestalt psychology that arrived in America was sometimes associated only with the study of perception, but the gestaltists also made important contributions to the psychology of thinking and problem solving, and their ideas influenced the later development of cognitive psychology.

The final portion of the chapter describes the life and work of Kurt Lewin. He was for a time associated with the gestaltists in Germany, and like Wertheimer and Köhler, he came to the United States to escape the Nazi menace. Lewin went beyond gestalt psychology, however, and developed a complex theory of human behavior that led him to make important contributions to developmental, social, and industrial psychology. Impatient with abstract laboratory studies, he developed "action research," aimed at making a direct impact on people's lives and solving social problems. After you finish this chapter, you should be able to:

- Describe the immediate antecedents of gestalt psychology, in the ideas of Brentano, Mach, and von Ehrenfels
- Describe Wertheimer's apparent motion study, and explain the significance of the study

- Summarize Koffka's contributions to gestalt psychology
- Describe and apply gestalt perceptual organizing principles
- Distinguish between geographical and behavioral environments, and describe the implications of the distinction
- Describe Köhler's research on problem solving in apes, and contrast his conclusions with those of Thorndike
- Describe Wertheimer's ideas about productive thinking and the general gestalt approach to thinking and problem solving
- Describe the essentials of Lewin's field theory
- Explain the Zeigarnik effect and show how it fits into Lewin's notion of equilibrium
- Describe the contributions made by Lewin to developmental and social psychology
- Describe the overall impact of gestalt psychology on American psychology, and explain why it did not become a dominant system in the United States

THE ORIGINS AND EARLY DEVELOPMENT OF GESTALT PSYCHOLOGY

The starting date for gestalt psychology is normally thought to be somewhere between 1910 and 1912, the years when German psychologist Max Wertheimer looked at a common perceptual phenomenon from a new perspective. As with all intellectual movements, however, starting dates are arbitrary, masking a more complicated lineage. The gestaltists were influenced indirectly by the German philosophical tradition of Kant, with its emphasis on how a priori perceptual and cognitive categories shape our experiences (see Chapter 2), and by the late 19th-century phenomenology of Edmund Husserl, which stressed the importance of relying on direct descriptions of our experiences over the artificial introspective accounts that attempted dissection when trying to understand the nature of these experiences. The gestaltists were also influenced by physics, especially the work of Max Planck (1858–1947), an important pioneer of field theory in physics, which emphasized how overall fields of force determine the nature of the relationships among components of the field. A magnetic field, for instance, represents a force that produces an overall pattern of interrelations among elements that cannot be understood by analyzing each of the elements within the total field.

Four direct influences on the creation of gestalt psychology were Ernst Mach, Christian von Ehrenfels, Franz Brentano, and Carl Stumpf. In a book on sensation written in 1886, Mach (1886/1914), a physicist, argued that certain "space-forms" resisted analysis into basic elements. For example, a square has the essential spatial feature of "squareness" that cannot be further reduced. The four lines that compose it can change in size, but the relationship among the four lines must stay the same for squareness to occur. The overall relationship is what counts when identifying squares, not the individual components. The Austrian philosopher Christian von Ehrenfels came to a similar conclusion. There are certain qualities of experience, he argued, that go beyond sensory elements and persist even if the elements are altered. A talented musician, von Ehrenfels used melody as an example. By playing a song in a different key or with a different instrument, the physical properties of every single note (element) might change, yet the melody itself does not change—it has a **form-quality** ("gestaltqualitat") different from the sum of the individual notes.

At about the same time that Wundt was publishing his *Physiological Psychology*, proclaiming the founding of a new science, the Viennese philosopher Franz Brentano (1838–1917) published

Psychology from an Empirical Standpoint (Brentano, 1874/1995). The title may be misleading to the modern reader, because the "empirical" seems to imply the collection of data. The book, however, is more of a philosophical treatise, but with important implications for psychology. As he used the term *empirical*, Brentano simply meant acquiring knowledge through direct experience and reflection on that experience. In the book, he argued that the important thing about studying the mind was not to examine its contents, or even to understand the underlying physiology, but to understand how the mind *operates* to create our experiences. When studying perception, for example, the important thing is not a detailed description of the sensations, images, and affects, as would occur in Titchener's lab, for example. Rather, from an empirical standpoint, the important thing is the act of perceiving, how the individual perceives the event, and what the event *means* to the individual. Brentano's system has been called an **act psychology** because of the emphasis on the mind as an active entity. Brentano had a direct influence on von Ehrenfels and Husserl, both students of his.

Like von Ehrenfels, Carl Stumpf (1848–1936) was a talented musician, capable of playing six instruments (Sprung, 1997). As a scientist, Stumpf (Figure 9.1) was noted for his work on the auditory perception of tones. This expertise led him into a spirited debate with Wundt over who was best qualified to be a subject in experiments about judging musical tones. At issue was an auditory phenomenon with a distinct gestalt theme. When listening to two pure tones simultaneously, the experience is of a unique new tone that does not seem to be a combination of its two components. Wundt believed that suitably trained laboratory workers would be capable of analyzing the phenomenon into its component tones, but Stumpf contended that skilled musicians were better observers and that the phenomenon resisted analysis. If a laboratory analysis contradicted the phenomenal experience of a trained musician, Stumpf

Photograph by Julius Cornelius Schaarwächter 1847–1904

FIGURE 9.1 Carl Stumpf (1848–1936), gestalt mentor.

argued, then the lab analysis was in error. Although not denying the importance of laboratory work, Stumpf and his followers urged the primacy of direct experience over abstract reductionism (Ash, 1985).

Stumpf was named professor at Berlin in 1894, where he soon helped create Berlin's Psychological Institute. Two of the original three gestaltists you are about to meet took their doctorates with Stumpf in Berlin, and the third studied with him for a time.

Max Wertheimer (1880–1943): Founding Gestalt Psychology

Max Wertheimer (Figure 9.2) was born in Prague and initially studied law at its university before his broad interests led him to switch to philosophy. He took courses with von Ehrenfels, where he learned about his teacher's concept of Gestaltqualitat; studied in Berlin for three semesters, where he encountered Stumpf; and then went to Würzburg, where he completed a doctorate with Oswald Külpe in 1904 (Newman, 1944). For the next few years, he studied informally in several Eastern European universities.

Somewhere around 1910, Wertheimer became fascinated by the perceptual problem of **apparent motion**. The phenomenon was well known at the time and the basis for the newly created motion picture industry. It can be illustrated with a simple example. In a darkened room, two adjacent small lights are flashed on and off in sequence. If the interval between the flashing of the two lights is just right (about 60 msec), the perception is not of two lights, each flashing on and then off, but of a single light that moves repeatedly from side to side. Thus, two separate sensory events occur, two flashing lights,

© UPI/Bettmann/Corbis

FIGURE 9.2 Max Wertheimer (1880–1943), gestalt psychology's founder.

but the perception is that of a single continuous event, one light moving.[1] In the space between the lights, the light is perceived to be moving even though there is no sensory basis for this perception. How could this occur?

Traditional explanations for this apparent motion centered on sensory-motor events or higher cognitive inferences. The first idea was that as the circles flashed alternately, the person would rapidly shift the eyes (without awareness) from left to right, over and over. Sensory stimulation resulting from the eye movements was said to produce the perceptual "fusion" that was experienced as movement. The second explanation, in the spirit of Helmholtz, was that the individual made an unconscious logical inference that if a light was in position A then in position B, it must have moved there. The perception, held to be illusory, was the result of this "reasonable" inference.

With the cooperation of Friedrich Schumann, laboratory director at the University of Frankfurt, Wertheimer acquired laboratory space and equipment to develop his ideas about apparent motion into a research project. He was aided by two young psychologists then working in Schumann's lab, Kurt Koffka and Wolfgang Köhler (both in Figure 9.3), who served as participants in the experiments (as did Koffka's wife). The outcome was a 1912 paper, "Experimental Studies on the Perception of Movement" (Wertheimer, 1912/1965), often considered the founding event of gestalt psychology.

In the research, Wertheimer and his colleagues demonstrated the phenomenon under a variety of conditions and raised serious questions about prevailing explanations. In one of their studies, for example, three lights in a straight line, A, B, and C, were used. If lights A and C were flashed on and off simultaneously, and then B was flashed after 60 msec, the perception was that two lights

Archives of the History of American Psychology, The Center for the History of Psychology —The University of Akron

FIGURE 9.3 Kurt Koffka (1886–1941) on the left and Wolfgang Köhler (1887–1967) at 9th International Congress of Psychology, held at Yale University in 1929, from Popplestone and McPherson (1994).

[1] If the interval between the flashing of the lights is too short, about 30 msec or less, the perception is that both lights are on at the same time and neither is moving. If the interval is longer than 200 msec, two separate flashing lights will be seen (Goldstein, 1996).

(A and C) had moved at the same time to the center point. This demonstration eliminated the eye movement explanation because the eyes cannot move in two directions at the same time. The inference explanation was rejected on the grounds that the movement perception occurred too quickly to involve such a complicated sequence of mental events and that the perception of motion was real, not illusory. Instead, Wertheimer argued that the phenomenon must stand on its own as a valid example of an immediately given phenomenological experience that does not require analysis into constituent parts. Indeed, because perception occurred in areas devoid of any sensory information (i.e., the space between the flashing lights), analysis into sensory elements could not possibly explain the phenomenon. Wertheimer referred to the perceived motion as the **phi phenomenon**; he disliked the term "apparent" motion because it implied that the motion was not really perceived (Henle, 1980). As he later concluded, we perceive whole, meaningful figures, not elements that somehow combine to form wholes. Not only is the whole different from the sum of its parts, but "the part-processes are themselves determined by the intrinsic nature of the whole" (Wertheimer, 1924/1967a, p. 2). The assault on atomism and structuralism had begun.

Wertheimer lectured and continued doing research at Frankfurt until 1916, then went to Berlin, where he became a central figure at the Berlin Psychological Institute until 1929.[2] In that year Schumann retired from Frankfurt, and Wertheimer returned there to chair the department. He probably would have remained at Frankfurt until his own retirement, but the rise of Nazi Germany changed everything. Shortly after Hitler came to power in 1933, the "Law for the Reestablishment of the Professional Civil Service" was enacted. Although the label sounds innocuous enough, its true intent was to remove anyone of Jewish heritage from professional positions funded by the state. Included were university professors. Soon, Jewish professors, including such luminaries as Wertheimer's close friend, Albert Einstein, began to be dismissed from their positions. Wertheimer, who was Jewish, saw the writing on the wall, gathered up his wife and three children, and fled to the United States, settling in New York.[3] There he joined a number of other German refugee–scientists at the recently created New School for Social Research. For the remaining 10 years of his life, he continued to work on perception and expanded an earlier interest in problem solving. The outcome was *Productive Thinking* (1945/1982) published posthumously, which will be described later in the section on the gestalt approach to cognition and learning.

Koffka (1886–1941) and Köhler (1887–1967): Cofounders

Kurt Koffka was born in Berlin and, except for a year spent at the University of Edinburgh in Scotland, educated there as well. He earned a PhD from Carl Stumpf at the University of Berlin in 1908, where he completed research in the perceptual topics of color contrast and auditory rhythm that would prepare the way for his acceptance of gestalt psychology (Harrower-Erickson, 1942). After completing his doctorate, Koffka studied physiology and then went to Würzburg for several years, where he worked in Külpe's laboratory, investigating imagery.

Starting in 1910 Koffka spent three semesters working in Schumann's lab at Frankfurt, and it was during this time that he encountered Wertheimer, participated in the famous apparent motion studies

---

[2]For a sense of the geography, refer again to the map of Germany at the beginning of Chapter 4.

[3]One of the children, Michael Wertheimer, is Professor Emeritus of psychology at the University of Colorado at Boulder. He is a prominent historian of psychology, nationally recognized as a master teacher by the APA, and a leader in Psi Chi, psychology's national honor society for students.

along with Köhler, and became a convert to gestaltist thinking. As he later wrote, the three young researchers "liked each other personally, had the same kind of enthusiasms, same kind of backgrounds, and saw each other daily discussing everything under the sun" (quoted in Ash, 1995, p. 120). Koffka left Frankfurt in 1911 to begin his first professorial job at the University of Giessen. He remained there until 1924, producing a modest but steady flow of experimental papers on such topics as sound localization and memory. He also extended gestalt ideas into the realm of developmental psychology.

Of the three early gestaltists, Koffka was primarily responsible for introducing the movement to the United States. He accomplished this first by writing an article in 1922 for *Psychological Bulletin* called "Perception: An Introduction to Gestalt-Theorie" (Koffka, 1922). It was an unfortunate choice of a title, however. Although the gestaltists thought of their movement as a new theory applicable to all psychology, the article implied that gestalt psychology was merely a new approach to the study of perception. This "misperception" lingers today—in modern introductory texts, discussion of gestalt psychology occurs almost exclusively in the perception chapter.

Koffka also spread the gestalt word in person starting in 1924, in a 30-campus lecture tour, in an invited address to the annual meeting of the APA in 1925, and in a pair of visiting professor appointments at Cornell and Wisconsin (Sokal, 1984). In 1927, he accepted a full-time academic position at Smith College in western Massachusetts, a private liberal arts college for women, where he remained until his death from a heart attack in 1941. At Smith, the absence of a graduate program curtailed Koffka's research productivity, but he influenced the careers of several talented women psychologists, including Eleanor Gibson (Chapter 14). In 1935, Koffka wrote his most important book, *Principles of Gestalt Psychology*. It established his reputation as gestalt psychology's major theorist, but also contributed to a growing impression among Americans that the gestaltists were more interested in theory than data. At a time when most American psychologists were firmly committed to active programs of experimental research, this tendency to emphasize theory was seen as a weakness. Koffka's arguments in his highly abstract book were also difficult to follow. The works of his more erudite gestalt colleague, Köhler, were more widely read.

Wolfgang Köhler was just a year younger than Koffka and 7 years younger than Wertheimer, but he outlived his peers by 25 years and 23 years, respectively. This longevity, combined with his deliberate promotion of gestalt ideas, made him the best-known gestaltist of the three originators, especially in America. In 1958, he became the only one of them to be elected president of the APA. His early career was not unlike Koffka's—he earned a doctorate from Stumpf in 1909. He then became Schumann's assistant at Frankfurt, just in time for the arrival of Wertheimer and Koffka and their fateful collaboration (Asch, 1968).

In 1913, an intriguing opportunity came Köhler's way in the form of an invitation to direct the research at a primate colony that the Prussian Academy of Sciences had created at Tenerife, largest of the Canary Islands, which lie off the northwest coast of Africa.[4] He accepted, arriving just before the outbreak of World War I, which marooned him on the island with his family and his small colony of apes. As this chapter's Close-Up relates, though, research might not have been his only activity during these years—some think he could have been a German spy. Regardless of the espionage claims, the Tenerife years made Köhler's reputation as a scientist. There he produced his most famous research, the studies of problem solving in apes. This research, chronicled in *The Mentality of Apes* (1917/1926), will be examined in more detail later in this chapter.

---

[4]Tenerife was chosen mainly because the climate would be favorable to the apes, but also because it was not too far from the African nation of Cameroon, a German colony at the time, where the animals could be captured (Teuber, 1994).

CLOSE-UP

A CASE OF ESPIONAGE?

Wolfgang Köhler's research on Tenerife during World War I established his scientific reputation. The insight studies he completed there are widely cited, even today, and not just in history texts. But was research into the mental capabilities of apes Köhler's only interest during these years? Perhaps not, according to psychologist Ronald Ley. During a visit to the island in 1975, attempting to locate the original site of Köhler's Research Station, he happened to meet 87-year-old Manuel González y García, who was none other than the animal handler and caretaker during Köhler's years on Tenerife. Despite the passage of years, González y García's memory of the work done at the Research Station and of the behavior of the apes appeared to be vivid. For instance, his recollections of the apes were not all fond. He remembered that Köhler's most famous ape, Sultan, almost bit off a finger, and he showed Ley the scars from encounters with other apes in the colony. Concerning Köhler, he indicated that the German scientist seemed to enjoy working with the animals, but that he never went into the animal enclosures alone; he made most of his observations from outside the cages. And one other thing—Köhler was a German spy.

Naturally, the espionage claim astounded the initially skeptical Ley, who eventually wrote *A Whisper of Espionage: Wolfgang Köhler and the Apes of Tenerife* (Ley, 1990), a scientific detective story that describes his search for information to verify the assertion by González y García. It took him from Tenerife to archival collections throughout Europe to the homes of Köhler's wife and son. Ley failed to find direct evidence that Köhler was a spy, but he was able to piece together some circumstantial evidence suggesting that Köhler might have contributed to the German war effort. Located close to allied shipping lanes, the mountainous Canary Islands had strategic importance. Observers could easily spot allied shipping and convey information about it to German U-boats. Throughout the war, the British, who had numerous ships sunk in the area, made repeated claims to Spain that German spies on the island were doing just that. The islands were owned by Spain, supposedly a neutral country, but friendly with Germany. The British claimed that German scientists on the island had the means (wireless telegraph) to conduct espionage. According to Ley, Köhler, who kept a wireless radio at the Research Station, might have been one of those scientists.

Ley's espionage claim is intriguing, but it has been criticized. According to Pastore (1990), the radio might simply have been for general communication with the mainland, Köhler's research and writing output would not have left much time for active spying, there were other German scientists on the island who were in a better location to report shipping activity (meteorologists), and the whole story might be nothing more than a rumor that eventually morphed into a "fact" in an old man's mind. Köhler himself had referred to such a rumor, writing that "certain Englishmen … take us for German spies, and are even so kind as to spread the rumors that the animals are just a pretext" (quoted in Pastore, 1990, p. 369). On the other hand, it would not be unusual for any young patriotic scientist, given the opportunity, to pass along information that might be of use to the homeland.

Ley's espionage claim might be debatable, but his research uncovered fascinating details about Köhler's years on Tenerife, including the role played by his first wife Thekla. While raising two young children, she managed to contribute substantially to the research. She was apparently more at ease with the apes than Köhler and, according to her daughter, "the one who pressed to continue the work during times when things were going poorly" (quoted in Ley, 1990, p. 226). A talented artist, she drew the profile sketch of one of the apes that appeared as the frontispiece for *The Mentality of Apes* (Figure 9.4), and she filmed the research. Köhler

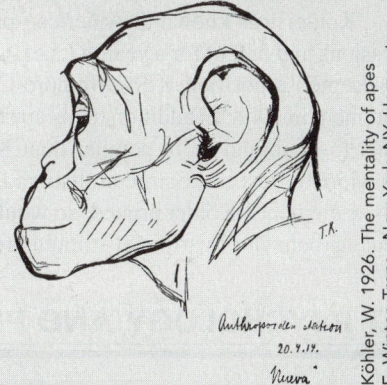

Köhler, W. 1926. The mentality of apes E. Winter, Trans... New York, NY: Harcourt, Brace. Original work published 1917; Sketch by Thekla Köhler 1914

FIGURE 9.4   This sketch of one of Köhler's apes was drawn by his first wife, Thekla, and appeared as the frontispiece to *The Mentality of Apes*.

recognized her value, writing to German authorities that Thekla was capable of running the Research Station herself and indicating that he wished her to be a coauthor of the book that summarized the research. He apparently changed his mind on the latter point, however. Thekla's initials below the sketch in the frontispiece are the only tangible sign of her contribution to the book.

Köhler returned to a war-ravaged Germany in 1920; within 2 years his status as a rising star in academia was confirmed when he was named to succeed the venerable Stumpf, his former mentor, as Director of the Psychological Institute at the University of Berlin. Wertheimer was also there, as was a young Kurt Lewin (discussed later in this chapter). Along with a talented group of students, the gestaltists created a "golden age" for their movement that lasted for about a decade (Henle, 1986). They produced important research, founded the journal *Psychologische Forschung* (*Psychological Research*) to promote their work, and sent their students throughout Germany to expand their influence. Then the Nazis arrived.

Of the three founding gestaltists, Köhler was the last to leave Germany when he emigrated in 1935. Because he was not Jewish, he did not face the kind of threat encountered by Wertheimer, but he was nonetheless appalled by the Nazi interference in academia, spoke out publicly, and paid for his activism. He was especially outraged by the passage of the law, mentioned earlier, that led to the wholesale dismissal of Jewish university professors. In April 1933, he wrote the last anti-Nazi article published during the Hitler years, denouncing the dismissals. In the article, he argued that "only the quality of a human being should determine his worth, that intellectual achievement, character, and obvious contributions to German culture retain their significance whether a person is Jewish or not" (quoted in Henle, 1986, p. 228). Although Köhler was not arrested for writing the article (to his and his students' surprise), his situation at the Institute rapidly deteriorated. He was forced to open lectures with a Nazi salute (which he did with notable sarcasm), Nazi sympathizer students began to "monitor" his lectures and "inspect" the laboratory, and some of Köhler's students (e.g., Karl Duncker, whose problem-solving research is described later in the chapter) were denounced as Communists. By early 1935, after refusing to sign a loyalty oath to Hitler, Köhler had had enough. He resigned his beloved directorship and wrote to colleagues that he "felt obliged to announce to all those who have taken a friendly interest in the Psychological Institute at Berlin that this institute does not exist anymore" (p. 236).

Köhler was known to American psychologists, having lectured in the United States on several occasions and taught for a year at Clark University in the mid-1920s. After leaving Berlin permanently, he accepted a position at Swarthmore College in eastern Pennsylvania, where he remained until his retirement in 1958. In addition to his ape book, Köhler wrote *Gestalt Psychology* in 1929. It was shorter, easier to read, and more popular than Koffka's dense text. It is notable for its assault on American behaviorism. Just as the structuralists and associationists had faltered by trying to analyze consciousness into its elements, Köhler argued, so would behaviorism fail because of its similar atomistic strategy of reducing behavior to artificial stimulus-response units.

GESTALT PSYCHOLOGY AND PERCEPTION

Wertheimer launched gestalt psychology with his research on a perceptual phenomenon, apparent motion, and the study of perception became an important part of the gestalt program. Much of the effort went into describing the basic rules determining how phenomena become organized into whole, meaningful figures. These so-called **gestalt organizing principles**, first articulated by Wertheimer

(1923/1967b), are now familiar fixtures in the perception chapters of general psychology texts. Here are some of the more important ones.

Principles of Perceptual Organization

One of our most basic perceptual tendencies is to separate whole figures from their backgrounds—it provides the foundation for all object perception (Goldstein, 1996). This **figure-ground** segregation was first described in detail in 1915 by Edgar Rubin, a Danish psychologist, who studied with G. E. Müller at Göttingen (Prentice, 1951). Rubin was not a gestalt psychologist, but the gestaltists used his figure-ground phenomenon to support their cause. According to Rubin's description, figures have distinct features that enable them to be isolated from backgrounds. The border seems to "belong" to the figure, for example, whereas the ground seems to extend behind the figure, and this perceptual impression is a strong one, even though we "know" otherwise. Also, the figure is more memorable than the ground and seems to have a substance that is lacking in the ground (Rubin, 1915/1958). In Figure 9.5*a*, for instance, observers usually perceive the segments with the straight, radiating lines as a figure against a background of concentric circles. The result is an overall perception of a type of cross that covers the circles.

With effort, it is possible to reverse the figure-ground relations in Figure 9.5*a*, making a cross with each arm, composed of arcs. This reversal is more easily accomplished in Figure 9.5*b*, the most famous part of Rubin's 1915 paper. By changing the focus of attention, the figure can either be a vase or two faces in profile. Note that only one of these perceptions can occur at a time. When the vase is the figure, the black area cannot be perceived as anything but an unformed background. When the faces are figures, the reverse happens. If you stare at Figure 9.5*b*, you will find your perception switching rapidly from one "whole" to another. One creative contemporary application of a figure-ground reversal is to be found in the logo for the Pittsburgh Zoo and Aquarium (Figure 9.5*c*); another is the FedEx logo (the next time you see it, look for the arrow).

Three other organizing principles are illustrated in Figure 9.6, taken from Wertheimer's 1923 paper on "Laws of Organization in Perceptual Forms" (Wertheimer, 1923/1967b). In Figure 9.6*a*, the first two dots seem to belong together, as do the next two, and so on. They are organized by the principle of **proximity**. Wertheimer (1923/1967b, p. 72) demonstrated the power of this simple principle by

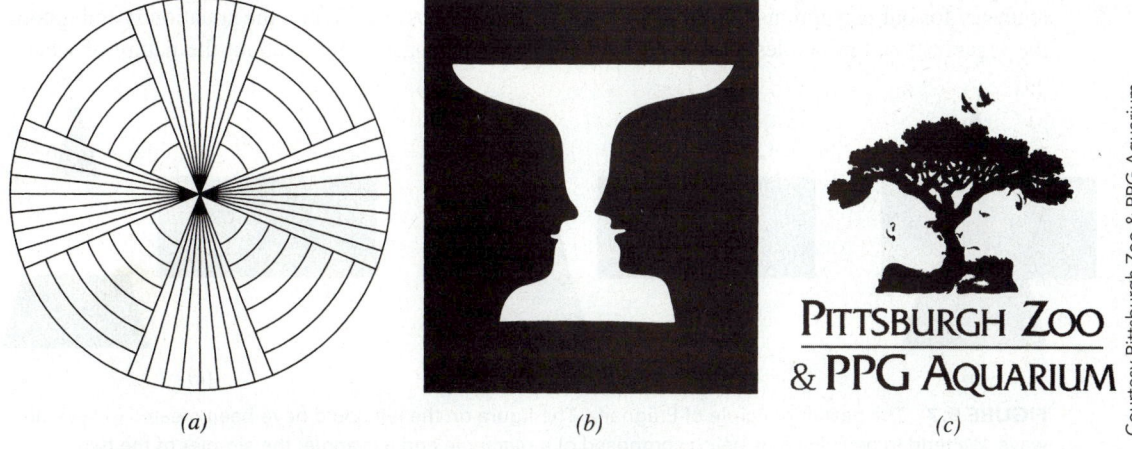

(a)   *(b)*   *(c)*

Courtesy Pittsburgh Zoo & PPG Aquarium

FIGURE 9.5 Reversible figure-ground illustrations (*a* and *b*), from Rubin (1915/1958), and (*c*) a modern application of a figure-ground reversal.

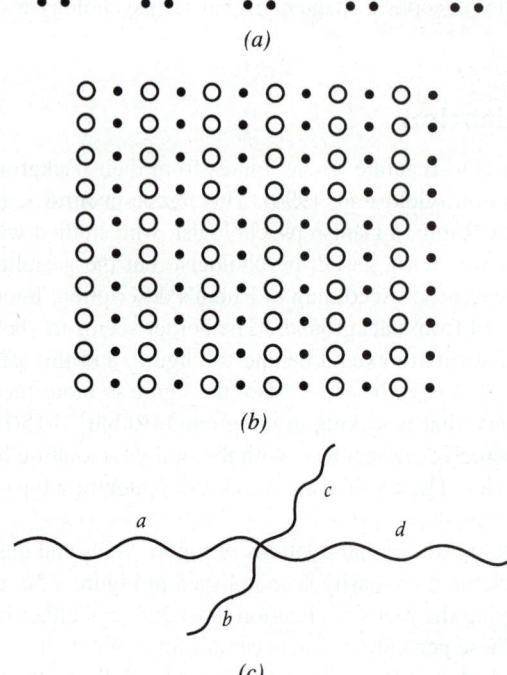

(a)

(b)

(c)

FIGURE 9.6 Gestalt perceptual organizing principles of (*a*) proximity, (*b*) similarity, and (*c*) good continuation, from Wertheimer (1923/1967b). Redrawn by John Wiley & Sons, Inc.

challenging readers to perceive the first dot as a unit, the second and third as another unit, and so on; he considered the task impossible. If proximity is held constant, then stimuli might be organized according to **similarity**, as shown in Figure 9.6*b*, and we are compelled to perceive alternating vertical columns of circles and dots. The third principle, **good continuation**, is a tendency to organize our perceptions in smoothly flowing directions. Thus, we perceive Figure 9.6*c* as two wavy lines a–d and b–c. It is difficult to perceive the figure as two lines that sharply change direction, a–b or c–d.

All the organizing principles have in common what is sometimes called the law of simplicity or what the gestaltists called **prägnanz** (rough translation: "simplest good figure"). It refers to the basic tendency for our perceptions to mirror reality as closely as possible. When the situation is ambiguous, the organizational principles work to provide the most reasonable guess about the nature of what is

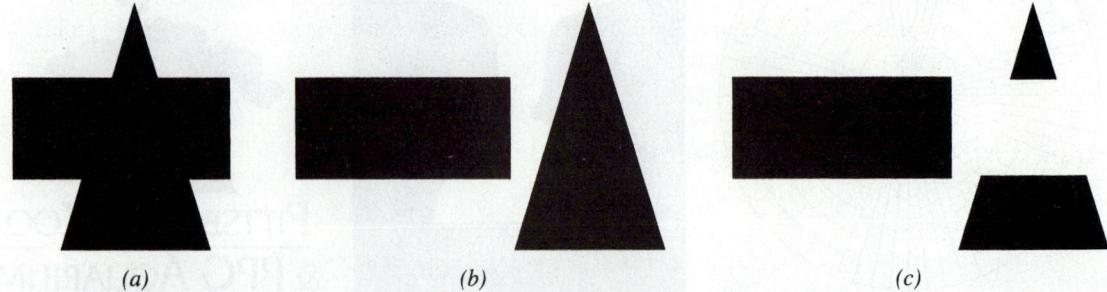

(a)　　　　　　*(b)*　　　　　　*(c)*

FIGURE 9.7 The gestalt principle of Prägnanz. The figure on the left could have been created in several ways. We tend to perceive it as being composed of a rectangle and a triangle, the simpler of the two possibilities shown on the right. Drawn by Dr. C. James Goodwin

FIGURE 9.8 Because of the gestalt principle of closure, we perceive these incomplete drawings as a dog, a giraffe, and Edgar Allen Poe.

being perceived. Thus, even though Figure 9.7 could have been created in several different ways, we tend to perceive the figure as being composed of an overlapping rectangle and a triangle, the simplest and most likely hypothesis. Similarly, when we encounter incomplete figures (e.g., Figure 9.8), we try to construct a "good figure" by filling in the gaps, a phenomenon called **closure**.

Behavioral versus Geographic Environments

The organizing principles might be designed to help us perceive the world as it is, but that is not to say that our perceptions mirror physical reality. The gestaltists, most notably Koffka in his *Principles of Gestalt Psychology* (1935) made an important distinction between the world as it is in reality, what he called the **geographical environment**, and the world as we perceive it, the **behavioral environment**. It is the latter perception that determines how we act. Koffka used an old German folktale to drive home the point. It concerned a weary traveler in the dead of winter who reached an inn after riding on horseback for hours over what seemed to be a vast open snow-covered plain. When he arrived, the innkeeper asked from which direction he had come. The rider pointed to the plain and the innkeeper, "in a tone of awe and wonder, said: 'Do you know that you have ridden across the Lake of Constance?' At which the rider dropped stone dead" (p. 28). Apparently, realizing that the behavioral environment ("this seems to be a wide open plain") does not match the geographical environment ("a frozen lake that could easily crack under the weight of a horse—I could have drowned!") can be rather stressful.

This distinction between physical reality and reality as perceived led Koffka to a point that would soon be elaborated by Kurt Lewin, with his concept of "life space" (see later discussion). If the behavioral and geographic environments differ, then two people in the same geographic environment are likely to perceive it differently. For instance, the perceptions of a walk in the woods by a geologist and a botanist will vary considerably.

THE GESTALT APPROACH TO COGNITION AND LEARNING

Although the title of Koffka's 1922 landmark article in *Psychological Bulletin* gave the impression that gestalt psychology was concerned only with perception, such was not the case. Rather, the gestalists conceived of their system as a general psychology, and they made specific contributions to the study of thinking, problem solving, and learning. The two best-known examples are Köhler's research on problem solving in apes and Wertheimer's posthumous book, *Productive Thinking* (1945/1982). Köhler's

The Mentality of Apes (1917/1926) was first published in German in 1917, and then translated into English in the 1920s.

Köhler on Insight in Apes

Early in his book, Köhler took dead aim at Thorndike's puzzle box experiments. As you recall from Chapter 7, Thorndike concluded that learning and problem solving were processes of trial and "acciden-tal success," with unsuccessful behaviors gradually being eliminated in favor of behaviors that worked. Köhler, however, disagreed that problem solving was such a mechanical, step-by-step process. Instead, in keeping with his gestalt orientation, he argued that solutions to problems occur when individuals can view the entire problem field and rearrange the elements of the problem into a new and meaningful con-figuration. Solutions have a perceptual quality to them, and they occur quickly, once the components have been reconfigured. Köhler used the term **insight** to label such a process. The main procedural problem with Thorndike's research, according to Köhler, was that the animals could never perceive the entire field. Hence, they were unable to see how the components of the apparatus related to each other in an overall configuration.[5] In Thorndike's studies, Köhler (1917/1926) wrote, "cats ... were frequently placed in cages containing the *extreme end* only of one or the other mechanism, or allowing a view of ropes or other parts of the mechanism, but from which a survey over the *whole* arrangement was not possible (p. 23, emphasis in the original). Köhler was determined not to make the same "mistake" in his research. His animals would have the entire field in front of them, and all of the elements needed to solve the problems would be in full view.

The most famous problem-solving experiment appearing in *The Mentality of Apes* appears in a chapter called "The Making of Implements." Two hollow bamboo sticks with slightly different diame-ters were available, each too short to get to a banana that was out of reach. Köhler wondered if one of his smartest chimpanzees, Sultan, could solve the problem by joining the sticks. Traditional accounts of this famous experiment portray a thoughtful animal carefully examining the problem and suddenly hit-ting on an insightful solution. Sultan's "solution" was not witnessed by Köhler, but by the ape's keeper (the same Manuel González y García mentioned in the Close-Up). The keeper's dramatic account is one of gestalt psychology's most quoted passages:

> Sultan first of all squats indifferently on the box, which has been left standing a little back from the railings; then he gets up, picks up the two sticks, sits down again on the box and plays carelessly with them. While doing this, it happens that he finds himself holding one rod in either hand in such a way that they lie in a straight line; he pushes the thinner one a little way into the opening of the thicker, jumps up and is already on the run towards the railings, to which he has up to now half turned his back, and begins to draw a banana towards him with the double stick. (Köhler 1917/1926, p. 132)

This description has all the components of Köhler's definition of insight—the solution occurs quickly, and it occurs when Sultan perceives the elements of the problem in a new configuration. But a close reading of the book, in the pages prior to the famous quote, reveals that Sultan was in fact rather slow in figuring out the solution and tried several strategies that failed. For example, he tried dragging a box to the side of the cage, apparently because of his experience in a box-stacking exper-iment, completed prior to the two-stick experiment. Another doomed strategy was to drop one stick

[5]Köhler criticized maze learning studies for the same reason, complaining that "American animal psychology makes animals (or people) seek their way out of mazes, over the whole of which there is no general survey from any point inside" (p. 18).

outside the cage, and then push it with the other stick. Sultan even failed to take the hint when an observer (probably Köhler) took the larger stick and pushed his finger into the open end, while Sultan was watching. In short, although Sultan might have displayed some degree of insight when eventually solving the problem, he also behaved in a way that would make sense to Thorndike—through trial and error.

Köhler's insight explanation did not go unchallenged by American psychologists, who questioned the methodological sophistication of Köhler's demonstrations and pointed out the trial-and-error evidence just described. Some attempts to replicate the research produced ambiguous results and suggested that the more prior experience the animal had with similar problems, the more likely a "quick" (i.e., insightful) solution would appear (Windholz & Lamal, 1985). On the other hand, Köhler's research introduced a new way of thinking into the debate about learning and problem solving and extended animal methodology beyond simple puzzle boxes and mazes.

Wertheimer on Productive Thinking

Köhler was not the only gestaltist studying cognition. Max Wertheimer had a long-standing interest in thinking and problem solving that culminated in *Productive Thinking* (1945/1982), which he sent to the publisher just before his death in 1943. Its topics ranged from how children learn arithmetic to how Einstein developed his theory of relativity. A good example of his use of gestalt principles can be found in his description of how to teach children about geometry. Wertheimer deplored the traditional approach to teaching math, which relied heavily on asking students to memorize rules and formulas without giving them insight into the concepts behind the symbols.

Early in the book, Wertheimer described his visit to a class in which the teacher was explaining how to find the area of parallelograms. Using the example in Figure 9.9a, the teacher explained the rules:

> "I drop one perpendicular line from the upper left corner and another perpendicular from the upper
> right corner."
> "I extend the baseline to the right."
> "I label the two new points e and f." (Wertheimer, 1945/1982, p. 14)

Because students had already memorized the rule for finding the area of rectangles, they could now determine the area of the parallelogram by multiplying its base (e–f) by its height (d–e). The teacher then gave the students several more problems, which they solved by going through the same steps.

The next day, Wertheimer again visited the class, and with the teacher's permission, gave students a slightly different parallelogram—the one in Figure 9.9b. Most students could not find its area. Some gave up immediately—"Teacher, we haven't had that yet" (Wertheimer, 1945/1982, p. 15)—whereas others tried applying the rules they had been taught, producing drawings like Figure 9.9c, but being unsure of how to proceed from that point. A few rotated the parallelogram 90°, and then applied their rules successfully. The teacher was not amused, claiming that Wertheimer had given his students "a queer figure. Naturally they are unable to deal with it" (p. 16).

Wertheimer believed that children would be more productive thinkers if they truly understood the concept of area. He suggested that teachers start with simple concrete examples. For instance, students could easily grasp the idea that two equivalent square fields would produce the same amount of some crop. Next, rectangular surfaces could be understood as combinations of square fields. With that knowledge, students could be shown that any parallelogram could be transformed into a rectangle by

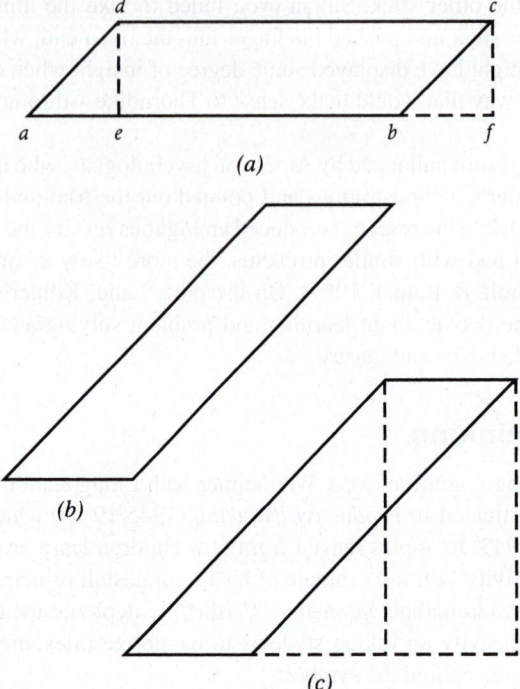

FIGURE 9.9 The area of a parallelogram: (*a*) diagram used to teach by formula; (*b*) problem presented by Wertheimer that caused difficulty for students taught by formula; (*c*) one solution attempt from students taught by formula, from Wertheimer (1945/1982). Redrawn by John Wiley & Sons, Inc.

chopping off one end and attaching it to the other. He demonstrated that children with such an insightful understanding had no trouble solving area problems like those on the left in Figure 9.10, what he called "A-Figures," while at the same time recognizing instantly that the procedure would fail for the problems on the right, the "B-Figures."

For Wertheimer, then, productive thinking in the classroom went far beyond memorizing rules and formulas for "correct" solutions. True understanding involved restructuring the problem to gain insight into its solution. By moving a portion of the parallelogram from one end to the other, children accomplished this "restructuring" and thereby created a "good gestalt," a simpler figure (rectangle) from which their understanding of squares and rectangles could be used to calculate area.

Other Gestalt Research on Cognition

As mentioned earlier, while at Berlin in the 1920s and early 1930s, the gestaltists attracted a talented group of students. Among them were Hedwig von Restorff, who lent her name to an important memory phenomenon, and Karl Duncker, whose studies of problem solving and insight are found routinely in general psychology texts today. Both worked as assistants to Köhler at Berlin, and both were dismissed during the conflict between Köhler and the Nazis. Little is known of von Restorff's fate after the dismissal, but Duncker came to the United States and reunited with Köhler at Swarthmore.

Hedwig von Restorff discovered that if people learned lists with a three-digit number embedded in a series of nonsense syllables, the number would almost always be recalled better than the syllables. In good gestaltist fashion, she interpreted the result as an extension of the figure-ground relationship—the

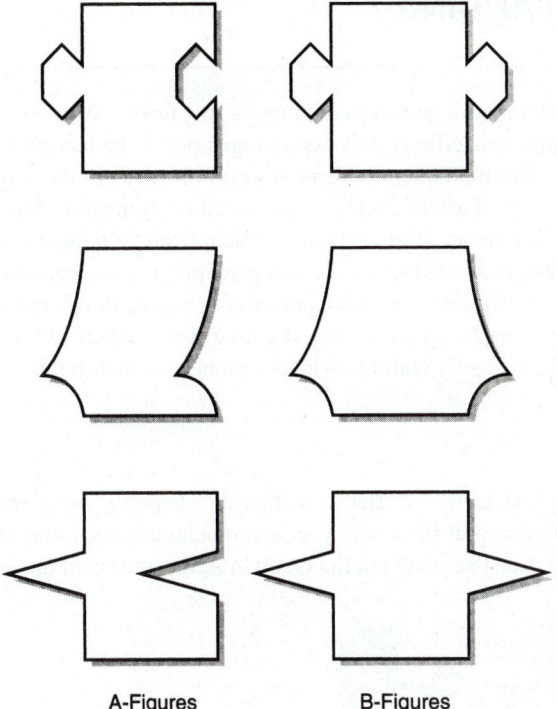

FIGURE 9.10 Sketches used by Wertheimer to illustrate productive thinking. Students with productive knowledge of area solve A-Figures and recognize the problem with B-Figures. For students who have learned area by rote, both types of figures seem unsolvable, from Wertheimer (1945/1982). Redrawn by John Wiley & Sons, Inc.

A-Figures   B-Figures

number provided a sharp figure against the background of nonsense syllables (Baddeley, 1990). Today, her result is called the **Von Restorff effect** (sometimes, the isolation effect). Anytime a stimulus in an information array stands out in some fashion, it will attract attention and be recalled more easily than the remaining information.

Although he died young (suicide at age 37), Karl Duncker produced a major work on thinking, extending Köhler's ideas about insight into the area of human problem-solving behavior. His innovative *Psychology of Productive Thought* appeared in German in 1935 and was translated into English 10 years later (Duncker, 1935/1945). It has been called by Hilgard (1987) "the most careful and analytical account of insight ever published" (p. 233). Duncker studied the cognitive processes of college students by asking them to think out loud while they were trying to solve problems. He then analyzed the transcripts of their protocols, searching for patterns of thinking and problem-solving strategies. He discovered, for instance, that students often solved problems creatively if they were able to imagine uses for objects that differed from typical uses. Duncker's famous candle problem illustrates the point. Subjects must mount a candle vertically on a wall so that it won't scorch the wall. They are given several objects, including a box of tacks. The correct solution involves seeing the box not as serving its normal function as a container, but as serving a different function—as a platform on which to mount the candle. Subjects who failed to solve the problem were said by Duncker to show **functional fixedness**, an inability to think beyond the typical function of an object. An everyday example is the person who thinks to use a dime as a screwdriver; that person has overcome functional fixedness.

KURT LEWIN (1890–1947): EXPANDING THE GESTALT VISION

Kurt Lewin[6] (Figure 9.11) was a contemporary of gestalt psychology's "big three," Wertheimer, Koffka, and Köhler. Although he did not consider himself a gestalt psychologist per se, he recognized his debt to "these outstanding personalities.... The fundamental ideas of gestalt theory are the foundation of all our investigations in the field of the will, of affect, and of the personality" (quoted in Marrow, 1969, p. 76). Like the gestaltists, Lewin built his theory around concepts taken from field theory, and he borrowed freely from gestalt ideas. The gestaltists tended to focus on perception, learning, and cognition, whereas Lewin was more interested in motivation, emotion, personality and its development, and the influence of social forces on human action. Researchers investigating those topics today, especially developmental and social psychologists, typically claim Lewin as a pioneer in their fields.

Early Life and Career

Lewin earned a doctorate from the University of Berlin with this chapter's most recognizable mentor—Carl Stumpf. He finished his doctoral dissertation at a momentous time—the outbreak of World War I in 1914. As a loyal citizen, Lewin enlisted in the German Army and spent the next several

Courtesy of The Adolf-Würth-Center for the History of Psychology, University of Würzburg, Germany

FIGURE 9.11 Kurt Lewin (1890–1947).

[6]The correct German pronunciation of Lewin is "La-Veen" but he began pronouncing it "Loo-in" after arriving in America. Apparently, his children's peers and schoolmates used the latter Americanized pronunciation, and Lewin decided to save his children the aggravation of continually "explaining to their friends why the family name was spelled 'Lewin' but pronounced 'Laveen'" (Marrow, 1969, p. 177).

years trying to survive the brutal trench warfare that decimated a generation of European men. He entered as a lowly private, left as an officer, was seriously wounded, and earned Germany's Iron Cross. While on furlough to recover from his wounds in 1917, he reflected on his experiences and wrote "The War Landscape," an article containing the seeds of many of his later concepts. In a distinction similar to the one made later by Koffka between geographical and behavioral environments, for instance, Lewin pointed out that the same objects in the environment can be phenomenologically different, depending on whether they are part of the war landscape or the peace landscape. A narrow path in the woods, which might produce enjoyment and relaxation under peaceful circumstances, can be deadly in the war landscape because it can provide cover for the enemy.

Lewin returned to Berlin's Psychological Institute at the end of the war (1918), became an instructor in 1921, and remained there for 12 years. During these years, he developed his ideas and his research program, attracted talented graduate students, and began establishing an international reputation. He also befriended his Berlin colleagues Wertheimer and Köhler, and he got to know Koffka. As his biographer wrote, although "he was never a completely orthodox Gestaltist, he did become a vital force in the new movement and contributed to it his own special insights" (Marrow, 1969, p. 13).

As a veteran, Lewin was initially exempt from the 1933 law designed to remove Jews from professional positions. Before long, however, his status as war hero was not sufficient to overcome the liabilities of his heritage.[7] Like Wertheimer, Lewin thought the future looked bleak, writing to Köhler that he could not "imagine how a Jew is supposed to live a life in Germany at the present time that does justice to the most primitive demands of truthfulness" (quoted in Ash, 1995, p. 328). Lewin was already well known in the United States, after giving a stirring address at the 1929 International Congress at Yale and spending a 6-month leave as visiting professor in Terman's department at Stanford. In 1933, Cornell's Robert Ogden arranged for Lewin to spend 2 years at Cornell. Ogden was an early American convert to the gestalt vision and as responsible as anyone for bringing the gestaltists to America (Freeman, 1977). But Ogden was not the only American psychologist looking out for the welfare of European psychologists being threatened by the Nazis. Consider the case of Karl and Charlotte Bühler.

FROM THE MILES PAPERS...

MILES LEARNS ABOUT THE NAZI VERSION OF ACADEMIC FREEDOM

In 1938, Nazi Germany annexed its neighboring country, Austria. This was now 5 years after the passage of the law in Germany that started dismissing Jewish professors from universities. In those 5 years things had only gotten worse for Jewish citizens. As you will see in the following letter, even an association with Jews could get one into trouble. In this letter from Egon Brunswick to Miles, you will learn about the arrest of Karl Bühler, an eminent psychologist at the University of Vienna. Bühler was not Jewish, but he had hired Jewish assistants in his laboratory, and that was apparently reason enough to get

him tossed in jail. Fortunately, his wife (Charlotte Bühler), who was half Jewish, was out of the country at the time. Also, you will see that their children, by virtue of having some Jewish heritage, would have been denied an education, had they stayed in Austria.

Dear Dr. Miles:

I have just had a letter from Charlotte Bühler, who is on a lecture tour in Norway, indicating that Professor Karl Bühler has been imprisoned "because of the preference of Jewish assistants." She,

---

[7]While in America, and with the Nazi menace becoming more evident, Lewin desperately tried to arrange for his mother's emigration, first to the United States, and then to Cuba, but was unsuccessful. Sometime in 1943 she perished in one of the Nazi death camps (Marrow, 1969).

herself, who is of partly Jewish origin, was fortunately in England when Hitler captured Austria and she has not returned since that time. She actually sees no chance to place herself or her husband in England, Norway, or any other of the European states, nor does she have any kind of appointment in the United States.... Karl Bühler, who is a pure Aryan, had already announced his intention of leaving his post in Vienna to look for a position in the United States, before he was put in prison.

Do you see any chance to place them? They realize, of course, that it would be difficult for them to be placed in the same or in neighboring universities, and they would be perfectly willing to take positions independently in places far distant from each other....

The Bühlers' daughter and son, one about 18 and other about 20, though more than 50% Aryan, are not permitted to study in German or Austrian universities.

I am sending this letter to a small number of other psychologists who, I think, might be particularly interested in the Bühlers. (Brunswick, 1938)

A month after this appeal, Miles received a second letter asking for help, this time from Edward Tolman (Chapter 11), indicating that Karl Bühler had been "let out of prison but that is all we know, except that the psychological institute in Vienna is closed, Bühler's money taken, etc." (Tolman, 1938b). The Miles papers do not contain copies of any response by Miles to either of these letters.

Karl Bühler (1879–1963), who had worked for a time in Kulpe's lab at Wurzburg, had an important role in founding the Psychological Institute in Vienna. His ideas were gestaltist in spirit, and he made important contributions to the study of language and to our understanding of child development. Charlotte Bühler (1893–1974) was also a prominent psychologist, perhaps even better known than her husband. She made important contributions to child psychology, worked for a time as a clinical psychologist, and was a pioneer in the humanistic psychology movement. Egon Brunswick (1903–1955) was a student of Karl Bühler's in Vienna and eventually wound up with Tolman on the faculty at the University of California, Berkeley. He was known for his research on perception and for a brand of functionalism called probabilistic functionalism. In part, this approach argued that in trying to reach our goals and make good decisions, we have to realize that life is a probability estimate and act accordingly.

As for the Bühlers' fate, they did manage to get to the United States and were given faculty positions at a small school in Minnesota. A few years later, they moved west and joined the faculty at the University of Southern California, where they completed their professional lives.

After spending academic years 1933–1934 and 1934–1935 in Ithaca, Lewin and his family moved to Iowa in 1935, where he joined the Child Welfare Research Station, a research institute connected to the University of Iowa, but separate from the psychology department. The institute had been created in 1917 to study the development of normal children and train child development researchers (Ash, 1992). Lewin remained there for 9 years and then moved back east to Boston in 1944 after successfully lobbying for funding to create a Research Center for Group Dynamics, to be housed at the Massachusetts Institute of Technology. His work there had just begun when he died suddenly of a heart attack in February 1947.

Field Theory

Lewin contributed more empirical research than the three gestalt founders combined, but like them he was first and foremost a theorist—in response to the criticism that theories are sometimes far removed from useful applications, he once said that "[t]here is nothing as practical as a good theory" (quoted in Marrow, 1969, p. 128). Lewin called his theory a **field theory** because he believed that understanding a person's behavior required knowing about all the forces acting on a person at a given moment. Lewin named the particular field within which the person operates the **life space**. It is the pivotal concept in his theory, and he defined it as a psychological field that includes the "totality of facts which determine the behavior (B) of an individual at a certain moment . . . . [It] includes the person (P) and the environment (E)" (Lewin, 1936b, p. 216). Person factors include such things as personality variables, needs, goals, and beliefs, whereas environmental factors include things external to the person that directly affect him or her. Furthermore, echoing Koffka, it is not simply the physical environment, but the environment as perceived by the individual that influences behavior. Thus, all behavior is a joint function of the characteristics of the person behaving and the features of the psychological environment in which the person is behaving. Or as Lewin summarized it in a now-famous formula: $B = f(P,E)$.

Lewin symbolized the life space concept by borrowing from **topology**, a nonquantitative spatial geometry. He represented life spaces with various ovals, which contained symbols of features influencing the individual. Life space included everything within an oval (i.e., the person, P, and the environment as perceived, E). Outside the oval, which Lewin referred to as the **foreign hull**, could be found all the events, circumstances, and stimuli that had no effect on a person at a particular moment.

A major difference between the original gestaltists and Lewin was the latter's emphasis on motivational constructs and goal-directed behavior. He believed that people were complex energy systems, in which individual actions can be predicted with reference to "tension" in the system, which in turn is the consequence of the predominant needs being felt, the strengths of those needs, and the various obstacles in the life space. When all needs are satisfied, the individual is said to be in a state of **equilibrium**. The creation of a need produces disequilibrium, and a person is motivated to return to a steady state. Consider Figure 9.12 as an illustration. It represents a situation in which a hungry child desires a cookie sitting in an out-of-reach jar. The desire has created tension in the life space. The cookie is the desired object, or in Lewin's terms, it has a positive **valence** (symbolized by the plus signs). The arrow pointing from the child (P) toward the cookies is a **vector**—these arrows symbolize a push that is directed toward a specific desired goal, an approach tendency, or away from a goal to be avoided, an avoidance tendency. The arrow's length is proportional to the strength of the need. The vertical bar is a barrier (the out-of-reach cookie jar), which has a negative valence.

Lewin used his topological system to analyze conflicts, one of his best-known contributions. He described three common situations in which a conflict between needs occurs. In Lewin's scheme, a conflict exists whenever there are at least two vectors that are exerting pressure in different directions. In an **approach-approach** conflict, there are two desirable goals of equal strength from which to choose. For instance, a diner might have to decide between steak and lobster. Two equally undesirable goals characterize **avoidance-avoidance** conflicts, as when a student might be faced with the choice of studying one of two disliked topics. Third, in an **approach-avoidance** conflict, the person experiences simultaneous approach and avoidance tendencies with reference to a single goal. Thus, our decision about whether to order the hot fudge sundae will be influenced by both approach (it's good) and avoidance (it's fattening) tendencies.

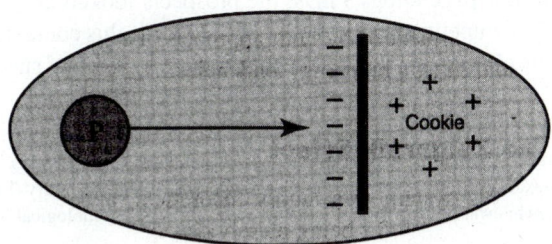

FIGURE 9.12 An example of a Lewin "egg," depicting a child desiring an out-of-reach cookie. Drawn by Dr. C. James Goodwin

The Zeigarnik Effect

Lewin's system was highly theoretical, and it was criticized for being merely descriptive. That is, the diagrams might be able to describe events, but they were said to be of little use in predicting behavior (Frank, 1978). Yet Lewin and his students did indeed conduct considerable research, and their studies produced results consistent with the theory. One famous example is a series of studies completed by one of Lewin's first students, the Russian psychologist Bluma Zeigarnik (1927/1967).[8]

Ideas for research often come from everyday observation, and that happened for Zeigarnik's research. In Berlin, Lewin gathered a team of active graduate students around him, typically 12 to 15 doctoral candidates (Marrow, 1969). Lewin's research group often met informally at a café across the street from the Institute, keeping their table by occasionally ordering refills on coffee and pieces of cake. In that setting, Lewin was impressed by a waiter who seemed to be able to keep track of what each student had ordered, without writing anything down. Soon after the bill was settled, however, the waiter had no memory of it. To Lewin the explanation was simple. As long as the bill was unpaid and the students remained at the café, the waiter's life space had tension in it, and he needed to keep the bill's contents in memory. Once the bill was paid, the tension dissipated, closure had been achieved, and equilibrium had been restored—no need to remember the order any more.

Zeigarnik's study assessed Lewin's interpretation by giving 164 teachers, students, and children between 18 and 22 simple tasks, each requiring a few minutes to finish. They included such things as constructing a cardboard box, making a clay figure, completing puzzles, and performing arithmetic and other mental tasks. Each subject was allowed to complete half of the tasks, but was interrupted and not allowed to finish the other half. To ensure that the interruption was clearly felt to be a disruption, Zeigarnik "always chose a time when the subject was most engrossed in his work" (1927/1967, p. 303). What she found was that the interrupted tasks were about twice as likely to be recalled as the uninterrupted ones. In Lewinian terms, the enhanced memory was the result of the unrelieved tension of the incomplete task. This phenomenon, that memory is better for incomplete rather than complete tasks, is today known as the **Zeigarnik effect**.

Lewin as Developmental Psychologist

Lewin arrived in New York in the fall of 1933, at a time when the United States was in the depths of economic crisis—the Great Depression. His position at Cornell, made possible through limited funds from a committee to help displaced European scholars, was not in the psychology department but in the School of Home Economics, and it was not a faculty appointment. This might not seem very impressive, in light of Lewin's growing international status, but it must be seen in light of the academic job market in the 1930s. One effect of the Depression was that few families could afford college, and with low enrollments, few colleges could afford new faculty. As a result, finding an academic position was virtually impossible. The depth of the problem was revealed in an APA survey, which found that in 1932, there were 32 positions available for 100 new psychology PhDs; the prospects looked even worse in 1933—46 jobs and 146 newly minted PhDs competing for them (Napoli, 1981). In this context, Lewin's appointment is perhaps an indication of his elevated stature rather than a puzzling loss of status.

---

[8]Bluma Zeigarnik (1901–1988) earned her doctorate with Lewin in Berlin in 1927. She then returned to Russia and had a long and productive career in the Soviet Union, specializing in abnormal psychology. Part of her time was spent working with the famed Russian psychologists Lev Vygotsky and Alexander Luria, researching the cognitive effects of brain injury (Luria, 1979). In 1983, she was the recipient of the Kurt Lewin award, given annually by the Society for the Psychological Study of Social Issues (SPSSI).

When Lewin arrived in the United States, American psychologists thought of him as a developmental psychologist whose approach contrasted sharply with (a) the evolving behaviorist movement, and (b) an increasing tendency to study groups of children and take statistical averages of their behavior (Ash, 1992). In contrast, Lewin believed that the behaviorists overemphasized the environment at the expense of personality factors. That is, in contrast to his balanced B = f(P,E), the behaviorists had too much E and not enough P. Methodologically, Lewin criticized the strategy of trying to identify some mythical average child; he preferred nonstatistical in-depth case studies of individual children.

The reputation of Lewin as a developmentalist was based on his much-discussed presentation at the Yale International Congress in 1929 and a chapter on developmental psychology that he wrote for the first edition of the *Handbook of Child Psychology* (Lewin, 1931). In the latter, he introduced his B = f(P,E) formulation to the American audience. His Yale talk was highlighted by a film that he showed of an 18-month-old girl trying to sit on a rock. She apparently thought that she would miss the target if she took her eyes off the stone, so she circled the rock several times trying to figure out how to sit on it accurately without removing her eyes from it. She finally devised the creative solution of putting her head between her knees and slowly backing up to the stone before sitting. In that way she could watch the stone while depositing herself on it. In his talk, Lewin described this simple event in terms of field forces, vectors, and valances and tied it to other research on reaching goals by making detours. Older children solve detour problems, according to Lewin, because they perceive the problem as a whole and recognize that the first step, a movement away from a goal (to get around the detour), is part of the overall structure of the solution. Thus, a solution can be achieved even if the initial vector points away from a goal. An older child would solve the rock-sitting problem as a detour problem, by recognizing that taking one's eyes off the rock, while seeming to be a step away from the goal, could be organized as part of the solution. The 18-month-old could not make that detour step, however, and was forced to rely on maintaining a simple goal-directed vector by not letting the rock out of sight. The difference between the younger and older child, according to Lewin, was that the older child had a greater degree of cognitive complexity or **differentiation**. For this older child, the life space had become more complex (differentiated) over time.

Lewin's 2 years at Cornell were busy. In addition to acclimating himself to a new environment and polishing his English, Lewin plunged into a research program on how social pressure affected the eating habits of children and, with the help of translators, published a collection of essays on personality theory (Lewin, 1935) and a book on his topological theory (Lewin, 1936b). He also organized a loose confederation of former and current students and colleagues into a "Topology Group." It first met in 1933 as a reunion of sorts, hosted by Koffka at Smith College. Its success produced its replication, and except for a few years during the World War II era, it met annually until 1965. In a manner reminiscent of Titchener's meetings of experimental psychologists, the sessions were marked by informality, camaraderie, and discussions of work in progress. Unlike Titchener's group, women were welcome at Topology Group meetings.

It was not until he moved to Iowa, however, and developed a research team at the Iowa Child Welfare Station, that Lewin was able to recreate an environment that reminded him of Berlin. He even found a substitute for the Berlin café where his observation of a waiter's memory inspired Zeigarnik's research. In Iowa City, Lewin and his students congregated at the Round Window Restaurant, where they dubbed their group the "Hot-Air Club" (Marrow, 1969). Lewin's research on children continued at Iowa and yielded one of his better-known studies—"Frustration and Regression: An Experiment with Young Children" (Barker, Dembo, & Lewin, 1941). Roger Barker came to Iowa from Stanford, where he had been a student (working with Miles) during Lewin's brief time there as visiting professor. Tamara Dembo, from Russia, was one of Lewin's most loyal students, with him at Berlin, Cornell, and Iowa.

The experiment evolved from some earlier research by Dembo in which children in detour problems sometimes became frustrated at not being able to reach the goal and gave up trying. Barker, Dembo, and Lewin decided to study the problem more systematically, the idea being to determine the effects of frustration on the quality of play for children just under 4 years of age.

Each of the 30 children in the study first encountered a "free play" period in a room where they could play with some simple toys. After 30 minutes, a partition was raised revealing a much richer play environment, which included a large doll house and "toy lake" complete with real water and boats. Each child spent up to 15 minutes in this enriched environment, then was led back to the front of the room and a wire mesh partition was lowered and secured. The child then spent a second 30-minute session with the same toys found in the original free play session. Unlike the first session, however, they could now see what they were missing. In Lewinian terms, the toys on the other side of the room had a much higher valence than the ones now available to them; the barrier had a negative valence and was producing tension. And the behavior of the children reflected their frustration. They tried to get around the barrier or out of the room entirely. Failing that, their play deteriorated significantly; they became destructive, easily distracted by what they could see across the room, and emotionally upset. Under high frustration, then, their behavior regressed to less constructive patterns.[9] Although increased age produces differentiation, Lewin pointed out that under stress, a temporary shift in the opposite direction, what he called **dedifferentiation**, could occur. The Barker, Dembo, and Lewin study became a classic in the developmental psychology literature, and it still appears in modern developmental psychology textbooks.

Lewin as Social Psychologist

Lewin's American colleagues might have identified him as a developmental psychologist, but his self-identity was much broader, as reflected in his general theory and research on such topics as prejudice, group influence, and leadership. These latter studies are the reason why he is considered one of the pioneers of modern social psychology. His leadership research, still frequently cited, grew out of his reflections on the state of the world in the mid-1930s. Mindful of the contrast between the democracy of his new home and the increasingly dictatorial environment of his old one, Lewin became interested in the consequences of different leadership styles. Along with Ronald Lippitt and Ralph White, he completed several experiments on the problem (Lewin, Lippitt, & White, 1939; Lippitt & White, 1943).

The basic procedure was to create different environments for five-person groups of boys (age 10), who were given various craft-making projects (e.g., making masks) to complete. The main experiment contrasted three different leadership styles—group leaders were authoritarian (no input from the boys), democratic (group decision making with the leader as mediator), and laissez-faire (virtually no leader participation). Each group of boys experienced all three styles, and their behavior was dramatically influenced by their leaders. When led by an autocratic leader, the boys quickly became submissive, failed to take any initiative, did not produce high-quality products, and showed little interest in the tasks. They also tended to be aggressive when the leader was out of the room, and they often made fun of disliked group members, a form of scapegoating. Those in the laissez-faire group did not fare much better. Because they were in an "unstructured field," they spent a great deal of time unsuccessfully trying to decide what to do. The lack of adult direction often led to confusion, frustration, and hostility.

---

[9]Although the experiment occurred long before the APA adopted an ethics code, Lewin was sensitive to the emotional states of his young subjects. After they finished the final 30 minutes of observation, the barrier was again raised, and the children were allowed to play with the high-valence toys for as long as they wished.

Under this form of leadership, nothing was accomplished. On the other hand, under a more democratic leader, the group became cohesive, task-oriented and motivated, and they produced more high-quality products. One disturbing finding was that when the boys switched from a democratic to an authoritarian environment, they quickly and with minimal protest succumbed to the tyranny. As Lewin later described it, "[t]here have been few experiences for me as impressive as seeing the expression on children's faces during the first day under an autocratic leader. The group that had formerly been friendly, open, cooperative, and full of life, became within a short half-hour a rather apathetic-looking gathering without initiative" (quoted in Marrow, 1969, p. 127). On the other hand, and equally troubling, those shifting from authoritarian to democratic settings had a difficult time overcoming the effects of being told what to do.

The broader implications of the leadership studies were obvious to Lewin. Although he recognized the problem of generalizing beyond the experimental setting, he saw the results as a strong endorsement of the democratic form of government and an indictment of anything short of it. They also reinforced his belief that scientists needed to be "in the arena" rather than confined to the rarified atmosphere of their laboratories. To that end, he became the prototype of the scientist–activist. He became a committed Zionist, vigorously advocating the creation of an independent Jewish state in Palestine, as a place for Jews to establish their own democratic system.[10] He also lobbied (unsuccessfully) for the creation of a psychological research institute at Hebrew University in Jerusalem. Third, Lewin became an early leader in the APA-affiliated Society for the Psychological Study of Social Issues (SPSSI), founded in 1936 and concerned with applying psychological knowledge to the solution of social problems. Activism pervaded his work, and much of his research was designed specifically to solve some real-world problems (Heims, 1978). He called this work "action research."

Action Research   The leadership research is just one example of a theme in Lewin's work—using science as a means of bringing about social change. Psychology must do more than just explain behavior, Lewin argued; it must "be equally concerned with discovering how people can change their ways so that they learn to behave better" (quoted in Marrow, 1969, p. 158). Much of Lewin's action research occurred in work settings, and for this reason he is important for the history of industrial/organizational psychology. For example, in a series of studies designed to increase worker productivity in an industrial setting, Lewin showed that letting workers set production goals after meeting in groups had the twofold effect of improving morale and increasing worker output. Group processes could also be used effectively to train managers and to overcome male prejudice against women workers.

To further his mission of using science to promote social change, Lewin in the late 1930s began planning for the creation of a research institute devoted to action research that would be affiliated with a university, yet autonomous. His aggressive pursuit of private funding paid off; in late 1944, he founded the Research Center for Group Dynamics, affiliated with the Massachusetts Institute of Technology (MIT) in Cambridge. There he quickly assembled an enthusiastic research team, most of them from the Iowa Hot-Air Club, and set out to study group processes and social action. At the same time, he accepted an invitation from the American Jewish Congress to organize a second action research initiative, the Commission on Community Interrelations (CCI), to be centered in New York City. Under Lewin's leadership, the CCI sponsored research on discrimination and prejudice (Marrow, 1969).

For the remaining 2 years of his life, Lewin immersed himself in the work of his two parallel projects, the MIT center for group dynamics and the CCI. The resulting studies, investigating such topics as interracial housing and in-group loyalty, combined with his other work on leadership and group dynamics, provide the foundation for modern experimental social psychology. The graduate students

---

[10]The state of Israel was created in 1948, a year after Lewin's death.

and colleagues who conducted the studies, such as Leon Festinger, Harold Kelley, Morton Deutsch, and Fritz Heider, became the recognized leaders of the field. Even today, their names figure prominently in social psychology textbooks.

Evaluating Lewin

When asked to describe Lewin's appeal for students, Jerome Frank, who studied with Lewin in Berlin, summed up his mentor's personality with a single word—"zest." He went on to describe Lewin as "a little man with an apparently inexhaustible supply of energy and a ruddy complexion that suggested vigorous health. Although he must often have been seated in my presence, in my memories he is almost always in motion" (Frank, 1978, p. 223). Other students had similar recollections of Lewin's passion for his work, their memories usually including images of Lewin filling the blackboard with his graphic representations of life space, "the air ... heavy with chalk dust" (Marrow, 1969, p. 137). Others recalled almost being overwhelmed by Lewin's work ethic. Roger Barker, who worked on the frustration-regression research, wrote: "I can remember being so tired I ached. He would go on and on. He never had any idea of when to stop" (quoted in Woodward, 2010, p. 120). Lewin's affection for his students is shown in a comment he once made in a letter to Walter Miles; after describing the nursery school exploits of his young children, Lewin added that his "old children, I mean Research Assistants, are doing quite satisfactory work" (Lewin, 1936a).

Lewin's topological theory, along with his egg-shaped illustrations, has disappeared from modern psychology, yet the research it generated makes him one of the leading psychologists of the 20th century. During his years in the United States, Lewin never landed a full-time academic position in the psychology department of a major university, yet he was able to surround himself with enthusiastic students (who were willing, like Barker, to ache) who turned his ideas into research and perpetuated his unique blend of basic and applied research long after his premature death in 1947. Ralph White, a Lewin student and one of the authors of the famous leadership study, acknowledged in a symposium in 1976 that field theory in its strictest sense was a thing of the past—few psychologists refer to "valences" or "vectors" anymore, and "one doesn't often see diagrams consisting of goals, paths, barriers, and little arrows, all within an elliptically-shaped outline" (White, 1978, p. 245). On the other hand, White argued that Lewin's influence could still be clearly felt:

> It is alive in the form of paying continual attention to the patterns of motivation and cognition that directly determine behavior.... It is alive in the form of a selective but fairly widespread use of Lewin's more specific theories and concepts, such as the approach-avoidance conflict and the differentiation of the cognitive field. It is alive in the very frequent quoting of Lewin's famous formula: $B = f(P,E)$. In other words, much of the substance of his field theory, though not usually in his words, is still very much alive. (pp. 245–246)

IN PERSPECTIVE: GESTALT PSYCHOLOGY IN AMERICA

During the 1920s, gestalt psychology flourished in Germany, especially at Berlin, but it also made its first inroads into American psychology in that decade. In Germany, the gestaltists established themselves by opposing what they believed to be the wrong way to study human conscious experience. It was fruitless to attempt analyzing experience into elementary units, they argued, because the whole of an experience had properties not evident in a description of component parts. When they came to America, the gestaltists perceived in behaviorism another form of the same elementist foe, and much of their writing was directed at the perceived shortcomings of this American psychology that seemed interested in analyzing behavior into S-R units. Gestalt psychology failed to become a major force in American psychology, but its influence was felt and is still being felt in many ways. Modern cognitive psychology, for example, which investigates such topics as the "organization" of information in memory, owes much to gestalt thinking.

Gestalt psychology's failure to become America's mainstream psychology stems in part from the historical circumstances of its early leaders. Its three originators found themselves in small schools without graduate programs to give birth to gestalt heirs, and of the four men highlighted in the chapter, three died in their early or mid-fifties. More fundamentally, however, the gestaltists were simply unable to convert most American psychologists to their message. Although a number of psychologists found the gestalt approach an appealing *addition* to the mix of competing viewpoints in psychology, few were convinced that *all* of psychology could be organized under the gestalt banner, and many were caught up in the new wave of behaviorism, the topic of the next two chapters. Pragmatic American psychologists, more comfortable with the concrete than the abstract, also viewed the gestalt movement as being long on theory and short on data and application. Furthermore, American psychologists were put off by the gestaltists' missionary zeal. Köhler, for example, recalled this about a conversation he once had with psychobiologist Karl Lashley, who was generally supportive of the gestalt position: "Once when we discussed the main tenets of gestalt psychology, he suddenly smiled and said, 'Excellent work—but don't you have religion up your sleeve?'" (Köhler, 1967/1969, p. 79).

Most American psychologists, reflecting a functional attitude receptive to any approach that helped explain human behavior and mental processes, tended to be more eclectic than would be acceptable to the gestaltists (Ash, 1985). Thus, when describing the new German movement in his *Schools of Contemporary Psychology*, first published in 1931, Robert Woodworth (Chapter 7) applauded their "great vitality" while at the same time gently chastising them for oversimplifying the ideas of their opponents. Specifically referring to Thorndike's trial-and-error learning and its law of effect, Pavlov's conditioned reflex research, and Köhler's insight studies, Woodworth argued that some truth could be found in all three and that "supporters of each interpretation could make out a plausible case for explaining all the facts in their own way" (Woodworth, 1931, p. 124). He closed the chapter by referring to gestalt psychology as "a strong and valuable addition to the varieties of psychology" (p. 125), and helped to perpetuate the idea that the movement was concerned mostly with perceptual phenomena by applauding them for emphasizing "the importance of the topic that has usually been called perception, neglected by the behaviorists and handled very meagerly by [others]" (p. 125).

In the final analysis, Wertheimer, Koffka, Köhler, and Lewin added considerable "insight" into our knowledge of the human experience and provided an important caution to those building psychological theories on the foundation of purely associationist principles. The tradition of understanding complexity through analysis was a strong one, however, as will be seen in the next two chapters.

SUMMARY

The Origins and Early Development of Gestalt Psychology

• The gestalt movement had it roots in the philosophical traditions of Kant and Husserl and in 19th-century developments in physics, in particular the work of Max Planck, a pioneer of field physics. Force fields can only be understood in terms of the overall patterns of relationships among objects in the field, he argued.

• The physicist Ernst Mach pointed out that some of our sensory experiences are of forms (e.g., squareness) that cannot be further reduced. Similarly, Christian von Ehrenfels used the example of a melody that changes key to illustrate the concept of form-qualities. A melody played in a new key retains its form-quality (gestaltqualitat) even though all the individual elements are different. The prominent philosopher/psychologist Carl Stumpf directed the dissertations of three of the four men featured in the chapter and briefly taught the fourth.

- Gestalt psychology was founded in 1912 when Max Wertheimer, with the help of Kurt Koffka and Wolfgang Köhler, completed research on apparent motion, which Wertheimer called the phi phenomenon. By flashing separated lights at certain intervals, observers perceived one light in motion, and the whole experience could not be analyzed into its component parts. Wertheimer concluded that the whole is different from and determines the nature of its component parts.

- Kurt Koffka earned his doctorate under Stumpf. He is known for introducing the gestalt movement to America, both through his publications and visits. He was the first gestaltist to move to the United States permanently, accepting a position at Smith College in 1927. He was gestalt's major theorist, and he extended gestalt ideas into the area of developmental psychology.

- Wolfgang Köhler also earned a doctorate with Stumpf. From 1913 to 1920 he studied primate behavior in the Canary Islands, where he completed research on insightful problem solving. He moved to the United States permanently in 1935, where he became gestalt's most influential spokesperson.

Gestalt Psychology and Perception

- Wertheimer described a number of basic principles that determine how our perceptions are organized. These gestalt organizing principles included figure-ground, grouping by proximity and similarity, and good continuation. Prägnanz, a tendency to organize perceptions into the simplest meaningful whole, governs our perceptions. We often construct such good figures by filling in gaps, a phenomenon called closure.

- Koffka made an important distinction between the world as it exists in reality, the geographical environment, and the world as perceived by the individual, the behavioral environment. Our behavior is most clearly influenced by the latter.

The Gestalt Approach to Cognition and Learning

- Köhler's *Mentality of Apes* summarized his research on problem solving in animals. He criticized Thorndike's mechanical trial-and-error explanation of animal learning and argued instead that animals could show insight and solve problems quickly if they were able to perceive all elements of the problem situation. In the two-stick problem, Köhler's apes were able build an instrument out of two bamboo poles to retrieve fruit that was out of the reach of each pole by itself.

- Wertheimer's *Productive Thinking* argued that thinking was inhibited by an educational system based on rote learning and rule memorization. Alternatively, the productive thinker had a true understanding of relationships and could solve novel problems. He used the example of figuring the area of a parallelogram as one illustration of the weakness of rule memorization and the advantage of his more insightful approach.

- Other gestaltists working on cognition included Hedwig von Restorff, who showed that memory was better for information that stood out from the background (the Von Restorff effect), and Karl Duncker, who investigated factors that inhibit insightful problem solving, such as functional fixedness, a tendency to think only of the normal uses for objects.

Kurt Lewin (1890–1947): Expanding the Gestalt Vision

- Like Koffka and Köhler, Lewin earned a doctorate with Stumpf; he joined Köhler and Wertheimer at Berlin's Institute of Psychology during the 1920s. He emigrated from Nazi Germany in 1933 and spent his remaining years at Cornell, the Child Welfare Research Station at Iowa, and the Research Center for Group Dynamics at MIT, which he founded shortly before his death.

- Lewin's field theory is centered on the concept of the life space, which includes all the factors influencing a person's actions in a given moment. These factors include those within the person (P) and those in the environment (E). Thus, $B = f(P,E)$. Lewin borrowed from topology to represent various life spaces symbolically. He emphasized the importance of motivation and the goal-directedness of behavior.

- Lewin used his system to describe various conflict systems (e.g., approach-avoidance). One of his students, Bluma Zeigarnik, showed that unresolved tension in the system could have behavioral consequences. The Zeigarnik effect states that memory will be greater for incomplete than for completed tasks.

- As a developmental psychologist, Lewin preferred studying individual cases over the "average child," and he considered development to be a process of increased differentiation. He studied the effects of frustration by giving children the opportunity to play with attractive toys and then removing the toys. The frustration resulted in the deterioration (regression) of their behavior.

- Lewin is considered a founder of modern social psychology. His most famous work in this area involved studying the consequences of different types of leadership styles. Adolescent boys were more effective when led by a democratic leader, than by either an autocratic or a laissez-faire leader.

- Much of Lewin's research has been called "action research" because of its social relevance. A committed activist, Lewin always believed that his research should contribute to the improvement of society. Examples of his action research include studies of prejudice and its reduction, in-group loyalty, and the effectiveness of group processes.

STUDY QUESTIONS

1. What did von Ehrenfels mean by a form-quality? Give an example.

2. Describe Wertheimer's apparent motion study. Explain his arguments against (a) an eye movement explanation and (b) the Helmholtz unconscious inference explanation.

3. For psychologists in America, gestalt psychology is sometimes assumed to involve only perception. What is the origin of this misperception?

4. What are the arguments for and against the idea that Köhler was a German spy in World War I?

5. What is figure-ground perception, and what are some of the characteristics of figures and grounds?

6. Describe any three gestalt organizing principles, and show how they all can be seen as variants of Prägnanz.

7. Use the Lake of Constance story, or Lewin's "war landscape" story, to illustrate the distinction between geographical and behavioral environments.

8. Explain Köhler's criticism of Thorndike's puzzle box research.

9. In gestalt terms, what was Köhler's explanation for Sultan's success in the two-stick problem?

10. Use the area of a parallelogram example to illustrate Wertheimer's ideas about thinking and problem solving.

11. What is the Von Restorff effect, and how does it relate to figure-ground?

12. What is functional fixedness, and how does it relate to insight?

13. In Lewin's field theory, use the example of a child desiring an out-of-reach cookie to illustrate his concepts of life space, foreign hull, valence, vector, and equilibrium.

14. Describe the three varieties of conflict examined by Lewin.

15. How did Zeigarnik investigate the effect named for her? How does the phenomenon relate to the Lewinian concept of equilibrium?

16. Describe Lewin's famous frustration and regression study and what he concluded from it.

17. Describe Lewin's famous leadership study and what he concluded from it.

18. Consider the impact of gestalt psychology on American psychology. Why was it not greater than the gestaltists hoped?

CHAPTER 10

THE ORIGINS OF BEHAVIORISM

> In a system of psychology completely worked out, given the response the stimuli can be predicted; given the stimuli the response can be predicted.
>
> —John B. Watson, 1913

PREVIEW AND CHAPTER OBJECTIVES

In the first two decades of the 20th century, psychologists in America became increasingly immersed in the kinds of applications described in Chapter 8. Near the end of this period, a new force arrived on the scene—behaviorism. The behaviorists set out to alter the direction of psychology in America, and to a large extent, they succeeded. The founder of behaviorism as a school of thought in American psychology was John Broadus Watson. Like Wundt, Watson has been awarded the title of "founder" by historians, not because he was the first to do the kind of research he did, but because he was a self-conscious promoter. For Watson, the thing to promote was a program with the seemingly impossible goal outlined in the quote that opens this chapter, taken from his 1913 "Behaviorist Manifesto."

The chapter will document the trends toward increased objectivity that led to the eventual acceptance of behaviorism by a majority of American psychologists. Then it will chronicle the life and work of the renowned Russian physiologist Ivan Pavlov; his conditioning research provided a methodology that some American behaviorists eventually adopted. Third, the chapter will look at Watson's life and work. Trained by Chicago functionalists, he quickly rose to the top of his profession at Johns Hopkins University, only to be forced out of academia by scandal at the height of his career. The chapter will examine his Behaviorist Manifesto and the reaction to it, his ideas about learning, and his research, including the (in)famous Little Albert experiment on conditioned fear. Most of Watson's middle adult years were spent in the world of advertising, where he became a living example of applied psychology. After you finish this chapter, you should be able to:

■ Recognize the similarities between British empiricist philosophy and 20th-century behaviorism

■ Describe the trends toward increased objectivity that preceded behaviorism

■ Describe the organization and operation of research in Pavlov's laboratory

■ Describe the basic conditioning phenomena studied by Pavlov

■ Describe Pavlov's relationship with the Soviets and why the Soviets valued his work

■ Describe Pavlov's influence on American psychologists

■ Describe Watson's research on animal behavior, from mazes to natural environments

■ Explain Watson's analysis of contemporary structural and functional psychology, and what he proposed instead, in his Behaviorist Manifesto

■ Describe Watson's research on basic emotions and the stimuli producing them

■ Describe and critically analyze Watson and Rayner's demonstration of conditioned fear

■ Show how Mary Cover Jones successfully eliminated a fear response and how her work relates to modern behavior therapy

■ Show how Watson brought his behaviorist ideas and scientific training to the world of advertising

■ Describe Watson's attempts to popularize the science of behavior

BEHAVIORISM'S ANTECEDENTS

American behaviorists often trace their roots to John B. Watson and in particular to his so-called **Behaviorist Manifesto**, a paper he tried out in a talk at Columbia University in February 1913 and soon published (Watson, 1913). Yet history seldom turns dramatically on such events—they are usually individual chapters of a more complex narrative. Long before Watson saw the inside of the psychology laboratory at the University of Chicago, forces were at work paving the way for behaviorist thinking to become accepted as the norm by American psychologists. Furthermore, the psychological world did not convert to behaviorism just because of Watson's "revolutionary" pronouncements. Rather, Watson contributed a strong voice to the growing dissatisfaction with introspective psychology. Few psychologists, however, were immediately converted to Watsonian behaviorism (Samelson, 1981). Indeed, it was not until Watson was far removed from the academic scene that behaviorism moved to the center of experimental psychology in the United States.

Behaviorism has an affinity with several of the philosophical movements described in Chapters 2 and 3. For example, the behaviorist's belief in the importance of the environment in shaping behavior resonates with the British empiricist/associationist dictum that experience is the all-important determiner of one's mind and character. There are also parallels between the behaviorist's stimulus-response connections and the concept of association. In Chapter 3, you learned about the influence of 19-century mechanistic and materialist thinking on physiologists; these philosophies are also congenial to behaviorist thinking. During the 19th century **positivism** also emerged, associated with the French philosopher Auguste Comte, and eventually taken as an article of faith by behaviorists. Comte argued that we could only be certain of knowledge resulting from publicly observable events. Positive knowledge was said to be the result of *objective* observations using the precise methods of science, to be made by unbiased observers. Truth, then, amounted to agreement among these scientific observers. Philosophical speculation (e.g., how do minds and bodies relate?) was considered to be a worthless exercise, according to the positivists, because such speculations could never be verified objectively. Positivists also valued "practical" knowledge, believing that an intimate connection existed between understanding nature and controlling it. Indeed, Comte argued that the ability to control nature was evidence that nature was understood—creating an effective steam engine, for instance, demonstrated understanding of several principles of physics. Comte's faith in science even led him to recommend the deliberate redesign of society. This theme of controlling nature, virtually identical to arguments made 200 years earlier by Sir Francis Bacon (Chapter 2), later became a centerpiece of behaviorist thinking. It appears, for instance, in B. F. Skinner's (Chapter 11) *Walden Two* (1948), a description of an ideal community based on principles of behavioral control. John Watson's prescriptions about child rearing, which you will encounter near the end of this chapter, also fall under the heading of using science to control nature.

At the start of the 20th century, psychologists were beginning to turn toward increased objectivity in their measures of psychological phenomena. One important influence was the rapid acceptance of evolutionary thinking among scientists and the resulting growth of animal psychology, as documented in Chapter 5. Animals cannot introspect, of course, so studying the relationship between human and animal consciousness required behavioral measures. Most 19th-century descriptions of animal behavior were unduly anthropomorphic, but as we have seen, Morgan established the principle that simpler explanations for animal behaviors were to be favored over unnecessarily complex ones. Explaining a dog's ability to open a gate in terms of trial-and-error learning, rather than by means of intelligence and planning, moved comparative psychology from anecdotes to more objective descriptions of stimuli and responses. Thorndike's puzzle box research (Chapter 7) is perhaps the clearest manifestation in America of the movement toward increased objectivity in animal psychology. In Czarist Russia at the same time, however, an even greater level of precision could be found in the laboratory of Ivan Pavlov. American psychologists did not immediately realize the value of the Russian's research for their own growing desire for an objective science, but the Russian's approach to research eventually became a model that many American behaviorists emulated.

As the new century unfolded, the trend toward greater objectivity led a number of American psychologists to become disillusioned with the state of experimental psychology, especially its reliance on introspection. Because introspective data were ultimately subjective, no independent way of evaluating each claim existed. As early as 1904, in an address delivered at a World's Fair in St. Louis, James McKeen Cattell declared that psychology should not be limited to the study of conscious experience and that introspection need not be the dominant method used by psychologists. In his words:

> [T]he rather widespread notion that there is no psychology apart from introspection is refuted by the brute argument of accomplished fact.
>
> It seems to me that most of the research work that has been done by me or in my laboratory is nearly as independent of introspection as work in physics or in zoology. The time of mental processes, ... individual differences, the behavior of animals and of children, these and other topics I have investigated without requiring the slightest introspection on the part of the subject ....
>
> It is certainly difficult to penetrate by analogy into the consciousness of the lower animals ... and of children, but the study of their behavior has already yielded much and promises much more. (Cattell, 1904, quoted in Woodworth, 1931, pp. 48–49)

Reflecting the positivist thinking just described, Cattell said that he saw "no reason why the application of systematized knowledge to the *control of human nature* may not in the course of the present century accomplish results commensurate with the 19th century applications of physical science to the material world" (p. 49, emphasis added).

In the same year that Cattell addressed the St. Louis World's Fair, another event marked a milestone in a career that was shifting from a fascination with the digestive system to a passion for discovering how the brain works. The event was the awarding of a Nobel Prize for physiology to the Russian scientist Ivan Petrovich Pavlov.

PAVLOV'S LIFE AND WORK

Pavlov earned the Nobel Prize for his painstaking and ingenious investigations of the physiology of digestion. In particular, he was known for inventing or perfecting a number of surgical techniques to facilitate this research. Yet when the 54-year-old scientist delivered his acceptance address in December of 1904 at the awards ceremony in Stockholm, Sweden, he did not have much to say about the work that won him the Nobel Prize. Rather, in an address entitled "The First Sure Steps along the Path of a New Investigation" (Babkin, 1949), Pavlov described research that had interested him for the past several years and would occupy the rest of his life. This research is familiar to you, bringing to mind images of salivating dogs. Pavlov's conditioning research eventually provided a model for American behavioral scientists, despite the fact that Pavlov himself always insisted that he was a physiologist, not a psychologist, and his regard for psychology was not high. He once pointed out that although the study of reflexes had been dominated historically by those taking a psychological (by which he meant introspective) approach, his more objective strategy offered the hope of these investigations of the reflex "being liberated from such evil influences" (Pavlov, 1906, p. 618).

The Development of a Physiologist

Ivan Petrovich Pavlov (1849–1936) was born into relative poverty in the small farming village of Ryazan in west central Russia. His father was a priest, and his mother was the daughter of a priest, but despite their resulting social status, feeding a large family was a constant struggle. Ivan was the firstborn of 11 children, 6 of whom died in childhood. His early schooling was geared toward following in his father's clerical footsteps, but while studying at the Ryazan Ecclesiastical Seminary, visits to a local library sparked an interest in science when he discovered (a) Darwin's *Origin of Species* and (b) *Reflexes of the Brain*, published in 1863 by Russia's leading 19th-century physiologist, Ivan Sechenov (1829–1905). Sechenov argued that all cortical processes involved complex relationships between excitatory and inhibitory processes in the nervous system and that "psychical" (psychological) events could be reduced to and explained by reflex action in the cortex. It was a model very much in tune with the mechanistic and materialistic climate of 19th-century science, and it was influenced by Sechenov's contact with some of Europe's leading physiologists. These ideas eventually became the cornerstone of Pavlov's model of nervous system functioning.

Pavlov left the seminary and enrolled as a student of physiology at St. Petersburg University in 1870, thereby trading a simple rural life for the glamour of Russia's most important city.[1] St. Petersburg, located in northwest Russia near the Gulf of Finland, was the cultural, political, and intellectual center of Russia in the late 19th century. It was also Russia's capital city until replaced by Moscow in 1918, following the Russian Revolution. In this high-powered environment, Pavlov completed a degree in medicine in 1883 and became a research physiologist. After additional years of study, several low-level research positions, and financial hardship, he was named director of the physiology division of St. Petersburg's Imperial Institute of Experimental Medicine in 1891 and professor at the nearby Military Medical Academy. It was during the 1890s that he systematically investigated the physiology of the digestive system, and this was the research that led to the Nobel Prize.

Working in Pavlov's Laboratory—The Physiology Factory

As director of the Institute of Experimental Medicine, Pavlov created a laboratory environment that resembled a smooth-running factory—the creation of surgically prepared research specimens (dogs),[2] tightly prescribed training procedures for worker–students, a research process that ran with clockwork

[1] After Lenin's death in 1924, the Soviets renamed the city Leningrad; in 1991, following the collapse of the Soviet Union, it was rechristened St. Petersburg, and that is its name today.

[2] Pavlov preferred dogs because their digestive system was similar to that of humans. He tried rabbits and pigs, but the rabbits often died in surgery, and the pigs were too nervous and excitable. He did not try cats, apparently because he thought of them as "loud and malicious" (Todes, 2000, p. 51).

precision, and the regular production of research output that resembled a factory assembly line (Todes, 1997b). Most of his students were military officers who had already qualified as physicians and were looking to add a doctorate in physiology (and a notable increase in their government salary) to their medical degree; between Pavlov's appointment in 1891 and the Nobel Prize year of 1904, no fewer than 100 physicians earned physiology doctorates in Pavlov's lab (Todes, 2000).

Large numbers of students required a well-structured training regimen, and Pavlov developed an effective one. Whenever a new student would enter the lab, Pavlov would assign an experienced worker to guide the newcomer through the standardized procedures and then give this person a problem that had already been investigated. Thus, the incoming student would learn experimental procedures without being under pressure to produce new findings, while also providing an ongoing program of **replication**. Once the earlier research had been replicated successfully, the worker would be given a new problem to investigate. A failure to replicate would trigger additional research to clear up the contradiction. Replication, of course, is a cornerstone of sound scientific research—results that cannot be repeated are of no value.

Pavlov studied digestion by isolating various parts of the digestive system and extracting digestive fluids. The quantities of the various fluids secreted were measured as a function of the type of substance fed to the animal. The research was noted for its precision and for the development of surgical techniques to isolate and collect digestive secretions in dogs that were otherwise functioning normally. One technique came to be called the "Pavlov pouch." He created it by segregating a small section of stomach and redesigning it as a miniature stomach. It was situated so that food could not enter when it reached the stomach from the esophagus. A small tube or fistula led from the pouch to the exterior, thereby providing a means to collect the fluids secreted by the mini-stomach. Uncontaminated by food, these pure gastric fluids could be accurately analyzed (Gray, 1979).

These fluids also provided Pavlov with a source of income. Although the Institute's budget was generous by Russian standards, Pavlov found it necessary to raise additional money through the sale of gastric juices taken from the dogs during his experiments. Pavlov marketed the vile-tasting fluid as an elixir for those suffering from various digestive ailments, especially those resulting from "an insufficient flow of the [their] own gastric juice" (Babkin, 1949, p. 69). It was also sold to laboratories throughout Europe for research purposes.[3]

In addition to investigating gastric secretions, Pavlov studied salivary responses, relating them to the type of food placed in the dog's mouth. He measured salivation with another type of fistula, this time a small tube directly connected to a salivary duct. Inevitably, as all dog owners know, the dogs would begin to salivate before food would reach their mouths. One of Pavlov's students, S. G. Vul'fson, studied the phenomenon in a study comparing salivation to moist versus dry foods. The main finding was that dogs salivated more to dry foods (less saliva needed for moist foods), but a secondary finding was that after a number of trials, the dogs began salivating *before* the food arrived, apparently in response to seeing Vul'fson holding the food (Windholz, 1997). The outcome presented Pavlov with a dilemma. On the one hand, these "psychic" secretions were a nuisance, reducing the accuracy of Pavlov's attempts to measure an exact amount of saliva in response to a specific amount of food. On the other hand, the animal's behavior was predictable, suggesting to Pavlov an objective way to study those "reflexes of

---

[3]Most of the fluid was collected during "sham feeding" experiments, in which a tracheal fistula was added to the stomach fistula. The dog would eat normally, but the food would exit through the tracheal fistula and never reach the stomach. Nonetheless, the action of chewing and swallowing stimulated the flow of gastric juices, which were then collected for analysis and sale. A typical dog could produce a liter of gastric juice a day. One visitor noted that "when first collected, this juice has a distinct odor of the dog but [Pavlov] found that by aspirating air through it, the smell is readily removed" (Benedict, 1907).

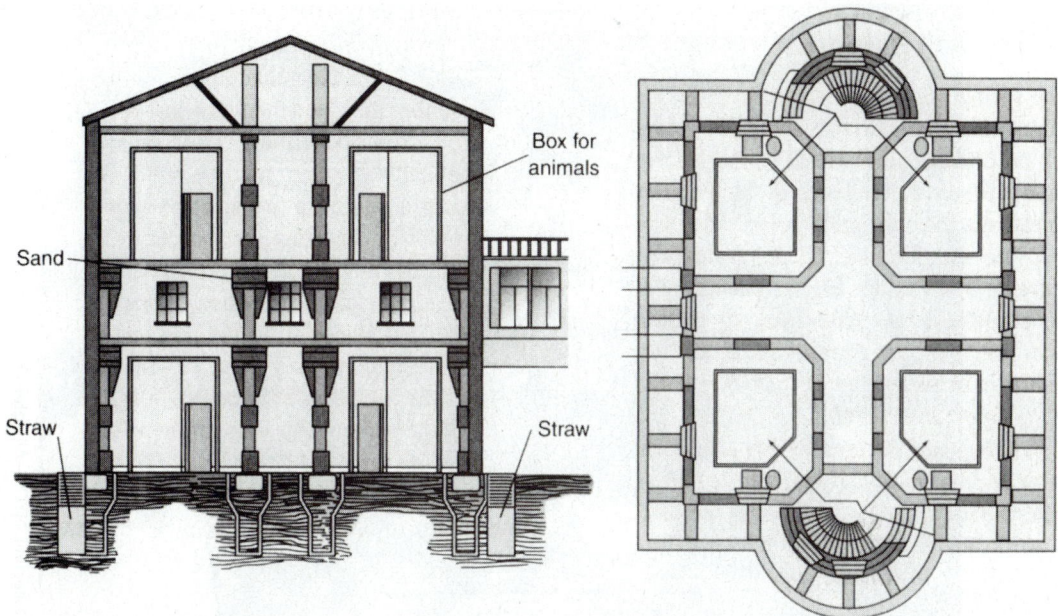

FIGURE 10.1 Cross-section and floor plan of Pavlov's "Tower of Silence" laboratory, from Pavlov (1928). From Pavlov, I. P. 1928. *Lectures on Conditioned Reflexes* W. H. Gantt, Trans. New York: International Publications.

the brain" that he had read about in Sechenov's book. Pavlov's decision to investigate these psychic secretions led to the research for which he is famous.

Beginning in 1910, the Institute built a special laboratory for Pavlov's new conditioning research. Sometimes known as the Tower of Silence, it featured extensive soundproofing techniques to ensure that the dogs would respond only to the stimulus being examined at the time and not to any extraneous stimuli. As Figure 10.1 shows, there were eight experimental chambers, four on each of two floors that were separated by an intermediate floor. Each research chamber was fully insulated and separated from other chambers by a corridor. Experimenters were separated from the dogs by the double wall, although they occasionally joined the dogs for photo opportunities (Figure 10.2). It was from the Tower of Silence that most of Pavlov's conditioning research was completed.

Pavlov's Classical Conditioning Research

In the spring of 1924, Pavlov organized a series of lectures that summarized about 25 years of his work on conditioning. He gave the lectures at the Military Medical Academy in St. Petersburg and then rewrote them for publication. Translated into English by G. V. Anrep, a British researcher and former student of Pavlov's, they were published as *Conditioned Reflexes: An Investigation of the Physiological Activity of the Cerebral Cortex* by the British Royal Society in 1927 (Pavlov, 1927/1960).

In his opening lecture, Pavlov (1927/1960) acknowledged his debt to Sechenov and Darwin, credited Thorndike (the puzzle box studies in Chapter 7) with doing pioneering research on the relationship between "visual and tactile stimuli on the one hand and the locomotor apparatus on the other" (p. 6), and then described the start of his own inquiries and his recognition that the problem had to be attacked from a physiological rather than a psychological standpoint. Pavlov believed that restricting

The Granger Collection, NYC — All rights reserved.

FIGURE 10.2 Pavlov (right center), students, and dog.

the investigation to specific external stimuli and measurable physiological responses was the only scientifically defensible strategy to use.

After a detailed description of basic reflex action, Pavlov concluded his opening lecture by referring to the accidental discovery of salivary conditioning that launched him into his 25 years of research:

> Let us return now to the simplest reflex from which our investigations started. If food … finds its way into the mouth, a secretion of saliva is produced. The purpose of this secretion is … to alter [the food] chemically. . . . But, in addition to this, a similar reflex secretion is evoked when these substances are placed at a distance from the dog and the receptor organs affected are only those of smell and sight. Even the vessel from which the food has been given is sufficient to evoke [a reflex] complete in all its details; and, further, the secretion may be provoked even by the sight of the person who brought the vessel, or by the sound of his footsteps. (Pavlov, 1927/1960, p. 13)

In his second lecture, Pavlov began by describing some of the technical details of his procedures and the measures taken to control experimental conditions. He explained that the dog presented with food shows both secretory (i.e., salivary) reflexes and motor reflexes. It drools, but it also turns its head, moves its mouth, and so on. That Pavlov decided to study the secretory reflex and ignore the motor reflexes is another indication of his concern over precise measurement and a desire to avoid anthropomorphic speculation about what the animal might be "trying to do."

Conditioning and Extinction Having set the stage, Pavlov described the basic procedure for acquiring a conditioned reflex. The essence of the technique is to pair a stimulus known to produce a particular response (i.e., salivation) with a neutral stimulus, such as a tone or a metronome.[4] During acquisition, then, the starting point is an already existing reflex. For Pavlov, this reflex was the **unconditioned reflex** (UCR) of salivating when food (the **unconditioned stimulus**, or UCS) was presented to the animal. Conditioning involved presenting a neutral stimulus, then the UCS. This neutral stimulus Pavlov called a **conditional stimulus** (later translated as conditioned stimulus), or CS, because the resulting reflex depended on (was "conditional" on) the CS-UCS pairing. This resulting reflex was called a **conditioned reflex**, or CR.

After describing acquisition, Pavlov showed how a CR could undergo **extinction** if the metronome (the CS) was sounded without being accompanied by food (the UCS). Pavlov let the metronome run for 30-second intervals every 2 minutes, recording the amount of saliva secreted and what he called the "latent period"—the amount of time between the starting of the metronome and the beginning of salivation. As Pavlov described it, the "weakening of the reflex to a conditional stimulus which is repeated a certain number of times without reinforcement may appropriately be termed experimental extinction of conditioned reflexes" (Pavlov, 1927/1960, pp. 48–49). With successive extinction trials, it took longer (i.e., greater latency) for the animal to begin salivating, and there was a steady decline in the amount of salivation.

Generalization and Differentiation Pavlov's subsequent lectures describe his procedures for demonstrating a wide range of conditioning phenomena, including many of the ones you learned about in your general psychology course. Two of the most familiar are generalization and discrimination (the latter referred to as differentiation by Pavlov). **Generalization** is in evidence when a response conditioned to stimulus A also occurs, to some degree at least, in response to stimuli that are similar to stimulus A. So if the CS of a 60 cps tone produces eight drops of saliva, the animal will also respond to a 70 cps tone, perhaps with six drops. A generalization gradient also exists—the amount of saliva secreted is proportional to the similarity of the CS and the tested stimulus. **Differentiation** results from pairing the 60 cps tone with food, while presenting the 70 cps tone without the food. Eventually, the dog salivates only to the 60 cps tone.

Pavlov also went to great lengths to incorporate Sechenov's constructs of cortical excitation and inhibition into his descriptions. For example, excitatory processes were said to be involved in acquisition and generalization, whereas inhibitory cortical processes contributed to extinction and differentiation. In general, Pavlov was not interested in the conditioning phenomena per se, but only in terms of the light they shed on how the brain operated.

Experimental Neurosis One interesting outgrowth of Pavlov's research on generalization and differentiation was his discovery of how a breakdown in differentiation could produce **experimental neurosis** or "pathological disturbance," as he put it in the title of his Lecture 17. He first projected a circle onto a screen in front of the dog's face, pairing its presentation with food. Soon, the circle became a normal CS for the CR of salivation. After creating this conditioned reflex, Pavlov then trained the dog to make an easy differentiation between the circle and an ellipse that had a 4:3 ratio between its two axes. The shape of the ellipse was then changed until it reached a 9:8 ratio; that is, the ellipse was made to look more and more like the circle. The dog showed the ability to discriminate at first, but it then failed, and eventually its behavior reached the point where it even had difficulty distinguishing an easy

---

[4]Ironically, although most students think that Pavlov's typical CS was a bell, Pavlov reported that "the violent ringing of a bell" was seldom effective as a CS because the dog tended to be startled by it (Pavlov, 1906, p. 616).

2:1 ellipse from the circle. For Pavlov, then, neurotic behavior meant a breakdown in the ability to make normal differentiations. The neurosis also manifested itself in other ways. As Pavlov described it,

> At the same time the whole behavior of the animal underwent an abrupt change. The hitherto quiet dog began to squeal in its stand, kept wriggling about, tore off with its teeth the apparatus for mechanical stimulation of the skin, and bit through the tubes connecting the animal's room with the observer, a behavior which never happened before. On being taken into the experimental room the dog now barked violently, which was also contrary to its usual custom; in short it presented all the symptoms of an acute neurosis. (Pavlov, 1927/1960, p. 291)

During the course of his research on experimental neurosis, Pavlov noticed that although all the dogs were adversely affected, they displayed differences in how they displayed their pathology. Furthermore, these variations seemed to reflect individual differences in the temperaments of the dogs. Thus, some dogs were generally more excitable than others—they tended to respond to the experimental neurosis procedure like the dog just described. Others, however, who were ordinarily of a more placid temperament, reacted to the procedure by becoming even more withdrawn. As he did with all his results, Pavlov interpreted these outcomes in terms of excitatory and inhibitory cortical processes. He believed that the individual differences in temperament related to whether excitatory or inhibitory processes were more dominant.

A Program of Research Pavlov's research is a classic example of how experiments seldom occur in isolation, but are embedded in an ongoing systematic program of research. The outcome of one study has interest in itself, but it also raises new questions and leads directly to the next study. For instance, the acquisition research led naturally to the question of the precise timing of the CS and UCS, and Pavlov and his students completed dozens of studies that carefully varied the timing and the sequencing of the CS-UCS interval. Similarly, research developed over the years on such topics as (a) higher order conditioning, which involved pairing a new CS with an already conditioned one; (b) the durability of extinction, in which it was found that if a dog was returned to the laboratory several days after extinction, the CR would occur to some degree (i.e., so-called spontaneous recovery occurred); and (c) the effectiveness of various types of conditional stimuli, in terms of how quickly conditioning could be established.[5]

Pavlov and the Soviets

Pavlov was the prototype of the scientist whose life was his work, a philosophy reflected in an article he wrote near the end of his life for a Soviet youth organization. He told them that scientists must be systematic, modest, and passionate about their work, and that "science demands of a man his whole life. And even if you could have two lives, they would not be sufficient. Science calls for tremendous effort and great passion" (quoted in Babkin, 1949, p. 110). While in the laboratory, and from September through May he was there virtually every day, Pavlov was completely absorbed in the research at hand and expected everyone else to share his passion. Thus, he was occasionally a stern taskmaster and was known for his frequent but short-lived outbursts of temper when mistakes were made. Nonetheless, his

---

[5]The productivity of Pavlov's lab made it easy to overlook other experimental demonstrations of the same type of conditioning that occurred at the time of or just before Pavlov's initial studies. Both the American psychologist E. B. Twitmyer and the Viennese physiologist Alois Kreidl produced conditioning in their labs (Logan, 2002). However, neither Twitmyer, who studied the knee jerk reflex, nor Kreidl, who was studying sensory capacity in fish, developed anything like the research program that Pavlov did.

workers were intensely devoted to him, knowing that his anger passed quickly and was not directed at them personally.

One famous story about Pavlov provides an indication of his single-minded devotion to his work. Although the story might be more mythical than real, it illustrates Pavlov's priorities. Pavlov is said to have admonished a worker for being late during the height of the 1917 Russian Revolution. When the worker told of bloody skirmishes in the streets, causing him to take a more circuitous route to the laboratory, Pavlov was not impressed. After all, he had made his customary 3 mile walk to the lab, arriving safely and promptly at nine o'clock. Pavlov made it clear to the worker that a mere revolution was not to interfere with the important work of the laboratory. The assistant was told to leave home earlier during the next revolution (Babkin, 1949).

Of course, the revolution of 1917 had a profound effect on everything in Russia, including Pavlov's work. Pavlov was initially hostile to the winners of the Soviet Revolution, Vladimir Lenin's Bolsheviks, once saying publicly that if "that which the Bolsheviks are doing with Russia is an experiment, for such an experiment I should regret giving even a frog" (quoted in Babkin, 1949, p. 161). He also complained to Joseph Stalin, Lenin's successor, about a policy to admit only communist professors to the Russian Academy of Science, telling the Russian leader: "On account of what you are doing I am ashamed to be called a Russian" (quoted in Gantt, 1973). Pavlov's ambivalent attitude was not hard to understand—the Soviets confiscated his Nobel Prize money, and when he requested permission to emigrate in the early 1920s, they refused.[6] Yet by the end of his life, Pavlov had come to accept the reality of the Soviet Union. According to Babkin, Pavlov's change of heart came about primarily because of the developing threat of the Nazis in Germany, who came to power in 1933. Fiercely patriotic, Pavlov recalled the huge Russian losses at the hands of Germany in World War I and feared (accurately) that the Nazis would bring more suffering to his beloved homeland. In that context, the Soviets clearly appeared to be the lesser of two evils.

Pavlov's gradual accommodation to the reality of the Soviet state also was aided by the strong backing the government gave to his work. As early as 1921, when Russia was immersed in civil war, conditions were generally chaotic, and Pavlov's laboratory was in dire straits, the Soviets saw to it that Pavlov's research continued with as much support as they could provide. For example, it was officially decreed that a special committee be formed "to create as soon as possible the most favorable conditions for safeguarding the scientific work of Academician Pavlov and his collaborators" (quoted in Babkin, 1949, p. 165). These conditions included extra rations and a pledge to equip Pavlov's laboratory.

It is easy to see why the Soviets were enamored of Pavlov. A major theme of his research was that controlling the environment could change behavior—actions could be "conditioned." That, of course, was exactly what the Soviets hoped to do on a broad scale, conditioning citizens to be comfortable with the Marxist–Leninist ideal whereby each should produce according to one's abilities and receive according to one's needs. Thus, although Pavlov had no interests beyond understanding the physiology of the brain, his research had propaganda value for the Soviets. This tolerance by the Soviets is shown

---

[6]It is important to keep in mind that Pavlov was 71 years old in 1920. He had many influential international colleagues, who tried in various ways to support him during the hard times of the Russian Civil war that occurred in the aftermath of the Bolshevik revolution of 1917 (e.g., fund raising, arranging food shipments for his dogs), According to Todes (1995), however, his friends were not able to arrange an academic appointment for him, mainly because of his age, so emigration would have meant retirement, an outcome that Pavlov would not have found palatable. Todes argued that Pavlov's talk of emigration was primarily a negotiating tool designed to improve conditions in his lab.

in a brief notice in an unidentified magazine article, which Walter Miles cut out and pasted into his diary in 1929. It said that Pavlov had

> refused an official celebration of his 80th birthday . . . . Said he: "I deplore the destruction of cultural values by illiterate Communists." Mindful that upon his research rests the behavioristic "Science of Marxism" . . . , the Soviet tolerates his slaps gently and without reproach, babies him. Birthday gifts from the Soviet to him include $50,000 endowment of his laboratory and an assurance that traffic would be diverted from the street near it so as not to disturb the conditioned reflexes of [his] dogs. (Miles, 1929b)

After Pavlov's death from pneumonia in 1936, the Soviets treated him like a war hero. A monument to him was erected in St. Petersburg, the Medical Institute was renamed the Pavlov Institute, his wife was given a generous pension, and his brain was preserved.

Pavlov and the Americans

Western scientists knew about Pavlov because of the Nobel Prize, but the impact of his conditioning research was slow in being felt. Most American psychologists were introduced to Pavlov through an article published in the *Psychological Bulletin* in 1909 by Robert Yerkes (Chapter 8), whose interests at that time were mainly in comparative psychology, and Sergius Morgulis, a Russian student. One feature of the article was a series of apparatus sketches that eventually resulted in mistaken portrayals of Pavlov's apparatus that continue to this day in textbooks (see this chapter's Close-Up).

Despite the Yerkes and Morgulis (1909) article, Pavlov's research had little immediate impact on American psychologists. The work was of interest to those studying animal behavior, but at a time when American psychology was still the science of human conscious experience, salivating dogs did not seem especially relevant. Most introductory psychology textbooks prior to 1920 either failed to mention Pavlov at all (including a 1911 text by Yerkes) or mentioned his work just briefly (Goodwin, 1991a). Even Watson, whose proclamation of behaviorism you will soon read, did not see the immediate relevance of Pavlov's work for his model of learning. Instead, Watson was initially more influenced by the conditioning work of another Russian physiologist, Vladimir Bekhterev (Skinner, 1981). Bekhterev investigated motor rather than salivary conditioning, in which muscle movements were conditioned to various stimuli. This lent itself more readily to Watson's interests in overt behavior, which of course relies on muscle action.

Pavlov's major impact on American psychology began in the 1920s, when much of his work was translated into English for the first time, in the lecture series described earlier. Pavlov also visited the United States twice, once in 1923 for a conference and lecture series at Rockefeller Institute in New York, and again in 1929 for the Ninth International Congress of Psychology at Yale University. At the latter he delivered one of the major invited addresses (Duncan, 1980), an impassioned description (in Russian) of his research on conditioning to a large audience of American and international psychologists. As one observer noted, "the audience was spellbound, and the following standing ovation brought little smiles and bows of appreciation from the Guest of Honor of the Congress" (Withington, quoted in Duncan, 1980). The event was especially memorable for Walter Miles, as you will learn by reading this chapter's "From the Miles Papers".

American psychologists, especially behaviorists, eventually understood the importance of Pavlov's research for their own theories of learning. A passage from Ernest Hilgard's well-known *Theories of Learning* (1948) shows that Pavlov's importance was taken for granted by the late 1940s. Hilgard pointed out that research on "conditioned salivary responses in dogs was carried out systematically by Pavlov over many years, and he discovered most of the relationships which later

CLOSE-UP

MISPORTRAYING PAVLOV'S APPARATUS

You probably recognize the sketch in Figure 10.3*a*. It shows up in one form or another in most general psychology texts, probably including the one you used, and it is usually identified as Pavlov's conditioning apparatus. It wasn't. Rather, it was devised by a German physiologist, G. F. Nicolai, who worked briefly in Pavlov's laboratory (Goodwin, 1991a). Nicolai wished to improve on how saliva was recorded in the early years in Pavlov's lab, when the drops of saliva were simply counted as they fell into the graduated cylinder attached to the salivary fistula, as portrayed in Figure 10.3*b*. How did the mistaken attribution of Nicolai's apparatus occur?

The article by Yerkes and Morgulis (1909), which introduced Pavlov's research to American psychologists, included both sketches. Neither was labeled, but the text of the article described Figure 10.3*b* as showing a dog prepared for conditioning research in Pavlov's lab, whereas Figure 10.3*a* was described as showing "the modification of experimental technique *which has been devised by Nicolai in Berlin*" (p. 259, emphasis added).

The distinction between Nicolai's and Pavlov's procedures was recognized by John Watson, who reproduced and correctly labeled both drawings in his comparative psychology text of 1914. The first erroneous attribution seems to have been in a popular introductory textbook by Walter Hunter (1919); it included only Figure 10.3*a*, referred to it as Pavlov's apparatus, and cited the Yerkes and Morgulis article. From this point on, the sketch of Nicolai's experimental setup became the standard depiction of Pavlov's apparatus, partly because it is consistent with Pavlov's eventual separation of dog and experimenter into two separate rooms, but also because it is simply more interesting than Figure 10.3*b*.

The perpetuation of this error over the years provides an important lesson for any writer—beware of relying too heavily on secondary sources. Many subsequent textbook authors probably included the wrong drawing simply because it had become so widely used by other writers. Seeing the same drawing over and over, it is easy to assume it must have depicted Pavlov's apparatus setup.

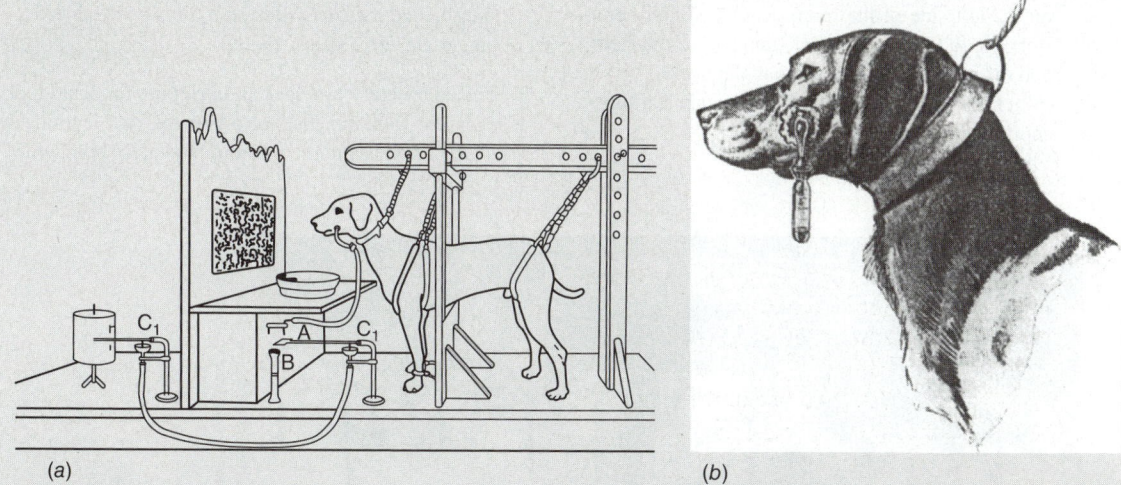

(a) (b)

FIGURE 10.3 (*a*) Conditioning setup developed by German physiologist Nicolai, but usually attributed to Pavlov; (*b*) Early fistula used by Pavlov for collecting salivary responses (both from Nicolai, 1907).

FROM THE MILES PAPERS...

MILES MEETS PAVLOV

Walter Miles was in the audience when Pavlov spoke at Yale Conference on the evening of September 2, 1929, writing to a colleague that "Pavlov delivered a rather notable address in Russian which was translated by Anrep who had no manuscript at his disposal" (Miles, 1929d). G. V. Anrep was a former student of Pavlov's and, as mentioned earlier, the translator of Pavlov's *Conditioned Reflexes* (Pavlov, 1927/1960). Miles got a much closer look at Pavlov the following evening.

James McKeen Cattell (Chapter 7), who presided over the conference, hosted a party for Pavlov on the evening of September 3. Just over a dozen psychologists and physiologists attended (one notable: Wolfgang Köhler), and the main event was the showing of two films made by Miles of rats in his laboratory navigating elevated mazes (Figure 10.4). One film showed normal rats; in the second, the rats had been given alcohol. As Miles described the "Pavlov–Cattell party" in his diary:

> Pavlov came in shirt sleeves, no coat or vest ... Pavlov and the three other Russians sat on the left side of the room. Köhler, Cattell, and Ebbecke [a German physiologist] sat on the right and the rest of the crowd were in the back.
> Film I. Elevated maze. Rats crossing gap, learning, short cut, memory.
> Film II. [illegible], alcohol.

There was much discussion. Points.

1. Pavlov wanted to know how the animal masters this thing. I took up tracking and eyes.
2. What is the effect of new wood? ...
3. What is the effect of turning the maze?
4. I stressed that the addition of obstruction [illegible] bring[s] out all that the animals were able to do.
5. They [said] that by different drugs perhaps we might find the difference between locomotion centers and the higher centers ...
6. Grünbaum asked the effect of changing an animal to a maze of increased size but no change in pattern.
7. Comments that alcohol made chiefly a motor disturbance ....

Pavlov was very appreciative and cordial and had lots to say. All of my remarks were translated for him, running continuously. Afterwards the Russians talked it all over. Between films I served iced ginger ale, etc. (Miles, 1929a)

This diary entry provides an intriguing firsthand look at scientific thinking. Seeing a film of rats learning a maze, the scientists in the room immediately bombarded

From the Walter Miles papers, Archives of the History of American Psychology, University of Akron

FIGURE 10.4   Rat (top center) navigating an elevated maze; still photo from film by Walter Miles.

Miles with question after question about the process of maze learning and made suggestions about altering the procedure slightly to determine the consequences of the change (e.g., turning the maze) on learning. Although Pavlov was generally critical of maze learning studies (no way to isolate stimuli and responses), he was clearly a gracious guest at the party and congenial with Miles, who he recognized as a fellow scientist.

studies have more fully explored. The translations of his terms have become common in the literature of learning" (Hilgard, 1948, p. 55).

Finally, Pavlov had a direct impact on the career choice of a young B. F. Skinner, whose decision to pursue behavioral research was strongly influenced by reading Pavlov's *Conditioned Reflexes* (1927/1960). Skinner once wrote that a guiding principle in his scientific life was Pavlov's simple dictum that if you "control your conditions ... you will see order" (Skinner, 1956, p. 223). Skinner was also excited by the writings of an American psychologist who shared with Pavlov a passion for research grounded in measurable behavior. This person was John B. Watson, usually considered to be the founder of the American school of thought that came to be known as behaviorism.

JOHN B. WATSON AND THE FOUNDING OF BEHAVIORISM

Near the beginning of the Chapter I mentioned that at the start of the 20th century, a number of American psychologists argued that psychology should adopt a more "objective" methodology than introspection. One example was the address by Cattell at the 1904 St. Louis World's Fair. Also at St. Louis and probably in the audience for Cattell's address was John B. Watson, a young psychologist with a brand new PhD from the University of Chicago. The developing trends toward objectivity in psychology were beginning to crystallize in the thinking and writing of this young man, and he would shortly become the mouthpiece for a movement that came to be called behaviorism.

The Young Functionalist at Chicago

Watson was born in 1878 in a rural area just outside Greenville, South Carolina, into a family that would earn the label "dysfunctional" today. His father was a marginally successful farmer whose interests included consuming large amounts of alcohol and brawling. Watson's mother was fiercely religious, enough so to name her son after a well-known Baptist preacher, John Broadus, and to insist that her son aspire to the ministry. Growing up in this environment, Watson understandably developed behavior problems; by midadolescence he was a known troublemaker and had been arrested at least twice. Nonetheless, he was known to be an intelligent young man when he entered nearby Furman University at the age of 16. He graduated with a master's degree in 1900.

Watson's mother died during his final year at Furman, releasing him from any obligation to pursue the ministry. Instead, he applied to and was accepted at the University of Chicago. Eight years old in 1900, the university was established with Rockefeller oil money and presided over by William Rainey Harper. As you recall from Chapter 7's discussion of functionalism, Harper envisioned a "practical" university that would produce leaders for an emerging class in America—the professional elite, experts who would manage society's improvement and industry's productivity. Watson was comfortable with the functionalist psychology prevalent at Chicago, and he was especially attracted to comparative psychology—not a surprise considering his rural background and familiarity with animals. Many years later, Watson's son rather painfully recalled that his father "preferred the company of animals to people most of the time" (Hannush, 1987, p. 150).

Watson's interests in animal behavior began to shape his beliefs about psychology in general. When reflecting on his Chicago years, he later wrote that he was always uncomfortable with introspective methods and human subjects but that with animals, he was "at home . . . . More and more the thought presented itself: Can't I find out by watching their behavior everything that the other students are finding out by using [humans]?" (Watson, 1936, p. 279). This belief was reinforced by Watson's contacts with Jacques Loeb and Henry Donaldson. Loeb was a German physiologist who studied **tropisms**, movements of plants or animals that are forced automatically by some aspect of the environment. For example, a flower that moves to face the sun is said to be showing a positive heliotropism (helio = sun). Loeb was an uncompromising materialist and mechanist who believed that organic life could be understood as a series of automatic responses to stimuli. Donaldson was a neurologist specializing in the nervous system of white rats.

Watson's doctoral dissertation, codirected by Donaldson and James Angell (Chapter 7), was a study of the relationship between cortical development and learning in young white rats. It was an important study because at the time many leading physiologists believed that immature rats were incapable of true associative learning. Through a series of studies that showcased his developing talent as a scientist, Watson demonstrated that rats showed minimal learning ability for approximately the first 3 weeks of their lives, but that their ability to form associations improved dramatically in their fourth week. Furthermore, these associations were correlated with physical development in the cortex. Watson borrowed $350 from Donaldson and had his results published as *Animal Education: An Experimental Study of the Psychical Development of the White Rat, Correlated with the Growth of Its Nervous System* (Watson, 1903). It earned him the doctorate and an offer to remain at Chicago as an instructor. Watson accepted.

The Watson–Carr Maze Studies

Watson remained on the Chicago faculty from 1903 to 1908, building a reputation as a good teacher and a careful scientist. His most important research during this time involved studying rats in mazes; the studies were completed with Harvey Carr, then a graduate student at Chicago, later an important leader in the functionalist movement, and eventually chair of Chicago's psychology department (Chapter 7).

The goal of the Watson/Carr studies (Carr & Watson, 1908; Watson, 1907) was to determine which senses were needed for a rat to learn a maze. Watson was intrigued by the maze studies done at Clark by Willard Small (Close-Up—Chapter 6), but believed that Small had not been very systematic in his research. For example, Small's willingness to let the rats live in the maze at night made it impossible to evaluate how quickly the learning occurred. Watson and Carr remedied that problem and others, producing a methodologically brilliant series of studies that established (at least for a time) the importance of the kinesthetic (muscle) sense for maze learning.

In their first study (Watson, 1907) Watson and Carr eliminated the ability of rats to use their senses when solving a modified version of the Hampton Court maze. Displaying skillful surgical techniques, Watson removed the eyes from some rats, the middle ears from others, and the olfactory bulbs from a third group. Deprived of their various senses, the rats nonetheless learned the maze with ease. Watson and Carr also found that learning ability was not markedly hindered by removing whiskers or anesthetizing feet. By a process of elimination (literally), Watson and Carr concluded that the only important factors in the formation of learned associations were "the kinesthetic impressions coupled with certain other intra-organic impressions" (Watson, 1907, p. 84). That is, the animals were learning to associate sequences of muscle movements with the various locations in the maze. In essence, they learned to take seven steps, turn right for another five steps, turn left, and so on.

Having ruled out several senses, Watson and Carr set out to provide direct evidence of their hypothesis about kinesthesis. In their second study (Carr & Watson, 1908), they hit on the clever idea of shortening or lengthening a maze that their rats had already learned, but keeping the overall design the same. Figure 10.5 shows the maze in its full-length version, with the piece that could be removed shaded. The effects were dramatic—rats initially trained in the full-length maze literally ran into the walls of the shortened maze. For example, Watson noted that one rat "ran into [the wall] with all her strength. Was badly staggered" (Carr & Watson, 1908, p. 39). Similarly, rats trained in the shortened maze and tested in the long version often started to turn at the point where the correct turn used to be.

The Watson/Carr studies are models of scientific research, arriving at a data-based conclusion by eliminating one alternative hypothesis after another and then producing a direct demonstration of the viability of the remaining (kinesthetic) hypothesis. They also provide a good illustration of how scientists can be naive about how their research will be accepted in the public eye. Watson might have thought he was simply pursuing an important question about learning, but in the public eye he became

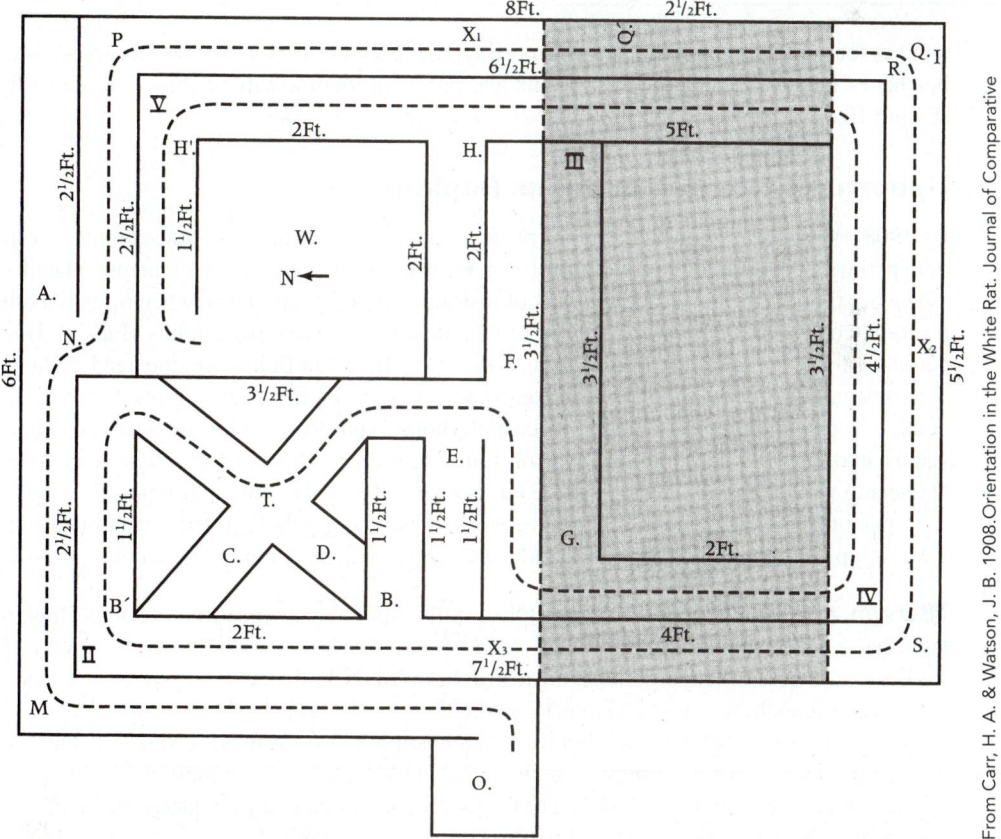

FIGURE 10.5 Maze used by Watson and Carr to test their kinesthetic model of maze learning; shaded piece could be removed to produce a shorter version of the maze.

From Carr, H. A. & Watson, J. B. 1908. Orientation in the White Rat. Journal of Comparative Neurology and Psychology, 18. 27–44.

This cartoon was attributed to the publishers of "Life" and was published in the "Journal of Zoophily" 1907, 166, p. 65. John Wiley & Sons Photo Library

FIGURE 10.6 Satirical antivivisectionist cartoon of Watson, after the Watson/Carr studies were publicized, from Dewsbury (1990a).

a target for antivivisectionists[7] and was portrayed in the *New York Times* on December 30, 1906, as a butcher of helpless rats, chopping out bits and pieces of them to satisfy some idle scientific curiosity (Figure 10.6).

Opportunity Knocks at Johns Hopkins

By 1908, Watson was known among his professional colleagues as an up-and-coming star in the world of experimental psychology (see Figure 10.7). He was also beginning to feel unappreciated at Chicago, where he still held the low academic rank of instructor after 5 years. Thus, when offered a full professor position, control of a laboratory, and more than double his salary from Johns Hopkins University, he could hardly refuse. Furthermore, within a year of his arrival in Baltimore, the head of the psychology department, James Mark Baldwin (Chapter 6), was fired for moral reasons (arrested in a police raid on a house of prostitution, he claimed ignorance of the house's purpose, but he also gave police a false name). Barely into his third decade, then, Watson found himself in charge of psychology at Johns Hopkins University. Over the next 12 years, before he also would be fired on moral grounds, he would (a) cement his reputation as a leading researcher in the world of animal psychology, (b) proclaim behaviorism, and (c) develop a program of research in child psychology, with an emphasis on emotional development.

Watson and Animal Behavior Once settled into his new position at Johns Hopkins, Watson launched a wide-ranging program of research in animal behavior. Like his dissertation and the maze studies with Carr at Chicago, some of the research was of the basic laboratory variety and included work in animal psychophysics. For example, he studied the visual abilities of several species by training them to make choices between pairs of slightly different stimuli (e.g., Watson, 1909). The logic of Watson's psychophysics research was simple—if an animal could be trained or conditioned to respond correctly to one stimulus (e.g., light red) while not responding to another (e.g., a darker shade of red), then the animal must be able to perceive the difference between the two.

[7]Like today's animal rights activists, antivivisectionists protested the use of animals for research purposes; their influence on early comparative psychology has been documented nicely by Dewsbury (1990a).

Archives of the History of American Psychology, The Center for the History of Psychology —The University of Akron

FIGURE 10.7 John B. Watson in 1908, at age 30.

Outside the laboratory, Watson completed a series of naturalistic studies, spending several summers on a small island near the Florida Keys observing the behavior of several species of terns. In contrast with Watson's later writings, which downplayed the importance of the instinctive control of behavior, especially human behavior, this research reads like an early version of the kind of ethological research later associated with names like Konrad Lorenz and Niko Tinbergen, emphasizing the importance of instinctive behavior for species survival (Dewsbury, 1994). Watson carefully documented the mating behaviors of the terns on Bird Key, their nest building and territoriality, and their behavior relating to the care of offspring, before and after their hatching (Todd & Morris, 1986). He also observed that recently hatched birds would often persistently follow him around the island. This of course is the same behavior studied by Spalding (Close-Up—Chapter 5) and later called imprinting by Lorenz.

Watson's Behaviorist Manifesto

In 1913, Watson accepted an invitation from Cattell to speak at Columbia University. By then he believed he had sufficient stature to proclaim what he had believed for at least 10 years—that it was time for the field to move away from the introspective psychology of consciousness and toward a psychology of behavior. His Columbia lecture, published later that year with the provocative title "Psychology as the Behaviorist Views It" (Watson, 1913), has come to be called the Behaviorist Manifesto. What did Watson proclaim? The opening sentences set the tone:

> Psychology as the behaviorist views it is a purely objective experimental branch of natural science. Its theoretical goal is the prediction and control of behavior. Introspection forms no essential part of its methods, nor is the scientific value of its data dependent upon the readiness with which they lend themselves to interpretation in terms of consciousness. (p. 158)

This is one of psychology's most quoted passages. In these first three sentences, Watson (a) firmly assigned psychology to the natural sciences, (b) articulated a set of goals for a scientific psychology, and (c) rejected the introspection-based research of most of his peers.

Watson quickly elaborated on his theme of discarding introspection and consciousness, pointing out the absurdity of a method that produced results that could never be independently verified (i.e., could never be objective) and where a failure to replicate some introspective result would be blamed on the inadequate training of introspectors. Consequently, Watson (1913) believed the time had come "when psychology must discard all reference to consciousness" (p. 163) and turn to behavior as the data to be observed. His attack was most clearly directed at Titchenerian structuralists, but he was also critical of his functionalist mentors. Although the functional approach had increased the diversity and scope of psychological research, it nonetheless had failed to reject introspection and the study of consciousness. The functionalists might be studying consciousness in a way that differed from the structuralists, Watson pointed out, but they were still studying it.

In place of psychology as the study of consciousness, Watson proposed that psychology become the science of behavior. Just as behavioral methods had increased our understanding of animals, he argued, so could they enhance our knowledge of humans. He set as a goal for psychology the prediction and control of behavior and boldly proclaimed that in a mature S-R system, "given the response the stimuli can be predicted; given the stimuli the response can be predicted" (Watson, 1913, p. 167). Even such activities as thinking could be reduced to stimuli and responses. According to Watson, thinking was in essence nothing more than **subvocal speech**, and the subject of this thinking would be determined by habits that he referred to as "laryngeal habits." He argued that as children, we talk to ourselves "out loud," but that as we get older, the talk eventually becomes silent. Thinking, then, might involve central (i.e., brain) processes, but it also manifests itself in peripheral actions that could be measured. Hence, even something as apparently nonbehavioral as thinking could in fact be measured as a behavior. Watson (1919) admitted that "the experimental evidence for this view is slight" (p. 362), but reported that several studies had attempted to measure the behavioral manifestations of thinking, by attaching a device for recording vibrations to a subject's neck in the region of the larynx, and then asking the subjects to read silently, do a math problem to themselves, or recall a poem. He reported some correlation between laryngeal movements and thinking, "but occasionally such records fail to appear even when a subvocal problem in arithmetic is worked out and the proper answer returned" (p. 326). Watson believed that better evidence would arrive when recording technology improved.[8] In an article written for the popular press, he later suggested (Watson, 1926), perhaps half-seriously, that some evidence in support of his position was the observation that our thinking tends to suffer when we experience a sore throat.

One thing that eventually made behaviorism popular among American psychologists was its insistence that behavioral principles must have applications to real life. Watson made the point in his manifesto as a way of contrasting his approach with introspective psychology, which seemed to him to be devoid of application. A behavioral strategy, he argued, was already making contributions to such applied topics as advertising, drug effects, the law, and education.

Watson's behaviorist manifesto was a powerful statement, sometimes seen as the starting point for a behaviorist "revolution" in psychology and as the vehicle that catapulted Watson to the presidency of the APA in 1915. Yet Samelson (1981) has shown that the immediate effect of the manifesto was that most psychologists ignored it or saw it as just one more instance of a growing discomfort with introspection. Only two psychologists—Titchener (1914) and Calkins (1913)—responded in print to it, and both were highly critical.[9] As for Watson's APA presidency, it was more likely the outcome of his

[8]In later years, the technology did improve, and Watson's argument about thinking collapsed. Studies showed, for example, that normal thinking could occur even when laryngeal muscles were completely paralyzed or had been removed surgically.

[9]Despite the obvious contrast between the psychologies of Titchener and Watson, they respected each other—after all, both were "laboratory men." They corresponded with some regularity and, when Watson hosted a meeting of Titchener's Experimentalists in 1910, Titchener was Watson's houseguest. When Watson was fired from John Hopkins in 1920, Titchener was one of the few psychologists who publicly supported his colleague (Larson & Sullivan, 1965).

already-existing status among his peers, earned by virtue of a decade of solid research, his friendships with influential APA members, his position as chair at Johns Hopkins, and his editorship of *Psychological Review*. Also, his nomination for the APA presidency occurred before the manifesto had been delivered (Samelson, 1981). On the other hand, although the manifesto might not have been a revolutionary event, it certainly energized Watson. For the remainder of the decade, he vigorously advocated behaviorism and eventually elaborated the manifesto into a book-length treatise—*Psychology from the Standpoint of a Behaviorist* (Watson, 1919). It was this book and Watson's promotional efforts in the 1920s, more than the earlier manifesto, that were responsible for the increased influence of behaviorism among American psychologists as the 1920s drew to a close (Todd, 1994).

Watson's APA Presidential Address Between the time of the 1913 manifesto and his 1915 APA Presidency, Watson worked hard to provide evidence to support his strong beliefs. As he put it in the opening paragraph of his Presidential address, "it is one thing to condemn a long-established practice, but quite another thing to suggest anything in its place" (Watson, 1916, p. 89). The method that Watson was eager to describe to his peers was the conditioning of two varieties of reflex, salivary and motor. As for the salivary reflex, which Watson appropriately credited to Pavlov, there was the need for surgery and the limitation (at that point) to research in dogs. Hence, Watson thought that the method had "no very wide sphere of usefulness or applicability" with humans (Watson, 1916, p. 93).

The second type of conditioning was of greater interest to Watson because it converged with his interests in measuring directly observable behavior. It was the motor reflex, a form of conditioning pioneered in Russia by the Vladimir Bekhterev, a colleague and rival of Pavlov's. A typical Bekhterev experiment consisted of using a mild electric shock to the heel of a subject's foot produce withdrawal, then pairing the shock with a neutral stimulus (e.g., tone). Soon the tone would produce the withdrawal of the foot. In his Presidential address, Watson (1916) indicated that "our own work has centered around the conditioned motor reflex of [Bekhterev], since we find for his method an immediate and widespread usefulness" (p. 94). Watson then described several experiments on the conditioned motor reflex underway in the Hopkins lab, both with animals and with humans. Watson made much of this research in his 1915 APA address, but it appears that the results were not always clear and that the conditioning procedure was abandoned after little more than a year (Rilling, 2000).

Studying Emotional Development In both his manifesto and Presidential address, Watson made substantial claims about the ability of behaviorism to deliver applications that would improve the quality of human life, based on conditioning. Yet by 1915, with a few exceptions, Watson's own research had been limited to animals. Thus, when an opportunity arose to study infants, Watson saw this as a chance to apply behaviorism in a way that would convince skeptics and secure Watson's position as a leader in the application of psychological principles to improve society. Furthermore, Watson was feeling some of the same pressure felt by other comparative psychologists (e.g., Yerkes), who were finding it increasingly difficult to maintain institutional support for their basic research in animal behavior. University administrators were becoming reluctant to supply budgetary support for research that seemed esoteric, was of little practical value, and required facilities with strong, unpleasant odors (Buckley, 1989).

The opportunity came to Watson in the form of an invitation from psychiatrist Adolf Meyer to set up a human laboratory in Meyer's clinic at the Johns Hopkins Medical School. The new lab was adjacent to the medical school's obstetrical ward, thereby providing Watson with a supply of infants for his research. The result was a series of studies investigating reflexes, basic emotions, and conditioned emotional responses.

The work on basic emotions was coauthored with J. J. B. Morgan. They set out to identify the most fundamental human emotional responses and the stimuli that produced these responses. They identified three: fear, rage, and love. According to Watson and Morgan (1917), the fear response, defined behaviorally as "a sudden catching of the breath, clutching randomly with the hands, ... blinking of the eye lids, puckering of the lips, then crying" (p. 166), occurred in response to either of two classes of stimuli, sudden loud noises (e.g., banging a steel bar with a hammer, right behind the baby's head) or a loss of support (e.g., dropping and then catching the infant). The second emotion, rage, resulted from hindering the infant's movements: "If the face or head is held crying results, quickly followed by screaming. The body stiffens and fairly well coordinated slashing or striking movements of the hands and arms result" (pp. 166–167). The third emotion, love, defined as smiling, gurgling, or cooing, resulted from gently stroking the infant's skin or gently rocking or patting the child.

The Zenith and the Nadir of a Career: Little Albert

From the infant research, Watson concluded that only a few stimuli would elicit the three instinctive emotions of fear, rage, and love. Then why do older children show these emotional responses to a much wider range of stimuli? For Watson, the answer was simple—conditioning. His attempt to demonstrate this produced the well-known Little Albert study. It was published as "Conditioned Emotional Reactions" in the *Journal of Experimental Psychology* in 1920, and it was coauthored by Watson and Rosalie Rayner, a graduate student at Johns Hopkins. As will be seen shortly, she played a pivotal role in another important event for Watson in 1920—his forced resignation from Johns Hopkins.

Watson and Rayner (1920) opened the article by stating their belief that emotional reactions develop through conditioning but that "direct experimental evidence in support of such a view has been lacking" (p. 1). Hence, the goal of their study was to provide just such evidence, using an 11-month old infant, Albert B. Albert was chosen for the study because "[h]e was on the whole stolid and unemotional. His stability was one of the principal reasons for using him as a subject in this test. We felt that we could do him relatively little harm" (pp. 1–2). Watson and Rayner evidently felt some ethical concern over the effect of the experiment on the young boy, but "[w]e decided finally to make the attempt, comforting ourselves by the reflection that such [fears] would arise anyway as soon as the child left the sheltered environment of the nursery for the rough and tumble of the home" (p. 3).

Before the experiment began, Albert was put through a series of tests—the same ones used in Watson's earlier infant research with Morgan. Albert showed no fear when presented "with a white rat, a rabbit, a dog, a monkey, with masks with and without hair, cotton wool, burning newspapers, etc." (p. 2). Unlike other infants, Albert did not show a fear response to the stimulus of a loss of support. Like the others, however, he was afraid of the loud noise produced by striking a metal bar with a hammer behind his head. Watson and Rayner's first session only lasted two trials:

1. White rat suddenly taken from the basket and presented to Albert. He began to reach for rat with left hand. Just as his hand touched the animal the bar was struck immediately behind his head. The infant jumped violently and fell forward, burying his face in the mattress. He did not cry, however.

2. Just as the right hand touched the rat the bar was again struck. Again the infant jumped violently, fell forward and began to whimper.
   In order not to disturb the child too seriously no further tests were given for one week. (Watson & Rayner, 1920, p. 4)

One week later, Albert experienced, in succession, the rat, three trials of the rat combined with the loud noise, the rat alone, two more "joint stimulations," and the rat alone again. One this last trial, this happened:

> Rat alone. *The instant the rat was shown the baby began to cry. Almost instantly he turned sharply to the left, fell over on one side, raised himself on all fours and began to crawl away so rapidly that he was caught with difficulty before reaching the edge of the table.* (p. 5, emphasis in the original)

With Albert now apparently fearful of the rat, Watson and Rayner's second goal was to see if the response would "transfer" to other stimuli (or "generalize," as Pavlov would say). Five days after the famous trials just described, Albert was returned to the lab and tested first with blocks and the rat. He played with the former and continued to avoid the latter. After showing that the conditioned response still existed, Watson and Rayner presented other stimuli, alternating them with occasions for the child to play with his blocks. Albert showed some degree of fear with a rabbit, a dog, and a fur coat. Also, in a trial that suggests Albert's primary fear might have been of the experimenter, Watson "put his head down to see if Albert would play with his hair. Albert was completely negative. Two other observers did the same thing. He began immediately to play with their hair" (Watson & Rayner, 1920, p. 7).

Believing that transfer (generalization) had been demonstrated, Watson and Rayner moved to a third research question: Would the response be retained for a significant period of time? The retention interval was limited to a month by a practical consideration—Albert was about to be removed from the hospital. During the interval, Albert was tested in other ways (e.g., in some research on handedness) and at the end of the month, he was once again shown the rat and some of the other stimuli used for generalization. He again showed fear responses, although they were not as strong as they had been a month earlier. Watson and Rayner (1920) concluded:

> These experiments would seem to show conclusively that directly conditioned emotional responses as well as those conditioned by transfer persist, although with a certain loss in the intensity of the reaction, for a longer period than one month. Our view is that they persist and modify personality throughout life. (pp. 10–12)

In the final section of their paper, Watson and Rayner addressed the question of how Albert's fear might have been alleviated, if additional time had been available. Although they gave the impression that they wished they could have had more time with Albert, it is clear that they knew of his forthcoming departure a month ahead of time and chose to test the persistence of the fear rather than to attempt its reversal. Nonetheless, they did make several suggestions about how the fear might be "unlearned."

> (1) Constantly confronting the child with those stimuli which called out the responses in the hopes that habituation would come in corresponding to "fatigue" of reflex when differential reactions are to be set up. (2) By trying to "recondition" by showing objects calling out fear responses (visual) and simultaneously stimulating the erogenous zones (tactual). We should try first the lips, then the nipples and as a final resort the sex organs. (3) By trying to "recondition" by feeding the subject candy or other food just as the animal is shown. This method calls for the food control of the subject. (4) By building up "constructive" activities around the object by imitation and by putting the hand through the motions of manipulation. (pp. 12–13)

Although Watson and Rayner made no attempt to alleviate Albert's fear, Watson later redeemed himself to some extent by supervising the research of Mary Cover Jones. Watson was by then out of academia and working in advertising (described later in the chapter), but his research with children inspired Jones, a young Columbia graduate student and friend of Rosalie Rayner. Working with several children who feared various objects, Jones (1924a) tried a number of methods, most of them unsuccessful. For example, fears were not reduced (a) simply through the passage of time, (b) through the method of verbal appeal (i.e., trying to convince the child that the fear was groundless), or (c) by having peers ridicule the child. What did work, however, was the third method that had been suggested in the Watson and Rayner paper. In a study often cited as a pioneering example of a behavior therapy technique that became known as **systematic desensitization**, Jones (1924b) reduced a young boy's fear of rabbits by placing the animal at some distance from the boy while he was eating, then gradually moving the rabbit closer. The pleasurable responses associated with eating apparently replaced the fear response associated with the rabbit.

The Little Albert study can be found in the chapters on learning in virtually all modern introductory psychology texts. The study is sometimes described as a "classic," displaying the power of behavioral principles to condition our emotions. If learning is a change in behavior brought about by experience (the typical textbook definition), then the study certainly illustrated learning of some kind. Yet the study had serious flaws. First, there is some question about whether the initial procedure actually produced a strong fear of animals in Albert (Harris, 1979). Films of Albert made by Watson show the infant a bit hesitant about the animals even before testing began; after testing, although he appears to be concerned about the animals, he does not seem to be in a panic. Second, during the start of generalization testing (transfer), his negative reactions were often so weak that they needed to be "freshened up" with additional pairings of the animal with the loud noise. These additional pairings constituted further learning trials, thus rendering the generalization test impossible to interpret. Third, even if one concedes that the child developed a fear, just what he was afraid of is not clear. As mentioned earlier, it is conceivable that Albert became afraid, not of the animals, but of Watson himself. Fourth, it is inappropriate to draw a general conclusion about fear conditioning on the basis of a study using a single baby. Research limited to individual subjects is fine, representing an important tradition in psychological research, but confidence in the generality of results only comes with replication. Yet several attempts to produce conditioned emotional responses in the 1920s and 1930s produced ambiguous results. For instance, English (1929) failed to condition a 14-month old to fear a wooden duck, primarily because the child did not react adversely to the loud noise. Also, Valentine (1930) failed to condition a child to fear opera glasses, but apparently succeeded with a caterpillar. Similarly, Bregman (1934) failed to condition fear to biologically neutral stimuli, including a curtain and some wooden blocks. Both the Valentine and Bregman studies were flawed methodologically, however, making it difficult to determine if replication occurred or not (Todd, 1994).

In summary, the Little Albert study cannot be considered a conclusive demonstration of the widespread applicability of conditioning principles. So why has it become so famous? One reason is political. For behaviorism to become recognized as an important force in American scientific psychology, it needed examples of the power of conditioning. It was one thing for Watson to proclaim behaviorism, but proof was needed. The Little Albert study seemed to fit the bill, and in subsequent descriptions of it by Watson and others sympathetic to behaviorism, the methodological weaknesses were ignored, and it eventually achieved the status of an unambiguous case of "conditioning in action" (Prytula, Oster, & Davis, 1977). A second reason for the study's popularity, related to the first, is that it has a certain dramatic appeal and applicability to one of life's importance tasks—how we raise our children. If their lives can be affected so strikingly by the experiences they encounter, then managing the child's environment becomes an important way to shape the child's future.

Thus, the Little Albert study served the important function of legitimizing the new behavioral approach that within a decade would become a dominant force in American psychology. Watson was not destined to be a major player during that decade of the 1920s, however. The year the Little Albert study was published, 1920, was also the year that Watson was fired from Johns Hopkins.

A New Life in Advertising

While a young bachelor instructor at the University of Chicago, Watson fell in love with Mary Ickes, a student in his introductory psychology class; he eventually married her. As an established experimental psychologist at Johns Hopkins, he had a similar experience with two major differences. This time the student was a graduate student (Rosalie Rayner) rather than an undergraduate; more important, this time Watson was already married—to the same woman who had been that undergraduate some 17 years earlier. The details of this unhappy situation can be found elsewhere (Buckley, 1989). It is enough to say that Watson's love for Rayner led to (a) his highly publicized divorce from Mary Ickes Watson, which featured the publication of love letters written by Watson to Rosalie and discovered by Mary; (b) his forced resignation from Johns Hopkins; and (c) his marriage to Rosalie.[10]

The exile from Johns Hopkins was devastating to Watson. Furthermore, the attendant publicity ruined any chance that he would secure another academic position. Instead, through the intercession of a friend, he joined the J. Walter Thompson advertising agency in New York City. After an apprenticeship, during which Watson served in all departments of the agency, he rose to the position of vice-president within 4 years (Buckley, 1989).

As an advertising executive (Figure 10.8), Watson had the opportunity to put into practice some of his claims about the applicability of behaviorism. For instance, he developed a number of advertising campaigns around themes derived from his research on the three basic emotions of fear, rage, and love. To sell a product to a consumer, Watson suggested, one must "tell him something that will tie [him] up with fear, something that will stir up a mild rage, that will call out an affectionate or love response,

Archives of the History of American Psychology, The Center for the History of Psychology —The University of Akron

FIGURE 10.8 Watson as an advertising executive.

[10]Even Watson's love letters identify him as a behaviorist, only interested in measurable stimuli and responses. An example: "[E]very cell I have is yours, individually and collectively. My total reactions are positive and towards you. So likewise each and every heart reaction" (quoted in Buckley, 1989, p. 112).

or strike at a deep psychological or habit need" (quoted in Buckley, 1989, p. 137). For example, an ad campaign for Johnson & Johnson baby powder sent a message designed to scare young parents into buying the product: If they failed to use baby powder, they risked exposing their children to serious infection. Watson also relied heavily on the use of testimonials by well-known personalities and experts to sell products. The baby powder campaign used testimony by doctors, for example.

Watson brought to his new career the same passion for scientific method that characterized his life in academia. In an autobiographical statement, for example, he claimed that "it can be just as thrilling to watch the growth of a sales curve of a new product as to watch the learning curve of animals or man" (Watson, 1936, p. 280). Indeed, his major contribution to consumer psychology was not the introduction of new advertising techniques—Coon (1994) has shown that he merely adopted strategies in use at the time. Rather, the more lasting impact was his applying scientific thinking to marketing (e.g., using demographic data to target certain consumers) and in the development of training programs and productivity evaluations for sales personnel.

Advertising did not occupy all of Watson's time during the 1920s, however. He lectured on behaviorism in New York at the New School for Social Research, joined the board of directors of Cattell's Psychological Corporation, and renewed his work on infants by supervising research financed through a grant from the Laura Spelman Rockefeller Memorial Fund (Buckley, 1989). The Fund provided $15,000 to Columbia University to continue the research begun at Johns Hopkins, and the experiments funded by the grant included the famous study mentioned earlier by Mary Cover Jones that successfully eliminated a learned fear. Watson also continued writing about behaviorism during the 1920s, securing his reputation as behaviorism's popular voice.

Popularizing Behaviorism

Watson began communicating with the general public early in his academic career, publishing articles in popular magazines (e.g., *Harper's Monthly*) with titles like "The New Science of Animal Behavior" (Watson, 1910). This activity blossomed in the 1920s, with additional magazine articles, radio broadcasts, a highly publicized debate ("The Battle of Behaviorism") in 1924 with British psychologist William McDougall, and two books: *Behaviorism* (1924/1930) and *Psychological Care of Infant and Child* (1928). The former became the most widely known statement of Watson's ideas. It was the book (along with Pavlov's translated lectures) that first interested a young B. F. Skinner in behaviorism. The book included one of Watson's most famous quotations, a reflection of his belief in the importance of the environment in shaping our lives:

> Our conclusion, then, is that we have no real evidence of the inheritance of traits. I would feel perfectly confident in the ultimately favorable outcome of careful upbringing of a healthy, well-formed baby born of a long line of crooks, murderers and thieves, and prostitutes . . . .
>
> I should like to go one step further now and say "Give me a dozen healthy infants, well-formed, and my own specified world to bring them up in and I'll guarantee to take any one at random and train him to become any type of specialist I might select—doctor, lawyer, artist, merchant-chief and, yes, even beggar-man and thief, regardless of his talents, penchants, tendencies, abilities, vocations, and race of his ancestors." (Watson, 1924/1930, pp. 103–104)

Watson admitted that he was going beyond the data in making his "dozen infants" claim, and he was probably overstating the case to contrast his views with those psychologists, including most of the mental testers (Chapter 8), who were promoting the role of inherited traits in individual behavior. Although Watson always recognized the interaction of nature and nurture in the production of behavior, his "dozen infants" quote has become a regular feature of introductory textbooks in psychology, and Watson is routinely portrayed as someone who denied the significance of the nature side of the nature–nurture dichotomy (Todd, 1994).

Watson's reputation as an extreme environmentalist was enhanced by some of the recommendations in his *Psychological Care of Infant and Child* (1928), written "with the assistance of Rosalie Rayner Watson" (frontispiece). The book contains Watson's strongest statements about how the technology of behavior could be brought to bear on that most important of tasks, the raising of children. He dedicated it to "the first mother who brings up a happy child" and began by stating the urgency of the task: Healthy babies can overcome the short-term effects of physiological deprivation, but "once a child's character has been spoiled by bad handling which can be done in a few days, who can say that the damage is ever repaired?" (p. 3).

Although Morris and Bigelow (2007) have shown that most of the recommendations in the book were innocuous and in line with other contemporary guides to raising children (e.g., avoiding physical punishment), one part of the book quickly became controversial. In a chapter entitled "The Dangers of Too Much Mother Love," Watson warned against being overly affectionate with children. The result would be "invalidism"—a failure of the child to become responsible, independent, and ultimately successful in life. He warned that there were "serious rocks ahead for the over-kissed child" (p. 71). What to do instead?

> There is a sensible way of treating children. Treat them as though they were young adults. Dress them, bathe them with care and circumspection. Let your behavior always be objective and kindly firm. Never hug or kiss them, never let them sit in your lap. If you must, kiss them once on the forehead when they say goodnight. Shake hands with them in the morning. Give them a pat on the head if they have made an extraordinarily good job of a difficult task. Try it out. In a week's time you will find how easy it is to be perfectly objective with your child and at the same time kindly. You will be utterly ashamed of the mawkish, sentimental way you have been handling it. (Watson, 1928, pp. 81–82)

Watson (1936) later said that he regretted writing the child-rearing book, that it was not sufficiently supported by data. Yet it stands as a perfect example of the faith that he had in the ability of behaviorism to affect daily living. More broadly, it illustrates the positivist belief that understanding and control go hand in hand.[11]

Evaluating Watsonian Behaviorism

In a certain sense, Watsonian behaviorism was a magnificent failure. The grand scheme of being able to predict all responses, given the stimulus, was never realized. Most of Watson's proclamations went far beyond the available empirical evidence—the data never caught up with the excessive claims. What, then, was the impact of Watson's system?

Watson's lasting importance for psychology derives from his propagandizing on behalf of his strong beliefs. As mentioned earlier, behaviorism certainly did not take hold immediately. Indeed, the initial reaction in academia was decidedly mixed. But Watson's forceful and repeated arguments started a process that by the mid-1930s brought behaviorism to the center of American experimental psychology. Thus, he deserves the title "founder" of behaviorism.

Second, by attacking introspective psychology directly and exposing its Achilles' heel, its lack of objectivity, Watson contributed to the gradual shift from psychology as the study of immediate

---

[11] In the opening paragraph of this chapter, Watson described how a woman approached him after hearing him lecture, saying to him, "Thank God, my children are grown—and that I had the chance to enjoy them before I met you" (Watson, 1928, p. 69).

conscious experience to psychology as the study of behavior. By making observable and measurable behavior the dependent variable, rather than an introspective report, Watson ultimately helped place the field of psychology on firmer scientific ground.

Third, Watson's popularity with the general public suggests that his ideas struck a responsive chord with Americans. His belief that the environment could be arranged to shape someone's future development was consistent with the American ideal that through proper child rearing and education, people could aspire to any goal. It was an especially appealing message in the 1920s, a time of prosperity in America and a time when average Americans were optimistic about their futures and had no comprehension that the Great Depression of the 1930s was just around the corner. Watson himself was a living example of this attitude, a poor farm boy who rose to the top of his profession twice—once in psychology and again in the business world. This message was much more inviting for average Americans than the one they were receiving from the mental testers. As you recall from Chapter 8, Terman and others were agitating for a meritocracy based on an IQ that was assumed to be largely innate.

Finally, Watson's behaviorism effectively bridged the gap between basic and applied psychology. Laboratory work in areas like conditioning and maze learning gradually became scientifically rigorous, thereby fulfilling the promise of a scientific psychology. At the same time, the possibilities for application, repeatedly stressed by Watson, also bore fruit as behaviorist ideas eventually influenced child rearing, education, industry, and even psychotherapy.

And what of Watson himself? His productivity as an advertising executive and as a popularizer of psychology declined precipitously in 1935 with the sudden death of Rosalie, the great love of his life (Figure 10.9). In that same year, he left J. Walter Thompson for a similar position with the William Esty Company and retired 10 years later. In his remaining years he became increasingly reclusive. In 1957, a year before his death, the American Psychological Association honored Watson at their annual convention, and although he traveled to the meeting in New York from his home in Connecticut, he

Courtesy of James B. Watson as published in: Kerry W. Buckley 1989, Mechanical Man: John Broadus Watson and the Beginnings of Behaviorism, New York: The Guilford Press

FIGURE 10.9 Watson and Rayner in happy times, 1930.

backed out at the last moment and did not attend the ceremony, sending his son in his place. According to his biographer, "Watson was afraid that in that moment his emotions would overwhelm him, that the apostle of behavior control would break down and weep" (Buckley, 1989, p. 182).

IN PERSPECTIVE: BEHAVIORISM'S ORIGINS

In Chapter 1's discussion of old versus new history, I introduced the concept of an *eponym*. Boring described these as historical periods or movements with labels referring to the names of people whose impact is thought to have had a determining influence on history—Darwinian biology would be an example. In an article entitled "Eponym as Placebo," Boring (1963a) cautioned that overusing eponyms might lead us to oversimplify history by ignoring the importance of the Zeitgeist. He argued that eponyms occur frequently, in part because we have limited cognitive abilities. History is enormously complex, so, for example, attributing crucial events in the 19th century to Darwinism simplifies matters cognitively, bringing "the historical subject matter within the range of comprehension and memory" (p. 21). The danger, of course, is that eponymy "magnifies those persons who are found above the threshold and diminishes those below it" (p. 24).

For the writer of a history of psychology text (me), there is a special challenge, especially in chapters like this one (and in Chapter 5, for instance, which has an eponymous title). Pavlov and Watson are unquestionably important in psychology's history, and psychology students cannot take a history course without learning about their work. Yet there is a danger that the student will leave the history course with some general understanding of "Pavlovian conditioning" or "Watsonian behaviorism" and little else about the roots and early development of behaviorist thinking. My hope is that after reading this chapter, and perhaps after hearing about the issue some more from your instructor, you will emerge from this chapter (and others) with an appreciation for the complexity of history and an understanding that historical context is inevitably intertwined with biography. Yes, Pavlov was a crucial figure, but the support of his work by the Soviets, hoping to reshape human behavior to their Communist ideal, made some of his work possible. Yes, Pavlov was initially skeptical of the Soviets, but his ultimate accommodation (and hence the continuance of his work) requires knowing about how Russians historically distrusted and feared Germans. Yes, Watson was a charismatic figure, but he also came along at a time when the problems with introspection were evident to an increasing number of psychologists, and his ideas found a receptive audience in a country where pragmatism ("What good is this?") was a value taken for granted and where the idea that the environment was an important force (anyone could become president) was part of the national psyche. Biography is important to history, but history transcends biography.

SUMMARY

Moving Toward Greater Objectivity

• Prior to Watson, many psychologists were becoming concerned about the objectivity of their measures. One influence was evolutionary theory, which led to the study of animal behavior. Studying animals meant developing behavioral measures, and American psychologists did just that (e.g., Thorndike's puzzle box studies).

• The philosophies of empiricism and associationism, which both emphasize the importance of experience, provided a foundation for behavioral thinking. Positivism, with its argument that inductive, systematic observation is the only path to valid knowledge, also contributed.

• Many psychologists became interested in objective measures because they were becoming increasingly critical of introspection.

Pavlov's Life and Work

• Pavlov thought of himself more as a physiologist than psychologist, and his 1904 Nobel Prize was for research on the physiology of digestion. He was especially known for developing surgical procedures (e.g., the Pavlov pouch) that allowed the digestive processes of live, intact animals to be studied.

• Pavlov's work on conditioning developed out of the digestion research, when he decided to investigate why his dogs would often salivate before food reached their mouths. He investigated a large number of conditioning phenomena, including acquisition, extinction, generalization, differentiation, and experimental neurosis (a breakdown in the ability to differentiate stimuli). He interpreted these phenomena in terms of the reciprocal brain processes of excitation and inhibition.

• Although initially hostile to the Soviet government, Pavlov accommodated when the threat from Nazi Germany developed. The Soviets saw Pavlovian conditioning as a foundation for shaping the modern communist citizen; consequently, the government heavily subsidized Pavlov's research.

• Pavlov's work was generally known to American psychologists from the early years of the 20th century, but not widely known and appreciated until his research was translated into English in the 1920s.

John B. Watson and the Founding of Behaviorism

• Watson was trained at the functionalist University of Chicago, where he developed a dislike for introspection and a love of animal research. His dissertation on the relationship between cortical development and the learning abilities of rats was followed by several important studies on how rats learned mazes by relying on their kinesthetic sense.

• After teaching at Chicago for several years following his doctorate, Watson moved to Johns Hopkins in 1908, where he stayed until 1920. His 1913 "Behaviorist Manifesto" proclaimed that introspective psychology, inherently subjective, should be replaced by a more objective behavioral psychology that specified the relationships between stimuli and responses. In his APA presidential address (1915), he showed how behaviors could be conditioned.

• In his final years at Johns Hopkins, Watson studied newborns and young children, especially their emotional development. He argued that fear, rage, and love were the fundamental emotions, each resulting from specific stimuli. More elaborate emotional responses resulted from conditioning.

• Watson attempted to demonstrate the conditioning of emotional responses in the Little Albert experiment. By pairing a loud noise with a white rat, Watson and Rayner apparently created a fear of the latter. The fear generalized to similar stimuli (e.g., rabbits) and lasted at least a month. Later, Mary Cover Jones (with Watson as consultant) demonstrated that fears could be unlearned.

• Watson spent his final professional years as an advertising executive, applying behavioral principles to marketing. During this time, he also became a popularizer of behaviorist philosophy, especially in the area of child rearing.

STUDY QUESTIONS

1. What are the similarities between John Locke's empiricist ideas and John Watson's behaviorist ideas?

2. What was positivism, and what was its significance for American psychology?

3. What was the influence of comparative psychology on the development of behaviorist thinking?

4. While being trained for the ministry, what influenced Pavlov to switch to science?

5. Describe the work that won Pavlov the Nobel Prize.

6. Describe the operation and organization of Pavlov's lab.

7. How did Pavlov demonstrate the basic phenomena of conditioning, extinction, generalization, and differentiation?

8. What did Pavlov mean by experimental neurosis, and how did he demonstrate its existence?

9. Explain why Pavlov's ideas were valued by the Soviets, and explain why Pavlov initially disliked the Soviets, but later made an accommodation.

10. How were Pavlov's ideas made known to American psychologists, and what was Pavlov's influence on American psychology?

11. What is the important point made about historiography made in the chapter's Close-Up?

12. Describe the factors that turned Watson into a behaviorist while at Chicago.

13. Describe the Watson/Carr maze studies from the standpoint of (a) methodology and (b) ethics.

14. In the Behaviorist Manifesto, what was the nature of Watson's criticism of structuralism and functionalism, and what did he propose instead?

15. In his manifesto, Watson described what could be called an S-R approach to psychology. Explain.

16. Describe how Watson determined that three fundamental emotions existed. What were the emotions, and what stimuli elicited them?

17. Describe and critically analyze the Little Albert study.

18. Watson and Rayner didn't even try to remove Albert's fear, but Jones showed that fear could be removed. How did she do it?

19. Describe how Watson influenced the world of advertising.

20. Describe a Watsonian approach to parenting.

CHAPTER 11

THE EVOLUTION OF BEHAVIORISM

> I believe that everything important in psychology ... can be investigated in essence through the continued experimental and theoretical analysis of the determiners of rat behavior at a choice-point in a maze.
>
> —Edward Chace Tolman, 1938a

PREVIEW AND CHAPTER OBJECTIVES

This chapter continues to describe the development of behaviorist thinking by focusing on the work of four psychologists (among many) who followed in Watson's footsteps—Edwin Guthrie, Edward Tolman, Clark Hull, and B. F. Skinner. But first it opens by examining the fate of Watsonian behaviorism and describes several trends (e.g., operationism) that prepared the way for behaviorism's rise in the 1930s. You will also learn, however, that not all prominent American psychologists were behaviorists during this time, and that behaviorism was largely an American phenomenon.

The learning theories to be considered here differed from each other substantially— concerning the definition and role of reinforcement in learning, for instance. All were grounded in research using animals as subjects, however, and all focused their research efforts on discovering the essential laws of learning/conditioning. Although not discounting the importance of biological factors, the neobehaviorists, in the tradition of the British empiricists, believed that understanding human action largely meant discovering how life's experiences (i.e., conditioning history) shaped the individual. After you finish this chapter, you should be able to:

- Distinguish between the myth of the behaviorist revolution and what really happened between Watson's 1913 manifesto and behaviorism's rise in the 1930s
- Describe how the relationship between logical positivism and operationism paved the way for the theorizing of the neobehaviorists Tolman and Hull
- Describe the beliefs held in common by neobehaviorists
- Explain why Guthrie's theory is the most parsimonious of those considered in the chapter
- Describe Guthrie's ideas for breaking bad habits and forming new ones
- Describe the major features of Tolman's theory of learning
- Describe and explain the significance of Tolman's research on latent learning, place learning, and cognitive maps
- Describe Hull's contributions to psychology prior to the development of his learning theory
- Describe the major features of Hull's hypothetico-deductive theory of learning, especially postulate number 4
- Describe how Skinner's approach to psychology differed from those of Guthrie, Tolman, and Hull

■ Describe the essential components of an experimental analysis of behavior, according to Skinner

■ Describe the work of the Brelands, which showed that operant conditioning could be profitable, but also showed that it had its (biological) limits

■ Evaluate the influence of neobehaviorism on the history of psychology

POST-WATSONIAN BEHAVIORISM

Traditional accounts of psychology's history often refer to Watsonian behaviorism as revolutionary. The bedtime story goes something like this: Before Watson, there was the darkness of introspective psychology. Because of its intensely subjective nature, introspectionism prevented psychology from being a truly "objective" science. Then came the mythical hero—Watson and his 1913 "Behaviorist Manifesto." Except for a few narrow-minded holdouts, psychologists everywhere saw the light, and psychology dramatically changed from the quasi science of consciousness to the true science of behavior. After Watson, behaviorism quickly became the only serious way of thinking among experimental psychologists. It is a dramatic plot, but not what happened. The actual story is infinitely more complex and considerably at odds with the origin myth.

As mentioned in the previous chapter, Watson's behaviorism did not catch on immediately, and the initial response to his 1913 manifesto was most likely to have been indifference, criticism, or "here's just another critique of introspection" (Samelson, 1981). Most American psychologists simply went about their business: if they were interested in attention, they continued to study it by combining cognitive tasks with introspection; if they were interested in the visual system, they continued to study phenomena like visual afterimages and illusions; if they were interested in comparative psychology, they continued to study animal behavior. After World War I, as we have seen, many psychologists became interested in mental testing and other areas of "applied" psychology. Furthermore, nonbehavioral approaches to psychology did not simply disappear after Watson's manifesto and during the 1920s. At least a dozen varieties of psychology were examined in Carl Murchison's *Psychologies of 1925* (Murchison, 1926) and *Psychologies of 1930* (Murchison, 1930), and gestalt psychology (Chapter 9) attracted considerable attention. As late as 1931, Robert Woodworth's widely read *Contemporary Schools of Psychology* preceded the chapter on behaviorism with one on introspective psychology, and included chapters on gestalt psychology, Freudian psychoanalysis, and "hormic" (i.e., focused on instincts) psychology. Woodworth (1931) correctly predicted that after 50 years, historians would assign much significance to the behaviorist movement, but he was "puzzled to guess exactly where [the historians] will find its significance to lie" (p. 89). He granted that behaviorism had an appeal to some of the younger psychologists, but he also pointed out that advocating objective methods was not unique to Watson, and that despite his arguments, introspective studies were still being carried out.

Beginning in the decade of the 1930s, however, behaviorism did begin to take hold in American experimental psychology. Watson played a role, especially with his consistent proselytizing on behalf of behaviorism, even after leaving academia. During the 1920s, his child-rearing advice, his numerous articles in popular magazines, and his *Behaviorism* (1924/1930), although "not one of his most scientific books from the psychologist's point of view" (Woodworth, 1931, p. 91), made great claims about shaping future generations during a decade of great optimism in America. In the so-called Roaring Twenties, the United States had emerged from World War I as a new world power, and it was not until the end of the decade that its confidence was shaken by the stock market crash that brought on the Great Depression. The *New York Times* said Watson's *Behaviorism* "marks an epoch in the intellectual history of man" (quoted in Woodworth, 1931, p. 92). Woodworth believed that behaviorism's significance would lie primarily in its appeal to those who believed that science could be used to improve the common good. To some extent, then, the development of behaviorism as a force in American psychology derived from an optimistic public's belief that a way had been found to raise their children efficiently; to improve their marriages, their businesses and their education; and in general to help them lead more productive lives.

Public enthusiasm for behaviorism cannot account for the whole story of its rise to power, however. Other events in the 1920s played important roles in bringing behaviorism to the forefront of American psychology. First, as pointed out in Chapter 10, Pavlov's conditioning research was translated into English for the first time. Americans knew about Pavlov, but before the 1920s, most experimental psychologists had little idea about the scope of his work, its precision, and its implications. If American psychologists were looking for a model of a systematic research program focusing on overt, measurable behavior, this was it.

Another event that paved the way for behaviorism was the publication of a book by a Harvard physicist. In *The Logic of Modern Physics* (1927), Percy Bridgman introduced American psychologists to operationism. Along with its close relation, logical positivism, operationism provided the intellectual foundation for neobehaviorism.

Logical Positivism and Operationism

Operationism appeared at about the same time a small group of philosophers, mathematicians, and scientists began meeting Thursday evenings in a Viennese coffeehouse to discuss the logic and philosophy of science. Known as the Vienna Circle, they promoted a version of positivist thinking that came to be known as **logical positivism** (Gillies, 1993). Since the 19th century, positivists had taken a strictly empiricist stance, maintaining that certain knowledge about natural phenomena could only result from the public observation of measurable events. This philosophy suited Watson just fine because it was consistent with his belief that psychology ought to be the study of observable behavior rather than subjective introspections. The difficulty was that even by focusing on observables, it is difficult if not impossible to avoid discussing unobservable concepts when developing a theory. For example, if you believe that human behavior can be motivated by the need to reduce a strong drive such as hunger, you are forced to address the question of just what is meant by hunger. Yet hunger is an unobservable event, seemingly limited to introspection ("my stomach just feels empty and I feel a bit light-headed"). The logical positivists, dealing with this problem in the context of physics—magnetism or gravity as forces also are not observed directly—resolved the issue to their satisfaction by distinguishing between observable and theoretical events and insisting that the two be closely tied to each other. Specifically, they allowed abstract concepts into a scientific theory, as long as these concepts were closely tied to observable events. Thus magnetism could be proposed as a theoretical force having specific properties if certain objects (e.g., metal filings) behaved in a predictable fashion and could be observed and measured objectively. Similarly, hunger could be used in a theory of motivation if it could be tied to observable behaviors. Operationism provided the link.

The essential idea of **operationism** was that scientific concepts were to be defined, not in absolute terms, but with reference to the operations used to measure them. The concept of length, for instance, would be defined by agreed-upon procedures. As Bridgman put it, in his *The Logic of Modern Physics* (1927), the "concept of length is … fixed when the operations by which length is measured are fixed; that is, the concept of length involves as much as and nothing more than a set of operations" (p. 5). Bridgman also discussed what he called *pseudoproblems*, questions that might be interesting, but were unanswerable by means of scientific observations. Whether or not time has a beginning or an end is an example.

A Harvard colleague of Bridgman's, experimental psychologist S. S. Stevens, was the most vocal promoter of operationism within psychology. Stevens was a doctoral student of E. G. Boring in the early 1930s and became the best-known 20th-century researcher in psychophysics. He also developed a way of classifying measurement scales (nominal, ordinal, interval, ratio) recognized by those who have survived a statistics course. His 1935 paper, "The Operational Definition of Concepts," was the first of several attempts to convince psychologists to adopt an operational strategy. For Stevens, operationism provided an answer to the problem confronted by the logical positivists—how to define scientific concepts that could not be observed directly. By using **operational definitions**, that is, definitions involving precise descriptions of procedures for measurement and for specifying the variables in an experiment, psychologists could study such seemingly invisible concepts as hunger, anxiety, and aggression, while remaining faithful to the dictates of a positivist philosophy. Researchers could now define a motivational state like hunger or a perceptual quality like loudness in terms of the set of operations that were assumed to bring them about. Thus, hunger could be defined as the outcome of a certain number of hours without food, perceived loudness could be defined as a series of discriminations of quantitatively different tones made by research participants, and so on.

Stevens also saw the relevance of Bridgman's pseudoproblems for experimental psychology. One of Bridgman's examples was the problem of whether person A's sensation of blue is the same as person B's sensation of blue. That can never be known for certain—the issue is a pseudoproblem. All that can be done is to determine if two persons make similar discriminations to a series of visual stimuli of measurable wavelengths. Thus, one outcome of operational thinking was to raise additional questions about the validity of introspective observations and to argue that they should be replaced with behavioral observations (i.e., discriminations between stimuli).

Operational definitions continue to be widely used among psychological scientists today, a fact known to every student who has taken a research methods course, but a rigid operationism did not last long in psychology. Bridgman's original conception of the operational definition is that the meaning of a concept does not go beyond the operations used to measure it (Green, 1992). Thus, hunger is *nothing more than* 24 hours without food. The problem was that researchers often disagreed on the "best" operational definition of a term. The idea that one definition could be better than another necessarily meant that researchers believed that the meaning of terms like hunger went beyond a mere set of operations (a belief not shared by Brigman). To complicate matters further, many of psychology's concepts resisted simple operational definitions. For instance, researchers studying aggression created operational definitions ranging from the delivery of shocks from one subject to another to horn honking among drivers at intersections. Is aggression being studied in both examples? Do widely different measures of a phenomenon measure the same thing? A strict operationist would have to argue that different operations measure different phenomena. Consequently, either all researchers would have to agree on a single definition of aggression, or all would have to agree that they are investigating different phenomena when using different measures.

Hilgard (1987) argued that the effect of operationism in psychology was simply to force experimental psychologists to define their terms more precisely. The chief advantage is *replication*. If terms are defined clearly enough, other researchers can repeat a particular study. Successful replications produce increased confidence in some research outcome; unsuccessful replications generate additional research to clear up the inconsistency. Furthermore, if researchers using slightly different operational definitions of terms nonetheless produce the same outcome (e.g., frustration tends to be followed by aggression), the generality of the outcome is increased. The phrase **converging operations** refers to this idea that our understanding of some psychological phenomenon is enhanced when several studies, each using different operational definitions, "converge" on the same basic conclusion. According to Hilgard, metaphysical arguments over the "real" meaning of phenomena in the world could be left to philosophers. Thus, he contended that the debate over the merits of operationism, and its philosophical cousin, logical positivism, was largely ignored by psychologists. For them, the take-home message was simply that variables needed to be defined carefully.

Neobehaviorism

Public enthusiasm for the promise of behaviorism, recognition of the importance of Pavlov's long series of conditioning studies, and the general acceptance of operationism and logical positivism, along with the emergence of several hard-working and highly creative experimental psychologists, converged in the late 1920s and early 1930s to produce a movement in psychology called **neobehaviorism**. The movement lasted roughly from 1930 to 1960.

Neobehaviorism was not a unified school of thought by any means; large differences existed among the psychologists that you are about to study. Nonetheless, there was a certain consensus among the neobehaviorists. First, all the neobehaviorists took for granted the evolutionary assumption of continuity among species. Laws of behavior that apply to one species should apply, at least to a degree that can be calibrated, to other species as well. Consequently, phenomena relevant for human behavior could be examined by using nonhuman subjects in research. Furthermore, Woodworth's famous text, the "Columbia bible" (Chapter 7), contributed to the increase in studies of animal behavior (Winston, 1990). Using the experimental method required having strict control over the variables of the study, often making animal studies more ethically and practically feasible than human studies. Thus, 24 hours without food, in a study of the effect of hunger on learning, is acceptable with rats but not with children. In experimental psychology, then, there was a substantial increase in the use of animal subjects for basic research on learning/conditioning during the period 1930–1960. Although said partly tongue-in-cheek during his APA presidential address, Edward Tolman's comment—"I believe that everything important in psychology ... can be investigated in essence through the continued experimental and theoretical analysis of the determiners of rat behavior at a choice-point in a maze" (Tolman, 1938a, p. 34)—reflected the neobehaviorist faith in the lessons to be learned by studying animal behavior. Tolman (1932) even dedicated his most important book to "M.N.A." (Mus Norvegicus Albinus—the white rat), and his bookplate further reflected his passion for animal research (Figure 11.1).

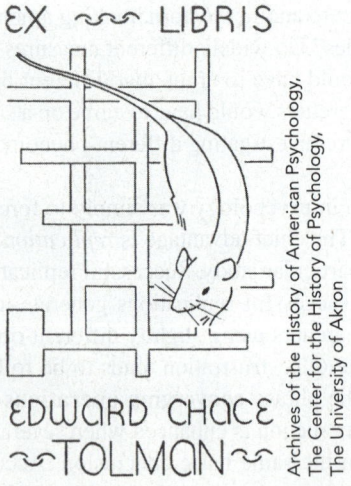

Archives of the History of American Psychology, The Center for the History of Psychology, The University of Akron

FIGURE 11.1 Tolman's bookplate.

The second belief held in common by neobehaviorists was that learning was central to understanding behavior. In simple terms, neobehaviorists leaned heavily toward the nurture end of the nature–nurture continuum, arguing that knowing why people do what they do requires a thorough analysis of the basic principles of how things are learned. This, of course, was one of Watson's guiding principles and the motivation for the Little Albert experiment. The emphasis on learning also provided a bridge between behaviorism and British empiricist thought. When John Locke resurrected the Aristotelian concept of the mind as a blank slate and proclaimed that "experience" was the writer, he was arguing the same point made by Watson when he claimed that fears were the result of learning. For the neobehaviorists, the world in which we live, that is, the environment, shapes our characteristic ways of behaving.

An emphasis on learning was also consistent with American psychology's fixation on practical applications. Watson's appeal with the general public was a result of his genius in showing how the principles of learning could be applied to improve education, child rearing, and sales figures. If we are what we learn, and if learning is the result of specific experiences in certain environments, then by arranging environments in certain ways, behavior can be shaped in any number of productive directions.

It is one thing to herald the importance of learning; it is quite another to know precisely how such learning comes about. Thus, during the era of neobehaviorism, the focus of research and theory was on the manner in which learning occurred. This fundamental issue produced the sharpest divisions among the neobehaviorists, but eventually yielded important knowledge about a variety of learning phenomena. We will examine the ideas of four prominent neobehaviorists: Guthrie, Tolman, Hull, and Skinner.

EDWIN R. GUTHRIE (1886–1959): CONTIGUITY, CONTIGUITY, CONTIGUITY

Perhaps reflecting his training in philosophy, which resulted in a PhD from the University of Pennsylvania in 1912, Edwin Guthrie's (Figure 11.2) professional focus in psychology was always on theory rather than research. In fact, he only produced one substantial research study, a study of escape behavior in cats (Guthrie & Horton, 1946). More on that study shortly. He spent his entire academic career at the University of Washington, starting in the philosophy department, switching to psychology, and finishing as Dean of the Graduate School.

Guthrie developed his learning theory in the 1930s and described it in a handful of papers and in his major work, *The Psychology of Learning* (Guthrie, 1935). The book is remarkable for its readability, its reliance on interesting and pertinent anecdotes to make theoretical points, its "penchant for the interjection of an irreverent brand of humor" (Sheffield, 1959, p. 647), and its virtual absence of empirical evidence. Guthrie's learning theory has a deceptive simplicity to it, based on one overriding principle, with many creative applications to a wide range of conditioning phenomena.

The central principle in Guthrie's theory is the old British empiricist concept of *contiguity*—the experiencing of things together. You might recall from Chapter 2 that contiguity was Hartley's principal way of accounting for the formation of associations. For Guthrie, contiguity was the foundation stone for conditioning. As he put it: "*A combination of stimuli which has accompanied a movement will on its recurrence tend to be followed by that movement*" (Guthrie, 1935, p. 26, emphasis in the original). That's it—if a stimulus is followed by a movement, the movement will be likely to occur again the next time the stimulus occurs. The stimulus and the movement have occurred contiguously, and that is all that is needed. It might seem to you that conditioning must be more complicated than this, an opinion shared by Guthrie's critics. Yet based on this one principle, Guthrie was able to build a coherent theory.

Courtesy of Pamela Guthrie

FIGURE 11.2   Learning theorist Edwin R. Guthrie (1886–1959).

One-Trial Learning

As mentioned earlier, Guthrie did not spend much time collecting data, but he believed the study he completed with Horton provided strong support for his basic idea. In that study, Guthrie and Horton (1946) studied cats as they escaped from a simple puzzle box. The box had clear glass walls and a pole in the middle of it. Tilting the pole opened the box, allowing escape. Any movement of the cat against the pole would trigger both the escape door and a camera. Figure 11.3 shows a sketch made from one of the photo sets. In it, cat "K" is shown hitting the pole with its rear haunch, an action that freed it. Thus, a connection was made between the stimulus, the pole as seen from a specific angle by the cat,

K9   K10   K11   K12

FIGURE 11.3   Four consecutive escapes by one of Guthrie and Horton's cats, from Guthrie and Horton (1946).

and a response, pushing against the pole. When returned to the box, the cat performed the same act to escape again. Learning had occurred, and it apparently happened in a single trial, the first time the cat pushed against the pole with its haunch.

Guthrie, then, believed that contiguity was both necessary and sufficient for learning to occur, and that S-R connections were made at full strength in just one trial. But how did he account for the fact that skilled behaviors require considerable practice (i.e., lots of trials)? The answer, argued Guthrie, comes from a distinction between movements and acts. Movements are simple muscular events that are connected in single trials to stimuli by contiguity. Acts, on the other hand, are complex sets of movements that eventually constitute a skill. Thus, learning a skill takes time and practice because there are a large number of S-R movements that make up that skill.

Guthrie's theory led him to some unorthodox ideas about such concepts as reinforcement, punishment, and forgetting, and it produced some interesting suggestions for breaking bad habits. We shall see shortly that reinforcement was central to some learning theorists (e.g., Hull, Skinner), but for Guthrie, the only function served by a reward was to change the stimulus situation, thereby preserving an S-R connection. Thus, when his cats were "rewarded" by getting out of the box, the "being out of the box" was a new stimulus situation, to be connected with new responses; the key S-R connection of "see the pole—hit the pole" was preserved. Punishment, Guthrie argued, worked because it encouraged new responses, not because of the pain of the punishment itself. For instance, "to train a dog to jump through a hoop, the effectiveness of the punishment depends on where it is applied, front or rear. It is what the punishment makes the animal do that counts, … not what it makes him feel" (Guthrie, 1935, p. 158). As for forgetting, Guthrie believed that memories never faded away; instead, all forgetting involved new learning. Hence, the professor who forgets student names does not have a leaky brain; it is just that those names were learned in a classroom situation, and the following semester's classroom produces new students and new names. On the other hand, if the stimuli in a set of S-R connections are not experienced for a long time, forgetting won't occur. Guthrie would say that is why we don't forget how to swim, even if it has been years since we have been in the water. Guthrie's advice on how to break bad habits was based on the idea that habits are behaviors that occur in response to a wide range of stimuli. The key to breaking a bad habit is to identify all the stimuli that elicit the habit and substitute new responses to those stimuli. Hence, the smoker has developed, over the years, a large number of stimuli that have led to smoking behavior. Breaking the habit, according to Guthrie simply meant identifying all those stimuli producing the bad behavior (e.g., morning coffee prompting a cigarette) and doing something else instead (e.g., morning coffee prompting eating a piece of fruit).

Evaluating Guthrie

There is appeal in simplicity, and Guthrie's theory certainly meets that criterion. It is perhaps for that reason that the theory was the starting point for several mathematical models of learning. And certain aspects of the theory "make sense"—why we never forget how to swim, for instance. On the other hand, simplicity sometimes overlooks necessary complexity (e.g., the biology of nicotine addiction). Also, critics argued that Guthrie's definitions were often vague. Hilgard (1948), for instance, argued that Guthrie's preference for everyday examples to illustrate his theory resulted in a failure to define the theory's most essential terms (e.g., stimulus and response), making it difficult to develop a systematic program of research. As pointed out earlier, Guthrie himself completed virtually no research. Furthermore, the one experiment associated with him, the Guthrie and Horton (1946) study, has been criticized for ignoring explanations based on instinct. Rubbing against the pole looks suspiciously similar to a cat's species specific behavior of "flank rubbing," a greeting and marking behavior well known to cat owners. Moore and Stuttard (1979) found that the Guthrie and Horton result replicated when human observers were close to the puzzle box, but failed to replicate in the absence of observers.

EDWARD C. TOLMAN (1886–1959): A PURPOSIVE BEHAVIORISM

Edward Chace Tolman was born into an upper-middle-class environment near Boston. As a youth, he learned the virtues of perseverance and hard work from his father, a successful business executive, and the need for a reflective life with a strong moral foundation from his mother, a Quaker. He graduated from the Massachusetts Institute of Technology (MIT) in 1911 with a degree in electrochemistry, but did not pursue a career in this field, apparently to avoid competing with his talented older brother (Crutchfield, 1961). Richard Tolman became a well-known physicist who contributed to the development of the atomic bomb during World War II. Another reason for Edward's shift away from physics and chemistry was his discovery of William James (who else?) during his senior year. *The Principles* gave Tolman's life a new direction.

After graduating from MIT, Tolman enrolled in two summer classes at Harvard, a philosophy course and an introductory psychology course taught by Robert Yerkes. Yerkes sold him for good on psychology, and he entered graduate school at Harvard, earning his doctorate in 1915. While taking a second course from Yerkes, he worked his way through Watson's *Behavior: An Introduction to Comparative Psychology* (1914). Although he did not become immediately converted to the behaviorist point of view, Tolman saw behaviorism as an attractive alternative to the traditional introspective psychology he was struggling with in Hugo Münsterberg's laboratory. As he later put it, he was troubled by the problems with introspection, and the "introduction in Yerkes' course to Watson's behaviorism came as a tremendous stimulus and relief" (Tolman, 1952, p. 326). During his graduate school years, while visiting Germany to prepare for his foreign language competency examination, Tolman met Kurt Koffka and was introduced to gestalt psychology. The gestalt concept of "wholes" would come to play an important role in his version of neobehaviorism. (Figure 11.4 shows Tolman with Lewin and Koffka at a 1935 meeting of Lewin's Topology Group.) A final important influence on Tolman during his Harvard years was another of his teachers, psychologist Edwin Holt (1873–1946), whose leanings toward behaviorism were infused with the notions of goals and purpose. Holt believed that Watsonian behaviorism was too reductionistic, that behavior could not be meaningfully reduced to simple physical stimuli and muscular or glandular responses. He argued instead that behavior should be defined more broadly as actions that serve some purpose. That is, behavior is goal directed. These ideas would become the core of Tolman's theory of learning.

Tolman taught for 3 years at Northwestern University during the World War I years. He was dismissed in 1918, allegedly for a lack of teaching skills, but more likely because of his visible antiwar stance (Tolman, 1952). It would not be the only time that his moral convictions, reflecting his mother's Quaker influence, would affect his career.

Tolman joined the faculty at Berkeley in 1918 and remained there for the rest of his academic career. When given an opportunity to develop a new course shortly after his arrival, he remembered "Yerkes' course and Watson's textbook [and] proposed 'comparative psychology.' And it was this that finally launched [him] down the behavioristic slope" (Tolman, 1952, p. 329). The course led to some

FIGURE 11.4 Tolman (center) at a meeting of the Topology group in 1935, with Lewin (left) and Koffka, from Marrow (1969).

research in animal maze learning, and Tolman was soon attracting talented graduate students to his lab. He began developing his unique form of behaviorism in the early 1920s, publishing articles with titles like "A New Formula for Behaviorism" (Tolman, 1922). His major work, *Purposive Behavior in Animals and Men*, appeared in 1932. For the remainder of his career at Berkeley, Tolman continued to develop and revise his system and to generate research support for it.

Tolman's System

Tolman's writings illustrate the complex interplay between empirical research and theorizing in the tradition of logical positivism. A theory makes testable predictions that lead to research, the outcome of which supports or reshapes the theory, which leads to more research, and so on. Because such theories evolve as a consequence of research outcomes, Tolman's theory of learning changed with time, but there are some constant themes in Tolman's writings.

Molar versus Molecular Behavior

Taking cues from his gestalt friends, Tolman argued that the unit of study had to be larger than the "molecular" muscle movements or glandular responses emphasized by Watson (and Guthrie). One of Tolman's students, for example, showed that rats taught to swim through a maze were later able to run through it accurately (Macfarlane, 1930). Hence, what was learned could not be simply a series of individual muscle responses to specific stimuli. Rather, the animal must come to some general understanding of the pattern of the maze. As a gestaltist would say, the whole behavior is more than the sum of its stimulus–response units. **Molar behavior**, then, referred to broad patterns of behavior directed at some goal. Tolman provided several examples:

> A rat running a maze; a cat getting out of a puzzle box; a man driving home to dinner; a child hiding from a stranger; a woman doing her washing … ; a psychologist reciting a list of nonsense syllables; my friend and I telling one another our thoughts and feelings—*these are behaviors* (qua *molar*).
> And it must be noted that in mentioning no one of them have we referred to, or, we blush to confess it, for the most part have known, what were the exact muscles and glands, sensory nerves, and motor nerves involved. (Tolman, 1932, p. 8, italics in the original)

Tolman called his theory a **field theory** to distinguish it from the more molecular stimulus–response approach, which he likened to a telephone switchboard. Learning did not involve the mere strengthening and weakening of connections between incoming calls (stimulus information) and outgoing ones (motor responses), he argued. Instead, he proposed that the brain is more like a "map control room than it is like an old-fashioned telephone exchange" and that during learning, the animal develops a "field map of the environment" (Tolman, 1948, p. 192).

Goal-Directedness The preceding examples of molar behavior all have another feature: They are directed toward some goal. Influenced by Holt, Tolman argued that goal-directedness or **purposiveness** was a universal feature of the behavior we learn. Although the term *purpose* might seem like a return to a subjective, even introspective, psychology, Tolman merely meant that behavior "always seems to have the character of getting-to or getting-from a specific goal-object.... Thus, for example, the rat's behavior of 'running the maze' has as its first and perhaps most important identifying feature the fact that it is getting to food" (1932, p. 10). Tolman was obviously influenced by evolutionary thinking here; goal-directed behavior is adaptive and therefore has survival value. As a term, Tolman used *purposiveness* as descriptive, not causal. That is, it is merely a label for that which can be inferred from observing behavior, as when a hungry rat consistently worked its way through a maze until finding food. The causes of such behavior are to be found elsewhere, in the animal's specific learning history and its instinctive behaviors.

Intervening Variables To Tolman belongs credit for introducing a concept that has been widely used in psychology: the intervening variable. Stimulus conditions, or independent variables, are under the direct control of the experimenter; behaviors, or dependent variables, can be measured with precision by the experimenter. **Intervening variables** are hypothetical factors that are not seen directly but are inferred from the manner in which independent and dependent variables are operationally defined. They are assumed to "intervene" between stimulus and behavior in such a way as to influence learning. For instance, "thirst" is an intervening variable. It is never seen directly, but can be inferred to exist as a consequence of (a) creating some stimulus condition, such as not allowing an animal to drink water for 12 hours, or (b) measuring the completion of some behavior that leads to water, which is consumed by the animal. As you might guess from the discussion earlier in the chapter, Tolman's intervening variables reflect the influence of logical positivism, with its insistence that abstract, theoretical terms (i.e., intervening variables) be closely tied to observable events (i.e., stimuli and responses).

To show how Tolman tied his intervening variables to operationally defined stimuli and responses, consider the intervening variable of *expectancy*. Tolman believed that one result of maze learning was that the rat developed certain expectations. Rats finding food at the end of a maze expect to find food there in the future. Furthermore, it could be that they come to expect a particular type of food, a prediction tested in a clever study by Tolman's student M. H. Elliott (1928).

Using the 14-unit T-maze shown in Figure 11.5a, Elliott taught two groups of rats the maze. The experimental group found bran mash in the goal box, whereas the control group found sunflower seeds. Over the first nine days of the study (i.e., nine trials, one per day), both groups improved, although performance was better for the group fed with bran mash. On the tenth day, Elliott changed the reward for rats in the experimental group—they now found sunflower seeds at the goal instead of bran mash. As Figure 11.5b shows, their behavior was disrupted (errors increased). In Tolman's terms, they had come to expect bran mash; when that expectancy was violated, their behavior changed. In short, expectancy is a process intervening between stimulus and response, but closely tied to the stimulus features of the experiment (type of food) and the observed behaviors (errors).

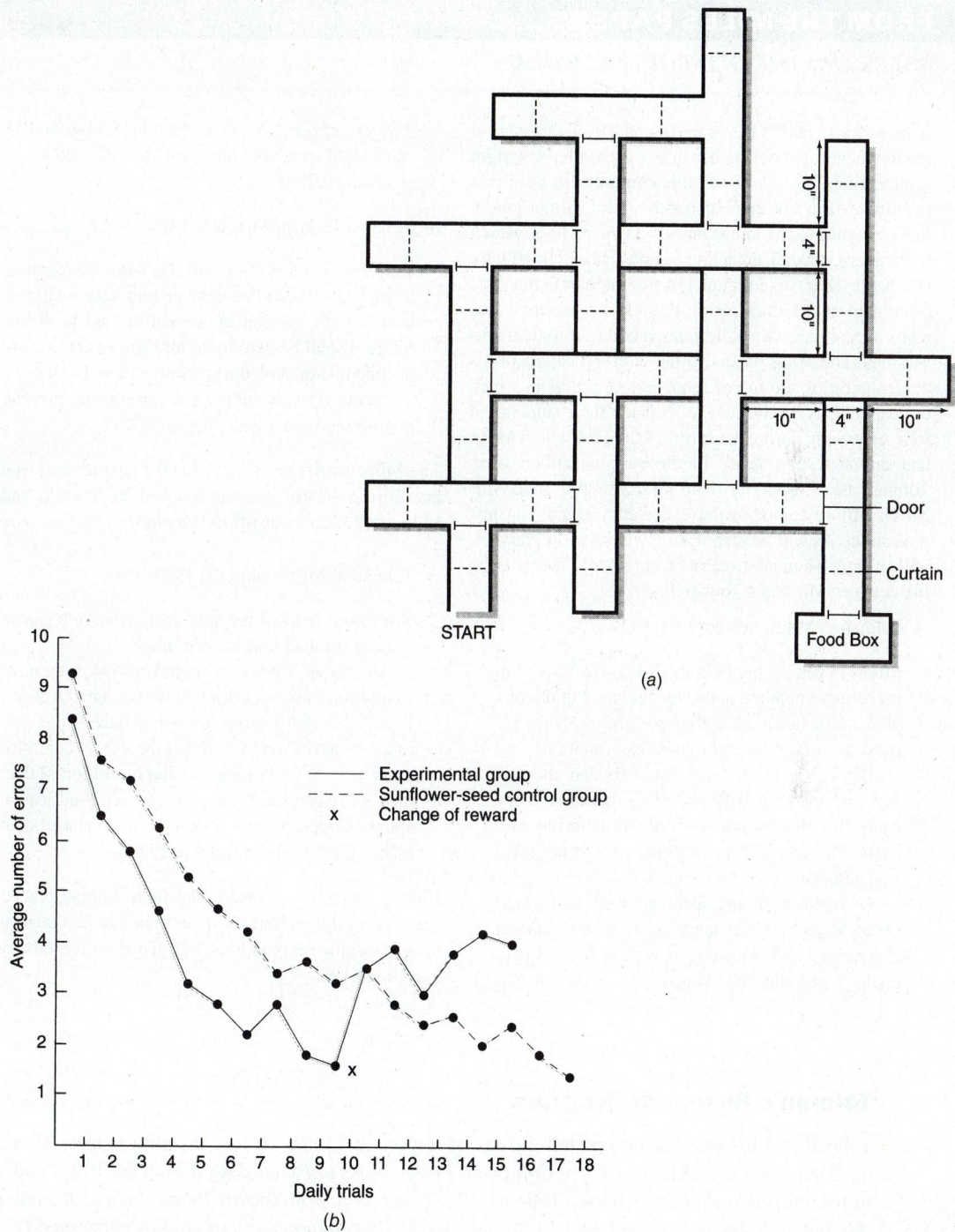

FIGURE 11.5 (*a*) Fourteen-unit multiple T-maze, used by Elliott to study expectancy, from Tolman 1932; (*b*) Results of Elliott's study of expectancy, from Tolman (1932).

FROM THE MILES PAPERS...

MILES AND THE OLD BOYS NETWORK

In many walks of life, it is an unfortunate truth that gainful employment often occurs because a person has the right "connections." In academia, this continues to hold true to some extent, but there also exist more formal guidelines designed to encourage fairness in hiring (e.g., search committees, federal guidelines against bias). In Miles's day, however, it was common practice, at least in the most prominent universities, for professors to place their students in positions with colleagues at other prominent universities. The Miles papers, along with the papers of his contemporaries, are full of sequences of letters in which correspondents discuss where to place their students in jobs, especially during the spring, a time for which Miles had an interesting label. In the case described here, Tolman asks Miles for help in finding a place for M. H. Elliott, author of the expectancy study you just read about. As will be seen, Elliott wound up at Harvard, with Boring. Here are excerpts from several letters passing between Miles and Tolman in 1929:

- Tolman to Miles, February 29, 1929

Elliott is getting his PhD this May. He is, as you probably remember, quite shy but has, I think, one of the best heads of the people around here. He passed a very good preliminary examination.

His thesis on the relation between motivation and learning with rats [i.e., the expectancy study] is going to turn out well. He is fertile with ideas. He has got the makings of a really A-1 psychologist ....

If you know of any opening I wish you would let us know. He has taken a lot of educational psychology and statistics, as well as animal psychology and abnormal psychology ... He has had

3 years' experience as a teaching fellow and is considered one of the best by the students. (Tolman, 1929a)

- Miles to Tolman, March 5, 1929

Thank you for writing me the letter concerning Elliott. Of course I remember him very well and have a high opinion of his ability and probable future. I shall be glad to do all I can to aid in connecting him up with the proper position. I will keep his name actively before me during this present mating season. (Miles, 1929c)

The Miles papers are silent over the next several weeks, but Boring clearly was approached by Tolman and/or Miles, and Elliott was off to Harvard.

- Tolman to Miles, May 23, 1929

Yes Elliott is fixed for next year. You are a peach to have still had him in your mind.

He has an instructorship at Harvard. I am now trembling in my boots for fear he won't make good. But I think that Boring quite understands the sort of a person [Elliott] is and that there is no commitment on their part or expectation on [Elliott's] that they will keep him more than a year. And it is a splendid opportunity for him. I am convinced that he has the "goods." (Tolman, 1929b)

Elliott apparently rewarded the faith Tolman placed in him. Harvard kept him for more than that first year; university catalog records have him listed on the faculty at least up to 1936.

Tolman's Research Program

Tolman and his students completed dozens of important studies of rats learning mazes. These were reported in a series of *University of California Publications in Psychology* during the 1920s and 1930s, in the *Purposive Behavior* book (Tolman, 1932), and in a well-known *Psychological Review* paper, "Cognitive Maps in Rats and Men" (Tolman, 1948). Two famous sets of studies concerned (a) latent learning and (b) cognitive maps.

Latent Learning An important issue that divided neobehaviorists was the role of reinforcement in learning. Tolman believed that food discovered by the rat at the end of the maze did not affect learning at all; it merely influenced the animal's motivation to complete the maze quickly and accurately. That is, learning needed to be distinguished from performance, and reinforcement affected performance but not learning. Some degree of learning the overall layout of the maze occurred whenever the animal was running through the maze, even if no food was in the goal box. Tolman termed the phenomenon **latent learning** because it occurred "below the surface," that is, without being immediately apparent in the animal's performance.

Testing for latent learning required showing that learning occurred even if reinforcement didn't, and Tolman and Honzik (1930) accomplished this by testing three groups of rats (one trial per day) in the same 14-unit T-maze shown used by Elliott. The first group of rats (no reward or NR) never found food after completing the maze. The second group (R) was always rewarded with food.

As you can see from Figure 11.6, the error scores for these two groups were about what you would expect—lots of errors for NR and steady improvement for R. The third group was the key one, however. As suggested by their label—NR-R—rats in this group were not rewarded initially (i.e., the first 10 days), but starting on day 11, they found food in the goal box. Tolman reasoned that if reinforcement was necessary for learning, then no learning would occur on days 1–10. Rather, learning would start on day 11, and only then would performance gradually begin to improve. That pattern did *not* happen, though, as is clear from the graph. Instead, performance improved *immediately* after day 11 for the third group. For Tolman, the evidence was clear—the maze was being learned during those first 10 days, even though the learning was not reflected in performance. That is, the learning on days 1–10 was "latent." As Tolman (1948) put it:

> Interpreting these results anthropomorphically, we would say that as long as the animals were not getting any food at the end of the maze they continued to take their time in going through it—they continued to enter many blinds. Once, however, they knew they were to get food, they demonstrated

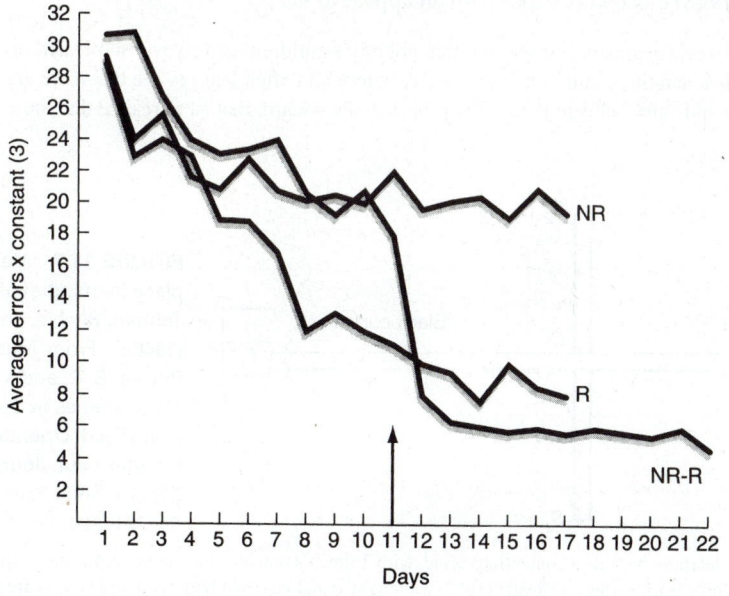

FIGURE 11.6 Results of Tolman and Honzik's study of latent learning, from Tolman (1932). From Tolman, E. C. 1932. Purposive Behavior in Animals and Men. New York: Appleton-Century-Crofts.

that during these preceding non-rewarded trials they had learned where many of the blinds were. They had been building up a "map," and could utilize the latter as soon as they were motivated to do so. (pp. 194–195)

Cognitive Maps This last sentence introduces a key concept for Tolman, a map. Tolman did not believe that rats learned stimulus–response connections when learning a maze. Rather, he argued, they created a **cognitive map** of the maze—an overall understanding of the maze's spatial pattern that gave them a general sense of where to go. A clever pair of studies demonstrated the operation of these maps. In one study (Tolman, Ritchie, & Kalish, 1946a), rats encountered the maze found in Figure 11.7 and were started at either S1 or S2. Some rats, the "response learning" group, always found food by turning right. Others, the "place learning" group, always found food in the same location, F1. Tolman et al. (1946a) found that rats in the place learning group learned faster, a result supporting Tolman's theory that the rats learn a map rather than a series of responses to specific stimuli.[1]

In the second study (Tolman, Ritchie, & Kalish, 1946b), rats first learned to run the simple maze in Figure 11.8a. Starting at A, they ran across an open circular table to C, the only part of the maze with sidewalls, then eventually to the goal box, G. A light was on at H. There were no errors to be made, so the rats soon learned to move quickly from A to G. After 12 trials, the simple maze was replaced with the one in Figure 11.8b. Now the path down C was blocked, and the rats had to choose another route to the food. An S-R behaviorist might expect the rats to choose either 9 or 10, the routes most similar to the original path at C, but Tolman, Ritchie, and Kalish reported that path 6, the best choice to get to the general location of the food, was the most frequently chosen. As with the place learning study, this outcome supported Tolman's argument that the rats were learning the overall configuration of a maze, not a series of turns.

In the last section of his 1948 "Cognitive Maps in Rats and Men" paper, Tolman tried to show how his maze learning studies were relevant for human behavior. Revealing the idealism and moral sensitivity that were never far from his thoughts, as well as his penchant for viewing the world as a large maze, Tolman (1948) closed his paper with an appeal to the

child-trainers and world-planners [to] see to it that nobody's children are too over-motivated or too frustrated. Only then can these children learn to look before and after, learn to see that there are often round-about and safer paths to their quite proper goals—learn, that is, to realize that the

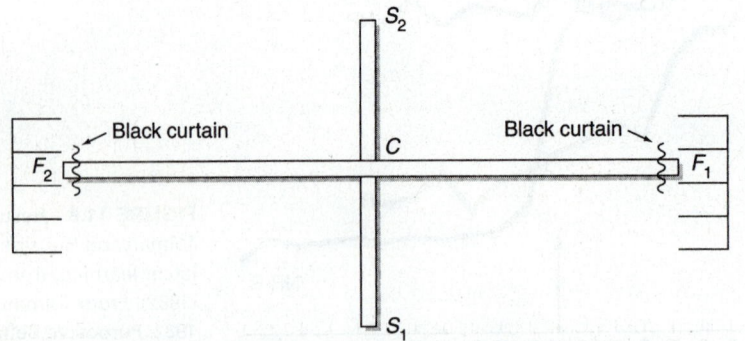

FIGURE 11.7 Maze used in place learning experiment by Tolman, Ritchie, and Kalish (1946a). From Tolman, E. C., Ritchie, B. F., and Kalish, D. 1946. Studies in Spatial Learning. I. Orientation and the Short-cut. Journal of Experimental Psychology, *36*, 221–229.

[1] "Place" versus "response" learning became a contentious issue, with Tolman's outcome not always replicated, especially by those supportive of Clark Hull's learning theory. Restle (1957) eventually concluded that both types of learning are possible, the outcome depending on whether place or response cues are more dominant in a particular situation.

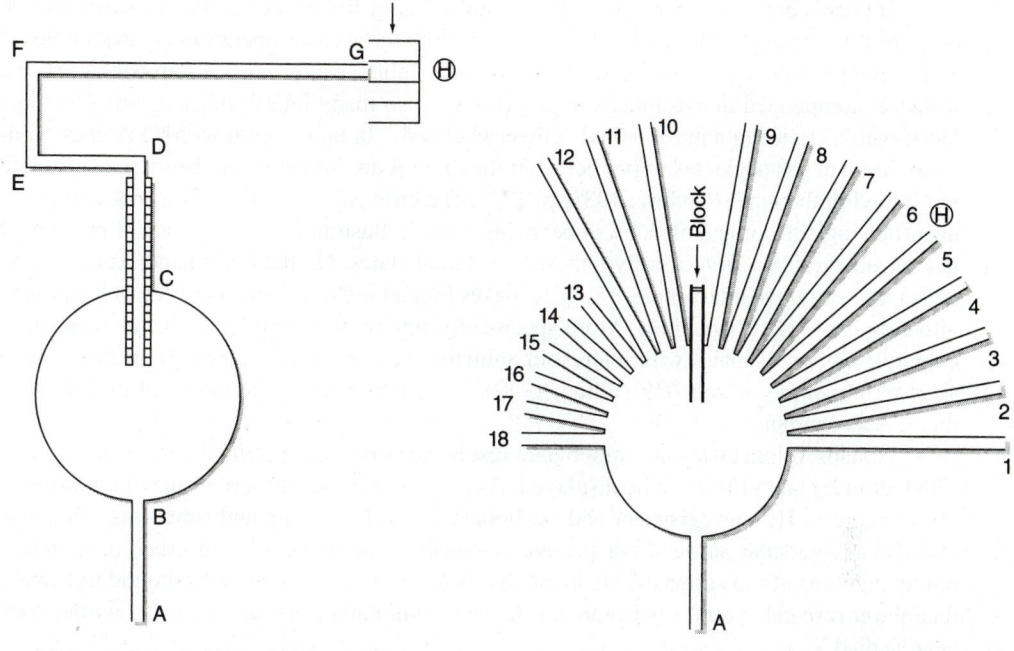

(a) Apparatus used in preliminary training   (b) Apparatus used in the test trial

FIGURE 11.8   (a) Apparatus used in the first phase of Tolman, Ritchie, and Kalish's experiment on the spatial abilities of rats. From Tolman 1948; (b) "Sunburst" apparatus for studying spatial learning, from Tolman (1948).

> well-beings of White and of Negro, of Catholic and of Protestant, of Christian and of Jew, of American and of Russian (and even of males and females) are mutually interdependent . . . .
>
> We must, in short, subject our children and ourselves (as the kindly experimenter would his rats) to the optimal conditions of moderate motivation and of an absence of unnecessary frustrations, whenever we put them and ourselves before that great God-given maze which is our human world . . . . (p. 208)

Evaluating Tolman

During the heyday of neobehaviorism, Tolman's research and his theorizing commanded attention, especially from the followers of Clark Hull (see later discussion), with whom Tolman disagreed on practically everything except the usefulness of intervening variables and the general precepts of logical positivism. The complexity of his theory contributed to its lack of lasting influence, but Tolman's research program was creative and helped to institutionalize the maze as standard research apparatus. His students were intensely loyal to him, and he in turn treated them as equals. On the other hand, despite their loyalty and devotion, few of Tolman's students continued doing research in "the Tolman tradition" when they left Berkeley. Whereas academia became crowded in the 1940s, 1950s, and 1960s with Hullians and Skinnerians, the "Tolmanian" was a rare creature. Furthermore, Tolman's research with rats in mazes did not produce much in the way of practical application. His plea for training children to have broad cognitive maps, for instance, gave little explicit guidance to parents. Instead of demonstrating the applicability of Tolman's work for everyday problems, the example seemed more like a good illustration of the dangers inherent in extrapolating far beyond one's data.

Tolman's emphasis on purposiveness and his heavy use of mentalistic variables were both criticized by his contemporaries. Tolman was careful to tie these terms operationally to stimulus conditions and responses, but some critics saw his use of such subjective terms as a step backward. Guthrie, for instance, complained that Tolman's theory proposed so many intervening cognitive factors that a rat faced with a choice in a maze would be overwhelmed: "In his concern with what goes on in the rat's mind, Tolman has neglected to predict what the rat will do. So far as the theory is concerned the rat is left buried in thought" (Guthrie, 1935, p. 172). The criticism is unfair—Tolman's writings are full of data showing rats doing quite a bit of behaving—but it illustrates the preference of many neobehaviorists for observable action over hypothesized internal states. On the other hand, Tolman's willingness to propose cognitive intervening variables makes him an important link between behaviorism and cognitive psychology (Chapter 14). More specifically, among those studying animal behavior, Tolman's cognitive theory resonates with interest in animal cognition. Olton's research on spatial behavior and short-term memory in rats (e.g., Olton, 1979), using a radial maze reminiscent of Tolman's sunburst maze, is an example.

Perhaps Tolman's lasting importance results not from his specific theory of learning but from a set of attitudes and values that he displayed. As a researcher, he was serious about his work and careful in executing it. He was persistent and passionate about developing and supporting his theory. Yet he also had a remarkable sense of perspective that enabled him to be fully absorbed in his research while not taking himself too seriously. He knew that better theories than his were bound to come along and that newer research would supersede his. As he said in one of the last pieces he wrote, published the year he died,

> The system may well not stand up.... But I do not much care. I have liked to think about
> psychology in ways that have proved congenial to me. Since ... psychology [is] still immersed in
> such tremendous realms of the uncertain and the unknown, the best that any individual
> scientist ... can do seems to be to follow his own gleam and his own bent, however inadequate they
> may be. In fact, I suppose that actually this is what we all do. In the end, the only sure criterion is to
> have fun. And I have had fun. (Tolman, 1959, p. 152)

In addition to his healthy sense of perspective, Tolman had one other enduring trait—his strong sense of morality. It led him to protest the U.S. involvement in World War I, thus contributing to his dismissal from Northwestern in 1918. In the midst of World War II, his strong feelings about war resurfaced, this time motivating him to write *Drives Toward War* (1942), in which he combined some of his ideas with those of Freud to explain what leads to warfare and to make some recommendations to eliminate the problem. One of his suggestions, which he granted was unlikely to occur, was the creation of a "World-Federation" that would replace nationalist boundaries and encourage cooperation among the peoples of the world rather than competition. The histories of the League of Nations and of the United Nations have made it clear just how difficult it is to overcome nationalist sentiment.

Near the end of his active career, Tolman's convictions faced a final test. In the early 1950s, America was at the beginning the so-called cold war, its long ideological struggle with the Soviet Union. The Soviets' expressed desire to spread the gospel of Marxist/Leninist doctrine created images of one country after another being subverted and falling (like dominoes) into Communist hands. Holding the line against Communism meant defending South Korea in the 1950s and South Vietnam in the 1960s.

It was also feared that Communists would infiltrate the United States, corrupt its youth, and eventually take over the country. In the 1950s, these fears were fueled by Senator Joseph McCarthy of Wisconsin, who claimed to know of Communists who had infiltrated the government. Senate hearings, laced with rumor and innuendo, ruined the careers of anyone who was merely accused of being a "Red."

McCarthy also hinted that Communists were infiltrating the film industry (dangerous because movies influence attitudes) and higher education (even greater influence—our children!).

In this climate, professors at California universities were told by those running the university system to sign oaths of loyalty to the United States and to declare that they were not members of the Communist Party. Professors were told to sign or resign. As a senior faculty member at Berkeley and by then one of America's leading psychologists, Tolman, offended by the demand, could easily have left Berkeley and been welcomed anywhere. Yet he stayed, and courageously refused to sign the oath, on the general principle that it violated the First Amendment's right of free speech. Also, not content with just his individual action, he led a fight that successfully repealed the oath in California and preserved the concept of academic freedom. In 1957, Tolman received the Distinguished Scientific Contribution Award from the APA and, just before his death in 1959, the Board of Regents of the University of California recognized the significance of his fight for academic freedom by awarding him an honorary degree (Crutchfield, 1961).

CLARK HULL (1884–1952): A HYPOTHETICO-DEDUCTIVE SYSTEM

The life and career of Clark Leonard Hull is a case study in how perseverance and hard work can overcome seemingly insurmountable odds. Born into poverty on a farm in New York, raised on a "good but unimproved" farm in Michigan, and educated in a one-room schoolhouse, Hull grew up under "pioneer conditions" (Hull, 1952b, p. 143). In addition to these trying circumstances, he almost died from typhoid fever just before starting college, and after his second year at Alma College in Michigan, he contracted polio, which left him partially paralyzed at age 24. At the time, he was aiming for a life as a mining engineer, but the polio made it impossible for him to meet the physical demands of that career.

After spending a year at home, during which his health improved, he decided on a career in psychology. Why psychology? In his words, he was searching for a field related to philosophy that would involve theoretical work, and "one which was new enough to permit rapid growth so that a young man would not need to wait for his predecessors to die before his work could find recognition, and ... would provide an opportunity to design and work with automatic apparatus" (Hull, 1952b, p. 145). The quote reveals two of Hull's enduring features: his strong ambition and his talent with the design and construction of experimental apparatus. The latter first manifested itself during the polio episode, when Hull designed his own leg brace.

Hull finished college at the University of Michigan. His most memorable experience was a year-long course in experimental psychology, taught jointly by John Shepard, who had studied with Watson, and Walter Pillsbury, a student of Titchener's. After being rejected for graduate school at Cornell and Yale, Hull was accepted to the University of Wisconsin, where he earned a PhD under the tutelage of Joseph Jastrow, a former student of G. Stanley Hall.

Doctoral dissertations often find their way into the far reaches of filing cabinets, but Hull's (1920) eventually became a well-known study of the processes involved in learning new concepts.[2] For stimuli, Hull used Chinese characters, including those in Figure 11.9. Notice that the characters in each row have

---

[2]The study was initially ignored by other researchers, which discouraged Hull greatly. However, a brief description of it appeared in a popular general psychology text in the late 1920s, and due to the tendencies of textbook authors to borrow from each other, it became increasingly cited thereafter (Hilgard, 1987).

Four of the Chinese radicals that Hull used are shown here. First, the subject was shown a Chinese character and guessed its "name" (for example, oo), then the experimenter gave the correct name, and so on. Characters with the same radicals always were given the same name so that after going through several packs of characters, the subjects improved their performances and were eventually able to correctly name characters they had never seen before.

Name	Concept	Pack I	Pack II	Pack III	Pack IV	Pack V	Pack VI

From Hull (1920)

FIGURE 11.9 Chinese characters used as stimulus materials in Hull's doctoral dissertation on concepts learning, from Hull (1920).

a common feature, called a "radical." Hull's subjects had to learn to associate a nonsense sound with each radical (e.g., "oo" for the radical that looks like a large check mark). Over the course of several sets of stimuli, subjects learned to look at a character and give the correct nonsense sound; eventually they could identify stimuli they had not seen before. There were a number of findings in the study, but the one that impressed Hull the most was the shape of the learning curve—performance improved gradually but steadily. The idea of learning being the result of a gradual increase in "habit strength" eventually became a salient feature of Hull's learning theory.

Hull completed the doctorate in 1918 and remained at Wisconsin for another decade. Early in his career, he was asked to teach a course in psychological testing. Although he knew little about the topic, the subject interested him, especially the correlational math involved in test validation. He immersed himself in the topic and within a few years produced an authoritative text called *Aptitude Testing* (Hull, 1928). Displaying mechanical aptitude again, he built a machine to automatically calculate correlations, saving himself the tedium of calculating by hand the numerous correlations needed to validate tests. The machine was delicate, however, a problem that prevented its widespread use.[3]

Shortly after Hull began teaching the testing course, he was asked to teach introductory psychology to premedical students. Because he believed that suggestion and physician authority influenced the outcome of many medical treatments, he decided to incorporate the topic into his lectures. This led him to hypnosis, and to the understatement that "the subject has largely tended to attract experimenters with a

[3]In a diary entry after traveling by train with Hull to a conference in 1928, Walter Miles of Stanford reported that Hull had built three of the machines but "they are hard to keep in shape and [he] will not send one far away." Consequently, an order that Miles had placed for one had to be canceled (Miles, 1928a).

peculiarly unscientific type of approach" (Hull, 1952b, p. 152). Determined to correct the problem, Hull spent about 10 years examining the phenomenon methodically, eventually producing another authoritative text, *Hypnosis and Suggestibility: An Experimental Approach* (Hull, 1933). He concluded that hypnosis was a state of hypersuggestibility and a reduction in analytical thought, brought on by hypnotically induced relaxation. He also decided that the medical community overestimated the therapeutic value of hypnosis. For example, he found that, contrary to the medical community's widely held belief, memory was not notably improved by hypnosis.

Although working primarily on aptitude testing and hypnosis in the 1920s, Hull did not lose sight of his dissertation topic of learning. Indeed, although Hull's interests in aptitude testing, hypnosis, and learning are often portrayed as three distinct periods in his life, they were intertwined, and all three reflected Hull's analytic approach to research (Triplett, 1982). During the 1920s, Hull was well aware of Watson's writings and was familiar with the research being done by Tolman. Learning became the primary focus of his life, however, after he read the translations of Pavlov's research in the late 1920s. The topic captured his full attention soon after 1929, the year he left Wisconsin to undertake (at age 45) a new challenge at Yale University.

When he arrived as president of Yale University in 1921, James Angell, one of the leaders of the Chicago functionalists (Chapter 7), found that psychology at Yale could only be described as moribund. The psychologists were still part of the philosophy department, virtually no research was being done, and only 8 psychology doctorates had been awarded between 1903 and 1921, compared with 46 at Columbia and 51 at Chicago (Morawski, 1986). With the aid of Robert Yerkes, Angell established the Institute of Psychology in 1924. In 1929, the Institute expanded into the multidisciplinary Institute of Human Relations (IHR), which had as its lofty goal "to correlate knowledge and coordinate technique in related fields that greater progress may be made in the understanding of human life" (quoted in Morawski, 1986, p. 219). It was populated with professors from a range of disciplines, including psychology, law, sociology, anthropology, and economics; their teaching duties at Yale were reduced to a minimum so they could devote the bulk of their time to the Institute and research. One of the psychologists assigned to IHR was Clark Hull, who had just been recruited from Wisconsin. Hull spent the rest of his career at Yale, dying of a second heart attack just weeks from his retirement. While there, he developed his theory of learning and created a small army of "Hullians," students and colleagues who extended the research program far beyond New Haven. The best known was Kenneth Spence (1907–1967), who got to know Hull while studying at Yale with Yerkes. Spence made contributions significant enough for Hull's theory to become known as the Hull–Spence theory among devotees. At the University of Iowa, Spence perpetuated the Hullian legacy by producing no fewer than 73 PhD students between 1940 and 1963 (Hilgard, 1967).

Hull's System

One of Hull's heroes was Sir Isaac Newton. He kept a copy of Newton's *Principia Mathematica* on his desk, and he urged graduate students to read it so they would understand that Hull's approach to research mirrored Newton's. Newton viewed the universe as a giant machine controlled by precise mathematical laws; Hull thought of humans in the same way. Indeed, he believed that an ultimate understanding of human behavior could only occur if a machine could be built that would be indistinguishable from a human. The attitude was undoubtedly influenced by Hull's own highly developed skill as a machine-builder.

Newton also influenced Hull's beliefs about progress in science and the importance of theory. For Hull, science advanced by developing sophisticated theories, then testing them, modifying them, testing the revisions, and so on. This system, also used by Tolman and consistent with the dictates of logical positivism, is called a **hypothetico-deductive system**. At the core of this type of theory of human behavior is a set of postulates, statements about behavior based on accumulated knowledge from research and logic. From these postulates specific hypotheses can be deduced, and these lead directly to experiments. The results of these experiments support or fail to support the postulates and, by extension, the theory. Over time, the theory evolves as a function of empirical support or nonsupport.

In addition to emulating Newton, Hull was also motivated to develop his theory by what he saw as a relative absence of theory building among American psychologists, compared to the extensive work on theory compiled by the gestaltists (Mills, 1988). It was time for American psychology to catch up. As Hull put it,

> these Gestalt people are so terrifyingly articulate. Practically every one of them writes several books. The result is that whereas they constitute a rather small proportion of the psychological population of this country, they have written ten times as much in the field of theory as Americans have. (Hull, 1942, quoted in Mills, 1988, p. 393)

Hull worked on the theory right up to his death, and the final account of it, *A Behavior System* (1952a), appeared posthumously. The best-known version of the system, however, can be found in *Principles of Behavior* (1943); it includes a set of 16 postulates, presented both verbally and mathematically, along with descriptions of research supporting the theory. A complete description of Hull's theory is well beyond the scope of this chapter segment, but some insight can be gained by examining his most famous postulate, number 4.

Postulate 4: Habit Strength Postulate 4 reveals the core of Hull's belief about the conditions necessary for learning to occur. It also illustrates the extent to which Hull aimed for theoretical precision—*Principles of Behavior* was not meant to be light reading. Here is just a portion of the fourth postulate:

> Whenever an effector activity ($r \rightarrow R$) and a receptor activity ($S \rightarrow s$) occur in close temporal contiguity ($_sC_r$), and this $_sC_r$ is closely associated with the diminution of a need ($\dot{G}$) or with a stimulus which has been closely and consistently associated with the diminution of a need ($\dot{G}$), there will result an increment to a tendency (Δ_sH_R) for that afferent impulse on later occasions to evoke that reaction. The increments from successive reinforcements summate in a manner which yields a combined habit strength ($_sH_R$) which is a simple positive growth function of the number of reinforcements (N). (Hull, 1943, p. 178)

The key elements here are contiguity and reinforcement. According to Hull, learning occurs when there is a close contiguity between stimulus and response. A rat learns to associate a location X in a maze, for instance, with the response "turn right." This contiguity is necessary, but it is not sufficient, however. In addition, reinforcement must be present for learning to occur. Reinforcers for Hull were stimuli that reduce drives; food reduces hunger, for example. Together, S-R contiguity and reinforcement gradually increase $_sH_R$, or **habit strength**. Thus, by repeatedly reaching X, turning right, and finding food, the rat accumulates habit strength with each reinforced trial. To learn is to increase $_sH_R$. That learning is incremental ("a simple positive growth function"), rather than sudden, echoes the results of Hull's dissertation on concept learning. The importance to Hull of the ideas in postulate 4 may be inferred from Figure 11.10, a portrait completed late in Hull's career. The graph in the background is a theoretical learning curve—notice that habit strength increases gradually.

For Hull, then, reinforcement was defined in terms of drive reduction ("diminution of a need"), and his theory is sometimes known as a **drive reduction** theory as a result. Primary drives are those

Archives of the History of American Psychology, The Center for the History of Psychology -The University of Akron

FIGURE 11.10   Portrait of Clark Hull.

connected directly with survival, and they can be reduced with **primary reinforcers** like food and water. But Hull also described **secondary reinforcers**, stimuli he described in postulate 4 as those that have been associated with primary reinforcers. A tone that has been paired with the primary reinforcer of food can itself become a reinforcer, for instance.

Reaction Potential   Although Hull rejected the type of intervening variables used by Tolman, he acknowledged that he borrowed the concept from his fellow neobehaviorist (Hull, 1943, p. 31). An important intervening variable for Hull was what he called **reaction potential**, or $_sE_R$. Introduced in postulate 7, $_sE_R$ refers to the probability ("potential") that a response ("reaction") will occur at a given time and can be inferred from several kinds of measurable behaviors (e.g., "response latency"—how long it takes an animal to respond). Hull believed that $_sE_R$ was influenced by several factors, with drive and habit strength being the most important. That is, a response will be most likely to occur if both habit strength *and* drive are high. And Hull argued that the relationship was multiplicative ($_sE_R = D \times {_sH_R}$) rather than additive. Thus, if either drive or habit strength is zero, the response won't occur. Rats will run a maze correctly only if they are motivated (e.g., hungry) *and* if they have a sufficient number of reinforced trials under their belts.

Evaluating Hull

Throughout the 1940s and into the early 1950s, Clark Hull's work was cited more often than that of any other psychologist (far more frequently than Tolman's work), and his students (and their students) spread the Hullian gospel far and wide. Between 1941 and 1950, for example, approximately 70% of all research articles published in the areas of learning and motivation referred to and referenced Hull's work (Spence, 1952). For the psychologists of Hull's era, his theory met the need for a clear direction into the future. Introspective psychology had met its demise in the 1920s, but there was nothing to replace it. Watsonian behaviorism appeared, but so did gestalt psychology, Freudianism, mental testing, and a host of other variants. Searching for maturity and respectability as a science, psychologists seized on what appeared to be just the kind of formalized theory that characterized the older sciences, especially physics.

   Paradoxically, today's college students not only fail to appreciate Hull's stature, they seldom even recognize his name. Hull's rise and abrupt fall are illustrated dramatically in an analysis by Guttman

(1977). He examined the reference sections of all of the articles published in the *Journal of Experimental Psychology* in 1940, 1950, 1960, and 1970, counting up the number of references to the work of Hull or Spence. For those 4 years, respectively, the percentages of articles citing Hull and/or Spence were 4%, 39%, 24%, and 4%.

There are several reasons for the collapse of Hull's theory. For one thing, it was overambitious, attempting to build a theory of extraordinary complexity and mathematical precision on what turned out to be a very narrow empirical base—the behavior of simple organisms (usually rats) in artificial, highly controlled, simple environments (a typical apparatus was a "straight maze"—no turns, no dead ends, with the time to run from one end to the other the typical dependent variable). Hullians countered that other sciences do the same thing; biologists, for instance, use isolated tissue cultures to study cellular processes, even though those cultures are "artificial" relative to real-life biological environments. Also, Hull was planning a major work that extended his system to complex human behavior, but was never able to get very far with it before his death. On the other hand, several of his students, along with other members of Yale's IHR, did manage to combine Hullian and Freudian ideas into a testable theory of human aggression. In *Frustration and Aggression* (Dollard, Doob, Miller, Mowrer, & Sears, 1939), Hull's students developed the well-known frustration–aggression hypothesis and tested it with both animal subjects and children.[4] The same group later produced *Social Learning and Imitation* (Miller & Dollard, 1941), which launched modern social learning theory, best known through the work of Albert Bandura (Bobo dolls and imitative aggression).

Another criticism of Hull's theory was that it overlooked the very human nature of research. Consistent with his underlying Newtonian assumption of human as machine, Hull took it for granted that disputes over the empirical support for the theory would be resolved by dispassionate and objective scientists listening to their data. There was faith that "crucial experiments" would decide the "truth" of some issue, but contentious issues never seemed to go away. For example, Hull and Tolman engaged in a series of skirmishes over the nature of learning. Tolman's group would produce a study that seemed to question some aspect of Hull's theory; Hull's group would then rush to the barricades and produce some data that seemed to explain away Tolman's results while simultaneously maintaining the Hullian model. Tolman would then respond. And so on. Followers of each theorist felt they had the data on their side, but to those outside both camps, it appeared that little was being resolved. Furthermore, the failure to settle these disputes about learning contributed to the growing suspicion that behaviorism might be flawed as a system, and questions about the adequacy of behaviorism contributed to the development of cognitive psychology in the 1960s (Segal & Lachman, 1972), as will be seen in Chapter 14.

One final problem for Hull was shared by Guthrie and Tolman and was perhaps the most important reason why all three men faded into relative obscurity in the latter half of the 20th century. The problem was the rising star of B. F. Skinner, who combined the brashness and entrepreneurial spirit of John Watson with the creativity, work ethic, and ability to attract talented students to match Guthrie, Tolman, or Hull.

---

[4]One member of this team was Neal Miller, a doctoral student of Walter Miles, who became one of the best-known experimental psychologists of his time. In a memo prepared for Miles in 1937, Miller summarized his work during the previous year; this work included: "Spent a great deal of time and energy cooperating with various members of the Institute in attempting to lay the theoretical foundations for integrated research. In particular, (a) collaborated with Dr. Dollard in a preliminary formulation of the problem of frustration with particular reference to aggression; (b) collaborated with Dr. Sears and Dr. Hovland in formulating a more elaborate system of hypotheses concerning frustration, aggression, and substitute response; (c) prepared for Dr. Hull's seminar a sample system of postulates and deductions based on that part of Freudian theory dealing with 'identification'" (Miles, 1937).

B. F. SKINNER (1904–1990): A RADICAL BEHAVIORISM

Burrhus Frederick Skinner was a product of small-town America (Susquehanna, Pennsylvania) during the Progressive era. He grew up at a time when optimism within the emerging white middle class was high in America—the country had just emerged from difficult economic times in the 1890s, and it had just beaten the overmatched Spanish in the Spanish-American War. The president, Theodore Roosevelt, was the dashing hero of the war and the youngest man ever to hold the office at that time. Parents, unless poor and/or nonwhite, had every reason to expect endless opportunity for their children. Skinner's father was a moderately successful lawyer; his mother stayed at home and cultivated in young Fred the Protestant values of hard work and concern about "what other people might think."

Hard work indeed characterized Skinner's life, but concern about what others thought did not become one of his enduring features. On the contrary, independent thinking and an unwillingness to accept the "wisdom of elders" unless accompanied by sound evidence was more his style. It emerged early—his high school principal wrote him a strong recommendation to New York's Hamilton College, but cautioned that young Fred was "passionately fond of arguing with his teachers. He is quite a reader and although I do not think he actually supposes himself wiser than his teachers, I have found him [to give] that impression … " (quoted in Bjork, 1993, p. 28).

Skinner was initially unhappy in the fraternity/sorority-dominated atmosphere of Hamilton, but he soon found his niche and developed a passion for creative writing. He even sent some stories to the poet Robert Frost, whom he had met at a writers' conference. Frost's praise led to a career decision. Determined to be an author, Skinner informed his parents that he wished to take a year off after graduation and simply write. This of course created problems for Skinner's parents, who were naturally concerned about what people would think of the new college graduate who was living at home but did not seem to have an actual job. It's not hard to imagine the pressure he felt from his parents to be productive ("And what did you write today, Fred?") and, as the year passed, he had a growing sense that he would never match the achievements of the famous writers whose works he was reading. Although Skinner later referred to this time as his "Dark Year," some of what he read eventually led him to graduate studies in psychology. For instance, during this time he read a number of popular articles on behaviorism, and this led him to Watson and Pavlov. He became intrigued by behaviorism and, in the fall of 1928, he was off to Harvard. Figure 11.11 shows Skinner working in the Harvard laboratory a few years later.

Skinner developed his system of behaviorism while at Harvard, first as a graduate student, then as a prestigious University Fellow. There was no noticeable change in his general attitude toward authority. He was not impressed by the work of E. G. Boring, the head of the laboratory and, of course, Titchener's best-known student. He referred to Boring's perception course as "simply painful" (Skinner, 1979, p. 47) and lamented that Boring spent three entire lectures explaining a single visual illusion.[5] Boring, in turn, was not inclined toward behaviorism and removed himself from Skinner's doctoral committee. During the defense of his doctoral dissertation, when the noted personality theorist Gordon Allport (Chapter 14) asked him to describe what he thought to be the shortcomings of behaviorism, Skinner replied that he could not think of any (p. 75).

Skinner's first book, *The Behavior of Organisms* (1938), summarized his research at Harvard. After stints at the University of Minnesota and Indiana University, Skinner returned to Harvard in 1948,

---

[5]Skinner did not elaborate, but the illusion in question was probably the moon illusion—a full moon looks huge on the horizon, but smaller when high in the sky. Research on this illusion was probably Boring's most important contribution to experimental psychology, and he completed several studies in the 1930s that attempted to explain the illusion (e.g., Holway & Boring, 1940).

© UPI/Bettmann/Corbis

FIGURE 11.11 B. F. Skinner as a graduate student at Harvard in 1930.

where he remained active, even after his retirement in 1974. Just days before his death from leukemia in 1990, he addressed the opening session of the APA's annual meeting in Boston. I was in the audience that evening and recall that he needed assistance from his daughter getting on stage and walking to the podium (you can just see the top of her head in Figure 11.12), but once there he barely glanced at his notes while delivering an articulate and impassioned plea for his brand of behaviorism and an attack on what he viewed as the misguided efforts of cognitive psychologists. The talk was published shortly after Skinner's death as "Can Psychology Be a Science of the Mind?" (Skinner, 1990).

The Experimental Analysis of Behavior

In chapters on learning, introductory psychology textbooks typically have a major section on "classical" or Pavlovian conditioning (probably accompanied by the wrong picture of Pavlov's apparatus), followed by an equally large section on "operant" conditioning. Skinner is responsible for making the distinction, and operant conditioning is sometimes referred to as Skinnerian conditioning.

In *The Behavior of Organisms* (1938), Skinner distinguished between Type S and Type R conditioning. **Type S conditioning** is the Pavlovian model: An identifiable stimulus elicits an identifiable response through the procedure of pairing two *stimuli*, one that initially elicits the response (e.g., food) and one that initially does not (e.g., a tone). It is called Type "S" because in this case an association is formed between two stimuli (food, the UCS, and tone, the CS), with both eventually producing the same response (dogs drooling). Type S conditioning accounts for a certain type of behavior, but Skinner

Courtesy of Kathleen Davis

FIGURE 11.12 Skinner's final public appearance, at APA's annual meeting in Boston, August, 1990.

argued that it cannot explain a great deal of behavior that seems to have no easily identifiable stimulus. That is, some behavior is *emitted* by the organism and is controlled by the immediate consequences of the behavior, not by an eliciting stimulus. In **Type R conditioning**, or **operant conditioning**, a behavior is emitted, it is followed by some consequence, and the future chances of that behavior occurring are determined by those consequences. If the consequences are positive, a behavior being rewarded, for example, the behavior is strengthened. If the consequences are negative, a behavior being punished, for example, the behavior is weakened. Skinner called operant conditioning Type "R" because in this case a consequence (e.g., a child getting a toy) is associated with the emitted *response* that preceded it (e.g., a child throwing a tantrum in a toy store). Skinner chose the term **operant** to describe this form of behavior because the behavior "operates" on the environment—when the behavior happens, it produces a predictable outcome.

Skinner, like Watson, believed that psychology should have but two goals—the prediction and control of behavior. This would be accomplished through an "experimental analysis of behavior," that is, through a full description of operant behaviors, the environments in which these behaviors occurred, and the immediate consequences of the behaviors. While recognizing that behaviors are influenced by an individual's innate behavioral tendencies and capabilities, Skinner focused on how behaviors were shaped by the environment. Hence, he made contact with the British empiricists, the environmentalism of Watson, and he provided a clear example of neobehaviorism's emphasis on learning.

Operant Conditioning: A Primer Skinner spent his life fleshing out the details of operant conditioning. The best full description can be found in his 1953 book, *Science and Human Behavior*, and reasonably thorough descriptions appear in textbooks on the psychology of learning. Here are some of the basics.

Skinner investigated operant conditioning by creating a highly structured environment that enabled him to follow what he considered the good advice of Pavlov. As he put it: "I had the clue from Pavlov: Control your conditions and you will see order" (Skinner, 1956, p. 223). Figure 11.13 shows this controlled environment, as designed for rats. It consists of a chamber with a small lever on one wall that can be pressed by the rat, a food trough for the delivery of positive consequences (food), devices for the presentation of visual and/or auditory stimuli, and a set of parallel bars as a floor, through which electrical current can pass, for the delivery of negative consequences (mild shock). A similar apparatus exists for pigeons, with a circular disk to be pecked substituting for the lever. Skinner called the apparatus an operant chamber, but Clark Hull referred to it as a Skinner box, and the name stuck. Behavior in a Skinner box is recorded by means of a cumulative recorder As paper is fed out at a constant rate, thereby producing time on an *X*-axis, a pen moves across the paper by a small distance every time the bar is pressed or a key is pecked. Rate of response, which for Skinner was the only important measure of behavior, can be determined by looking at the slope of the line. Whenever a specific behavior is reinforced (e.g., followed by food), the pen makes a short downward vertical line. When the pen reaches the top of the paper, it quickly returns to the baseline to start over. Figure 11.14 shows an example of a cumulative record.

With an operant chamber and a cumulative recorder, Skinner was in a position to examine operant conditioning in depth. Just as Pavlov was able to demonstrate such phenomena as extinction in his classical conditioning paradigm, so Skinner was able to demonstrate them with an operant procedure. With a rat that had been conditioned to bar press for food, for instance, Skinner could demonstrate *extinction* by withholding the reinforcer. In fact, Skinner's initial demonstration of extinction appeared by accident. In his words (which also reveal something about Skinner's passion for his work),

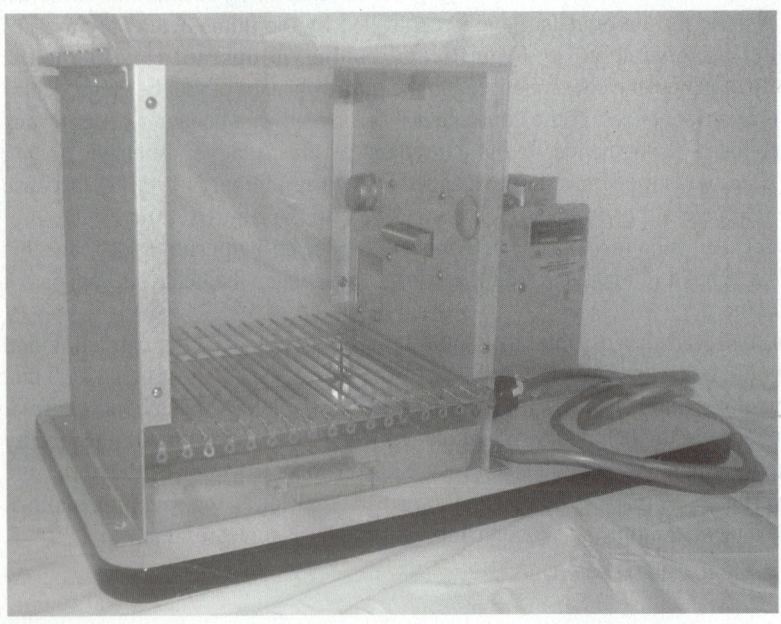

Courtesy of Dr. C. James Goodwin

FIGURE 11.13 A typical Skinner box for rats.

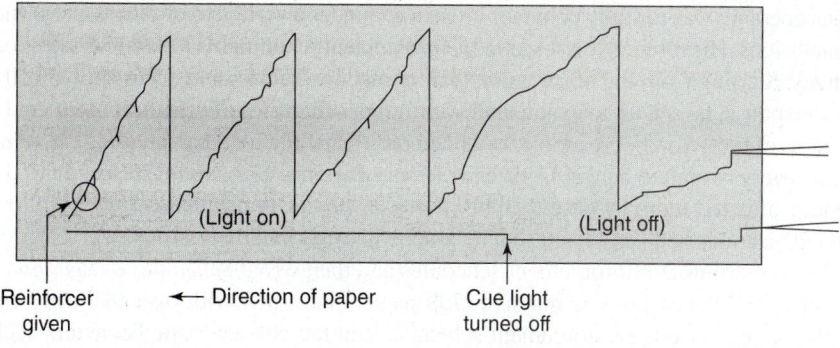

FIGURE 11.14 A sample cumulative record, initially showing a high rate of response, then a decline to no responding (perhaps the result of an extinction procedure).

> My first extinction curve showed up by accident. A rat was pressing the lever in an experiment on satiation when the pellet dispenser jammed. I was not there at the time, and when I returned I found a beautiful curve....
>
> The change was more orderly than the extinction of a salivary reflex in Pavlov's setting, and I was terribly excited. It was a Friday afternoon and there was no one in the laboratory who I could tell. All that weekend I crossed streets with particular care and avoided all unnecessary risks to protect my discovery from loss through my accidental death. (Skinner, 1979, p. 95)

The extinction curve that Skinner found would have looked something like the right-hand side of Figure 11.14—a high rate of response while the rat was being reinforced for bar pressing, followed by a gradual lessening of the response rate, eventually resulting in no responses.

In addition to extinction, Skinner demonstrated a variety of other conditioning phenomena. For example, while a rat was being conditioned to bar press, a light would typically be on in the operant chamber. By dimming the light the rate of response slowed. This was Pavlov's *generalization*—behavior occurring in one environment also occurred in a similar environment. By reinforcing bar presses with the light on, but not when the light was off, the rat would eventually bar press only when the light was on—this was what Pavlov called *differentiation* (Skinner called it *discrimination*, the term used today). Together, these phenomena illustrated what Skinner called **stimulus control**. In operant conditioning, the environment in which a behavior is reinforced (i.e., a Skinner box with the light on) comes to exert control over the rat's behavior. In an experimental analysis, then, understanding behavior involves being able to specify the behavior being studied, the immediate consequences of that behavior, and the environment where the behavior occurs. Notice that Skinner's two main goals are thereby accomplished—behavior can now be predicted, knowing the environment and the reinforcement history of the organism, and it also can be controlled (e.g., by turning a light on and off).

Skinner and Theory

Skinner's philosophy of science differed fundamentally from that of Hull and Tolman. Rather than deducing hypotheses from theoretical statements, designing studies to test these hypotheses, and then adjusting a complex theory depending on the research outcome, Skinner preferred an inductive approach to research, studying samples of behavior and looking for regularities that could become general principles. His reference to Pavlov and the search for orderly behavior hints at the strategy. This freedom from the dictates of theory is also evident in his recommendation to researchers that "[w]hen you find something fascinating, drop everything else and study it" (Skinner, 1956, p. 223).

Skinner's modus operandi was to study behavior intensively under a variety of circumstances, and then draw general conclusions. His research on so-called reinforcement schedules is a classic illustration of this inductive strategy. Starting from the observation that, in real life, reinforcers occur sporadically rather than after every response, he set out to examine how different **schedules of reinforcement** could produce different patterns of behavior. For example, in a fixed ratio schedule for a bar-pressing rat, reinforcement might follow every twentieth bar press instead of every bar press (i.e., an FR20 schedule). In a fixed interval schedule, affected more by time than by responses per se, reinforcement might follow the first response after 20 seconds had passed (i.e., an FI20 schedule). Skinner and his student, Charles Ferster, examined dozens of different reinforcement schedules and then wrote *Schedules of Reinforcement* (Ferster & Skinner, 1957). The book is massive (739 pages) and filled with over 900 different cumulative records illustrating various reinforcement schedules and the characteristic behaviors each produces (e.g., higher rates of responding for FR than for FI schedules). The book is not much fun to read, but for Skinnerians, it became an indispensable reference source for information about how behavior can be predicted from knowledge of various reinforcement schedules.

Skinner and the Problem of Explanation   We have learned that both Tolman and Hull proposed the existence of intervening variables to help account for learned behavior, and these variables were carefully tied to stimuli and responses via operational definitions. Skinner avoided intervening variables, however, mainly because he thought it opened the door to what he called **explanatory fictions**. These refer to a tendency to propose some hypothetical internal factor mediating between observable stimuli and measurable behaviors and then later to use the factor as a pseudoexplanation for the behavior. It is something that we do all the time, at least informally. For example, suppose your new roommate stays up late at night studying and seems to spend more time in the library than anyone else you know. You ask his friends about him. They say that he has a high need for achievement. According to Skinner, at this point we might make the mistake of thinking that we have explained the studying behavior by attributing it to the high need for achievement. In fact, however, this "need for achievement" is an explanatory fiction, merely a label that summarizes the studying and library-going behaviors and adds nothing to our understanding of what causes the behavior. The explanation, Skinner would contend, lies in the person's overall learning history and the specific reinforcement contingencies in place when the behavior occurs.

The problem with explanatory fictions led Skinner to be critical of physiological psychologists, who sought to explain behavior by reducing it, in his view, to nervous system activity. Although Skinner recognized the importance of studying brain function and nervous system activity, he was certain that a thorough experimental analysis of behavior was possible without reference to the nervous system, and he would not be impressed by modern neuroscience. In this regard, Skinner mirrored the attitude of the Harvard physiologist W. J. Crozier, with whom Skinner studied.[6] Similarly, he rejected most of contemporary cognitive psychology, on the grounds that it also resorted to explanatory fictions (e.g., attributing memory failures to short-term memory capacity limits).

This is not to say that Skinner denied the obvious fact that thinking, memory, and language occur. He rejected the idea that there was a qualitative distinction between public and private events and, as some behaviorists argued, that private events could not be studied scientifically. He argued instead that both public and private events can be understood through an experimental analysis of them (Skinner,

---

[6]W. J. Crozier (1892–1955) was a professor of physiology at Harvard and follower of Loeb, who had a strong influence on Watson. Crozier (like Loeb) believed that behavior could be interpreted in purely mechanical terms and without reference to the nervous system. Skinner (1956) once wrote that it "had been said of Loeb, and might have been said of Crozier, that he 'resented the nervous system.' Whether this was true or not, the fact was that both these men talked about animal behavior without mentioning the nervous system and with surprising success" (pp. 222–223).

1953). Running is a public event and problem solving is a private event, but they are both things that humans do and are therefore subject to the contingencies of reinforcement and stimulus control. A Skinnerian analysis of problem solving, for instance, would focus on how different problem-solving behaviors occur in different environments and how these behaviors have been reinforced in the individual's learning history. Skinner first outlined his views about public and private events in a 1945 paper called "The Operational Analysis of Psychological Terms." In that paper he explicitly labeled his approach a "radical behaviorism," a label that continues to be associated with him.

A Technology of Behavior

Skinner's inductive strategy was in the tradition of Sir Francis Bacon, and Skinner often referred to Bacon as his model (Smith, 1996a). As you recall from Chapter 2, Bacon argued that understanding nature required making careful observations of it without a preconceived theoretical framework. General principles would emerge from these observations. Bacon also believed that the control of nature was an important goal for science.

Bacon provided the prototype of what Smith (1992) has referred to as the *technological ideal*—a scientist who desires not merely to understand nature but to control it. In fact, Bacon argued that true understanding only occurred if one could demonstrate control over some phenomenon, either by manipulating some aspect of the environment and observing a predicted outcome or by creating some technology that worked reliably. Thus, a thorough understanding of physics can be demonstrated by creating machines that rely on various physical laws. For Skinner, the extrapolation to psychology was easy. He would show that behavior could be predicted, and he would create a technology of behavior, based on reinforcement principles, to show how behavior could be controlled.

Skinner's first attempt to develop a behavioral technology was known as Project Pigeon (Skinner, 1960), undertaken while he was at the University of Minnesota. During World War II, he obtained modest funding to develop a guidance system using pigeons to direct missiles. Along with a dedicated team of students, he was able to train pigeons to key peck at a target screen. As they pecked at the target, the missile would change direction until the target remained in the crosshairs of the screen. As a backup measure, each nose cone was fitted with three pigeons, each with its own target. The pigeons, of course, would make just one trip. Skinner was able to build a sophisticated prototype and to demonstrate its effectiveness, but the military killed the project.[7] Many years later, though, operant conditioning did make its way into a missile project, although Skinner was not involved directly. On at least two of early flights during the NASA space program that began in the 1960s, chimpanzees spent their time in space learning various operant tasks. One psychologist involved in the project wrote that "[e]very technique, schedule, and programming and recording device we used then and subsequently can be traced to [Skinner] or his students" (Rohles, 1992, p. 1533).

Despite the military's lack of enthusiasm for guiding missiles with pigeons, the experience convinced Skinner that his brand of behaviorism was applicable outside the laboratory. At a 1947 symposium on current trends in psychology, he pointedly argued for "extending the practices of an experimental science to the world at large. We can do this as soon as we wish to do it" (quoted in Capshew, 1996, p. 144). Good to his word, Skinner would, in subsequent decades, (a) follow Watson's

[7]One of the persons involved in killing Project Pigeon was Tolman's physicist brother, who was involved with the National Defense Research Committee. Skinner apparently believed that Richard Tolman's "lack of respect … for his brother's behavioral psychology" (Bjork, 1993, p. 123) contributed to the demise of the project.

lead and delve into the areas of child development and parenting, (b) challenge educational practice and develop a programmed teaching machine to facilitate learning, long before the development of personal computers, and (c) satisfy his long-held desire to write fiction with *Walden Two* (Skinner, 1948), which described a utopian community based on operant principles. Other Skinnerians extended his ideas into the areas of psychotherapy and business. And applying Skinner's ideas to animal training yielded outcomes familiar to anyone who has been to Sea World, but also demonstrated that operant conditioning has its limits.

CLOSE-UP

THE IQ ZOO AND THE "MISBEHAVIOR OF ORGANISMS"

Two of the Minnesota graduate students who worked with Skinner on Project Pigeon were Keller and Marian Breland. The experience changed their lives. Rather than following the normal path from grad school to an academic career, they decided to make a life for themselves by using what they knew of operant conditioning to train animals. They created a business called Applied Behavior Enterprise (ABE) and quickly landed a contract with General Mills, Inc., which called for the training of chickens in advertisements for one of their products, Larro Farm Feed. The hens tap danced and rolled wooden eggs down a chute and into a basket. Success with chickens led to bigger and better things, including "Priscilla the Fastidious Pig," who was able to turn on a radio, push around a vacuum cleaner, and select her favorite feed product (Larro, naturally), among other things (Breland & Breland, 1951).

The Brelands moved ABE south to Arkansas in the early 1950s and, in 1955, opened the "IQ Zoo" in Hot Springs. It quickly attracted tourists, drawn by such acts as chickens walking tightropes, parrots riding bicycles, raccoons playing basketball, and rabbits playing pianos (Figure 11.15). Over the next decade, 60,000 visitors a year paid 50 cents to tour the zoo (Drumm, 2009). The Brelands also became involved with dolphin training, and between 1955 and 1965, they consulted with Marineland of the Pacific (no longer exists, but was a model for today's SeaWorld). They wrote the first training manuals for conditioning dolphins, developed scripts for early dolphin shows, and trained others in basic operant principles (Gillaspy & Bailey, 2008).

One of the beliefs held by ardent behaviorists was that conditioning principles, both the classical and operant variety, were so powerful that virtually any type of behavior could be conditioned. The Brelands were certainly convinced, at least early in their career. In 1951, for instance, they wrote an article called "A field of applied animal behavior" (Breland & Breland, 1951), in which they enthusiastically described their promising new business (ABE) and lamented that their new applied field was "so vast … that we cannot begin to develop one-tenth of the projects we have thought of" (p. 204). Ten years later, though, they were less convinced of the universality of conditioning principles, writing an article that represents their most important contribution.

The article was called "The misbehavior of organisms" (Breland & Breland, 1961), the first published description of what came to be referred to the "biological constraints on learning" or "biological preparedness." In the article, they described some occasional frustrations in training animals to do certain tricks, experiencing "a persistent pattern of discomforting failures" (p. 681). For example, they attempted to train a raccoon to pick up wooden coins and deposit them in a piggy bank. It was not difficult to shape the animal to pick up a coin by simply reinforcing the behavior. It was also not too difficult to train the raccoon to place a single coin in the bank. The big problem occurred when they introduced a second coin, training the raccoon to pick up and deposit both. As the Brelands described it,

> Now the raccoon really had problems (and so did we). Not only could he not let go of the coins, but he spent seconds, even minutes, rubbing them together (in a most miserly fashion), and dipping them into the container. He carried on this behavior to such an extent that the practical application we had in mind—a display featuring a raccoon

(a)

Bob Bailey Animal Behavior Enterprises

(b)

FIGURE 11.15 (*a*) Keller and Marianne Breland and a musical friend; (*b*) a poster for the IQ Zoo.

putting money in a piggy bank—simply was not feasible. The rubbing behavior became worse and worse as time went on, in spite of nonreinforcement. (p. 682)

The experience (and four similar ones described in the article) shook the Brelands' faith in the power of pure conditioning, but it led them to the important insight that conditioning principles could sometimes be trumped by instinct. That is, they discovered that if the animals were asked to behave in a way that interfered with any of their naturally occurring instinctive behaviors, then the instinct would take over. They referred to it as *instinctive drift*. So the raccoon was showing a "washing response," an instinctive tendency to wash or prepare food (e.g., raccoons apparently rub crayfish together to remove the

exoskeletons). Animals, then, simply cannot be conditioned to produce any behavior a trainer wishes. What can be trained is limited by the animal's instinctive or species-specific behaviors.

Keller Breland (1915–1965) died suddenly in 1965, but Marian (1920–2001) carried on the work. Eleven years later she married Bob Bailey, a zoologist with a strong entrepreneurial spirit. Together they continued and expanded ABE, eventually developing behavioral exhibits with more than 150 species and gaining such clients as Opryland, Six Flags, Mobil Oil, and U.S. Department of Defense (Gillaspy & Bihm, 2002). Perhaps the best-known of the Breland–Bailey ABE programs was Bird Brain—a chicken who could play Tic-Tac-Toe and *never* lost to a human. On one occasion, it even beat none other than B. F. Skinner.

Evaluating Skinner

Unlike Guthrie, Tolman, and Hull, Skinner was never elected president of the American Psychological Association (perhaps the electorate got wind of his Tic-Tac-Toe loss). His research is seldom referenced in mainstream APA journals like the *Journal of Experimental Psychology*. He attracted many enthusiastic graduate students and many remained devoted operant researchers, but their relative numbers (compared with cognitive psychologists for instance) were small. Scattered across a number of universities there are still true believers and programs with a strong behavioral slant, and the two primary operant-based journals (*Journal of the Experimental Analysis of Behavior* and the *Journal of Applied Behavior Analysis*) remain vigorous, but Skinner's radical behaviorism was (and remains) outside the mainstream of American psychology. Today, few psychology departments have more than a single "operant" person (Robinson & Woodward, 1996).[8] Skinner himself was concerned about the longevity of his brand of behaviorism, fearing that it would fade after his death. As early as 1974, he wrote about what he perceived to be "the lack of young operant conditioners" (quoted in Bjork, 1993, p. 224) and the difficulty they had in finding jobs during a time when cognitive psychology was "in." Yet it is clear that his impact on psychology surpasses that of Guthrie, Tolman, or Hull, as well as most of the psychologists you have read about in this text. In a survey by Korn, Davis, and Davis (1991), for example, department chairs and historians were asked to rank order psychologists in terms of eminence. Two sets of rankings were obtained: one for the top 10 "contemporary" psychologists and another for an "all-time" top 10. Among contemporary psychologists, both chairpersons and historians ranked Skinner no. 1; on the "all-time" list, Skinner again ranked no. 1 among chairpersons, but dropped to no. 8 among historians. Although Skinner's rating was probably inflated by the proximity of the survey to his death in 1990, it is nonetheless clear that psychologists and historians alike consider him to be one of the discipline's premier figures. Incidentally, neither Guthrie, Tolman, nor Hull made any of the final top 10 lists.

Throughout this history of modern psychology, we have seen that American psychologists have felt pressured to show that their systems could be applied to improve the general welfare. This is one reason for the failure of Titchenerian psychology and the general success of functional and behavioral psychologies. In this regard, Skinner's contributions are unmatched in the history of psychology. His early research at Harvard, leading to *The Behavior of Organisms*, and his work in the 1950s, which produced *Schedules of Reinforcement*, fall into the category of basic laboratory research, but the bulk of his writing was directed at convincing the world that an experimental analysis of behavior is the only hope for the future welfare of the human species. This, of course, makes Skinner the true heir to Watson, who also labored long and hard to spread the "good word" of behaviorism. His strong and consistent advocacy made Skinner a controversial figure,[9] but it also resulted in his ideas being applied in more ways than ever imagined by Guthrie, Tolman, or Hull.

---

[8]One Skinnerian even postponed retirement to ensure that operant work at a major research university continued—"On a personal note, rather than retire I feel compelled to retain my position at UCSD in order to keep the faculty line in behavior analysis and to insure that the undergraduate laboratory in operant psychology (a pigeon lab) that I have taught for 40 years can continue to be offered" (Fantino, 2008, p. 126).

[9]Skinner never wavered in his beliefs, and his strong advocacy led many to consider him to be arrogant, condescending, and out of touch with core American values. Yet, Rutherford (2003) argued convincingly that Skinner's ideas for improving society occasionally meshed with contemporary cultural values and were applauded. His post–World War II attempt to build a market for an improvement on a baby's crib, for instance, was viewed favorably by many, in the context of a time when technological improvements to aid life at home were valued. Also, those who knew Skinner consistently described him as a warm, considerate, unassuming, and gentle man. He was also far from the narrow-minded scientist whose work occupied his every waking hour—he was widely read, a published poet, a big opera fan, and part of a Cambridge play-reading group (Smith, 1996b).

IN PERSPECTIVE: NEOBEHAVIORISM

Behaviorism has been a powerful force in American psychology. It produced some of psychology's most famous persons (Watson, Skinner), it dominated the research scene for several decades in the middle of the 20th century, and its applications continue to have widespread use in business, education, psychotherapy, and even daily life. Yet it is important to make two qualifications. First, behaviorism has largely been an American phenomenon. Behaviorist thinking was not widely influential in Europe, for example. Despite the heritage of British empiricism, there was not much of a British community of committed behaviorists, and in Europe, the movement has had little impact. We have already seen, in the discussion of Thorndike and his argument with Wells over laboratory methods (Chapter 7), for example, that European animal psychologists (e.g., Lorenz, Tinbergen) were much more inclined than Americans to study animal behavior in its natural environments than in the lab, and they were much more interested in instinctive than learned behavior. A key reason for behaviorism being more American-centered has to do with its applicability. We have seen over and over again that American pragmatism has played a strong role in shaping American psychology.

The second caveat is that although it is true that behaviorism dominated American experimental psychology in the '30s, '40s, and into the '50s, there was a nonetheless a great deal of research being done in American laboratories that had little to do with behaviorism, and a substantial number of experimental psychologists were doing important research that had nothing to do with conditioning. During the years of behaviorist hegemony, the pages of the leading journals still contained numerous articles describing research on such cognitive topics as memory, perception, attention, language, and thinking. Among many others, they included, in 1935, one of psychology's most famous papers, a summary of three experiments by an obscure graduate student at George Peabody College in Tennessee, J. Ridley Stroop (1935/1992). The "Stroop effect," a problem in which color naming is hindered by interference from automatic reading processes (e.g., the word RED is printed in green ink and the correct response to it is "green" not "red"), has been called psychology's most replicated finding (MacLeod, 1992). So not all the research during the heyday of behaviorism involved rats in mazes or pigeons in Skinner boxes.

In the opening paragraph of his book on the alleged mid-20th century cognitive revolution in psychology, Baars (1986) made the observation that behaviorism "is often referred to in the past tense" (p. 1) and that not too many psychologists refer to themselves as behaviorists anymore. There is a grain of truth to this assertion—as we will learn in Chapter 14, behaviorism with a capital "B" has been on the wane for decades, and cognitive psychology, which returned the study of mental processes to scientific respectability, has to a certain extent replaced behaviorism as American psychology's predominant conceptual framework. Yet Baars's assertion overstates the case. It overlooks the fact that research on learning and conditioning continues to occur at virtually every major university in America, and that behavioral principles continue to form the basis for many successful applications (e.g., behavior therapy). More important, and as an indication of just how influential behaviorism has been, the central message of behaviorism is now taken for granted by every research psychologist. That is, regardless of whether researchers consider themselves "behaviorists," they all are careful to operationally define psychological concepts in behavioral terms, and even if they are interested in internal, unobservable processes (e.g., insight in problem solving), they limit their evidence to behavioral phenomena (e.g., solutions to problems). Furthermore, I know of no introductory textbook that fails to include the term *behavior* in its definition of psychology. Baars recognized this himself in the preface to his book, writing that, in the sense just described, "we are all behaviorists" (p. ix).

SUMMARY

Post-Watsonian Behaviorism

• Contrary to traditional historical accounts, American psychology did not become predominantly behaviorist as the immediate result of Watson's program. Behaviorism did begin to take hold in the 1930s, however, partly because of Watson's continued propagandizing but also because full translations of Pavlov's research became available for the first time.

• Logical positivism, which allowed for theories to include abstract concepts but insisted that these concepts be tied to observable events, created a fertile climate for the evolution of behaviorism. Operationism, originating in physics in the late 1920s, also helped to create an environment conducive to objective, behaviorist thinking. Operational definitions define concepts in terms of a set of operations, under the control of the researcher, that are assumed to bring about the term in question (e.g., 24 hours without food brings on hunger). Confidence in the generality of some research outcome increases when various studies, each using a slightly different operational definition, nonetheless converge on the same outcome.

• Neobehaviorists disagreed on a number of issues, but agreed that (a) continuity among species allowed for general rules of behavior to be derived from nonhuman species, (b) understanding behavior required a thorough knowledge of how the organism learns, and (c) research results should have practical applications.

Edwin R. Guthrie (1886–1959): Contiguity, Contiguity, Contiguity

• Contiguity was the central principle in Guthrie's theory. Stimuli occurring contiguously with movement responses would result in a fully formed (i.e., one-trial learning) S-R bond. Skills, which require more than one-trial learning, involved building numerous S-R bonds.

• The effect of rewards was not to strengthen behavior, but to remove the animal from the original situation, thereby preserving the S-R connection. Punishment only works if a new behavior results, and forgetting involves replacing one S-R connection with another.

• Bad habits can be changed by identifying all the stimuli that lead to the habitual response and substituting new responses.

Edward C. Tolman (1886–1959): A Purposive Behaviorism

• According to Tolman, rats in a maze do not learn a series of S-R connections; rather, they learn an overall cognitive map of the maze. This spatial ability can be shown in latent learning studies, in which animals can be shown to be learning a maze even though the learning is not reflected in their performance until reinforcement is made available, and in place learning, in which animals learn to go to a location more quickly than they learn to make a specific response.

• Tolman believed that behavior was goal directed or purposive and that molar rather than molecular behavior should be the unit of study. He did not think that reinforcement was necessary for learning to occur. He developed the concept of the intervening variable, a hypothetical factor internal to the organism that intervenes between stimulus and response and is defined operationally. Many of the intervening variables in Tolman's system (e.g., expectancy) were cognitive.

Clark Hull (1884–1952): A Hypothetico-Deductive Behaviorism

• Although known primarily for his theory of learning based on animal studies, Hull also studied the development of concept learning in humans, aptitude testing, and experimental hypnosis, producing a doctoral dissertation on the first and books on the latter two topics.

• Modeled on Newtonian physics and consistent with the dictates of logical positivism, Hull's hypothetico-deductive system of behavior involved the development of a theory in which experiments were created to test hypotheses that were derived from highly formalized postulates. Research outcomes then strengthened faith in the postulates or brought about their revision.

• Hull's learning theory is a drive-reduction theory. Postulate 4 proposes that learning (i.e., an increase in habit strength) involves stimulus–response contiguity accompanied by reinforcement. Reinforcers are stimuli that reduce drives. They can be primary or biologically based (e.g., food), or secondary (learned through association with primary reinforcers).

• Hull used a large number of intervening variables. The most important one was reaction potential, $_sE_R$, the probability that a response will occur at a given time. It was said to be influenced by a number of factors, including drive (D) and habit strength ($_sH_R$), both of which Hull believed were necessary for learned behavior to occur.

B. F. Skinner (1904–1990): A Radical Behaviorism

• Skinner rejected the more formal theories of both Tolman and Hull and argued for a more inductive, descriptive behaviorism. He is best known for developing the distinction between classical and operant conditioning and for investigating the latter. To do so, he created the Skinner box, an experimental chamber in which the rate of some response (e.g., bar pressing) is recorded continuously by a cumulative recorder. Psychology's goals were to be the prediction and control of behavior, and the understanding of behavior, according to Skinner, occurred through an experimental analysis of behavior. Operant conditioning occurs when behavior is shaped by its immediate consequences. If the consequences are positive, the behavior occurring in a specific environment is more likely to occur in that environment in the future; if they are negative, the behavior becomes less likely to occur. Patterns of behavior vary as a function of various reinforcement schedules.

• Skinner rejected the use of what he called explanatory fictions, hypothetical factors that appear to explain a phenomenon but actually do nothing more than relabel it. Hence, he was critical of nervous system explanations of behavior, and he never accepted the idea that explanations for behavior would be found by cognitive psychologists.

• Skinner called for a technology of behavior to improve child rearing, education, and society as a whole through the use of behavioral techniques. Two of his students, Keller and Marian Breland, became famous as animal trainers, using operant techniques. They also discovered that not all behaviors were equally conditionable—an animal's instinctive behaviors could limit the power of conditioning.

STUDY QUESTIONS

1. Describe the "myth" of the behaviorist revolution.

2. Describe the events of the 1920s that paved the way for neobehaviorism to become dominant in the 1930s.

3. Explain how logical positivism, combined with operationism, dealt with the issue of how to study abstract nonobservable phenomena (e.g., hunger) objectively.

4. Give an example to show that you know what is meant by an operational definition, and explain the importance of using operational definitions in psychological research.

5. There was a degree of consensus among neobehaviorists on two important issues issues. Describe them.

6. Of all the learning theories considered in this chapter, Guthrie's is the most parsimonious. Explain.

7. Describe the Guthrie and Horton (1946) study, and explain how Guthrie thought it supported his theory.

8. Describe the influence of (a) gestalt psychology and (b) Edwin Holt on Tolman's theory of learning.

9. Define intervening variable, and use examples to show how the concept was used by (a) Tolman and (b) Hull.

10. Describe Tolman's latent learning study and explain what Tolman thought it demonstrated about the role of reinforcement in maze learning.

11. Describe Tolman's research on cognitive maps, and show how it fits into his theory of learning.

12. Describe Tolman's place learning experiment, and explain its significance.

13. Describe Hull's doctoral dissertation on concept learning, and show how it connected with his subsequent theory of learning.

14. Describe how research is conducted using a hypothetico-deductive approach.

15. Describe Hull's postulate 4.

16. What was the importance of reaction potential to Hull's theory, and what was the significance of the relationship between drive and habit strength being multiplicative rather then additive?

17. Explain why Hull was a leading figure in American psychology in the '40s and '50s and virtually forgotten today.

18. Describe the influence of Sir Francis Bacon on B. F. Skinner's ideas.

19. How did Skinner's approach to science differ from Hull's and Tolman's?

20. What is the distinction between Type S conditioning and Type R conditioning?

21. What did Skinner mean by an experimental analysis of behavior?

22. Describe the danger that Skinner saw with explanatory fictions. Use an example.

23. Write a brief essay that connects these concepts: technological ideal, Project Pigeon.

24. Describe the work of the Brelands and the significance of their 1961 paper on the "misbehavior of organisms."

25. In his book on the history of cognitive psychology, Baars concluded, "we are all behaviorists." Explain.

CHAPTER 12

MENTAL ILLNESS AND ITS TREATMENT

Our hysterical patients suffer from reminiscences. Their symptoms are residues … of particular (traumatic) events.

—Sigmund Freud, 1909

PREVIEW AND CHAPTER OBJECTIVES

When students first begin to explore psychology, they typically identify the field with the diagnosis and treatment of "mental illness." Of course, they quickly discover that psychology is a much broader subject—in a normal introductory course, they must wade through a dozen or so chapters on such topics as the brain and behavior, perception, motivation, emotion, learning, and cognition, before they get to the chapters on psychopathology and its treatment. Similarly, most histories of psychology, including this one, focus on how the discipline began applying scientific methods to age-old philosophical questions and how it developed as a science in an academic environment. Yet no history of psychology can be complete without describing, if briefly, the various ways that mental illness has been conceived of and treated over the years. Most of this chapter is devoted to Sigmund Freud's creation and his promotion of psychoanalysis—although trained as a physician, Freud pioneered the use of a nonmedical approach to treatment. We will explore the origins and evolution of some of his well-known concepts.

Prior to the detailed discussion of Freud, however, the chapter examines some early conceptions of mental illness and its treatment, beginning with the Enlightenment-era "moral treatment" strategy pioneered by Phillipe Pinel in France and William Tuke in England, and a more biological approach taken by America's Benjamin Rush. This is followed by a description of the 19th-century asylum movement and the asylum reform efforts by Dorothea Dix and Clifford Beers. Leading directly into the discussion of Freud is a description of the use of hypnotism as a therapeutic tool, starting with the magnetic personality of Anton Mesmer, and ending with the legendary Jean Charcot who, for a brief time, taught Freud. After you finish this chapter, you should be able to:

■ Show how Enlightenment thinking influenced reforms in the treatment of the mentally ill

■ Describe the features of the moral treatment approach, as used by Pinel in France and Tuke in England, and then imported to the United States

■ Describe the medical approach to treatment pioneered by Rush

■ Describe the development of the asylum movement and the influence of architecture (e.g., the Kirkbride model) on the philosophy of treatment for mental illness

■ Describe the reform efforts of Dix and Beers, and the outcomes of their work

- ■ Describe Kraepelin's early efforts at the classification and diagnosis of mental illness
- ■ Describe Mesmer's approach to treating hysteria, and explain why it was occasionally successful
- ■ Contrast the theories of hypnosis posed by Liebeault and Bernheim and by Charcot
- ■ Describe the "Freudian myth," and show how it was promoted
- ■ Show how Freud's ideas were influenced by materialist and evolutionary thinking
- ■ Describe and criticize the traditional description of the Anna O. case, and explain what Freud believed he had learned from it
- ■ Summarize the essential features of Freud's approach to therapy, in particular his strategies for accessing the unconscious
- ■ Describe the alternatives to psychoanalytic theory proposed by Adler and Jung
- ■ Critically analyze Freud's contributions to psychology

EARLY TREATMENT OF THE MENTALLY ILL

Every society must deal with people whose thoughts, emotions, and behaviors mark them as deviant. For much of recorded history, such persons, so different from the rest of "us," have sometimes been a source of fear and loathing, their treatment less than humane. At times, they have been regarded as evil or possessed by the devil, to be punished by being tortured and put to death, perhaps by being burned at the stake or drowned as a "witch." Alternatively, they have been considered either morally deficient and dangerous to society because of their transgressions, or incurable nuisances, and in need of being locked away from decent folks, perhaps chained to a wall, with no hope of being freed. Out of sight, out of mind. On the other hand, the picture is not as uniformly bleak as portrayed in standard histories of mental illness (e.g., Zilboorg, 1941). Treatises proposing reasonable biological causes for mental illness existed in medieval times, at the same time that demonology was a competing hypothesis, and there is evidence that the insane frequently were treated with compassion in their communities and through organized governmental intervention (Kroll, 1973; Neugebauer, 1978). As is true today, however, community size and socioeconomic status were important predictors of care. The mentally ill poor, especially those living in larger population areas, received the worst treatment, if they received any help at all.

"Enlightened" Reform: Pinel, Tuke, Rush

Several efforts at improving treatment of the mentally ill occurred in the late 18th and early 19th centuries, a product of the Enlightenment, a time of "spreading light into the dark corners of the human mind" (Appleby, Hunt, & Jacob, 1994, p. 36). As you recall from Chapter 3, the hallmark of Enlightenment thinking was a belief in the ideas of progress and reform and a strong faith in the ability of science to improve society. It was the kind of thinking that helped produce political revolutions both in the United States and France, and it elevated "science," the engine of progress, to the status of religion. In that context, mental illness came to be viewed in naturalistic terms as being biologically based and amenable to treatment.

An important reformer during this era was the French physician Phillipe Pinel (1745–1826), who instituted humane reforms in Paris, while working at both major hospitals there—the Bicêtre for men (1793) and the Salpêtrière for women (1795). Pinel's most dramatic action was to remove the chains from mentally ill patients who had been restrained, in some instances, for years. A famous painting by Tony Robert-Fleury commemorated the event (Figure 12.1). Although it has been shown (Micale,

FIGURE 12.1 Robert-Fleury's painting of Pinel ordering the removal of restraints at the Salpêtrière.

1985) that the number of liberated patients was relatively small, about 15 percent of the total hospital population, Pinel nonetheless deserves credit for bringing the concept of reform to institutions housing the mentally ill. He called his program *traitement moral* **moral treatment**, and it featured improvements in nutrition, hygiene, and general living conditions, and an early form of behavior modification, using rewards and punishments to bring order to patients' lives. Pinel's efforts, occurring in the context of the French Revolution, provide an example of the combined effects of an "enlightened" approach to insanity and an assault on institutions perceived to be repressing individual freedom. His reforms united the Enlightenment faith in progress and the revolutionary desire to liberate the oppressed.

At about the same time that Pinel was effecting change in France, similar reforms occurred in England, led by William Tuke (1732–1822). As a Quaker, Tuke was predisposed to provide relief for the downtrodden (the Society of Friends also became leaders in the antislavery movement, both in Great Britain and in the United States), and those suffering from mental illness were in special need of care. In 1792, Tuke founded the York Retreat in the north of England, dedicated to the benevolent treatment of the insane; the Retreat would be "a place in which the unhappy might obtain a refuge; a quiet haven in which the shattered bark might find the means of reparation and safety" (Beam, 2001, p. 11). Set in a rural environment and designed to resemble a working farm, the Retreat established a treatment program similar in spirit to the one used by Pinel. Good nutrition and hygiene were priorities, and patients were given freedom of movement within the Retreat property, allowed regular visitors, and given opportunities for recreation and work, all contingent on good behavior. The building was set on high ground, providing residents with a pleasant and relaxing view of the surrounding countryside. The Retreat's origins in the Society of Friends meant that Quakers in other parts of the world who had similar reform motives would know about the York Retreat and its philosophy of treatment. According to Grob (1994), Tuke's York Retreat became the model for at least half of the private mental hospitals created in the United States in the first quarter of the 19th century (e.g., the Friends Asylum, just outside of Philadelphia, established in 1813).

In addition to moral treatment, "enlightened" medical approaches to psychopathology developed during this time. The person credited with being the first in America to bring a medical strategy to the treatment of the mentally ill was Benjamin Rush, a prominent signer of the Declaration of Independence and surgeon general to the Continental Army of the American Revolution. He has been called the "father" of modern psychiatry, largely on the basis of his *Medical Inquiries and Observations upon the Diseases of the Mind*, which went through five editions between 1812 and 1835. One of the few "doctors" of this era with actual university training in medicine,[1] Rush became a strong advocate of a contemporary belief that disease resulted from abnormalities in the blood and circulatory system. Accordingly, a common remedy was to remove diseased or (especially) excess blood, and Rush became a promoter of **bloodletting** as a cure for a wide range of illnesses. These included mental ones, which Rush believed stemmed from "hypertension in the brain's blood vessels" (Bell, 1980, p. 9). Reducing the tension, then, involved opening veins and removing blood until the person reached a more tranquil state. This often worked rather well as a temporary means of calming violent patients, perhaps because these unfortunate individuals, down a few pints, were too weak to be hyperactive. Placebo effects may also have been involved.

In addition to bloodletting, Rush also created several devices designed to calm or redistribute the blood. For example, the *tranquilizer*, shown in Figure 12.2, was a chair with straps for restraining arms and legs, and a boxlike device that fit tightly over the head. By restricting movement, the goal was to reduce pulse rate, thereby calming the patient. The chair and similar restraining devices became common forms of treatment in postrevolutionary America, and although they might seem cruel to us today, it is important to recognize that they reflected an important new idea at the time—a belief that the mentally ill could benefit from treatment.

The 19th-Century Asylum Movement

In the United States, institutions created specifically for the mentally ill were rare prior to the 19th century. The first such asylum was the Eastern State Hospital, completed in 1773 in Williamsburg, Virginia. It was concerned more with confinement and public safety than with care, however, designed for "a poor unhappy set of people who are deprived of their senses and wander about the country, terrifying the rest of their fellow creatures" (Gamwell & Tomes, 1995, p. 20). Other than at places like Williamsburg, however, the mentally ill in the late 18th and early 19th centuries typically would find themselves at home, hidden away from neighbors if possible; in prison, if their behavior seemed to threaten the community; in the back wards or cellars of hospitals, which began to appear in the United States in the mid-18th century; or in an "almshouse," originally planned as a refuse for the poor and/or elderly in a community (Grob, 1973). In virtually all cases, treatment would be nonexistent.

As the 19th century progressed, however, especially as the population of urban areas began to increase, the need for institutions devoted to the mentally ill became increasingly apparent. Private asylums began to appear, many of them based on the York model and funded by Quakers. Yet private

---

[1]His medical training included a stop at the university in Edinburgh, Scotland. As was mentioned in Chapter 5, Edinburgh was Great Britain's foremost center for medical education, the locus of Darwin's unsuccessful attempt to become a doctor.

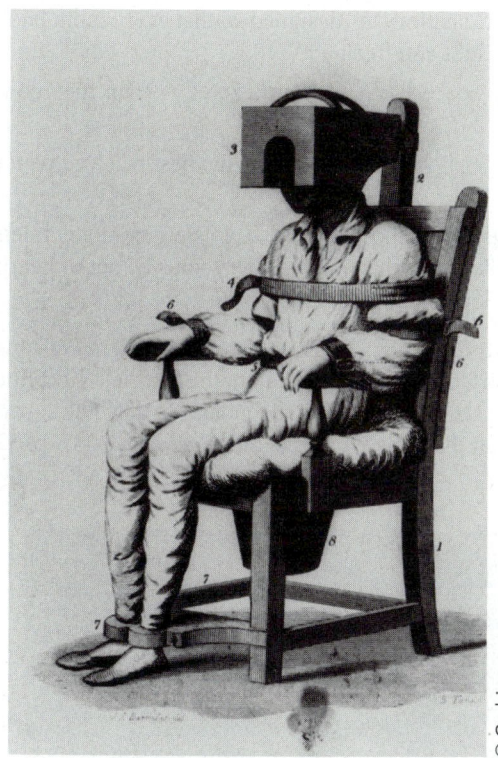

© Corbis

FIGURE 12.2 The tranquilizer chair, devised by Benjamin Rush for restraining and "calming" agitated mental patients.

asylums could handle just a fraction of those in need. They were either too small (Philadelphia's Friends Asylum housed about 30 patients), or they were beyond the means of most Americans. Cost was a major consideration at the McLean Asylum, just outside of Boston (founded 1818), for instance. Populated largely by the affluent mentally ill, it housed a yearly average of around 50 patients during its first dozen years of existence and had a staff-to-patient ratio of approximately 2:1, compared with a ratio of (at best) 10:1 in public institutions (Beam, 2001). The need for publicly funded institutions for the mentally ill, which would have greater capacity and would be affordable, became increasingly evident.

An important pioneer in the design of larger state-funded institutions was the physician Thomas Kirkbride (1809–1863). A Quaker and a firm believer in moral treatment, Kirkbride thought that architecture could be an important element of treatment. His ideas about the design of asylums, articulated in *On the Construction, Organization, and General Arrangements of Hospitals for the Insane with Some Remarks on Insanity and Its Treatment* (Kirkbride, 1854), established a standard that was widely copied in the second half of the 19th century (Grob, 1983). The "Kirkbride design" included these elements:

- Built in a rural environment, in imitation of the York plan, and placed on high ground, to provide patients with relaxing panoramic views of the countryside
- A central structure (the "center main") to house administrative offices and parlors for family to visit patients
- A series of wings on either side of the center main, with males housed on one side and females on the other; each wing to have a relatively small number of rooms and common rooms for recreation

- The wings set back from each other in a "shallow V," designed so that every room had a view of the countryside and was exposed to sunlight and fresh air

- Wide corridors in each wing, allowing space for patients to exercise when they could not go outside (e.g., in bad weather)[2]

- Three to four stories in height, with upper floors designated for the best behaved patients (good behavior earned a better view)

- In some cases, separate smaller buildings for the most disruptive, noisiest, or more violent patients (better control, but also in response to pleas like this one: "let her rooms be out of hearing of any shrieking you might have" (Yanni, 2007, p. 39)

Figure 12.3 shows an example of a Kirkbride design, St. Elizabeth's Hospital in Washington, DC. It dates from 1855 and was originally called the Government Hospital for the Insane.[3] Kirkbride asylums were typically designed to hold 250 patients, a size considered small enough so that "the superintendent could visit all the male patients and his wife all the female patients daily" (Yanni, 2007, p. 52). By the

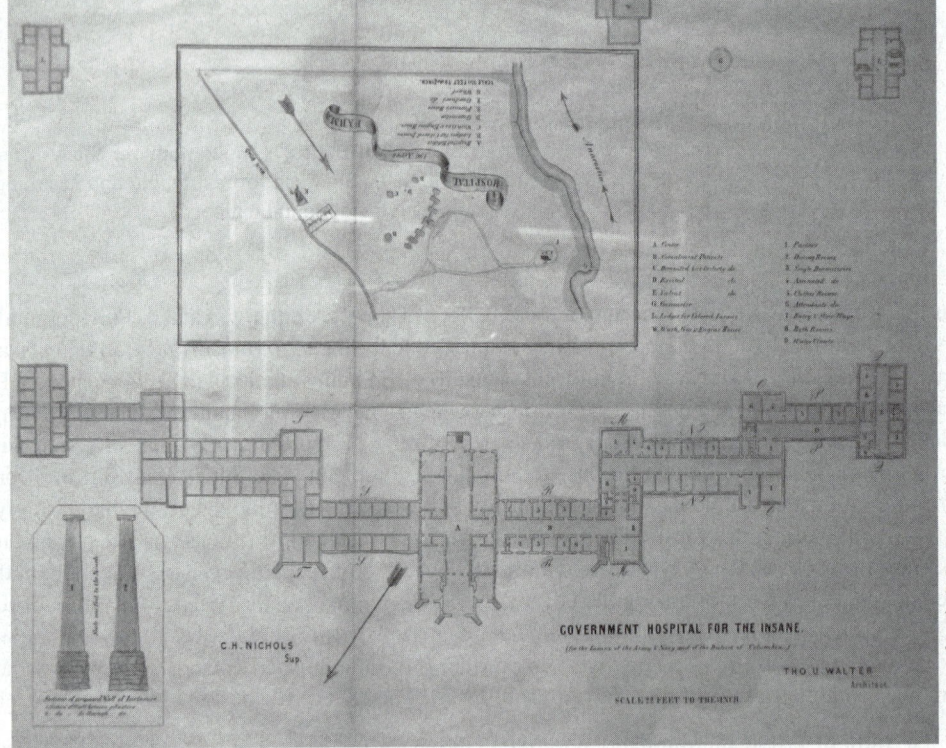

FIGURE 12.3 A Kirkbride design for St. Elizabeth's Hospital, Washington, DC.

Courtesy of Ludy T. Benjamin, Jr.

[2]This feature eventually had an unfortunate negative side effect—as asylums became overcrowded in the 20th century, these wide corridors provided space for additional beds.

[3]The hospital exists today, and its most prominent resident is John Hinckley, Jr., who attempted to assassinate President Reagan in 1981; Hinckley was judged not guilty by reason of insanity.

end of the century, however, an association of asylum superintendents had approved expansion of the Kirkbride design to sprawling buildings holding 600 patients (no more daily visits by the superintendent and his wife). By the early 20th century, these buildings often housed considerably more than 600.

Reforming Asylums: Dix and Beers

Kirkbride's contribution was substantial, but there were others whose advocacy for the mentally ill contributed to the creation, development, and reform of the 19th-century asylum. One such crusader was Dorothea Dix (1802–1887). Dix (Figure 12.4) was a New England educator whose general concern for the less fortunate led her to examine the conditions for treating those housed in public institutions. In Massachusetts in 1841, she began an 18-month tour of the state's jails, hospitals, and almshouses, and any other location that might house the mentally ill poor. What she encountered was an alarming level of abuse and neglect—instances where the mentally ill were chained to the walls of unheated closet-sized rooms, poorly fed and clothed, sometimes beaten into submission, and generally abandoned. On her return home, she wrote a scathing indictment of the system. Her case was presented to the Massachusetts legislature and led to a series of reforms, including an increase of funds to improve the state's public asylum in Worcester.[4] This success prompted her to repeat her modus operandi in other states—a thorough tour of institutions followed by a detailed exposé. By 1848, the Dix crusade had logged some 60,000 miles of travel, observing in the process "more than nine thousand idiots, epileptics, and insane … destitute of appropriate care and protection" (quoted in Viney, 1996, p. 22).

© Corbis

FIGURE 12.4 Dorothea Dix, crusader for mental health reform.

[4]The Worcester asylum dated from the early 1830s. After the expansion following Dix's report, the asylum quickly became overcrowded, and a major expansion was undertaken in the 1870s, which adapted the Kirkbride design. This building burned in a massive fire in 1991.

Her efforts played a role in the creation of 47 mental hospitals (many using the Kirkbride design) and schools for the feebleminded (Viney & Zorich, 1982). Although many of these institutions over the years grew to sizes that prevented effective care and led in the 20th century to a renewal of problems with overcrowding and abuse, her efforts on behalf of the mentally ill dramatically improved the living conditions of those powerless to help themselves. That she was able to accomplish what she did in the face of her own poor health (probably tuberculosis), difficult traveling conditions, and the generally accepted belief that women were not worth listening to, is nothing less than extraordinary.

Another avenue for asylum reform came from within the asylum itself. It took the form of a remarkable book published in 1908, written by a former mental patient, Clifford Beers (1876–1943). Beers was a graduate of Yale and had settled into a position in a New York City insurance company when a suicide attempt, followed by a year of depression, landed him in the first of three mental institutions that he would inhabit for just over 3 years. After being released from the third one in 1903, Beers compiled his notes into a book describing the day-to-day life of a hospitalized mental patient. Five years later, he published *A Mind That Found Itself* (Beers, 1908), complete with a prefatory letter from William James, who had read the manuscript and wished to support the cause of reform. Beers was critical of the doctors he had encountered, believing them to be generally incompetent and too willing to use punitive measures, but he saved his heaviest invective for the attendants in charge of the day-to-day operation of the wards. He documented the constant verbal and occasional physical abuse suffered at the hands of the staff and called for improved conditions and professional training for attendants.

Because Beers had experienced mental institutions and lived to write about them, a second message of his book was that mental illness was curable. This was an important idea at a time when the many in the medical community had come to believe that little hope existed for the institutionalized mentally ill. In 1909, Beers founded the National Committee for Mental Hygiene to further the cause of prevention, and he spent his remaining years informing the public of his beliefs about mental illness, promoting programs to enhance mental health, and lobbying for the creation of mental hygiene clinics (Williams, Bellis, & Wellington, 1980).

Progress in the treatment of mental illness necessarily implies improvements in the diagnosis of mental illness. You might know about the modern version of this, the *DSM-V*. This chapter Close-Up provides some background and a connection to Wundt.

CLOSE-UP

DIAGNOSING MENTAL ILLNESS

As you might recall from your general psychology course, or a course in abnormal psychology, one of the most valuable tools for psychiatrists and clinical psychologists is *DSM-V*, short for *Diagnostic and Statistical Manual of Mental Disorders*, now in its fifth edition (American Psychiatric Association, 2013). It includes detailed descriptions of symptoms for the various disorders, based on the accumulated research of decades. It is encyclopedic, including more than 400 psychiatric diagnostic categories. *DSM-V* is just the most recent of a long line of attempts to categorize mental illness. A major advance in diagnosis was made by the German physician

Emil Kraepelin (1856–1926), who appears to have used some of what he learned in Wundt's laboratory to provide the first clear insight into a disorder that he named *dementia praecox*, and that we now call schizophrenia.

Kraepelin earned a medical degree from the Würzburg in 1878, specializing in psychiatry. While working as a resident in Munich, he learned of the new laboratory psychology being developed at Leipzig, and he traveled there in 1882 to experience Wundt's laboratory firsthand. While at Leipzig, he was involved in several research projects during the 2 years he was there, but he did not complete a doctoral degree with Wundt. After several brief appointments at asylums and universities in the 1880s, his big break arrived in 1890—a position as professor of psychiatry in the clinic at Heidelberg University. The prestigious clinic afforded Kraepelin a large patient base, enabling him to begin a process of sorting patients into discrete categories, based partly on symptoms, but primarily on the kinds of outcomes (prognosis) that could be expected. He became known for his massive collections of individual note cards on which he recorded the details of each case, from the information collected from the initial intake to the final outcome. Kraepelin remained at Heidelberg for 13 years and then finished his career in Munich as director of the university clinic there.

Kraepelin began his efforts to build a classification scheme for mental illness in 1883, and his "textbook" went through nine editions, the last one appearing the year after his death. His first effort, published when he was only 27, has been described as a "slim *Compendium* of no particular merit" (Shorter, 1997, p. 102), but in fact it ran to 400 pages and began to establish Kraepelin's reputation. By the time he died, the ninth edition had expanded to two volumes and 2,425 pages (Menninger, 1963).

Kraepelin's sixth edition, appearing in 1899, is the best known. In it he identified 13 categories of mental illness, ranging from those that were relatively mild and had a promising prognosis (e.g., "fright neurosis") to the more serious disorders. Among the most debilitating were two that he labeled manic-depressive psychosis and dementia praecox (Havens, 1965). Mania and depression had been known for some time, and "circular states" had been described as well, but Kraepelin provided the first comprehensive description of the disorder that today is known as bipolar disorder. But it was his description of **dementia praecox** that made Kraepelin famous. He used the name, which translates roughly as "premature dementia," to reflect the fact that this incapacitating mental disorder tended to appear relatively early in life, often during late adolescence. The symptoms included "disturbances in apprehension, … in orientation, … of attention, … of memory, … of the train of thought, … of the emotional field," and "hallucination" (quoted in Sahakian, 1968, p. 323). Note that several of these symptoms reflect the kinds of cognitive processes that Kraepelin learned about as a student in Wundt's laboratory. Kraepelin believed that one of the defining attributes of dementia praecox was an inability to focus attention, and his theory is similar to modern attentional theories of the disorder. He argued that the thought processes of those with dementia praecox lacked the normal apperceptive ability and their attentional capacity was severely limited. Whereas normal people could focus their attention and direct their mental activity along meaningful paths (i.e., they can *apperceive*, to use Wundt's term), those with dementia praecox could not. Hence, their mental activity resembled random associations. This accounts for one of the common symptoms: the meaningless strings of phrases often emitted by those suffering from the disorder.

Kraepelin also believed that the prognosis was so poor for this form of dementia that any chance for recovery was virtually hopeless. It wasn't long before this fatalistic prognosis was challenged by psychiatrists who pointed to cases where improvement did occur. One such researcher was Eugene Blueler (1857–1939), who renamed the disorder *schizophrenia*, the name used today.

Dementia praecox was not the only form of mental deterioration that interested Kraepelin. He also investigated a form of dementia that mysteriously appeared in adults of late middle age that was similar in form to that shown by the very elderly. This premature dementia was later studied in greater depth by a close friend and research colleague of Kraepelin's at Heidelberg, Aloys Alzheimer (1864–1915), for whom this terrifying disease is named.

MESMERISM AND HYPNOSIS

Superintendents of asylums usually were psychiatrists, so treatments there, when they existed, tended to be based on a medical model, although the moral treatment ideal had a strong psychological aspect to it (e.g., behave and you get a better room). Other strategies for treating mental illness based on a psychological approach evolved through the years, and one of them became very popular in the early 20th century, when Sigmund Freud invented psychoanalysis. First, though, it is necessary to set the stage for

Freud by briefly describing the history of hypnosis, a technique that Freud learned about in Paris and tried for a while, eventually abandoning it for other methods. The origins of hypnosis lie with an eccentric Viennese physician who created an occasionally effective therapy based on the idea that illness, mental or otherwise, was the consequence of misaligned magnetic forces within the distressed person.

Mesmerism and Animal Magnetism

The start of Franz Anton Mesmer's (1734–1815) professional career was conventional enough. He earned a medical degree at the prestigious University of Vienna in 1766 and quickly established a thriving practice. Through a fortunate marriage, he entered into Vienna's highest social circles, counting the young composer Wolfgang Amadeus Mozart among his friends. As a scientist, Mesmer was aware of current developments and was especially intrigued by recent discoveries of such forces such electricity and magnetism. He became convinced that magnetism affected humans directly, with good health being the consequence of properly aligned internal magnetic forces. Were these forces to become misaligned, however, ill health (either physical or mental) would result. If you can imagine the effects of trying to push together the plus poles of two magnets, you can get an idea of Mesmer's disease concept. Illness resulted from the disharmony of forces opposing each other. The cure, then, involved straightening out these forces within the body. Thus Mesmer found that he could help many of his patients, especially those suffering from disorders with psychological roots, by giving them medicine containing heavy doses of iron, then passing magnets over their bodies. Patients would fall into a "crisis state," a type of trance, and when they emerged, would find their health improved. He called his theory of illness and cure **animal magnetism**. He did not know it, but he had inadvertently demonstrated the power of suggestion on human behavior, and he had discovered what would later be renamed hypnosis.

Mesmer soon learned that he could produce cures without the magnets. Convinced that he had magnetic powers himself, he discarded the magnets and began treating patients directly by passing his hands over them. He would also massage parts of a patient's body that were causing distress (e.g., an apparently paralyzed arm), following the path of the nerves and suggesting that things would improve (Winters, 1950). He would also occasionally place one hand on the patient's stomach and another on the small of the back, "in order to saturate the trunk with magnetic fluid" (Forrest, 1999, p. 19). Mesmer had some success and became convinced that he was quite special, but he aroused the ire of the generally conservative medical community in Vienna. The fact that most of his patients were women and his therapy was quite "hands-on" contributed to the concern. After becoming embroiled in several heated controversies over the effectiveness of his cures and the appropriateness of his technique, he found himself no longer welcome in Vienna. In May of 1777, he was expelled from the medical faculty of the University of Vienna and ordered to stop practicing medicine in the city (Hoffeld, 1980). It was time to move on.

Hoping to find a more open-minded environment, Mesmer moved his magnetic therapy to Paris in 1778. Aided by his promotional skills and his "magnetic" personality, he soon began attracting more patients than he could easily handle. His solution to the overcrowding was to create perhaps the first version of group therapy. In an expensively decorated clinic in one of the most fashionable neighborhoods in Paris, small groups of patients would congregate around Mesmer's famous *baquet*. This was a type of wooden tub that contained various chemicals and had iron rods protruding from it in all directions. Patients would encircle the baquet and grab hold of an iron rod, while Mesmer would pass among them and encourage them to enter the crisis state. There was much moaning and swooning, with many individuals undoubtedly influenced by a form of group contagion. Once the mass crisis passed, patients recovered their composure, pronounced themselves much better, and then left the clinic to spread the good word. Indeed, many patients seemed to be cured, especially those suffering from a variety of what we would today call psychosomatic complaints (e.g., headaches, fainting spells, digestive problems). Although most of Mesmer's patients had the financial means to pay for treatment, others didn't, and Mesmer responded by providing free magnetism—he magnetized a large oak tree in a Paris park, where those in need could go and receive some benefit by holding onto ropes attached to the tree (Forrest, 1999).

As in Vienna, however, the medical community was not impressed. Paris in the prerevolutionary years was a place of much uncertainty and flux, and it was full of faith healers and others promising simple answers to the anxieties of the day (Hoffeld, 1980). In this context, Mesmer seemed to be just another quack. The question of the validity of **mesmerism**, as Mesmer's technique was now called, was taken up by a distinguished commission of the French Royal Academy of Sciences, appointed by the king. At its head was the renowned Benjamin Franklin, the American ambassador to France and a distinguished scientist in his own right, a pioneer in the study of electricity and the inventor of a remarkable new device, the lightning rod (Cohen, 1995). The Franklin committee concluded that mesmerism had no scientific foundation. It recognized that some patients had been helped by Mesmer, but attributed any cures to the patient's beliefs rather than to Mesmer's "magnetizing" powers.

From Mesmerism to Hypnosis

Mesmer gradually faded from the scene after the Franklin commission's report, but mesmerism itself spread throughout Europe, mainly at the level of entertainment. Much like today's stage hypnotists, mesmerists toured the countryside giving dramatic demonstrations that wowed the locals. Few scientists paid attention, but one who did was John Elliotson (1791–1868), a professor of medicine at University College, London, and senior physician at the teaching hospital affiliated with the college. He was intrigued by the demonstrations of apparent anesthesia, during which mesmerized people would show no signs of pain, even while being poked with sharp needles. Elliotson was one of those open-minded scientists who often antagonizes the establishment—he was already under suspicion for promoting a new contraption that most other doctors refused to use, the stethoscope (Boring, 1950). Thus, eyebrows were raised when he began mesmerizing patients. When Elliotson proposed researching the anesthetic effects of mesmerism in the late 1830s, the storm broke. He was denied permission by his hospital board, which also outlawed any use of mesmerism at the hospital. Elliotson resigned in protest and spent his remaining years promoting mesmerism.

Meanwhile other physicians were starting to use mesmerism to reduce the pain of surgery. In the 1840s, for example, there were numerous reported cases of amputations being done while the patient was in a trance. As a witness to an 1842 case of an amputated leg reported:

> The placid look of his countenance never changed for an instant; his whole frame rested, uncontrolled, in perfect stillness and repose; not a muscle was seen to twitch. To the end of the operation, including the sawing of the bone, securing the arteries, and applying the bandages, occupying a period of upwards of twenty minutes, he lay like a statue. (quoted in Forrest, 1999, p. 180)

The largest study of the effects of mesmeric effects on pain was completed by James Esdaile (1808–1859), a Scottish surgeon working in India. In 1845, he summarized the results of several hundred surgeries using mesmerism-induced anesthesia. He reported a mortality rate of less than 5 percent as a result of the surgery, at a time when mortality was normally 40 percent (Gravitz, 1988). Keep in mind that these were the days before the existence of chemical anesthetics such as ether, and surgery was a brutal business that prized speed over precision, with screaming patients firmly secured to the operating table. Thus, any procedure for pain reduction was a welcome development. Nonetheless, the medical community as usual was slow to change, and the prevailing medical wisdom was that pain, because it was a naturally occurring phenomenon, was good and even necessary for surgery to succeed. As one contemporary medical treatise put it, "pain is a wise provision of nature, and patients ought to suffer pain while their surgeon is operating; they are all the better for it, and recover better" (quoted in Forrest, 1999, p. 181).

Mesmerism finally began to gain respectability in the late 1840s, in part by changing its name. The Scottish physician James Braid (1795–1860), a respected member of the conservative medical establishment, initially set out to demolish mesmerism, but came to recognize the validity of some of its effects. Because he thought the trance state was similar to a state of sleep, he coined a new term for the phenomenon. **Neurypnology**, a contraction of "neuro-hypnology," combined Greek terms for nervous (neuro) and sleep (hypnos) and was defined by Braid as a "nervous sleep." Soon the initial part of the term began to be dropped, and the phenomenon came to be called hypnology or **hypnotism**. Braid discovered that the hypnotic trance could be induced by having patients stare fixedly at an object just above their line of vision, and he came to believe that a general fixation of attention was behind the phenomenon. He also emphasized the importance of suggestion in producing hypnotic effects. By 1860, when the discovery of ether and chloroform rendered surgical use of hypnosis unnecessary, the phenomenon had been recognized in the scientific community as legitimate and worthy of study. Further developments, and controversy, occurred in France.

The Hypnotism Controversies

Hypnotism achieved a degree of legitimacy with Braid, but little consensus existed over its explanation. Two opposing views about the nature of hypnotism developed in France, with a pair of physicians working in the provincial city of Nancy (180 miles east of Paris) on one side of the sometimes acrimonious debate, and the powerful director of the famous Salpêtrière Hospital in Paris on the other.

The so-called Nancy School of hypnosis originated from the curiosity of Auguste Liebeault (1823–1904), an unassuming country doctor practicing just outside Nancy, who decided to give hypnosis a try after being intrigued by an old book on mesmerism. He recruited patients for hypnotic treatment by charging no fees for it, and his success produced a legendary local reputation. He soon attracted the attention of a nationally known physician living nearby, Hippolyte Bernheim (1840–1919), who traveled to Liebeault's clinic expecting to discover and expose fakery. Instead, he became a convert.

The central feature of the Liebeault–Bernheim theory of hypnosis was **suggestion**, which they defined as the ability to uncritically accept an idea or a command suggested by a hypnotist and transform the suggestion into an action (Ellenberger, 1970). They considered suggestibility to be a personality trait, with every person having it to some degree. Hypnotic susceptibility was therefore considered to be a normal phenomenon, experienced by different people with varying degrees of strength. In their medical practices, Liebeault and Bernheim induced hypnosis by having the patient stare into the doctor's eyes while being told to relax deeply. Once in a sleeplike trance, the doctor would suggest to the patient that the symptoms (e.g., headache) would go away. The symptoms often did just that.

Meanwhile, the sprawling Salpêtrière Hospital in Paris had become the European center for the study of hypnosis. Its director, Jean-Martin Charcot (1825–1893), was known throughout Europe for his pioneering work on epilepsy; he was the first to identify the features of grand mal seizures and to distinguish them from petit mal seizures. Charcot was also an expert in the study of **hysteria**, a disorder characterized by a wide range of symptoms that appeared to indicate neurological malfunction, but without apparent damage to the nervous system. Some patients experienced epilepsy-like seizures, others developed paralyses that were neurologically impossible (e.g., only the hand), and still others had nervous tics, headaches, sensory loss (e.g., deafness), or severe memory lapses. Charcot's contribution was to take hysteria seriously as a disorder and search for its cause. Contemporary medical opinion, grounded in the materialistic belief that true disorders had a physical basis, was that hysterics were simply malingerers, making up their symptoms. Charcot's willingness to tackle the problem head-on eventually earned him the title of "Napoleon of the Neuroses" (Ellenberger, 1970, p. 95).

Because Charcot observed that many of the symptoms of hysteria were the same as phenomena demonstrated under hypnosis, he came to believe that hysteria and the ability to be hypnotized shared the same underlying pathology. Thus, although the hypnotists at Nancy considered suggestibility a normal trait and therefore generally useful as a therapy tool, Charcot declared that hypnotism was dangerous if it was used indiscriminately. Furthermore, he argued, susceptibility to hypnosis was an indication of underlying hysteric tendencies, which Charcot believed were the result of an inherited nervous system disorder. Hypnotism, then, was an "innately predisposed reaction on the part of [hysterics] to stroking, fixations of the sensory apparatus, and various other means of hypnotic induction" (Sulloway, 1979, p. 46). Hypnotism could be useful, Charcot proclaimed, primarily as a means of investigating and influencing the symptoms of those suffering from hysteria. Furthermore, because some patients were indeed malingerers, hypnosis was the means of separating the true hysterics from the fakes. Only true hysterics could be hypnotized, Charcot believed.

At the Salpêtrière, Charcot was famous for his elaborate and spectacular clinical demonstrations of hysteria. He would pick his "best" hysteric patients, hypnotize them, and suggest various symptoms to them. Charcot's patients apparently competed with each other for the privilege of being "on stage." Predictably, they performed as expected. Figure 12.5 portrays Charcot giving a clinical demonstration of hypnosis on Blanche Wittman, whose dramatic performances earned her the title among her peers of "Queen of the Hysterics" (Fancher, 1990). Charcot also used hypnosis to suggest the removal of hysteric symptoms in his patients and claimed some success.[5]

FIGURE 12.5 Painting of Charcot lecturing on hysteria at the Salpêtrière, with Blanche Wittman as the hypnotized patient, from Gay (1988). Freud bought an engraving of the piece and hung it in his consulting room (look carefully at Figure 12.7).

Courtesy of National Library of Medicine

[5]Chapter 8 briefly described some research on hypnosis that embarrassed a young Alfred Binet, in which his apparent success in producing effects with magnets was shown to be the result of suggestion. This study was conducted under Charcot's direction at the Salpêtrière, and the patient was none other than Blanche Wittman (Fancher, 1990).

The doctors from Nancy disagreed sharply with Charcot's beliefs about hypnosis, arguing that his dramatic clinical demonstrations merely showed the effects of suggestion. Charcot's patients knew exactly what was expected of them, it was argued, and they delivered. A fierce debate erupted in the mid-1880s, and between 1888 and 1893, one bibliography listed 801 publications in journals and magazines on the nature of hypnosis (Sulloway, 1979). By the mid-1890s, most observers had rejected Charcot's ideas about the connection between hysteria and hypnosis in favor of the Nancy model emphasizing suggestibility.

During the height of his fame, young physicians from all over Europe came to the Salpêtrière to experience Charcot and learn from his brilliant lectures and demonstrations. One such man was a young doctor from Vienna whose ideas reverberated through the 20th century.

SIGMUND FREUD (1856–1939): FOUNDING PSYCHOANALYSIS

That Sigmund Freud has had a profound influence on Western culture is widely recognized. What is less known is the manner in which his ideas evolved and the sources of influence on him. Indeed, students in introductory and personality courses often encounter a distorted description of Freud that perpetuates what Sulloway (1979) called the "myth of the hero." This Freudian myth encompasses two components, according to Sulloway. First, it includes the image of Freud as a solitary heroic figure fighting for his ideas against all odds, in a uniformly hostile environment. Second, it maintains the illusion that the hero's theories were original to him, without serious precedent. Both aspects of this Freudian myth have been brought into question by recent historical scholarship. As will be seen: (a) Freud was indeed controversial but his ideas were not nearly as revolutionary as is normally portrayed, and (b) all his major concepts have traceable origins to related or identical ideas in existence in the late 19th and early 20th centuries. Freud's genius was not in creation but in synthesis and advocacy—in weaving ideas together into a unified theory of human behavior and in vigorously promoting this theory in the medical community.

Interestingly enough, Freud played a role in creating his own myth, in part by hand-picking his first biographer, Ernest Jones, but also by destroying his papers and correspondence on at least two occasions (1885 and 1907), thereby making it difficult to trace the roots of his ideas. After the first of these events, Freud wrote this to his fiancée:

> One intention ... I have almost finished carrying out, an intention which a number of as yet unborn and unfortunate people will one day resent ... : my biographers. I have destroyed all my notes of the past fourteen years, as well as letters, scientific excerpts, and the manuscripts of my papers.... I couldn't have matured or died without worrying about who would get hold of those old papers.... As for the biographers, let them worry, we have no desire to make it too easy for them. Each one of them will be right in his opinion of "The Development of the Hero," and I am already looking forward to seeing them go astray. (quoted in Sulloway, 1979, p. 7)

This is a remarkable letter. Who was this young man, not yet 30 years old, who was certain that he would someday have biographies written about him?

Early Life and Education

Freud spent most of his life in Vienna, Austria. His father moved a growing family there in 1860, when young Sigmund was four, and Freud left only when the Nazi threat to his personal safety took him to London in 1938, a year before his death. Freud's intellectual promise appeared early. He was a precocious young child in a large household of moderate means, the only one of his siblings given a room of his own for study. He was also given a generous book-buying allowance, and legend has it that when he once complained about the distractions of a younger sister's noisy piano lessons, they ended, and the piano was banished from the house.

Freud was the first of eight children produced by the marriage of Jacob and Amalia Freud. Amalia was Jacob's third wife and half his age (20 versus 40). Freud developed a strong emotional attachment to his young mother, while his father was more distant and appeared more grandfatherly than fatherly—the family dynamics almost certainly played a role in Freud's later thinking about parent–child relationships, especially his advocacy of the Oedipal complex (Kramer, 2006). Although the Freud family was Jewish, religious practice was not at the center of family life, and Freud would later recall that his father "allowed [him] to grow up in complete ignorance of everything that concerned Judaism" (quoted in Gay, 1988, p. 6). One aspect of Judaism that Freud did experience, however, was Vienna's pervasive anti-Semitism. The period of Freud's youth saw a steady rise in the Jewish population in Vienna, from 2 percent of the population in 1857 to 10 percent by 1880 (Gay, 1988). Although reforms made life easier for Jews in the 1860s, a serious economic depression in 1873 led to an all too familiar scapegoating scenario: Jews were blamed for Vienna's problems and became the objects of political (and physical) attack and discrimination. In that same year, Freud entered the University of Vienna's famed medical school, where he quickly became an academic star.

Although he was a medical student, Freud had no intention of practicing medicine—research was his passion. Through his mentor, Ernst Brücke, director of the university's Physiological Institute, Freud became immersed in the 19th-century materialist-mechanist-determinist zeitgeist in physiology. Brücke had been a student of the great Johannes Müller, and together with Helmholtz and other students of Müller, he was a leader in the movement that sought to explain all living action by reducing it to physical, mechanical forces. Although Freud's interest in searching for the physiological mechanisms underlying psychological processes diminished over the years, he never wavered in his belief that all events have causes that can be identified through science. His later ideas that dreams were not random events, but had deep underlying meanings, and that even events seeming to be accidents (i.e., Freudian slips) are nonetheless meaningful, are just two examples of his strong faith in the essential orderliness and predictability of psychological events.

Freud's immersion in research was the main reason it took him 8 years instead of the typical 5 to earn his medical degree. Working in Brücke's laboratory from 1876 to 1882, he published articles on the nervous systems of various species; he also developed an important research technique for staining nerve fibers (similar to the stains developed by Golgi and Ramon y Cajal, described in Chapter 3). Much of his comparative neurological research carried with it strong evolutionary implications, for Darwin's monumental text was less than 20 years old, and its ideas affected the thinking of all physiologists during the era. Indeed, Darwin's thinking would eventually influence Freud profoundly. First, Darwin's basic insight that human nature is rooted in its animal past provided support for Freud's beliefs about the importance of biological instincts in motivating behavior and the fact that behavior is not always "rational." Second, Freud's belief in the importance of sexual motivation follows logically from the rather obvious point that sex, with the resulting perpetuation of the species, is at the core of evolutionary theory.

Freud had every intention of continuing as a researcher when he completed his medical degree in 1883, but by then he was also in love and faced with a financially uncertain future as a laboratory researcher. And as a Jew, few academic positions would be open to him. If he wished to marry, establishing a medical practice would be necessary. Hence, on Brücke's advice, he reluctantly began to prepare for life as a practitioner by taking 3 years of instruction at Vienna's General Hospital. For part of this time, he came under the tutelage of Theodor Meynert, a famous brain anatomist and professor of psychiatry. Freud's earlier research with Brücke led him to be especially interested in disorders of the nervous system, and the time spent with Meynert confirmed in him the decision to specialize in that area. Patients with neurological problems also included hysterics, of course, and it was through his experience with Meynert that Freud first began to encounter the type of patient who would soon become the focus of his life's work. In 1885, he broadened his knowledge of hysteria and began to learn something about hypnosis, when he earned a travel grant to study for 6 months with Charcot at the Salpêtrière. He later used hypnosis in the early years of his practice, but eventually abandoned it as ineffective, for him at least.

Breuer and the Catharsis Method Another important contact that Freud made while in medical school was with the eminent physician Joseph Breuer (1842–1925), known for his discovery of the role played by the semicircular canals of the inner ear in maintaining balance and equilibrium. From 1880 to 1882, while Freud was still finishing medical school, Breuer had treated a perplexing case of hysteria that was destined to become one of the defining events in the history of psychoanalysis—the **Anna O. case**. It is also just one example of how the story of psychoanalysis has become distorted over the years.

Anna O. was the pseudonym that Breuer created for Bertha Pappenheim, an intelligent woman in her early twenties with a bewildering array of hysteric symptoms.[6] At various times her right (then her left) side appeared to be paralyzed and anesthetic, she had a persistent nervous cough, experienced both visual and auditory deficits, developed bizarre eating habits (e.g., living solely on oranges for a period of several weeks), lost the ability to speak German for a time (while retaining the ability to speak English), and experienced dissociative states that she called "absences" (Sulloway, 1979). The problems appeared to be precipitated by the long-term nursing care she had given to her dying father, although Anna's general frustrations about her situation in life contributed as well. An intelligent young woman, Anna was raised in a family and cultural context that consistently stifled her intellect and ambition.

According to the traditional (and mythical) description of the case, Breuer found success with what he called the method of **catharsis**. He discovered that if Anna could be made to trace a particular symptom back to the occasion of its first appearance, she would experience an emotional release, which Breuer referred to as a "catharsis," and she would gain symptom relief. Anna referred to it as her "talking cure." For example, for a time she was unable to drink water from a glass and thought the practice disgusting. Breuer got her to trace her hydrophobia back to a situation in which Anna had witnessed a woman at a dinner party who shared the same glass of water with her dog. Once the initial memory had been retrieved, she achieved a catharsis and the hydrophobia disappeared. In like manner, so the story goes, Breuer worked his way laboriously through Anna's remaining symptoms, seeing her almost every evening for more than a year.

The Anna O. case is a compelling story, but clever detective work by Ellenberger (1972) showed that the case was not as straightforward as it appears in most descriptions. Although the cathartic method had some success, relief of Anna's symptoms was often just temporary, and the initial diagnosis of hysteria was only a small part of her problem (she also had psychotic symptoms and possibly a dissociative disorder). She began to recover only after spending several lengthy confinements in a sanatorium after Breuer ended her treatment. Also, several of the events reported in traditional descriptions were factually wrong. For example, according to the account in the Jones biography of Freud, Breuer's wife was

---

[6]The family of Bertha Pappenheim (1859–1936) was not pleased when Ernest Jones revealed her identity in the first volume of his biography of Freud (Jones, 1953).

not happy about the amount of time he was spending with this attractive young woman, and when Anna developed a false pregnancy and named Breuer as the father, he did his catharsis magic to relieve the symptom and then terminated the therapy in a mild panic. The very next day he whisked his wife off to a second honeymoon to Venice where they conceived a daughter (and they all lived happily ever after). Ellenberger, however, showed that none of Breuer's case notes mentioned a false pregnancy, and the birth date of his daughter conflicts with the second honeymoon story.

An interesting side note to this story is that after her eventual recovery, Anna (Bertha Pappenheim) became a prominent advocate for women's rights in Germany; she once wrote that "if there is any justice in the next world, women will make the laws and men will bear the children" (quoted in Sulloway, 1979, p. 57). She became famous enough to warrant the issuance of a stamp in her honor in 1954, on the 50th anniversary of her death (Figure 12.6).

Breuer told his younger colleague Freud about the case, and it eventually became featured as the first of several cases described in their coauthored *Studies on Hysteria* (Breuer & Freud, 1895/1955). This book is often considered the founding event for psychoanalysis. For Freud, the case demonstrated that (a) memory of a traumatic event might be actively repressed into the unconscious, but it will continue to influence the person's behavior as a hysteric symptom; (b) the form of a hysterical symptom bears a symbolic relationship to the traumatic event that caused it, as in the hydrophobia example; and (c) a symptom can be alleviated if the person gains insight into the originating event. As Freud would later say in the first of a series of lectures given at Clark University, "[o]ur hysterical patients suffer from reminiscences. Their symptoms are residues … of particular (traumatic) events" (1909/1977, p. 16).

Freud also believed he detected a strong undercurrent of sexuality in the case. Anna seemed to be unusually attached to her father and, near the end of therapy, developed a strong attachment to Breuer as well. Freud would eventually refer to this attachment for the therapist as **transference** and would consider it an important step on the road to recovery. Breuer, while recognizing that sexuality was involved in the case, rejected Freud's argument that hysteria had sexual origins and split with Freud over the issue, thus ending a long friendship. It would not be the only time that Freud's insistence on the importance of sexual motivation would cost him a colleague.

Courtesy of Ludy T. Benjamin, Jr.

FIGURE 12.6 German stamp honoring Bertha Pappenheim (Anna O.).

Creating Psychoanalysis

From the mid-1880s to the mid-1890s, Freud developed his clinical practice, specializing in the treatment of hysteria. He was not at a loss for patients. Vienna was like other European cities in the Victorian era—sex in marriage was considered a necessary evil, good only for producing heirs, whereas sex for pleasure was confined to males visiting prostitutes and/or mistresses. The results included frustrated sexual needs for the faithful wife, lingering guilt for the wandering husband, and good incomes for therapists like Freud. The picture was more complicated, of course—historians continue to debate whether the Victorian female was sexually inhibited (e.g., Sterns, 1985). Nonetheless, neurotic symptoms seemed plentiful at a time when Freud was trying to establish his practice. He tried everything with his patients, from conventional medical treatments such as hydrotherapy (i.e., similar to a modern whirlpool bath, presumably designed to soothe the nerves) to hypnosis to a procedure in which he pressed on a patient's forehead while insisting that they retrieve repressed memories. He eventually discovered a technique that became the centerpiece of psychoanalytic practice—**free association**. Patients were placed in a relaxed position (hence, the famous couch—Figure 12.7) and encouraged to say whatever came into their minds, without censoring anything. This often proved difficult for patients, who would display what Freud called **resistance**—they would be unable or unwilling to mention some topics. Freud welcomed resistances, believing they were a sure sign that he was getting to the root of the patient's problem. For example, if a depressed female patient resisted telling the therapist that she was attracted to her brother-in-law, who looked a bit like her father and shared some of Dad's mannerisms, Freud would immediately begin thinking about how her problems might stem from unresolved feelings toward her father.

©AP/Wide World Photos

FIGURE 12.7 Freud's couch. Freud sat in the chair by the patient's head. The painting above the couch should look familiar.

In addition to free association, Freud used **dream analysis** as a means to explore the unconscious. He went as far as to describe dreams as the "royal road" to the unconscious. He first hit on the idea while searching for a way to perform psychoanalysis on himself, a task he undertook in the late 1890s. He could recall his dreams in great detail, and he discovered that they provided a rich source of information, both on their own and as a starting point for further free association. He published what is widely considered his most important book, *The Interpretation of Dreams*, in 1900. Freud believed that dreams were disguised wishes, and he distinguished between the *manifest* content of a dream (our verbal description of it, what the dream appears to be about) from the *latent* content (its true unconscious meaning, usually having to do with sex and/or aggression). Through the process of *dream work*, latent content is transformed through symbolism into manifest content. A dream that is truly about a frustrated desire for sex, for example, might be disguised (thinly) as a dream about a model train set with lots of tunnels. By interpreting dreams, Freud argued, we could achieve insight into our genuine but unconscious wishes (Freud, 1900/1938a).

The Importance of Sex As Freud's experience with hysteria grew, he became convinced that unresolved sexual problems were at the heart of the matter for his troubled patients. Patients exploring their past by way of free associations and dream reports often seemed to have experienced some type of sexual trauma at a young age. By the mid-1890s, Freud had heard enough of this theme to propose what became known as his **seduction hypothesis**. Hysteria, he argued, was the result of childhood sexual abuse by a parent or other adult. Because the young child had no understanding of what was happening, Freud believed, the experience was forgotten, buried in the unconscious. Sometime after puberty, when the person began to understand about and experience mature sexuality, the long-buried memory would resurface in the form of one or more hysterical symptoms (Gleaves & Hernandez, 1999).

Freud first presented his seduction theory in public at an 1896 meeting of the Vienna Society for Psychiatry and Neurology, which was presided over by Richard von Krafft-Ebbing, the era's leading authority on sexual pathology. The talk was not well received by the medical community, and Krafft-Ebbing called Freud's theory a "scientific fairy tale" (Gay, 1988, p. 93). Freud himself soon began to doubt the strength of the abuse–hysteria connection, partly because some of his patients' stories didn't seem to stand up to other evidence. Also, Freud was bothered by the idea that it was only sexual traumas in childhood that led to later problems. What about all the other, nonsexual traumas (e.g., severe illness, dog bites) that children experience? Why didn't they lead to later hysteria? It seemed impossible, Freud later wrote, "to suppose that distressing sexual effects so greatly exceed all other unpleasurable effects in intensity. It must be another characteristic of sexual ideas that can explain how it is that sexual ideas are alone subjected to [pathological] repression" (quoted in Sulloway, 1979, p. 111).

Tradition has it that Freud's great intellectual breakthrough was to abandon his seduction theory and replace it with the idea that sexual events in childhood were not real but imagined and that sexuality did not begin in adolescence but existed in some form from infancy. This insight about universal childhood sexuality supposedly emerged from Freud's self-analysis in the late 1890s. There is probably some truth to Freud's "heroic" account of how, entirely on his own and without the influence of contemporary ideas, he came to abandon his seduction hypothesis and develop his famous Oedipal complex. However, this is an area where the Freudian myth has also been at work. Freud was not operating in an intellectual vacuum here, creating ideas that were unique. For instance, several other noted "sexologists" (e.g., Havelock Ellis) were also proposing that sexual strivings extended into infancy and that repressed sexuality was connected with later psychopathology. Indeed, the 1890s witnessed an outpouring of books on sex, childhood and otherwise, and Freud was fully aware of them (Sulloway, 1979). Hence, the origins of the concept of infantile sexuality include Freud's self-analysis, but go much deeper to include the intellectual context of late 19th-century Europe.

Psychoanalysis Enters the 20th Century By the turn of the 20th century, Freud was launched on his career as a psychoanalyst specializing in the treatment of hysteria. With *The Interpretation of Dreams*, he also began developing his general theory of behavior, which continued to evolve for the rest of his life. A year after the dream book, in 1901, he published *The Psychopathology of Everyday Life* (Freud, 1901/1938b), which featured the analysis of events that later came to be called Freudian slips.[7] In 1905 two books appeared: *Three Contributions to the Theory of Sex* (Freud, 1905/1938c) and *Wit and Its Relation to the Unconscious* (Freud, 1905/1938d. With these publications (four books in 5 years), Freud's reputation grew, slowly but steadily, throughout the first decade of the 20th century. In America, his theories caught the enthusiastic attention of G. Stanley Hall of Clark University. As you recall from Chapter 6, Hall's enormous range of interests included the study of children and adolescents, including their sexual development. He described Breuer and Freud's work on hysteria in his two-volume book on adolescence, and he was offering courses on sexuality as early as 1904 (Rosenzweig, 1992).

In 1909, to celebrate the 20th anniversary of Clark University's founding, Hall invited Freud to Worcester to receive an honorary degree and to lecture on psychoanalysis. Several other prominent scientists also gave talks and were awarded degrees at the celebration, including Titchener, the noted anthropologist Franz Boas, and Carl Jung, who accompanied Freud on the trans-Atlantic voyage. Still other psychologists came to hear the talks, including James, Cattell, and Goddard (look back to Figure 6.5 for the famous group photo). It was Freud's only visit to the United States, and he returned with a healthy dislike of the country, especially its food. Nonetheless, he was forever grateful to Hall, crediting him with enhancing the international reputation of psychoanalysis and providing "the first official recognition of our endeavors" (quoted in Gay, 1988, p. 207).

The Evolution of Psychoanalytic Theory

Freud was already 54 years old when he delivered his lectures at Clark, but he was just beginning to develop his general theory of human behavior and mental processes. Over the next 20 years, this theory evolved considerably; indeed, many of the concepts most frequently associated with Freud did not appear until after World War I, when he was in his late sixties.

One major postwar change in Freud's theorizing was his conviction that destructive tendencies were just as powerful as sexual ones in motivating behavior. Freud did not ignore aggression in the years prior to World War I. Male feelings of hostility toward the father were an integral part of the Oedipal complex, and the sex act itself contains elements of male aggression, he believed. Yet the war, with its seemingly unending brutality and appalling loss of life, had a profound impact on Freud's thinking (Gay, 1988). In 1920, he produced *Beyond the Pleasure Principle*, in which he proposed a distinction between **eros**, the life instinct, manifested in sexual motivation, and **thanatos**, a death instinct, which showed itself in the form of aggression and self-destruction. Hence, he came to believe that human behavior was jointly motivated by life-enhancing (sexual) and life-destroying (aggressive) instincts.

[7]Here are two slips that Freud described. First, when a lecturer referred to the "Freuer–Breudian" theory of hysteria instead of "Breuer–Freudian," when referring to their jointly authored book, Freud suggested that a hostile motive was behind the mistake. In second example, a patient who couldn't recall (i.e., had repressed) where a man had touched her, quickly changed the subject to her summer home. When asked where the home was located, she said "near the mountain loin" instead of "mountain lane."

Although his reflections on the world war were the immediate stimulus for his proposal that we all have destructive tendencies, the concept of a death instinct was also rooted in a lifelong preoccupation that Freud had with death, and his conviction of its reality was strengthened by events in his life during the 1920s. Shortly after he wrote *Beyond the Pleasure Principle* (Freud, 1920/1959a), for instance, one of his three daughters died during an influenza outbreak. Soon after that, a favorite grandson died and a niece committed suicide. Then in 1923, Freud, who smoked up to 20 cigars a day, was diagnosed with cancer of the mouth and saw his own demise coming. Over the next 16 years, he endured 33 painful surgeries and had to live with a series of increasingly bulky denture-like prostheses to replace parts of his palate and jaw. Freud saw all these events as confirmation that death instincts go hand in hand with life instincts.

Other well-known Freudian concepts also developed in his later years. These include his structural analysis of personality and his description of the relationship between anxiety and ego defense mechanisms. Freud first wrote about his familiar tripartite structure of personality—id, ego, and superego—in *The Ego and the Id*, which appeared in 1923 (Freud, 1923/1959b). The *ego*, partly conscious and partly unconscious, lies at the center of personality, Freud wrote, trying to maintain a balance between three conflicting forces: the id, the superego, and reality. The *id*, repository of the instinctive drives of sex and aggression, constantly demands that its needs be satisfied. On the other hand, the *superego*, the person's learned moral values, works to inhibit the free expression of the instincts. The ego must also take into account the environmental factors operating in the real world. For Freud, the properly functioning ego serves as a mediator, channeling id-based needs in directions that are both realistic and consistent with moral values.

The constant demands made on the ego produce anxiety. Freud distinguished three forms of it, one for each of the forces pressuring the ego. *Objective anxiety* (or "realistic" anxiety) is a normal reaction to a perceived threat from the external world, based on the person's memories of past situations of danger. Thus, sailors observing a "red sky in the morning" know they must "take warning" because it means a storm is on the horizon. More interesting to the analyst, however, were the other two forms of anxiety, neurotic and moral. In *neurotic anxiety*, the person fears that id-based impulses will get out of control. In *moral anxiety*, feelings of guilt and shame arise from a sense that one is about to violate the strict moral code of the superego.

The feeling of anxiety serves as a signal to the ego that it is under attack, Freud reasoned, and it responds through defense. The response to objective anxiety is to deal with the situation realistically (e.g., the sailors prepare the ship for a storm). Because neurotic and moral anxieties are generated internally, however, the responses must also come from within, and they do so in the form of **ego defense mechanisms**. The most common form of defense is **repression**, in which unwanted impulses are actively forced from awareness and into the unconscious. Repression is also an element in the other defenses. In *projection*, for example, personal faults cannot be accepted, so they are attributed to some other person. People who cannot accept the hostility within them, for example, might convince themselves that those around them are the hostile ones. That is, they repress their own hostility and project it onto others (Hall, 1954). *Sublimation* is a successful defense, Freud thought, for it channels instinctive urges into activities that have social value. Aggression is channeled into athletics, for example, and sex is channeled into art (both sex and art are "creative").

Freud's thinking about defense mechanisms was aided significantly by his daughter and fellow analyst, Anna Freud (1895–1982; Figure 12.8). She was a pioneer in extending psychoanalytic practice to children through the use of *play therapy*. Children lack the verbal fluency for normal analysis, of course, so Anna probed children's psyches by giving them various materials (e.g., Mommy and Daddy dolls) and asking them just to play. She also helped her father develop his own theory, especially the

Mary Evans Picture Library/Sigmund Freud Copyrights

FIGURE 12.8 Freud and his daughter Anna, in 1928, the year of Anna's book on child psychoanalysis.

relationship between anxiety and defense. In fact, the lists of defense mechanisms (projection, etc.) normally found in introductory texts are more the result of her work than her father's. She articulated them in *The Ego and Mechanisms of Defense* (A. Freud, 1937). After Freud's death, Anna became a fierce protector of her father's reputation and a collaborator in the "Freudian myth," according to Sulloway (1979).

Freud's Followers: Loyalty and Dissent

By the turn of the 20th century, Freud had begun attracting the interest of other physicians in Vienna. In 1902, he asked four of them to join him on Wednesday evenings to discuss issues related to psychoanalysis. The group expanded to about 20 by 1908 and began calling itself the Vienna Psychoanalytic Society. Discussions were spirited, but the authoritarian and dogmatic Freud dominated the meetings and made it clear that his word was to be law. As might be expected, although some members remained intensely loyal to Freud for years, others were not so compliant. The first major defector was one of the original five who met in 1902.

Alfred Adler (1870–1937) was trained in ophthalmology and general medical practice at the University of Vienna. He was attracted to Freud's ideas on reading *The Interpretation of Dreams*, and he became an enthusiastic charter member of the Wednesday evening group. Soon, however, he began to question Freud's obsession with sexual motivation. Instead, Adler drew on his own troubled childhood and proposed the **inferiority complex** as the basis for an alternative theory. All infants are inherently inferior in their abilities, he argued, and life could be viewed as an attempt to compensate for this inferiority. He also pointed out that as we grow, the social environment places obstacles in our paths that also create feelings of inferiority to be overcome. Adler's emphasis on the importance of social factors over biological ones, along with his writings on inferiority and his belief that behavior was determined as much by conscious planning for the future as by the repressed events of one's past, alienated him from Freud. The official break came in 1911, when he was tossed out of the Vienna Psychoanalytic Society, taking several followers with him. He went on to create a rival school of psychoanalysis that he called **individual psychology**. Adler and Freud never reconciled; indeed Gay (1988) described their subsequent relationship as one of mutual hate, and when Adler died suddenly in 1937, Freud was evidently delighted to learn that he had outlived his rival.

An equally bitter split occurred between Freud and the Swiss psychiatrist Carl Jung (1875–1961), known for his pioneering work with schizophrenia. The two met in Vienna in 1907 after exchanging some earlier correspondence in which Jung's praise for Freud's dream theory was matched by Freud's enthusiasm for a **word association** task that Jung had developed. The procedure involved giving patients a prepared list of words and asking them to respond to each with the first word that came to mind. Also, their reactions were timed, and some physiological measures were recorded (Watson & Evans, 1991). Jung assumed that longer reaction times and arousal (e.g., increased breathing) would indicate that a particular word had important emotional implications, a rationale similar to the one later used to justify the polygraph's validity as a lie detector.

Jung accompanied Freud to America and the Clark conference of 1909, where he lectured on his word association procedure. In 1911, Freud arranged to have Jung named the first president of the newly formed International Psychoanalytic Society, in part because Freud believed that naming Jung, who was neither Viennese nor Jewish, would make the association appear to be more international and broad-based than it really was. Meanwhile, Freud began thinking of Jung in father–son terms, even writing to him as his "successor and crown prince" (quoted in McGuire, 1974, p. 218). But trouble was brewing and, by 1913, Jung went the way of Adler, expelled from the inner circle.

Like Adler, Jung questioned Freud's emphasis on sex, and he also had some ideas of his own. Over the rest of his career, Jung developed what came to be called **analytical psychology**, to be distinguished from Freud's psychoanalysis. He went beyond Freud in some ways. For example, to the concept of a "personal" unconscious, similar to Freud's use of the term, Jung added the concept of the **collective unconscious**, said to include the collective experiences of our ancestors. He believed that the common themes found in mythology reflected a shared human legacy. Jung also contributed to personality theory with his distinction between what he saw as two major personality types: introverts and extroverts.

After the defections of Adler, Jung, and some others, Freud closed ranks. At the suggestion of Ernest Jones (1879–1958), destined to be Freud's handpicked biographer, Freud formed a secret group of five called the "Committee." The group vowed to "write nothing contradictory to Freud's theories, would publish nothing without each other's approval, and would sniff out heresy wherever it might begin" (Maddox, 2006, p. 102). Freud even gave each member of his new inner sanctum a gold ring. Their task was to safeguard orthodox Freudianism, respond to critics, control the various psychoanalytic organizations; in essence, their job was to perpetuate the Freudian myth (Sulloway, 1979).

Psychoanalysis in America

The 1909 Clark lectures put Freud on the intellectual map in America, although, as seen in Chapter 6, some attendees were more impressed than others. Over the next few years, American psychologists had the opportunity to learn more about Freud. Reviews of Freud's work and articles on psychoanalysis appeared frequently, but many academic psychologists found psychoanalysis either tangential to their research interests, or annoyingly "unscientific". Robert Woodworth of Columbia (Chapter 7), who might have been congenial to the Freudians because of his own interest in motivation and his general eclecticism, attacked psychoanalysis as being more religion than science (Woodworth, 1917). He was especially annoyed at a clever strategy used by analysts—whenever attacked, they would attribute the criticism to an unconscious resistance on the part of the attacker, thereby providing pseudosupport for a key Freudian concept. Thus, analysts could claim support for Freud's ideas regardless of whether critics praised or condemned them. For Woodworth, this attitude was scientifically unconscionable. Equally galling to American psychologists was the analysts' claim that to truly understand psychoanalysis and to criticize it, one had to undergo a complete psychoanalysis oneself (Hornstein, 1992).

As mentioned in Chapter 11, in the late 1930s some behaviorally inclined psychologists (i.e., John Dollard and Neal Miller)[8] tried to assimilate psychoanalysis by reinterpreting it in terms understandable to them. Repression, for instance, rather than being some mysterious force that wrestled with unacceptable ideas and shoved them into the unconscious, could be considered "more rationally" as a response of nonthinking about certain events that were associated in one's learning history with negative emotions. It was simply a matter of avoidance conditioning—nonthinking about some event was reinforced by the elimination of anxiety associated with that event. Other psychologists tried to bring Freudian concepts into the laboratory and subject them to operational definitions. Repression, for example, could be defined in terms of whether or not people recognized "dirty words" that were flashed at threshold level (e.g., McGinnies, 1949). This research on perceptual defense was interesting in its own right, but whether it adequately tested Freud's ideas was another question.

Freudian psychoanalysis might not have played well within academia, but it had a strong impact on the medical practice of psychiatry, and it caught the imagination of the general public. Between 1912 and 1918, some 170 articles relating to psychoanalysis appeared in medical journals, and about 50 articles appeared in popular magazines ranging from *The Ladies' Home Journal* to *The New Republic* (Green & Reiber, 1980). By the 1920s, psychoanalysis was popular enough to be the subject of light satire. In "A Manual of the New Mentality," for example, Leacock (1924) noted the frequent "references to psychoanalysis, auto-suggestion, hypnosis, hopnoosis, psychiatry, inebriety, and things never thought of a little while ago" (p. 471). A more sarcastic tone was taken by Grace Adams, a former student of Titchener. Referring to the Clark conference in an *Atlantic Monthly* article, she noted that the psychologists in the audience didn't realize they were listening to the wave of the future; rather, they thought "they were merely listening to a bearded foreigner make some altogether preposterous remarks" (Adams, 1934, p. 85). Adams went on to lament the intrusion of psychoanalysis into everyday life, with "its majestic verbiage and high-minded meddlesomeness" (p. 88).

Despite the criticism and the satire, psychoanalysis persevered. It made significant inroads in the medical community, and by the 1930s, training in psychiatry and neurology typically included a strong dose of Freud (Hale, 1971). In addition, psychoanalytic institutes were created in urban areas, especially in the eastern United States, and catered to MDs who wished further certification as professional psychoanalysts.

Evaluating Freud

Near the end of his life, Freud was once again reminded of his Jewish heritage. Ominous signs occurred soon after the Nazis rose to power in 1933 when, as you recall from the gestalt chapter, Jewish professors began to be fired. In addition, psychoanalysis was branded "Jewish science" and outlawed within Germany. Soon, Freud's writings were publicly burned, along with other books by Jews (e.g., Einstein). Freud wryly noted that the world seemed to be making progress: "In the Middle Ages they would have burnt me; nowadays they are content with burning my books" (quoted in Gay, 1988, pp. 592–593). Then in March of 1938, the Nazis occupied Austria, and Vienna became a scene of beatings and even of cold-blooded murders of Jews on its streets. Freud was reluctant to leave Vienna, but became convinced that it was time to go after Nazi sympathizers searched his home and the Gestapo briefly detained

[8]Neal Miller, a student of Walter Miles, travelled to Vienna in 1935 and underwent psychoanalysis (not with Freud, however); on his return, Miles wrote to Boring that Miller "seems to me to exhibit mighty little change from his former patterns and attitudes" (Miles, 1936).

his daughter Anna.[9] He left Vienna with his family in June of 1938 and resettled in London, where his cancer finally claimed him on September 23, 1939.

The value of Freud's contributions to psychology has been a matter of considerable debate. Scholars dissecting Freud's published case histories have found scant evidence of the effectiveness of psychoanalysis as therapy; indeed, there is evidence that he bent the facts of his case histories to suit theories he had already decided on (Kramer, 2006). He has also been chastised for missing the opportunity to expose widespread childhood sexual abuse when he abandoned his original seduction theory (Gay, 1988). Defenders, on the other hand, argue that Freud is responsible for some of the most important ideas of the 20th century and that his influence spreads beyond psychology and deeply into Western culture. This issue will not be resolved here, of course, or at any time in the near future. What can be enumerated are some aspects of Freud's influence and some of the typical criticisms that are made of his work.

Contributions As we have seen, historians have uncovered many of the sources and antecedents of Freud's ideas. As a result, his ideas are recognized as considerably less than original (Sulloway, 1979). Nonetheless, any attempt to understand human nature must include serious consideration of his work. First, although Freud did not discover the unconscious, he popularized the concept, and components of unconscious thinking such as repression, defense, and the "Freudian slip" have become part of the psychological (and popular) lexicon. Freud's emphasis on unconscious motives also raised awareness of the general need to study motivational processes and of the fact that human behavior is not always rational. Second, we now take it for granted that the events of early childhood can significantly affect later development. We might take issue with the Freudian model of early development, especially the Oedipal complex and its ramifications, but there is no question that he made us more aware of the vulnerability of the young mind. Third, at a time when the medical community favored biological explanations of mental disorders and their treatment, Freud showed that some problems were psychological in origin and, therefore, could be treated with psychological means, through psychoanalysis.

Criticisms Many of Freud's conflicts with peers concerned the degree of emphasis he placed on sexual motivation. Breuer, Jung, and Adler all disagreed with him over the issue, and we now recognize that human behavior is too complex to be reduced to single broad motives. Psychoanalysts in the post-Freudian era have paid increasing attention to the roles of interpersonal relationships and the social environment in shaping personality (Pervin, 1991). The criticism of Freud's overemphasis on sex is part of a broader problem—he often overstated the case. Thus, although childhood is clearly an important determiner of later personality, it is an exaggeration to say, as Freud did, that the personality structure is essentially determined during childhood. A third frequent criticism of Freud, often delivered by those accustomed to laboratory control over variables, concerns the "scientific status" of his work. Freud has been criticized for relying on a limited sample of case studies, for excessive bias in bending the data from his patients into shapes that suited him, and for defining terms too loosely for his theory to be adequately tested. Freud's dogmatic insistence on his point of view and his demands of loyalty from his followers have also been said to be at odds with the "objectivity" expected of scientists. Finally, Freud has been widely criticized for his theoretical views about female psychology, although one must

---

[9]Freud never seemed to grasp the precariousness of his situation, and like most people living during that era, he had no idea of the extent of the evil to come. Included among the six million killed in the Nazi death camps were four of his sisters (Fancher, 1990).

be careful to recognize that few people can step away from the social context in which they live. Thus, Freud was a typical Victorian male with a typical Victorian attitude about the second-class status of most women, and it showed in his work. He believed, for example, that superego development was never complete in women, that they envied the status of men ("penis envy"), and that a woman's best hope for fulfillment was to produce male children. Anatomy, Freud declared, was destiny. In fairness, Freud never hindered and even encouraged the development of competent female analysts, most obviously his daughter Anna. And he occasionally acknowledged his meager understanding of the female psyche, once asking plaintively "What does a woman want?" (quoted in Gay, 1988, p. 501).

Freud's theory may not have held together over the years, but many of his insights have stood the test of time. As early as 1910, this conclusion about Freud was recognized by his contemporary, Havelock Ellis, and is a fitting way to close the book on Freud: "But if … Freud sometimes selects a very thin thread, he seldom fails to string pearls on it, and these have value whether the thread snaps or not" (Ellis, 1910, p. 523).

IN PERSPECTIVE: TREATING MENTAL ILLNESS

This chapter has covered considerable ground, from early attempts to treat the mentally ill in a humane fashion, through Freud's monumental effort to treat the mentally ill while simultaneously building a general theory of behavior. What you have read here is just a small part of a much larger story, a story that will continue in the next chapter, when we will examine (a) medical strategies for treating mental illness in the early 20th century, and (b) an early version of "clinical psychology" that emerged from the laboratory of an American experimental psychologist, and then dramatically changed its identity in the aftermath of World War II.

You might have been surprised to see that a relatively small proportion of this book has been devoted to the diagnosis and treatment of the mentally ill. After all, when most people think of psychology, they think of the psychologist-as-therapist stereotype, with an image that might include a couch. By now, however, and perhaps through your other courses in psychology, you should know that psychology is a much wider endeavor. Its history, at least in the United States, has primarily been a history of psychology becoming and establishing itself as a new scientific discipline, primarily in an academic environment. This in turn has meant that most psychologists have been trying to increase our understanding of behavior and mental processes through scientific research, and, through various applications, to improve society through this increased understanding. Treatment of the mentally ill, on the other hand, has a history that overlaps considerably with the history of medicine, a portion of which you will read about in the next chapter. That is, for the most part, issues surrounding the diagnosis and treatment of mental illness have occurred outside the academic environment, at least until World War II (with a notable exception, as you will see in the next chapter). Most modern departments of psychology continue with this mission of research and application, so it is perhaps not surprising that your academic course in the history of psychology (and the text used for it) is a history that emphasizes the academic side.

SUMMARY

Early Treatment of the Mentally Ill

• Near the end of the 18th century, Enlightenment thinkers pressed for reform in the ways of treating the mentally ill. In France, Phillipe Pinel introduced the concept of moral treatment, in which institutional living conditions were improved, the tendency to rely exclusively on physical restraint of patients was reduced, and direct efforts were made to improve the behavior of patients. Similar reforms were undertaken at the York Retreat in England by William Tuke. His model was copied extensively in the United States in the 19th century. Benjamin Rush, considered to be the founder of modern psychiatry, introduced a medical model as a way of explaining mental illness and developed an approach to treatment that emphasized "improving" the condition of patients' blood and circulatory systems.

• In the middle of the 19th century, large-scale asylums were built to house the mentally ill, many following the Kirkbride design, which emphasized several architectural features (e.g., pleasant views from all rooms) that were thought to promote mental health. Dorothea Dix successfully urged the reform of asylums and better treatment for the mentally ill poor. At the turn of the 20th century, Clifford Beers, a former mental patient, agitated for similar reforms; he was also a pioneer in the Mental Hygiene movement, which emphasized prevention.

• The classification of mental illnesses took a major leap forward with the work of Emil Kraepelin, a psychiatrist who also studied with Wundt. Among other things, Kraepelin is known for his description of dementia praecox (later renamed schizophrenia) and his description of it in attentional terms.

Mesmerism and Hypnosis

• In the mid-1700s, Franz Anton Mesmer developed a procedure for treating hysteria (apparent nervous system disorders with no true organic damage), based on his belief that the disorder was the result of disturbed magnetic forces in the body. Believing that he had magnetic powers, he treated patients and effected some cures by "mesmerizing" them. Although he didn't know it, his successes were the result of the power of suggestion; Mesmer had discovered a procedure that would eventually be known as hypnosis.

• Before the discovery of such drugs as ether in the 19th century, mesmerism was championed by the British doctor John Elliotson as an anesthetic for surgery and used in India by another British doctor, James Esdaile. It gained further scientific credibility in the hands of James Braid, who renamed the procedure "neurypnology," which soon came to be called hypnology or hypnotism.

• In France in the mid-19th century, two schools of thought developed about the nature of hypnotism. According to Liebeault and Bernheim of the "Nancy" school, hypnotism was a normal phenomenon that had its effects through the power of suggestion; people differed in their levels of suggestibility. According to Charcot in Paris, however, hypnotic effects mirrored the symptoms of hypnosis, and suggestibility was a sign of hysterical neurosis.

Sigmund Freud (1856–1939): Founding Psychoanalysis

• Freud is one of psychology's best-known figures. Over the years, a Freudian myth has developed, a false belief that Freud was the solitary hero fighting for his ideas against overwhelming opposition, and that his ideas were original to him, without important antecedent. Recent scholarship has questioned both aspects of the myth.

• Freud was trained in neurology and influenced, through his contact with Ernst Brücke, by the prevailing materialism and determinism of 19th-century physiology. Financial problems led him to the private practice of neurology, where he became interested in the treatment of hysteria. In the 1880s, he studied with two of the leading experts of the problem, Meynert and Charcot. He was also greatly influenced by Darwin's work.

• Through his association with Josef Breuer, Freud learned of the Anna O. case, in which hysteric symptoms were shown to be related to repressed memories, and successful treatment occurred (apparently) if the patient would retrieve memories of the events surrounding the first appearance of a symptom. The recall produced an emotional release or catharsis. With Breuer, Freud published *Studies on Hysteria* in 1895, normally considered the founding event for psychoanalysis.

• Freud believed that hysteria resulted from the repression of trauma, real or imagined, into the unconscious, and the purpose of psychoanalysis was to bring repressed memories back to the surface so that insight into the causes of the patient's problem could be gained. To explore the unconscious, Freud developed the procedures of free association, in which a person said whatever came to mind, and dream analysis. All dreams reflected some disguised wish fulfillment, Freud argued. He also believed that all events have causes; even accidents or slips of the tongue (Freudian slips) can be traced to unconscious purposes.

• Freud believed that sexual problems were a critical determinant of hysteria. He initially believed that hysteria resulted from the effects of childhood sexual abuse, but he later abandoned this "seduction" hypothesis, arguing that the memories of abuse were actually the results of imagined sexual feelings originating in childhood. This led to his theory of infantile sexuality and the Oedipal complex.

• Freud cultivated an inner circle of followers loyal to psychoanalysis. Two early converts, Alfred Adler and Carl Jung, both broke with Freud over the issue of sex and established their own schools of thought, individual psychology (Adler) and analytical psychology (Jung). Two of Freud's most loyal followers were his daughter Anna, known for extending psychoanalysis to the treatment of children, and Ernest Jones, Freud's handpicked biographer.

● After World War I, Freud's theory evolved to include the proposals that (a) both life (sex) and death (aggression) instincts are part of human nature; (b) personality structure centers on the ego, which mediates between the instinctive demands of the id, the moral restrictions of the superego, and reality constraints; and (c) that each of the three sources of pressure on the ego can create anxiety, and the ego reacts through defense mechanisms (e.g., projection).

● Freud's ideas were treated with skepticism by academic psychologists and were more influential in the medical community and with the general public. His contributions include the concepts of the unconscious and repression, his emphasis on the importance of early childhood, and his insistence on the psychological nature of mental disorders. Critics have cited his overemphasis on sex, problems with the scientific status of psychoanalysis, and his description of female psychology.

STUDY QUESTIONS

1. Explain how Pinel was influenced by the general ideals of the Enlightenment.

2. Describe the practice of "moral treatment" as it appeared in the work of Pinel and Tuke.

3. Describe what it might be like to be a patient of Benjamin Rush.

4. Describe the Kirkbride plan for asylums, and explain how various aspects of the design were assumed to help the mentally ill.

5. As crusaders for mental health reform, describe the work of (a) Dorothea Dix and (b) Clifford Beers.

6. Describe the contribution of Emil Kraepelin to the classification of mental disorders.

7. What was the theory behind "mesmerism"? Why did the treatment sometimes "work"?

8. Describe the origins of the term hypnotism.

9. What was the theory of hypnotism developed by the Nancy school, and why did Charcot consider the theory dangerous? Which approach prevailed?

10. Describe the two main components of the so-called Freudian myth. What role did Freud play in perpetuating the myth?

11. How were Freud's ideas influenced by (a) 19th-century materialist thought and (b) Darwinian theory?

12. Describe the traditional version of the Anna O. case, what really happened, and what Freud learned from the case (or thought he learned).

13. Describe the methods used by Freud to probe the unconscious.

14. Freud's deterministic beliefs are evident in his dream theory and in his description of "Freudian slips." Explain.

15. Describe Freud's seduction hypothesis and what happened to it.

16. Describe the evolution of Freud's theory after World War I.

17. What were Anna Freud's contributions to her father's theories?

18. What were the alternatives to Freudian psychoanalysis proposed by (a) Alfred Adler and (b) Carl Jung?

19. What was the effect of Freudian psychoanalysis on America, both in the general public and in academic circles?

20. Write an analysis of the contributions of Freud to 20th-century psychology, and the ways in which he has been criticized.

CHAPTER 13

PSYCHOLOGY'S PRACTITIONERS

One brief way of describing the change which has taken place in me is to say that in my early professional years I was asking the question, How can I treat, cure, or change this person? Now I would phrase the question this way: How can I provide a relationship which this person may use for his own personal growth?

—Carl Rogers, 1961b

PREVIEW AND CHAPTER OBJECTIVES

The chapter opens with a continuation of the question of how best to treat those suffering with mental illness, focusing on the medical strategy and several "great and desperate cures" that developed in the 1920s and 1930s (e.g., electroshock, lobotomy). We then consider the history of clinical psychology in the United States. The story begins in an academic setting, the laboratory of experimental psychologist Lightner Witmer, who adapted existing laboratory procedures and created new ones to diagnose and treat children with various problems hindering their performance in school. Clinical psychology took a dramatic turn after World War II, when psychiatrists were overwhelmed by the caseload. The war transformed clinical psychologists from psychiatric assistants, engaged mainly in administering psychological tests, into highly trained professionals, diagnosing and treating the full range of mental and behavioral disorders. Also after the war, traditional psychotherapy based on the Freudian psychoanalytic model came under fire for its questionable effectiveness, spawning alternative therapies. The alternatives to be considered here are behavior therapy, based on behaviorist conditioning principles, and therapies deriving from an approach that called itself the Third Force. This humanistic psychology created its distinct identity by contrasting itself with psychology's other two forces, psychoanalysis and behaviorism. Its most visible advocates were Abraham Maslow, vigorous promoter of self-actualization, and Carl Rogers, creator of client-centered therapy.

The professional practice of psychology extended beyond clinical psychology, of course. One major focus of application, as you recall from Chapter 8, was in business and industry. Modern industrial/organizational psychology continues the tradition begun by such pioneers as Scott, Münsterberg, and Bingham. The chapter will continue Chapter 8's discussion of psychology as it applied to business and industry, highlighted by an examination of a famous series of studies at a plant that manufactured components for telephone systems in Hawthorne, Illinois. After you finish this chapter, you should be able to:

■ Describe the various forms of therapy (fever, insulin coma, metrazol shock, electroshock) that emerged in the 1920s and 1930s as medical treatments for mental illness

■ Describe the history of the lobotomy as a medical tool for treating severe mental illness

■ Describe the causes and the various treatments for shell shock in World War I, and the contributions of British psychologists Myers and Rivers

- Summarize Witmer's contribution to clinical psychology, and explain why he is also considered a pioneer of school psychology
- Describe the state of clinical psychology in the United States in the years prior to World War II
- Describe the effect of World War II on the development of modern clinical psychology
- Compare the Boulder and Vail models of graduate training for clinical psychologists, and describe the status of both approaches
- Describe the Eysenck studies of psychotherapy effectiveness and their impact on clinical psychology
- Describe behavior therapy, especially the history of systematic desensitization, and show its connection to behaviorist principles
- Explain why humanistic psychology was called the "third force" in psychology
- Describe the development of the concept of self-actualization in the work of Maslow and how it fit into the philosophy of humanistic psychology
- Describe the essence of the client-centered therapy, developed by Rogers, showing how the therapeutic atmosphere is crucial for personal growth of the client
- Evaluate the influence and current status of humanistic psychology
- Describe the impact of the text by Viteles on the development of industrial/organizational psychology
- Describe the Hawthorne experiments, and critically analyze them

THE MEDICAL APPROACH TO MENTAL ILLNESS

In the late 19th century, psychiatric practice centered on the asylum and the treatment of patients who were seriously mentally ill. As we saw in Chapter 12, the Kirkbride design and the moral treatment philosophy of care attempted to improve the lives of those confined to asylums. Yet by the turn of the 20th century, it had become clear that architecture could not provide cures and that moral treatment, although laudatory, was not very effective with the severely mentally ill. Little could be done for these poor souls beyond custodial care, and "treatment" often amounted to restraint, sedation, and warm baths. With the advent of Freudian psychoanalysis, psychiatrists began to start private practices, treating patients with manageable psychological disorders, and shifting from medical treatment to a psychological analysis. Yet the seriously disturbed, their numbers steadily increasing in the 20th century, remained in asylums and hospitals, with little hope for improvement. In the 1920s and 1930s, however, several new medical treatments appeared on the scene, with the promise of providing some relief. Psychiatrists, partly due to the pressure they were feeling to justify their fees during the Depression era of the 1930s, welcomed these procedures that seemed to have beneficial effects (Grob, 1983).

It is easy to dismiss some of these therapies as the misguided ideas of quack doctors. But remember the dangers of presentist thinking—it is important to keep in mind that psychiatrists were honestly attempting to provide some needed relief to patients, at the time when nothing else seemed to work and the patients were clearly suffering. Nonetheless, some techniques, referred to as "great and desperate cures" in a book by that name (Valenstein, 2010), seemed to come into fairly widespread practice even though there was a surprising lack of scientific basis for their implementation and little evidence for their effectiveness.

A Shock to the System: Fever, Insulin, Metrazol, and Electricity

One early therapeutic breakthrough came in the form of "fever" therapy, pioneered by the Austrian psychiatrist Julius Wagner-Jauregg. Having noticed a decline in pathological symptoms among mental patients who had developed typhoid fever, Wagner-Jauregg developed the hypothesis that high fever somehow had a beneficial effect on the mentally ill, especially those suffering from general paresis, a debilitating condition caused by late-stage neurosyphilis. Its symptoms, which could appear any time from 10 to 20 years after a patient first contracted syphilis, ranged from anxiety to depression to psychotic-like delusions. After experimenting with several forms of fever-inducing substances, Wagner-Jauregg hit on the idea of injecting live malaria cells into patients and published a report in 1917 showing that malarial fever seemed to improve mental stability in several cases of paresis (four of eight cases improved). The technique spread—general paresis was considered incurable at the time, so any treatment suggesting improvement was seized on. As for the patient's resulting malaria, it could be treated with quinine. Manageable malaria, so the argument went, was better than incurable mental suffering. Fever therapy's popularity declined in the 1930s, in part because research began to question its effectiveness, but mainly because penicillin was found to be an effective cure for syphilis. The discovery of fever therapy won Wagner-Jauregg the Nobel Prize in 1927 (Shorter, 1997).

Two other medical therapies arrived on the scene in the 1930s that were also pioneered by Europeans. They were (a) insulin coma therapy, developed by the Viennese physician Manfred Sakel, and (b) metrazol shock therapy, created in Budapest by Ladislaus Meduna. In insulin coma therapy, patients would be injected with insulin, which lowered their blood sugar enough to send them into a coma that typically lasted 20 minutes. Injections of glucose (sugar) then brought them out of the coma and into a state of symptom relief, at least for a time. The sequence was repeated daily and usually continued until about 20 comas had been achieved (Shorter, 1997). Metrazol shock therapy emerged from Meduna's observation that patients with epilepsy seldom showed schizophrenic symptoms. Thinking that convulsive seizures might work to prevent psychotic symptoms, he injected patients with metrazol, a powerful seizure-inducing drug. As with insulin coma therapy, the metrazol treatment lasted over multiple sessions. Both the insulin and metrazol treatments had a measure of success, although the reasons for the improvement were a mystery, and the improvement tended to be just short term. In the context of large populations of patients suffering from what seemed to be hopeless and incurable disorders, however, it is not hard to understand the enthusiasm that psychiatrists felt for treatments that seemed to have some positive effect. Both insulin coma and metrazol shock quickly spread to the United States—by the late 1930s, more than half the mental institutions in America were using insulin and two-thirds were using metrazol regularly (Valenstein, 2010). But a new form of shock therapy was rapidly becoming the treatment of choice.

This form of medical therapy involved electricity, and it continues in use today. **Electroshock therapy** (ECT), in which a burst of electricity is applied at the patient's temples and produces a convulsive seizure, also had its origins in Europe, in the Rome laboratory of physician Ugo Cerletti. After experimenting on dogs and pigs to discover a voltage range that would produce convulsions but not death, Cerletti and his team performed the first ECT treatment on a human in April 1938 (Kneeland & Warren, 2002). A 39-year-old Milanese engineer showing schizophrenic symptoms (e.g., hallucinations, delusions, talking meaninglessly to himself) was the patient. With a rubber tube in his mouth to keep him from biting his tongue, the patient had electrodes placed against each temple, and electric current was applied in short bursts. The result was a grand mal seizure. After recovery, the patient seemed improved, although he had no memory of the session. Eleven ECT treatments later, he was discharged from the hospital, apparently much improved. On follow-up he seemed to be better (held a job), but his wife reported that after 3 months "he resumed his jealous attitude toward her, and that sometimes during the night he would speak as though in answer to voices" (quoted in Shorter, 1997, p. 221).

ECT spread quickly throughout Europe and then to America, primarily through the promotional efforts of Lothar Kalinowsky, a member of Cerletti's team. Kalinowski had fled Hitler's Germany in 1933 (he was half Jewish) and gone to Rome. He later spent time in Paris and Coulson (just south of London), vigorously promoting ECT, and then came to New York, where he created an ECT treatment center at the New York State Psychiatric Institute, which was affiliated with Columbia University (Shorter, 1997). ECT became a popular treatment in the 1940s and 1950s, its use expanding to a range of symptoms and becoming especially likely to be used for patients suffering from severe depression. The procedure also became more refined and less dangerous to the patient—muscle relaxants reduced the dangers of injury (e.g., broken bones) during convulsion, for example. The procedure came under attack in the 1960s and 1970s (part of a general skepticism of psychiatry and the medical model of mental illness) and declined in use for a time. It regained status in the 1980s, partly for economic reasons (shorter hospital stays), and ECT continues to be used today (Kneeland & Warren, 2002).

ECT is assumed to work because of the resulting convulsion, not because of the electricity per se. However, there was a time when electric shock was delivered to humans for the purpose of "curing" their mental disorders. These involved cases of "shell shock," a disturbing consequence of the horrific trench warfare of World War I. This chapter's Close-Up examines this terrifying disorder, a misguided therapy that tried to shock people out of it, and the efforts of two pioneering British psychologists to treat the problem more humanely.

CLOSE-UP

SHELL SHOCK

Much has been written about the way in which barbed wire, machine guns, artillery, shrapnel, and trenches, prominent features of World War I, changed the nature of modern warfare. Nations learned the hard way that infantry charges across contested ground were suicidal, and during the 4 years of the war, 1914–1918, a generation of young men died. In addition to an appalling death toll, a significant number of soldiers suffered severe psychological damage, a condition that came to be called **shell shock**. Its symptoms varied dramatically, from nervous tremors and apparent paralysis to terror-filled dreams, waking hallucinations, and what we would today call panic attacks. It was first thought that the symptoms resulted from physical damage to the nervous system, resulting from the repeated shock of being exposed to thunderous artillery shelling. It soon became clear, however, that cases were occurring in soldiers who had not been in the vicinity of exploding shells, and the problem was therefore more of a psychological affliction than a physical one. And it quickly became a serious

problem—in the British army, for instance, about 7 to 10 percent of officer casualties in 1914 were shell shock cases, there were an estimated 80,000 such cases in the military overall, and as late as 1921, 65,000 ex-soldiers were getting disability payments for the problem (Hearn-shaw, 1964).

Once it had been established that shell shock was not the result of exploding artillery shells, it was thought by military authorities to involve nothing more than malingering and cowardice (Bogacz, 1989). One early form of treatment, based on the idea that shell shock involved a willful decision to fake symptoms, was the use of electricity. The primary advocate of this "therapy" was Lewis Yealland, a Canadian physician who used shock and verbal exhortation to treat shell shock. In one notable case, a young man rendered mute by his war experience was told that he would be given electric shocks to his tongue until he started talking and that he could not leave the room until he was cured. Yealland reported that all of the "malingering" symptoms disappeared after just four (!) hours (Jones & Wessely, 2005).

A more humane approach characterized the work of two British psychologists, Charles S. Myers, and William H. R. Rivers. Myers (1873–1946), too old for active duty in the war, managed to get himself a position in a hospital near Paris. There he encountered a number of shell shock victims. The term had originated among soldiers at the front, but it became "official" in a 1915 article by Myers in the British medical journal *Lancet*. His developing expertise led to his appointment as Consulting Psychologist to the Army. He argued that shell shock was a defensive response to extreme trauma, in which soldiers repressed the horrific memory and developed symptoms to help maintain the repression. He had some success treating individual cases with hypnosis, but his main contribution was institutional—on his recommendation, the British army set up several treatment centers, far removed from the sounds of artillery, designed to help those suffering from shell shock.

Rivers (1864–1922; Figure 13.1), a close colleague of Myers, developed a treatment program for shell-shocked British officers at the Craiglockhart War Hospital, just outside Edinburgh, Scotland. (Rivers's time at Craiglockhart was the subject of a 1997 film, *Behind the Lines*.) Adopting essentially the same trauma model used by Myers, Rivers treated his psychologically wounded officers with a version of psychoanalysis. Rivers was not a fan of Freudian theory, with its emphasis on sexual motivation, but he did agree with Freud about the effects of severe trauma and the unconscious mind's attempts to cope (Shephard, 2001). Rivers had a measure of success, but the nature of psychoanalysis meant he treated just a small number of men, and because he treated only officers, his patients tended to be more educated and

FIGURE 13.1 William H. R. Rivers on duty at Craiglockhart War Hospital during World War I.

Courtesy of Rob Ruggenberg

articulate than the typical shell shock victim. On the whole, neither Myers nor Rivers did much to treat the overwhelming number of shell shock cases, but they were instrumental in starting a process that gradually changed military and public opinion about the problem. When a royal commission investigating shell shock issued a report in 1922, it recognized that the shell shock was more than simple dereliction of duty, and that psychological expertise was needed to both recognize and treat the problem (Bogacz, 1989).

Of course, this problem known as shell shock in World War I was not unique to that war; it has appeared at different times with different labels. In the American Civil War, for example, it was called irritable heart or soldier's irritable heart, and in World War II and the Korean War it was called battle fatigue or battle exhaustion. Currently, it is most likely to be labeled combat stress reaction.

No Reversal: Lobotomy, Transorbital and Otherwise

The therapies based on creating fever, brief comas or convulsive shocks were stressful to patients, but they were in some cases beneficial, at least for a time. The permanence of their effects pales in comparison, however, with surgical procedures that produce irreversible brain destruction. Consider the lobotomy. The story begins with a paper presented at the Second International Congress on Neurology, held in London in 1935. It included some interesting research by two American scientists, Carlyle Jacobsen and John Fulton, who reported that surgical damage to the frontal lobes of chimpanzees could have a beneficial effect. Prior to the surgery, the animals had been quite aggressive, but the aggression seemed to disappear after the surgery, and the animals' mental functions seemed otherwise unimpaired. By severing the connections between frontal lobes and lower brain centers affecting emotional behavior, the researchers seemed to have found a way to calm the easily agitated chimps. In the audience that day was a Portuguese neuropsychiatrist, António Egas Moniz. He was already well known and highly respected, having been nominated for a Nobel Prize for his discovery of methods to create images of cerebral blood flow. It occurred to Moniz that the Jacobsen/Fulton procedure might be worth trying with his seriously disturbed (and agitated) psychotic patients (Grob, 1983).

With no science other than the Jacobsen and Fulton primate study for support, and knowing that destruction of brain tissue was irreversible, Moniz developed a procedure that he called a *prefrontal leucotomy* (roughly means a cutting of brain tissue in the prefrontal area of the cortex), carried out with a device he created called a *leucotone*. After small holes had been drilled in both sides of the skull, just in front of the temples, the thin leucotone would be inserted successively into each hole to a fixed depth and moved side to side, thereby severing brain tissue that connected the frontal and prefronatal lobes with lower brain centers. By early 1936, Moniz had tried the procedure on 20 patients, those with manic-depression or obsessive-compulsive disorders that were severe enough that they were suicidal or showed signs of being dangerous. Moniz reported (without substantial supporting data) that the procedure was mostly successful (seven "recovered," seven "improved," six "unchanged"; Valenstein, 2010). Although many of the patients later became listless, apathetic, and emotionally passive after recovering from the surgery, Moniz believed it was a small price to pay for the relief from their severe, even life-threatening symptoms. To his credit, Moniz urged that the procedure not be used except in extreme cases and only after all alternative methods of helping a patient had failed. For this work he was awarded the Nobel Prize in 1949; over the years, Portugal issued at least three stamps in his honor.

If Moniz was conservative about the use of his new procedure, two American neurologists were not. Walter Freeman and James Watt thought the Moniz procedure was a major breakthrough in the treatment of a wide range of psychiatric disorders, and they set about to spread the good news far and wide, while at the same time completing as many of these surgeries as they could. They renamed the procedure **lobotomy**. In 1946, Freeman invented a new procedure that he called a *transorbital lobotomy*. It involved inserting a device similar in design to an ice pick through the eye sockets and into the prefrontal and frontal lobes. Compared with the Moniz technique, the new procedure could be completed more quickly, and it enabled a greater number of fibers to be cut. Freeman was undeterred by the occasional death (about 2.5 percent of patients), however, and became a passionate advocate for the new procedure, partly because of how quickly it could be done and the fact that it could be completed on an outpatient basis (i.e., more lobotomy income per unit of time). Freeman's enthusiasm caused a split with Watt, who appeared increasingly nervous about Freeman's crusading zeal for the procedure (Watt was a trained surgeon; Freeman was not). Freeman soldiered on, even traveling around the country in a small RV that came to be called the lobotomobile, doing demonstrations like the one pictured in Figure 13.2, in which he can be seen tapping his transorbital leucotone into the eye of a patient, while nurses hold onto the patient and onlookers carefully observe (note the absence of surgical gloves and masks). By himself, Freeman was responsible for just under 3,000 transorbital lobotomies.

By 1951, more than 18,000 patients had undergone various types of lobotomy, according to one estimate (Grob, 1991), despite growing uneasiness about the procedure. A lobotomy was certainly effective in calming agitated patients, but it often resulted in permanent changes in personality and extreme lethargy. Also, the procedure was occasionally used simply to manage unruly or disagreeable patients, a situation portrayed disturbingly well in *One Flew Over the Cuckoo's Nest*, a 1962 novel by Ken Kesey that was made into a movie in 1975 and dominated the Oscars the following year.[1]

---

[1] The film won for Best Picture (another contender was *Jaws*), Best Director, Best Actor (Jack Nicholson), Best Actress (Louise Fletcher), and Best Adapted Screenplay.

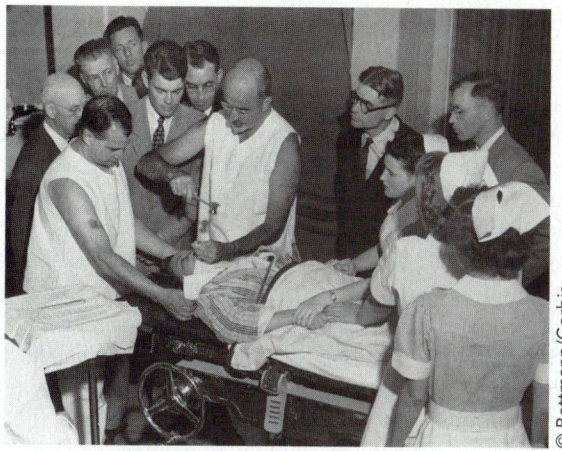

© Bettmann/Corbis

FIGURE 13.2 A demonstration of a transorbital lobotomy by Walter Freeman in 1949.

Lobotomies quickly went out of fashion in the mid-1950s, with the discovery of a number of effective antipsychotic drugs, especially thorazine, which was enthusiastically marketed as a "chemical" lobotomy, but without the mess.

CLINICAL PSYCHOLOGY BEFORE WORLD WAR II

Today, those trained in **clinical psychology** specialize in the diagnosis and treatment of all types of mental disorders, and they are at the forefront of research concerning these problems. In contrast with psychiatrists, clinical psychologists train in graduate school rather than medical school and earn PhDs (or PsyDs) rather than MDs. Many have their own private practice, whereas others work in Veterans Administration (VA) hospitals or in private clinics. Some combine their practice with academic positions at colleges and universities. Some incorporate Freudian concepts into their practice, but most do not. Today, they comprise a highly influential group among those providing mental health services. This type of clinical psychologist began to emerge at the end of World War II, when the astounding number of psychological casualties created a need that the medical community (i.e., psychiatry) could not meet. In one sense, then, clinical psychology as we know it today is about 50 years old.

On the other hand, a portion of the APA's 1996 annual meeting was devoted to a celebration of clinical psychology's *centennial*. Much was made of a clinic created on the campus of the University of Pennsylvania in 1896 by the director of the psychology laboratory there, Lightner Witmer. The event was undoubtedly important, as will be elaborated shortly, and it set in motion circumstances that eventually led to modern clinical psychology. Yet the clinical psychology that existed prior to World War II was quite different from the discipline that emerged in the postwar era. The APA's centennial celebration is an interesting example of how the historical significance of some event can be created long after the event has occurred, through the decisions of historians and others (e.g., convention planners) who may be motivated by more than just a desire for historical truth. Thus, although the centennial of Witmer's clinic deserved a celebration on its own merits, it is probably no coincidence that it came at a time when clinicians were struggling to maintain their status in the face of cost-conscious health-care providers who sometimes questioned the value of paying for clinical services. One hundred years as a profession looks more substantial and enduring than 50.

Lightner Witmer (1867–1956): Creating Psychology's First Clinic

Like a number of other American applied psychologists, Lightner Witmer (Figure 13.3) was trained in basic laboratory research, but made his reputation by applying psychology to solve real-world problems. A native Philadelphian, Witmer stayed close to home for most of his life, earning a bachelor's degree at the nearby University of Pennsylvania in 1888 and then taking graduate courses there while teaching at a local college preparatory school. His shifting interests eventually settled on psychology, and for a time he served as the laboratory assistant for Penn's new psychology professor, James McKeen Cattell. He then followed Cattell's example and went to Leipzig, completing a doctorate in Wundt's laboratory in 1892 (same year as his Leipzig classmate, E. B. Titchener). On his return to the United States, Witmer was named laboratory director at the University of Pennsylvania, Cattell having moved to Columbia the year before. Witmer became a vigorous advocate of the new laboratory psychology, revealing his passion for research in an amusing letter to Hugo Münsterberg in 1893 (quoted in the Chapter 7 Close-Up), in which he described a study on the psychology of memory and pain that he had undertaken by deliberately letting a horse throw him (Witmer, 1893). The episode apparently was in character—one friend later recalled that when on holiday in New York's Adirondacks, Witmer liked to ride his brakeless bicycle "down steep hills … with [his] legs on the handlebar" (Collins, 1931, p. 9).

Although fiercely committed to a scientific psychology, Witmer, like most American psychologists, believed that psychology should be able to improve people's lives. Thus, he was intrigued when a

Courtesy of Lightner Witmer and the Beginning of Clinical Psychology, University of Pennsylvania Museum

FIGURE 13.3 Lightner Witmer (1867–1956), experimentalist and creator of psychology's first clinic.

local schoolteacher, who knew Witmer from taking a summer course with him, came into the laboratory in March of 1896. She brought along one of her students, a 14-year-old who had trouble spelling, even though he was reasonably competent otherwise. Witmer, always willing to try something new, agreed to help and quickly discovered that part of the problem was poor eyesight. Once corrected, the boy was able to undertake a training program, and his spelling improved. This episode, and a second one involving a child with a speech disorder, turned a portion of Witmer's laboratory into a makeshift clinic and launched what came to be known as clinical psychology, the eventual outcome being several days of symposia and celebrations at the 1996 APA convention.

Word of the clinic spread, and soon Witmer began seeing other cases of children with physiological, cognitive, and behavioral problems related to school performance, about two dozen during the rest of 1896 (McReynolds, 1987). In December of that year, he read a paper at the APA's annual meeting in Boston, in which he called for increased research on the kinds of problems he was encountering and the creation of training programs to increase the number of experts able to solve such problems. In 1907 he founded the journal, *The Psychological Clinic*, which included descriptions of case studies, research reports, and theoretical articles. The first issue contained a lead essay by Witmer; its title, "Clinical Psychology," gave a name to the emerging new specialty (Witmer, 1907/1931). In the article, he described the first 10 years of the clinic's development and again called for increased research and training. He urged the creation of "a new profession—that of the psychological expert, who should find his career in connection with the school system, through the examination and treatment of mentally and morally retarded children" (p. 346). Thus, clinical psychology began with a relatively narrow focus—diagnosing and treating children with school-related problems. Today, that area of expertise is associated with **school psychology**. In fact, school psychologists also consider Witmer one of their pioneers, and the APA's Division for School Psychology gives an annual "Lightner Witmer Award" to a promising young school psychologist (Baker, 1988).

By 1909, Witmer's clinic had expanded and had developed a team approach. A child entering the program would be given a thorough medical examination by a consulting physician, a social worker would compile a family and school history, and Witmer or one of his assistants would do the mental testing, using a battery of tests for such things as memory, attention, and motor coordination (Fernberger, 1931). Witmer disliked paper-and-pencil tests of intelligence, and although he believed that Binet-style assessments could yield interesting information, he thought they were overused, and he saw little value in IQ scores (McReynolds, 1996). After compiling all the information, the children would be classified as (a) experiencing some correctable medical condition (e.g., defective vision) but not needing special training, (b) possibly experiencing some medical problem but more clearly requiring some special training program or other environmental intervention (e.g., improved nutrition), or (c) being severely retarded, untreatable, and requiring custodial care (Baker, 1988).

Unlike many of his contemporaries, Witmer was skeptical of the claims being made for the heritability of traits like mental defectiveness. He clearly recognized individual differences in ability in the students he saw, and he conceded that some degree of deficiency was inherent and unalterable. Severely retarded children, he believed, should be segregated from society in special institutions and prevented from having children. Yet the very existence of his clinic demonstrated his firm belief that some deficiencies could be corrected through proper training and/or control of the environment. Hence, Witmer shared with behaviorists the belief that the environment could shape behavior. He believed that if past environmental influences produced the problem behavior observed in the clinic, then future intervention could alter behavior and make the child more productive as a student. He considered his approach to be an optimistic one, arguing that to emphasize heredity is to give up hope of change: "To ascribe a condition to the environment, is a challenge to do something for its ameliorization or cure; to ascribe it to heredity often means that we fold our hands and do nothing" (Witmer, 1911, p. 232).[2] Witmer introduced the term **orthogenics** to refer to this strategy of "investigat[ing] retardation and deviation and the *methods of restoring to normal condition* those who are found for one reason or another to be retarded or deviate" (Witmer, 1909, p. 122, emphasis added).

Witmer's clinic grew rapidly in the early decades of the 20th century, its total case files numbering just under 10,000 by 1931 (Fernberger, 1931). It also added several specialized functions to its general role of diagnosing and treating problems in school-aged children. One was a clinic for speech disorders, developed by E. B. Twitmyer in 1914.[3] Another was a vocational clinic where adolescents and adults could go for testing and advice about careers; it was run by Morris Viteles, whose important work in industrial psychology will be described later in this chapter. Witmer's clinics also spawned numerous copies and variants, about two dozen by the start of World War I (Sexton, 1965). Meanwhile other forces were at work that eventually would yield modern clinical psychology.

Clinical Psychology Between the World Wars

Chapter 8 chronicled the evolution of the mental testing movement, Chapter 12 described the drive for mental hygiene that originated with the efforts of Clifford Beers, and this chapter just described Witmer's clinic. All these events contributed to clinical psychology's history. In addition, during the period between the two World Wars, there were several organizational efforts within the APA to professionalize the work of the clinician. It was a difficult struggle. One problem was that psychology's increasing popularity and the apparent success of the World War I mental testing program prompted many unqualified people to claim that they could deliver psychological services. An illustration of the dilemma was the effect of a resolution the APA passed in 1915 requiring that testing be done only by those trained to do so. Most people administering the tests did not belong to APA, however, so the resolution had little effect (Napoli, 1981). And the issue of qualification was not resolved quickly—over 20 years later Woodworth (1937) remained concerned that "[u]nqualified practitioners will continue to operate for some time and to besmirch the name of psychology by the harm they do to people" (p. 5). A second problem was that clinicians did not always feel welcome in an APA that was centered in the academic environment and maintained strict scholarly requirements for membership. A final problem for clinicians was that unless they worked in clinics like Witmer's, they generally had low status in their work environments, which were often hospitals or private clinics. There they were usually limited to administering mental tests under close supervision, while psychiatrists completed the major diagnostic and therapy work. Naturally, the medical community had no wish to yield its authority or status.

The first serious effort toward forming an identity for clinicians within APA was made at the 1917 annual convention, when J. E. Wallace Wallin organized a meeting "to consider the advisability of establishing a new association to 'encourage and advance professional service in the field of clinical psychology'" (Wallin, 1966, p. 107). The seven people (including Leta Hollingworth—see Chapter 8's Close-Up) who met that winter in Pittsburgh formed the American Association of Clinical Psychologists

---

[2]This is exactly the same argument made by John Stuart Mill, when he criticized William Hamilton's nativist philosophy in 1869—see Chapter 2.

[3]Twitmyer's dissertation, under Witmer's direction, was an examination of the knee-jerk reflex (Twitmyer, 1905). During the course of his investigation, he discovered that knee jerks could be elicited by stimuli associated with stimulation of the patellar tendon. That is, shortly after Pavlov discovered classical conditioning in Russia, Twitmyer was making the same discovery in the United States. Pavlov justifiably gets the credit, however, because of the massive research program that he undertook. Twitmyer, on the other hand, after being ignored when presenting his research at the 1904 APA meeting, abandoned conditioning and focused his efforts on Witmer's clinic.

(AACP). APA's leadership was not amused, however, fearing an eventual split with APA. A compromise was reached in 1919 when the APA created a "section" for clinical psychology within the Association, and the AACP members abandoned their new organization and joined it. During the 1920s, the Clinical section pursued a number of professional issues, including training, certification, and ethics, but little came of their efforts. The only major effect of their growing presence was that the APA relaxed its membership requirements in the mid-1920s, creating two categories: full member and associate member. By the end of the decade, associates, many of them clinicians, outnumbered full members (Napoli, 1981).

During the 1930s, clinical psychologists (and other psychologists with applied interests) kept pushing for recognition in an APA that continued to be dominated by academic interests. Even the most firmly entrenched academician had to face the reality of the Great Depression, however. As you recall from the discussion of Lewin's experiences in the 1930s (Chapter 9), academic positions became increasingly difficult to find during the Depression years, making nonacademic employment a growing necessity for young psychologists. The APA created such committees as the Committee on the Social Utilization of Unemployed Psychologists and the Committee on Psychology and the Public Service. Despite these efforts, however, applied psychologists still felt the need for their own organization, and they created one in 1937—the American Association for Applied Psychology (AAAP). By 1940 it claimed more than 600 members, compared to approximately 4,000 in APA, and it included sections in clinical, educational, consulting, and industrial psychology (Hilgard, 1987).

The AAAP remained in existence until the end of World War II, independent of the APA, but not in direct competition with it—in fact, around 90 percent of AAAP members also belonged to the APA (Capshew, 1999). The organization made some progress on the issues of training and standards, but the advent of a second world war within a generation once more transformed psychology. The national spirit of unity and interdependence fostered a degree of cooperation between academicians and practitioners that had not existed before (and has not existed since). The outcome was a complete reorganization of the APA to incorporate both scientific and applied interests. It emerged from an "intersociety" convention held in New York in 1943, chaired by E. G. Boring, which brought together 25 delegates from several different organizations, but mainly from APA and AAAP. They approved a new structure for the APA, one that continues today. The structure was an umbrella organization that included special interest "Divisions," and a revised purpose. Whereas the original APA described its primary goal as the advancement of psychology as a "science," the expanded vision added advancement as a "profession" and as a "means of promoting human welfare" to its list of purposes (Napoli, 1981, p. 127).

THE EMERGENCE OF MODERN CLINICAL PSYCHOLOGY

As we have seen, clinical psychologists struggled to establish their status as independent professionals prior to World War II. In the 1930s, for example, they tended to be employed in mental hospitals or clinics, under the supervision of psychiatrists; their "practice" was limited primarily to administering mental tests. Because there was virtually nothing in the way of formal clinical training available to them, they developed their skills on the job or in internship-like arrangements (Capshew, 1999). The cruel circumstances of the war, however, created a permanent place for clinicians, who were among those providing professional services to the mentally wounded.

Organized psychiatry, which had controlled the delivery of therapeutic services to the mentally ill prior to the war, was overwhelmed by the need for therapy. As in the first world conflict, applied psychologists in the United States contributed their services through various testing programs, but in the second war they also gained experience treating those who were damaged psychologically by their war experiences. And the need was great. During the vicious Pacific battle for Guadalcanal in 1942, for example, 40 percent of the casualties that were serious enough to require evacuation were psychological breakdowns (Herman, 1995). Furthermore, of the first 1.5 million soldiers given medical discharges, about 675,000 (45 percent) were for psychiatric reasons (Vandenbos, Cummings, & DeLeon, 1992). When the war ended, there were approximately 44,000 veterans who were in Veterans Administration hospitals suffering from various mental disorders resulting from the war, compared with 30,000 hospitalized with physical wounds (Sexton, 1965). In the face of this overwhelming need, psychiatry simply could not manage the caseload and was forced to abandon its therapeutic monopoly. In addition, the federal government, recognizing the problem, launched an aggressive program to support the training of graduate students in clinical psychology. In the academic year 1946–1947, for instance, the VA funded training programs in 22 universities that enrolled 200 students (Capshew, 1999).

Out of these circumstances the modern clinical psychologist emerged—no longer limited to testing, but gradually recognized as an expert diagnostician and therapist; no longer limited to children and juveniles in school settings, but now capable of delivering services to anyone in need of them; no longer restricted to a clinic setting, but now more likely to develop a private practice; no longer under the supervision of psychiatrists, but increasingly on a par with them. As this new clinician emerged, however, the need for a standardized training program and an accreditation system became clear.

The Boulder Model

In 1947, with the financial support of the federal government, through the Veterans Administration and the U.S. Public Health Service, the APA formed a Committee on Training in Clinical Psychology (CTCP). It was chaired by David Shakow (1901–1981), who already had been quite active in promoting his ideas about the training of clinical psychologists. As chief psychologist at Worcester State Hospital in Massachusetts, Shakow (Figure 13.4) had been an active member of the original AAAP (American

Photographed by Thomas Joy; National Institute of Health/Archives of the History of American Psychology, The Center for the History of Psychology, The University of Akron

FIGURE 13.4 David Shakow (1901–1981), the person primarily responsible for the shape of the scientist–practitioner (Boulder) model for training in clinical psychology.

Association of Applied Psychologists) and, just before World War II, had served on their committee for the training of clinicians. Shakow's influence on the CTCP is evident from the fact that their committee report is usually referred to as the "Shakow Report" (Baker & Benjamin, 2000). It formed the backbone for deliberations about clinical training held during an intensive 15-day conference that attracted 71 clinical psychologists and other professionals to the University of Colorado in Boulder the late summer of 1949.

Out of the Boulder conference came a blueprint for clinical training that was designed to balance what Shakow saw as the three primary types of expertise that any clinical psychologist should have—they should be experts in the diagnosis of mental disorders, they should be skilled therapists, and they should be able to complete high-quality research on clinically relevant topics. The "Boulder model," because it combined training in the science and in the practice of psychology, came to be known as the **scientist–practitioner model** of clinical training. The training was to include a thorough grounding in basic knowledge of the principles of psychology and in the research methods for generating these principles; a thorough understanding of psychometrics (psychological testing), psychopathology, and psychotherapy; a data-based doctoral dissertation; and a yearlong internship at a professional clinic, VA hospital, or similar setting. Total preparation would take 4 to 5 years and lead to a PhD in clinical psychology. With this training model in place and a strong need for their services, clinical psychologists rapidly increased their numbers throughout the 1950s and 1960s.

The Eysenck Study: Problems for Psychotherapy

The conference at Boulder provided a new ideal for the training of clinical psychologists. At about the same time, the ability of clinicians to deliver effective therapy was enhanced by the development of new forms of psychotherapy. Two of these approaches, behavior therapy and client-centered therapy, will be featured here. They developed and prospered in the context of a time when the effectiveness of traditional psychoanalytic and other "insight" therapies was being questioned. The doubts were magnified by a brief (six pages) article that appeared in 1952, written by British psychologist Hans Eysenck, with the title: "The Effects of Psychotherapy: An Evaluation." In the article, Eysenck examined the efficacy of traditional insight approaches to psychotherapy by combining the results reported in 19 other studies—5 of them evaluating psychoanalytic (Freudian) therapy and the remaining 14 evaluating what he called "eclectic" therapy, which integrated a variety of theoretical approaches. In the absence of a control group not receiving therapy, Eysenck combined the results of two other studies that examined improvement among "neurotics" in the absence of formal psychotherapy (e.g., from insurance claims of disability). While recognizing problems with this comparison group, Eysenck claimed an improvement rate of about 72 percent in the absence of therapy, over the course of 2 years. When he looked at the 2-year recovery rates for patients undergoing psychotherapy, however, he found that the reported percentage improved in Freudian psychoanalysis was a paltry 44 percent. A recovery rate of 64 percent for the eclectic therapy was better, but still less than the rate for those receiving *no therapy at all*. Eysenck (1952) concluded there "appears to be an inverse relationship between recovery and psychotherapy; the more psychotherapy, the smaller the recovery rate" (p. 322). Later research (e.g., Bergin 1971) uncovered methodological problems that moderated Eysenck's stark conclusion, but the damage was done. Throughout the 1950s and 1960s, psychologists proposing alternatives to traditional psychoanalysis often pointed to Eysenck's work as evidence that new strategies were needed. Two of those new approaches were therapies deriving from behaviorism and those coming from what came to be called humanistic psychology.

Behavior Therapy

We learned in Chapter 10 that one reason for the popularity of the behaviorist ideas of promoters like John Watson was the promise of application to daily life, through such things as the improvement of child-rearing practices. If behaviors are primarily the result of learning, then presumably dysfunctional behaviors could be unlearned and replaced with more adaptive ones. This rationale was part of Watson's thinking as he formulated the Little Albert study. As you recall from Chapter 10, although he and Rayner made no attempt to remove Albert's fear of rats, they made several suggestions about how to do so, based on conditioning principles. Furthermore, some of these ideas were tested in the 1920s, especially by Mary Cover Jones. She tried Watson's suggestions and several of her own ideas on a number of different children and is remembered for one particular case (Jones, 1924b) in which she removed a young boy's fear of rabbits by gradually moving the rabbit closer to the child while he was eating, using a procedure that she called "direct conditioning."

During the 1920s and 1930s, there were several other demonstrations of how conditioning principles could be applied to alter behavior in a clinical setting. In Russia, for example, researchers applied Pavlovian principles to treat alcoholism by pairing alcohol (CS) with electric shock (UCS), and hysteria by conditioning movement in limbs that appeared initially to be paralyzed (Kazdin, 1978). In the United States, O. Hobart and Willie M. Mowrer developed a treatment program for bed-wetting based on conditioning principles by creating a crib pad that rang a bell as soon as it became wet. The Mowrers used the success of their procedure to attack psychoanalytic concepts of bed-wetting, which relied on the usual deep-seated unconscious conflicts to explain the problem. Instead, the Mowrers argued, it is much simpler to assume that the problem results from a failure to recognize the stimulus cues connected with bladder tension. If conditioning is the problem, they believed, it is also the solution (Mowrer & Mowrer, 1938).

Behavior therapy gained impetus in the 1950s through (a) the work of Eysenck and his colleagues in London, and (b) the development of an effective therapy technique similar to the method used by Mary Cover Jones. At Maudsley Hospital in London, Eysenck followed his 1952 critique of traditional psychotherapy by assembling a team of colleagues to examine the possibility of developing a new therapy approach, one based on the conditioning principles of Pavlov and Hull. By 1960, he and his group had accumulated a sufficient number of applications of conditioning principles to justify producing a book (Eysenck, 1960) that was the first to include the term *behavior therapy* in the title (Glass & Arnkoff, 1992). Three years later Eysenck launched behavior therapy's first journal, *Behaviour Research and Therapy*, with a title that made clear Eysenck's belief that therapies should not be used unless they can be empirically validated.

In the 1950s, Joseph Wolpe, a South African at the University of Witwatersrand, created a procedure that he called **systematic desensitization** (Wolpe, 1958). It remains one of the best-known and most effective behavior therapy techniques. Wolpe, a medical doctor, was trained in traditional psychoanalytic procedures but became dissatisfied with them. He began studying learning theory, especially Hull's, and benefited from the presence in South Africa of an American psychologist who had studied with Kenneth Spence, Hull's alter ego.

Wolpe began exploring behavioral techniques by studying the phobic reactions of cats. After creating fears by shocking the animals whenever they reached for food, he tried to eliminate the fear. Like Mary Cover Jones, he assumed that fear and eating were incompatible responses, so he tried to replace the fear responses by substituting eating responses. Wolpe accomplished this by feeding the animal first in a room that vaguely resembled the original room where the shock occurred, then in a room that more closely resembled the original room, and so on. That is, the fear response was gradually weakened, replaced by the approach to food (Kazdin, 1978).

Wolpe discovered a way to apply this procedure to phobic humans after reading a book by the Chicago physiologist Edmund Jacobson, which described a technique called **progressive relaxation** (Jacobson, 1929). Jacobson had been using relaxation to treat patients with nervous disorders; Wolpe viewed the procedure as a substitute for the eating response he had used with cats. In essence, Wolpe's systematic desensitization procedure involved relaxation training, then the creation of an "anxiety hierarchy," a list of situations that created increasingly greater levels of anxiety. Patients would become relaxed and imagine the situation of least anxiety, then gradually ascend the hierarchy. Wolpe found that after just a few sessions, patients could remain relaxed in the presence of their most feared objects.

With additional modifications over the years, Wolpe's procedure was shown to be highly effective with certain types of anxiety problems (Paul, 1966). A number of other behavior therapy techniques evolved over the years, ranging from token economy/reinforcement systems based on an operant model, to cognitive-behavior therapy, which synthesizes learning theory and the insights from cognitive psychology. A good summary can be found in Kazdin (1978).

The Humanistic Approach to Psychotherapy

Humanistic psychology started as a revolt. It came to be known as psychology's "Third Force," rejecting what it believed to be the "mechanistic, impersonal, hierarchical, elitist psychoanalytic establishment and [the] overly scientific, cold, removed behaviorism" (Cushman, 1992, p. 55). Humanistic psychologists criticized the ideas that human behavior could be reduced to repressed biological instincts or simple conditioned reflexes, rejected the idea that individuals' past histories inevitably limited what their futures could be, and denied the deterministic assumptions of the other two "forces" in psychology, psychoanalysis and behaviorism. Instead, they proposed that the qualities best characterizing humans are free will and a sense of responsibility and purpose, a forward-looking lifelong search for meaning in one's life, and an innate tendency toward growth and personal development. The two American psychologists most closely associated with humanistic psychology were Abraham Maslow and Carl Rogers.

Abraham Maslow and the Goal of Self-Actualization Maslow (1908–1970; Figure 13.5) was trained as an experimental psychologist and researched dominance behavior in primates with Harry Harlow (well known to students for his surrogate mother studies), but later exchanged what he saw as a sterile and reductionist scientific approach for the more wholistic humanistic strategy. He once wrote that laboratory psychology was fine for the laboratory, but that it was "useless at home with your

The Granger Collection, NYC— All rights reserved

FIGURE 13.5 Humanistic psychologist pioneer Abraham Maslow (1908–1970).

kids and wife and friends ... It's not a guide to living, to values, to choices" (quoted in Grogan, 2013, p. 58).

After completing a lab-based doctorate in 1934, Maslow came to New York and eventually settled into a faculty position at Brooklyn College, where he stayed until 1951, when he moved to Brandeis University (near Boston) and completed his career. During this time, and strongly influenced by his discovery of gestalt psychology, Maslow made his shift from experimental to humanistic psychology. Maslow is now known to all students in general psychology for his hierarchy of needs, a model that proposed a series of need systems, arranged in a pyramid, with lower level and more primitive needs at the bottom and culminating with the goal of **self-actualization** at the top. Achieving self-actualization required satisfying all the needs below it—physiological needs, safety needs, the need for love and belonging, and the need for self-esteem, in that order. As he once wrote,

> healthy people have sufficiently gratified their basic needs for safety, belongingness, love, respect, and self-esteem, so that they are motivated primarily by ... self-actualization, defined as ongoing actualization of potentials, capacities and talents, as fulfillment of mission ... , as a fuller knowledge of, and acceptance of, the person's own intrinsic nature, as an unceasing trend toward unity, integration or synergy within the person. (Maslow, 1971, p. 25)

Maslow argued that studying self-actualization, in contrast with a strategy focusing on psychological disorders (e.g., as Freud did), would produce a healthier psychology. As he put it in a famous quote, "the study of crippled, stunted, immature, and unhealthy specimens can yield only a cripple psychology .... The study of self-actualizing people must be the basis for a more universal science of psychology" (Maslow, 1954, p. 234). Maslow followed his own advice and examined the concept of self-actualization more closely, identifying real historical individuals who seemed to be self-actualized, and then looking for commonalities among them. The work began informally, with his reflections about two people that he had come to know in New York—the anthropologist Ruth Benedict and the gestalt psychologist Max Wertheimer (Chapter 9). He later reported that when studying Benedict and Wertheimer, he realized "their two patterns could be generalized. I was talking about a kind of person, not about two incomparable individuals ... I tried to see whether this pattern could be found elsewhere" (Maslow, 1971, pp. 41–42). It could. Through a variety of techniques, Maslow identified a number of people who seemed to share some of the attributes of Benedict and Wertheimer. Maslow found that self-actualizers perceived reality accurately, were highly independent and creative, were spontaneous and natural around others, thought of their work as a career or a calling rather than a job, had a strong moral code, and were problem centered rather than ego centered. Actualizers also would occasionally experience what Maslow called **peak experiences**—moments of intense enjoyment or pure joy that seem almost spiritual in nature. Peak experiences were available to anyone, Maslow believed, but they were more frequently encountered by self-actualizers.

Carl Rogers and Client-Centered Therapy

Humanistic psychology's other main character was Carl Rogers (1902–1987), the creator of **client-centered therapy**, an approach that appealed to a large number of clinicians in the 1960s and 1970s. Rogers (Figure 13.6) was the fourth of six children, raised in a Chicago suburb in an extremely conservative Protestant family that valued hard work and considered all pleasures sinful. As Rogers (1961a) later recalled: "[E]ven carbonated beverages had a faintly sinful aroma, and I remember my slight feeling of wickedness when I had my first bottle of 'pop'" (p. 5). When Rogers was 12, his father moved the family to a Wisconsin farm, in part to remove his children from the evils of suburbia. He was determined to run the farm according to the principles of "scientific agriculture," and Carl developed a keen appreciation for science from the experience. It

© Bettmann/Corbis

FIGURE 13.6 Carl Rogers (1902–1987), creator of client-centered therapy.

led him to enroll in the college of agriculture at the University of Wisconsin, but the enthusiasm soon faded as the sheltered young man discovered a bright new world of people and ideas. He switched to studying history and, determined to be a minister, entered New York's Union Theological Seminary after graduating from Wisconsin in 1924. The theology students at Union were encouraged to think for themselves, and Rogers (1961a) "thought [himself] right out of religious work" (p. 8) and into psychology.

Rogers began taking courses across the street from Union at Columbia's Teachers College, where he came under the influence of Leta Hollingworth. She sparked his interest in working with children, and he began to think about being a professional psychologist. He completed an internship at the Freudian-based Institute for Child Guidance in New York, where he gained some insights about unconscious processes but developed a distaste for psychoanalysis. After earning a doctorate from Columbia (1931), Rogers took a position as a staff psychologist at a child guidance clinic in Rochester, New York, where he began developing his unique brand of therapy. Professionally, he attended APA meetings, but found them "full of papers on the learning processes of rats and laboratory experiments which seemed ... to have no relation to what [he] was doing" (Rogers, 1961a, p. 12). When the American Association for Applied Psychology (AAAP) formed in 1937, he quickly became an active member, and in 1939 he advocated a training model for clinicians that reduced the heavy emphasis on research and increased the opportunities for supervised practice in the craft of diagnosis and therapy. Academia ignored his proposal, but the idea was in essence identical to the one that emerged 30 years later in the form of the PsyD degree (Napoli, 1981).

Rogers entered academia himself in 1940, accepting a position at The Ohio State University. There the stimulus provided by critically thinking graduate students sharpened his ideas about therapy and personality and resulted in his first book, *Counseling and Psychotherapy* (Rogers, 1942). Rogers went to the University of Chicago as a professor of psychology and director of the counseling center in 1945. In the following year he was elected president of the APA, the second president following the big postwar reorganization, and a clear sign to research-oriented academicians that the APA had begun to shift in the practitioner direction. Rogers spent 12 years at Chicago and then 4 back at Wisconsin, where he had a joint appointment in psychology and psychiatry. The Wisconsin years were not happy ones—his client-centered therapy had come under attack as being relevant only for articulate people with mild problems, and Rogers wanted to show that more seriously disturbed clients could benefit as well. He launched an ambitious project to apply the therapy to schizophrenic patients at a local hospital, but the results were at best "equivocal" (Lakin, 1996). That outcome, combined with a cool reception from the experimentally oriented psychology department at Wisconsin, led Rogers to look for greener pastures. He found them in California in 1961, where he joined the staff at the Western Behavioral Sciences Institute at La Jolla. Several years later, he founded the Center for the Study of the Person in La Jolla, where he extended his client-centered therapy to a group therapy setting.

The essence of Rogers's client-centered therapy is not difficult to grasp. Consistent with one of humanistic psychology's cornerstone ideas, Rogers rejected the notion that it was important to delve into the client's past history for therapy to be effective. Rather, the formula for success was for the therapist to create the right kind of therapeutic environment; this, in turn, would allow the client to be able to take control of his or her life and begin to grow in the direction of self-actualization. This ideal therapeutic atmosphere included three components. First, the therapist must be "genuine" and honest with the client (Rogers avoided the word *patient*, with its medical overtones). This genuineness enables the therapist to act as a model for the kind of emotional health being sought in the client. Second, Rogers believed that the therapist must accept the client as a person, meaning "a warm regard for him as a person of unconditional worth—of value no matter what his condition, his behavior, or his feelings" (p. 34). This means accepting a person as having value simply by virtue of being a human being.

The third component of an effective therapist–client relationship is **empathy**, and it follows from the humanistic philosophy proposing that reality is the reality as perceived and experienced by a person. Hence, understanding someone else requires trying to understand how that person views things. Rogers recognized that completely understanding another person was impossible, but it was the effort that counted. This effort included a technique developed by Rogers called **reflection**. It meant taking something said by the client and rephrasing it in a way that leads the client to think "this therapist understands what I'm saying."

If the therapist succeeded in establishing the proper therapeutic environment, good things would happen, according to Rogers. That is, the client "shows fewer of the characteristics which are usually termed neurotic or psychotic, and more of the characteristics of a healthy, well-functioning person" (Rogers, 1961b, p. 36). One final point is that Rogers believed that what he had to say about the therapeutic environment applied to *all* human relationships.

> Thus it seems reasonable to hypothesize that if the parent creates with his child a psychological climate such as we have described, then the child will become more self-directing, socialized, and mature. To the extent that the teacher creates such a relationship with his class, the student will become a self-initiated learner, more original, more self-disciplined, less anxious and other-directed. If the administrator, or military or industrial leader, creates such a climate within his organization, then his staff will become more self-responsible, more creative, better able to adapt to new problems, more ... cooperative. (p. 37)

As an alternative to Freudian-based insight therapies, in which the therapist played the controlling role, client-centered therapy quickly became popular among clinical psychologists and counselors.

In contrast with analytic approaches, it was easier to grasp conceptually, and it actually seemed to help people. It was also based on a more optimistic assessment of human potential for change, reflecting Rogers's own ability to take control of his life and a general midwestern faith that things can be improved if one works hard enough. Also, Rogers was able demonstrate the therapy's effectiveness. Perhaps stemming from his earlier experiences with scientific agriculture, Rogers took great pleasure in completing empirical research on therapy outcomes, complete with comparisons between those in treatment and those in waiting list control groups. He was able to show that his approach brought about measurable positive changes in people's lives (e.g., Rogers, 1954).

Evaluating Humanistic Psychology Humanistic psychology enjoyed great popularity in the 1960s and 1970s. A *Journal of Humanistic Psychology* appeared 1961, largely through Maslow's efforts; the American Association of Humanistic Psychology was created a year later. Maslow was elected APA president in 1968, and the APA created a division for humanistic psychology (Division 32) in 1972. That it was popular during this period of American history is no surprise. As a rebellion against the forces of psychoanalysis and behaviorism, it fit well into the context of a time marked by numerous challenges to existing authority in the wider American culture. And as a philosophy centered on the individual person (e.g., SELF-actualization), it was consistent with some of the values of the 1970s, a decade sometimes referred to as the "Me Decade" (Schulman, 2001). Despite its popularity, however, the humanistic movement has always been on the fringe of psychology. It has been faulted for overemphasizing the self at the expense of the importance of the community and for being clearer about what it was against than what it proposed as an alternative (e.g., Farson, 1978; Wertheimer, 1978). Nonetheless, it has had an important impact on the clinical practice of psychology, especially through the work of Rogers, and it provided some of the inspiration for today's research-based *positive psychology* movement.[4]

The Vail Conference and the PsyD Degree

Before leaving this section of the chapter on clinical psychology, it is worth noting how the Boulder model fared over the years and how a significant alternative to it developed. As you recall, the Boulder model was designed to produce a synthesis of scientist and practitioner, someone able to conduct high-quality research and also able to be an effective clinician. Although the model continues to be the main approach to clinical training, it is not clear that it always reached its ideal. In their analysis of Boulder's first 50 years, for example, Benjamin and Baker (2000) reported that it "is a model that has been much praised, much maligned, and according to some, rarely if ever tried" (p. 233). What were the problems?

First, because academic departments of psychology controlled the clinical training programs, in many cases the scientist side of the training received much greater emphasis than the practitioner side, despite Shakow's vision of a 50–50 split between research and practice training (Cautin, 2006). By the late 1950s, many PhD clinicians were complaining that they were unprepared for the actual practice of psychology, and because they were working mostly in clinical settings and not in academia, they were

---

[4]Humanistic psychology and positive psychology share many values, but the relationship between humanistic psychologists and positive psychologists has not always been congenial (Waterman, 2013). For example, one prominent leader in the positive psychology movement, Martin Seligman, criticized humanistic psychology for its failure to provide much empirical support for their ideas; positive psychology, on the other hand, is firmly grounded in experimental research on such topics as the factors contributing to human happiness ("subjective well-being"). Humanistic psychologists have argued that positive psychologists sometimes forget their historical roots and don't give humanistic psychology enough credit for paving the way for positive psychology.

not getting much use out of their research skills. A second and related problem was that professors of clinical psychology, according to the Boulder recommendations, were expected to "maintain their clinical skills by continuing some clinical practice" (Raimy, 1950, p. 130). Most did, but only to a limited extent. In the academic environment, professors of clinical psychology were under the usual pressure to publish, making it difficult for them to maintain their clinical skills. As a result, graduate students did not always get the best training in how to do clinical work. Many departments took the attitude that students would develop all the needed clinical skills when they did their yearlong internship, but the original Boulder model made it clear that training in clinical practice should occur throughout the 4- to 5-year program and that the internship should not be seen as a "repair shop" for a prior lack of experience (Stricker & Cummings, 1992).

Criticisms of the Boulder model led to considerations of an alternative, one that emphasized the practice of clinical psychology more than research. It was an idea that preceded Boulder. For example, in the mid-1920s, Crane (1925) wrote an article called "A Plea for the Training of Psychologists." Written at a time when there were *no* doctoral training programs for clinical psychologists (Capshew, 1999), he argued that the typical PhD training in psychology, with its emphasis on basic research in traditional topic areas (e.g., perception, learning), was inappropriate. Instead, aspiring clinicians ought to be given much more instruction in the actual practice of psychology, and he suggested the creation of a new kind of degree that he called a "Doctor of Psychology" degree (Peterson, 1992). At a time when clinical psychologists had little status, however, the proposal went nowhere. The same was true for a similar idea, mentioned earlier, floated by Carl Rogers in 1939.

By the 1960s, however, dissatisfaction with the Boulder model was beginning to produce new proposals for the way in which clinicians should learn their craft. And the general atmosphere of dissent that permeated the 1960s led to several attempts to create a new direction for training. First, an APA committee on training recommended, in 1967, that alternatives to the scientist–practitioner model be explored, including one that would accentuate clinical practice and lead to a new degree, a Doctor of Psychology, or **PsyD**, degree. Second, the University of Illinois decided to implement the recommendation, thereby creating, in 1968, the first university-based PsyD program. The prestige of the University of Illinois immediately gave the PsyD some respectability, and other universities soon began developing similar programs. Third, PsyD programs began developing at freestanding schools of professional psychology, not affiliated with universities. The first one was created in California—the California School of Professional Psychology. It opened with two campuses (San Francisco and Los Angeles) in 1970, and added two more (San Diego and Fresno) in 1972.

Just as the need for training guidelines for the new postwar clinical psychologist led to the Boulder conference in 1949, the need for some degree of standardization in the training of the new PsyD clinician led to its own conference, held at Vail, Colorado, in 1973. The goal of the Vail conference was to legitimize the PsyD degree and provide a clear distinction between it and programs yielding a PhD. In essence, the PhD was designed to produce the traditional scientist–practitioner, whereas the PsyD would produce a practitioner–scientist, knowledgeable about research, but primarily trained to deliver psychological services. It took some time for PsyD programs to attain perceived legitimacy, and for many Boulder model clinicians, the quality of PsyD training remains an issue. PhD programs are considerably more selective, for instance, typically accepting about 10% of applicants, compared with up to 50% for PsyD programs (Norcross, Castle, Sayette, & Mayne, 2004). The APA provides full accreditation for both PhD Boulder model programs and PsyD Vail model programs, however.

A major part of the postwar story of clinical psychology has been its increased status in the community of mental health care providers. As you recall from Chapter 12, clinical psychologists prior to World War II had relatively low standing among health-care professionals and were often under the direct supervision of psychiatrists. Since the war, however, organized psychiatry's hegemony has gradually diminished. Over the past half century, sometimes after intense legal battles, clinical psychologists have gained the rights to (a) admit and release patients from mental hospitals, (b) serve as expert witnesses in court (e.g., insanity and child custody cases), and (c) receive third-party payments from insurance companies. At present, organized psychology and psychiatry are skirmishing over prescription privileges, with a few states (e.g., New Mexico) allowing clinical psychologists to prescribe medicine. There is every indication that before too long, this major distinction between psychiatrists and clinical psychologists will disappear (Wiggins, 1994).

PSYCHOLOGY AND THE WORLD OF BUSINESS AND INDUSTRY

We have already seen (Chapter 8) that it did not take psychology long to become involved in the business world. Soon after the turn of the 20th century, Walter Dill Scott was writing on the application of psychology to advertising and how business could be made more efficient; Hugo Münsterberg was doing the consulting work that would produce his *Psychology and Industrial Efficiency*; Walter Bingham was creating his Division of Applied Psychology at the Carnegie Institute in Pittsburgh and consulting with local businesses; the Gilbreths were establishing their successful industrial consulting business; and the Hollingworths were discovering that drinking Coca-Cola late at night was not such a hot idea.

During the 1920s, a period of growth, prosperity, and optimism in America (until the Stock Market crashed in 1929), these kinds of activities increased significantly. Following the highly visible Army testing program in World War I, psychologists began developing tests as quickly as they could be printed, for applications in education as well as business, and many businesses and industries hired psychologists to revamp their personnel departments, primarily by developing tests for the selection and evaluation of workers. Many of these efforts produced tests of questionable quality, but problems with reliability and validity didn't slow the momentum of the testing "boom" until the late 1920s, and the apparent success of the enterprise spawned a new development in the 1920s—companies designed to provide psychological consulting services.

Walter Dill Scott created the first one, the Scott Company (see the announcement of its creation in Figure 13.7), shortly after the end of World War I; it only lasted a few years, mainly because Scott's leadership disappeared when he was named president of Northwestern University in 1920. A second attempt, which floundered initially but eventually prospered, was the Psychological Corporation. It was the brainchild of James McKeen Cattell, who, as you recall from earlier chapters, was a doctoral student of Wundt, a promoter of the failed Galtonian approach to mental testing, and chair of the psychology department at Columbia during a time when it became a leading graduate school in psychology (two of his students were Thorndike and Woodworth). In the early 1920s, Cattell no longer worked in academia, having been fired from Columbia for his antiwar views. He continued as editor-in-chief of the journal *Science*, but he was looking for a way to return to prominence among fellow psychologists. He was also concerned about the growing number of people fraudulently claiming expertise in psychology and cashing in on the widespread interest in psychological testing (Sokal, 1981a). His idea for the company was to create a nationwide network of PhD psychologists with expertise in testing and methodology. The Corporation would be a central clearing house; for instance, a business in St. Louis, in need of psychological assessment in its personnel department, would contact the Psychological Corporation in

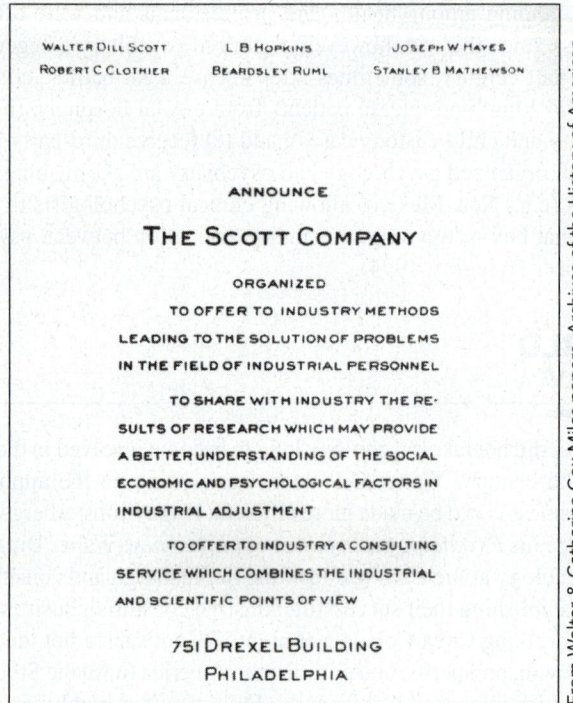

| WALTER DILL SCOTT | L B HOPKINS | JOSEPH W HAYES |
| ROBERT C CLOTHIER | BEARDSLEY RUML | STANLEY B MATHEWSON |

ANNOUNCE

THE SCOTT COMPANY

ORGANIZED

TO OFFER TO INDUSTRY METHODS
LEADING TO THE SOLUTION OF PROBLEMS
IN THE FIELD OF INDUSTRIAL PERSONNEL

TO SHARE WITH INDUSTRY THE RE-
SULTS OF RESEARCH WHICH MAY PROVIDE
A BETTER UNDERSTANDING OF THE SOCIAL
ECONOMIC AND PSYCHOLOGICAL FACTORS IN
INDUSTRIAL ADJUSTMENT

TO OFFER TO INDUSTRY A CONSULTING
SERVICE WHICH COMBINES THE INDUSTRIAL
AND SCIENTIFIC POINTS OF VIEW

751 DREXEL BUILDING
PHILADELPHIA

From Walter & Catherine Cox Miles papers, Archives of the History of American Psychology, The Center for the History of Psychology, The University of Akron

FIGURE 13.7 Announcing the Scott Company, the first consulting company for business organized by professional psychologists.

New York (or one of its planned branch offices) and would be referred to a local expert psychologist who had signed on with the Corporation. The psychologist would perform the service and collect a fee, half of which went back to the Corporation.

The Psychological Corporation began in 1921, with Cattell as its first president. It was a fine idea in principle, but almost immediately it ran into difficulty, primarily because of Cattell's leadership. He was never clear about precisely what services would be offered, making businesses hesitant about signing contracts, and he did not have a good head for business. As late as 1925, for instance, the Corporation's net income was $51.75, while it was renting offices in prime New York real estate and paying $2,500 to the person in charge of day-to-day operations. To keep the operation afloat, Cattell had to contribute $5,000 of his own money (Sokal, 1981a). This wouldn't do—by 1926, Cattell was ousted by his Board of Directors. He was replaced by Walter Van Dyke Bingham, who had solid connections in the business world because of his experiences running the applied psychology operation at the Carnegie Institute in Pittsburgh. Although the Psychological Corporation suffered during the Great Depression of the 1930s, as most businesses did, it survived, and then flourished, especially after World War II. In the year that a publishing house purchased the corporation, 1969, it was worth $2.5 million in total assets and was selling about $5 million in psychological tests per year (Sokal, 1981a).

The field of industrial psychology achieved a substantial increase in perceived legitimacy with the publication of a large (652 pages) and important textbook in 1932 by Morris Viteles of the University of Pennsylvania. He called it *Industrial Psychology*, thereby giving the field an agreed-upon name for the first time (Thompson, 1998).[5] It had three main sections, one detailing the history and foundations of the field (7 chapters), one on employee testing and selection (8 chapters), and one concerning a range of topics from worker safety to training and management issues (12 chapters). Viteles had been Lightner Witmer's best-known doctoral student, earning his degree at 1921 with a study, reminiscent of Münsterberg, on competency testing for streetcar employees (McReynolds, 1997). Two years later, Witmer named Viteles director of a new branch of the Psychological Clinic, named the Vocational Guidance Clinic. It offered testing and consulting services to businesses, but it was primarily for the purpose of helping high school and college students prepare for and enter the world of work. Viteles spent the rest of his career at the Clinic, while also working as a consultant to various businesses and industries in the Philadelphia area and writing his famous book. His consulting work went far beyond the typical employee selection realm—Viteles conducted valuable studies on safety and accident prevention for the Yellow Cab Company, and for the Bell Telephone Company, he developed a program to help managers develop leadership skills and participate more effectively in corporate decision making (Hilgard, 1987).

The Hawthorne Studies

An important event for industrial psychology in the 1920s was the start of a series of research studies that stretched into the 1930s. The research led to the naming of an effect that was (supposedly) demonstrated over and over in the studies, and today appears regularly in textbooks in industrial psychology, social psychology, and research methodology—the Hawthorne effect. The name derives from the Illinois city where the research occurred, the home of the Western Electric Plant. The plant manufactured communication equipment for the American Telephone and Telegraph Company (AT&T).

The experiments at Hawthorne began in 1924 with a series of studies, extending over 3 years, to examine the effects of lighting on worker productivity. The studies were sponsored in part by the electrical industry, which hoped to find evidence of a correlation between lighting and productivity—the more light in the work space, the higher the productivity (Gillespie, 1991). Such evidence, of course, would help sell lightbulbs. Unfortunately for the industry, however, the research failed to show any consistent relationship between lighting and work output. Productivity remained about the same, regardless of lighting level, even when the lighting was poor. We now know that productivity is highly complex, influenced by a variety of factors. But at Hawthorne the outcome of the lighting study was the conclusion that the physical environment was not as important for productivity as the "human factor." Workers knew they were in a study and that the results were important, so their productivity remained high because they felt valued. At least that is the standard interpretation. What was not mentioned was that several other factors surely contributed to the high level of productivity—for instance, the level of direct supervision was increased during the lighting experiments (Gillespie, 1991).

The findings of the illumination experiments were confirmed, or at least that is the standard line, in the most famous of the Hawthorne studies, the Relay Assembly Test Room (RATR) studies. In these experiments, six female workers were selected from a larger group in the plant. Their job was to assemble electrical relays for telephones. Five workers did the actual assembly, and the sixth kept them supplied with parts. Figure 13.8 shows the workroom from two angles. The assembly was a time-consuming, labor-intensive, repetitive job, requiring the assembly of some 35 parts per relay.

---

[5]Today, the field is known as Industrial–Organizational or I/O Psychology, made official in 1973 by APA's Division 14 (Society for Industrial and Organizational Psychology). According to Vinchur (2007), Viteles was also responsible for this expansion of the field, popularizing it his 1953 book, *Motivation and Morale in Industry*.

Courtesy of AT&T Archives and History Center

FIGURE 13.8 The working arrangements in the Relay Assembly Test Room experiment at the Hawthorne plant.

Western Electric produced about seven million relays a year (Gillespie, 1988), so naturally they wished to maximize productivity.

The first relay studies ran from May 1927 through September 1928. During that time, several workplace variables were studied. At various times there were changes in the scheduling of rest periods, total hours of work, and bonuses paid for certain levels of production. The standard account, similar to the outcome for the lighting studies, has it that productivity for this small group quickly reached high levels and stayed there even when working conditions worsened. One example always mentioned concerned the "12th test period" when workers were informed that the workweek would increase from 42 to 48 hours per week, and that rest periods and free lunches would be discontinued (Gillespie, 1988). Virtually all research methods textbooks describe the results somewhat like this:

> With few exceptions, no matter what changes were made—whether there were many or few rest periods, whether the workday was made longer or shorter, and so on—the women tended to produce more and more telephone relays. (Elmes, Kantowitz, & Roediger, 2003, p. 138)

Supposedly, the workers remained productive because they believed they were a special group and the focus of attention—they were part of an experiment. This, along with the similar outcome of the lighting studies, is the origin of the concept called the **Hawthorne effect**, the tendency for performance to be affected because people know they are being studied in a research project.

The effect may be genuine in a research context, but whether it happened at Western Electric is uncertain. A close look at what actually happened reveals some interesting alternative explanations. First, although accounts of the RATR study typically emphasize how delighted the women were to be in this special testing room, the fact is that of the five original assemblers, two had to be removed from the room for insubordination and low output. One was said to have "gone Bolshevik" (Bramel & Friend, 1981). Remember, the Soviet Union was brand new then, and the "red menace" was a threat to industrial America, resulting in things like a fear of labor unions by those in management. Of the two replacement workers, one was especially talented and enthusiastic and quickly became the group leader. She apparently was selected because she "held the record as the fastest relay-assembler in the regular department" (Gillespie, 1988, p. 122). Her efforts certainly contributed to the high level of productivity.

A second problem with interpreting the relay data is a simple statistical problem. In the famous 12th test period, productivity was recorded as output per week rather than output per hour, yet workers were putting in an extra 6 hours per week compared to the previous test period. If the more appropriate output per hour is used, productivity actually *declined* slightly (Bramel & Friend, 1981). Also, the women were apparently angry about the change, but afraid to complain lest they be removed from the test room, thereby losing bonus money (there were not-so-subtle hints to them that such an outcome could occur if they messed up). Last, it could have been that in the RATR, as well as in some of the other Hawthorne experiments, increased worker productivity could have been simply the result of feedback about performance, along with concrete rewards for productivity (Parsons, 1974).

As you know by now, historical events must be understood within their entire political, economic, and institutional context, and the Hawthorne studies are no exception. Painting a glossy picture of workers unaffected by specific working conditions and more concerned with being considered special ushered in a human relations movement in industry and led corporations to emphasize the humane management of employees to create the impression of one big happy family of labor and management. Paying attention to the well-being of workers was a significant advance, in the context of the long history of workers' needs being ignored by management. However, such a picture also helps to maintain power at the level of management and impede efforts at unionization, which some historians (e.g., Bramel & Friend, 1981) believe were among the true motives behind the studies completed at Western Electric.

IN PERSPECTIVE: PSYCHOLOGY'S PRACTITIONERS

We have seen that World War II was responsible for the creation of modern clinical psychology. The war also provided an impetus to other areas of applied psychology as well. As was the case during the first world conflict, psychologists were heavily involved in developing tests for such tasks as the selection of officers and the placement of soldiers into military jobs that suited them. The first war produced Army Alpha and Beta; the second war produced a much more sophisticated test, the Army General Classification Test (AGCT). It graded soldiers into five ability levels, had adequate reliability as a test, and had a degree of validity in that it correlated reasonably well with educational level (Capshew, 1999). The war also gave a boost to applied psychologists whose work examined the relationship between humans and machines, and the war produced a new specialty within psychology—**engineering psychology**. This field has as its goals the creation of machines that were designed for efficient human use. A well-engineered airplane cockpit, for example, has seats that reduce fatigue and instruments that avoid perceptual errors. As you recall from Chapter 8, an important pioneer in this field, was Lillian Gilbreth.

The focus of this chapter has been on the application of psychology to the diagnosis and treatment of those with mental illness (psychiatry and clinical psychology) and the use of psychological principles to improve business (industrial psychology). It is important to note that applied psychology extends to other areas that have not been a part of this chapter, however. These include counseling, school, forensic, and educational psychology. A good historical analysis of these other applied areas can be found in *From Séance to Science: A History of the Profession of Psychology in America* (Benjamin & Baker, 2004).

The reorganization of APA after World War II ushered in a period of tremendous growth for psychology in America. Applied psychology was the beneficiary of APA's new charter, which added advancing psychology as a profession to its original goal of advancing the science of psychology. The scientific side of psychology also prospered in the years after World War II, especially in the form of a major postwar movement called cognitive psychology. The story of cognitive psychology's postwar ascendance, along with discussion of other important historical landmarks in other subdisciplines of psychology during this time, will be told in the next chapter.

SUMMARY

The Medical Approach to Mental Illness

• In the 1920s and 1930s, in the face of overcrowded asylums and bleak prognoses, several medical approaches to therapy developed. These included fever therapy, insulin coma therapy, and metrazol shock therapy. They were popular for a time, but gave way to electroshock therapy, a procedure that continues in use today.

• Charles Myers and William Rivers, two British psychologists, played important roles in changing opinions about the many shell shock victims of World War I. Instead of being signs of cowardice or malingering, shell shock came to be recognized as a severe psychological disorder.

• A controversial medical strategy for treating mental illness, the lobotomy, was created in the 1930s by Egas Moniz. The procedure was based on the idea that by severing the connections between the frontal lobe and lower brain centers, the person would be better able to exert control over emotions. Walter Freeman developed a more efficient but controversial procedure, the transorbital lobotomy, by entering through the eye socket. The procedure fell out of favor in the 1950s—it had limited effectiveness, it was sometimes used for questionable reasons, and better forms of treatment (drugs) appeared.

Clinical Psychology before World War II

• Lightner Witmer is usually credited with establishing, in 1896, the first clinic for the treatment of psychological disorders in the United States. His clinic focused on "psycho-educational" problems similar to those encountered by modern school psychologists—physiological, cognitive, and behavioral problems related to school performance. He believed that the problems he studied could be cured, and he called his treatment program orthogenics.

• Prior to World War II, clinical psychologists for the most part provided mental testing services and did not have high status, either in clinical settings, which were dominated by psychiatrists, or in the APA, which was controlled by academics. The American Association for Applied Psychology was formed in 1937 as a way of professionalizing the practice of psychology. The APA reorganized at the close of World War II and expanded its mission, beyond science, to include the professional practice of psychology.

The Emergence of Modern Clinical Psychology

• Modern clinical psychology emerged from the terrible necessity of World War II. Psychiatry, up to then in control of treatment for mental illness, could not keep up with the caseload. Shortly after the war, a conference on the training of clinical psychologists was held at Boulder, under the leadership of David Shakow. The outcome was a training model featuring a combination of scientific expertise along with expertise in the diagnosis and treatment of mental disorders. The clinical psychologist earned a PhD degree and had to complete a research-based doctoral dissertation.

• A study by Eysenck in 1952 questioning the effectiveness of traditional insight forms of psychotherapy (e.g., Freudian psychoanalysis), focused attention on the need for high-quality research on therapy effectiveness and led to the development of several new approaches to therapy, most notably behavior therapy and a variety of humanistic therapies.

• Behavior therapy is based on the idea that many of life's problems are the result of learning and that experiences influence the kinds of disorders that develop. Therapies based on behaviorist principles existed well before World War II, but after the war they came into their own, especially with the work of Joseph Wolpe, who developed a form of therapy called systematic desensitization.

• Humanistic psychology is sometimes called psychology's "third force" because it rejected the determinism of psychoanalysis and behaviorism and proposed that humans are free to develop and control their own lives, rather than being tied to their past. Humanistic psychologists believe that all humans have the potential for personal growth and self-actualization, a concept investigated by Abraham Maslow, who studied real-life exemplars of self-actualized people (e.g., Max Wertheimer). Self-actualizers perceive reality accurately; are independent, creative, spontaneous, moral, and natural; are devoted to a career; and have occasional peak experiences.

• Carl Rogers rejected traditional psychotherapy and developed a humanistic approach to treatment. The emphasis in client-centered therapy is on positive growth in a client, said to occur if the therapeutic atmosphere is healthy. The job of the therapist is to create this atmosphere, which includes being a model of the self-actualized person ("genuine"), showing unconditional positive regard for the client, and displaying empathy. The therapeutic technique of reflection is designed to aid the process.

• In 1973, the Vail conference produced a new training model for clinicians, one that focused more on practice than on research and did not necessarily require a research-based dissertation. It resulted in a PsyD degree (doctorate of psychology), rather than the traditional PhD Today, APA accredits programs based on both models.

Psychology and the World of Business and Industry

• During the 1920s, many psychologists worked as consultants to business and industry, a development fueled in part by the great interest in testing in the 1920s. Psychologists also joined together to form consulting businesses that would provide a range of services. The Scott Company was the first, but did not survive the 1920s. The Psychological Corporation, under the wayward leadership of James McKeen Cattell, did survive, and eventually prospered, but not until Cattell was ousted. An important 1932 textbook by Morris Viteles institutionalized the name for the field of industrial psychology.

• The Hawthorne studies, extending from 1924 to 1933, have traditionally been seen as providing evidence that productivity will be high if workers are cared for and given healthy work conditions. Productivity did not seem to be affected by such things as lighting conditions and changes in work breaks; what seemed to matter was that workers felt important because they were part of an experiment (i.e., the traditional Hawthorne effect). Historians have shown, however, that the traditional version of what happened at Hawthorne is questionable, and that the Hawthorne studies had the effect of maintaining management control over the workplace.

• World War II contributed to the creation and growth of engineering psychology—a form of applied experimental psychology that examines the relationship between humans and machines, the goal being the development of machines that humans can use efficiently, comfortably, and safely.

STUDY QUESTIONS

1. Describe the similarities and differences among fever, insulin coma, and metrazol shock therapy.

2. Describe the origins and evolution of electroshock as a therapy for mental illness. Why did it outlast the three strategies listed in item 1?

3. Define shell shock, describe the military's initial explanation for it, and describe the various approaches taken to treat it.

4. What was the scientific basis for the development of the lobotomy, and how did Freeman alter the procedure invented by Moniz? Why did lobotomies more or less disappear after the mid-1950s?

5. Lightner Witmer is sometimes considered the founder of clinical psychology in America. What is the basis for the claim? Why could he be considered the founder of school psychology instead?

6. Describe the typical work done by a clinician in the period prior to World War II.

7. How did the activities of clinical psychologists after World War II differ from their activities prior to the war? What brought about the change?

8. Compare the two major training models for clinicians—the Boulder model and the Vail model. What were the problems with the former that led to the creation of the latter?

9. What did Hans Eysenck find in his analysis of studies that evaluated psychotherapy? What was the impact of the Eysenck study?

10. Describe Wolpe's systematic desensitization, and show how it relates to behaviorist principles.

11. Why is humanistic psychology sometimes referred to as psychology's "third force"?

12. Briefly summarize the basic beliefs of humanistic psychologists.

13. Describe Maslow's work with self-actualization. What did he conclude were the attributes of a self-actualized person?

14. Describe the three necessary conditions for therapy to be effective, according to Rogers.

15. Describe the therapy technique of reflection, as used by Rogers, and explain its purpose.

16. In addition to creating client-centered therapy, Rogers is also known for being interested in research on therapy effectiveness. Explain how his personal history might have contributed to that interest.

17. Humanistic psychology was popular in the 1960s and '70s, but then faded. Explain.

18. Describe the origins of the Psychological Corporation, how it was designed to operate, and what happened to it.

19. What was the original purpose of the Relay Assembly Test Room at Hawthorne, what was the outcome, and what is the traditional interpretation of the results? What really happened in the Relay Assembly Test Room?

20. The Hawthorne studies were said to show that relationships with workers were the key to productivity, but historians have interpreted the Hawthorne studies differently. Explain.

CHAPTER 14

PSYCHOLOGY'S RESEARCHERS

The basic reason for studying cognitive processes has become as clear as the reason for studying anything else: because they are there.... Cognitive processes surely exist, so it can hardly be unscientific to study them.

—Ulric Neisser, 1967

PREVIEW AND CHAPTER OBJECTIVES

A key development in academic psychology after World War II was the emergence of modern cognitive psychology. During the 1950s and especially the 1960s, American psychologists began to shift their research and theoretical interests. Whereas in the 1930s and 1940s behaviorism and the search for basic laws of conditioning occupied the attention of most laboratory researchers, the postwar period saw a rebirth of interest in studying cognitive processes—perception, memory, attention, and thinking. The shift was evolutionary rather than revolutionary, and not everyone joined in; behaviorists, especially Skinnerians, remained active and productive in the face of the shift toward cognitive psychology. Nonetheless, the academic psychology of 1970 was quite different from the 1950 version. This chapter will examine the rise of cognitive psychology and its influence on other subdisciplines of psychology. Then it will examine four other prominent areas of research and theory—physiological, perceptual, social, and personality psychology. For each of these subdisciplines, the influence of two historically prominent psychologists will be highlighted. After you finish this chapter, you should be able to:

- Describe examples of cognitive research that occurred during the era of neobehaviorism, especially the work of Europeans unaffected by behaviorism, Sir Frederick Bartlett and Jean Piaget
- Describe the factors within psychology and in fields external to psychology that influenced the development of cognitive psychology
- Critically examine the question of whether a "cognitive revolution" occurred in psychology
- Describe some of the landmark research (e.g., STM capacity) that established cognitive psychology
- Describe the influence of Neisser's first book on cognitive psychology and compare its emphasis with that of Neisser's second book, which advocated ecological validity
- Describe the contributions of Karl Lashley and Donald Hebb to the study of the relationship between brain and behavior
- Describe the contributions of James and Eleanor Gibson to the study of perceptual psychology
- Describe the contributions of Leon Festinger and Stanley Milgram to the study of social psychology
- Describe the contributions of Henry Murray and Gordon Allport to the study of the psychology of personality

COGNITIVE PSYCHOLOGY ARRIVES (AGAIN)

When psychology began to identify itself as a separate discipline in the latter half of the 19th century, it aimed at a scientific understanding of human conscious experience, and Ebbinghaus, Wundt, Wertheimer, Titchener, and other pioneers studied such mental phenomena as memory, attention, perception, and thinking. Psychologists in America also took up these same topics, gave them a functional twist, and investigated them vigorously in the early years of the 20th century. Then Watson appeared and said that the study of mental life was unscientific and that everyone should be a behaviorist, studying the relationships between environmental stimuli and the individual's responses. Not everyone listened, of course, and Watson's message took a while to produce noteworthy effects. By the mid-1930s, however, neobehaviorism had become a force in American psychology, and the prototypical image of the psychology laboratory in those days included rats in mazes. After World War II, however, interests began to shift again, and the study of cognitive processes came once more to the forefront. This time the methods were different from those of Titchener's day, and the models were based on a new technological breakthrough—the computer. But the topics of interest were the same. Some psychologists began calling themselves cognitive psychologists, and a new movement, which was in a sense a return to an old one, was born. During the latter half of the 20th century, cognitive psychology became the dominant conceptual framework in American psychology.

The Roots of Modern Cognitive Psychology

Despite Watson's best promotional efforts, American psychology did not become behaviorist overnight; even when behaviorism was "in" among American psychologists, not everyone joined the party. In the 1920s, '30s, and '40s, the pages of leading journals still contained numerous articles describing research on such cognitive topics as memory, perception, attention, language, and thinking. Among others, they included the famous "Stroop effect" study (Stroop, 1935/1992), mentioned briefly in Chapter 11, and a study by Jenkins and Dallenbach (1924) that still appears regularly in general psychology books. Their experiment examined the effect of cognitive interference on memory, showing that after studying verbal materials, recall could be improved if sleep (i.e., minimal interference) intervened between study and recall. Books dealing with cognitive topics also appeared during behaviorism's heyday, even including one with the title *Cognitive Psychology* (Moore, 1939). Although its treatment of cognition was more of a look back to the earlier years of the century than a call for a new approach to cognition (Knapp, 1985), it dealt with many of the same topics that would concern cognitive psychologists two decades later. On the theoretical front, the gestaltists promoted the study of cognition and argued with behaviorists throughout the 1930s and 1940s.

As you recall from Chapter 11, behaviorism was mostly an American phenomenon, and hence it is not surprising to learn that there were several notable European psychologists doing cognitive work during behaviorism's glory years. Most American experimental psychologists, however, focused intently on whether their rat was going to turn left or right in a maze, paid little attention to this ongoing cognitive research. These Europeans included the Swiss developmental psychologist Jean Piaget, whose ideas about cognitive development first appeared in the 1920s (Piaget, 1923/1959), and England's Sir Frederick Bartlett, who took memory research in a distinctly non-Ebbinghaus direction.

Jean Piaget (1896–1980): A Genetic Epistemology

All students who have taken a course in developmental psychology will recognize the name Jean Piaget and will probably recall seeing a photo in their text of a child staring at the water levels in two different-sized containers. Piaget was a master at creating simple demonstrations of complex cognitive phenomena, and his conservation of volume task, in which "preoperational" children typically fail to recognize that the volume of a liquid remains constant when it is transferred to a taller or shorter container, is among the better known of them.

Jean Piaget was a native of Switzerland and spent most of his life there. Much like John Stuart Mill and Francis Galton before him, he was a precocious child. He developed a strong interest in biology as a schoolboy, and at the age of 10, he managed to publish a one-page description of an albino sparrow in a local natural history journal. He spent most of his adolescence collecting and classifying mollusks, publishing several articles, and even being offered a job as curator of mollusks at a reputable museum in Geneva, which he had to decline because he was still in high school (Piaget, 1952). Piaget completed his college degree at age 18. Within another 3 years, in 1918, he had earned a PhD in biology and had an international reputation as an expert on mollusks.

During his school years, Piaget also became interested in the philosophical problems of epistemology, especially the question of how we obtain our knowledge of the world. He read widely in philosophy and psychology (including William James and Sigmund Freud) and, after finishing his biology doctorate, decided to examine the problem more closely. An opportunity arose in 1919 when he met Théodore Simon, of Binet-Simon fame, who asked the young biologist to work on intelligence testing in Binet's Paris laboratory. Hence, Piaget spent the next few years studying verbal intelligence in school-aged children. His initial task was to standardize a test of reasoning, but while doing so, he discovered that he was less interested in whether the children answered questions correctly than in the thinking processes they used to answer the questions. To explore these strategies, Piaget began interviewing the children about how they solved the problems. From this experience, he concluded that children's cognition differs from adult cognition not just quantitatively, but qualitatively. That is, children do not just know less than adults, they think in an entirely different manner. Eventually, this insight led to Piaget's well-known stage theory of cognitive development.[1]

Following his experience in the Binet lab, Piaget was offered a position as director at a research institute for the study of children in Geneva in 1921. During the 1920s, he also taught at the universities of Geneva and Neuchâtel (his hometown) and published numerous articles and five books. The first of the five, *The Language and Thought of the Child* (1923/1959), gave Piaget an international reputation while he was still in his late twenties (Brainerd, 1996).

Piaget and his wife also had three children during this time, daughters in 1925 and 1927, and a son in 1931. Piaget was not about to miss an opportunity, so he and his wife made careful observations of their three children as they grew. One important lesson for Piaget was that the verbal interviews he used in the Binet laboratory were useless for preverbal infants—other observational procedures had to be used. For instance, he inferred that infants were learning about cause and effect by observing their tendency to repeat their actions ("circular reactions"), and he developed his concept of "object permanence" by noting whether or not infants would search for objects that were out of sight. It was during these years, the decade of the 1930s, that Piaget developed some of his most famous demonstrations of children's cognition and formulated his stage theory of cognitive development (Brainerd, 1996). He referred to his approach as a **genetic epistemology**, using the term *genetic* to refer to developmental processes, not heredity (i.e., in the same way that G. Stanley Hall had used the term a generation earlier). That is, Piaget's focus was on determining precisely how knowledge, as represented by hypothetical mental structures that he called **schemata** (plural of "schema"), developed within the individual. You can think of a schema as similar to a "concept." Piaget believed that children were active formulators

---

[1] As you may recall, the stages are sensorimotor (0–2), preoperational (2–7), concrete operational (7–11), and formal operational (11–adult). For details, refer to any textbook of developmental psychology.

of their knowledge rather than passive recipients of their experiences, and he believed that knowledge structures formed "wholes" that could not be reduced to their elements. This latter point connects with gestalt psychology, of course, and Piaget was well aware of and appreciative of the gestaltists for showing him that he was not alone in formulating a theory based on "structures-of-the-whole." As he put it, "contact with the work of Köhler and Wertheimer made [an] … impression on me . . . . I had the distinct pleasure of concluding that my previous research was not sheer folly, since one could design on such a central hypothesis of the subordination of the parts to the organizing whole not only a consistent theory, but also a splendid series of experiments" (Piaget 1952, p. 248).

In the early 1950s, Piaget established a research institute at the University of Geneva, the International Center for Genetic Epistemology, and remained its director for his remaining years (Voyat, 1981). Despite his reputation in Europe, however, he was still relatively unknown in the United States, partly because not all his work was being translated into English, but also because of the American preoccupation with behaviorism. He was not completely unknown in America—he had been among the group of young international psychologists participating in the famous 1929 International Congress at Yale,[2] and Harvard had given him an honorary degree at a conference celebrating its three-hundredth birthday in 1936 (Kessen, 1996). Also, the editors of the prestigious *History of Psychology in Autobiography* series (including E. G. Boring) saw fit to include Piaget in their fourth edition, which appeared in 1952. Nonetheless, his work was not widely known in the United States until the 1960s, when cognitive psychology was becoming more visible in American experimental psychology. Following a 1960 conference devoted to his work, sponsored by the Social Science Research Council (Kessen & Kuhlman, 1962), and the publication of Flavell's *The Developmental Psychology of Jean Piaget* (1963), Piaget's ideas exploded onto the scene, and he began accumulating the status he retains today as one of the 20th century's most influential psychologists (Kessen, 1996).

Frederick C. Bartlett (1886–1969): Constructing Memory

In 1932, a brief book appeared, with the simple title of *Remembering: A Study in Experimental and Social Psychology*. It was written by a psychologist from England's Cambridge University, Frederick Bartlett. In the United States, the book was ignored, and an American reviewer concluded a generally dismissive review by saying that the book would "find a place upon the shelves of those who study remembering, but it will not be in the special section reserved for those investigators whose writings have become landmarks in the advance towards the comprehension of this important problem" (Jenkins, 1935, p. 715). The reviewer probably had Ebbinghaus in mind as a "landmark." Today, Bartlett's book is recognized as being equal to Ebbinghaus's in importance.

Frederick Bartlett was educated at Saint John's College of Cambridge University, graduating in 1914. He remained at Cambridge for graduate studies and completed the research on memory as his doctoral thesis, shortly after World War I. Thus, the studies described in *Remembering* were completed more than a decade before they were published (Oldfield, 1972). During the 1920s, Bartlett became head of the Psychology Laboratory at Cambridge and set about establishing one of the few centers of experimental psychology in Great Britain. He directed the laboratory until his retirement in 1952, producing research on topics ranging from pilot fatigue to animal learning. He also adapted some of the

---

[2]Instead of its normal annual meeting in 1929, APA combined its meeting with the Ninth International Congress at Yale. This was the meeting where Miles showed off his movies of rats in mazes at the party for Pavlov; other notable international psychologists at the meeting were Charles Spearman, Kurt Lewin, William Stern, Wolfgang Köhler, and Karl and Charlotte Bühler.

methods used in his memory book to the study of thinking, the result being *Thinking: An Experimental and Social Study* (Bartlett, 1958a). It was the memory book that made his reputation, however.

Bartlett opened his memory book by questioning the usefulness of research in the Ebbinghaus tradition, which emphasized the effects of rote repetition on memorizing highly artificial stimuli, the famous nonsense syllables.

> I endeavored, in this series of experiments, to avoid as far as possible the artificiality which hangs over laboratory experiments in psychology. I therefore discarded the use of nonsense syllables and throughout employed material a part of which, at least, might fairly be regarded as interesting and sufficiently normal. (Bartlett, 1932/1967, p. 47)

Also, in contrast with the meticulous Ebbinghaus, Bartlett described his results in narrative form, not as summary statistics, and his descriptions of methodology were often vague. As one reviewer pointed out, Bartlett's studies are better conceived of as "controlled demonstrations, rather than true experiments" (Roediger, 1997, p. 489).

Bartlett believed that the memorizer, rather than passively accumulating associative strength as the result of practice and repetition, *actively* organized the material into meaningful wholes that he referred to as *schemata*, the same term (and used in essentially the same way) by Piaget. Bartlett defined these schemata as "active organisation[s] of past reactions, or of past experiences, which must always be supposed to be operating in any well-adapted organic response" (1932/1967, p. 201). For example, as a result of our experiences, we will develop a schema relating to the concept of death. This schema will in turn influence our current and future perceptions of death and dying and affect our memory of these experiences. People with different experiences and from different cultures will have different schemata about death.

To provide empirical support for his arguments, Bartlett developed several memory tasks, the most famous of which used what he called the "method of repeated reproduction." Participants were given a 328-word story of a Native American folk tale called *The War of the Ghosts*. The story reflected a culture quite different from that of early 20th-century England, and the tale had certain elements that would not "make sense" to a typical Britisher. The concepts of life, death, and the nature of "ghosts" seemed odd to many of Bartlett's 20 participants, for instance. Fifteen minutes after reading the story, subjects were asked to reproduce as much of the story as they could. Additional reproductions were elicited at later intervals ranging from hours to months.

Bartlett reported the results by reproducing dozens of the actual recalled stories, then summarizing the kinds of errors found. Total recall declined with the passage of time, of course, but what was more intriguing to Bartlett was the quality of the reproductions. Participants did not just recall less—what they recalled was shaped by their need to form a coherent, understandable story within the context of their own cultural schemata. Thus, "something black coming out of his mouth," a phrase appearing at the end of the story that seemed to indicate the death of one of the characters, was transformed to "foaming at the mouth" for one participant and the soul leaving the body for another. Also, there was ambiguity about the ghosts—some of the characters seemed to be ghosts, yet it appeared that they were subsequently killed in the story; if they were *already* ghosts, how could this happen?. To resolve the question, one subject decided that "Ghosts" was just a label for a particular tribe. This transformation (or *rationalisation*, as Bartlett called it) "made the whole thing more comprehensible" (Bartlett, 1932/1967, p. 68). Others recalled erroneously, but logically for their death schema, that the "ghosts" appeared only *after* some Indians were killed in the battle. In all, then, subjects recalled the story within the framework of their own British cultural schemata about battle and death and the afterlife. Thus, memory was not merely an act of reproducing intact memory traces; rather, it was an active process of *construction*. As Bartlett put it,

> In the many thousands of cases of remembering which I collected, ... literal recall was very rare. With few exceptions, ... reexcitement of individual traces did not look to be in the least what was happening .... In fact, if we consider the evidence rather than presupposition, remembering appears to be far more decisively an affair of construction rather than one of mere reproduction. (pp. 204–205)

Bartlett's ideas about memory did not make much of a stir in the United States, appearing during the height of neobehaviorism. It was only in the 1960s, after cognitive psychology had emerged from multiple sources, that the significance of the work began to be appreciated. His notion of memory as constructive is now widely accepted and essential to the understanding of such phenomena as false memory (e.g., Roediger & McDermott, 1995) and eyewitness memory (e.g., Loftus, 1979).

A Convergence of Influences

The influences that produced modern cognitive psychology came both from within psychology, in the form of a growing suspicion about the adequacy of conditioning principles, and outside psychology, through several disciplines that received their initial impetus during World War II or developed after the end of the conflict (Segal & Lachman, 1972).

Influences within Psychology   Among psychologists during the 1940s and 1950s, there was growing concern that conditioning and associationist principles could not adequately account for all human behavior, especially language. Although some behaviorists had either reduced mental events to subtle muscular responses to stimuli (Watson) or viewed them merely as internal behavior under the control of reinforcement contingencies (Skinner), Tolman and Hull had attempted to address the problem of "representation." That is, both recognized that individuals acted as if they were influenced by internal representations or conceptions of the external world (e.g., memories). Hull dealt with the issue by avoiding mentalistic concepts and proposing internal sequences of stimuli and responses that became chained together through reinforced learning trials. Tolman went further and proposed that such internal constructs as cognitive maps and expectancies served to guide behavior. Both approaches fell short when it came to explaining distinctly human behavior such as language, however, and attempts to force language into conditioning terms failed.

The adequacy of associationism's principles was also called into question, most notably by the neuropsychologist Karl Lashley (more on him later in the chapter), a former colleague of Watson's at Johns Hopkins, but a longtime critic of simple Watsonian S-R formulations. In 1948, Lashley participated in the Hixon Symposium, an interdisciplinary meeting that brought together psychologists, mathematicians, neurologists, and psychiatrists to consider the general topic of the relationship between the brain and behavior. Lashley's talk dealt with the problem of serial order and the general failure of association theory to account for it (Lashley, 1951). Simply stated, the **serial order problem** concerns the question of how to explain, in terms of cerebral mechanisms, linear sequences of behavior, ranging from the series of finger movements while playing the violin to the memorization of a list of words to the production of language in sentences. A basic tenet of association theory was that adjacent elements in a sequence become associated or "chained" together because they are experienced together (i.e., contiguously). Lashley argued that such a formulation was inadequate. In complex motor skills such as playing the violin, for example, the sequence of behaviors occurs much too rapidly for one element to depend on the neurological analysis of the preceding element and be the stimulus for the next element. Also, the oral production of a sentence is more complex than a simple linear sequencing of words, as illustrated by the rules of syntax and slips of the tongue. Thus, two sentences, one in the active voice and the other in the passive, have completely different sequences yet convey the same meaning. And certain errors of speech, called Spoonerisms, involve anticipations of words or word segments that were meant to occur later in the sentence.[3] Instead of a cortical model based on the concept of linear associative chains, Lashley argued that the brain was a more complex system that exercised organizational control over patterns of behavior.

Lashley's paper was well received, but like Bartlett's work, its significance for the development of cognitive psychology was not immediately recognized (Bruce, 1994). References to the article accumulated at a leisurely pace throughout the 1950s and then increased substantially in the mid-1960s, the decade in which cognitive psychology was building momentum. Thus, the serial order paper was a bit ahead of its time. Nonetheless, it contributed to the critical mass that was developing in the postwar years that eventually led to cognitive psychology's appearance.

Influences External to Psychology Developments in disciplines outside psychology had a profound impact on the shift toward an interest in cognition. One of the most critical was the development of computer science, which was accelerated in the 1940s by the military needs of World War II, with its demands for such things as automated radar-tracking systems (Baars, 1986). Of course, philosophers and psychologists have a long history of using contemporary technology as metaphors relating to human behavior. Examples range from Descartes' use of hydraulic garden figures in his model of the nervous system to Watson's belief that the telephone switchboard paralleled the S-R connections underlying the relationship between stimulus and action. In the postwar era, it wasn't long before scientists began to see parallels between the computer and the brain.

The computer is essentially a device for taking in information from the environment, processing it internally, and producing some output. By analogy, the brain could be seen as doing the same thing. The mathematician John von Neuman explicitly developed this metaphor in the opening address given at the Hixon Symposium in 1948. The analogy reappeared on occasion in the 1950s, and by the 1960s it was commonplace to hear cognitive phenomena described in computer language and its models portrayed as computer flowcharts. The best-known example, soon to be a regular feature in the memory chapters of introductory psychology books, was the model proposed by Atkinson and Shiffrin (1968). Some form of the flowchart in Figure 14.1, a simplified version of theirs, is probably familiar to you. It introduced the well-known distinctions between the limited capacity short-term memory (STM) system, analogous to a computer's RAM, and the unlimited capacity long-term memory (LTM), likened to a computer's hard drive. And the Atkinson/Shiffrin model freely used computer jargon. Thus, humans don't just memorize things, they "transfer information from STM to LTM," and they don't just remember things, they "retrieve information from LTM."

One advantage of the computer metaphor was that it provided a scientifically respectable way to discuss complex internal mental processes, thus muting behaviorism's criticisms that psychological scientists shouldn't be dealing with mysterious unobservable entities that intervene between stimulus and response, and avoiding the old problems with introspection. Further respectability came from a

---

[3] An example of a Spoonerism might be saying "Let me sew you to your sheets" instead of the intended "Let me show you to your seats."

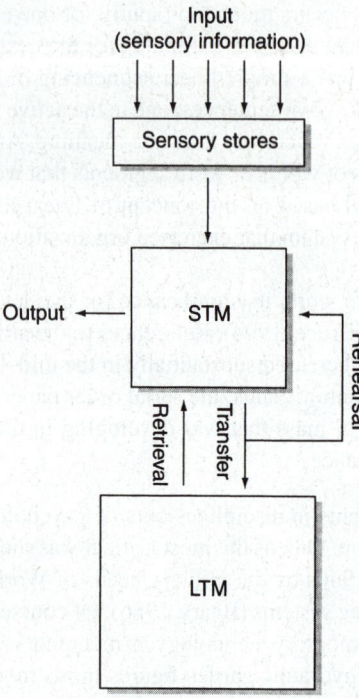

FIGURE 14.1   An example of a computer flow chart used to illustrate the two-stage model of memory like the Atkinson and Shiffrin (1968) model.

refinement in the way of describing the flow of information through the system. This occurred with the publication of *The Mathematical Theory of Communication* (Shannon & Weaver, 1949), which introduced **information theory** and the concept of the **bit**, an abbreviation of "binary digit." An electrical engineer, Shannon recognized a connection between the logical operators of "true" and "false" and the two states, "on" and "off," of any electromagnetic relay. Working with Weaver, he defined the bit as the amount of information that would enable a decision between two equally likely alternatives. Thus, information reduces uncertainty. A coin toss, for instance, contains one bit of information because it tells us which of two possible outcomes is true. Each time the number of alternatives doubles, one additional bit of information is added: With four alternatives, it takes two bits of information to reduce uncertainty, with eight alternatives, it takes three bits, and so on. The significance of the concept was that it provided a way of standardizing units of information, regardless of the form that the information took (e.g., coin toss, dice throw, numbers, letters). The bit wound up being more important for computer science than for cognitive psychology, but in the 1950s it added further legitimacy to the scientific study of the mind.

Another area of development outside psychology, but relating to the assault on behaviorism within psychology, was linguistics. Led by Noam Chomsky (b. 1928) of the Massachusetts Institute of Technology (MIT), theories of language structure and language production began to proliferate in the 1950s, and they went beyond anything conceivable to behaviorists. Chomsky came to the attention of psychologists in 1959, when he wrote a highly critical review of *Verbal Behavior*, B. F. Skinner's (1957) creative attempt to put language into operant terms (Chomsky, 1959). Language development occurs too rapidly for conditioning to be relevant, he argued. Even if we could learn a sentence per second, there are not enough seconds in a lifetime to learn all the sentences that we are capable of producing. Furthermore, people routinely create and/or understand sentences they have never experienced before. Language was simply too complex for what Chomsky took to be an overly simplistic behaviorist explanation.

As the result of the work of Chomsky and other linguists, language came to be viewed not as verbal behavior that was the outcome of conditioning and associative learning, but as the result of the application of a hierarchical set of rules called a **grammar**. These rules allow the individual to generate a virtually infinite number of grammatical sentences, while also enabling the person to immediately identify nongrammatical sentences. For instance, to use one of Chomsky's favorite examples (Gardner, 1985), we easily recognize "Colorless green ideas sleep furiously" as perfectly grammatical, if silly, whereas we have no difficulty rejecting these same words in a different order, "Sleep ideas green colorless furiously," as ungrammatical. The sentences we use cannot be the result of simple learning, Chomsky argued, but must follow from the application of a grammar. Furthermore, this ability to use grammar is instinctively human—Chomsky believed that language was the attribute that most clearly distinguished humans from other species. He believed that all languages shared common principles, which he called **linguistic universals**, and that the human brain is structured to be able to understand these universals quickly (Chomsky, 1966). Chomsky and other linguists supported their nativist arguments about language by pointing out that (a) as with other species-specific behaviors, there appears to be a critical period for language development, and (b) attempts to teach language skills to other species (e.g., through the use of sign language) have failed.[4]

Questions about behaviorism, along with developments in computer science, information theory, and linguistics, helped to change the intellectual climate among experimental psychologists. Some even referred to the events at this time as a scientific revolution, an issue that is examined in this chapter's Close-Up.

CLOSE-UP

WHAT REVOLUTION?

There is little doubt that more experimental psychologists in America were interested in studying cognitive processes in the 1960s than in the prior two decades and, except for diehard Skinnerians, behaviorism began to decline at the same time. Some have referred to the change as a "revolution" in psychology (e.g., Segal & Lachman, 1972; Sperry, 1993), and at least two books chronicling the shift to cognition include *cognitive revolution* in their titles (Baars, 1986; Gardner, 1985). On the other hand, Leahey (1992) argued that the development of cognitive psychology does not meet any of the accepted criteria for being a scientific revolution. Resolving the issue requires some understanding of what is meant by a "revolution" in science.

In 1962, a brief (172 pages) but momentous book entitled *The Structure of Scientific Revolutions* appeared on the academic scene, proposing a new way to look

at progress in science. Its author, physicist-turned-historian Thomas Kuhn, questioned the traditional Enlightenment-based notion that scientific progress involves a steady accumulation of objective knowledge over time. Rather, in Kuhn's view, science proceeds through history by establishing agreed-upon "paradigms" that guide scientists and then shifts from one paradigm to another. When such a shift occurs, a scientific revolution has happened.

According to Kuhn, all sciences begin in a "preparadigmatic stage." During this time there are competing schools of thought within a disciple, and they argue over fundamental conceptual and definitional issues. Eventually, one of those schools gains a majority of adherents and becomes established as a **paradigm**. A Kuhnian paradigm is an all-embracing worldview within the scientific community that organizes what is known into

---

[4]Chimpanzees and other primates have been successful at learning to use sign language, but the general consensus among both linguists and cognitive psychologists is that their learning is imitative and does not show evidence of the use of a true rule-bound grammar (see Anderson, 1990, for a review).

a grand theory, determines how terms are defined and what problems are to be solved by scientists, and dictates appropriate research methods. Newtonian physics is the typical example. Once a paradigm has been established, there exists a period of **normal science**, during which the paradigm guides research designed to provide empirical evidence for it. Because all paradigms have some truth to them, much of this research indeed supports the paradigm, but not all of it does. Anomalous findings can usually be ignored or explained away, but sometimes predictions keep failing and the science enters a "crisis" period, during which confidence in the paradigm starts to wane. Eventually, a creative scientist or two will come up with a new idea that explains the anomalies along with everything else explained by the paradigm-in-crisis. If this new idea is sufficiently powerful and well promoted, it can become a new paradigm, replacing the old one. If so, a revolution is said to have occurred. The replacement of Newtonian physics with Einsteinian physics is the typical example.

Kuhn's ideas have been applied to psychology. Kirsch (1977), for example, claimed that psychology's first paradigm could be called "mentalism," and it encompassed Wundtian, structuralist, and functionalist thinking. Its guiding interest was the scientific study of human conscious experience. Methodological problems (i.e., introspection) led to a paradigm crisis, however, leading to a behaviorist revolution. Similar arguments were made by Palermo (1971), who believed that psychology in the 1960s was in the midst of a second revolution, from behaviorism to cognitive psychology. The shifts from mentalism to behaviorism and then to cognitive psychology have a certain intuitive appeal, and there is a degree of truth to Kirsch's and Palermo's arguments.

According to Leahey (1992), however, clothing psychology's history in Kuhnian garb can oversimplify complex events and perpetuate myths. Concerning the so-called cognitive revolution, for instance, he argued

that (a) behaviorists disagreed on too many fundamental issues (e.g., the role of reinforcement) for behaviorism to be anything close to a Kuhnian paradigm; (b) any shift from behaviorism to cognition was too gradual for the term *revolutionary* to have any meaning; (c) the early research in cognition was not motivated primarily by the perception of a "crisis" in behaviorism, but by a variety of other factors (e.g., the computer–brain metaphor); and (d) cognitive psychologists themselves disagreed on too many fundamentals for cognitive psychology to resemble a Kuhnian paradigm.

Leahey (1992) also made the interesting suggestion that the 1962 appearance of Kuhn's book *by itself* helped to create the "myth" that a cognitive revolution was in progress. Reflecting on that era, researcher James Jenkins recalled it as a "tremendously exciting time. The basic assumption was that things were boiling over, and … a new day was coming. And of course, everyone toted around their little copy of Kuhn" (quoted in Baars, 1986, p. 249). Although not denying that changes were indeed occurring, Leahey concluded "*there was no awareness of revolution until Kuhn's book suggested it*" (p. 315, emphasis in the original). It is worth noting that all of this was going on during a particularly turbulent time in American history. In the 1960s, protests against the war in Vietnam and the civil rights and women's movements produced a climate in which talk of overthrowing the existing order, not trusting anyone over 30, and rejecting institutional authority was commonplace on university campuses. As a graduate student in cognitive psychology myself at that time, I can recall how Kuhn's message of revolutionary change seemed to resonate with my professors and peers. For instance, the book was the first one we had to read in a seminar on "higher mental processes," and it colored the discussion for the whole semester. By formulating a new way of looking at the history of science, then, in a culture awash with calls for change, Kuhn's book might have helped to create the idea that a "cognitive revolution" was occurring.

Magical Numbers, Selective Filters, and TOTE Units

Whether revolutionary or evolutionary, it is clear that change was occurring in experimental psychology. Perhaps the first psychologist to recognize this was George A. Miller (1920–2012). As a research fellow in Harvard's Psycho-Acoustic Laboratory from 1944 to 1948, Miller (Figure 14.2) investigated speech perception, a problem that derived from a military context—the difficulty in hearing spoken messages while sitting in loud airplanes (Hilgard, 1987). Out of this research came a course offered to

Archives of the History of American Psychology, The Center for the History of Psychology, The University of Akron

FIGURE 14.2   George Miller (1920–2012), of 7±2 fame.

Harvard undergraduates called "The Psychology of Speech and Communication," and from the course came Miller's first book, *Language and Communication* (1951). Shortly after Shannon and Weaver (1949) produced their groundbreaking work, Miller introduced information theory to psychologists in a *Psychological Review* article (Miller & Frick, 1949). Then, in 1956, he published an article with a title more whimsical than normally found in stuffy academic journals—"The Magical Number Seven, Plus or Minus Two: Some Limits on Our Capacity for Processing Information" (Miller, 1956). The conclusions of the paper were destined to become a standard feature in the memory chapters of introductory psychology textbooks, and the article itself became the most frequently cited paper in the first 100 years of the *Psychological Review* (Kintsch & Cacioppo, 1994).

In the article, Miller showed how information theory concepts such as bits and channel capacity could be used to describe limits on our ability to process information in several kinds of tasks. The last portion of the paper contains the most frequently cited information, Miller's analysis of the limited capacity of immediate memory. Depending on the type of information being memorized, he argued that people could only process between five (for monosyllabic words) and nine (for binary digits) items at a time. Recognizing that the amount of information in bits varies dramatically, depending on the type of material being studied, Miller introduced a new term, the **chunk**, to refer to the information being held in immediate memory. Hence, the capacity limit on STM was identified as seven, plus or minus two, chunks of information, the chunk being a small, meaningful unit of information. Further, Miller applied the information theory concept of **recoding** to take into account the fact that humans have the ability to reorganize data, thereby squeezing in more information per chunk. Miller used the example of learning Morse code to drive home the point. The learner first hears each dot and dash as an individual unit. With experience, however, combinations of these sounds are recoded ("chunked") as whole letters, then words, then phrases, so that the experienced operator can, in effect, keep many more dots and dashes in immediate memory than the novice.

The 1950s also saw the publication of several works from England that applied information theory ideas to attention, a cognitive phenomenon largely neglected since Wundtian times. The prime mover was a student of Bartlett's at Cambridge, Donald Broadbent (1926–1993), who first became interested in psychology during World War II, while being trained as a pilot in the Royal Air Force. Although impressed by the technical complexity of the aircraft he was flying, he was frustrated by the failure of engineers to take the human pilot into account when designing the cockpit instrumentation and controls. The similarity of gauges often induced perceptual and attentional errors—for instance, Broadbent recalled that while landing on one occasion, he thought he was flying at 2,000 feet, only to discover that he was attending to the wrong gauge and that he was actually flying at 2,000 rpm (Broadbent, 1980).

After the war, Broadbent went to Cambridge, studied with Bartlett, and was eventually named director of Bartlett's laboratory. During the 1950s, he and Colin Cherry, a professor of telecommunications, pioneered modern research on attention by using a **dichotic listening** procedure, in which research participants would experience two channels of information at the same time, one sent to each ear via headphones. They were able to document limits on the ability to use multiple communication channels, showing, for instance, that while attending to one message, very little of a second message could be recalled (e.g., Cherry, 1953). Broadbent summarized this research in *Perception and Communication* (1958) and proposed a **selective filter** model of attention. When confronted with two streams of information, he suggested, our limited capacity system filters out one message and selects the other for attention and further processing. The problem of selective attention, which introductory textbooks soon began labeling the "cocktail party phenomenon" because the task resembled that of trying to listen to two conversations at once, remains an important and vigorous area of research in cognitive psychology.

A third example of the shift toward cognitive psychology in the 1950s took the form of a book. Entitled *Plans and the Structure of Behavior*, it appeared in 1960, the outcome of a collaboration between Miller, of 7±2 fame; Eugene Galanter, a Harvard experimental psychologist with expertise in math and computers; and Karl Pribram, a prominent neuroscientist. The book centered on the idea of a "plan," defined as "any hierarchical process in the organism that can control the order in which a sequence of operations is to be performed" (Miller, Galanter, & Pribram, 1960, p. 16). In keeping with the computer metaphor that was rapidly coming into vogue, the authors explicitly likened a plan to the program written for a computer.

Plans and the Structure of Behavior is perhaps best remembered for applying the concept of feedback to human systems. In a radical departure from behaviorist/associationist tradition, the book proposed that a feedback system could be substituted for the reflex as the basic unit of behavioral control. In a feedback system, the operation of one part of the system produces results that are fed back and monitored by the system, thereby affecting its future operation. The thermostat and furnace, for instance, operate together as a simple feedback system. On a cold day, the thermostat sends a signal to the furnace to start, which increases the air temperature, which is read by the thermostat, which eventually tells the furnace to stop. The temperature then drops, triggers another signal from the thermostat to restart the furnace, and so on. In the long run, the feedback system produces a "steady state," a temperature that does not vary much from the thermostat setting. For human feedback systems, Miller and his colleagues created the basic concept of the **TOTE unit**, TOTE being an acronym for Test-Operate-Test-Exit.

It begins with a Test phase that looks for incongruities in the system (e.g., in the thermostat example, a difference between the desired temperature and the actual temperature). If there are no incongruities, nothing happens, but if there are, an operation occurs to reduce the incongruity. Another Test then occurs, and so on until no incongruity exists. For humans, these TOTE units are organized hierarchically, as in the example shown in Figure 14.3, which represents the authors' example of a two-level system for hammering a nail. The first Test is to see if the nail is sticking up. If not, no hammering is needed; if so, the second level TOTE units engage to alter the state of the nail.

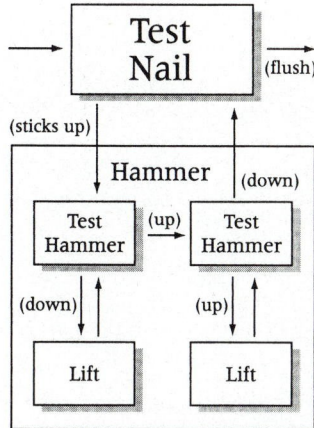

FIGURE 14.3 TOTE units arranged to illustrate a hierarchical plan for hammering nails, from Miller, Galanter, and Pribram (1960).

Neisser and the "Naming" of Cognitive Psychology

Miller's 7±2 paper, the British work on attention, and *Plans* were just three prominent examples of events that marked an important shift in experimental psychology during the 1950s, legitimizing the study of heretofore frowned-on mentalistic topics. The momentum continued to build in the 1960s, a tumultuous decade in which change from the existing order became a familiar theme (refer again to this chapter's Close-Up). In addition, experimental psychology benefited from increased government funding of all scientific research, part of the attempt during the cold war to reestablish American scientific supremacy in the wake of Soviet successes in space (e.g., launching the first satellite—"Sputnik"—into orbit in 1957). By the mid-1960s, sufficient research existed to warrant book-length summaries, and texts in cognitive psychology began to appear, most notably Ulric Neisser's *Cognitive Psychology* in 1967. What the Viteles text did for industrial psychology in 1932, Neisser's text accomplished in 1967—it gave the subdiscipline a name. Neisser would later recall getting "letters from people saying that they were glad that I had given [the movement] a name, because they were interested in all the topics I considered, but the area had not had a theoretical identity" (quoted in Baars, 1986, p. 278). After Neisser, it did.

As an undergraduate at Harvard, Neisser (1928–2012; Figure 14.4) studied with George Miller, later recalling that Miller's course on speech and communication "covered some pretty unusual topics ... [such as] linguistics, acoustics, articulatory physiology, and engineering mathematics" (Neisser, 1988, p. 82). Neisser's interest in cognition was aroused by the experience, and he went on to earn a doctorate in psychoacoustics at Harvard in 1956. He subsequently taught at Brandeis, Cornell, and Emory.

In the opening chapter of *Cognitive Psychology*, Neisser (1967) began by pointing out that the times had changed in psychology:

> A generation ago, a book like this one would have needed at least a chapter of self-defense against the behaviorist position. Today, happily, the climate of opinion has changed, and little or no defense is necessary. Indeed, stimulus-response theorists themselves are inventing hypothetical mechanisms with vigor and enthusiasm and only faint twinges of conscience. The basic reason for studying cognitive processes has become as clear as the reason for studying anything else: because they are there . . . . Cognitive processes surely exist, so it can hardly be unscientific to study them. (p. 5)

Courtesy of Emory Photo Video

FIGURE 14.4 Ulric Neisser (1928–2012), whose 1967 book gave cognitive psychology a name.

As for the question of what cognitive psychology actually meant, Neisser considered it to be the experimental study of all cognitive process, and by cognition, he meant

> *all the processes by which the sensory input is transformed, reduced, elaborated, stored, recovered, and used.* It is concerned with these processes even when they operate in the absence of relevant stimulation, as in images and hallucinations. Such terms as sensation, perception, imagery, retention, recall, problem-solving, and thinking, among many others, refer to hypothetical stages or aspects of cognition. (p. 4, emphasis in the original)

The content chapters of Neisser's *Cognitive Psychology* are full of rich experimental detail about some of the ways that the human information processor can transform information. Reflecting the novelty of cognitive psychology, about 60 percent of the book's 321 references are to research published in the decade of the 1960s (Weaver, 1998). The bulk of the book concerns the processing of visual and auditory information, but there are also chapters on memory, language, and a brief concluding chapter on the relationship between memory and thought.

The Evolution of Cognitive Psychology

Interest in cognitive psychology continued to grow rapidly after the publication of Neisser's 1967 book. Psychology departments rushed to create cognitive laboratories and to hire cognitive psychologists, conferences on cognition were held, their contents later published in edited books (e.g., the Loyola Symposium, in Solso, 1973), and informal networks such as SWIM (Southeastern Workers in

Memory) appeared. Traditional journals such as the *Journal of Experimental Psychology* featured more cognitive research, and new journals appeared—*Cognitive Psychology* in 1970, *Cognition* in 1972, *Cognitive Science* in 1977, and *Memory and Cognition* in 1983. In addition, cognitive psychology spread to psychology's other subdisciplines, such as developmental, social, personality, and abnormal psychology. Even animal psychology was not immune, as researchers began investigating "animal cognition" (e.g., Flaherty, 1985).

Within cognitive psychology itself, changes occurred in the 1970s, once again led by Neisser. In *Cognition and Reality* (1976), he argued that the laboratory tradition in cognitive psychology, although producing important results, nonetheless had failed to yield knowledge about information processing in real-world contexts. He was even critical of his own 1967 text for being top heavy with basic laboratory research. Instead, explicitly recognizing the influence of Bartlett, Neisser called for more research concerning what he called **ecological validity**—research with relevance for the everyday cognitive activities of people adapting to their environment. Experimental psychologists, Neisser (1976) urged, "must make a greater effort to understand cognition as it occurs in the ordinary environment and in the context of natural purposeful activity. This would not mean an end to laboratory experiments, but a commitment to the study of variables that are ecologically important rather than those that are easily manageable" (p. 7).

Neisser's call to arms was embraced by many cognitive researchers, and the 1980s and 1990s saw increased research in such topics as eyewitness memory (e.g., Loftus, 1979), the long-term recall of topics learned in school (e.g., Bahrick, 1984), and autobiographical memory, the memory for the events of one's life (e.g. Kennedy, Mather, & Carstensen, 2004). This turn to everyday cognition should not be surprising, given what we know about the history of functionalist thinking in American psychology. Research that helps us to understand how the individual adapts to the environment and has practical applications is the type of research that has always resonated with American psychology's functional/pragmatic spirit.

In addition to the interest in ecological validity, another aspect of the evolution of interests among research psychologists was the development of **cognitive science**, an interdisciplinary field that includes cognitive psychology, linguistics, computer science, cultural anthropology, and epistemology. Gardner (1985) defined the field broadly as an "empirically based effort to answer long-standing epistemological questions—particularly those concerned with the nature of knowledge, its components, its sources, its development, and its deployment" (p. 6). The term *cognitive science* began to appear in the mid-1970s and became institutionalized with the naming of a journal devoted to it in 1977. In the opening editorial for *Cognitive Science*, Collins (1977) pointed out that the discipline could have been called "applied epistemology or intelligence theory, but someone on high declared it should be cognitive science and so it shall" (p. 1). A major topic of interest among cognitive scientists has been in the interface between humans and computers—computer simulations of cognitive processes and the development of artificial intelligence have been topics of frequent interest to cognitive scientists.

It is worth noting that although the label is relatively new, cognitive science is not. The initial stirrings of the new discipline can be seen in the postwar era, when the aforementioned "influences external to psychology" (information theory, computer science, linguistics) contributed to the emergence of what psychologists began calling "cognitive psychology." From a broader perspective, however, it is clear that something more than a new type of psychology was developing back then, and that some of the key players were aware of it. George Miller, for instance, traced the origins of cognitive science to a 1956 symposium on information theory, held at MIT (Baars, 1986), and in 1960, Miller and Jerome Bruner cofounded the Center for Cognitive Studies at Harvard, designed explicitly to foster the interdisciplinary study of cognition. Bruner later recalled that he and Miller decided "that psychology was too complicated a field to leave to the psychologists, [so] what we needed was an alliance with colleagues from other disciplines who were, each in his or her own context, concerned about how humans acquired and used knowledge" (Bruner, 1988, p. 92).

Evaluating Cognitive Psychology

Although some have considered cognitive psychology to be an all-encompassing framework, even a "paradigm," for modern psychology, the movement has also been sharply criticized. Understandably, the most vocal critic was B. F. Skinner, the leading behaviorist of the second half of the 20th century. Skinner objected to the creation of hypothetical mental mechanisms (e.g., STM), which all too easily could become reified, he believed, into *explanatory fictions*. That is, instead of looking for the causes of behavior in the environment and one's learning history, where they belonged (in Skinner's view), the cognitive psychologist turned these hypothetical mechanisms into real, causal entities. Attributing failures of recall to limited STM capacity hardly explains the phenomenon, he argued. Skinner deplored the spread of cognitive ideas throughout the field of psychology, sarcastically observing that a graph showing the use of the term *cognitive* in psychology's literature would show exponential growth after 1960—"Is there any field of psychology today in which something does not seem to be gained by adding that charming adjective to the occasional noun?" (Skinner, 1987, p. 783).

A second general criticism of cognitive psychology derives from the computer metaphor, with its human-as-machine implication. Such a view ignores significant aspects of human behavior, critics charge, such as emotion and motivation (e.g., Zajonc, 1980), or intentionality (Searle, 1980). Hilgard (1980), referring to an ancient tripartite division of mental activities—the cognitive, the affective (emotional), and the conative (motivational/behavioral)—made a similar argument that cognitive psychology addresses only a portion of the whole. A related criticism has been that cognitive psychologists sometimes ignore neurological reality, building models of mental processing that contradict what is known about how the nervous system operates.

Despite the problems, the study of cognitive processes has worked its way into virtually every area of modern psychological investigation. The pervasiveness of cognitive factors is perhaps an indication of how important such processes have always been to psychology, even when prominent behaviorists may have questioned their importance, and how central they are to the very definition of what it means to be human.

OTHER RESEARCH AREAS

In Descartes' time, the first half of the 17th century, serious scholars believed that it was possible to gain a complete understanding of all scientific knowledge. Descartes himself made that his goal with the writing of his *The World* (completed in 1633 but not published until after his death), which included topics ranging from anatomy to meteorology. Today, of course, in an age of information explosion and specialization, nobody could hope to have a thorough knowledge of a single science, never mind all science. Even within a particular science such as psychology, comprehensive knowledge is impossible. The cognitive psychologist who studies eyewitness memory, for example, probably knows very little about developmental psychology's research on children's attachment behavior. In fact, the cognitive psychologist studying eyewitness memory finds it difficult to keep up with the literature in other areas of cognitive psychology.

We have just seen that cognitive psychology came to dominate the interests of many psychological scientists in the second half of the 20th century. Concepts from cognitive psychology also had important influences on a variety of other subdisciplines in psychology. In social psychology, for example, a great deal of research on "social cognition" began appearing in the 1980s (e.g., Fiske & Taylor, 1984). These specialized subdisciplines have their own histories, and a comprehensive analysis of them is beyond the scope of this book. Instead, let us briefly examine some of the history of four of psychology's subdisciplines. Instead of attempting to string together a sentence or two about a list of contributors to each of these areas (and the list is long for each), the focus will be on two well-known persons from each area. The areas to be considered involve the (a) study of the relationship between brain and behavior, which used to be called physiological psychology and is now usually referred to as neuroscience or neuropsychology; (b) perceptual psychology, the experimental study of how we interpret sensory information in meaningful ways; (c) social psychology, the study of how behavior is influenced by social factors; and (d) personality psychology, the study of individual differences in various personal traits.

The Brain and Behavior

One of psychology's enduring mysteries concerns the relationship between stimulus events that produce physical changes in the body, especially in the nervous system, and the psychological experience of those events. Research psychologists long ago gave up on the idea of solving the mind–body problem through science—it is a philosophical question. Thus, although researchers might be able to specify in extraordinary detail how the operation of certain combinations of neurons in the striate cortex is correlated with the perception of a line shown to someone at a certain angle, they cannot answer the question: But how does the firing of these neurons actually result in the psychological experience of the tilted line? Recognizing this fundamental limitation, physiological psychologists have concentrated their attention on the search for relationships between physical and mental events by examining the functioning of the brain and nervous system and how the activity of these structures corresponds to experience and behavior. Two of the 20th century's most prominent physiological psychologists were Karl Lashley and his student, Donald Hebb.

Karl Lashley (1890–1958) Karl Lashley (Figure 14.5) was trained as a biologist, earning a PhD from noted Johns Hopkins zoologist H. S. Jennings in 1911. More important for psychology's history, while at Hopkins, Lashley also came under the influence of the behaviorist John Watson and S. I. Franz, a psychologist at a nearby mental hospital, who was interested in the effects of brain damage on behavior. With Watson, Lashley conducted field studies of animal behavior, laboratory experiments on the sensory abilities of various species, and research on the conditioning of salivary and motor responses. The conditioning research was especially noteworthy because it marked the point at which Lashley decided that his future would not be in biology, but in the intersection between biology and psychology (Bruce, 1986). This decision was cemented when he completed postdoctoral research on the effects of brain injury on behavior with Franz. By 1920, Lashley knew he would be an experimental psychologist specializing in how learning and memory affect the brain.

The year 1929 was an important one for Lashley. His peers elected him president of the American Psychological Association, recognizing the value of research he had been engaged in during the 1920s; this series of experiments was characterized at the time of his death as being "without equal in recent experimental psychology" (Hebb, 1959, p. 142). The research was summarized in his *Brain Mechanisms and Intelligence*, which also appeared in 1929. Lashley defined intelligence in an animal learning context, using it to cover the behavior of rats learning to negotiate mazes and solve

Courtesy of the Department of Psychology, Harvard University

FIGURE 14.5 Karl Lashley (1890–1958), pioneer neuropsychologist.

simple discrimination and puzzle box problems. He readily admitted that his choice of tests could be criticized: "They all deal with some aspect of the learning process, [but their] relation to the problem of intelligence is not yet clearly established" (Lashley, 1929, p. 14). Nonetheless, he argued that simple S-R explanations of learning, such as the ones proposed by Watson and Pavlov, were inadequate to capture the complexity of how animals went about solving the kinds of problems that enabled them to survive in their environments (a criticism similar to the one he made concerning the serial order problem, described earlier in the chapter). Thus, Lashley considered the tasks presented to his rats to be sufficiently intricate to bear at least some relation to the intelligent, adaptive behavior found in the animals' real-world environments.

Lashley's procedures were in the tradition of the great French physiologist Flourens (Chapter 3)— he observed the effects of brain ablation on behavior, systematically destroying different amounts of cortex and observing the effects on the learning and retention of three types of mazes that differed in complexity. He discovered that for both the learning of mazes and the retention of mazes already learned, the rat's performance (especially on complex mazes) was dramatically affected by the extent of damage to the cortex, but the location of the damage was not critical. Thus, Lashley reached two related conclusions very similar to the ones arrived at by Flourens nearly a century earlier. First was the principle that Lashley called **equipotentiality**, a term "used to designate the apparent capacity of any intact part of a functional area to carry out, with or without reduction in efficiency, the functions which are lost by destruction of the whole" (Lashley, 1929, p. 25).

Equipotentiality—different parts of the cortex had "equal potential" to control learning— was a strong argument against cerebral localization of function, at least within the broad area of learning and in those cortical areas not known to govern specific sensory-motor functions. It was supplemented by the law of **mass action**, "whereby the efficiency of performance of an entire complex function may be reduced in proportion to the extent of brain injury" (Lashley, 1929, p. 25). Thus, although the process of learning did not seem to be localized in any specific cortical location (equipotentiality), learning efficiency was proportional to the amount of destruction (mass action).

The principles of equipotentiality and mass action were Lashley's key findings, but he was also interested in the general process of maze learning. He was well aware of the maze research of his former colleague John Watson, for example, and disagreed with Watson's belief that maze learning involved the kinesthetic sense and the conditioning of a chain of specific motor responses. Lashley argued that Watson's model could not account for the strange behavior of those animals with lesions affecting their motor movements. They could still make it through the maze, even if their motor movements were considerably altered:

> One drags himself through with his forepaws; another falls at every step but gets through by a series of lunges; a third rolls over completely in making each turn, yet manages to avoid rolling into a cul-de-sac and makes an errorless run . . . . If the customary sequence of movements employed in reaching the food is rendered impossible, another set ... may be directly and efficiently substituted. (Lashley, 1929, p. 136)

Lashley's conclusions about how the rat learned the maze were similar to those drawn by Tolman (Chapter 11), who argued that rats developed a "cognitive map" of the maze and thus knew the general direction of the goal. When describing such maps, Tolman (1948, p. 203) referred specifically to Lashley's work for support.

Lashley's distinguished career included stops at the University of Minnesota, the University of Chicago, and Harvard University (recruited by Boring). In 1942, he became director of the Yerkes Primate Laboratory in Florida, where his research on animal behavior bridged the laboratory-based comparative psychology favored by American scientists and the field-based, naturalistic approach of European ethologists (Bruce, 1991). He died of heart failure in 1958, while on holiday in France. Some idea of his daily laboratory life can be seen in an excerpt from the Walter Miles diaries.

FROM THE MILES PAPERS...

MILES VISITS LASHLEY

During the years that Walter Miles was at Stanford (1922–1932), he often took long train trips to the east, usually in connection with meetings of APA or Titchener's Experimentalists. To get as much as he could out of these trips, Miles would typically visit the laboratories of colleagues, catching up on their latest research. One such trip occurred in the spring of 1928, and it included a stop in Chicago and a visit to Lashley's lab on March 28. Here are some of the observations that Miles reported in his diary, including a critical comment about the use of mazes as apparatus and some support for Tolman's concept of cognitive maps.

[Lashley] thinks the maze has taught us nothing about learning <u>as such</u> but a very useful tool to reveal comparative factors. Rat certainly gets the general orientation of place of food and can go over the top of [the maze to reach the goal]; the linear maze important here. Asked about one rat teaching another; thinks not.

And then some practical issues with specific types of rats:

<u>Non-runner</u>, puts in another rat to start one that sits still long time in corner . . . .

<u>Wildness</u>, a little gray means some wildness, thinks wildness goes with coat color, the more white the less bite ... he thinks the coat color and the wildness a good problem to work on in inheritance ...

<u>Kinesthesis</u>, by cutting the cord at two different levels one on one side and the other on the other,

he pretty well destroys the usual kinesthesis but the rats learn.

Shortcut work, he expressed much interest in the work I have done with shortcuts and alternate paths, etc. (Miles, 1928a)

The entry ends with a set of drawings of rats' ears with small holes punched in them ("get a small chicken marking punch [from] Sears Roebuck"), illustrating a system for identifying individual rats.

Donald O. Hebb (1904–1985) Ironically, Lashley's 1929 conclusions about mass action and equipotentiality had a dampening effect on brain research that focused on localization. Furthermore, during the heyday of neobehaviorism, many researchers agreed with Skinner's arguments that explanations of behavior could be achieved without reference to the nervous system. Interest in the brain and behavior was rekindled, however, by a Canadian student of Lashley's, Donald Hebb. Hebb earned a master's degree at Montreal's McGill University, where he encountered two former students of Pavlov and learned Pavlovian conditioning techniques. Like Pavlov, Hebb wondered about the relationship between brain and behavior, but he became skeptical of Pavlov's model of the cortex. After earning his master's degree in 1934, Hebb was encouraged to apply to Chicago and study with Lashley, who was at the height of his reputation. Lashley accepted the young Canadian, and when the mentor moved to Harvard the following year, he took Hebb with him. Hebb completed his doctorate there in 1938. Job prospects were bleak, however, a combination of the lingering effects of the Depression and the fact that "[p]hysiological psychology was in its long period of decline, between 1930 and 1950" (Hebb, 1980, p. 287).

Returning to his native Canada, Hebb landed a job as research assistant to McGill University's Wilder Penfield. Penfield was just beginning his famous research on the surgical treatment of epilepsy, in which some patients reported what appeared to be intact memories during electrical stimulation of the temporal lobe (Penfield & Perot, 1963). Hebb was right in the center of this research, and it had a profound effect on him—it "set the main course for all my subsequent work" (Hebb, 1980, p. 290). Two fruitful years with Penfield were followed by 3 years of teaching at Ontario's Queen's University. In 1942, Hebb returned to Lashley, who had just been appointed director of the Yerkes Laboratory of Primate Biology in Florida, and studied primate behavior for 5 years. In 1947, his career came full circle when he was appointed to a professorship at McGill. Within a year, Hebb was named department chair, and he finished his distinguished career at McGill.

Hebb is best known for his 1949 book, *The Organization of Behavior*, which revived interest among American psychologists in the relationship between brain and behavior (Glickman, 1996). From the title, it is clear that the book is more than just a description of nervous system functioning. Rather, Hebb was aiming at a theory that would fully integrate physiology and psychology, not simply reduce the psychological to the physiological. As he later wrote, in criticism of such reductionist thinking, it was "not possible to substitute neurophysiological conceptions for psychological ones, either now or in the future, but it is possible to maintain liaison (translatability of terms) between the two universes of discourse" (Hebb, 1960, p. 744).

Hebb proposed that cortical organization occurs through the development of what he called "cell assemblies" and "phase sequences." A **cell assembly** is the basic unit, a set of neurons that become associated with each other because they have been activated together by repeated experiences. Hebb (1949) recognized the associationist roots of his construct, writing that the "general idea is an old one, that any two cells or systems of cells that are repeatedly active at the same time will tend to become 'associated,' so that activity in one facilitates activity in the other" (p. 70). **Phase sequences** are higher levels of organization involving the incorporation of several cell assemblies; for Hebb, they were the physiological equivalent of thinking. Taken together, cell assemblies and phase sequences accounted for the fact that environmental stimuli do not simply produce behavioral responses in a simple S-R fashion, but are mediated by the brain. You will recognize this as similar to the "O" in the S-O-R formulation of Robert Woodworth (Chapter 7), the intervening variables of the neobehaviorists Tolman and Hull (Chapter 11), and the opinion of Hebb's mentor, Lashley.

To account for the effects of experience and hence to provide a physiological account of learning, Hebb proposed that cell assemblies and phase sequences are formed because the repeated stimulation of adjacent cells produces structural changes at the synaptic level. Thus, according to Hebb (1949), "[w]hen an axon of cell A is near enough to excite cell B and repeatedly … takes part in firing it, some growth process or metabolic change takes place in one or both cells such that A's efficiency, as one of the cells firing B, is increased" (p. 62). This idea has come to be called "Hebb's rule," and synapses that change as the result of experience are often called **Hebb synapses**. Hebb applied his theory to topics ranging from attention to emotion to mental illness, and his book, combined with such technological advances as the electroencephalograph (EEG) for measuring brain waves, triggered a renewal of interest in the relationship between brain and behavior.

The Psychology of Perception

How we come to perceive the world around us has long been a topic of interest both to philosophers and psychological scientists. To the British empiricists (e.g., Locke), as you recall, it was central to understanding how we accumulate our knowledge of the world—nothing in the mind not first in the senses, as they put it. For the early experimental psychologists, topics in sensation and perception were often a focus of attention, with efforts ranging from Titchener's attempt to identify the elementary sensory attributes of perception to the gestaltist argument that an analytic approach necessarily fails and that we perceive meaningful wholes, not parts. Among the prominent 20th-century experimental psychologists interested in perception, two of them had the additional attribute of being married to each other.

James J. Gibson (1904–1979) You might recall from Chapter 7 the story of Titchener's Experimentalists, the like-minded experimental psychologists who met every spring to discuss current research. As a way to bring promising young scientists into the fold, Titchener encouraged his peers to bring their best graduate students to the meetings, and one of them can be seen in the group photo in Figure 7.5, taken at the 1926 meeting at the University of Pennsylvania. He is in the back row on the far left, and hatless. This is James J. Gibson, and he was a Princeton doctoral student of H. S. Langfeld, one of the Experimentalist regulars. After finishing his PhD at Princeton with a dissertation on form perception, Gibson landed a position at Smith College, a prominent women's college in western Massachusetts (alma mater of Mary Calkins), where he taught for just over 20 years. In 1949, he moved to Titchener's old stomping ground, Cornell, where he became legendary, referred to in an obituary as the "seer of Ithaca" (Restle, 1980).

During World War II, on leave from Smith, Gibson served in the Army Air Corps, first developing standard paper-and-pencil selection tests for pilots, and then creating films for training and selection purposes. The idea was to test pilots' abilities to judge distance and motion during simulated flight landings. The war experience changed Gibson's ideas about how best to study perception (E. Gibson, 2002). Whereas traditional laboratory research typically used stationary participants perceiving various stationary stimuli, Gibson realized that in real-world perception, persons are usually in motion, and objects in the environment seem to flow as the person moves through the environment. Out of this insight came a research program and a theoretical stance that became known as **ecological perception**—perception while navigating through realistic environments and perception that emphasized environmental factors rather than the internal attributes of the perceiver. Instead of looking at perception from the standpoint of what was happening on the person's retina, that is, the focus for Gibson shifted to what was happening in the environment (Reed, 1988). To illustrate the strength of Gibson's conviction, consider what he had to say about the tachistoscope. The "T-scope" has a long history and had become a standard apparatus in the perception laboratory; it is a device in which stationary participants peer into a box that presents simple stimuli to be judged in some way (e.g., compared for size or distance from the viewer). Gibson was not impressed:

> What experimenters have been trying to do is to impoverish the stimulation so as to allow the processes of perception to manifest themselves in purer form.... Hence the tachistoscope is used to reduce the flow of stimulation to a snapshot ... Is the tachistoscope an achievement? It seems to me to be a calamity. Far from reducing visual experience to its simplest form, it prevents the visual system from operating normally. (p. 228)

This quote hints strongly at Gibson's plan, which was to describe perception as it occurred in the complexity of the real world. The tone of the quote also helps you understand why his ideas were not always welcomed by more "traditional" perception researchers. Gibson's theories about perception reached their final form in the year he died, with the publication of *The Ecological Approach to Visual Perception* (J. Gibson, 1979). His ideas contributed significantly to Ulric Neisser's *Cognition and Reality* (1976)—as you recall from earlier in the chapter, Neisser (a close friend of Gibson) called for a more ecological strategy when studying cognition.

To illustrate Gibson's ecological approach, consider what he called environmental *invariances*. He argued that some aspects of the environment are constant and provide valuable information to perceivers navigating the real world. One such invariance is produced by *texture gradients* in the environment. Imagine, for example, that you are standing at the end of a long corridor that has a floor with a checkerboard pattern, black and white tiles that are each 6″ square. You look straight down, and then you move your gaze down the corridor to the other end. At your feet the texture is highly detailed (you can clearly make out the sharp edges of the squares) but as your gaze moves down the corridor, your ability to detect that level of detail decreases. In Gibson's terms, the texture gradient changes as our gaze shifts from a near to a far distance. Now suppose you place a foot-tall cylinder midway down the corridor and an identical cylinder toward the far end of the corridor. The retinal image for the closer cylinder will be larger, but the two cylinders will appear to be the same size, with one of them just being farther away. They appear to be the same size, Gibson would say, because each cylinder covers exactly the same amount of texture (same number of tiles). So this phenomenon, known as size constancy, occurs because the relationship between the object and its surrounding texture remains the same (i.e., is invariant), and they will remain the same even as you move along the corridor.

One final point about Gibson is that his years at Smith College, in addition to giving him his start as a respected teacher and researcher, had one other life-changing outcome. It was at Smith where he met and fell in love with one of his students, eventually marrying her. Eleanor Jack became Eleanor Jack Gibson, and she was one of the 20th century's most prominent psychologists, in some ways even surpassing her husband. It was Eleanor, for instance, and not James, standing in the Rose Garden of the White House in 1992, receiving the National Medal of Science from President George H. W. Bush. The medal is the highest honor a president can confer on a scientist.

Eleanor Gibson (1910–2002) Gibson's medal was for a lifetime of research on topics ranging from the development of depth perception to the basic processes involved in reading. Only nine other psychologists had earned this award up to that time (Kent, 1992). Today, students are most likely to recall Gibson as the creator of the "visual cliff," used to study the development of depth perception in infants. Her career is a case study in perseverance.

Gibson (Figure 14.6) first became interested in psychology at Smith, where she took a course from Smith's German professor, Kurt Koffka (Chapter 9), but found the experience less than enthralling—the gestaltist did little more than read notes from his forthcoming book on gestalt psychology. She had better luck in a yearlong laboratory course taught by a newly hired experimental psychologist, James Gibson. Eleanor fell in love with both the laboratory and the professor. She remained at Smith for a year after graduation, earned a master's degree, and then married her favorite teacher in 1932. Smith hired her as an instructor, and the Gibsons settled down to an academic life.

Full of enthusiasm for research in psychology, Gibson wanted to earn a doctorate, so she went to Yale in 1935, eager to work in the primate lab of the famous Robert Yerkes (Chapter 8). She managed with some difficulty to get an appointment to see Yerkes, who seemed curious about why she was there. When she said that she wished to work for him, "[h]e stood up, walked to the door, held it open, and said, 'I have no women in my laboratory'" (E. Gibson, 1980, p. 246). Although angered and somewhat disillusioned, Gibson stubbornly refused to leave Yale and eventually managed to convince the neobehaviorist Clark Hull (Chapter 11) of her abilities and earned a doctorate under his direction in 1938. She was then welcomed back to Smith, where she taught for several years before following her husband to Ithaca when James was hired by Cornell University in 1949. Antinepotism rules, a major problem for many women psychologists married to professors, kept her from employment at Cornell,

FIGURE 14.6 Eleanor Gibson (1920–2002) and her visual cliff apparatus.

Photograph by Russ Hamilton, Cornell University Photography. Division of Rare and Manuscript Collections, Cornell University Library

© Topham Picturepoint/The Image Works

yet she persevered once again. For 16 years, she labored as an unpaid "research associate," earning her keep by winning a series of competitive and prestigious research grants. It was during these years that she created the visual cliff and completed the pioneering studies on depth perception with Richard Walk (e.g., Gibson & Walk, 1960).

The visual cliff research emerged from some perceptual development research with rats that she was doing with a Cornell colleague, Richard Walk. They were both curious about depth perception. In the military, Walk had studied training programs for parachute jumpers, and at Cornell's "Behavior Farm," Gibson had marveled at the ability of newborn goats to avoid falling from a raised platform. While doing some research comparing rats that were either reared in the dark or in the light, they decided to add a depth perception element to the project. With a lab assistant, Gibson "hastily put together a contraption consisting of a sheet of glass held up by rods, with a piece of wallpaper under one side of it and nothing under the other side except the floor many feet below" (Gibson, 1980, p. 259). A narrow strip of wood was put at the border between the "shallow side" and the "deep side." They first tested rats that had been reared in a normal light-filled environment, putting them on the wood in the middle of the apparatus. None of the rats walked onto the deep side—they all went to the shallow side. Then they tested the rats who had never been exposed to daylight. Their response? Gibson and Walk "watched in fascination as every one of them repeated the behavior of the light-reared animals" (Gibson, 2002, p. 80); they too avoided the deep side.

Excited by their results, Gibson and Walk replicated the procedure with a number of species, discovering that animals that relied on vision seemed to be competent at perceiving depth as soon as they were mobile. The next step was to test human infants. Parents of 36 infants, ranging in age from 6 to 14 months, responded to newspaper ads asking for "crawling infants." Placed on the center board of the visual cliff, virtually all the infants crawled onto the shallow side and avoided the deep side, even when receiving tactile information from their hands that the deep side was safe (some of the youngest infants, new to crawling, ventured onto the deep side). Also, the infants gladly crawled toward Mom when she was on the shallow side, but not when she was on the deep side. These results are probably familiar to you—they routinely appear in textbooks in general and developmental psychology, along with photos like the one on the right side of Figure 14.6.

Like her husband, Gibson was a pioneer investigator of perceptual processes. In addition to the visual cliff work, she also investigated the general topic of perception and learning, in essence examining the nature–nurture issue with regard to how we come to perceive the world the way we do. This effort resulted in a well-received book, *Principles of Perceptual Learning and Development* (Gibson, 1969). And although James Gibson will always be known strictly for his work as a perceptual psychologist, Eleanor Gibson became just as famous as a developmental psychologist (perhaps even more so) than as a perceptual psychologist.

Social Psychology

Social psychology began to develop as an identifiable subdiscipline of psychology through the efforts of Floyd Allport (1890–1978), whose brother Gordon will be highlighted in this chapter's section on personality psychology. Floyd studied with Hugo Münsterberg at Harvard and earned a doctorate in 1919 (directed by Herbert Langfeld, who subsequently went to Princeton and mentored James Gibson). Allport's dissertation research was on social facilitation, the influence of others on the behavior of an individual, and this research set the tone for his approach to social psychology. It was behaviorist in spirit, and Allport deliberately contrasted his social psychology, with its emphasis on the behavior of the individual being influenced by the social environment, and a different version that evolved into modern

sociology, which had more of an emphasis on group processes (Parkovnick, 2000). For example, when studying group problem solving, Allport insisted that the explanation for the behavior that occurred was to be found in the actions of the individuals making up the group. From a more group-oriented standpoint, emphasis might be on some "group process" that would influence the solution to the problem at hand. Allport criticized the tendency to explain behavior by referring to group processes as the "group fallacy" (Danziger, 2000). Allport promoted his view in his 1924 text, *Social Psychology* (F. Allport, 1924), a text said to have created social psychology as a course routinely found in department of psychology course listings (Hilgard, 1987).

Leon Festinger (1919–1989)

Allport's emphasis on the individual in social psychology was challenged by the work of Kurt Lewin. We have already seen that in addition to his many other contributions, Lewin (Chapter 9) was an important pioneer in social psychology, through his studies of leadership and much of his action research. The gestalt influence was evident in Lewin's concepts of group processes—to apply the gestalt anthem to social psychology, one could say that group behavior is more than the sum of the behaviors of the group's individual members. Lewin's influence was widespread, and he had a direct effect on his most famous student, Leon Festinger.

Leon Festinger was born and raised in New York City, the son of Jewish immigrants. When he graduated from City College of New York in 1939, he already had a publication (with one of his college teachers) in the prestigious *Journal of Experimental Psychology* (Hertzman & Festinger, 1940). This professor also introduced Festinger to Lewin's ideas, prompting Festinger to apply to graduate school at the University of Iowa to study with Lewin. Festinger earned a PhD with Lewin in 1942 and remained connected with his mentor until the Lewin's early death in 1947. During World War II, Festinger served as a statistician for the Committee on Selection and Training of Aircraft Pilots. Then, after the war, he rejoined Lewin at MIT in Boston, where Lewin had just inaugurated the Research Center for Group Dynamics. After Lewin's early death, Festinger was part of the group that moved the Center to the University of Michigan. He went from Michigan to the University of Minnesota in 1951, then Stanford in 1955, and then returned home to New York in 1968, where he finished his career at the New School for Social Research (Zajonc, 1990). It was during his Stanford tenure that Festinger made his reputation and attracted students who became prominent social psychologists themselves (best known: Elliott Aronson). Over the years, his students remained fiercely loyal to him, even though he could be a hard taskmaster and was not tolerant of imprecise thinking (Brehm, 1998).

Festinger is best remembered for developing what could be the most important theory that social psychology has yet seen, the theory of **cognitive dissonance**. Festinger drafted a version of it in 1954 and then produced the first thorough description in book form 3 years later (Festinger, 1957). One criterion of a good theory is that it produces research; by that measure, Festinger's dissonance theory has been a great theory, generating hundreds of experiments and being applied to situations ranging from the consequences of decision making to the effects of hypocrisy (Harmon-Jones & Mills, 1999). A social psychology text will give you a better description of the theory and its numerous well-known studies, but in general, dissonance theory assumes that we try to be consistent in our thoughts, feelings, and actions. Holding inconsistent thoughts, or behaving in a way that is inconsistent with beliefs, creates cognitive dissonance, however, a state of emotional and cognitive discomfort. In various ways, we try to reduce dissonance and return to a balanced state.

To illustrate, consider an example that Festinger frequently used, the intelligent person who smokes. Like everyone, the smoker desires to be consistent in thought and action. Yet there are two thoughts that are inconsistent—"I am smoking" and "Research shows that smoking will kill me." These thoughts create dissonance, which the person is then motivated to reduce. This can be accomplished in several ways: The person could stop smoking, could question the validity of the evidence, or might add other elements to the situation, saying, for instance, that everyone has to die and, although the smoking might not be ideal, it helps with weight control.

Festinger's research is important because it created an experimental tradition in social psychology that was distinctive in its use of elaborately staged research settings (Aronson, 1991). These research environments were designed to involve research participants in the experiment so that their honest reactions to dissonance-arousing situations could be measured and the theory given a strong test. Perhaps the most famous example was a study by Festinger and a Stanford undergraduate, Merrill Carlsmith (Festinger & Carlsmith, 1959). Students who signed up for the study first spent an hour completing several boring tasks; then, through an elaborate deception, they were induced to tell the person who seemed to be the next participant that the study was really interesting. Thus, Carlsmith (who ran the study) convinced participants to lie, a situation producing dissonance—"I am an honest person" is dissonant with "I just told someone that a very boring experiment was actually interesting." Participants were paid either $1 or $20 to lie. Afterwards, apparently as part of a survey (another deception), participants were asked what they *really* thought of the experiment. The results? Those paid $20 still thought the experiment was boring, but those paid just $1 shifted their attitude and decided the study was pretty interesting after all. Festinger and Carlsmith concluded that when faced with the dissonance about lying, participants in the $20 group justified it by saying it was a small lie and worth the money. Those paid $1, however, did not have sufficient justification for the lie, so they convinced themselves that they had not really lied—the study really was actually kind of interesting.

Typically, research participants were completely taken in and reacted as if they were really involved in the scenarios Festinger created. Of course, that meant participants in Festinger's studies were routinely deceived about the true purpose of the studies, which made Festinger's research the object of numerous discussions about the ethics of deception in research (e.g., Korn, 1997). Festinger later indicated that he stopped doing research in social psychology in 1964, mainly because he was looking for a new challenge (he found it in the study of archeology), but also because he found the increased concern about research ethics annoying. Festinger was not insensitive to the problem, harshly criticizing Army research that gave unwitting soldiers LSD to see their reactions. Compared to that, however, he saw little danger "in temporarily deceiving persons in order to study some important question" (Festinger, 1980, p. 249). Nonetheless, Festinger's procedures set the tone, and social psychological research in the 1960s and 1970s became infamous for its high level of deception.

Another legacy of the Festinger research program concerned research design. Although influenced by Lewin in terms of the topics he studied, Festinger thought Lewin's approach to design was rather casual, and he set out to increase control and be more systematic in the manipulation of independent variables (e.g., $1 vs. $20) and the measurement of dependent variables. He also relied heavily on the analysis of variance (ANOVA), developed by British statistician Sir Ronald Fisher, and becoming widely used in the 1950s as the way to analyze data (Rucci & Tweney, 1980).[5] As Danziger (2000) observed, by applying ANOVA logic to his social psychology research, Festinger helped enhance the scientific reputation of his subdiscipline, which was not always held in high esteem by traditional experimentalists.

---

[5]Fisher developed the ANOVA in the context of agricultural research, in which he would examine, for instance, the effects of some type or some amount of fertilizer on corn production. He published his work on ANOVA in a general text in statistics in the 1920s (Fisher, 1925), but his most elaborate description of the technique appeared a decade later (Fisher, 1935). If you are familiar with the technique from a statistics class, and remember calculating an "F ratio," or reading one from an SPSS printout, you have probably already guessed that the "F" stands for the test's inventor.

Festinger, a heavy smoker, died of liver cancer in 1989. Perhaps thinking of his often-quoted dissonance example of the smoker, and perhaps reducing dissonance to the end, he is said to have announced during his illness, "Make sure everyone knows it wasn't lung cancer!" (quoted in Zajonc, 1990, p. 662).

Stanley Milgram (1933–1984) Not long after taking a general psychology course, most students forget much of the course content. One thing they are likely to recall, however, is one of psychology's most famous series of studies—the obedience research by Stanley Milgram (Figure 14.7). Even if they don't recall Milgram's name, a photo of the shock apparatus will be sufficient as a retrieval cue.

After graduating from Queen's College in New York with a degree in political science in 1954, Milgram was accepted into the graduate program at Harvard's Department of Social Relations, an interdisciplinary program that included social and clinical psychologists, sociologists, and anthropologists. There he encountered Henry Murray and Gordon Allport, both featured in this chapter's next section. Allport directed Milgram's dissertation, a cross-cultural study comparing conformity in Norway and France, but the future for Milgram was determined more by Solomon Asch than by Allport (Blass, 2004). In the 1950s, Asch had completed a series of studies on conformity that have become classics—in the face of social pressure, subjects would make errors in a line-judging task that they never made when judging lines without group pressure. Looking for a more realistic scenario than a line-judging task, Milgram eventually hit on the idea of asking how far subjects would go in responding to strong demands made by an authority figure. Obedience to authority had special meaning for Milgram, who was Jewish—he had a strong desire to understand the "I was only obeying orders" defense used by Nazi war criminals who participated in the horrors of the Holocaust (Benjamin & Simpson, 2009).

With doctorate in hand, Milgram began his academic career in the fall of 1960 at Yale. There he designed and carried out the obedience research with which you are familiar (Milgram, 1963).

Courtesy of Alexandra Milgram

FIGURE 14.7 Stanley Milgram (1933–1984), with the apparatus that made him famous.

Male subjects were put into the role of teachers in a study that was said to concern the effects of punishment on memory. The learner, apparently just another subject but in fact in Milgram's employ, was in an adjacent room and was to be shocked by the teacher whenever he made an error. At least the teachers were led to believe that real shocks were being given—no shock actually occurred. Milgram's apparatus (now on display at the Center for the History of Psychology at the University of Akron) had 30 switches, each corresponding to voltage levels ranging from 15 to 450 volts, with 15 volt increments. With each successive error by the learner (and the learner made quite a few), the shock level delivered by the teacher would increase by 15 volts. Milgram wished to learn how high the voltage would go before the teacher would disobey the experimenter's authority and refuse to administer what seem to be very painful shocks. Based on feedback from colleagues and his own intuition, Milgram expected that subjects would disobey fairly early in the game, especially when the learner began to show signs of discomfort. Instead, the teacher–subjects obeyed to a remarkable extent. In the first study, 26 of 40 subjects (65%) continued to deliver shocks (or so they thought) until the voltage level reached the maximum, 450 volts, and they only reason they stopped there was that the experimenter halted the study. Despite showing great discomfort themselves, the teachers obeyed to a remarkable extent.[6]

Milgram published the initial study in 1963, then completed 17 more variations on the original procedure and published them in the book *Obedience to Authority: An Experimental View* (Milgram, 1974). In these additional studies, he examined a variety of factors affecting obedience. For instance, he established the fact that obedience depended on the proximity of teacher and learner—obedience levels decreased when the learner was in the same room with the teacher and even further when the teacher had to deliver the shocks by forcing the learner's hand onto an insulated "shock plate." In another variation, Milgram showed that obedience depended on the perception that the experimenter was a legitimate professional authority. Obedience levels were high when the study was conducted in Milgram's lab at prestigious Yale University, but declined when the study was moved to a storefront in Bridgeport and said to be run by a private company sponsored by business interests.

Like the Festinger studies of cognitive dissonance, Milgram's obedience research was criticized on ethical grounds, both for the deception and the possible damage done to subjects. Milgram argued that in follow-up studies, his subjects were fine and were happy to have participated (dissonance reduction?) and that the scientific value of the research justified the temporary deception. The main value of the research, Milgram believed, was that it demonstrated the power of the situation over the personality attributes of the subjects. Everyday people, he argued, could behave in ways they would not imagine possible, if put into a situation with powerful demands on their behavior. In the last sentence of his book, Milgram (1974) wrote that the take-home message of the research was that "often, it is not so much the kind of person a man is as the kind of situation in which he finds himself that determines how he will act" (p. 205).

Milgram's name has become synonymous with his obedience research, but it wasn't his only contribution to social psychology. He invented the "lost letter technique" as a way to measure attitudes behaviorally; he originated research on the "small world phenomenon," showing that there are often just "six degrees of separation" between any two individuals; and he created the term "familiar stranger," a reference to that person seen on the way to work every day, with whom we have a nodding acquaintance, but never really make the effort to know (Blass, 2004).

---

[6] In light of the subsequent storm over the ethics of the study, Milgram might have regretted how he phrased one sentence of his 1963 article, in which he wrote that he had "observed a mature and initially poised businessman enter the laboratory smiling and confident. Within 20 minutes he was reduced to a twitching, stuttering wreck" (Milgram, 1963, p. 377).

After 3 years at Yale, Milgram returned to Harvard's Department of Social Relations, but was bitterly disappointed when he was turned down for tenure there. He returned home to New York in 1967 and finished his academic career at the City University of New York (CUNY) Graduate Center. He died in 1984 at age 51, after the last of five heart attacks.

Personality Psychology

For most of the research encountered in this chapter, the goal has been to understand some general principles about behavior or cognition. Thus, when Milgram found that obedience levels differed as a function of proximity of learner and teacher, he was describing a principle that presumably affected people in general. This is an approach to science that is known as a **nomothetic** one. On the other hand, there is an alternative strategy that focuses on detailed analyses of unique individuals and examines ways of determining how one individual differs from another. A strategy that concentrates on the unique individual is said to reflect an **idiographic** approach. Two strong advocates of the idiographic approach to the study of personality were Henry Murray and Gordon Allport, two Harvard colleagues.

Henry Murray (1893–1988) A substantial attempt to bring psychoanalytic concepts into the academic environment was made by Henry Murray (1893–1988; Figure 14.8), who became director of the Harvard Psychological Clinic in 1928. Murray had a background in medicine and a strong interest in the unconscious—he studied briefly with Carl Jung. He brought to the Clinic a penchant for in-depth analyses of individual cases, and his *Explorations in Personality* (Murray, 1938), based on detailed descriptions of 50 college-aged men, became a landmark example of a **case study** approach to personality (Barenbaum, 2006). Along with Christiana Morgan, Murray also developed a personality

Courtesy of the Harvard University Archives, Harvard University

FIGURE 14.8 Personality theorist Henry Murray (1893–1988).

assessment tool that remains in use today—the Thematic Apperception Test, or TAT. Individuals taking the test see a series of ambiguous drawings and are instructed to create a story describing what they believe to be happening in the drawing. The TAT is an example of a projective personality test, one in which responses to ambiguous stimuli are assumed to reflect important personality attributes. For example, one famous TAT card shows a young boy gazing at a violin. So if a person wrote a story about the boy dreaming to be a concert violist, the interpretation might be that the person had a strong need for achievement. A story centering on the boy's thoughts about hitting his sister over the head with the violin might be interpreted in terms of a need for aggression.

Based on his case studies, and using the TAT to provide evidence, Murray developed a theory of personality that he referred to as a **personology**, a term reflecting his belief in the importance of studying individual persons in depth—the ideographic strategy. Murray's theory had strong ties to psychoanalytic theory, emphasizing the importance of (a) early experiences on later personality, and (b) the unconscious as a source of motivation. The theory is best known for its emphasis on motivation, expressed with a catalog of needs that could be assessed with the TAT. The number of important needs varied as the theory evolved, but was typically around 20. Examples include the needs for achievement (abbreviated by Murray as "nAch"), affiliation, autonomy, order, and dominance. Individuals could have various needs in different strengths, and the combination determined their overall personality. These needs were also influenced by the environments that individual found themselves in (e.g., an abusive parent)—Murray used the term "press" to refer to these environmental pressures. Thus, in a manner reminiscent of Lewin's B = f(P,E), Murray argued that behavior is a joint function of the individual's dominant needs and the press of the environment in which the person lives.

Murray was a charismatic figure, attracting a number of young scholars to the clinic. His abnormal psychology course was among the most popular at Harvard. However, he was often at odds with the more traditional academicians at Harvard, especially Boring, who lorded over the psychology department in the 1930s, insisting on his rigorous brand of experimental psychology. That Murray and Boring would clash was inevitable, given Boring's uncompromising beliefs and Murray's equally strong feeling that laboratory psychology as it existed in the 1930s was sterile. In one often-quoted remark, Murray complained that psychology was misdirected—by studying such basic processes as sensation, perception, and memory in the laboratory, it had failed to understand real human beings:

> The truth which the informed are hesitant to reveal and the uninformed are amazed to discover is that academic psychology has contributed practically nothing to the knowledge of human nature. It has not only failed to bring light to the great, hauntingly recurrent problems, but it has no intention, one is shocked to realize, of attempting to investigate them. (quoted in Barenbaum, 2006, p. 170)

You will not be surprised to learn that such sentiments did not endear Murray to his more traditional colleagues, who did all they could to prevent him from earning tenure at Harvard when he became eligible in 1936. Lashley, for instance, threatened to resign if Murray was tenured (Barenbaum, 2006). Murray was promoted in 1937 but not given tenure, which was finally granted in 1948. Despite the strength of Murray's own personality, his psychoanalytically based personology never gained a strong foothold at Harvard, although one of his needs, nAch, became the focus of a major research effort examining the characteristics and the development of a need for achievement (Atkinson & Feather, 1966; McClelland, 1961).

Gordon Allport (1897–1967)

Social psychology and personality psychology have important historical connections, including a family link. Gordon Allport was born in Indiana and raised in Cleveland, Ohio, the last of his parents' four boys. One of his brothers, Floyd, was the noted social psychologist you read about earlier in the chapter—his 1924 social psychology text was an important step in the creation of modern social psychology. Gordon had the same effect on personality psychology when he published *Personality: A Psychological Interpretation* (G. Allport, 1937).

Allport was both an undergraduate and a graduate student at Harvard. Following his brother's suggestion, he chose the emerging topic of personality as his dissertation topic. That his topic was away from mainstream experimental psychology became evident to him in 1921, when he presented his work on personality to a meeting of Titchener's Experimentalists at Clark University, invited by his mentor Herbert Langfeld.[7] As Boring (1967) later reported:

> There was a long discussion of David Katz's modes of appearance of colors, and after that Langfeld was asked for a report and he put up Gordon Allport to tell about his analysis of personality. Allport's communication was followed by a long silence, and then Titchener said: "As we were saying, the modes of appearance of colors are . . . . " Social psychology and personality were as much taboo at the Experimentalists as animal psychology. "What did you let him work on that for?" Titchener later asked Langfeld. (p. 323)

Undeterred, Allport completed his doctorate on personality in a mere 2 years, in 1922. He then toured Europe on a study grant before returning to Harvard as an instructor. There he developed a course in personality that eventually led to his famous text (Allport, 1937); many years later, his mature views on personality appeared in *Pattern and Growth in Personality* (Allport, 1961). He stayed at Harvard briefly, went to Dartmouth for 4 years, and then was enticed to return to Harvard in 1930, where he finished his career.

Although he contributed research in the nomothetic tradition, Allport was a champion of the idiographic ideal that everyone was a unique personality and that much could be learned by the careful study of individuals (Pettigrew, 1969). In Allport's conception of personality, the basic unit of individual personality was the **trait**, which for him meant a particular pattern of thinking, feeling, and behaving that was characteristic of a person and a means of distinguishing that person from others. Allport identified three varieties of traits—cardinal, central, and secondary. **Cardinal traits**, not possessed by everyone, were attributes that were dominant in a person, to the point where describing a person's cardinal trait would identify that person to others, and most of what that person would do was related to the trait. Napoleon, for instance, might be described by a cardinal trait of a need for power. **Central traits** were those dozen or so attributes that provide a reasonably accurate summary description of an individual. For example, they are the kinds the terms typically appearing in letters of recommendation (Hilgard, 1987). **Secondary traits** were less important characteristics, manifested in relatively few behaviors.

In line with his idiographic sentiments and like Murray, Allport advocated the case study, an in-depth analysis of a person, as a way to study personality. Although he completed just one detailed case study himself, it was a famous one: *Letters from Jenny* (Allport, 1965). The book-length study described the personality of "Jenny Masterson" (fictitious name), based on a close analysis of 301 letters written over a 12-year period by a middle-aged woman (Hall & Lindzey, 1970). Allport was also involved in the development of a popular paper-and-pencil personality test. With Philip Vernon,

---

[7]You have probably noticed that Herbert Langfeld appears several times in this chapter, directing the doctoral dissertations of three of the prominent psychologists featured—James Gibson and both Allports. Langfeld (1879–1958) earned his PhD at Berlin in 1909, under Carl Stumpf (mentor to several gestaltists) and then joined the faculty at Harvard, where he remained until 1924, when he moved to Princeton and became director of the laboratory there. He was APA president in 1930. With Boring and H. P. Weld, he published a successful introductory psychology text that went through several editions. And he developed a close friendship with another major character in this chapter, F. C. Bartlett—they often played golf together during Langfeld's frequent visits to England (Bartlett, 1958b).

a visiting professor from England who had been a student of Bartlett, Allport developed *A Study of Values* (G. Allport & Vernon, 1931), a test measuring the strength of six potential value systems—theoretic, aesthetic, social, political, economic, and religious.

Allport came to prominence at a time when Freud's psychoanalytic theories were popular in America, but, unlike his Harvard colleague Henry Murray, Allport was no fan of psychoanalytic theory. He did not reject the concept of the unconscious, but he simply did not think it was essential for understanding someone's personality. He also thought Freud's emphasis on sex was excessive, and he rejected the idea that our past history had an overwhelming effect on our present and future. He also was not impressed with the psychoanalytic strategy for measuring personality with projective tests like the TAT or the inkblot test developed by Hermann Rorschach in 1921 (the latter popular enough to have 38 articles written about it in the 1920s and about 230 more in the 1930s; Klopfer, 1973). Such tests assumed that people were not capable of giving accurate descriptions of their personality on a self-report because much of the personality was said to be buried in the unconscious. After giving responses to ambiguous stimuli (TAT pictures, inkblots), the "true" personality could only be inferred through a process of interpretation, so the argument went. Allport did not buy it. Instead, he firmly believed people capable of knowing themselves and therefore able to respond accurately to self-report personality inventories.

Allport's criticism of Freudian psychoanalysis was genuine, but his dislike might also have been influenced by a brief meeting that he had with Freud during a visit to Vienna. After brashly making an appointment to see Freud, and being ushered into the famous office, Allport found himself at a loss for a way to open the conversation in a way that might impress the great man. Hoping to get a quick Freudian interpretation, he described an incident he witnessed in which a small boy seemed to be overly concerned about dirt: "He kept saying to his mother, 'I don't want to sit there ... don't let that dirty man sit beside me'" (Allport, 1967, p. 8). Allport apparently expected Freud to give an analysis of the relationship between mother and son, but instead, he "fixed his kindly therapeutic eyes upon me and said, 'And was that little boy you?'" (p. 8).

Allport is accurately considered the father of modern personality theory, and the title of his biography, *Inventing Personality* (Nicholson, 2003), is apt. It was Allport who was primarily responsible for taking the 19th-century study of "character" and turning it into the 20th-century study of "personality." He also made important contributions to his brother's area of social psychology (*The Nature of Prejudice*, 1954b) and his deep spirituality led him to write on the psychology of religion (*The Individual and His Religion*, 1950).

IN PERSPECTIVE: PSYCHOLOGY'S RESEARCHERS

Chapter 13 focused on psychology's practitioners, and this chapter has concerned psychology's researchers and theorists. For both chapters, it is important to note that the surface has barely been scratched. Chapter 13 concentrated on clinical and industrial psychology, but left out other major areas of application: school psychology, community psychology, rehabilitation psychology, and forensic psychology, just to name a few. Similarly, this chapter opened with cognitive psychology, then sampled from physiological, perceptual, social, and personality psychology. A glimpse at any modern introductory text will tell you that much was omitted. But my goal was never to be comprehensive in these descriptions of psychology during the 20th century. Rather my purpose was partly to give you a glimpse of the tremendous diversity of interests among psychologists, partly to show some of the interconnections among them, and partly to entice you to become interested in these topics and study them in more depth. The final chapter elaborates on the theme of diversity and ends with a brief discussion of whether there is one psychology or many.

SUMMARY

Cognitive Psychology Arrives (Again)

• After World War II, psychologists became increasingly involved in studying mental processes, a topic that had been a key interest for psychology's earliest pioneers. This cognitive psychology movement in America developed gradually during the 1950s, 1960s, and 1970s, while behaviorism became a less powerful force. The change was more evolutionary than revolutionary.

• During the period when behaviorism dominated American psychology (the 1930s and 1940s), some American researchers (e.g., Stroop) still investigated cognitive topics, and European psychologists, who never became as enamored of behaviorism as the Americans did, made important contributions to the understanding of mental processes. One of the Europeans was Jean Piaget, whose genetic epistemology (i.e., an interest in understanding the growth and development of knowledge within an individual) and stage theory of cognitive development eventually became influential in America, after American psychologists turned from behavior to an interest in cognitive processes.

• A second prominent European psychologist was Frederick Bartlett. He criticized the laboratory-based, nonsense-syllable type of memory research and proposed instead that research on memory should emphasize real-life situations. He believed that memory was constructive and was influenced by schemata, that is, one's basic concepts about the phenomenal world.

• Within American psychology, the cognitive movement gained momentum from problems that developed within the behaviorist/associationist tradition. At the Hixon Symposium in 1948, Lashley showed that associationist principles could not explain the problem of serial order, and behaviorism seemed incapable of explaining language behavior, which seemed to be more species specific than the outcome of conditioning.

• Outside psychology, developments in the disciplines of computer science, information theory, and linguistics contributed to the evolution of cognitive psychology. Researchers began to create models of cognitive processes that used the computer program as a metaphor and emphasized the concept of the individual as an information processor rather than as a responder to stimuli.

• During the decade of the 1950s, several landmark works appeared. These included Miller's paper on the limited capacity of information processing in immediate memory (7±2), Broadbent's research on selective attention, and the book by Miller, Galanter, and Pribram on "plans," which featured the idea of information feedback in the form of TOTE units as a replacement for the reflex arc concept.

• The first major summary of laboratory research in cognitive psychology appeared in 1967 with Neisser's book; the book also produced a self-identification of the field as "cognitive psychology." About a decade later, Neisser questioned cognitive psychology's emphasis on basic laboratory research and, in the spirit of Bartlett, called for an increase in research on cognitive processes as they operate in the everyday world to help individuals adapt to their environments (i.e., research having ecological validity).

• Cognitive psychology has spread to other specialty areas within psychology. In addition, the interdisciplinary field of cognitive science evolved in parallel with cognitive psychology. Cognitive science includes psychology, computer science (e.g., artificial intelligence), linguistics, anthropology, and epistemology.

Other Research Areas

• In addition to the area of cognitive psychology, there were important developments in other research topics of interest to psychologists. Advances were made in understanding (a) the relationship between the brain and behavior, (b) the nature of human perception, (c) the effect of the social environment on individual behavior, and (d) the nature of human personality.

• Two of the 20th century's most prominent neuropsychologists were Karl Lashley and his student, Donald Hebb. Lashley's principles of mass action and equipotentiality showed that learning and memory were proportional to the amount of brain loss and that when part of the cortex was damaged, other cortical areas could take over the lost functioning. Hebb's model of the brain centered on the cell assembly, an interrelated combination of associated neurons, and the phase sequence, an organization of cell assemblies and the neurological equivalent of thinking. Hebb synapses are synapses that have undergone structural change as a result of some learning process.

• For most of the history of research on the nature of human perception, the emphasis has been on the attributes of the perceiver, but James Gibson, promoting his ecological view of perception, argued that the important factors affecting human perception (e.g., perceptual invariances, optic flow) lie in the environment, not within the person. Eleanor Gibson completed important research on the relationship between perception and learning, and her visual cliff studies have become classic studies of the development of depth perception.

• Floyd Allport and Kurt Lewin are important pioneers in social psychology, but Leon Festinger (a student of Lewin) developed the most important social psychological theory of the 20th century, the theory of cognitive dissonance. Festinger's experiments were known for the precision and elegance of their design, their use of complex statistical analysis (ANOVA), and their extensive use of deception. Stanley Milgram's obedience studies, showing that situational pressures can overcome individual personality, are among psychology's most famous studies.

• Henry Murray was a champion of the idiographic tradition, which emphasizes the in-depth study of individuals, as opposed to the nomothetic tradition, the study of general principles. His personology emphasized the interaction between an individual's needs (e.g., nAch) and environmental press, and he created the well-known projective personality test, the TAT. More than anyone, Allport is responsible for making personality psychology a topic of study in psychology. He believed that people could be characterized with reference to their cardinal, central, and secondary traits.

STUDY QUESTIONS

1. Why did Piaget call himself a genetic epistemologist? Why was the importance of his work late in achieving recognition in the United States?

2. Describe Bartlett's criticism of the Ebbinghaus approach to memory. How did his methodology differ?

3. Explain why Bartlett believed memory to be constructive. Be sure to work the term "schema" into your answer.

4. What was the serial order problem, and why did it create a problem for behaviorism?

5. Describe how the development of cognitive psychology was influenced by computer science and information theory.

6. Chomsky argued that behaviorism failed to explain language. What were his arguments?

7. Describe how scientific revolutions occur, according to Thomas Kuhn's model.

8. The Close-Up argues that a cognitive "revolution" did *not* really occur. Explain.

9. What did George Miller discover about the nature of STM?

10. Describe how Broadbent studied selective attention and what he concluded about it.

11. What was the influence of the "Plans" book on cognitive psychology?

12. Consider the two books by Neisser that are described in the chapter. What was the influence of each?

13. What is the difference between cognitive psychology and cognitive science?

14. Describe Lashley's research and how he arrived at his principles of mass action and equipotentiality.

15. Describe Hebb's ideas about cortical organization and the effects of experience on the brain.

16. How did James Gibson's ecological approach to perception differ from traditional perception research?

17. What did Gibson mean by "invariance"? Give an example.

18. Describe the method, results, and conclusions of Eleanor's Gibson's visual cliff studies.

19. Floyd Allport and Kurt Lewin had different ways of conceptualizing social psychology. How did they differ?

20. Describe Festinger's theory of cognitive dissonance.

21. Describe Festinger's impact on the nature of research in social psychology.

22. Describe Milgram's research and what he concluded about the nature of obedience.

23. Distinguish between nomothetic and idiographic approaches to psychology.

24. Describe Murray's personology and how he used to TAT to assess needs.

25. Describe Gordon Allport's influence on personality psychology. Why is he said to have "invented" personality?

CHAPTER 15

PSYCHOLOGY IN THE 21ST CENTURY

But there is a sense in which we are nothing if not our history. Our history is our binding force.

—Sigmund Koch, 1992

PREVIEW AND CHAPTER OBJECTIVES

Now that we are in the second decade of the 21st century, a reasonable way to conclude this survey of psychology's history would be to examine the current state of the field. I argued in Chapter 1 that the present cannot be understood without knowing the past, so I hope what you now know about psychology's history will help put this chapter in perspective. We will look at the diversity of modern psychology, describe some trends that have developed in recent years, and finish with a discussion of whether psychology is (and ever has been) a unified discipline. After you finish this final chapter, you should be able to:

■ Describe the uneasy relationship between two broad categories of psychologist: researchers and practitioners

■ Describe the indicators of increased diversity in modern psychology

■ Summarize five current trends in psychology, and show how their understanding requires knowing some history

■ Understand why it can be argued that psychology is many disciplines, not just one

■ Understand the role of history as a unifying force in psychology

RESEARCHERS AND PRACTITIONERS

In Chapter 13, after the discussion of Lightner Witmer, you learned about the first hints of a professional identity for clinical psychologists. They formed the short-lived American Association of Clinical Psychologists in 1917, had a section created for them in the APA, and then joined other applied psychologists in forming a vigorous association, the American Association for Applied Psychology (AAAP), in 1937. Near the end of World War II, they played a major role in the reorganization (recreation, actually) of APA. The new APA would no longer focus only on science; it would now have the additional stated goals of advancing psychology as a profession and promoting human welfare (Hilgard, 1987). Prior to World War II, academic psychology had dominated APA, but after the war, the power began to shift, and a turning point occurred in 1962, when APA members working in nonacademic jobs outnumbered those working in colleges and universities for the first time (Tryon, 1963).

For research psychologists working in an academic environment, this shift was a big change from the prewar years, when they held all the power, and the change was not a welcome one. Long before practitioners outnumbered academician/researchers in 1962, the latter group had become distressed about the direction the reorganized APA was taking. They were especially concerned about the makeup of the annual meeting, which, after the war, seemed to be increasingly devoted to practice issues. As early as 1949, the chair of APA's Policy and Planning Board noted that the APA's annual program was shifting in the direction of increased attention to the practice of psychology (Peatman, 1949). As just a small example of the growing rift between practitioners and researchers, in 1959 the APA decided not to allow slides to be shown during any of the presentations, a move that infuriated experimentalists, who were accustomed to using slides to present their data (Dewsbury & Bolles, 1995). This seemingly trivial incident helped bring about a major defection of experimental psychologists from the APA, who formed the Psychonomic Society near the end of the 1950s. It held its first meeting in 1960, devoted to the presentation of research (including slides), and it continues today as an important organization for experimentalists.

Most members of the Psychonomic Society remained members of APA, however, and continued to agitate for conditions favorable to the researcher/academician. The APA, however, kept shifting its resources toward the practice of psychology and focused much of its energy on issues relevant for practitioners (e.g., payment for therapy from insurance companies). Researchers agitated for a new reorganization of APA in the mid-1980s that would restore some of their status, and when the effort failed, a group of prominent experimental psychologists banded together and formed the American Psychological Society (APS) in 1988. Membership reached more than 5,000 within the first 6 months, indicating that the group had struck a chord, and the APS quickly became a strong advocate for psychological research, created a group of high-quality journals (e.g., *Psychological Science*), and developed an annual convention entirely devoted to research. When it celebrated its 25th anniversary in 2013, it had reached a membership of about 26,000. In 2006, the group retained its acronym, but brought its mission into clearer focus and enhanced its international visibility by changing its name to the Association for Psychological Science.

This researcher–practitioner split, reflected in the histories of APA and APS, can easily be overstated. Many APS members also belong to APA, APA has a vigorous "Science Directorate," and most of the APA journals are devoted to research. Also, two of the APS journals are of value to both researchers and practitioners. In 2001, APS launched *Psychological Science in the Public Interest*, a journal that includes research-based articles on topics of relevance for the practice of psychology. More recently (2013), the APS began publishing *Clinical Psychological Science*, a journal devoted to research of relevance for clinicians. Yet the division between researcher/academicians and practitioners is a real one, representing different value systems and different interests. Gaining a clear understanding of psychology in the 21st century requires knowing about this issue and its history.

THE GROWTH AND DIVERSITY OF PSYCHOLOGY

The number of both practitioners and researchers has increased substantially over the years. Data for the growth of the APS is impressive. As for the APA, its growth over the past 120 years has also been substantial. From its origins in G. Stanley Hall's study in 1892 until the mid-1920s, APA showed steady but unspectacular expansion. The initial 31 charter members rose to about 125 by the turn of the 20th century and to about 375 by the end of World War I (Fernberger, 1932). With the creation of the associate member status in 1925, however, the growth curve changed direction. After World War II, the total membership stood at approximately 5,000, and it has climbed steadily since that time, reaching the 70,000 mark by 1990 (Bulatao, Fulcher, & Evans, 1992). With the 21st century now underway, full APA membership has surpassed 100,000. The future, for both APA and APS, promises continued growth—psychology is among the most popular majors on campus, new graduate programs appear each year, and applications to graduate school far outnumber available places.

Along with the expansion reflected in membership rolls, psychology has also become more diverse over the years. One form of this diversity has been specialization. As you know from the last two chapters, psychologists are no longer just psychologists, they are developmental psychologists, social psychologists, industrial psychologists, clinical psychologists, and personality psychologists, among many others. Even these labels are too broad. Developmental psychologists, to take just one example, cannot hope to be knowledgeable about their entire subfield, but must specialize further within it, perhaps by establishing expertise in infant concept development, adolescent peer relations, or autobiographical memory in the elderly. A second form of psychology's increased diversity is in various types of persons who enter the field. After the 1980s, psychologists were more likely than ever to be female and/or nonwhite.

Women in Psychology's History

The problems for women in psychology have been examined several times in this book. From Chapter 6, you recall the difficulties experienced by such pioneering women as Mary Calkins, Margaret Washburn, and Christine Ladd-Franklin, who were either unable to secure full-time academic positions (Ladd-Franklin) or were limited to teaching at small women's colleges without graduate programs (Calkins and Washburn). This latter problem actually got worse in the 1920s, when many of these small colleges began replacing female professors with males to "enhance" their prestige (Diehl, 1992). We also saw that Leta Hollingworth was held back for a time because she was unable to teach and be married at the same time, and that Eleanor Gibson (a) was shown the door by Robert Yerkes and (b) could not be hired at Cornell for many years because of antinepotism laws.

Another significant barrier to advancement was that women were excluded from the all-important informal communication network of scientific psychologists, as described in Chapter 7. Although allowing women into his graduate program at Cornell, in part because of a university requirement, E. B. Titchener kept them out of his Experimentalists "club." After Titchener's death in 1927, the group reorganized as the Society of Experimental Psychologists (SEP) and voted to include women, but the de facto obstacles remained. Two women, Washburn and June Downey of Wyoming (who died before attending any meetings), were made charter members of the new group, and Washburn even hosted an SEP meeting at Vassar in 1931.[1] Yet photos of the group in the 1940s and early 1950s don't include female faces, and no other woman was elected until 1958 (Furumoto, 1988), when Eleanor Gibson was voted into the group. Although relatively small in number, the SEP constituted a closed network that influenced academic hiring and advancement. The SEP exists today, primarily as an honor society for esteemed experimental psychologists. The number of women in the group is increasing, but they remain underrepresented—there are about 200 members, about 30 of them women. Most of the women members were elected in the 1990s (Goodwin, 2005).

---

[1] At that meeting, Walter Miles reported a conversation with Washburn, in which she confided that Titchener was better as a lecturer than as a researcher and that he wasn't much of a mentor to her: "Miss W was his first grad student, he gave her little, according to her, they were too near the same age. Miss W says that her loyalty, admiration, and devotion are all to Cattell" (Miles, 1931). As you might recall from Chapter 6, Washburn first went to Columbia and Cattell, but Cattell recommended she go to Cornell because Cornell could grant her a PhD but Columbia would not.

Today, women undergraduate majors in psychology outnumber men by about two to one, about three quarters of graduate students are female, and the majority of doctorates in psychology are awarded to women. Although most senior faculty teaching in psychology departments continue to be male, changes are on the way—the proportion of women faculty in departments of psychology (with graduate programs) shifted from about 20% in the mid-1980s to 33% a decade later to 45% in 2009–2010 (Pagano, Wicherski, & Kohout, 2010; "Sex, Race/Ethnicity Data," 1995).

Minorities in Psychology's History

Like women, members of minority groups have been on the outside looking in for most of psychology's history. Unlike the case for women, however, significant gains for blacks and most other minorities were not made in the years following World War II, and minorities continue to be underrepresented in psychology. In 1991, for example, only 14 percent of all bachelor's degrees, 11 percent of master's degrees, and 9 percent of doctoral degrees were granted to minorities ("Sex, Race/Ethnicity Data," 1995). Of these, about one half went to African-American students, a quarter to Hispanic students, and the remainder to Asian Americans and Native Americans. In 2009–2010, for psychology departments offering graduate programs, just 13% of faculty members were from minority groups. Change is coming, however—in 2009–2010, minorities comprised 28% of the graduate student population (Finno, Wicherski, & Kohout, 2010).

Despite barriers at least as high as those confronting women, minority psychologists have made important contributions to psychology's history. We have already seen that displaced European Jewish psychologists such as Wertheimer and Lewin made important contributions to American psychology. They did so in the face of an anti-Semitism that, though less virulent than the version found in Nazi Germany, occurred in subtle ways nonetheless. The gestaltists were already well enough known to secure positions, but job searches were not quite so easy for other Jewish psychologists, especially during the Great Depression when all jobs were scarce. As Winston (1996a) has shown, for example, letters of recommendation during the 1930s frequently reinforced the stereotype of Jewish persons as being shrewd and calculating, oversensitive to perceived slights, argumentative, clannish, and defensively aggressive. Candidates for academic positions could be doomed by a letter indicating that they possessed these attributes, and their chances were hardly improved if they were praised by saying, in effect, that although they might be Jewish, they were not like a "typical" Jew. In recommending one of his students, for example, Robert Woodworth wrote that "as his name indicates, [he is] a Jew, but I am sure you would find him a very satisfactory colleague ... cooperative and eager to fit into the group" (quoted in Winston, 1996a, p. 30).

The difficulties faced by Jews paled in comparison to those encountered by African Americans, however. At least nobody accused Jews of lacking intellectual ability. Blacks, on the other hand, have often had their basic abilities questioned, and this was especially true during psychology's formative years. As you recall from Chapter 6, scholars such as Francis Sumner faced enormous obstacles when trying to obtain graduate education and then employment in academia. Sumner eventually found his way to Howard University in Washington, D.C., where he established the best-known psychology program at a historically black university. As you recall, two of his most prominent students were Kenneth and Mamie Phipps Clark, authors of the famous doll study.

Although minority group members are not as well represented in psychology today as they could be, the APA has made a number of attempts over the years to create a climate of inclusiveness. In 1950, for instance, APA's Council passed a resolution that it would only hold its annual meeting in cities free from overt discriminatory practices. The 1957 meeting, for instance, was moved from Miami to

New York, after it was learned that some Miami hotels would not register blacks (Smith, 1992). And in 1963, APA created an Ad Hoc Committee on Equality of Opportunity in Psychology (CEOP) for the purpose of "explor[ing] the possible problems encountered in training and employment in psychology as a consequence of race" (quoted in Holliday, 2010, p. 1). Yet in the late 1960s, a survey of 398 African-American psychologists found them dissatisfied with their status as professional psychologists (Wispe et al., 1969). This dissatisfaction led to the creation of the Association of Black Psychologists at the 1968 APA convention in San Francisco. Today this group has about 1,400 members and publishes the *Journal of Black Psychology*.

Mainly through the efforts of Kenneth Clark during his APA presidency (1971), the APA followed up on the CEOP by creating the Board of Social and Ethical Responsibility for Psychology in 1972 (Pickren & Tomes, 2002); it in turn spawned today's Board of Ethnic Minority Affairs. The APA's Minority Fellows Program began awarding financial aid for graduate study in 1974, and in 1987, Division 45, the Society for the Psychological Study of Ethnic Minority Issues, was created.

TRENDS IN MODERN PSYCHOLOGY

Chapter 1 included the argument that understanding psychology's present requires knowing something of its past, a point made eloquently by E. G. Boring (1963a) when he wrote that "the seats on the train of progress all face backwards: you can see the past but only guess about the future. Yet a knowledge of history, although it can never be complete and fails miserably to foretell the future, has a huge capacity for adding significance to the understanding of the present" (p. 5). I hope that what you have learned from your history of psychology course and from this book have combined with the knowledge accumulated in other psychology courses to enhance your understanding of psychology's present. This next-to-last segment of the book briefly identifies five contemporary trends in psychology, none of which can be properly understood without knowing something about psychology's history. As I see them, these trends are

1. *The accelerated study of the relationship between the brain and behavior*, with the term *neuroscience* being added to an increasing number of subdisciplinary labels (e.g., cognitive neuroscience) and the 1990s being called "the decade of the brain." Dramatic technological innovations have fueled this development, but our current understanding rests on a long history of studying the brain (Chapter 3), and the basic issues involved (e.g., the mind–body question; localization of function) remain deeply rooted in the histories of philosophy and physiology (Chapters 2 and 3).

2. *The vigorous return of evolutionary thinking*, accompanied by a shift toward the nature end of the nature–nurture issue. Chapter 5 told the story of Darwin and his influence during psychology's formative years. One aspect of that influence was the tendency to explain some behaviors with reference to evolutionary mechanisms and, consequently, to take the nature side of the nature–nurture issue. Evolutionary explanations went out of vogue in American psychology during the era of behaviorism, which produced a shift to the nurture side of the debate. In recent years, however, the balance has shifting back again. Much attention is being given to behavior genetics, the study of genetic influences on behavior and mental processes, and evolutionary psychology has reached the status of a course in the psychology curriculum, with several textbooks now available (e.g., Buss, 1999).

3. *Significant changes in research brought about by the capacities of modern computers.* The history of research methodology is a topic worthy of its own text, but you have encountered some

elements of it—Titchener's Manuals (Chapter 7), Woodworth's "Columbia bible" (Chapter 8), and the influence of ANOVA on Festinger's research designs in social psychology (Chapter 14). One effect of both the Woodworth text and ANOVA had been a relative neglect of correlational research designs, but they have become increasingly commonplace (and more sophisticated) in recent years with the development of statistical software capable of performing highly complex multivariate analyses (e.g., multiple regression, factor analysis) quickly.

4. *The increased professionalization of psychological practitioners.* As you know, there is a history of uneasiness between academician/researchers and those who practice psychology professionally. Knowing something of that history helps understand tensions between these groups (e.g., APS and APA) and puts into perspective any attempts to bridge the gap between them.

5. *The increased fragmentation of psychology.* This requires a section of the chapter of its own, one that will close the book.

THE FUTURE: PSYCHOLOGY OR PSYCHOLOGIES?

Clearly, psychology has demonstrated enormous growth and increased specialization over the past 120 years; it is therefore worth considering whether the field can be said to be unified in any way. A little over a decade into the 21st century, is there a field of psychology or are there multiple psychologies?

First, the question implies that psychology was once unified, yet it is unclear if psychology has *ever* been a coherent discipline. It may have approached unity in its early years, when it was trying to forge an identity separate from physiology and philosophy, but it is evident that strong disagreements existed even then. The conflicts between Titchener and others (e.g., Watson) over psychology's very definition illustrate the point, as do the long-standing squabbles among various constituencies, especially among practitioners and researchers, reflected today in the split between APA and APS. In terms of its professional organizations, psychology seems to be characterized more by disunity than unity.

When addressing the issue of fragmentation at an APA symposium celebrating the centennial of Wundt's laboratory in 1979, George Miller, the prominent cognitive psychologist (Chapter 14), "discovered several other psychologies, all claiming proprietary rights to the label, all competing for disciples, and each contemptuous of the others. In short, I discovered that psychology is an intellectual zoo" (Miller, 1992, p. 40). Some understanding of the range of species in this zoo can be achieved by examining the specialties of just a few of the 54 divisions of the APA:

  3 Experimental Psychology

14 Industrial/Organization Psychology

12 Clinical Psychology

16 School Psychology

25 Behavior Analysis

26 History of Psychology

28 Psychopharmacology and Substance Abuse

30 Psychological Hypnosis

36 Psychology of Religion

38 Health Psychology

47 Exercise and Sport Psychology

52 International Psychology

56 Trauma Psychology[2]

Many psychologists belong to more than one division, but it is clear that widely divergent interests are represented under the APA's broad umbrella. Also, some of the experimental psychology areas represented by the APS extend the range of specialties even further. It is difficult to imagine a neuropsychologist studying the effects of neurotransmitter X on memory, a developmental psychologist studying parallel play in children, a social psychologist developing social facilitation, and a perception psychologist examining illusions having much in common.

As for modern psychology as an academic discipline, the field appears to have a fragile sense of unity, reflected in the standard definition found in all introductory textbooks (some version of "psychology is the science of behavior and mental processes") and manifested in the institutional organization of "psychology departments." Yet some academic psychologists have specialties that lead them to other departments. This phenomenon led Spence (1987) to worry about

> a decimation of institutional psychology as we know it. Human experimental psychologists desert to the emerging discipline of cognitive science; physiological psychologists go happily to departments of biology and neuroscience; industrial/organizational psychologists are snapped up by business schools; and psychopathologists find their home in medical schools. (p. 237)

What concerned Spence in 1987 has occurred to a degree, but virtually all university campuses still have departments called "psychology departments," and these departments employ the vast majority of academic psychologists (just as campuses have biology, chemistry, and physics departments, even though these disciplines have experienced even greater specialization than psychology, and over a longer period of time). It is worth noting, however, that some of departments have changed their names, in part to reflect either psychology's increased coordination with biology (e.g., Dartmouth College's department is now the Department of Psychological and Brain Sciences) or to reinforce psychology's scientific nature (e.g., both the University of Missouri and Northern Kentucky University have departments of "Psychological Science").

Perhaps it is most reasonable to assume that psychology is not a single discipline but a collection of them. One of psychology's foremost theoreticians, Sigmund Koch (1917–1996), argued this point for years, recommending that the term *psychology* be replaced with the more pluralistic label of *psychological studies* (Koch, 1993). He viewed this as a historical process similar to that found in other sciences—biology, for instance, encompasses a wide range of "biological studies" (e.g., botany, zoology). Similarly, memory researcher and former APS president Gordon Bower, in a 1992 APA symposium on "The Fragmentation of Psychology," suggested that a more positive connotation results from labeling the phenomenon "specialization" rather than "fragmentation" (Bower, 1993). Although the term *psychology* has not been replaced with *psychological studies*, most psychologists would agree with Koch's and Bower's essential point that psychology today is really a plurality of subdisciplines, each a specialty in its own right. Bower used the metaphor of a growing tree to make his point, likening the growth and diversity of psychology to the growth process of a tree, with age producing increased branching. He compared the individual psychological scientist to a "small bug feeding on a succulent

---

[2]If you go to the APA website you will see a list of divisions that reach to number 56. However, there are no divisions 4 or 11; hence there are 54 total divisions. Division 4 had been called the Psychometric Society, but it disbanded in 1948, and most members joined Division 5 (Evaluation, Measurement, and Statistics). Division 11 was the division for "Abnormal Psychology and Psychotherapy," but it lasted just a year, its members migrating to Division 12 (Society of Clinical Psychology) for the most part.

leaf at one end of a very tiny branch and perhaps talking to the other bugs feeding on the same leaf" (p. 905).

If there is any sense of a unifying force in modern psychology, other than the institutional one deriving from the academic category of "psychology department," and the definitional one found in general psychology texts, one could argue that it derives from psychology's history. As Koch (1992a) put it, "there is a sense in which we are nothing if not our history. Our history is our binding force" (p. 966). Regardless of one's modern specialty, there are common origins (to follow the tree metaphor, one trunk and one root system) and familiar themes, many of which have been discussed in this book. I hope that what you have read in those pages will entice you to learn more about what connects psychologists and will deepen your understanding of psychology's rich heritage.

SUMMARY

Researchers and Practitioners

• One result of the reorganization of the APA in 1945 was increased visibility for professional practitioners of psychology. This did not sit well with academic psychologists, whose primary activities were teaching and research, and who had controlled the APA in the years between the world wars.

• Believing the APA was becoming too focused on professional practice, psychological scientists formed the Psychonomic Society in 1960 and, in 1988, the American Psychological Society (APS), which was renamed the Association for Psychological Science in 2006.

The Growth and Diversity of Psychology

• Psychology has shown vigorous growth during its one-hundred-plus years of existence as an independent discipline, and as it has grown, the interests of psychologists have become more specialized. Throughout most of its history, leading psychologists were white and male, a situation that is now changing, especially as more women enter the field.

• Minority groups, including Jews and African Americans, also have faced discrimination throughout psychology's history. Blacks in particular had to confront the prejudices deriving from the early 20th-century belief in the inherited racial superiority of white males.

Trends in Modern Psychology

• There are five major trends evident in modern psychology—increased interest in neuroscience, the development of evolutionary psychology, the expanding impact of computers, an increased level of professionalization, and increased specialization. None of them can be thoroughly understood without knowing something about history.

Psychology or Psychologies?

• Psychology in the early 21st century is not a unified discipline, and with its recurring debates over fundamental issues, it may never have been one. Modern psychology is marked by increased specialization, and it might be more appropriate to replace the idea of a single field of psychology with Koch's concept of there being a set of psychological studies. One unifying force in psychology lies in the discipline's history, however.

STUDY QUESTIONS

1. Describe the conflict between scientists and practitioners that led to the creation of the Psychonomic Society and the APS.

2. Describe some of the problems encountered by women and minorities in psychology's history.

3. Describe five trends that are evident in modern psychology.

4. Explain why it might be better to use the term "psychologies" instead of "psychology."

5. Despite increased specialization, what factors tend to unify psychology?

REFERENCES

A stash in the stacks. (1996, August/September). *Civilization, 3*(4), 15.

Adams, G. (1934, January). The rise and fall of psychology. *The Atlantic Monthly,* 82–92.

Albrecht, F. M. (1970). A reappraisal of faculty psychology. *Journal of the History of the Behavioral Sciences, 6,* 36–40.

Allport, F. H. (1924). *Social psychology.* Boston, MA: Houghton Mifflin.

Allport, G. A. (1954a). The historical background of social psychology. In G. Lindzey (Ed.), *Handbook of social psychology* (Vol. I, pp. 3–56). Reading, MA: Addison-Wesley.

Allport, G. W. (1937). *Personality; A psychological interpretation.* New York, NY: Holt.

Allport, G. W. (1950). *The individual and his religion.* New York, NY: Macmillan.

Allport, G. W. (1954b). *The nature of prejudice.* Cambridge, MA: Addison-Wesley.

Allport, G. W. (1961). *Pattern and growth in personality.* New York, NY: Holt, Rinehart, & Winston.

Allport, G. W. (1965). *Letters from Jenny.* New York, NY: Harcourt, Brace, & World.

Allport, G. W. (1967). Gordon Allport. In E. G. Boring & G. Lindzey (Eds.), *A history of psychology in autobiography* (Vol. 5, pp. 3–25). New York, NY: Appleton-Century.

Allport, G. W., & Vernon, P. E. (1931). *A study of values.* Boston, MA: Houghton.

American Psychiatric Association. (2013). *Diagnostic and statistical manual of mental disorders* (5th ed.). Washington, DC: American Psychiatric Association.

Anastasi, A. (1954). *Psychological testing.* New York, NY: Macmillan.

Anastasi, A. (1993). A century of psychological testing: Origins, problems, and progress. In T. K. Fagan & G. R. VandenBos (Eds.), *Exploring applied psychology: Origins and critical analyses* (pp. 13–36). Washington, DC: American Psychological Association.

Anderson, J. R. (1990). *Cognitive psychology and its implications* (3rd ed.). New York, NY: Freeman.

Angell, J. R. (1904). *Psychology.* New York, NY: Holt.

Angell, J. R. (1948). The province of functional psychology. In W. Dennis (Ed.), *Readings in the history of psychology* (pp. 439–456). New York, NY: Appleton-Century-Crofts. (Original article published 1907)

Angell, J. R., & Moore, A. W. (1896). Reaction time: A study in attention and habit. *Psychological Review, 3,* 245–258.

Appleby, J., Hunt, L., & Jacob, M. (1994). *Telling the truth about history.* New York, NY: Norton.

Armstrong, P. (1993). An ethologist aboard the *H. M. S. Beagle*: The young Darwin's observations on animal behavior. *Journal of the History of the Behavioral Sciences, 29,* 339–344.

Arnett, J. J., & Cravens, H. (2006). G. Stanley Hall's Adolescence: A centennial reappraisal. Introduction. *History of Psychology, 9,* 165–171.

Aronson, E. (1991). Leon Festinger and the art of audacity. *Psychological Science, 2,* 213–217.

Aronson, E. (1999). *The social animal* (8th ed.). New York, NY: Freeman.

Asch, S. E. (1968). Wolfgang Köhler: 1887–1967. *American Journal of Psychology, 81,* 110–119.

Aserinsky, E., & Kleitman, N. (1953). Regularly occurring periods of eye motility and concomitant phenomena during sleep. *Science, 118,* 273–274.

Ash, M. G. (1985). Gestalt psychology: Origins in Germany and reception in the United States. In C. E. Buxton (Ed.), *Points of view in the modern history of psychology* (pp. 295–344). New York, NY: Academic Press.

Ash, M. G. (1992). Cultural contexts and scientific change in psychology: Kurt Lewin in Iowa. *American Psychologist, 47,* 198–207.

Ash, M. G. (1995). *Gestalt psychology in German culture, 1890–1967: Holism and the quest for objectivity.* Cambridge, UK: Cambridge University Press.

Atkinson, J. W., & Feather, N. T. (1966). *A theory of achievement motivation*. New York, NY: Wiley.

Atkinson, R. C., & Shiffrin, R. M. (1968). Human memory: A proposed system and its control processes. In K. W. Spence & J. T. Spence (Eds.), *The psychology of learning and motivation: Advances in research and theory* (pp. 89–195). New York, NY: Academic Press.

Averill, L. A. (1982). Recollections of Clark's G. Stanley Hall. *Journal of the History of the Behavioral Sciences, 18,* 341–346.

Baars, B. J. (1986). *The cognitive revolution in psychology*. New York, NY: Guilford Press.

Babkin, B. P. (1949). *Pavlov: A biography*. Chicago, IL: University of Chicago Press.

Bache, R. M. (1895). Reaction time with reference to race. *Psychological Review, 2,* 475–486.

Baddeley, A. (1990). *Human memory: Theory and practice*. Boston, MA: Allyn & Bacon.

Bahrick, H. P. (1984). Semantic memory content in permastore: 50 years of memory for Spanish learned in school. *Journal of Experimental Psychology: General, 113,* 1–29.

Bakan, D. (1966). The influence of phrenology on American psychology. *Journal of the History of the Behavioral Sciences, 2,* 200–220.

Baker, D. B. (1988). The psychology of Lightner Witmer. *Professional School Psychology, 3,* 109–121.

Baker, D. B., & Benjamin, L. T., Jr. (2000). The affirmation of the scientist-practitioner: A look back at Boulder. *American Psychologist, 55,* 241–247.

Balance, W. D. G., & Bringmann, W. G. (1987). Fechner's mysterious malady. *History of Psychology Newsletter, 19*(1, 2), 36–47.

Baldwin, J. M. (1895). *Mental development in the child and the race*. New York, NY: Macmillan.

Baldwin, J. M. (1896). A new factor in evolution. *American Naturalist, 30,* 441–451.

Baldwin, J. M. (1897). *Social and ethical interpretations in mental development*. New York, NY: Macmillan.

Baldwin, J. M. (1913). *History of psychology: A sketch and an interpretation*. New York, NY: Putnam.

Barenbaum, N. B. (2006). Henry A. Murray: Personology as biography, science, and art. In D. A. Dewsbury, L. T. Benjamin, Jr., & M. Wertheimer (Eds.), *Portraits of pioneers in psychology* (Vol. 6, pp. 169–187). Washington, DC: American Psychological Association.

Barker, R., Dembo, T., & Lewin, K. (1941). Frustration and regression: An experiment with young children. *University of Iowa Studies in Child Welfare, 18, No. 1.*

Barone, D. F. (1996). John Dewey: Psychologist, philosopher, and reformer. In G. A. Kimble, C. A. Bonneau, & M. Wertheimer (Eds.), *Portraits of pioneers in psychology* (Vol. II, pp. 47–61). Washington, DC: American Psychological Association.

Bartlett, F. C. (1958a). Herbert Sidney Langfeld: 1879–1958. *American Journal of Psychology, 71,* 616–619.

Bartlett, F. C. (1958b). *Thinking: An experimental and social study*. London, UK: Allen & Unwin.

Bartlett, F. C. (1967). *Remembering: A study in experimental and social psychology*. Cambridge, UK: Cambridge University Press. (Original work published 1932)

Baugh, F. G., & Benjamin, L. T., Jr. (2006). Walter Miles, Pop Warner, B. C. Graves, and the psychology of football. *Journal of the History of the Behavioral Sciences, 42,* 3–18.

Bayton, J. A. (1975). Francis Sumner, Max Meenes, and the training of black psychologists. *American Psychologist, 30,* 185–186.

Beam, A. (2001). *Gracefully insane: The rise and fall of America's premier mental hospital*. New York, NY: Perseus Books.

Beck, H. P., Levinson, S., & Irons, G. (2009). Finding Little Albert: A journey to John B. Watson's infant laboratory. *American Psychologist, 64,* 605–613.

Beers, C. W. (1908). *A mind that found itself*. New York, NY: Longmans Green.

Bell, C. (1965). Bell on the specificity of sensory nerves, 1811. In R. J. Herrnstein & E. G. Boring (Eds.), *A sourcebook in the history of psychology* (pp. 23–26). Cambridge, MA: Harvard University Press. (Original work published 1811)

Bell, L. V. (1980). *Treating the mentally ill: From colonial times to the present*. New York, NY: Praeger Publishers.

Benedict, F. G. (1907). *Report of Investigation of Foreign Laboratories, 1907*. Francis G. Benedict papers, Center for the History of Medicine, Francis A. Countway Library of Medicine, Boston, MA.

Benjamin, L. T., Jr. (1993). *A history of psychology in letters*. Dubuque, IA: Brown & Benchmark.

Benjamin, L. T., Jr. (1996). Harry Hollingworth: Portrait of a generalist. In G. A. Kimble, C. A. Bonneau, &

M. Wertheimer (Eds.), *Portraits of pioneers in psychology* (Vol. II, pp. 119–135). Washington, DC: American Psychological Association.

Benjamin, L. T., Jr. (2000). Hugo Münsterberg: Portrait of an applied psychologist. In G. A. Kimble & M. Wertheimer (Eds.), *Portraits of pioneers in psychology* (Vol. IV, pp. 112–129). Washington, DC: American Psychological Association.

Benjamin, L. T., Jr. (2003). Harry Hollingworth and the shame of applied psychology. In D. B. Baker (Ed.), *Thick description and fine texture: Studies in the history of psychology* (pp. 38–56). Akron, OH: The University of Akron Press.

Benjamin, L. T., Jr., & Baker, D. B. (2000). Boulder at 50: Introduction to the section. *American Psychologist, 55,* 233–236.

Benjamin, L. T., Jr., & Baker, D. B. (2004). *From séance to science: A history of the profession of psychology in America.* Belmont, CA: Wadsworth.

Benjamin, L. T., Jr., & Crouse, E. M. (2002). The American Psychological Association's response to *Brown v. Board of Education. American Psychologist, 57,* 38–50.

Benjamin, L. T., Jr., & Simpson, J. A. (2009). The power of the situation: The impact of Stanley Milgram's obedience studies on personality and social psychology. *American Psychologist, 64,* 12–19.

Benjamin, L. T., Jr., & Vandenbos, G. R. (2006). The window on psychology's literature: A history of *Psychological Abstracts. American Psychologist, 61,* 941–954.

Benjamin, L. T., Jr., Durkin, M., Link, M., Vestal, M., & Accord, J. (1992). Wundt's American doctoral students. *American Psychologist, 47,* 123–131.

Benjamin, L. T., Jr., Rogers, A. M., & Rosenbaum, A. (1991). Coca-Cola, caffeine, and mental deficiency: Harry Hollingworth and the Chattanooga trial. *Journal of the History of the Behavioral Sciences, 27,* 42–55.

Bergin, A. E. (1971). The evaluation of therapeutic outcomes. In A. E. Bergin & S. L. Garfield (Eds.), *Handbook of psychotherapy and behavior change: An empirical analysis.* New York, NY: Wiley.

Berkeley, G. (1948). An essay towards a new theory of vision. In A. A. Luce & T. E. Jessup (Eds.), *The works of George Berkeley, Bishop of Cloyne. Vol. 1.* London, UK: Thomas Nelson & Sons. (Original work published 1709)

Berkeley, G. (1957). *Treatise concerning the principles of human knowledge.* Indianapolis, IN: Bobbs-Merrill. (Original work published 1710)

Binet, A., & Henri, V. (1965). Alfred Binet (1857–1911) and Victor Henri (1872–1940) on the psychology of individual differences. In R. J. Herrnstein & E. G. Boring (Eds.), *A sourcebook in the history of psychology* (pp. 428–433). Cambridge, MA: Harvard University Press. (Original work published 1895)

Binet, A., & Simon, T. (1916). *The development of intelligence in children* (E. S. Kite, Trans.). Baltimore, MD: Williams and Wilkins.

Bingham, W. V. (1952). Walter Van Dyke Bingham. In E. G. Boring, H. S. Langfeld, H. Werner, & R. M. Yerkes (Eds.), *A history of psychology in autobiography* (Vol. 4, pp. 1–26). Worcester, MA: Clark University Press.

Bjork, D. W. (1983). *The compromised scientist: William James in the development of American psychology.* New York, NY: Columbia University Press.

Bjork, D. W. (1993). *B. F. Skinner: A life.* New York, NY: Basic Books.

Blass, T. (2004). *The man who shocked the world: The life and legacy of Stanley Milgram.* New York, NY: Basic Books.

Blum, D. (2006). *Ghost hunters: William James and the search for scientific proof of life after death.* New York, NY: Penguin.

Blumenthal, A. L. (1975). A reappraisal of Wilhelm Wundt. *American Psychologist, 30,* 1081–1088.

Blumenthal, A. L. (1980). Wilhelm Wundt and early American psychology: A clash of cultures. In R. W. Reiber & K. Salzinger (Eds.), *Psychology: Theoretical-historical perspectives* (pp. 25–42). New York, NY: Academic Press.

Blumenthal, A. L. (2001). A Wundt primer: The operating characteristics of consciousness. In R. W. Reiber & D. K. Robinson (Eds.), *Wilhelm Wundt in history: The making of scientific psychology* (pp. 121–144). New York, NY: Kluwer Academic.

Boakes, R. (1984). *From Darwin to behaviourism: Psychology and the minds of animals.* New York, NY: Cambridge University Press.

Bogacz, T. (1989). War neurosis and cultural change in England, 1914–1922: The work of the War Office Committee of Inquiry into "shell-shock." *Journal of Contemporary History, 24,* 227–256.

Boorstin, D. J. (1971). *Democracy and its discontents: Reflections on everyday America.* New York, NY: Random House.

Boorstin, D. J. (1983). *The discoverers.* New York, NY: Vintage Books.

Boring, E. G. (1928a). *Letter to Walter R. Miles, January 5, 1928*. Walter R. Miles papers. Archives of the History of American Psychology, University of Akron, Akron, OH.

Boring, E. G. (1928b). *Letter to Walter R. Miles, February 21, 1928*. Walter Miles papers, Archives of the History of American Psychology, University of Akron, Akron, OH.

Boring, E. G. (1928c). *Letter to Walter R. Miles, March 10, 1928*. Walter Miles papers, Archives of the History of American Psychology, University of Akron, Akron, OH.

Boring, E. G. (1929). *A history of experimental psychology*. New York, NY: Century.

Boring, E. G. (1942). *Sensation and perception in the history of experimental psychology*. New York, NY: Appleton-Century-Crofts.

Boring, E. G. (1950). *A history of experimental psychology* (2nd ed.). Englewood Cliffs, NJ: Prentice-Hall.

Boring, E. G. (1961a). Edward Bradford Titchener, 1867–1927. In E. G. Boring (Ed.), *Psychologist at large: An autobiography and selected essays* (pp. 246–265). New York: Basic Books.

Boring, E. G. (1961b). Psychologist at large. In E. G. Boring (Ed.), *Psychologist at large: An autobiography and selected essays* (pp. 3–83). New York, NY: Basic Books.

Boring, E. G. (1963a). Eponym as placebo. In R. I. Watson & D. T. Campbell (Eds.), *History, psychology, and science: Selected papers by Edwin G. Boring, Harvard University* (pp. 5–25). New York, NY: Wiley.

Boring, E. G. (1963b). Fechner: Inadvertent founder of psychophysics. In R. I. Watson & D. T. Campbell (Eds.), *History, psychology, and science: Selected papers by Edwin G. Boring, Harvard University* (pp. 126–131). New York, NY: Wiley.

Boring, E. G. (1963c). The influence of evolutionary theory upon American psychological thought. In R. I. Watson & D. T. Campbell (Eds.), *History, psychology, and science: Selected papers by Edwin G. Boring, Harvard University* (pp. 159–184). New York, NY: Wiley.

Boring, E. G. (1965). Edward Wheeler Scripture: 1864–1945. *American Journal of Psychology, 78,* 314–317.

Boring, E. G. (1967). Titchener's Experimentalists. *Journal of the History of the Behavioral Sciences, 3,* 315–325.

Boring, E. G., Langfeld, H. S., & Weld, H. P. (1939). *Introduction to psychology*. New York, NY: Wiley.

Bouchard, T. J., Jr., & McGue, M. (1981). Familial studies of intelligence. *Science, 212,* 1055–1059.

Bower, G. H. (1993). The fragmentation of psychology? *American Psychologist, 48,* 905–907.

Brainerd, C. J. (1996). Piaget: A centennial celebration. *Psychological Science, 7,* 191–195.

Bramel, D., & Friend, R. (1981). Hawthorne, the myth of the docile worker, and class bias in psychology. *American Psychologist, 36,* 867–878.

Brands, H. W. (1995). *The reckless decade: America in the 1890s*. New York, NY: St. Martin's Press.

Bregman, E. O. (1934). An attempt to modify the emotional attitudes of infants by the conditioned response technique. *Journal of Genetic Psychology, 45,* 169–198.

Brehm, J. W. (1998). Leon Festinger: Beyond the obvious. In G. A. Kimble & M. Wertheimer (Eds.), *Portraits of pioneers in psychology* (Vol. III, pp. 329–344). Washington, DC: American Psychological Association.

Breland, K., & Breland, M. (1951). A field of applied animal psychology. *American Psychologist, 6,* 202–204.

Breland, K., & Breland, M. (1961). The misbehavior of organisms. *American Psychologist, 16,* 681–684.

Brentano, F. (1995). *Psychology from an empirical standpoint*. London, UK: Routledge. (Original work published 1874)

Breuer, J., & Freud, S. (1955). *Studies on hysteria*. New York, NY: Basic Books. (Original work published 1895)

Brewer, W. F., & Schommer-Aikins, M. (2006). Scientists are not deficient in mental imagery: Galton revised. *Review of General Psychology, 10,* 130–146.

Bridgman, P. W. (1927). *The logic of modern physics*. New York, NY: Macmillan.

Brigham, C. C. (1923). *A study of American intelligence*. Princeton, NJ: Princeton University Press.

Bringmann, W. G., Balance, W. D. G., & Evans, R. B. (1975). Wilhelm Wundt 1832–1920: A brief biographical sketch. *Journal of the History of the Behavioral Sciences, 11,* 287–297.

Bringmann, W. G., Bringmann, N. J., & Balance, W. D. G. (1980). Wilhelm Maximilian Wundt 1832–1920: The formative years. In W. G. Bringmann & R. D. Tweney (Eds.), *Wundt studies: A centennial collection* (pp. 13–32). Toronto, Canada: C. J. Hogrefe.

Broadbent, D. E. (1958). *Perception and communication*. London, UK: Pergamon Press.

Broadbent, D. E. (1980). Donald E. Broadbent. In G. Lindsey (Ed.), *A history of psychology in autobiography* (Vol. 7, pp. 39–73). San Francisco, CA: Freeman.

Broca, P. (1965). Paul Broca (1824–1880) on the speech center, 1861. In R. J. Herrnstein & E. G. Boring (Eds.), *A sourcebook in the history of psychology* (pp. 223–229). Cambridge, MA: Harvard University Press. (Original work published 1861)

Brown, R., & McNeill, D. (1966). The tip of the tongue phenomenon. *Journal of Verbal Learning and Verbal Behavior, 5,* 325–327.

Browne, J. (1995). *Charles Darwin: Voyaging.* New York, NY: Knopf.

Browne, J. (2002). *Charles Darwin: The power of place.* Princeton, NJ: Princeton University Press.

Brubacher, J. S., & Rudy, W. (1976). *Higher education in transition: A history of American colleges and universities, 1636–1976* (3rd ed.). New York, NY: Harper and Row.

Bruce, D. B. (1986). Lashley's shift from bacteriology to neuropsychology, 1910–1917, and the influence of Jennings, Watson, and Franz. *Journal of the History of the Behavioral Sciences, 22,* 27–44.

Bruce, D. B. (1991). Integrations of Lashley. In G. A. Kimble, M. Wertheimer, & C. L. White (Eds.), *Portraits of pioneers in psychology* (Vol. I, pp. 306–323). Washington, DC: American Psychological Association.

Bruce, D. B. (1994). Lashley and the problem of serial order. *American Psychologist, 49,* 93–103.

Bruner, J. S. (1968). Gordon Willard Allport: 1897–1967. *American Journal of Psychology, 81,* 279–284.

Bruner, J. S. (1988). Founding the Center for Cognitive Studies. In W. Hirst (Ed.), *The making of cognitive science: Essays in honor of George A. Miller* (pp. 90–99). New York, NY: Cambridge University Press.

Brunswick, E. (1938). *Letter to Walter R. Miles, April 22, 1938.* Walter Miles papers, Archives of the History of American Psychology, University of Akron, Akron, OH.

Buckley, K. W. (1989). *Mechanical man: John Broadus Watson and the beginnings of behaviorism.* New York, NY: Guilford Press.

Bulatao, E. Q., Fulcher, R., & Evans, R. B. (1992). Appendix: Statistical data on the American Psychological Association. In R. B. Evans, V. S. Sexton, & T. C. Cadwallader (Eds.), *The American Psychological Association: A historical perspective* (pp. 391–394). Washington, DC: American Psychological Association.

Burnham, J. C. (1972). Thorndike's puzzle boxes. *Journal of the History of the Behavioral Sciences, 8,* 159–167.

Buss, D. M. (1999). *Evolutionary psychology: The new science of the mind.* Boston, MA: Allyn & Bacon.

Buss, D. M. (2009). The great struggles of life: Darwin and the emergence of evolutionary psychology. *American Psychologist, 64,* 140–148.

Cairns, R. B. (1994). The making of a developmental science: The contributions and intellectual heritage of James Mark Baldwin. In R. D. Parke, P. A. Ornstein, J. J. Reiser, & C. Zahn-Waxler (Eds.), *A century of developmental psychology* (pp. 127–143). Washington, DC: American Psychological Association.

Calkins, M. C. (1930). Mary Whiton Calkins. In C. Murchison (Ed.), *A history of psychology in autobiography* (Vol. 1, pp. 31–62). Worcester, MA: Clark University Press.

Calkins, M. W. (1894). Association I. *Psychological Review, 1,* 476–483.

Calkins, M. W. (1896). Association II. *Psychological Review, 3,* 32–49.

Calkins, M. W. (1906). A reconciliation between structural and functional psychology. *Psychological Review, 13,* 61–81.

Calkins, M. W. (1907). *The persistent problems of philosophy.* New York, NY: Macmillan.

Calkins, M. W. (1913). Psychology and the behaviorist. *Psychological Bulletin, 10,* 288–291.

Camfield, T. M. (1973). The professionalization of American psychology, 1870–1917. *Journal of the History of the Behavioral Sciences, 9,* 66–75.

Capaldi, N. (2004). *John Stuart Mill: A biography.* Cambridge, UK: Cambridge University Press.

Capshew, J. H. (1996). Engineering behavior: Project Pigeon, World War II, and the conditioning of B. F. Skinner. In L. D. Smith & W. R. Woodward (Eds.), *B. F. Skinner and behaviorism in American culture* (pp. 128–150). Bethlehem, PA: Lehigh University Press.

Capshew, J. H. (1999). *Psychologists on the march: Science, practice, and professional identity in America, 1929–1969.* New York, NY: Cambridge University Press.

Capshew, J. H., & Hearst, E. (1980). Psychology at Indiana University: From Bryan to Skinner. *Psychological Record, 30,* 319–342.

Carmichael, L. (1957). Robert Mearns Yerkes, 1876–1956. *Psychological Review, 64,* 1–7.

Carr, H. A. (1925). *Psychology: A study of mental activity.* New York, NY: Longmans, Green.

Carr, H. A. (1935). *An introduction to space perception.* New York, NY: Longmans, Green.

Carr, H. A., & Watson, J. B. (1908). Orientation in the white rat. *Journal of Comparative Neurology and Psychology, 18,* 27–44.

Cashman, S. D. (1993). *America in the gilded age* (3rd ed.). New York, NY: New York University Press.

Cattell, J. M. (1886). The time it takes to see and name objects. *Mind, 11,* 63–65.

Cattell, J. M. (1895). Report of the Secretary and Treasurer for 1894. *Psychological Review, 2,* 149–152.

Cattell, J. M. (1948a). The influence of the intensity of the stimulus on the length of the reaction time. In W. Dennis (Ed.), *Readings in the history of psychology* (pp. 323–325). New York, NY: Appleton-Century-Crofts. (Original article published 1885)

Cattell, J. M. (1948b). Mental tests and measurements. In W. Dennis (Ed.), *Readings in the history of psychology* (pp. 347–354). New York, NY: Appleton-Century-Crofts. (Original work published 1890)

Cautin, R. L. (2006). David Shakow: Architect of modern clinical psychology. In D. A. Dewsbury, L. T. Benjamin, Jr., & M. Wertheimer (Eds.), *Portraits of pioneers in psychology* (Vol. 6, pp. 207–221). Washington, DC: American Psychological Association.

Cherry, E. C. (1953). Some experiments on the recognition of speech with one and with two ears. *Journal of the Acoustical Society of America, 25,* 975–979.

Chomsky, N. (1959). Review of Skinner's Verbal Behavior. *Language, 35,* 26–58.

Chomsky, N. (1966). *Cartesian linguistics.* New York, NY: Harper & Row.

Clark, K., & Clark, M. (1947). Racial identification and racial preferences in Negro children. In T. M. Newcomb & E. L. Hartley (Eds.), *Readings in social psychology* (pp. 169–178). New York, NY: Holt.

Cohen, E. (1991, Fall). Psychology's attic. *Akron, 6*(1), 12–19.

Cohen, I. B. (1995). *Science and the founding fathers.* New York: Norton.

Collins, A. (1977). Why cognitive science? *Cognitive Science, 1,* 1–2.

Collins, J. (1931). Lightner Witmer: A biographical sketch. In R. A. Brotemarkle (Ed.), *Clinical psychology: Studies in honor of Lightner Witmer* (pp. 3–9). Philadelphia, PA: University of Pennsylvania Press.

Colp, R., Jr. (1986). "Confessing a murder:" Darwin's first revelations about transmutation. *Isis, 77,* 9–32.

Conley, J. J. (1984). Not Galton, but Shakespeare: A note on the origin of the term "nature and nurture." *Journal of the History of the Behavioral Sciences, 20,* 184–185.

Coon, D. J. (1992). Testing the limits of sense and science: American experimental psychologists combat spiritualism, 1880–1920. *American Psychologist, 47,* 143–151.

Coon, D. J. (1994). "Not a creature of reason": The alleged impact of Watsonian behaviorism on advertising in the 1920s. In J. T. Todd & E. K. Morris (Eds.), *Modern perspectives on John B. Watson and classical behaviorism* (pp. 37–63). Westport, CT: Greenwood Press.

Costall, A. (1993). How Lloyd Morgan's Canon backfired. *Journal of the History of the Behavioral Sciences, 29,* 113–122.

Cottingham, J. (1986). *Descartes.* New York, NY: Basil Blackwell.

Crane, L. (1925). A plea for the training of psychologists. *Journal of Abnormal and Social Psychology, 20,* 228–233.

Cravens, H. (1992). A scientific project locked in time: The Terman genetic studies of genius, 1920s–1950s. *American Psychologist, 47,* 183–189.

Croce, P. J. (1995). *Science and religion in the era of William James: Eclipse of certainty, 1820–1880.* Chapel Hill, NC: University of North Carolina Press.

Cronbach, L. J. (1957). The two disciplines of scientific psychology. *American Psychologist, 12,* 671–684.

Cronbach, L. J., Hastorf, A. H., Hilgard, E. R., & Maccoby, E. E. (1990). Robert R. Sears (1908–1989). *American Psychologist, 45,* 663–664.

Crutchfield, R. S. (1961). Edward Chace Tolman: 1886–1959. *American Journal of Psychology, 74,* 135–141.

Cushman, P. (1992). Psychotherapy to 1992: A historically situated interpretation. In D. K. Freedheim (Ed.), *History of psychotherapy: A century of change* (pp. 21–64). Washington, DC: American Psychological Association.

Dallenbach, K. M. (1913). The measurement of attention. *American Journal of Psychology, 24,* 465–507.

Danziger, K. (1980). The history of introspection reconsidered. *Journal of the History of the Behavioral Sciences, 16,* 241–262.

Danziger, K. (1988). A question of identity: Who participated in psychological experiments? In J. G. Morawski (Ed.), *The rise of experimentation in American psychology* (pp. 35–52). New Haven, CT: Yale University Press.

Danziger, K. (2000). Making social psychology experimental: A conceptual history, 1920–1970. *Journal of the History of the Behavioral Sciences, 36,* 329–347.

Darwin, C. (1839). *Journal of researches into the geology and natural history of the various countries visited by the H.M.S. Beagle.* London, UK: Henry Colburn.

Darwin, C. (1871). *The descent of man, and selection in relation to sex.* London, UK: Murray.

Darwin, C. (1872). *The expression of the emotions in man and animals.* London, UK: Murray.

Darwin, C. (1877). A biographical sketch of an infant. *Mind, 2,* 285–294.

Darwin, C. (1958a). Autobiography. In F. Darwin (Ed.), *The autobiography of Charles Darwin and selected letters* (pp. 5–58). New York, NY: Dover. (Original work published 1892)

Darwin, C. (1958b). *On the origin of species by means of natural selection, or the preservation of favoured races in the struggle for life.* New York, NY: Mentor Books. (Original work published 1859)

Degler, C. N. (1991). *In search of human nature: The decline and revival of Darwinism in American social thought.* New York, NY: Oxford University Press.

Dennis, P. M. (1984). The Edison questionnaire. *Journal of the History of the Behavioral Sciences, 20,* 23–37.

Dennis, W. (Ed.). (1948). *Readings in the history of psychology.* New York, NY: Appleton-Century-Crofts.

Denny-Brown, D. (1952). Charles Scott Sherrington: 1857–1952. *American Journal of Psychology, 65,* 474–477.

Descartes, R. (1960). *Discourse on method* (L. J. Lafleur, Trans.). Indianapolis, IN: Bobbs-Merrill. (Original work published 1637)

Descartes, R. (1969). Passions of the soul. In E. S. Haldane & G. R. T. Ross (Trans.), *The philosophical works of Descartes* (Vol. I, pp. 329–427). New York, NY: Cambridge University Press. (Original work published 1649)

Desmond, A., & Moore, J. (1991). *Darwin: The life of a tormented evolutionist.* New York, NY: Norton.

Desmond, A., & Moore, J. (2009). *Darwin's sacred cause: How a hatred of slavery shaped Darwin's views on human evolution.* Boston, MA: Houghton Mifflin.

Dewey, J. (1886). *Psychology.* New York, NY: Harper.

Dewey, J. (1899). *The school and society.* Chicago, IL: University of Chicago Press.

Dewey, J. (1900). Psychology and social practice. *Psychological Review, 7,* 105–124.

Dewey, J. (1948). The reflex arc concept in psychology. In W. Dennis (Ed.), *Readings in the history of psychology* (pp. 355–365). New York, NY: Appleton-Century-Crofts. (Original work published 1896)

Dewsbury, D. A. (1984). *Comparative psychology in the twentieth century.* Stroudsburg, PA: Hutchinson Ross.

Dewsbury, D. A. (1990a). Early interactions between animal psychologists and animal activists and the founding of the APA committee on precautions in animal experimentation. *American Psychologist, 45,* 315–327.

Dewsbury, D. A. (1990b). Whither the introductory course in the history of psychology? *Journal of the History of the Behavioral Sciences, 26,* 371–377.

Dewsbury, D. A. (1992). Triumph and tribulation in the history of comparative psychology. *Journal of Comparative Psychology, 106,* 3–19.

Dewsbury, D. A. (1994). John B. Watson: Profile of a comparative psychologist and proto-ethologist. In J. T. Todd & E. K. Morris (Eds.), *Modern perspectives on John B. Watson and classical behaviorism* (pp. 141–144). Westport, CT: Greenwood Press.

Dewsbury, D. A. (1996). Robert M. Yerkes: A psychobiologist with a plan. In G. A. Kimble, C. A. Bonneau, & M. Wertheimer (Eds.), *Portraits of pioneers in psychology* (Vol. II, pp. 87–105). Washington, DC: American Psychological Association.

Dewsbury, D. A. (2006). *Monkey farm: A history of the Yerkes laboratories of primate biology in Orange Park, Florida, 1930–1965.* Lewisburg, PA: Bucknell University Press.

Dewsbury, D. A., & Bolles, R. C. (1995). The founding of the Psychonomic Society. *Psychonomic Bulletin and Review, 2,* 216–233.

Diamond, I. T. (1985). A history of the study of the cortex: Changes in the concept of the sensory pathway. In G. A. Kimble & K. Schlesinger (Eds.), *Topics in the history of psychology* (Vol. 1, pp. 305–387). Hillsdale, NJ: Erlbaum.

Diehl, L. A. (1992). The discovering of Iva Lowther Peters: Transcending male bias in the history of psychology. In J. C. Christer & D. Howard (Eds.), *New directions in feminist psychology: Practice, theory, and research* (pp. 101–115). New York, NY: Springer.

Dollard, J., Doob, L. W., Miller, N. E., Mowrer, O. H., & Sears, R. R. (1939). *Frustration and aggression*. New Haven, CT: Yale University Press.

Donnelly, M. E. (Ed.). (1992). *Reinterpreting the legacy of William James*. Washington, DC: The American Psychological Association.

Dorn, H. (1972). Ernst Heinrich Weber. In C. C. Gillespie (Ed.), *Dictionary of scientific biography*. Vol. XIV. New York, NY: Charles Scribner's Sons.

Douthat, R. (2006, December). They made America. *The Atlantic, 298*, 59–78.

Drumm, P. (2009). Applied animal psychology at an American roadside attraction: Animal Behavior Enterprises and the IQ Zoo of Hot Springs, Arkansas. *American Journal of Psychology, 122*, 537–545.

Duncan, C. P. (1980). A note on the 1929 International Congress of Psychology. *Journal of the History of the Behavioral Sciences, 16*, 1–5.

Duncker, K. (1945). On problem solving. *Psychological Monographs, 58, Whole No. 270*. (Original work published 1935)

Ebbinghaus, H. (1908). *Psychology: An elementary textbook* (M. Meyer, Trans.). Boston, MA: D. C. Heath.

Ebbinghaus, H. (1964). *Memory: A contribution to experimental psychology* (H. A. Ruger & C. A. Bussenius, Trans.). New York, NY: Dover. (Original work published 1885)

Ebbinghaus, H. (1965). Hermann Ebbinghaus (1850–1909) on the completion test. In R. J. Herrnstein & E. G. Boring (Eds.), *A sourcebook in the history of psychology* (pp. 433–437). Cambridge, MA: Harvard University Press. (Original work published 1897)

Eiseley, L. (1958). *Darwin's century: Evolution and the men who discovered it*. New York, NY: Doubleday.

Ellenberger, H. F. (1970). *The discovery of the unconsciousness*. New York, NY: Basic Books.

Ellenberger, H. F. (1972). The story of "Anna O": A critical review with new data. *Journal of the History of the Behavioral Sciences, 8*, 267–279.

Elliott, M. H. (1928). The effect of change of reward on the maze performance of rats. *University of California Publications in Psychology, 4*, 19–30.

Ellis, H. (1910). Review of *a psycho-analytic study of Leonardo da Vinci. Journal of Mental Science, 56*, 522–523.

Elmes, D. G., Kantowitz, B. H., & Roediger, H. L., III. (2003). *Research methods in psychology* (7th ed.). St. Paul, MN: West.

Emde, R. N., Plomin, R., Robinson, J., Corley, R., DeFries, J., Fulker, D. W., Resnick, J. S., Campos, J., Kagan, J., & Zahn-Waxler, C. (1992). Temperament, emotion, and cognition at fourteen months: The MacArthur longitudinal twin study. *Child Development, 63*, 1437–1455.

English, H. B. (1929). Three cases of "conditioned fear response." *Journal of Abnormal and Social Psychology, 24*, 221–225.

Estes, W. K. (1981). The bible is out. *Contemporary Psychology, 26*, 327–330.

Evans, R. B. (1972). E. B. Titchener and his lost system. *Journal of the History of the Behavioral Sciences, 8*, 168–180.

Evans, R. B. (1984). The origins of American academic psychology. In J. Brozek (Ed.), *Explorations in the history of psychology in the United States* (pp. 17–60). Lewisburg, PA: Bucknell University Press.

Evans, R. B., & Koelsch, W. A. (1985). Psychoanalysis arrives in America: The 1909 psychology conference at Clark University. *American Psychologist, 40*, 942–948.

Eysenck, H. J. (1952). The effects of psychotherapy: An evaluation. *Journal of Consulting Psychology, 16*, 319–324.

Eysenck, H. J. (Ed.). (1960). *Behaviour therapy and the neuroses*. London, UK: Pergamon.

Fancher, R. E. (1983). Alphonse de Candolle, Francis Galton, and the early history of the nature-nurture controversy. *Journal of the History of the Behavioral Sciences, 19*, 341–352.

Fancher, R. E. (1985). *The intelligence men: Makers of the IQ controversy*. New York, NY: Norton.

Fancher, R. E. (1987). Henry Goddard and the Kallikak family photographs: "Conscious skullduggery" or "Whig history"? *American Psychologist, 42*, 585–590.

Fancher, R. E. (1990). *Pioneers of psychology* (2nd ed.). New York, NY: Norton.

Fancher, R. E. (2009). Scientific cousins: The relationship between Charles Darwin and Francis Galton. *American Psychologist, 64*, 84–92.

Fantino, E. (2008). Behavior analysis is thriving, but what about its future? *Journal of the Experimental Analysis of Behavior, 89,* 125–127.

Farr, R. M. (1983). Wilhelm Wundt (1832–1920) and the origins of psychology as an experimental and social science. *British Journal of Social Psychology, 22,* 289–301.

Farson, R. (1978). The technology of humanism. *Journal of Humanistic Psychology, 18,* 5–35.

Faust, D. G. (2008). *This republic of suffering.* New York, NY: Knopf.

Fearing, F. (1930). *Reflex action: A study in the history of physiological psychology.* New York, NY: Hafner.

Fechner, G. T. (1996). *Elements of psychophysics.* New York, NY: Holt, Rinehart, & Winston. (Original work published 1860)

Fernberger, S. W. (1931). The history of the psychological clinic. In R. A. Brotemarkle (Ed.), *Clinical psychology: Studies in honor of Lightner Witmer* (pp. 10–36). Philadelphia, PA: University of Pennsylvania Press.

Fernberger, S. W. (1932). The American Psychological Association: A historical summary, 1892–1930. *Psychological Bulletin, 29,* 1–89.

Ferrier, D. (1876). *The functions of the brain.* New York, NY: Putnam.

Ferster, C. B., & Skinner, B. F. (1957). *Schedules of reinforcement.* New York, NY: Appleton-Century-Crofts.

Festinger, L. (1957). *A theory of cognitive dissonance.* Evanston, IL: Row, Peterson, & Co.

Festinger, L. (1980). Looking backward. In L. Festinger (Ed.), *Retrospections on social psychology* (pp. 236–254). New York, NY: Oxford University Press.

Festinger, L., & Carlsmith, J. M. (1959). Cognitive consequences of forced compliance. *Journal of Abnormal and Social Psychology, 58,* 203–211.

Finger, S. (2000). *Minds behind the brain: A history of the pioneers and their discoveries.* New York, NY: Oxford University Press.

Finno, A. A., Wicherski, M., & Kohout, J. L. (2010). *First-Year Students in U.S. and Canadian graduate departments of psychology: 2009–2010.* Center for Workforce Studies, American Psychological Association.

Fisher, R. A. (1925). *Statistical methods for research workers.* London, UK: Oliver & Boyd.

Fisher, R. A. (1935). *The design of experiments.* London, UK: Oliver & Boyd.

Fiske, S. T., & Taylor, S. E. (1984). *Social cognition.* Reading, MA: Addison-Wesley.

Flaherty, F. C. (1985). *Animal learning and cognition.* New York, NY: McGraw-Hill.

Flavell, J. H. (1963). *The developmental psychology of Jean Piaget.* Princeton, NJ: Van Nostrand Reinhold.

Flourens, P. (1978). Phrenology examined (C. D. Meigs, Trans.). In D. N. Robinson (Ed.), *Significant contributions to the history of psychology. Series E. Volume II.* Washington, DC: University Publications of America. (Original work published 1846)

Forrest, D. W. (1974). *Francis Galton: The life and work of a Victorian genius.* New York, NY: Taplinger.

Forrest, D. W. (1999). *Hypnotism: A history.* New York, NY: Penguin.

Frank, J. D. (1978). Kurt Lewin in retrospect—A psychiatrist's view. *Journal of the History of the Behavioral Sciences, 14,* 223–227.

Freeman, F. N. (1922). The mental age of adults. *Journal of Educational Research, 6,* 441–444.

Freeman, F. S. (1977). The beginnings of Gestalt psychology in the United States. *Journal of the History of the Behavioral Sciences, 13,* 352–353.

Freud, A. (1928). *Introduction to the technique of child analysis.* New York, NY: Nervous and Mental Disease Publishing Co.

Freud, A. (1937). *The ego and mechanisms of defense.* New York, NY: International Universities Press.

Freud, S. (1938a). *The interpretation of dreams.* In A. A. Brill (Ed. & Trans.), *The basic writings of Sigmund Freud* (pp. 179–549). New York, NY: Random House. (Original work published 1900)

Freud, S. (1938b). *The psychopathology of everyday life.* In A. A. Brill (Ed. & Trans.), *The basic writings of Sigmund Freud* (pp. 33–178). New York, NY: Random House. (Original work published 1901)

Freud, S. (1938c). *Three contributions to the theory of sex.* In A. A. Brill (Ed. & Trans.), *The basic writings of Sigmund Freud* (pp. 551–629). New York, NY: Random House. (Original work published 1905)

Freud, S. (1938d). *Wit and its relation to the unconscious.* In A. A. Brill (Ed. & Trans.), *The basic writings of Sigmund Freud* (pp. 631–803). New York. NY: Random House. (Original work published 1905)

Freud, S. (1959a). *Beyond the pleasure principle* (J. Strachey, Trans.). New York. NY: Bantam Books. (Original work published 1920)

Freud, S. (1959b). *The ego and the id* (J. Strachey, Trans.). New York, NY: Bantam Books. (Original work published 1923)

Freud, S. (1977). *Five lectures on psycho-analysis* (J. Strachey, Trans.). New York, NY: Norton. (Original work published 1909)

Fritsch, G., & Hitzig, E. (1965). Gustav Fritsch (1838–1927) and Eduard Hitzig (1838–1907) on cerebral motor centers, 1870. In R. J. Herrnstein & E. G. Boring (Eds.), *A sourcebook in the history of psychology* (pp. 229–233). Cambridge, MA: Harvard University Press. (Original work published 1870)

Fuchs, A. H. (2000). Contributions of American mental philosophers to psychology in the United States. *History of Psychology, 3,* 3–19.

Fuchs, A. H., & Viney, W. (2002). The course in the history of psychology: Present status and future concerns. *Journal of the History of the Behavioral Sciences, 5,* 3–15.

Furumoto, L. (1979). Mary Whiton Calkins (1863–1930): Fourteenth president of the American Psychological Association. *Journal of the History of the Behavioral Sciences, 15,* 346–356.

Furumoto, L. (1988). Shared knowledge: The Experimentalists, 1904–1929. In J. G. Morawski (Ed.), *The rise of experimentation in American psychology* (pp. 94–113). New Haven, CT: Yale University Press.

Furumoto, L. (1989). The new history of psychology. In I. S. Cohen (Ed.), *The G. Stanley Hall lecture series* (Vol. 9, pp. 9–34). Washington, DC: American Psychological Association.

Furumoto, L. (1991). From "paired associates" to a psychology of self: The intellectual odyssey of Mary Whiton Calkins. In G. A. Kimble, M. Wertheimer, & C. L. White (Eds.), *Portraits of pioneers in psychology* (Vol. I, pp. 56–72). Washington, DC: American Psychological Association.

Furumoto, L. (1992). Joining separate spheres—Christine Ladd-Franklin, woman-scientist (1847–1930). *American Psychologist, 47,* 175–182.

Galef, B. G., Jr. (1998). Edward Thorndike: revolutionary psychologist, ambiguous biologist. *American Psychologist, 53,* 1128–1134.

Gall, F. J. (1965). Franz Joseph Gall (1758–1828) on phrenology, the localization of the functions of the brain, 1825. In R. J. Herrnstein & E. G. Boring (Eds.), *A sourcebook in the history of psychology* (pp. 211–220). Cambridge, MA: Harvard University Press. (Original work published 1825)

Gallistel, C. R. (1981). Bell, Magendie, and the proposals to restrict the use of animals in neurobehavioral research. *American Psychologist, 36,* 357–360.

Galton, F. (1874). *English men of science: Their nature and nurture.* London, UK: Macmillan.

Galton, F. (1883). *An inquiry into human faculty and its development.* London, UK: Macmillan.

Galton, F. (1908). *Memories of my life.* London, UK: Methuen.

Galton, F. (1950). *Hereditary genius: An inquiry into its laws and consequences.* London, UK: Watts & Co. (Original work published 1869)

Galton, F. (1965). Galton on mental capacity, 1883. In R. J. Herrnstein & E. G. Boring (Eds.), *A sourcebook in the history of psychology* (pp. 421–423). Cambridge, MA: Harvard University Press. (Original work published 1883)

Gamwell, L., & Tomes, N. (1995). *Madness in America: Cultural and medical perceptions of mental illness before 1914.* Ithaca, NY: Cornell University Press.

Gantt, W. H. (1973). Reminiscences of Pavlov. *Journal of the Experimental Analysis of Behavior, 20,* 131–136.

Gardner, H. (1985). *The mind's new science: A history of the cognitive revolution.* New York, NY: Basic Books.

Garrett, H. E. (1951). *Great experiments in psychology* (3rded). New York, NY: Appleton-Century-Crofts.

Gay, P. (1988). *Freud: A life for our time.* New York, NY: Norton.

Gibson, E. J. (1969). *Principles of perceptual learning and development.* New York, NY: Appleton-Century-Crofts.

Gibson, E. J. (1980). Eleanor Gibson. In G. Lindsey (Ed.), *A history of psychology in autobiography* (Vol. 7, pp. 239–271). San Francisco, CA: Freeman.

Gibson, E. J. (1994). Has psychology a future? *Psychological Science, 5,* 69–76.

Gibson, E. J. (2002). *Perceiving the affordances: A portrait of two psychologists.* Mahwah, NJ: Erlbaum.

Gibson, E. J., & Walk, R. D. (1960). The "visual cliff." *Scientific American, 202,* 64–71.

Gibson, J. J. (1979). *The ecological approach to visual perception.* Boston, MA: Houghton Mifflin.

Gibson, J. J. (1992). Conclusions from the century of research on sense perception. In S. Koch & D. E. Leary (Eds.), *A century of psychology as a science* (2nd ed., pp. 224–230). Washington, DC: APA.

Gilbreth, F. B., & Gilbreth, L. M. (1916). *Fatigue study: The elimination of humanity's greatest unnecessary waste*. New York, NY: Sturgis & Walton.

Gilbreth, F. B., & Gilbreth, L. M. (1917). *Applied motion study*. New York, NY: Sturgis & Walton.

Gilbreth, F. B., Jr., & Carey, E. G. (1949). *Cheaper by the dozen*. New York, NY: Bantam.

Gilderhus, M. T. (2000). *History and historians: A historiographic introduction* (4th ed.). Upper Saddle River, NJ: Prentice Hall.

Gillaspy, J. A., & Bailey, R. E. (2008, August). *Expansion of operant psychology into animal training (1955–1965)*. Boston, MA: American Psychological Association.

Gillaspy, J. A., & Bihm, E. M. (2002). Marian Breland Bailey (1920–2001). *American Psychologist, 57,* 292–293.

Gillespie, R. (1988). The Hawthorne experiments and the politics of experimentation. In J. G. Morawski (Ed.), *The rise of experimentation in American psychology* (pp. 114–137). New Haven, CT: Yale University Press.

Gillespie, R. (1991). *Manufacturing knowledge: A history of the Hawthorne experiments*. New York, NY: Cambridge University Press.

Gillies, D. (1993). *Philosophy of science in the twentieth century: Four central themes*. Oxford, UK: Blackwell Press.

Glass, C. R., & Arnkoff, D. B. (1992). Behavior therapy. In D. K. Freedheim (Ed.), *History of psychotherapy: A century of change* (pp. 587–628). Washington, DC: American Psychological Association.

Gleaves, D. H., & Hernandez, E. (1999). Recent formulations of Freud's development and abandonment of his seduction theory: Historical/scientific clarification or a continued assault on truth? *History of Psychology, 2,* 324–354.

Glickman, S. E. (1996). Donald Olding Hebb: Returning the nervous system to psychology. In G. A. Kimble, C. A. Bonneau, & M. Wertheimer (Eds.), *Portraits of pioneers in psychology* (Vol. II, pp. 227–244). Washington, DC: American Psychological Association.

Goddard, H. H. (1910). Four hundred feeble-minded children classified by the Binet method. *Journal of Genetic Psychology, 17,* 387–397.

Goddard, H. H. (1912). *The Kallikak family: A study in the heredity of feeble-mindedness*. New York, NY: Macmillan.

Goddard, H. H. (1913). The Binet tests in relation to immigration. *Journal of Psycho-Asthenics, 18,* 105–107.

Goddard, H. H. (1917). Mental tests and the immigrant. *Journal of Delinquency, 2,* 243–277.

Goddard, H. H. (1928). Feeblemindedness: A question of definition. *Journal of Psycho-Asthenics, 33,* 219–227.

Goldstein, E. B. (1996). *Sensation and perception* (4th ed.). Pacific Grove, CA: Brooks/Cole.

Goodenough, F. L. (1949). *Mental testing*. New York, NY: Holt, Rinehart, & Winston.

Goodenough, F. L. (1950). Edward Lee Thorndike: 1874–1949. *American Journal of Psychology, 63,* 291–301.

Goodwin, C. J. (1985). On the origins of Titchener's Experimentalists. *Journal of the History of the Behavioral Sciences, 21,* 383–389.

Goodwin, C. J. (1987). In Hall's shadow: Edmund Clark Sanford (1859–1924). *Journal of the History of the Behavioral Sciences, 23,* 153–168.

Goodwin, C. J. (1991a). Misportraying Pavlov's apparatus. *American Journal of Psychology, 104,* 135–141.

Goodwin, C. J. (1991b). Using psychologists' letters to teach about introspection. *Teaching of Psychology, 18,* 237–238.

Goodwin, C. J. (2003). An insider's look at experimental psychology in America: The diaries of Walter Miles. In D. B. Baker (Ed.), *Thick description and fine texture: Studies in the history of psychology* (pp. 57–75). Akron, OH: The University of Akron Press.

Goodwin, C. J. (2005). Reorganizing Titchener's Experimentalists: The origins of the Society of Experimental Psychology. *History of Psychology, 8,* 347–361.

Goodwin, C. J. (2009). E. W. Scripture: The application of "new psychology" methodology to athletics. In C. D. Green & L. T. Benjamin, Jr. (Eds.), *Psychology gets in the game: Sport, mind, and behavior, 1880–1960* (pp. 78–97). Lincoln, NE: University of Nebraska Press.

Goodwin, C. J. (2010). The 1928 Carlisle conference: Knight Dunlap and a National Laboratory for psychology. *History of Psychology, 13,* 378–392.

Goodwin, C. J., & Royer, L. (Eds.). (2010). *Walter Miles and his 1920 grand tour of European physiology and psychology laboratories*. Akron, OH: The University of Akron Press.

Gould, S. J. (1981). *The mismeasure of man*. New York, NY: Norton.

Gravitz, M. A. (1988). Early uses of hypnosis as surgical anesthesia. *American Journal of Clinical Hypnosis, 30,* 201–208.

Gray, J. A. (1979). *Ivan Pavlov.* New York, NY: Viking.

Gray, P. H. (1962). Douglas Alexander Spalding: The first experimental behaviorist. *Journal of General Psychology, 67,* 299–307.

Green, C. D. (1992). Of immortal mythological beasts: Operationism in psychology. *Theory and Psychology, 2,* 291–320.

Green, C. D. (2004). The hiring of James Mark Baldwin and James Gibson Hume at the University of Toronto in 1889. *History of Psychology, 7,* 130–153.

Green, C. D. (2009). Darwinian theory, functionalism, and the first American psychological revolution. *American Psychologist, 64,* 75–83.

Green, C. D., & Benjamin, L. T., Jr. (Eds.). (2009). *Psychology gets in the game: Sport, mind, and behavior, 1880–1960.* Lincoln, NE: University of Nebraska Press.

Green, M., & Rieber, R. W. (1980). The assimilation of psychoanalysis in America. In R. W. Rieber & K. Salzinger (Eds.), *Psychology: Theoretical-historical perspectives* (pp. 263–304). New York, NY: Academic Press.

Greenwood, J. D. (2003). Wundt, Volkerpsychologie, and experimental social psychology. *History of Psychology, 6,* 70–88.

Grmek, M. D. (1972). François Magendie. In C. C. Gillespie (Ed.), *Dictionary of scientific biography. Vol. IX.* New York, NY: Scribner.

Grob, G. N. (1973). *Mental institutions in America: Social policy to 1875.* New York, NY: Free Press.

Grob, G. N. (1983). *Mental institutions and American society: 1875–1940.* Princeton, NJ: Princeton University Press.

Grob, G. N. (1991). *From asylum to community: Mental health policy in modern America.* Princeton, NJ: Princeton University Press.

Grob, G. N. (1994). *The mad among us: A history of the care of America's mentally ill.* New York, NY: Free Press.

Grogan, J. (2013). *Encountering America: Humanistic psychology, sixties culture, and the shaping of the modern self.* New York, NY: Harper Perennial.

Gundlach, H. U. K. (1986). Ebbinghaus, nonsense syllables, and three-letter words. *Contemporary Psychology, 31,* 469–470.

Guthrie, E. R. (1935). *The psychology of learning.* New York, NY: Harper and Brothers.

Guthrie, E. R., & Horton, G. P. (1946). *Cats in a puzzle box.* New York, NY: Rinehart & Co.

Guthrie, R. V. (1976). *Even the rat was white: A historical view of psychology.* New York, NY: Harper & Row.

Guttman, N. (1977). On Skinner and Hull: A reminiscence and projection. *American Psychologist, 32,* 321–328.

Haines, H., & Vaughan, G. M. (1979). Was 1898 a "great date" in the history of experimental social psychology? *Journal of the History of the Behavioral Sciences, 15,* 323–332.

Haldane, J. B. S. (1954). Introducing Douglas Spalding. *British Journal of Animal Behavior, 2,* 1–11.

Hale, N. G., Jr. (1971). *Freud and the Americans: The beginnings of psychoanalysis in the United States, 1876–1917.* New York, NY: Oxford University Press.

Hall, C. S. (1954). *A primer of Freudian psychology.* New York, NY: World Publishing Company.

Hall, C. S., & Lindzey, G. (1970). *Theories of personality* (2nd ed.). New York, NY: Wiley.

Hall, G. S. (1887). Editorial. *American Journal of Psychology, 1,* 3–4.

Hall, G. S. (1890–1891). Review of "The Principles of Psychology." *American Journal of Psychology, 3,* 578–591.

Hall, G. S. (1904). *Adolescence.* New York, NY: Appleton.

Hall, G. S. (1922). *Senescence: The last half of life.* New York, NY: Appleton.

Hall, G. S. (1923). *Life and confessions of a psychologist.* New York, NY: Appleton.

Hall, G. S. (1948). The contents of children's minds. In W. Dennis (Ed.), *Readings in the history of psychology* (pp. 255–276). New York, NY: Appleton-Century-Crofts. (Original work published 1883)

Hannush, M. J. (1987). John B. Watson remembered: An interview with James B. Watson. *Journal of the History of the Behavioral Sciences, 23,* 137–152.

Harlow, J. M. (1868). *Recovery from the passage of an iron bar through the head.* Boston, MA: Clapp.

Harmon-Jones, E., & Mills, J. (Eds.). (1999). *Cognitive dissonance: Progress on a pivotal theory in social psychology.* Washington, D.C.: American Psychological Association.

Harris, B. (1979). Whatever happened to Little Albert? *American Psychologist, 34,* 151–160.

Harris, B. (2010). Letting go of Little Albert: Disciplinary memory, history, and the uses of myth. *Journal of the History of the Behavioral Sciences, 47,* 1–17.

Harrower-Erickson, M. R. (1942). Kurt Koffka: 1886–1941. *American Journal of Psychology, 55,* 278–281.

Hartley, D. (1971). *Observations on man, his frame, his duty, and his expectations. Volume I.* New York, NY: Garland. (Original work published 1749)

Haupt, E. J. (1998). The origins of American psychology in the work of G. E. Müller: Classical psychophysics and serial learning. In R. W. Reiber & K. D. Salzinger (Eds.), *Psychology: Theoretical-historical perspectives* (2nd ed., pp. 17–75). Washington, DC: American Psychological Association.

Havens, L. L. (1965). Emil Kraepelin. *Journal of Nervous and Mental Disease, 141,* 16–28.

Hawkins, H. (1960). *Pioneer: A history of the Johns Hopkins University, 1874–1899.* Ithaca, NY: Cornell University Press.

Hearnshaw, L. S. (1964). *A short history of British psychology, 1840–1940.* London: Butler and Tanner.

Hebb, D. O. (1949). *The organization of behavior.* New York, NY: Wiley.

Hebb, D. O. (1959). Karl Spencer Lashley (1890–1958). *American Journal of Psychology, 72,* 142–150.

Hebb, D. O. (1960). The American revolution. *American Psychologist, 15,* 735–745.

Hebb, D. O. (1980). D. O. Hebb. In G. Lindsey (Ed.), *A history of psychology in autobiography* (Vol. 7, pp. 273–303). San Francisco, CA: Freeman.

Heidbreder, E. (1933). *Seven psychologies.* New York, NY: Appleton-Century-Crofts.

Heims, S. (1978). Kurt Lewin and social change. *Journal of the History of the Behavioral Sciences, 14,* 238–241.

Helmholtz, H. (1965). Hermann Ludwig Ferdinand von Helmholtz (1821–1894) on the three-color theory of vision and visual specific nerve energies, 1860. In R. J. Herrnstein & E. G. Boring (Eds.), *A sourcebook in the history of psychology* (pp. 40–44). Cambridge, MA: Harvard University Press. (Original work published 1860)

Helson, H. (1972). What can we learn from the history of psychology? *Journal of the History of the Behavioral Sciences, 8,* 115–119.

Henle, M. (1980). The influence of Gestalt psychology in America. In R. W. Rieber & K. Salzinger (Eds.),

Psychology: Theoretical-historical perspectives (pp. 177–190). New York, NY: Academic Press.

Henle, M. (1986). One man against the Nazis—Wolfgang Köhler. In M. Henle (Ed.), *1879 and all that: Essays in the theory and history of psychology* (pp. 225–237). New York, NY: Columbia University Press.

Herbart, J. F. (1824–1825). *Psychology as a science* (Vols. 1 and 2). Königsberg, Germany: Unger.

Herman, E. (1995). *The romance of American psychology: Political culture in the age of experts.* Berkeley, CA: University of California Press.

Hertzman, M., & Festinger, L. (1940). Shifts in explicit goals in a level of aspiration experiment. *Journal of Experimental Psychology, 27,* 439–452.

Hess, U., & Thibault, P. (2009). Darwin and emotional expression. *American Psychologist, 64,* 120–128.

Hicks, L. H., & Ridley, S. E. (1979). Black studies in psychology. *American Psychologist, 34,* 597–602.

Hilgard, E. R. (1948). *Theories of learning.* New York, NY: Appleton-Century-Crofts.

Hilgard, E. R. (1957). Lewis Madison Terman: 1877–1956. *American Journal of Psychology, 70,* 472–479.

Hilgard, E. R. (1964). *Introduction to Dover Edition of "Memory: A contribution to experimental psychology".* New York, NY: Dover.

Hilgard, E. R. (1967). Kenneth Wartinbee Spence: 1907–1967. *American Journal of Psychology, 80,* 314–318.

Hilgard, E. R. (1980). The trilogy of mind: Cognition, affection, and conation. *Journal of the History of the Behavioral Sciences, 16,* 107–117.

Hilgard, E. R. (1982). Robert I. Watson and the founding of Division 26 of the American Psychological Association. *Journal of the History of the Behavioral Sciences, 18,* 308–311.

Hilgard, E. R. (1987). *Psychology in America: A historical survey.* San Diego, CA: Harcourt Brace Jovanovich.

Hindeland, M. J. (1971). Edward Bradford Titchener: A pioneer in perception. *Journal of the History of the Behavioral Sciences, 7,* 23–28.

Hoffeld, D. R. (1980). Mesmer's failure: Sex, politics, personality, and the zeitgeist. *Journal of the History of the Behavioral Sciences, 16,* 377–386.

Hofstadter, R., & Hardy, C. D. (1952). *The development and scope of higher education in the United States.* New York, NY: Columbia University Press.

Holliday, B. G. (2010, April). *Communiqué: Ethnic minority recruitment, retention, and training.* Office of Ethnic Minority Affairs, American Psychological Association.

Hollingworth, H. L. (1916). *Vocational psychology: Its problems and methods.* New York, NY: D. Appleton and Company.

Hollingworth, H. L. (1990). *Leta Stetter Hollingworth: A biography.* Bolton, MA: Anker Publishing. (Original work published 1943)

Hollingworth, L. S. (1926). *Gifted children: Their nature and nurture.* New York, NY: Macmillan.

Holway, A. H., & Boring, E. G. (1940). The moon illusion and the angle of regard. *American Journal of Psychology, 53,* 109–116.

Horley, J. (2001). After "The Baltimore affair": James Mark Baldwin's life and work, 1908–1934. *History of Psychology, 4,* 24–33.

Hornstein, G. A. (1992). The return of the repressed: Psychology's problematic relations with psychoanalysis, 1909–1960. *American Psychologist, 47,* 254–263.

Hothersall, D. (1995). *History of psychology* (3rd ed.). New York, NY: McGraw-Hill.

Hubel, D. H., & Wiesel, T. N. (1963). Receptive fields of cells in the striate cortex of very young, visually inexperienced kittens. *Journal of Neurophysiology, 26,* 994–1002.

Hull, C. L. (1920). Quantitative aspects of the evolution of concepts. *Psychological Monographs, 28, No. 123.*

Hull, C. L. (1928). *Aptitude testing.* Yonkers-on-Hudson, NY: Word Book.

Hull, C. L. (1933). *Hypnosis and suggestibility: An experimental approach.* New York, NY: Appleton-Century.

Hull, C. L. (1943). *Principles of behavior.* New York, NY: Appleton-Century-Crofts.

Hull, C. L. (1952a). *A behavior system.* New Haven, CT: Yale University Press.

Hull, C. L. (1952b). Clark L. Hull. In E. G. Boring, H. S. Langfeld, H. Werner, & R. M. Yerkes (Eds.), *A history of psychology in autobiography* (Vol. 4, pp. 143–162). Worcester, MA: Clark University Press.

Hull, D. L. (1979). In defense of presentism. *History and Theory, 18,* 1–15.

Hume, D. (1969). *A treatise of human nature* (E. C. Mossner, Ed.). Baltimore, MD: Penguin. (Original work published 1739–1740)

Hunter, W. S. (1919). *General psychology.* Chicago, IL: University of Chicago Press.

Hunter, W. S. (1949). James Rowland Angell, 1869–1949. *American Journal of Psychology, 62,* 439–450.

Irmscher, C. (2013). *Louis Agassiz: Creator of American science.* Boston, MA: Houghton Mifflin Harcourt.

Izard, C. E. (1977). *Human emotions.* New York, NY: Plenum.

Jacobson, E. (1929). *Progressive relaxation.* Chicago, IL: University of Chicago Press.

James, H. (Ed.). (1920). *The letters of William James. Vol. 2.* Boston, MA: Atlantic Monthly Press.

James, W. (1891). *Letter to M. W. Calkins, December 20, 1891.* Calkins Papers, Wellesley College, Wellesley, MA.

James, W. (1950a). *Principles of psychology. Vol. 1.* New York, NY: Dover. (Original work published 1890)

James, W. (1950b). *Principles of psychology. Vol. 2.* New York, NY: Dover. (Original work published 1890)

James, W. (1961). *Psychology: The briefer course.* New York, NY: Harper & Row. (Original work published 1892)

Jaynes, J. (1969a). Edwin Garrigues Boring: 1886–1968. *Journal of the History of the Behavioral Sciences, 5,* 99–112.

Jaynes, J. (1969b). The historical origins of "ethology" and "comparative psychology." *Animal Behaviour, 17,* 601–606.

Jenkins, J. G. (1935). Review of *Remembering* by F. C. Bartlett. *American Journal of Psychology, 47,* 712–715.

Jenkins, J. G., & Dallenbach, K. M. (1924). Minor studies from the psychological laboratory of Cornell University: Oblivescence during sleep and waking. *American Journal of Psychology, 35,* 605–612.

Jenkins, K. (1991). *Re-thinking history.* London, UK: Routledge.

Johnson, M. G., & Henley, T. B. (Eds.). (1990). *Reflections on "The Principles of Psychology."* Hillsdale, NJ: Erlbaum.

Johnston, T. D. (2003). Three pioneers of comparative psychology in America, 1843–1890. *History of Psychology, 6,* 14–51.

Jonçich, G. (1968). *The sane positivist: A biography of Edward L. Thorndike.* Middletown, CT: Wesleyan University Press.

Jones, E. (1953, 1955, 1957). *The life and work of Sigmund Freud (Vols. 1–3).* New York, NY: Basic Books.

Jones, E., & Wessely, S. (2005). *Shell shock to PTSD: Military psychiatry from 1900 to the Gulf War.* New York, NY: Psychology Press.

Jones, M. C. (1924a). A laboratory study of fear: The case of Peter. *Pedagogical Seminary, 31,* 308–315.

Jones, M. C. (1924b). The elimination of children's fears. *Journal of Experimental Psychology, 7,* 382–390.

Joynt, R. J. (1973, October). Phrenology in New York State. *New York State Journal of Medicine,* 2382–2384.

Jung, C. G. (1919). *Studies in word association.* New York, NY: Moffat-Yard.

Kant, I. (1952). *Critique of judgment* (J. C. Meredith, Trans.). Oxford, UK: Oxford University Press. (Original work published 1790)

Kant, I. (1959). *Critique of practical reason.* (T. K. Abbott, Trans.). New York, NY: Longmans, Green. (Original work published 1788)

Kant, I. (1965). *Critique of pure reason.* (N. K. Smith, Trans.). New York, NY: St. Martin's. (Original work published 1781)

Kazdin, A. E. (1978). *History of behavior modification: Experimental foundations of contemporary research.* Baltimore, MD: University Park Press.

Kennedy, Q., Mather, M., & Carstensen, L. L. (2004). The role of motivation in the age-related positivity effect in autobiographical memory. *Psychological Science, 15,* 208–214.

Kent, D. (1992, September). E. Gibson, A. Newell receive National Medal of Science. *APS Observer, 5*(1), 14–15.

Kent, D. (1994, July/August). Interview with APS President-elect Richard F. Thompson. *APS Observer, 7*(4), 4, 10.

Kent, G. H. (1911). Experiments on habit formation in dementia praecox. *Psychological Review, 18,* 375–410.

Kent, G. H., & Rosanoff, A. J. (1910). A study of association in insanity. *American Journal of Insanity, 67,* 37–96, 317–390.

Kessen, W. (1996). American psychology just before Piaget. *Psychological Science, 7,* 196–199.

Kessen, W., & Kuhlman, C. (Eds.). (1962). Thought in the young child: Report of a conference on intellective development with particular attention to the work of Jean Piaget. *Monographs of the Society for Research in Child Development, 27 (Serial No. 83).*

Kevles, D. J. (1968). Testing the Army's intelligence: Psychologists and the military in World War I. *Journal of American History, 55,* 565–581.

Kimble, G. A. (1991). Psychology from the standpoint of a mechanist: An appreciation of Clark L. Hull. In G. A. Kimble, M. Wertheimer, & C. L. White (Eds.), *Portraits of pioneers in psychology.* Washington, DC: American Psychological Association.

King, D. B. (1992). Evolution and revision of the Principles. In M. E. Donnelly (Ed.), *Reinterpreting the legacy of William James* (pp. 67–75). Washington, DC: The American Psychological Association.

Kinnaman, A. J. (1902). Mental life of two Macacus rhesus monkeys in captivity. II. *American Journal of Psychology, 13,* 173–218.

Kintsch, W. (1985). Reflections on Ebbinghaus. *Journal of Experimental Psychology: Learning, Memory, and Cognition, 11,* 461–463.

Kintsch, W., & Cacioppo, J. T. (1994). Introduction to the 100th anniversary issue of the *Psychological Review. Psychological Review, 101,* 195–199.

Kirkbride, T. S. (1854). *On the construction, organization, and general arrangements of hospitals for the insane with some remarks on insanity and its treatment.* Philadelphia, PA: J. B. Lippincott.

Kirsch, I. (1977). Psychology's first paradigm. *Journal of the History of the Behavioral Sciences, 13,* 317–325.

Klein, A. G. (2002). *Forgotten voice: A biography of Leta Stetter Hollingworth.* Scottsdale, AZ: Great Potential Press.

Klein, D. B. (1970). *A history of scientific psychology: Its origins and philosophical background.* New York, NY: Basic Books.

Kline, L. W. (1899). Suggestions toward a laboratory course in comparative psychology. *American Journal of Psychology, 10,* 399–430.

Klopfer, W. G. (1973). The short history of projective techniques. *Journal of the History of the Behavioral Sciences, 9,* 60–65.

Kluger, R. (1987). *Simple justice: The history of* Brown v. Board of Education *and black America's struggle for equality.* New York, NY: Knopf.

Knapp, T. J. (1985). Contributions to the history of psychology: XXXIX. T. V. Moore and his Cognitive Psychology of 1939. *Psychological Reports, 57,* 1311–1316.

Kneeland, T. W., & Warren, C. A. B. (2002). *Pushbutton psychiatry: A cultural history of electroshock in America.* Walnut Creek, CA: Left Coast Press.

Koch, S. (1992a). Postscript: The second century of psychology at age 12 and the American Psychological Association at age 100. In S. Koch & D. E. Leary (Eds.), *A century of psychology as science* (2nd ed., pp. 951–968). Washington, DC: American Psychological Association.

Koch, S. (1992b). Wundt's creature at age zero—and as centenarian: Some aspects of the institutionalization of the "new psychology." In S. Koch & D. E. Leary (Eds.), *A century of psychology as science* (2nd ed., pp. 7–35). Washington, DC: American Psychological Association.

Koch, S. (1993). "Psychology" or "the psychological studies"? *American Psychologist, 48,* 902–904.

Koelsch, W. A. (1987). *Clark University, 1887–1987: A narrative history.* Worcester, MA: Clark University Press.

Koffka, K. (1922). Perception: An introduction to Gestalt-theorie. *Psychological Bulletin, 19,* 531–585.

Koffka, K. (1935). *Principles of Gestalt psychology.* New York, NY: Harcourt, Brace.

Köhler, W. (1926). *The mentality of apes* (E. Winter, Trans.). New York, NY: Harcourt, Brace. (Original work published 1917)

Köhler, W. (1947). *Gestalt psychology.* New York, NY: Liveright. (Original work published 1929)

Köhler, W. (1969). Gestalt psychology. In D. L. Krantz (Ed.), *Schools of psychology: A symposium* (pp. 69–85). New York, NY: Appleton-Century-Crofts. (Original work published 1967)

Korn, J. H. (1997). *Illusions of reality: A history of deception in social psychology.* Albany, NY: SUNY Press.

Korn, J. H., Davis, R., & Davis, S. F. (1991). Historians' and chairpersons' judgments of eminence among psychologists. *American Psychologist, 46,* 789–792.

Kramer, P. D. (2006). *Freud: Inventor of the modern mind.* New York, NY: HarperCollins.

Krantz, D. L. (1969). The Baldwin-Titchener controversy. In D. L. Krantz (Ed.), *Schools of psychology: A symposium* (pp. 1–19). New York, NY: Appleton-Century-Crofts.

Kroll, J. (1973). A reappraisal of psychiatry in the Middle Ages. *Archives of General Psychiatry, 29,* 276–283.

Kuhn, T. S. (1962). *The structure of scientific revolutions.* Chicago, IL: University of Chicago Press.

Ladd, G. T. (1887). *Elements of physiological psychology.* New York, NY: Scribner's.

Ladd, G. T., & Woodworth, R. S. (1911). *Elements of physiological psychology* (revised ed.). New York, NY: Scribner's.

Lakin, M. (1996). Carl Rogers and the culture of psychotherapy. *The General Psychologist, 32,* 62–68.

Lal, S. (2002). Giving children security: Mamie Phipps Clark and the racialization of child psychology. *American Psychologist, 57,* 20–28.

Landy, F. J. (1992). Hugo Münsterberg: Victim or visionary? *Journal of Applied Psychology, 77,* 787–802.

Landy, F. J. (1993). Early influences on the development of industrial/organizational psychology. In T. K. Fagan & G. R. VandenBos (Eds.), *Exploring applied psychology: Origins and critical analyses* (pp. 83–118). Washington, DC: American Psychological Association.

Larson, C., & Sullivan, J. J. (1965). Watson's relation to Titchener. *Journal of the History of the Behavioral Sciences, 1,* 338–354.

Lashley, K. S. (1929). *Brain mechanisms and intelligence.* Chicago, IL: University of Chicago Press.

Lashley, K. S. (1951). The problem of serial order in behavior. In L. A. Jeffress (Ed.), *Cerebral mechanisms in behavior: The Hixon symposium* (pp. 112–146). New York, NY: Wiley.

Lathem, E. C. (Ed.). (1994). *Bernard Bailyn on the teaching and writing of history: Responses to a series of questions.* Hanover, NH: University Press of New England.

Leacock, S. (1924, March). A manual of the new mentality. *Harper's Monthly Magazine, 47,* 480.

Leahey, T. H. (1979). Something old, something new: Attention in Wundt and modern cognitive psychology. *Journal of the History of the Behavioral Sciences, 15,* 242–252.

Leahey, T. H. (1981). The mistaken mirror: On Wundt's and Titchener's psychologies. *Journal of the History of the Behavioral Sciences, 17,* 273–282.

Leahey, T. H. (1992). The mythical revolutions of American psychology. *American Psychologist, 47,* 308–318.

Leary, D. E. (1992). William James and the art of human understanding. *American Psychologist, 47,* 152–160.

Leary, D. E. (2006). G. Stanley Hall, a man of many words: The role of reading speaking, and writing in his psychological work. *History of Psychology, 9,* 198–223.

Leibniz, G. W. (1982). *New essays on human understanding* (P. Remnant & J. Bennett, Trans.). New York, NY: Cambridge University Press. (Original work published 1765)

Lesch, J. E. (1972). George John Romanes. In C. C. Gillespie (Ed.), *Dictionary of scientific biography. Vol. XI.* New York, NY: Scribner.

Lewin, K. (1931). Environmental forces in child behavior and development. In C. Murchison (Ed.), *Handbook of child psychology* (pp. 94–127). Worcester, MA: Clark University Press.

Lewin, K. (1935). *A dynamic theory of personality* (D. K. Adams & K. E. Zener, Trans.). New York, NY: McGraw-Hill.

Lewin, K. (1936a). *Letter to Walter R. Miles, January 13, 1936.* Walter Miles papers, Archives of the History of American Psychology, University of Akron, Akron, OH.

Lewin, K. (1936b). *Principles of topological psychology* (F. Heider & G. M. Heider, Trans.). New York, NY: McGraw-Hill.

Lewin, K., Lippitt, R., & White, R. (1939). Patterns of aggressive behavior in experimentally created "social climates." *Journal of Social Psychology, 10,* 271–299.

Lewis, R. W. B. (1991). *The Jameses: A family narrative.* New York, NY: Farrar, Straus, & Giroux.

Ley, R. (1990). *A whisper of espionage.* Garden Park, NY: Avery Publishing Group.

Leys, R., & Evans, R. B. (1990). *Defining American psychology: The correspondence between Adolf Meyer and Edward Bradford Titchener.* Baltimore, MD: The Johns Hopkins University Press.

Lippitt, R., & White, R. K. (1943). The "social climate" of children's groups. In R. G. Barker, J. S. Kounin, & H. F. Wright (Eds.), *Child behavior and development* (pp. 485–508). New York, NY: McGraw-Hill.

Lippmann, W. (1922a). The abuse of tests. *New Republic, 32,* 297–298.

Lippmann, W. (1922b). A future for tests. *New Republic, 33,* 9–10.

Locke, J. (1960). *Two treatises on government.* New York, NY: Cambridge University Press. (Original work published 1690)

Locke, J. (1963a). *An essay concerning human understanding.* Germany: Scientia Verlag Aalen. (Original work published 1690)

Locke, J. (1963b). *Some thoughts concerning education.* Germany: Scientia Verlag Aalen. (Original work published 1693)

Loftus, E. F. (1979). *Eyewitness testimony.* Cambridge, MA: Harvard University Press.

Logan, C. A. (2002). When scientific knowledge becomes scientific discovery: The disappearance of classical conditioning before Pavlov. *Journal of the History of the Behavioral Sciences, 38,* 393–403.

Luria, A. R. (1979). *The making of mind: A personal account of Soviet psychology* (M. Cole & S. Cole, Eds.). Cambridge, MA: Harvard University Press.

Macfarlane, D. A. (1930). The role of kinesthesis in maze learning. *University of California Publications in Psychology, 4,* 277–305.

Mach, E. (1914). *Analysis of sensations.* La Salle, IL: Open Court. (Original work published 1886)

MacLeod, C. M. (1992). The Stroop task: The "gold standard" of attention measures. *Journal of Experimental Psychology: General, 121,* 12–14.

Macmillan, M. (1986). A wonderful journey through skull and brain: The travels of Mr. Gage's tamping iron. *Brain and Cognition, 5,* 67–107.

Macmillan, M. (2000). *An odd kind of fame: Stories of Phineas Gage.* Cambridge, MA: MIT Press.

Maddox, B. (2006). *Freud's wizard: Ernest Jones and the transformation of psychoanalysis.* Cambridge, MA: Perseus.

Madigan, S., & O'Hara, R. (1992). Short-term memory at the turn of the century: Mary Whiton Calkins's memory research. *American Psychologist, 47,* 170–174.

Magendie, F. (1965). François Magendie (1783–1855) on spinal nerve roots, 1822. In R. J. Herrnstein & E. G. Boring (Eds.), *A sourcebook in the history of psychology* (pp. 19–22). Cambridge, MA: Harvard University Press. (Original work published 1822)

Malone, J. C. (1991). *Theories of learning: A historical approach.* Belmont, CA: Wadsworth.

Mankill, H. (2011). *The troubled man.* New York, NY: Knopf.

Marrow, A. J. (1969). *The practical theorist: The life and work of Kurt Lewin.* New York, NY: Basic Books.

Maslow, A. H. (1971). *The farther reaches of human nature.* New York, NY: Viking.

Maslow, A. H. (1954). *Motivation and personality.* New York, NY: Harper.

Mazlish, B. (1975). *James and John Stuart Mill: Father and son in the nineteenth century.* New York, NY: Basic Books.

McClelland, D. C. (1961). *The achieving society.* Princeton, NJ: Van Nostrand.

McCullough, D. (1992). *Brave companions: Portraits in history*. New York, NY: Simon & Schuster.

McDougall, W. (1908). *Introduction to social psychology*. London, UK: Methuen.

McGinnies, E. (1949). Emotionality and perceptual defense. *Psychological Review, 56,* 244–251.

McGuire, W. (Ed.). (1974). *The Freud/Jung letters*. Princeton, NJ: Princeton University Press.

McReynolds, P. (1987). Lightner Witmer: Little-known founder of clinical psychology. *American Psychologist, 42,* 849–858.

McReynolds, P. (1996). Lightner Witmer: The father of clinical psychology. In G. A. Kimble, C. A. Bonneau, & M. Wertheimer (Eds.), *Portraits of pioneers in psychology* (Vol. II, pp. 63–71). Washington, DC: American Psychological Association.

McReynolds, P. (1997). *Lightner Witmer: His life and times*. Washington, DC: American Psychological Association.

Meischner-Metge, A., & Meischner, W. (1997). Fechner and Lotze. In W. G. Bringmann, H. E. Lück, R., Miller, & C. E. Early (Eds.), *A pictorial history of psychology* (pp. 101–106). Chicago, IL: Quintessence Publishing.

Menand, W. (2011, March 14). Wild thing: Did the O.S.S. help win the war against Hitler? [Review of the book *Wild Bill Donovan* by Douglas Waller], *The New Yorker,* 69–73.

Menninger, K. (1963). *The vital balance: The life process in mental health and illness*. New York, NY: Viking Press.

Merton, R. K. (1961). Singletons and multiples in scientific discovery: A chapter in the sociology of science. *Proceedings of the American Philosophical Society, 105,* 470–486.

Micale, M. S. (1985). The Salpêtrière in the age of Charcot: An institutional perspective on medical history in the late nineteenth century. *Journal of Contemporary History, 20,* 703–731.

Miles, W. R. (1920). *Letter to Carl Seashore, September 3, 1920*. Walter R. Miles papers. Archives of the History of American Psychology, University of Akron, Akron, OH.

Miles, W. R. (1922). Static equilibrium as a useful test of motor control. *Journal of Industrial Hygiene, 3,* 316–331.

Miles, W. R. (1927). *Letter to Raymond Dodge, September 7, 1927*. Walter R. Miles papers. Archives of the History of American Psychology, University of Akron, Akron, OH.

Miles, W. R. (1928a). *Diary entry, March 28, 1928*. Walter R. Miles papers, Archives of the History of American Psychology, The University of Akron, Akron, Ohio.

Miles, W. R. (1928b). *Diary entry, March 30, 1928*. Walter Miles papers, Archives of the History of American Psychology, University of Akron, Akron, OH.

Miles, W. R. (1929a). *Diary entry, September 3, 1929*. Walter Miles papers, Archives of the History of American Psychology, University of Akron, Akron, OH.

Miles, W. R. (1929b). *Diary insertion*. Walter R. Miles papers, Archives of the History of American Psychology, The University of Akron, Akron, Ohio.

Miles, W. R. (1929c). *Letter to Edward C. Tolman, March 5, 1929*. Walter Miles papers, Archives of the History of American Psychology, University of Akron, Akron, OH.

Miles, W. R. (1929d). *Letter to Francis G. Benedict, October 14, 1929*. Walter Miles papers, Archives of the History of American Psychology, University of Akron, Akron, OH.

Miles, W. R. (1930). On the history of research with rats and mazes: A collection of notes. *Journal of General Psychology, 3,* 324–337.

Miles, W. R. (1931). *Diary entry, April 1, 1931*. Walter R. Miles papers, Archives of the History of American Psychology, The University of Akron, Akron, Ohio.

Miles, W. R. (1932). *Letter to B. C. Graves, February 19, 1932*. Walter R. Miles papers. Archives of the History of American Psychology, University of Akron, Akron, OH.

Miles, W. R. (1936). *Letter to E. G. Boring, December 4, 1936*. Walter Miles papers, Archives of the History of American Psychology, University of Akron, Akron, OH.

Miles, W. R. (1937). *Memorandum from Neal Miller on "Research for 1936–1937."* Walter Miles papers, Archives of the History of American Psychology, University of Akron, Akron, OH.

Miles, W. R., & Graves, B. C. (1931). Studies in physical exertion: III. Effects of signal variation on football charging. *Research Quarterly, 2,* 14–31.

Milgram, S. (1963). Behavioral study of obedience. *Journal of Abnormal and Social Psychology, 67,* 371–378.

Milgram, S. (1974). *Obedience to authority: An experimental view*. New York, NY: Harper & Row.

Mill, J. (1948). Analysis of the phenomena of the human mind. Excerpt in W. Dennis (Ed.), *Readings in the history of psychology* (pp. 140–154). New York, NY: Appleton-Century-Crofts. (Original work published 1829)

Mill, J. S. (1869). *The subjection of women*. London, UK: Longmans, Green, Reader, and Dyer.

Mill, J. S. (1987). *The logic of the moral sciences*. LaSalle, IL: Open Court Classics. (A reprinting of the sixth book of Mill's A system of logic, ratiocinative and inductive, being a connected view of the principles of evidence, and the methods of scientific investigation; Original work published 1843)

Mill, J. S. (1989). *Autobiography*. London, UK: Penguin. (Original work published 1873)

Miller, G. A. (1951). *Language and communication*. New York, NY: McGraw-Hill.

Miller, G. A. (1956). The magic number seven plus or minus two: Some limits on our capacity for processing information. *Psychological Review, 63*, 81–97.

Miller, G. A. (1992). The constitutive problem of psychology. In S. Koch & D. E. Leary (Eds.), *A century of psychology as science* (pp. 40–45). Washington, DC: American Psychological Association.

Miller, G. A., & Frick, F. C. (1949). Statistical behavioristics and sequences of responses. *Psychological Review, 56*, 311–324.

Miller, G. A., Galanter, E., & Pribram, K. H. (1960). *Plans and the structure of behavior*. New York, NY: Holt.

Miller, N. E., & Dollard, J. (1941). *Social learning and imitation*. New Haven, CT: Yale University Press.

Mills, E. S. (1974). George Trumbull Ladd: The great textbook writer. *Journal of the History of the Behavioral Sciences, 10*, 299–303.

Mills, J. A. (1988). The genesis of Hull's *Principles of Behavior*. *Journal of the History of the Behavioral Sciences, 24*, 392–401.

Mills, W. (1899). The nature of animal intelligence and the methods of investigating it. *Psychological Review, 6*, 262–274.

Minton, H. L. (1987). Lewis M. Terman and mental testing: In search of the democratic ideal. In M. M. Sokal (Ed.), *Psychological testing and American society, 1890–1930* (pp. 95–112). New Brunswick, NJ: Rutgers University Press.

Minton, H. L. (1988). *Lewis M. Terman: Pioneer in psychological testing*. New York, NY: New York University Press.

Monastersky, R. (1997, March 1). The call of catastrophes. *Science News, 151*, 20.

Montague, H., & Hollingworth, L. S. (1914). The comparative variability of the sexes at birth. *American Journal of Sociology, 20*, 342.

Moore, B. R., & Stuttard, S. (1979). Dr. Guthrie and *Felis domesticus* or: Tripping over the cat. *Science, 205*, 1031–1033.

Moore, T. V. (1939). *Cognitive psychology*. Philadelphia, PA: Lippincott.

Moorehead, A. (1969). *Darwin and the Beagle*. New York, NY: Harper & Row.

Morawski, J. G. (1986). Organizing knowledge and behavior at Yale's Institute of Human Relations. *Isis, 77*, 219–242.

Morgan, C. L. (1890). *Animal life and intelligence*. London, UK: Edward Arnold.

Morgan, C. L. (1903). *An introduction to comparative psychology*. London, UK: Walter Scott. (Original work published 1895)

Morgan, M. J. (1977). *Molyneux's question*. New York, NY: Cambridge University Press.

Morison, S. E. (1965). *The Oxford history of the American people*. New York: Oxford University Press.

Morris, E. K., & Bigelow, K. M. (2007, July). *Childrearing as the behaviorist views it: John B. Watson's advice in perspective*. Cheiron Society, University College, Dublin, Ireland.

Moskowitz, M. J. (1977). Hugo Münsterberg: A study in the history of applied psychology. *American Psychologist, 32*, 824–842.

Mowrer, O. H., & Mowrer, W. M. (1938). Enuresis—a method for its study and treatment. *American Journal of Orthopsychiatry, 8*, 436–459.

Münsterberg, H. (1908). *On the witness stand*. New York, NY: The McClure Company.

Münsterberg, H. (1909). *Psychotherapy*. New York, NY: Moffat, Yard.

Münsterberg, H. (1913). *Psychology and industrial efficiency*. New York, NY: Houghton Mifflin.

Murchison, C. (Ed.). (1926). *Psychologies of 1925*. Worcester, MA: Clark University Press.

Murchison, C. (Ed.). (1930). *Psychologies of 1930*. Worcester, MA: Clark University Press.

Murphy, G., & Ballou, R. O. (Eds.). (1960). *William James on physical research*. New York, NY: Viking.

Murray, H. A. (1938). *Explorations in personality: A clinical and experimental study of fifty men of college age*. New York, NY: Oxford University Press.

Napoli, D. S. (1981). *Architects of adjustment: The history of the psychological profession in the United States*. Port Washington, NY: Kennikat Press.

Neisser, U. (1967). *Cognitive psychology*. New York, NY: Appleton-Century-Crofts.

Neisser, U. (1976). *Cognition and reality*. San Francisco, CA: Freeman.

Neisser, U. (1988). Cognitive reflections. In W. Hirst (Ed.), *The making of cognitive science: Essays in honor of George A. Miller* (pp. 81–88). New York, NY: Cambridge University Press.

Neugebauer, R. (1978). Treatment of the mentally ill in medieval and early modern England: A reappraisal. *Journal of the History of the Behavioral Sciences, 14,* 158–169.

Newman, E. B. (1944). Max Wertheimer: 1880–1943. *American Journal of Psychology, 57,* 428–435.

Nicholson, I. A. M. (2003). *Inventing personality: Gordon Allport and the science of selfhood*. Washington, DC: American Psychological Association.

Nicolai, G. F. (1907). Die physiologische methodik zur erforschung der tierpsyche, ihre möglichkeit und ihre anwendung [The physiological method for research in animal psychology, its method and application]. *Journal für Psychologie und Neurologie, 10,* 1–27.

Nicolas, S., & Sanitioso, R. B. (2012). Alfred Binet and experimental psychology at the Sorbonne laboratory. *History of Psychology, 15,* 328–363.

Norcross, J. C., Castle, P. H., Sayette, M. A., & Mayne, T. J. (2004). The PsyD: Heterogeneity in practitioner training. *Professional Psychology: Research and Practice, 35,* 412–419.

O'Donnell, J. M. (1979a). The clinical psychology of Lightner Witmer: A case study of institutional innovation and intellectual change. *Journal of the History of the Behavioral Sciences, 15,* 3–17.

O'Donnell, J. M. (1979b). The crisis of experimentalism in the 1920s: E. G. Boring and his uses of history. *American Psychologist, 34,* 289–295.

O'Donnell, J. M. (1985). *The origins of behaviorism: American psychology, 1870–1920*. New York, NY: New York University Press.

Ogden, R. M. (1951). Oswald Külpe and the Würzburg school. *American Journal of Psychology, 64,* 4–19.

Okrent, D. (2010). *Last call: The rise and fall of Prohibition*. New York, NY: Scribner.

Oldfield, R. C. (1972). Frederick Charles Bartlett: 1886–1969. *American Journal of Psychology, 85,* 133–140.

Olds, J., & Milner, P. (1954). Positive reinforcement produced by electrical stimulation of septal area and other regions of rat brain. *Journal of Comparative and Physiological Psychology, 47,* 419–427.

Olton, D. S. (1979). Mazes, maps, and memory. *American Psychologist, 34,* 583–596.

O'Sullivan, J. J., & Quevillon, R. P. (1992). 40 years later: Is the Boulder model still alive? *American Psychologist, 47,* 67–70.

Pagano, V., Wicherski, M., & Kohout, J. L. (2010). *Faculty in U.S. and Canadian graduate departments of psychology: 2009–2010*. Center for Workforce Studies, American Psychological Association.

Palermo, D. (1971). Is a scientific revolution taking place in psychology? *Science Studies, 1,* 135–155.

Palmer, R. R. (1964). *A history of the modern world* (2nd ed.). New York, NY: Alfred A. Knopf.

Parkovnick, S. (2000). Contextualizing Floyd Allport's *Social Psychology*. *Journal of the History of the Behavioral Sciences, 36,* 429–441.

Parsons, H. M. (1974). What happened at Hawthorne? *Science, 183,* 922–932.

Pastore, N. (1990). Espionage. *Journal of the History of the Behavioral Sciences, 26,* 366–371.

Paul, G. L. (1966). *Insight vs. desensitization in psychotherapy*. Palo Alto, CA: Stanford University Press.

Pavlov, I. P. (1906, November). The scientific investigation of the psychical faculties or processes in the higher animals. *Science, 24,* 613–619.

Pavlov, I. P. (1928). *Lectures on conditioned reflexes* (W. H. Gantt, Trans.). New York, NY: International Publications.

Pavlov, I. P. (1960). *Conditioned reflexes: An investigation of the physiological activity of the cerebral cortex* (G. V. Anrep, Trans.). New York, NY: Dover. (Original work published by Oxford University Press in 1927)

Peatman, J. G. (1949). Policy and plans of APA. IV. How scientific and how professional is the American Psychological Association? *American Psychologist, 4,* 486–489.

Pegram, T. R. (1998). *Battling demon rum: The struggle for a dry America, 1800–1933*. Chicago, IL: Irvin R. Dee.

Penfield, W., & Perot, P. (1963). The brain's record of auditory and visual experience. *Brain, 86,* 595–696.

Perloff, R., & Naman, J. L. (1996). Lillian Gilbreth: Tireless advocate for a general psychology. In G. A. Kimble, C. A. Bonneau, & M. Wertheimer (Eds.), *Portraits of pioneers in psychology* (Vol. II, pp. 107–116). Washington, DC: American Psychological Association.

Perloff, R., & Perloff, L. S. (1977). The fair—an opportunity for depicting psychology and for conducting behavioral research. *American Psychologist, 32,* 220–229.

Pervin, E. J. (1991). *Introduction to personality* (5th ed.). New York, NY: HarperCollins.

Peterson, D. R. (1992). The doctor of psychology degree in professional psychology. In D. K. Freedheim (Ed.), *History of psychotherapy: A century of change* (pp. 829–849). Washington, DC: American Psychological Association.

Pettigrew, T. F. (1969). Gordon Willard Allport, 1897–1967. *Journal of Personality and Social Psychology, 12,* 1–5.

Philbrick, N. (2006). *Mayflower*. New York, NY: Viking.

Phillips, L. (2000). Recontextualizing Kenneth B. Clark: An Afrocentric perspective on the paradoxical legacy of a model psychologist-activist. *History of Psychology, 3,* 142–167

Piaget, J. (1952). Jean Piaget. In E. G. Boring, H. S. Langfeld, H. Werner, & R. M. Yerkes (Eds.), *A history of psychology in autobiography* (Vol. 4, pp. 237–256). New York, NY: Russell & Russell.

Piaget, J. (1959). *The language and thought of the child*. London, UK: Routledge and Kegan Paul. (Original work published 1923)

Pick, H. L., Jr. (1994). Eleanor J. Gibson: Learning to perceive and perceiving to learn. In R. D. Parke, P. A. Ornstein, J. J. Rieser, & C. Zahn-Waxler (Eds.), *A century of developmental psychology* (pp. 527–544). Washington, DC: American Psychological Association.

Pickren, W. E., & Tomes, H. (2002). The legacy of Kenneth B. Clark to the APA: The Board of Social and Ethical Responsibility for Psychology. *American Psychologist, 57,* 51–59.

Pillsbury, W. B. (1955). Harvey A. Carr: 1873–1954. *American Journal of Psychology, 67,* 149–151.

Poffenberger, A. T. (1940). Leta Stetter Hollingworth: 1886–1939. *American Journal of Psychology, 53,* 299–301.

Poffenberger, A. T. (1962). Robert Sessions Woodworth: 1869–1962. *American Journal of Psychology, 75,* 677–689.

Popplestone, J. A. (1975). Retrieval of primary sources. *Journal of the History of the Behavioral Sciences, 11,* 20–22.

Popplestone, J. A. (1987). The legacy of memory in apparatus and methodology. In W. Traxel (Ed.), *Ebbinghaus-Studien 2* (pp. 203–215). Passau, Germany: Passavia Universitätsverlag.

Popplestone, J. A., & McPherson, M. W. (1984). Pioneer psychology laboratories in clinical settings. In J. Brozek (Ed.), *Explorations in the history of psychology in the United States* (pp. 196–272). Lewisburg, PA: Bucknell University Press.

Popplestone, J. A., & McPherson, M. W. (1994). *An illustrated history of American psychology*. Dubuque, IA: Brown & Benchmark.

Porter, J. P. (1904). A preliminary study of the psychology of the English sparrow, *American Journal of Psychology, 15,* 313–346.

Prentice, W. C. H. (1951). Edgar John Rubin: 1886–1951. *American Journal of Psychology, 64,* 608–609.

Prytula, R. E., Oster, G. D., & Davis, S. F. (1977). The "rat rabbit" problem: What did John B. Watson really do? *Teaching of Psychology, 4,* 44–46.

Radbill, S. X. (1972). Robert Whytt. In C. C. Gillespie (Ed.), *Dictionary of scientific biography. Vol. XIV*. New York, NY: Scribner.

Raimy, V. C. (Ed.). (1950). *Training in clinical psychology*. Englewood Cliffs, NJ: Prentice-Hall.

Ramón y Cajal, S. (1999). *Advice for a young investigator*. (Trans. N. Swanson & L. W. Swanson). Cambridge, MA: MIT Press.

Raphelson, A. C. (1973). The pre-Chicago association of the early functionalists. *Journal of the History of the Behavioral Sciences, 9,* 115–122.

Reed, E. S. (1988). *James J. Gibson and the psychology of perception*. New Haven, CT: Yale University Press.

Reed, J. (1987). Robert M. Yerkes and the mental testing movement. In M. M. Sokal (Ed.), *Psychological testing and American society, 1890–1930* (pp. 75–94). New Brunswick, NJ: Rutgers University Press.

Reel, M. (2013). *Between man and beast: An unlikely explorer, the evolution debates, and the African adventure that took the Victorian world by storm*. New York, NY: Doubleday.

Restak, R. (1984). *The brain*. Toronto, Canada: Bantam Books.

Restle, F. (1957). Discrimination of cues in mazes: A resolution of the "place-vs.-response" question. *Psychological Review, 64,* 217–228.

Restle, F. (1980). The seer of Ithaca. *Contemporary Psychology, 25,* 291–293.

Richards, R. J. (1983). Why Darwin delayed, or interesting problems and models in the history of science. *Journal of the History of the Behavioral Sciences, 19,* 45–53.

Richardson, J. T. E. (2003). Howard Andrew Knox and the origins of performance testing on Ellis Island, 1912–1916. *History of Psychology, 6,* 143–170.

Richardson, R. D. (2007). *William James: In the maelstrom of American modernism.* Boston: Houghton Mifflin.

Rilling, M. (2000). How the challenge of explaining learning influenced the origins and development of John B. *Watson's behaviorism. American Journal of Psychology, 113,* 275–301.

Risse, G. B. (1976). Vocational guidance during the depression: Phrenology versus applied psychology. *Journal of the History of the Behavioral Sciences, 12,* 130–140.

Robinson, D. N. (1981). *An intellectual history of psychology* (2nd ed.). New York, NY: Macmillan.

Robinson, J. K., & Woodward, W. R. (1996). Experimental analysis of behavior at Harvard: From cumulative records to mathematical models. In L. D. Smith & W. R. Woodward (Eds.), *B. F. Skinner and behaviorism in American culture* (pp. 254–272). Bethlehem, PA: Lehigh University Press.

Roediger, H. L., III, & McDermott, K. B. (1995). Creating false memories: Remembering words not presented in lists. *Journal of Experimental Psychology: Learning Memory, and Cognition, 21,* 803–814.

Roediger, H. L., III. (1997). Remembering. *Contemporary Psychology, 42,* 488–492.

Roediger, H. L., III. (1985). Remembering Ebbinghaus. *Contemporary Psychology, 30,* 519–523.

Rogers, C. R. (1942). *Counseling and psychotherapy.* Boston, MA: Houghton Mifflin Company.

Rogers, C. R. (1954). Changes in the maturity of behavior as related to therapy. In C. R. Rogers & J. A. Precker (Eds.), *Psychotherapy and personality change* (pp. 215–237). Chicago, IL: University of Chicago Press.

Rogers, C. R. (1961a). Some hypotheses regarding the facilitation of personal growth. In C. R. Rogers (Ed.), *On becoming a person* (pp. 31–38). Boston, MA: Houghton Mifflin.

Rogers, C. R. (1961b). This is me. In C. R. Rogers (Ed.), *On becoming a person* (pp. 3–27). Boston, MA: Houghton Mifflin.

Rohles, F. H., Jr. (1992). Orbital bar pressing: A historical note on Skinner and the chimpanzees in space. *American Psychologist, 47,* 1531–1533.

Romanes, G. J. (1886). *Animal intelligence.* New York, NY: D. Appleton. (Original work published 1882)

Rosenzweig, S. (1992). *The historic expedition to America (1909): Freud, Jung, and Hall the king-maker.* St. Louis, MO: Rana House.

Rosnow, R. L., & Rosenthal, R. (1993). *Beginning behavioral research.* New York, NY: Macmillan.

Ross, D. (1969). The "zeitgeist" and American psychology. *Journal of the History of the Behavioral Sciences, 5,* 256–262.

Ross, D. (1972). *G. Stanley Hall: The psychologist as prophet.* Chicago, IL: University of Chicago Press.

Rubin, E. (1958). Figure and ground. In D. C. Beardslee & M. Wertheimer (Eds.), *Readings in perception* (pp. 194–203). Princeton, NJ: Van Nostrand. (Original work published 1915)

Rucci, A. J., & Tweney, R. D. (1980). Analysis of variance and the "second discipline" of scientific psychology: A historical account. *Psychological Bulletin, 87,* 166–184.

Ruch, F. L. (1935). *Letter to Walter R. Miles, December 18, 1935.* Walter Miles papers, Archives of the History of American Psychology, University of Akron, Akron, OH.

Ruch, F. L. (1937). *Psychology and life.* Glenview, IL: Scott, Foresman.

Ruse, M. (1979). *The Darwinian revolution: Science red in tooth and claw.* Chicago, IL: University of Chicago Press.

Russo, N. F. (1988). Women's participation in psychology: Reflecting and shaping the social context. In A. N. O'Connell & N. F. Russo (Eds.), *Models of achievement: Reflections of eminent women in psychology* (Vol. 2, pp. 9–27). Hillsdale, NJ: Erlbaum.

Rutherford, A. (2003). B. F. Skinner's technology of behavior in American life: From consumer culture to counterculture. *Journal of the History of the Behavioral Sciences, 39,* 1–23.

Ryan, W. C. (1939). *Studies in early graduate education.* New York, NY: Carnegie Foundation.

Sahakian, W. S. (1975). *History and systems of psychology.* New York, NY: Wiley.

Sahakian, W. S. (Ed.). (1968). *History of psychology: A source book in systematic psychology*. Itasca, IL: F. E. Peacock.

Samelson, F. (1981). Struggle for scientific authority: The reception of Watson's behaviorism in 1913. *Journal of the History of the Behavioral Sciences, 17,* 399–425.

Samelson, F. (1985). Organizing for the kingdom of behavior: Academic battles and organizational policies in the twenties. *Journal of the History of the Behavioral Sciences, 21,* 33–47.

Sanford, E. C. (1910). *Letter to E. B. Titchener, August 8, 1910.* Titchener papers, Cornell University, Ithaca, NY.

Satariano, W. A. (1979). Immigration and the popularization of social science, 1920 to 1930. *Journal of the History of the Behavioral Sciences, 15,* 310–320.

Satel, S., & Lilienfeld, S. O. (2013). *Brainwashed: The seductive appeal of mindless neuroscience*. New York, NY: Basic Books.

Scarborough, E., & Furumoto, L. (1987). *Untold lives: The first generation of American women psychologists*. New York, NY: Columbia University Press.

Schlereth, T. J. (1991). *Victorian America: Transformations in everyday life*. New York, NY: HarperCollins.

Schulman, B. J. (2001). *The seventies: The great shift in American culture, society, and politics*. Cambridge, MA: Perseus.

Schultz, D. P. (1981). *A history of modern psychology* (3rd ed.). New York, NY: Academic Press.

Schultz, D. P., & Schultz, S. E. (1987). *A history of modern psychology* (4th ed.). San Diego, CA: Harcourt, Brace, Jovanovich.

Scott, W. D. (1903). *The theory of advertising*. Boston, MA: Small & Maynard.

Scott, W. D. (1908). *The psychology of advertising*. Boston, MA: Small & Maynard.

Scott, W. D. (1911). *Increasing human efficiency in business*. New York, NY: Macmillan.

Scott-Kakures, D., Castagnetto, S., Benson, H., Taschek, W., & Hurley, P. (1993). *History of philosophy*. New York, NY: HarperCollins.

Scripture, E. W. (1895). *Thinking, feeling, doing*. New York, NY: Chautauqua-Century Press.

Searle, J. R. (1980). Minds, brains, and programs. *Behavioral and Brain Sciences, 3,* 417–424.

Sechenov, I. M. (1965). *Reflexes of the brain*. Cambridge, MA: MIT Press. (Original work published 1863)

Sechzer, J. A., (1983). The ethical dilemma of some classical animal experiments. *Annals of the New York Academy of Sciences, 406,* 5–12.

Segal, E. M., & Lachman, R. (1972). Complex behavior or higher mental processes: Is there a paradigm shift? *American Psychologist, 27,* 46–55.

Sex, race/ethnicity data available. (1995, Winter). *Trends in Education: APA Education Directorate News, 2*(1), 2–3.

Sexton, V. S. (1965). Clinical psychology: An historical survey. *Genetic Psychology Monographs, 72,* 401–434.

Shakow, D. (1930). Hermann Ebbinghaus. *American Journal of Psychology, 42,* 505–518.

Shannon, C. E., & Weaver, W. (1949). *The mathematical theory of communication*. Urbana, IL: University of Illinois Press.

Sheffield, F. D. (1959). Edwin Ray Guthrie: 1886–1959. *American Journal of Psychology, 72,* 642–650.

Shephard, B. (2001). *A war of nerves: Soldiers and psychiatrists in the twentieth century*. Cambridge, MA: Harvard University Press.

Sherrington, C. S. (1906). *The integrative action of the nervous system*. New Haven, CT: Yale University Press.

Shields, S. A. (1982). The variability hypothesis: History of a biological model of sex differences in intelligence. *Signs: Journal of Women in Culture and Society, 7,* 769–797.

Shorter, E. (1997). *A history of psychiatry: From the era of the asylum to the age of Prozac*. New York, NY: Wiley.

Simon, L. (1998). *Genuine reality: A life of William James*. Chicago, IL: University of Chicago Press.

Simonton, D. K. (1994). *Greatness: Who makes history and why*. New York, NY: Guilford Press.

Singer, C. A. (1957). *A short history of anatomy and physiology from the Greeks to Harvey*. New York, NY: Dover.

Skinner, B. F. (1938). *The behavior of organisms: An experimental analysis*. New York, NY: Appleton-Century-Crofts.

Skinner, B. F. (1945). An operational analysis of psychological terms. *Psychological Review, 52,* 270–277.

Skinner, B. F. (1948). *Walden two*. New York, NY: Macmillan.

Skinner, B. F. (1953). *Science and human behavior*. New York, NY: Macmillan.

Skinner, B. F. (1956). A case history in scientific method. *American Psychologist, 11,* 221–223.

Skinner, B. F. (1957). *Verbal behavior*. New York, NY: Appleton-Century-Crofts.

Skinner, B. F. (1960). Pigeons in a pelican. *American Psychologist, 15,* 28–37.

Skinner, B. F. (1979). *The shaping of a behaviorist.* New York, NY: Knopf.

Skinner, B. F. (1981). Pavlov's influence on psychology in America. *Journal of the History of the Behavioral Sciences, 17,* 242–245.

Skinner, B. F. (1987). Whatever happened to psychology as the science of behavior? *American Psychologist, 42,* 780–786.

Skinner, B. F. (1990). Can psychology be a science of the mind? *American Psychologist, 45,* 1206–1210.

Small, W. S. (1901). Experimental study of the mental processes of the rat. II. *American Journal of Psychology, 12,* 206–239.

Smith, L. D. (1992). On prediction and control: B. F. Skinner and the technological ideal of science. *American Psychologist, 47,* 216–223.

Smith, L. D. (1996a). Conclusion: Situating B. F. Skinner and behaviorism in American culture. In L. D. Smith & W. R. Woodward (Eds.), *B. F. Skinner and behaviorism in American culture* (pp. 294–315). Bethlehem, PA: Lehigh University Press.

Smith, L. D. (1996b). Knowledge as power: The Baconian roots of Skinner's social meliorism. In L. D. Smith & W. R. Woodward (Eds.), *B. F. Skinner and behaviorism in American culture* (pp. 56–82). Bethlehem, PA: Lehigh University Press.

Smith, L. D., Best, L. A., Cylke, V. A., & Stubbs, D. A. (2000). Psychology without *p* values: Dada analysis at the turn of the century. *American Psychologist, 55,* 260–263.

Smith, M. B. (1992). The American Psychological Association and social responsibility. In R. B. Evans, V. S. Sexton, & T. C. Cadwallader (Eds.), *The American Psychological Association: A historical perspective* (pp. 327–345). Washington, DC: American Psychological Association.

Sobel, D. (1995). *Longitude: The true story of a lone genius who solved the greatest scientific problem of his time.* New York: Walker.

Sobel, D. (2000). *Galileo's daughter: A historical memoir of science, faith, and love.* New York, NY: Penguin.

Sokal, M. M. (1971). The unpublished autobiography of James McKeen Cattell. *American Psychologist, 26,* 626–635.

Sokal, M. M. (1980). Biographical approach: The psychological career of Edward Wheeler Scripture. In J. Brozek & L. J. Pongratz (Eds.), *Historiography of modern psychology: Aims, resources, approaches* (pp. 255–278). Toronto, Canada: C. J. Hogrefe.

Sokal, M. M. (1981b). The origins of the Psychological Corporation. *Journal of the History of the Behavioral Sciences, 17,* 54–67.

Sokal, M. M. (1984). The Gestalt psychologists in behaviorist America. *American Historical Review, 89,* 1240–1263.

Sokal, M. M. (1987). James McKeen Cattell and mental anthropometry: Nineteenth-century science and reform and the origins of psychological testing. In M. M. Sokal (Ed.), *Psychological testing and American society* (pp. 21–45). New Brunswick, NJ: Rutgers University Press.

Sokal, M. M. (1992). Origins and early years of the American Psychological Association, 1890–1906. *American Psychologist, 47,* 111–122.

Sokal, M. M. (2009). James McKeen Cattell, Nicholas Murray Butler, and academic freedom at Columbia University, 1902–1923. *History of Psychology, 12,* 87–122.

Sokal, M. M. (Ed.). (1981a). *An education in psychology: James McKeen Cattell's journal and letters from Germany and England, 1880–1888.* Cambridge, MA: The MIT Press.

Sokal, M. M., & Rafail, P. A. (1982). *A guide to manuscript collections in the history of psychology and selected areas.* Millwood, NY: Kraus International.

Solso, R. L. (Ed.). (1973). *Contemporary issues in cognitive psychology: The Loyola symposium.* Washington, DC: V. H. Winston.

Spalding, D. A. (1873). Instinct, with original observations on young animals. *Macmillan's Magazine, 27,* 282–293.

Spence, J. T. (1987). Centrifugal versus centripetal tendencies in psychology: Will the center hold? *American Psychologist, 42,* 1052–1054.

Spence, K. W. (1952). Clark Leonard Hull: 1884–1952. *American Journal of Psychology, 65,* 639–646.

Sperry, R. W. (1961). Cerebral organization and behavior. *Science, 133,* 1749–1757.

Sperry, R. W. (1993). The impact and promise of the cognitive revolution. *American Psychologist, 48,* 878–885.

Spillman, J., & Spillman, L. (1993). The rise and fall of Hugo Münsterberg. *Journal of the History of the Behavioral Sciences, 29,* 322–338.

Sprung, H. (1997). Carl Stumpf. In W. G. Bringmann, H. E. Lück, R.,Miller, & C. E. Early (Eds.), *A pictorial history of psychology* (pp. 247–250). Chicago, IL: Quintessence Publishing.

Spurzheim, J. G. (1978). Outlines of phrenology. In D. N. Robinson (Ed.), *Significant contributions to the history of psychology. Series E. Volume* II. Washington, DC: University Publications of America. (Original work published 1832)

Sterns, C. Z. (1985). Victorian sexuality: Can historians do it better? *Journal of Social History, 18,* 625–634.

Stetson, G. R. (1897). Some memory tests of whites and blacks. *Psychological Review, 4,* 285–289.

Steudel, J. (1972). Johannes Peter Müller. In C. C. Gillespie (Ed.), *Dictionary of scientific biography. Vol. IX.* New York, NY: Scribner.

Stevens, S. S. (1935). The operational definition of concepts. *Psychological Review, 42,* 517–527.

Stocking, G. W., Jr. (1965). On the limits of "presentism" and "historicism" in the historiography of the behavioral sciences. *Journal of the History of the Behavioral Sciences, 1,* 211–217.

Stricker, G., & Cummings, N. A. (1992). The professional school movement. In D. K. Freedheim (Ed.), *History of psychotherapy: A century of change* (pp. 801–828). Washington, DC: American Psychological Association.

Stroebe, W. (2012). The truth about Triplett (1898), but nobody seems to care. *Perspectives on Psychological Science, 7,* 54–57.

Stroop, J. R. (1992). Studies of interference in serial verbal reactions. *Journal of Experimental Psychology: General, 121,* 15–23. (Original work published 1935)

Strunk, O., Jr. (1972). The self-psychology of Mary Whiton Calkins. *Journal of the History of the Behavioral Sciences, 8,* 196–203.

Sulloway, F. J. (1979). *Freud: Biologist of the mind.* New York, NY: Basic Books.

Sulloway, F. J. (1982). Darwin and his finches: The evolution of a legend. *Journal of the History of Biology, 15,* 1–53.

Swazey, J. P. (1972). Charles Scott Sherrington. In C. C. Gillespie (Ed.), *Dictionary of scientific biography. Vol. XII.* New York, NY: Scribner.

Taylor, D. W. (1972). Santiago Ramón y Cajal. In C. C. Gillespie (Ed.), *Dictionary of scientific biography. Vol XI.* New York, NY: Scribner.

Temkin, O. (1947). Gall and the phrenological movement. *Bulletin of the History of Medicine, 21,* 275–321.

Terman, L. M. (1906). Genius and stupidity: A study of some of the intellectual processes of seven "bright" and seven "stupid" boys. *Pedagogical Seminary, 13,* 307–373.

Terman, L. M. (1924). The mental test as a psychological method. *Psychological Review, 31,* 93–117.

Terman, L. M. (1925). *Genetic studies of genius: Vol. 1. Mental and physical traits of a thousand gifted children.* Stanford, CA: Stanford University Press.

Terman, L. M., & Oden, M. H. (1947). *Genetic studies of genius: Vol. 4. The gifted child grows up: Twenty-five years' follow-up of a superior group.* Stanford, CA: Stanford University Press.

Terman, L. M., & Oden, M. H. (1959). *Genetic studies of genius: Vol. 5. The gifted group at mid-life: Thirty-five years' follow-up of the superior child.* Stanford, CA: Stanford University Press.

Teuber, M. L. (1994). The founding of the primate station, Teneriffe, Canary Islands. *American Journal of Psychology, 107,* 551–581.

Thompson, A. S. (1998). Morris S. Viteles. *American Psychologist, 53,* 1153–1154.

Thomson, K. S. (1975). HMS *Beagle,* 1820–1870. *American Scientist, 63,* 664–672.

Thorndike, E. L. (1899). A reply to "The nature of animal intelligence and the methods of investigating it." *Psychological Review, 6,* 412–420.

Thorndike, E. L. (1900). Comparative psychology. *Psychological Review, 7,* 424–426.

Thorndike, E. L. (1913). *Educational psychology.* New York, NY: Teacher's College.

Thorndike, E. L. (1914). *Educational psychology: The briefer course.* New York, NY: Teacher's College.

Thorndike, E. L. (1936). Edward Lee Thorndike. In C. Murchison (Ed.), *A history of psychology in autobiography* (Vol. 3, pp. 263–270). Worcester, MA: Clark University Press.

Thorndike, E. L. (1948). Animal intelligence. In W. Dennis (Ed.), *Readings in the history of psychology* (pp. 377–387). New York, NY: Appleton-Century-Crofts. (Original work published 1898)

Thorndike, E. L. (2000). *Animal intelligence: Experimental studies*. New Brunswick, NJ: Transaction Publishers. (Original work published 1911)

Thorndike, E. L., & Woodworth, R. S. (1901). The influence of improvement in one mental function upon the efficiency of other functions. I. *Psychological Review, 8,* 247–261.

Thorndike, R. L. (1991). Edward L. Thorndike: A professional and personal appreciation. In G. A. Kimble, M. Wertheimer, & C. L. White (Eds.), *Portraits of pioneers in psychology* (pp. 139–151). Washington, DC: American Psychological Association.

Titchener, E. B. (1895). Note. *American Journal of Psychology, 7,* 448–449.

Titchener, E. B. (1897). *Letter to Walter Pillsbury, October 26, 1897*. Titchener papers, Cornell University, Ithaca, NY.

Titchener, E. B. (1898a). *Letter to Hugo Münsterberg, October 12, 1898*. Titchener papers, Cornell University, Ithaca, NY.

Titchener, E. B. (1898b). Postulates of a structural psychology. *Psychological Review, 7,* 449–465.

Titchener, E. B. (1898c). A psychological laboratory. *Mind (n.s.), 7,* 311–331.

Titchener, E. B. (1899). *An outline of psychology*. New York, NY: Macmillan. (Original work published 1896)

Titchener, E. B. (1901). *Experimental psychology: A manual of laboratory practice: Vol. 1. Qualitative experiments. Part 1: Student's manual; part 2: Instructor's manual*. New York, NY: Macmillan.

Titchener, E. B. (1905a). *Experimental psychology: A manual of laboratory practice: Vol. 2. Quantitative experiments. Part 1: Student's manual; part 2: Instructor's manual*. New York, NY: Macmillan.

Titchener, E. B. (1905b). Review [of Thorndike's Elements of Psychology]. *Mind, 56,* 552–554.

Titchener, E. B. (1906). *Letter to L. N. Wilson, June 6, 1906*. Wilson Papers, Clark University, Worcester, MA.

Titchener, E. B. (1909). *A text-book of psychology*. New York, NY: Macmillan.

Titchener, E. B. (1914). On "Psychology as the behaviorist views it." *Proceedings of the American Philosophical Society, 53,* 1–17.

Titchener, E. B. (1921a). George Trumbull Ladd. *American Journal of Psychology, 32,* 600–601.

Titchener, E. B. (1921b). Wilhelm Wundt. *American Journal of Psychology, 32,* 161–178.

Todd, J. T. (1994). What psychology has to say about John B. Watson: Classical behaviorism in psychology textbooks, 1920–1989. In J. T. Todd & E. K. Morris (Eds.), *Modern perspectives on John B. Watson and classical behaviorism* (pp. 75–107). Westport, CT: Greenwood Press.

Todd, J. T., & Morris, E. K. (1986). The early research of John B. Watson: Before the behavioral revolution. *The Behavior Analyst, 9,* 71–88.

Todes, D. (2000). *Ivan Pavlov: Exploring the animal machine*. New York, NY: Oxford University Press.

Todes, D. P. (1995). Pavlov and the Bolsheviks. *History and Philosophy of the Life Sciences, 17,* 379–418.

Todes, D. P. (1997a). From the machine to the ghost within: Pavlov's transition from digestive physiology to conditional reflexes. *American Psychologist, 52,* 947–955.

Todes, D. P. (1997b). Pavlov's physiological factory. *Isis, 88,* 205–246.

Tolman, E. C. (1922). A new formula for behaviorism. *Psychological Review, 29,* 44–53.

Tolman, E. C. (1929a). *Letter to Walter R. Miles, February 26, 1929*. Walter Miles papers, Archives of the History of American Psychology, University of Akron, Akron, OH.

Tolman, E. C. (1929b). *Letter to Walter R. Miles, May 23, 1929*. Walter Miles papers, Archives of the History of American Psychology, University of Akron, Akron, OH.

Tolman, E. C. (1932). *Purposive behavior in animals and men*. New York, NY: Appleton-Century-Crofts.

Tolman, E. C. (1938a). The determiners of behavior at a choice point. *Psychological Review, 45,* 1–41.

Tolman, E. C. (1938b). *Letter to Walter R. Miles, May 28, 1938*. Walter Miles papers, Archives of the History of American Psychology, University of Akron, Akron, OH.

Tolman, E. C. (1942). *Drives toward war*. New York, NY: D. Appleton-Century Company.

Tolman, E. C. (1948). Cognitive maps in rats and men. *Psychological Review, 55,* 189–208.

Tolman, E. C. (1952). Edward Chace Tolman. In E. G. Boring, H. S. Langfeld, H. Werner, & R. M. Yerkes (Eds.), *A history of psychology in autobiography* (Vol. 4, pp. 323–339). Worcester, MA: Clark University Press.

Tolman, E. C. (1959). Principles of purposive behavior. In S. Koch (Ed.), *Psychology: A study of a science. Study 1* (Vol. 2, pp. 92–157). New York, NY: McGraw-Hill.

Tolman, E. C., & Honzik, C. H. (1930). Introduction and removal of reward, and maze performance in rats. *University of California Publications in Psychology, 4,* 257–275.

Tolman, E. C., Ritchie, B. F., & Kalish, D. (1946a). Studies in spatial learning. I. Orientation and the short-cut. *Journal of Experimental Psychology, 36,* 13–24.

Tolman, E. C., Ritchie, B. F., & Kalish, D. (1946b). Studies in spatial learning. II. Place learning versus response learning. *Journal of Experimental Psychology, 36,* 221–229.

Tolstoy, L. (1942). *War and peace* (L. Maude & A. Maude, Trans.). New York, NY: Simon and Schuster. (Original work published 1869)

Triplett, N. (1898). The dynamogenic factors in pacemaking and competition. *American Journal of Psychology, 9,* 507–533.

Triplett, R. G. (1982). The relationship of Clark L. Hull's hypnosis research to his later learning theory: The continuity of a life's work. *Journal of the History of the Behavioral Sciences, 18,* 22–31.

Tryon, R. C. (1963). Psychology in flux: The academic-professional polarity. *American Psychologist, 18,* 134-143.

Turing, A. M. (1950). Computing machinery and intelligence. *Mind, 59,* 433–460.

Turner, R. S. (1972). Hermann von Helmholtz. In C. C. Gillespie (Ed.), *Dictionary of scientific biography.* Vol. VI. New York: Scribner.

Twitmyer, E. B. (1905). Knee-jerks without stimulation of the patellar tendon. *Psychological Bulletin, 2,* 43–44.

Valenstein, E. S. (2010). *Great and desperate cures: The rise and decline of psychosurgery and other radical treatments for mental illness.* Ann Arbor, MI: Elliot Valenstein.

Valentine, C. W. (1930). The innate bases of fear. *Journal of Genetic Psychology, 37,* 394–420.

Vandenbos, G. R., Cummings, N. A., & DeLeon, P. H. (1992). A century of psychotherapy: Economic and environmental influences. In D. K. Freedheim (Ed.), *History of psychotherapy: A century of change* (pp. 65–102). Washington, DC: American Psychological Association.

van Drunen, P. (1997). Psychotechnics. In W. G. Bringmann, H. E. Lück, R. Miller, & C. E. Early (Eds.), *A pictorial history of psychology* (pp. 480–484). Chicago, IL: Quintessence Books.

van Strien, P. J. (1998). Early applied psychology between essentialism and pragmatism: The dynamics of theory, tools, and clients. *History of Psychology, 1,* 205–234.

Veysey, L. R. (1965). *The emergence of the American university.* Chicago, IL: University of Chicago Press.

Vinchur, A. J. (2007). Early contributions to the science and practice of industrial psychology. In L. L. Koppes (Ed.), *Historical perspectives in industrial and organizational psychology* (pp. 37–58). Mahwah, NJ: Erlbaum.

Viney, W. (1996). Dorothea Dix: An intellectual conscience for psychology. In G. A. Kimble, C. A. Bonneau, & M. Wertheimer (Eds.), *Portraits of pioneers in psychology* (Vol. II, pp. 15–31). Washington, DC: American Psychological Association.

Viney, W., & Zorich, S. (1982). Contributions to the history of psychology: XXIX. Dorothea Dix and the history of psychology. *Psychological Reports, 50,* 211–218.

Viteles, M. S. (1932). *Industrial psychology.* New York, NY: Norton.

Voyat, G. (1981). Jean Piaget: 1896–1980. *American Journal of Psychology, 94,* 645–648.

Vrooman, J. R. (1970). *René Descartes: A biography.* New York, NY: Putnam.

Wade, N. J. (1994). Hermann von Helmholtz. *Perception, 23,* 981–989.

Wallin, J. E. W. (1966). A red-letter day in APA history. *Journal of General Psychology, 75,* 107–114.

Warner, L. H., & Warden, C. J. (1927). The development of a standardized animal maze. *Archives of Psychology, 15 (No. 92).*

Warr, P. (2007). Some historical developments in I-O psychology outside the United States. In L. L. Koppes (Ed.), *Historical perspectives in industrial and organizational psychology* (pp. 81–107). Mahwah, NJ: Erlbaum.

Warren, R. M. (1984). Helmholtz and his continuing influence. *Music Perception, 1,* 253–275.

Washburn, M. F. (1908). *The animal mind.* New York, NY: Macmillan.

Washburn, M. F. (1932). Margaret Floy Washburn. In C. Murchison (Ed.), *A history of psychology in autobiography* (Vol. 2, pp. 333–358). Worcester, MA: Clark University Press.

Washburn, M. F. (1935). James Mark Baldwin (1861–1934). *American Journal of Psychology, 47,* 168–169.

Waterman, A. S. (2013). The humanistic psychology—positive psychology divide. *American Psychologist, 68,* 124–133.

Watson, J. B. (1903). *Animal education: An experimental study of the psychical development of the white rat, correlated with the growth of its nervous system.* Chicago, IL: University of Chicago Press.

Watson, J. B. (1907). Kinesthetic and organic sensations: Their role in the reactions of the white rat to the maze. *Psychological Review Monograph Supplements, 8 (#33).*

Watson, J. B. (1909). Some experiments bearing upon color vision in monkeys. *Journal of Comparative Neurology and Psychology, 19,* 1–28.

Watson, J. B. (1910, February). The new science of animal behavior. *Harper's Monthly Magazine, 120,* 346–353.

Watson, J. B. (1913). Psychology as the behaviorist views it. *Psychological Review, 20,* 158–177.

Watson, J. B. (1914). *Behavior: An introduction to comparative psychology.* New York, NY: Holt.

Watson, J. B. (1916). The place of the conditioned reflex in psychology. *Psychological Review, 23,* 89–116.

Watson, J. B. (1919). *Psychology from the standpoint of the behaviorist.* Philadelphia, PA: Lippincott.

Watson, J. B. (1926, June). How we think: A behaviorist's view. *Harper's Monthly Magazine, 153,* 40–45.

Watson, J. B. (1928). *Psychological care of infant and child.* New York, NY: Norton.

Watson, J. B. (1930). *Behaviorism* (2nd ed.). New York: Norton. (Original work published 1924)

Watson, J. B. (1936). Autobiography. In C. Murchison (Ed.), *A history of psychology in autobiography* (Vol. 3, pp. 271–281). Worcester, MA: Clark University Press.

Watson, J. B., & Morgan, J. J. B. (1917). Emotional reactions and psychological experimentation. *American Journal of Psychology, 28,* 163–174.

Watson, J. B., & Rayner, R. (1920). Conditioned emotional reactions. *Journal of Experimental Psychology, 3,* 1–14.

Watson, R. I. (1953). A brief history of clinical psychology. *Psychological Bulletin, 50,* 321–346.

Watson, R. I. (1960). The history of psychology: A neglected area. *American Psychologist, 15,* 251–255.

Watson, R. I., & Evans, R. B. (1991). *The great psychologists: A history of psychological thought* (5th ed.). New York, NY: HarperCollins.

Weaver, K. A. (1998). Capturing the fervor of cognitive psychology's emergence. *Teaching of Psychology, 25,* 136–138.

Webb, M. E. (1988). A new history of Hartley's "Observations on Man." *Journal of the History of the Behavioral Sciences, 24,* 202–211.

Weiner, J. (1994). *The beak of the finch.* New York, NY: Vintage Books.

Weiten, W., & Wight, R. D. (1992). Portraits of a discipline: An examination of introductory psychology textbooks in America. In A. E. Puente, J. R. Matthews, & C. L. Brewer (Eds.), *Teaching psychology in America: A history* (pp. 453–504). Washington, DC: American Psychological Association.

Wertheimer, M. (1965). Experimental studies on the seeing of motion. In R. J. Herrnstein & E. G. Boring (Eds.), *A sourcebook in the history of psychology* (pp. 163–168). Cambridge, MA: Harvard University Press. (Original work published 1912)

Wertheimer, M. (1967a). Gestalt theory. In W. D. Ellis (Ed.), *A source book of Gestalt psychology* (pp. 1–11). London, UK: Routledge and Kegan Paul. (Original talk delivered 1924)

Wertheimer, M. (1967b). Laws of organization in perceptual forms. In W. D. Ellis (Ed.), *A source book of Gestalt psychology* (pp. 71–88). London, UK: Routledge and Kegan Paul. (Original work published 1923)

Wertheimer, M. (1978). Humanistic psychology and the humane but tough-minded psychologist. *American Psychologist, 33,* 739–745.

Wertheimer, M. (1982). *Productive thinking.* Chicago, IL: University of Chicago Press. (Original work published 1945)

White, M. (1997). *Isaac Newton: The last sorcerer.* Reading, MA: Perseus Books.

White, R. K. (1978). Has "field theory" been "tried and found wanting"? *Journal of the History of the Behavioral Sciences, 14,* 242–246.

Whytt, R. (1751). *Essay on the vital and other involuntary motions of animals.* Edinburgh, UK: Hamilton, Balfour, & Neill.

Wiggins, J. G. Jr. (1994). Would you want your child to be a psychologist? *American Psychologist, 49,* 485–492.

Williams, D. H., Bellis, E. C., & Wellington, S. W. (1980). Deinstitutionalization and social policy: Historical perspectives and present dilemmas. *American Journal of Orthopsychiatry, 50,* 54–64.

Willis, T. (1965). *The anatomy of the brain.* Montreal, CA: McGill University Press. (Original work published 1664)

Windholtz, G. (1990). Pavlov and the Pavlovians in the laboratory. *Journal of the History of the Behavioral Sciences, 26,* 64–74.

Windholz, G. (1986). A comparative analysis of the conditional reflex discoveries of Pavlov and Twitmyer, and the birth of a paradigm. *Pavlovian Journal of Biological Science, 21,* 141–147.

Windholz, G. (1997). Ivan P. Pavlov: An overview of his life and psychological work. *American Psychologist, 52,* 941–946.

Windholz, G., & Lamal, P. A. (1985). Köhler's insight revisited. *Teaching of Psychology, 12,* 165–167.

Winston, A. S. (1990). Robert Sessions Woodworth and the "Columbia Bible": How the psychological experiment was redefined. *American Journal of Psychology, 103,* 391–401.

Winston, A. S. (1996a). "As his name indicates": R. S. Woodworth's letters of reference and employment for Jewish psychologists in the 1930s. *Journal of the History of the Behavioral Sciences, 32,* 30–43.

Winston, A. S. (Ed.). (1996b). *Defining difference: Race and racism in the history of psychology.* Washington, DC: American Psychological Association.

Winters, B. (1950). Franz Anton Mesmer: An inquiry into the antecedents of hypnosis. *Journal of General Psychology, 43,* 63–75.

Wispe, L., Awkward, J., Hoffman, M., Ash, P., Hicks, L. H., & Porter, J. (1969). The Negro psychologist in America. *American Psychologist, 24,* 142–150.

Wissler, C. (1965). Clark Wissler (1870–1947) on the inadequacy of mental tests. In R. J. Herrnstein & E. G. Boring (Eds.), *A sourcebook in the history of psychology* (pp. 442–445). Cambridge, MA: Harvard University Press. (Original work published 1901)

Witmer, L. (1893). *Letter to Hugo Münsterberg, July 14, 1893.* Münsterberg papers, Boston Public Library, Boston, MA.

Witmer, L. (1909). The study and treatment of retardation: A field of applied psychology. *Psychological Bulletin, 6,* 121–127.

Witmer, L. (1911). Criminals in the making. *The Psychological Clinic, 4,* 221–238.

Witmer, L. (1931). Clinical psychology. In R. A. Brotemarkle (Ed.), *Clinical psychology: Studies in honor of Lightner Witmer* (pp. 341–352). Philadelphia, PA: University of Pennsylvania Press. (Original work published 1907)

Wolpe, J. (1958). *Psychotherapy by reciprocal inhibition.* Palo Alto, CA: Stanford University Press.

Woodward, W. R. (2010). Russian women émigrés in psychology: Informal Jewish networks. *History of Psychology, 13,* 111–137.

Woodworth, R. S. (1917). Some criticisms of the Freudian psychology. *American Journal of Psychology, 12,* 174–194.

Woodworth, R. S. (1918). *Dynamic psychology.* New York, NY: Columbia University Press.

Woodworth, R. S. (1921). *Psychology.* New York, NY: Holt.

Woodworth, R. S. (1931). *Contemporary schools of psychology.* New York, NY: Ronald Press.

Woodworth, R. S. (1932). Robert S. Woodworth. In C. Murchison (Ed.), *A history of psychology in autobiography* (Vol. 2, pp. 359–380). Worcester, MA: Clark University Press.

Woodworth, R. S. (1937). The future of clinical psychology. *Journal of Consulting Psychology, 1,* 4–5.

Woodworth, R. S. (1938). *Experimental psychology.* New York, NY: Holt.

Woodworth, R. S. (1958). *Dynamics of behavior.* New York, NY: Holt.

Woodworth, R. S., & Schlosberg, H. (1954). *Experimental psychology* (2nd ed.). New York, NY: Holt.

Wozniak, R. H. (2009). Consciousness, social heredity, and development: The evolutionary thought of James Mark Baldwin. *American Psychologist, 64,* 93–101.

Wozniak, R. H., & Santiago-Blay, J. (2013). Trouble at Tyson Alley: James Mark Baldwin's arrest in a Baltimore bordello. *History of Psychology, 16,* 227–248.

Wright, R. (1994). *The moral animal.* New York, NY: Random House.

Wundt, W. (1862). *Contribution to a theory of sense perception.* Leipzig, Germany: Winter.

Wundt, W. (1897). *Outlines of psychology* (C. H. Judd, Trans.). Leipzig, Germany: Wilhelm Engelman.

Wundt, W. (1904). *Principles of physiological psychology* (5th ed.) (E. B. Titchener, Trans.). New York, NY: Macmillan. (Original work published 1873–1874)

Wundt, W. (1907). *Lectures on human and animal psychology* (J. Creighton & E. B. Titchener, Trans.). New York, NY: Macmillan. (Original work published 1863)

Yanni, C. (2007). *The architecture of madness: Insane asylums in the United States.* Minneapolis, MN: University of Minnesota Press.

Yerkes, R. M. (1911). *Introduction to psychology.* New York, NY: Holt.

Yerkes, R. M. (Ed.). (1921). Psychological examining in the United States Army. *Memoirs of the National Academy of Sciences, 15,* 1–890.

Yerkes, R. M., & Morgulis, S. (1909). The method of Pawlow in animal psychology. *Psychological Bulletin, 6,* 257–273.

Yoakum, C. S., & Yerkes, R. M. (1920). *Army mental tests.* New York, NY: Holt.

Young, R. M. (1972). Franz Joseph Gall. In C. C. Gillespie (Ed.), *Dictionary of scientific biography. Vol. V.* New York, NY: Scribner.

Youniss, J. (2006). G. Stanley Hall and his times: Too much so, yet not enough. *History of Psychology, 9,* 224–235.

Zajonc, R. B. (1980). Feeling and thinking: Preferences need no inferences. *American Psychologist, 35,* 151–175.

Zajonc, R. B. (1990). Leon Festinger (1919–1989). *American Psychologist, 45,* 661–662.

Zeigarnik, B. (1967). On finished and unfinished tasks. In W. D. Ellis (Ed.), *A source book of Gestalt psychology* (pp. 300–314). London, UK: Routledge and Kegan Paul. (Original work published 1927)

Zenderland, L. (1988). Education, evangelism, and the origins of clinical psychology: The child-study legacy. *Journal of the History of the Behavioral Sciences, 24,* 152–165.

Zenderland, L. (1998). *Measuring minds: Henry Herbert Goddard and the origins of American intelligence testing.* New York, NY: Cambridge University Press.

Zilboorg, G. (1941). *A history of medical psychology.* New York, NY: Norton.

GLOSSARY

Ablation   Method of studying the brain, pioneered by Flourens, in which the function of some brain area is assessed after that portion of the brain has been destroyed.

Accommodation   Visual phenomenon described by Berkeley; the tendency of the lens of the eye to change shape as objects move toward and away from the person.

Act psychology   Brentano's position that psychology should be the study of mental acts, not mental contents; with the perception of some event, for example, one should not analyze it into its elements, but examine the act of perception (how the individual perceives the event and what the event means to the individual).

Analytical Psychology   Jung's theory of psychology, which differed from Freud's in a number of ways, including a decreased emphasis on sex.

Anecdotal Evidence   Research method in which evidence takes the form of an accumulation of examples supporting some principle or theory; associated with Romanes and the origins of comparative psychology; also used by phrenologists; heavy reliance on such evidence leads one to ignore counterinstances that might disprove a hypothesis.

Animal Magnetism   Belief held by Mesmer and contemporaries that living organisms were influenced by magnetic forces and that cures for illness could result from the proper use of magnets.

Animal Spirits   Hypothetical essence once believed (e.g., by Descartes) to inhabit the nervous system and to be the driving force behind muscle movement.

Anna O. Case   Famous case of hysteria treated by Breuer and reported by Breuer and Freud in *Studies on Hysteria*; gave Freud the insight that hysterics suffer from their memories of traumatic events; details distorted over the years.

Anthropomorphism   Tendency to attribute human characteristics to nonhuman entities; associated with Romanes and the origins of comparative psychology.

Antithesis   Darwin's principle of emotional expression, stating that some emotions that were the opposite of each other were reflected in expressions that were likewise opposed.

Apparent Motion   Phenomenon studied by Wertheimer in which stationary stimuli appear to move under certain circumstances.

Apperception   A high level of awareness, in which we focus our full attention on some object and apprehend it fully; associated with Leibniz originally; central concept for Wundt's psychology.

Apperceptive Mass   Term used by Herbart for an interrelated group of ideas at the forefront of consciousness.

Approach–Approach Conflict   For Lewin, a situation in which a conflict exists within a person, resulting from having to make a choice between two goals with a positive valence.

Approach–Avoidance Conflict   For Lewin, a situation in which a conflict exists within a person, occurring when a goal elicits both approach and avoidance tendencies.

Archive   A repository of unpublished data of use to historians.

Argument from Design   Explained the great complexity in nature by arguing that it required a superior being (i.e., God) to produce it; associated with Reverend Paley.

Army Alpha   Group intelligence test developed by Yerkes for testing the abilities of literate soldiers in World War I.

Army Beta   Group intelligence test developed by Yerkes for testing the abilities of illiterate soldiers in World War I.

Association   For Locke, analogous to Newtonian gravity; a force that attracts ideas.

Associationism   Philosophical school of thought, related to empiricism, which emphasizes the rules by which relationships between ideas and experiences are formed.

Atomism   Belief that nature can be understood best by reducing complexity to its smallest, most fundamental elements (opposed to holism).

Attributes   In Titchener's system, these were the ways of classifying the various elements of conscious experience; for example, the element of sensation had the attributes of quality, intensity, duration, and clarity.

Attrition   Methodological problem in longitudinal research, when participants drop out of the study; notably low in Terman's longitudinal study of giftedness.

Avoidance–Avoidance Conflict   For Lewin, a situation in which a conflict exists within a person, resulting from having to make a choice between two goals with a negative valence.

Baldwin Effect   James Mark Baldwin's idea that certain forms of learning, especially social learning, could be subject to natural selection.

Behavioral Environment   For the gestaltists, this referred to the environment as perceived, as contrasted with the physical environment (the geographical environment).

Behaviorist Manifesto   Watson's 1913 paper that argued for a behaviorist approach to psychology.

Bell–Magendie Law   A statement that the posterior roots of the spinal cord controlled sensation, whereas the anterior roots controlled motor movement; sometimes considered an example of a "multiple."

Binocular Vision   Vision involving the use of two eyes; aids in depth perception.

Bit   Abbreviation of "binary digit"; the amount of information that enables a choice between two alternatives.

Bloodletting   Medical technique promoted by Benjamin Rush; drawing blood was believed to relieve, among other things, mental disorders brought about by excessive tension in the circulatory system.

Brass Instrument Psychology   Term used (sarcastically) by William James to describe the German reaction time and psychophysics research, which relied heavily on apparatus made of brass.

Cardinal trait   For Allport, the most essential traits that characterize an individual.

Cartesian Dichotomy   From Descartes, the distinction between humans (mind + body) and animals (only a mechanical body).

Case Study   Research method involving an in-depth analysis of a single individual; advocated by Allport as a way to investigate personality.

Catastrophism   Theory in geology that geological change occurred infrequently and as a consequence of such catastrophic events as the Biblical flood.

Catharsis   In Freudian psychoanalysis, an emotional release that occurs when one gains insight into the unconscious origins of some problem; key part of the Anna O. case.

Cause and Effect   One of Hume's laws of association; Hume argued that we cannot be certain of the fundamental causes of events, only that events occur together regularly.

Cell Assembly   For Hebb, a basic unit in the nervous system, a set of neurons that become associated with each other because they have been repeatedly activated together.

Central trait   For Allport, a set of traits that sum up an individual's personality, aside from cardinal traits.

Chain of Being   Belief that all species on earth could be placed on a linear scale with reference to their level of complexity.

Chunk   For Miller, a meaningful unit of information; short-term memory capacity said to be 7±2 chunks of information.

Client-Centered Therapy   Humanistic approach to psychotherapy created by Rogers; it assumed that responsibility for therapeutic change ultimately belonged to the client, whereas the therapist's responsibility was to create an atmosphere conducive to such change.

Clinical Method   Method of studying the brain, pioneered by Broca, in which existing behavioral or cognitive deficits are correlated with brain damage upon autopsy.

Clinical Psychology   Field of psychology concerned with the diagnosis and treatment of mental and behavioral disorders; named by Witmer.

Closure   Gestalt organizing principle, a tendency to fill in missing gaps in our perception to perceive whole figures.

Cognitive Dissonance   In a theory proposed by Festinger, a state of cognitive discomfort resulting from the experience of holding two inconsistent thoughts simultaneously or behaving in a way that is inconsistent with one's beliefs.

Cognitive Map   For Tolman, a hypothetical spatial memory of a maze, acquired simply as a result of experiencing the maze (i.e., reinforcement not needed).

Cognitive Science   An interdisciplinary field that includes cognitive psychology, linguistics, computer science, cultural anthropology, and epistemology.

Collective Unconscious   Jung's concept that the unconscious included the collective experiences of our ancestors; reflected in the common themes that occur in the mythology of various cultures.

Comparative Psychology   Study of the similarities and differences among species; originated from the implication of Darwin's theory of evolution that continuity existed among species.

Complex Idea   For Locke, ideas that were combinations of simple ideas.

Complication Experiment   A 19th-century reaction time experiment, typically using the Donders subtractive method, in which reaction times for simple tasks were subtracted from reaction times for more "complicated" tasks.

Concomitant Variation   From Mill's *Logic*, method that examines whether changes in event *X* are associated with changes in event *Y*.

Conditional Stimulus   Any stimulus in Pavlovian conditioning that will be paired with an unconditioned stimulus to produce a conditioned response (e.g., tone).

Conditioned Reflex   The outcome of Pavlovian conditioning; by pairing a conditioned (conditional) stimulus (e.g., tone) with an unconditioned stimulus (e.g., food), the conditioned stimulus eventually elicits a conditioned response or reflex.

Connectionism   Thorndike's model of learning, emphasizing the development and strengthening of connections between stimulus situations and responses that became stronger with trial and error learning.

Conscious Attitudes   In the Würzburg school, referred to such mental processes as hesitation and doubt; occurred during the imageless thought studies.

Consciousness   Sense of awareness; how to study it became a contentious issue in the late 19th and early 20th centuries.

Conservation of Energy   Associated with Helmholtz and used by him to combat vitalism; proposed that the total energy within a system remains constant, even if changes occur within the system.

Contiguity   One of Hume's laws of association and Hartley's fundamental law; events experienced together, either simultaneously (spatial contiguity) or successively (temporal contiguity), become associated with each other.

Convergence   Visual phenomenon described by Berkeley; the tendency of the eye muscles to make the eyes move in the direction of "crossing" as objects move closer to the person.

Converging Operations   Refers to a series of studies, each with different operational definitions of the main constructs that nonetheless lead to the same general conclusion.

Correlation   Statistical tool that assesses the degree of relationship between two variables; concept originated with Galton and his studies of intelligence.

Critical Period   Certain instinctive behaviors (e.g., imprinting) must develop within a limited time frame, if they are to develop at all; associated with Lorenz and other European ethologists, but also proposed by Spalding.

Dedifferentiation   For Lewin, a process that occurs under stress, in which a person reverses the normal differentiation process and reverts to an earlier, more primitive way of behaving; similar to Freudian regression.

Dementia Praecox   Term used by Kraepelin that literally means a premature dementia, a disorder later named schizophrenia.

Dependent Variable   Any variable in research that is measured as an outcome of an experimental study; this usage introduced by Woodworth.

Derived Ideas   For Descartes, ideas that result from one's experiences in the world.

Determinism   Philosophical position that all events in the universe have prior causes.

Dichotic Listening   A procedure in research on selective attention in which a person wearing headphones hears one message in one ear and a second message in the other ear.

Differentiation   For Lewin, a developmental process in which a child's life space becomes more complex; for Pavlov, refers to discrimination, the ability to distinguish between two stimuli.

Direct Action of the Nervous System   Darwin's principle of emotional expression, stating that some expressions (e.g., blushing) are the side effects of the physiological arousal accompanying strongly felt emotions.

Doctrine of the Skull   The phrenological belief that skull contour reflected brain shape; enabled measurement of faculties by measuring contour of the skull.

Dream Analysis   A cornerstone of Freudian psychoanalysis; for Freud, dreams were the "royal road" to the unconscious; surface or manifest content of dreams needed to be analyzed for their deeper, or latent, content.

Drill Courses   Instructional courses in basic laboratory techniques, predominant in American universities in the late 19th century.

Drive Reduction   Central to Hull's theory of learning; learning required reinforcers, which were any stimuli (e.g., food) that reduced a strong drive (e.g., hunger).

Dualist   On the mind–body problem, someone (e.g., Descartes) who believes that mind and body are two separate and distinguishable essences.

Ecological Memory   Study of memory as it occurs in everyday situations.

Ecological Perception   Gibson's approach to the study of perception, which emphasized perception while navigating in realistic environments; the emphasis is on environmental factors guiding perception rather than the internal perceptual systems of the perceiver.

Ecological Validity   In cognitive psychology, research that is relevant for understanding everyday cognitive activities is said to have ecological validity.

Ego Defense Mechanisms   In Freudian theory, ways of behaving or thinking that serve to defend the ego against anxiety.

Electroshock Therapy   A medical approach to the treatment of severe mental illness, developed in the 1930s and in use today, in which electric shock is used to produce convulsions.

Empathy   Ability to understand, both cognitively and emotionally, what another person is experiencing; important prerequisite for therapy success, according to Rogers.

Empiricist   Someone who believes that our knowledge of the world is constructed from our experiences in it; school of thought associated with such British philosophers as Locke, Berkeley, and Mill.

Engineering Psychology   That branch of psychology concerned with the design of objects to improve their use by humans (e.g., by reducing perceptual errors, by reducing fatigue).

Enlightenment   Historical period from mid-18th century to late 19th century, characterized by a belief that true knowledge could be found through the use of science and reason and that progress was inevitable and good.

Epistemology   Branch of philosophy concerned with studying the nature of and the origins of human knowledge.

Eponyms   Historical periods or movements named with reference to some important historical person (e.g., Darwinian biology).

Equilibrium   For Lewin, a steady state in which all needs have been satisfied for the moment.

Equipotentiality   Principle associated with Lashley, proposing that if some portion of the brain is destroyed, other areas will be able to serve the same function (to a degree).

Ergonomics   Study of how systems and equipment can be best designed to avoid human error; pioneered by Gilbreth.

Eros   In Freudian theory, the name given to the life instinct and manifested in the sex drive.

Ethology   The study of animal behavior in its natural surroundings; associated with Lorenz, but with roots in Spalding's work.

Eugenics   Term created by Galton, referring to a variety of methods (e.g., selective breeding) for enhancing the quality of a species, especially humans.

Evolutionary Psychology   Late 20th-century development in psychology, with roots in Darwinian thinking; proposes that virtually all human behavior, especially social behavior, must be understood in an evolutionary context, as the product of natural selection.

Experimental Neurosis   In Pavlovian conditioning, an emotional response that occurs after training a discrimination between two stimuli, then making the stimuli too similar to be discriminated.

Explanatory Fictions   For Skinner, hypothetical constructs proposed as mediators between stimuli and responses that erroneously become used as explanations for behavioral phenomena (e.g., recalling only a few words because of limited short-term memory).

External History   A history that examines factors external to a discipline (e.g., social, political, institutional, economic) that influence the history of that discipline.

Extinction   In Pavlovian conditioning, the gradual elimination of a conditioned response following the repeated presentation of a conditioned stimulus in the absence of an unconditioned stimulus.

Faculty Psychology   Prevalent early and mid-19th-century approach to psychology, derived from Scottish Realism; emphasized real existence of mind, which they believed held a number of innate attributes ("faculties"), such as intelligence and judgment.

Field Theory   Associated with Lewin and Tolman; for Lewin, derived from his belief that to understand behavior requires knowing about all the forces acting on a person at a particular time; for Tolman, reflected the extent to which his neobehaviorism was influenced by the gestaltists.

Figure-Ground   Gestalt organizing principle stating that a fundamental perceptual tendency is to separate whole figures from their backgrounds.

Foreign Hull   For Lewin, all events outside the person's life space, and therefore having no effect on the individual at a given moment.

Forensic Psychology   The application of psychology to the law, pioneered by Münsterberg.

Form-Quality   As described by von Ehrenfels, the overall quality of some entity (e.g., a melody, a square) that exists over and above its individual components (e.g., notes, lines).

Fractionation Procedure   Developed in Külpe's laboratory in Würzburg, in which complicated events were broken down into sections ("fractionated"); then separate introspections were accomplished for each section.

Free Association   In Freudian psychoanalysis, a procedure to probe the unconscious, in which patients describe whatever occurs to them without internal censorship.

Functional Fixedness   Failure to solve a problem because of an inability to think of using some object in a manner different from its normal function.

Functionalism   School of psychology favored by most early American psychologists; focused on the study of human conscious experience from an evolutionary perspective, concerned with studying the adaptive value of various mental and behavioral processes.

Generalization   The tendency for a response learned to one stimulus to occur after the presentation of a second stimulus similar to the first.

Genetic Epistemology   Piagetian psychology, which examined the manner in which knowledge developed within the individual.

Genetic Psychology   Approach that emphasizes the evolution and development of the mind, including developmental psychology, comparative psychology, and abnormal psychology; associated with Hall.

Geocentric   Ancient astronomical viewpoint that placed earth at the center of the known universe.

Geographical Environment   For the gestaltists, this referred to the physical environment, as contrasted with the environment as perceived (the behavioral environment).

Gestalt Organizing Principles   Perceptual principles described by the gestaltists that summarize the ways in which sensory phenomena become organized into a whole, meaningful figure.

Good Continuation   Gestalt organizing principle, a tendency to organize perceptions in a smoothly flowing direction.

Grammar   Set of rules allowing for (a) the production of all possible sentences in a language and (b) the recognition and rejection of nonsentences.

Habit Strength   For Hull, an intervening variable influencing behavior that was a direct function of the number of reinforced trials ($_SH_R$).

Hawthorne effect   Tendency for the performance of subjects in an experiment to be influenced by their knowledge that they are under observation; based on the Hawthorne studies.

Hebb Synapses   For Hebb, synapses that change their structure as a result of learning.

Heliocentric   Astronomical viewpoint proposed by Copernicus and elaborated by Galileo that placed the sun at the center of the known universe.

Historicist   An interpretation of historical events made from the vantage point of the knowledge and values in place at the time of the events.

Historiography   The writing of history; historical methodology and theory.

Holism   The philosophical assumption underlying gestalt psychology; argues that wholes (e.g., complex ideas) are more than the sum of their constituent elements (e.g., sensations, simple ideas); opposed to atomism.

Humanistic Psychology   Movement pioneered by Rogers, Maslow, and others as a reaction to the deterministic assumptions of behaviorism and psychoanalysis; assumed that humans are characterized by free will, a search for meaning, and the potential for self-actualization.

Hypnotism   State of heightened suggestibility, pioneered by Mesmer, Elliotson, and named by Braid.

Hypothetico-Deductive System   General approach taken by Hull in which hypotheses for research are deduced from the formal postulates of the theory, and the outcomes of research support the theory or lead to its modification.

Hysteria   Disorder in which a number of symptoms (e.g., paralysis) indicate neurological damage, but no such damage exists.

Ideas   For Hume, ideas were "faint copies" of sensory impressions.

Idiographic   A research tradition emphasizing an in-depth analysis of individual cases; also examines differences from one individual to another; contrasted with a nomothetic strategy.

Imageless Thought   Any thought process that could not be further reduced to mental images; considered nonexistent by Titchener, who believed that all thought included images.

Impressions   For Hume, these were basic sensations, the raw data of experience.

Imprinting   Instinctive tendency for newly hatched ducklings (and other related species) to follow the first moving object they encounter; associated with Lorenz, but also observed by Spalding and Watson.

Independent Variable   Any variable in research that can be directly manipulated by an experimenter; this usage introduced by Woodworth.

Individual Differences   Originally referring to the individual variation among members of a particular species, became for psychology the more general study of the characteristics that differentiated one person from another (e.g., intelligence).

Individual Psychology   Label used by both Binet and Adler; for Binet, psychology should focus on ways of identifying and measuring individual differences (e.g., mental testing) rather than on general laws; for Adler, individual psychology was his version of psychoanalysis, which emphasized social factors in the development of the individual.

Inductive   An approach to knowledge that emphasizes that general scientific principles are generalizations made after the collection of large amounts of data; associated with Sir Francis Bacon.

Inferiority Complex   Concept associated with Adler, who believed that much of human behavior could be viewed as an attempt to compensate for feelings of inferiority.

Information Theory   An influence external to psychology that helped develop cognitive psychology; concerns the manner in which information is structured (bits) and processed.

Inheritance of Acquired Characteristics   Theory that characteristics developed as a result of experience during one's lifetime could be passed on biologically to offspring; associated with Lamarck.

Innate Idea   Idea that exists or can be deduced in the absence of direct experience, through reasoning (the idea of a material object's "extension" in space was used by Descartes as an example).

Insight   For the gestaltists, a sudden problem solution that occurred when the individual reorganized the elements of the problem situation into a new configuration.

Instinct   Behavior is said to be instinctive when alternative explanations in terms of learning or experience can be ruled out; pioneering work done by early comparative psychologists, especially Spalding.

Intelligence Quotient   Term invented by Stern and used by Terman in the Stanford–Binet tests; "IQ" equaled mental age divided by chronological age, the result multiplied by 100.

Interactionist   A dualist who believes that body and mind directly influence each other.

Internal History   A history of the ideas, theories, and findings of a discipline, without regard for the influence of external, contextual factors.

Internal Perception   Wundt's version of introspection, in which "observers" would give brief verbal responses to controlled stimuli (e.g., in reaction time or psychophysics experiments).

Intervening Variables   Used by Tolman and Hull; referred to hypothetical internal factors (e.g., cognitive map for Tolman; habit strength for Hull) that intervened between stimulus and response.

Introspection   Method of experiencing some phenomenon, then giving a description of the conscious experience of the phenomenon.

Introspective Habit   The result of extensive practice with introspection, this was a dissociative ability to make mental notes about an experience while the experience was occurring.

James–Lange Theory of Emotion   Theory that held that the strong emotions were in essence the physiological reaction that followed the perception of some emotion-eliciting event.

jnd   Or just noticeable difference; point where the difference (in weight, color, pitch, etc.) between two stimuli becomes just barely detectable.

Joint Method   J. S. Mill's combination of the methods of agreement and difference.

Latent Learning   For Tolman, learning that occurred but was not reflected in an animal's performance.

Law of Effect   Thorndike's principle that behaviors that were effective in problem solving would be strengthened (stamped in), while behaviors that were not effective would be weakened (stamped out).

Law of Exercise   Thorndike's principle that learned connections between stimuli and responses were strengthened with additional practice.

Life Space   For Lewin, a field within which a person operates; includes all the factors that influence a person's behavior at a certain moment.

Linguistic Universals   For Chomsky, common principles shared by all languages, the existence of which supports the notion that language is innate to the human species.

Lloyd Morgan's Canon   Principle stating that the best explanation for some behavioral phenomenon was the one with the fewest unnecessary assumptions; Morgan did not deny the use of mental processing when explaining animal behavior, but argued that there was no need to propose mental capabilities beyond the level needed for survival in a given species.

Lobotomy   Surgical procedure pioneering by Moniz in the 1930s that involves severing connections between the cortex and lower brain centers; originally designed to treat severe mental illness but abandoned when found to be of marginal effectiveness and often abused.

Localization of Function   Concerns the issue of whether specific parts of the brain have specific functions.

Logical Positivism   Philosophical movement associated with the Vienna Circle that extended positivist thinking; distinguished between theoretical and observable events and described ways of connecting the two through operational definitions.

Mass Action   Principle associated with Lashley, proposing a limit on equipotentiality; the greater the amount of brain destroyed, the greater the difficulty for remaining areas of the brain to take over brain function.

Materialism   Philosophical position that the only reality is physical reality and that living matter can be reduced to physical and chemical properties; held by most physiologists of the 19th century; opposed to vitalism.

Mechanist   Someone who explains bodily actions in mechanical terms.

Memory Drum   Device for presenting verbal stimuli in a memory experiment; invented by G. E. Müller.

Mental Age   Mistranslation of Binet's mental level; indicated a child's level of mental ability, reported in terms of years.

Mental Chronometry   Name given to 19th-century reaction time research, in which the goal was to measure the time taken for various mental events.

Mental Level   Term used by Binet to indicate a child's level of mental functioning; those in need of remediation scored two levels below the norm for their chronological age.

Mental Set   In the Würzburg laboratory, referred to the effect of giving observers some instructions that predispose them to think in certain ways; for the gestaltists, a fixed, habitual way of thinking.

Mental Test   Any test designed to measure mental activity or ability; term introduced in 1890 by Cattell.

Meritocracy   A model of society based on the idea that the most mentally competent should be the leaders; championed by most American mental testers, especially Terman.

Mesmerism   Early version of hypnotism, associated with Mesmer; held that hysteria and other disorders could be cured through the use of magnets.

Method of Adjustment   Method of psychophysics, described by Fechner, in which the subject directly controls a physical stimulus, adjusting it until it is just barely detected.

Method of Agreement   From Mill's *Logic*, a method in which a proposed cause is present whenever the effect is also present.

Method of Constant Stimuli   Method of psychophysics, described by Fechner, in which stimuli of varying physical intensities are presented in random order.

Method of Difference   From Mill's *Logic*, a method in which the absence of a proposed effect is always accompanied by the absence of a proposed cause.

Method of Limits   Method of psychophysics, described by Fechner, which alternates ascending trials (stimulus is first below threshold, then increased until detected) and descending trials (stimulus is first well above threshold, then decreased until no longer detected).

Molar Behavior   For Tolman, broad patterns of behavior that were goal directed, in contrast with the molecular behavior that was the result of a reductionist model of behavior.

Monads   For Leibniz, the fundamental elements of both physical and mental reality.

Moral Treatment   For Pinel and for Tuke, an approach to treating mental illness that included improved nutrition and living conditions, and rewards for productive behavior.

Moron   Term invented by Goddard as a label for adolescents or adults scoring at a mental age of 8 through 12.

Motor Aphasia   Found in Broca's patient Tan; speech apparatus normal, intelligence normal, but a serious inability to express ideas verbally.

Multiple   The simultaneous or near simultaneous discovery of some phenomenon, used to support the importance of the zeitgeist and a naturalistic approach to history.

Nativism   An extreme nationalist tendency, in which outsiders are considered inferior and dangerous; characterized United States in 1920s, contributing to restrictions placed on immigration.

Nativist   Someone who argues for the existence of innate ideas or, more generally, believes that some knowledge, faculties, or abilities are innate.

Naturalistic   An approach to history that emphasizes the importance of environmental and situational forces in shaping history.

Natural Selection   Central idea in Darwin's theory of evolution; held that in the struggle for existence, those organisms with adaptive variations would be most likely to survive (i.e., be selected by nature) and pass their attributes on to the next generation.

Neobehaviorism   Behaviorist movement that emerged in the 1930s, associated with Tolman, Hull, and others.

Neurypnology   Term created by Braid to reflect his belief that hypnotism was related to the state of sleep.

Nomothetic   A research strategy that focuses on discovering general principles that apply, to a calibrated degree, to all individuals; contrasted with an idiographic strategy.

Nonsense Syllables   Consonant-vowel-consonant combinations, invented by Ebbinghaus as stimulus materials in his studies on the formation and retention of associations.

Normal Science   In Kuhn's approach to the history of science, this is a period during which a paradigm is in control and a scientist's activities are shaped by the constraints of the paradigm.

Observer   Name used for someone participating in a psychological experiment in the late 19th and early 20th centuries, so-called because the primary activity was observing one's mental activities through introspection.

Operant   Any behavior emitted by an organism and controlled by the immediate consequences of the behavior.

Operant Conditioning   Skinnerian conditioning in which a behavior occurs, and the immediate consequences of the behavior determine its future probability of occurrence.

Operational Definition   A definition in terms of a specific, observable set of operations (e.g., hunger = 24 hours without food); more generally, defining scientific terms with precision.

Operationism   Philosophical position that scientific concepts were to be defined in terms of a set of operations used to measure those concepts.

Ophthalmoscope   Device for examining the retina, invented by Helmholtz.

Origin Myths   Descriptions of the beginning points for ideas, research findings, theories, or movements in psychology that oversimplify the complexity of origins and are often used to give the impression that origins go back further than they really do.

Orthogenics   Witmer's term for his therapeutic strategy of helping those with school-related problems (e.g., learning disabilities) to recover.

Paired-Associate Learning   Popular learning procedure in which pairs of stimuli are presented; after a study time, stimuli are presented and the associated response must be given; invented by Calkins.

Paradigm   In Kuhn's approach to the history of science, an all-encompassing theory that determines which problems are to be solved and the methods used to solve them.

Parallelism   Dualistic position on the mind–body problem, associated with Hartley, Leibniz, and others; asserts that mind and body are separate and noninteracting, but in perfect harmony.

Peak Experience   In humanistic psychology, a rare experience of extreme joy, pleasure, or accomplishment.

Periodic Function   Concept used in the early 20th century to refer to a women's alleged incapacity during the time of menstruation.

Personal Equation   Calibrating the reaction of one astronomer against another astronomer; needed because different reaction times among astronomers yielded different astronomical measurements.

Personalistic   An approach to history that emphasizes persons and their roles in shaping historical events.

Personology   The theoretical approach to personality taken by Henry Murray, one that emphasized the study of the individual person in depth.

Petites Perceptions   For Leibniz, perceptions below the level of awareness, but essential for higher levels of perception.

Phase Sequences   For Hebb, a higher level of cortical organization than the cell assembly, in which combinations of assemblies are formed.

Phi Phenomenon   Wertheimer's term for apparent motion, chosen to avoid the connotation that "apparent" motion was not really perceived, but was illusory.

Phrenology   The first serious localization of function theory; proposed that "faculties" were located in specific brain locations, that the strength of a faculty was proportional to the amount of brain assigned to it, and that faculties could be assessed by measuring skull contours.

Pineal Gland   Portion of the brain selected by Descartes as the locus for mind–body interactions.

Positivism   Philosophical position associated with Comte, who argued that the only certain knowledge is obtained through objective, publicly observable events.

Pragmatism   Position taken by several late 19th-century American philosophers, most notably William James; judged the value of ideas by their usefulness in helping someone adapt to the environment.

Pragnänz   Gestalt organizing principle of perception (translation—"good figure"), a tendency for our perceptions to mirror reality as closely as possible.

Presentist   An interpretation of historical events made from the vantage point of present-day knowledge and values.

Primary Qualities   For Locke, attributes of some object that are inherent to that object that exist regardless of perception (e.g., extension in space).

Primary Reinforcers   For Hull, unlearned reinforcers (e.g., food).

Primary Source   Materials written or created at or near the time of some historical event, such as correspondence, diaries, speeches, minutes of meetings, university records.

Problem of Perception   For Helmholtz, it was the dilemma posed by the fact that human perception is extraordinary, whereas the mechanisms (e.g., eye, ear) appeared to have design flaws.

Progressive Education   Associated with Dewey, an approach to education that emphasized making the student an active learner (learning by doing).

Progressive Relaxation   Technique of gradually and systematically relaxing major muscle groups; pioneered by Jacobson and used by Wolpe in systematic desensitization.

Proximity   Gestalt organizing principle of perception, a tendency to perceive that objects in close proximity "belong" together.

Psychophysics   Study of the relationship between physical stimuli and the perception of those stimuli; pioneered by Weber and (especially) Fechner.

Psychotechnics   Term used to identify a variety of applied psychology activities (mostly related to business) in Europe in the period between the world wars.

PsyD   Degree given to clinical psychologists trained with reference to the Vail model, which places a heavier emphasis on practice and a lighter emphasis on research expertise than does the Boulder, scientist–practitioner model.

Purposiveness   For Tolman, this referred to goal-directedness and was believed by him to be a universal feature of learned behavior.

Rationalist   Philosophical tradition emphasizing the use of reason and logic to arrive at truth; associated with Descartes.

Reaction Potential   For Hull, the probability that a response will occur at a given time, depending on such factors as drive and habit strength ($_sE_R$).

Recapitulation   Hall's theory, taken from a similar idea in biology, that the development of the individual mirrors the evolution of that individual's species.

Reciprocal Innervation   For Sherrington, the idea muscles work in coordinated pairs under the control of the nervous system—when one muscle flexes, a second, paired muscle, extends; the action allows complex and coordinated actions (e.g., walking).

Recoding　For Miller, a process of reorganizing information to increase the amount of information per chunk.

Reflection　Therapy technique used by Rogers to show that the therapist could empathize; involved rephrasing a client's comment in a way to show understanding.

Reflex Arc　Basic unit of behavior, reduced by physiologists into the stimulus producing sensation, the central processing producing an idea, and the motor response; analysis rejected by Dewey, who argued that the arc should be seen instead as a coordinated unit that adapted the individual to the environment.

Replication　Process of repeating an experiment to judge its validity and generality.

Repression　A Freudian defense mechanism in which unwanted impulses or traumatic memories are forced out of awareness and into the unconscious.

Resemblance　One of Hume's laws of association; objects similar to each other become associated with each other.

Resistance　In Freudian psychoanalysis, occurs when a person is unable to free associate, and indicates (to a Freudian) the presence of repressed material.

Resonance Theory　Theory of hearing associated with Helmholtz, which proposed that different frequencies of sound stimulated receptors located in different places along the basilar membrane of the cochlear (found in the inner ear).

Retroactive Inhibition　Interference from some activity that intervenes between the learning of a list of stimulus items and its recall.

Savings Method　Measure of memory used by Ebbinghaus, based on the difference between the amount of time to learn a list of nonsense syllables during original learning and the amount of time to relearn the list some time later.

Schedules of Reinforcement　Specification of the relationship between the number or pattern of responses and the delivery of reinforcers, whenever reinforcement does not follow each behavior.

Schemata　Term used both by Piaget and Bartlett to refer to hypothetical mental structures that represent knowledge.

Scholasticism　Educational tradition combining the careful use of reason with the received wisdom of the church and Aristotelian authority.

School Psychology　Field of psychology concerned with the development of programs for treating children and adolescents with school-related problems (e.g., learning disabilities); pioneered by Witmer, although he did not use the term.

Scientist–Practitioner Model　Training model for PhD in clinical psychology that emphasizes a research dissertation; also called the Boulder model.

Secondary Qualities　For Locke, attributes of some object that depend on perception for their existence (e.g., color).

Secondary Reinforcers　For Hull, reinforcers that are learned through association with primary reinforcers (e.g., money).

Secondary Source　Materials written or created some time after a historical event that serve to summarize or analyze that event.

Secondary Trait　For Allport, part of an individual personality, but not often displayed.

Seduction Hypothesis　Freud's original belief that hysteria originated from actual childhood sexual abuse.

Selective Filter　For Broadbent, a model of selective attention emphasizing our tendency to separate information on the basis of physical characteristics (e.g., pitch), then focus on one message, while filtering out other ones.

Self-Actualization　For humanistic psychologists, a state in which people have reached their full potential.

Self Psychology　Theoretical approach to psychology taken by Calkins, influenced by James; held that all consciousness is ultimately self-consciousness.

Sensory Aphasia　A disorder characterized by the inability to comprehend speech, and although there is no difficulty producing speech, the speech product is incoherent and/or illogical.

Serial Learning　Procedure used by Ebbinghaus that involved memorizing a list of verbal stimuli (e.g., nonsense syllables), then recalling them in the exact order of presentation.

Serial Order Problem　The problem of explaining sequences of behavioral events in neurological terms; posed by Lashley as a problem not solvable by traditional S-R behaviorist models.

Serviceable Associated Habits　Darwin's belief that emotional expressions were the product of evolutionary forces; certain expressions (e.g., sneer) originally had some survival function.

Sexual selection Darwin's theory, expressed in his *Descent of Man*, that mate selection is influenced by factors (e.g., coloration), not necessarily relevant for natural selection, that favor one male over another in the competition for females.

Shell Shock Name given to psychological trauma suffered by soldiers in World War I.

Similarity Gestalt organizing principle of perception, a tendency to perceive that objects resembling each other "belong" together.

Simple Ideas For Locke, ideas resulting from sensory experience or simple reflection.

Social Darwinism The belief that evolutionary forces were natural and inevitable and that any attempt to disrupt them (e.g., by creating programs for the poor) was misguided and doomed to failure; associated with Spencer.

S-O-R Model Proposed by Woodworth to recognize the importance of the organism intervening between stimulus and response.

Spatial Contiguity When experiencing two events simultaneously, they become associated, according to Hartley.

Spatial Summation Process described by Sherrington; individual stimuli fail to elicit a response, but several stimuli simultaneously in close spatial proximity to each other will produce one; supported Sherrington's proposal of the synapse.

Species Problem Problem of the origin of species, addressed by Enlightenment thinkers faced with increasing uncertainty over Biblical accounts.

Specific Energy of Nerves Doctrine proposed by Bell and Müller that different sensory nerves convey different qualities; pointed out that we perceive the world indirectly through the action of our nervous systems.

Spiritualism Popular 19th-century belief in the afterlife and in the ability to communicate with the dead; William James was a strong believer that spiritualist claims needed to be evaluated seriously.

Stimulus Control In a stimulus environment in which a behavior is reinforced regularly, the stimulus is said to gain stimulus control over the behavior.

Structuralism School of psychology, associated with Titchener that focused on identifying the structural elements of human conscious experience, primarily through basic laboratory and introspective methods.

Subjective Idealism For Berkeley, the philosophical position that the reality of the material world cannot be determined with certainty; we can be certain of the reality of our own perceptions, however.

Subtractive Method Method of measuring the duration of mental events, pioneered by Donders; reaction times for simple tasks were subtracted from reaction times for more "complicated" tasks.

Subvocal Speech Watson's definition of thinking.

Suggestion The ability to uncritically accept an idea or command from another; underlies hypnosis and was central to the view of hypnosis held by Liebeault and Bernheim of the Nancy School.

Survey Method Research method that originated with Darwin's questionnaires on emotion and Galton's questionnaires on a variety of topics; Galton normally credited with their creation.

Synapse Physical space between neurons, first proposed by Sherrington.

Systematic Desensitization Behavior therapy procedure in which fear response is replaced by an incompatible response (e.g., relaxation); pioneered by Jones and Wolpe, who named it.

Systematic Experimental Introspection Form of introspection associated with Külpe and Titchener, in which the experience of complex mental events was followed by detailed introspective descriptions; a more elaborate form of introspection than Wundt's.

Temporal Contiguity When experiencing two events in immediate succession, they become associated, according to Hartley.

Temporal Summation Process described by Sherrington; individual stimuli fail to elicit a response, but several stimuli in close temporal contiguity will produce one; supported Sherrington's proposal of the synapse.

Thanatos In Freudian theory, the name given to the death instinct and manifested in aggression.

Thresholds Points on a continuum of awareness where one passes from no conscious awareness to some awareness (absolute threshold) or from an awareness that one stimulus is noticeably different from another stimulus (difference threshold); associated with Leibniz and begun as a topic in experimental psychology by Weber and Fechner.

Topology Mathematical field of nonquantitative spatial geometry, used by Lewin as a basis for his field theory.

TOTE Unit Feedback unit (Test-Operate-Test-Exit) to replace reflex arc; proposed by Miller, Galanter, and

Pribram, and influenced by developments in cybernetics.

Trait a characteristic and distinctive attribute of a person.

Transfer The effect of learning in one situation on learning in a second situation; could be positive or negative; pioneer studies by Woodworth and Thorndike.

Transference In Freudian psychoanalysis, occurs when the patient develops a strong emotional attachment to the therapist.

Trial-and-Error Learning Thorndike's explanation for the behavior of his cats in puzzle boxes—they escaped by trying various behaviors until hitting on one that worked; also used by Morgan to provide a parsimonious explanation for the behavior of dogs escaping from yards.

Trichromatic Theory The Young-Helmholtz theory of color vision, which proposed the existence of three different color-sensitive cells in the eye, one for each of the primary colors (red, green, blue); color vision believed to result from various combinations of firings of these cells.

Tropisms Forced movements, automatic responses to specific stimuli, as studied by Loeb.

Twin Studies First suggested by Galton as a means of demonstrating the heritability of intelligence.

Two-Point Threshold Point where the perception of two points touching the skin changes from "one point perceived" to "two points perceived"; studied extensively by Weber.

Type R conditioning Skinner's term for operant conditioning, in which an association is formed between some behavior (R) and a consequence.

Type S conditioning Skinner's term for classical conditioning (Pavlov), in which two stimuli are associated, both producing the same response.

Unconditioned Reflex For Pavlov, any stimulus-response connection (e.g., food-salivate) that does not have to be learned.

Unconditioned Stimulus Any stimulus that will produce a specific reflex response (e.g., food elicits saliva).

Unconscious Inference For Helmholtz, a process, outside our awareness, by which our perceptions are influenced by past experiences.

Uniformitarianism Theory in geology, championed by Lyell, that geological change occurred gradually, over a long period of time, and as a consequence of such regular phenomena as erosion.

Valence For Lewin, term used to describe whether an object is valued by the person (positive valence) or not valued (negative valence).

Variability Hypothesis The idea that men had a greater degree of variability in most traits, compared to women, and were therefore at a selective advantage in evolutionary terms.

Vector For Lewin, refers to the direction of a desired goal.

Vitalism Belief that a "life force" or vital force existed that went beyond the physical and chemical components of living organisms; opposed to materialism.

Voluntarism Wundt's system of psychology, so-called because of his emphasis on the idea that the mind actively organizes information.

Von Restorff Effect Increased recall of information that stands out in some manner from other to-be-learned information.

Weber's Law As stimulus A increases in intensity, it takes progressively larger differences between stimulus A and stimulus B for a person to detect a difference between the two; the jnd divided by the size of the standard stimulus is a constant.

White Paper Locke's term, borrowed from Aristotle, for the nature of the mind at birth; knowledge acquired through experience is analogous to writing on this white paper.

Word Association Test Procedure associated with both Galton and Jung to investigate the nature of associations in the mind; involves responding to a stimulus word with the first response word that comes to mind.

Zeigarnik Effect Named for student of Lewin, refers to a tendency to be more likely to recall unfinished tasks than finished tasks.

Zeitgeist The overall intellectual, political, and cultural climate of a particular historical era.

INDEX

1800–1850

On October 22, Fechner's mind–body insight	**1850**	
	1849	Dickens: *David Copperfield*
Phineas Gage's accident	1848	Gold discovered in California; gold rush begins
	1847	
	1846	Irish potato famine begins
	1845	
American Psychiatric Association founded	1844	Morse sends first Morse code message
J. S. Mill: *Logic*; Flourens disproves phrenology	1843	Dickens: *A Christmas Carol*
	1842	Richard Owen coins term "dinosaur"
James Braid sees first demo of mesmerism	1841	P. T. Barnum opens "American Museum" in NY
	1840	
	1839	
Johannes Müller: *Elements of Physiology*	1838	Coronation of England's Queen Victoria
	1837	Agassiz proposes glaciation theory
Mesmerism introduced in U.S.	1836	
Darwin arrives at the Galapagos Islands	1835	Babbage invents a mechanical calculator
Weber publishes on "just noticeable differences"	1834	Hugo: *Hunchback of Notre Dame*
	1833	Whewell coins term "scientist"
Spuzheim (phrenologist) dies in U.S. tour	1832	
	1831	McCormick invents first successful reaper
	1830	
James Mill publishes in association	1829	Braille publishes reading system for the blind
	1828	
Thomas Upham: *Elements of Mental Philosophy*	1827	Audubon: *Birds of North America*
	1826	Cooper: *Last of the Mohicans*
	1825	Erie Canal connects New York City to Lake Erie
SPCA founded in London	1824	
	1823	
Magendie publishes on sensory/motor nerves	1822	
	1821	Napoleon I dies
	1820	Malthus: *Principles of Political Economy*
	1819	
	1818	Shelley: *Frankenstein*
Weber appointed docent in physiology (Leipzig)	1817	
	1816	Laënnec invents stethoscope
	1815	Napoleon I defeated at Waterloo
	1814	
First private mental hospital in the United States (Philadelphia)	1813	Austen: *Pride and Prejudice*
Benjamin Rush: first psychiatry textbook	1812	Cuvier argues species wiped out by catastrophes
	1811	Luddites destroy industrial machines in England
	1810	
Lamarck publishes on evolution	1809	Darwin and Lincoln born on same day (February 14)
	1808	
Hegel: *Phenomenology of Mind*	1807	England prohibits slave trade
Pinel: *Treatise on Insanity*	1806	
	1805	Admiral Nelson's victory at Trafalgar
	1804	Lewis and Clark expedition begins
	1803	
Thomas Young publishes theory of color vision	1802	German naturalist Treviranus coins term "biology"
Itard: *The Wild Boy of Aveyron*	1801	
Gall/Spurzheim phrenology collaboration begins	**1800**	Royal College of Surgeons founded, London

1850–1900

Small's maze learning study	**1900**	
	1899	Wilde: *The Importance of Being Earnest*
Thorndike's puzzle box research	1898	U.S. declares war on Spain over Cuba
Ellis: *Studies in the Psychology of Sex*	1897	
Dewey on reflex arc; Witmer's clinic started	1896	Beginning of Klondike gold rush (Alaska)
Breuer & Freud: *Studies on Hysteria*	1895	Roentgen discovers X-rays
Washburn's PhD with Titchener (1st woman PhD)	1894	
	1893	Chicago's Columbian Exposition opens
Hall founds APA; Titchener & Münsterberg arrive	1892	New immigration center opens on Ellis Island
	1891	Michelin brothers patent removable tire
James: *Principle of Psychology*	**1890**	Lakota Sioux attacked at Wounded Knee
	1889	London murders by "Jack the Ripper"
Cattell measured at Galton's Anthropometric Lab	1888	
Hall starts *American Journal of Psychology*	1887	Anne Sullivan begins teaching Helen Keller
	1886	Stevenson: *Dr. Jekyll and Mr. Hyde*
Ebbinghaus: *On Memory*	1885	German engineer Benz builds his first car
Galton's Anthropometric Lab opens (London)	1884	
Hall opens first lab in the United States (Johns Hopkins)	1883	Brooklyn Bridge opens in New York
	1882	Stevenson: *Treasure Island*
Freud completes MD at University of Vienna	1881	
Breuer begins treating Anna O.	**1880**	Rodin sculpts *The Thinker*
Official founding year for Wundt's lab at Leipzig	1879	Anti-Jesuit laws introduced in France
	1878	Gilbert & Sullivan: *HMS Pinafore*
Darwin: biographical sketch of infant son	1877	
Journal *Mind* established in England	1876	Bell invents telephone; Johns Hopkins opens
	1875	Twain: *The Adventures of Tom Sawyer*
Wundt: *Principles of Physiological Psychology*	1874	First Impressionist art exhibit in Paris
	1873	
Darwin: *Expressions of Emotions*	1872	First national park: Yellowstone
Darwin: *Descent of Man*	1871	Chicago's great fire
First electrical stimulation of brain (Fritsch/Hitzig)	**1870**	
J. S. Mill: *The Subjection of Women*	1869	Suez Canal opens
Donders publishes on reaction time	1868	Cro-Magnon man skeleton discovered in France
	1867	Russia sells Alaska to the United States for 7.2 million dollars
	1866	Nobel invents dynamite
James accompanies Agassiz to the Amazon	1865	
	1864	
Wundt: *Lectures on Human & Animal Psychology*	1863	Lincoln's Gettysburg Address
	1862	
Broca's autopsy on "Tan"	1861	U.S. Civil War begins (ends 1865)
Fechner: *Elements of Psychophysics*	**1860**	First British Open golf tournament
Darwin: *Origin of Species*	1859	
Wundt becomes assistant to Helmholtz	1858	Burton and Speke explore the Nile's origins
	1857	
	1856	Neanderthal skull discovered near Düsseldorf
Spencer: *Principles of Psychology*	1855	Florence Nightingale nurses in the Crimean War
Helmholtz on the speed of neural impulse	1854	Pope declares Immaculate Conception as dogma
	1853	
Congress funds first federal mental hospital (DC)	1852	Stowe: *Uncle Tom's Cabin*
	1851	Melville: *Moby Dick*
	1850	

1900–1950

	1950	North Korean forces invade South Korea
Boulder model for clinical training	1949	Gilbreth & Carey: *Cheaper by the Dozen*
Skinner: *Walden Two*	1948	State of Israel founded
	1947	
Nobel Prize for physics: Percy Bridgman	1946	
Wertheimer: *Productive Thinking*	1945	Atom bombs dropped on Japan: WWII ends
	1944	D-Day landings in Normandy
Hull: *Principles of Behavior*	1943	Academy Award for Best Picture: *Casablanca*
	1942	
Fromm: *Escape from Freedom*	1941	Pearl Harbor attacked; U.S. enters WWII
	1940	Hemingway: *For Whom the Bell Tolls*
Freud dies in London	1939	Germany invades Poland; WWII begins
Woodworth's "Columbia Bible"	1938	"War of the Worlds" broadcast creates panic
AAAP formed by applied psychologists	1937	
SPSSI founded	1936	Berlin Olympics: 4 gold medals for Jesse Owens
Koffka: *Principles of Gestalt Psychology*	1935	Richter invents measuring scale for earthquakes
	1934	
	1933	Hitler appointed Chancellor of Germany
Bartlett: *Remembering*	1932	
	1931	Al Capone convicted of tax evasion
Lewin introduces B = *f*(P,E)	**1930**	
Yale International Conference; Psi Chi formed	1929	U.S. stock market crashes
Sumner begins tenure at Howard University	1928	1st Mickey Mouse cartoon; bubble gum invented
Psychological Abstracts begins publication	1927	Babe Ruth hits 60 home runs
	1926	
Köhler: *Mentality of Apes*	1925	Scopes "monkey trial" in Tennessee
	1924	
Freud: *The Ego and the Id*	1923	Founding of *Time* magazine
Hall's *Senescence: The Last Half of Life*	1922	Joyce: *Ulysses*
	1921	Sacco and Vanzetti found guilty of murder
Watson & Rayner's Little Albert study	**1920**	
	1919	Spanish flu pandemic ends; 30 million die
Army testing program (Alpha and Beta)	1918	Red Sox win third World Series in 4 years
Army testing program begins	1917	U.S. enters WWI; Russian Revolution
Terman's Stanford-Binet IQ test	1916	
	1915	Einstein proposes general theory of relativity
	1914	WWI begins in Europe; Panama Canal opens
Watson's behaviorist manifesto	1913	Crossword puzzle invented
Wertheimer's apparent motion study	1912	*Titanic* hits iceberg, sinks
	1911	
	1910	W. E. B. Dubois founds NAACP
Freud's Clark lectures	1909	
Washburn: *Animal Mind*	1908	Foster: *A Room with a View*
Beers: *A Mind That Found Itself*	1907	Baden-Powell founds Boy Scouts
Angell's APA address on functionalism	1906	San Francisco earthquake
Calkins elected first female president of APA	1905	
Nobel Prize to Pavlov	1904	Barrie: *Peter Pan*
	1903	Wright brothers' flight at Kitty Hawk, NC
	1902	Doyle: *The Hound of the Baskervilles*
British Psychological Society created	1901	
Freud: *Interpretation of Dreams*	**1900**	Alois Alzheimer records case of dementia

1950–2000

2000s declared "Decade of Behavior"	**2000**	
First positive psychology summit, Lincoln, NE	1999	Columbine high school shootings
	1998	Good Friday peace accord, Ireland
	1997	Google registers domain name google.com
50 years for APA's original divisions	1996	Birth of Dolly the sheep, first cloned mammal
	1995	Federal building in Oklahoma City bombed
Herrnstein & Murray: *The Bell Curve*	1994	
Freud's fourth appearance on cover of *Time*	1993	First bombing of NY World Trade Center
APA centennial celebration	1992	
	1991	
Skinner's final pubic address, APA in Boston	**1990**	Nelson Mandela freed from South African prison
1990s declared "Decade of the Brain"	1989	Berlin Wall falls; *Exxon Valdez* oil spill
APS founded	1988	Pan AM 103 bombed over Lockerbie, Scotland
First international Alzheimer's conference (Miami)	1987	
	1986	Chernobyl nuclear disaster in USSR
PsycLIT on CD-ROM first available	1985	
First stamp for psychologist: Lillian Gilbreth	1984	Indian Prime Minister Indira Gandhi assassinated
	1983	
	1982	
Nobel Prizes for Hubel, Weisel, Sperry	1981	First space shuttle flight (*Columbia*)
	1980	Mount St. Helens explodes; John Lennon killed
Wundt laboratory centennial	1979	U.S. diplomats taken hostage in Iran
	1978	
	1977	Elvis found dead (apparently)
Guthrie: *Even the Rat Was White*	1976	
APA Minority Fellowship program initiated	1975	Nicklaus wins 5th Masters and 4th PGA titles
Public Law 93-348 (human Ss protection) signed	1974	Nixon resigns presidency
Vail conference on clinical training (PsyD)	1973	Academy Award: *The Godfather*
	1972	Terrorists kill Israeli athletes at Munich Olympics
	1971	
	1970	Student protesters shot at Kent State
National Medal of Science to Skinner	1969	Armstrong, first man on moon
Atkinson & Shiffrin's memory model (STM/LTM)	1968	Assassinations: M. L. King, R. Kennedy
Neisser: *Cognitive Psychology*	1967	
	1966	Capote: *In Cold Blood*
Head Start program announced	1965	
	1964	Civil Rights Act passes in the United States
First of Milgram's obedience studies published	1963	JFK assassinated; first *Doctor Who* episode
Kuhn: *The Structure of Scientific Revolutions*	1962	Carson: *Silent Spring*
First issue: *Journal of Humanistic Psychology*	1961	
Gibson & Walk's visual cliff article appears	**1960**	Hitchcock's *Psycho* in theaters
	1959	
Wolpe: *Psychotherapy by Reciprocal Inhibition*	1958	
Festinger: *A Theory of Cognitive Dissonance*	1957	Soviets launch first satellite, *Sputnik*
Miller's 7+2 paper	1956	
	1955	
Allport: *The Nature of Prejudice*	1954	*Brown* v. *Board of Education* decision
Skinner: *Science and Human Behavior*	1953	Watson & Crick map structure of DNA
Eysenck article evaluation psychotherapy	1952	Polio vaccine created
Rogers: *Client-Centered Therapy*	1951	
Gibson: *Perception of the Visual World*	**1950**	*Peanuts* cartoon strip introduced